Trial Technique and Evidence

Second Edition

Michael R. Fontham

Partner
Stone, Pigman, Walther, Wittmann & Hutchinson
New Orleans, Louisiana

Adjunct Professor of Law
Tulane University Law School
Louisiana State University Law Center

LexisNexis™
Matthew Bender®

ISBN#: 0-8205-5635-1

Editorial Offices
744 Broad Street, Newark, NJ 07102 (973) 820-2000
201 Mission St., San Francisco, CA 94105-1831 (415) 908-3200
701 East Water Street, Charlottesville, VA 22902-7587 (804) 972-7600
www.lexis.com

(Pub.03108)

ABOUT THE AUTHOR

Michael R. Fontham engages in a civil litigation practice as a partner in the New Orleans firm of Stone, Pigman, Walther, Wittmann & Hutchinson. His practice involves commercial disputes before state and federal courts and regulatory agencies and includes contract disputes, utility rate matters, and varied commercial cases.

Mr. Fontham is a graduate of the University of Virginia Law School. He teaches evidence as an adjunct professor at the Tulane University Law School and the Louisiana State University Law Center. He taught evidence as a visiting professor at the University of Virginia Law School. Mr. Fontham is an instructor in the Trial Advocacy Institute at the University of Virginia, has taught advocacy skills courses at the Law School at Loyola University, and has taught evidence in the Louisiana Judicial College. In addition to teaching evidence and trial advocacy, he has taught appellate advocacy, constitutional law, and antitrust law.

Mr. Fontham is the author of *Written and Oral Advocacy*, a treatise on brief writing, oral argument, and legal research. Along with Michael Vitiello and David W. Miller, he also authored *Persuasive Written and Oral Advocacy in Trial and Appellate Courts*, which expands and supplements the instruction in the original book. He has authored a number of articles and delivered numerous lectures on trial and appellate advocacy, evidence, and substantive law issues.

PREFACE

This book is designed to fill a gap in the literature for training lawyers; it provides instruction on trial technique and the evidence rules in the same volume. The second edition reorganizes and expands the original book, including additional material on electronic evidence, developments in the law governing expert testimony, changes in the Federal Rules of Evidence, jurisprudential developments, and additional instruction in trial technique. The structure of the book has been changed to combine evidence and trial technique more cohesively.

As a trial practitioner and teacher of evidence and advocacy, I have been amazed at the absence of evidence instruction in many trial advocacy courses and the omission of practical material in evidence courses. The failure to teach practice is a common defect in legal instruction, but it is most glaring when a course in "evidence" does not cover how to introduce it. Teaching evidence without trial technique is like teaching surgery without explaining how to use a scalpel.

Trial advocacy courses suffer the mirror image of the same problem; they focus on practice, but rarely link the practice with the evidence rules. Additionally, the instruction often centers on delivery and style without addressing content. As a result, lawyers and students often do not understand how to use evidence to support a compelling story, or how to make advocacy techniques comply with evidence requirements. With the enactment of the federal rules of evidence and the adoption of evidence codes in many states, evidence rules are ever more consistently applied in trial, and lawyers must understand them to be effective.

By combining evidence and trial technique in a single volume, I hope to provide an instruction manual that is useful to both lawyers and students. The sections on evidence explain the rules to show how they should be applied at trial. They cover the substantive evidence rules — those dealing with foundations, relevance, hearsay, privileges, and other matters — but in a practical context. The discussion of trial technique not only makes use of evidence theory but covers methods for a compelling presentation.

The text addresses the practical methods of presenting evidence — direct and cross-examination and introducing exhibits — in combination with the requirements of the evidence rules. I include sufficient theory to permit the reader to understand the purpose and application of each rule. I also review the practical steps for compliance with the rules and provide examples to facilitate the reader's understanding of how to use them. Additionally, I discuss how to achieve the aims of advocacy while complying with the evidence rules, an aspect of trial advocacy that sorely needs attention.

The text provides a relatively elaborate discussion of the strategy and tactics of trial advocacy. I review fundamentals, but also address the nuances of trial presentation, and discuss both in light of the evidence rules. I attempt to provide insight into the "why" and "how" associated with various techniques. The explanations are basic enough for the beginner to understand and apply, but also provide more sophisticated suggestions for practitioners who have trial experience.

I also provide an extensive discussion of *preparing* for various aspects of the trial. Most people know that preparation is essential to success, but do not have a clear grasp of exactly what to do to be prepared. They may spend time in what they imagine is "preparation," but the effort produces few results. Based on years of learning from others and instructing students and lawyers in advocacy, I provide an explanation of "how to prepare." This material explains how to identify goals in trial, select and emphasize thematic points, prepare direct and cross-examination, and prepare for argument.

One practical problem in teaching trial technique is the abstract level of most instruction. Rarely are techniques discussed in the context of a specific case. As a result, the instruction often focuses on style rather than content and fails to address methods to build a thematic and compelling fact presentation. To remedy this problem I use a mock case file — *Danielson v. ComputerCentre Associates* — and provide examples of various techniques based on the material in the file. The Danielson examples include trial preparation, identification of themes and points of proof, presenting opening statement, conducting direct and cross-examination, and presenting closing argument. Through the examples I hope to show the reader how to accomplish substantive objectives — establishing facts and persuading the trier they are true — as well as how to achieve an impressive style.

This book synthesizes a wealth of knowledge I learned from others. I owe a great deal to lawyers who give their time to train members of the bar. I am particularly indebted to the founders of the University of Virginia Trial Advocacy Institute, Herbert J. Stern and Stephen A. Saltzburg: Herb Stern for offering his common sense insights in persuasion, and Steve Saltzburg for sharing his immense knowledge of evidence. My colleagues at that institute over more than a decade provided the foundation for this book. I owe Fred Lane for introducing me to trial technique, instructors in many advocacy seminars for improving my knowledge, my partners and colleagues for sharing their experience, and my students for helping me learn how to teach.

In preparing the second edition, I am indebted to my student assistants, Suzanne Levert and Annie Miller, for researching points in the manuscript and ensuring its accuracy. Brenda Joseph worked long hours in revising and formatting the material, with the aid of Kathleen King and others in my law firm. Steve Baron offered helpful suggestions for dealing with witnesses on cross-examination, particularly experts. My editors, Diane Allen, Debra Landis, and Seth Schoenfeld, edited the manuscript and provided helpful suggestions.

For the first edition, I owe thanks to Jennifer Hayes and Eric Zentner, my student assistants, for their help in researching and preparing the manuscript; Joyce Weinstein and Susan Miller for working long hours to type and revise it; George Freeman and Laurie Barcelona for reviewing the manuscript and offering helpful suggestions; and to my students for their suggestions. I appreciate the work and support of Heather White and Michael Morgan, my editors, and others who participated in its publication.

For both editions the Tulane University Law School generously supported my research assistants, and Stone, Pigman, Walther, Wittmann & Hutchinson provided valuable administrative support. I especially thank my wife, Terry, for her patience and support during the periods in which I was consumed with this project and for her suggestions for improving the manuscript.

DEDICATION

To Jack and Michelle

TABLE OF CONTENTS

CONTENTS

CONTENTS

CHAPTER 6. HEARSAY **193**

I. HEARSAY RULE

CONTENTS

CONTENTS

CONTENTS

CONTENTS

II. DEMONSTRATIVE EXHIBITS

III. OBJECTIONS AND SUBMISSIONS OF EXHIBITS TO JURY

CONTENTS

IV. ORIGINAL WRITING RULE

CHAPTER 9. CROSS-EXAMINATION AND IMPEACHMENT 415

I. CROSS-EXAMINATION

CONTENTS

CONTENTS

II. IMPEACHMENT

CONTENTS

CONTENTS

CONTENTS

CHAPTER 1

TRIAL PREPARATION

---

§ 1-1.   Introduction.

This book is designed to help lawyers and students use both the tools of advocacy and the rules of evidence to present compelling cases in trial. Good advocacy not only requires knowledge of effective trial techniques, but an understanding of the rules of evidence. This book reviews how the two can work together to produce good advocacy; indeed, the rules of evidence often promote good technique and effective advocacy can easily accommodate evidentiary requirements. Lawyers should strive to understand both as they develop the skills they will use in trial.

Preparation is the most effective weapon in any litigator's arsenal. This chapter deals with preparing for trial. It assumes you have already completed preliminary trial preparation, including a thorough factual inquiry and complete discovery on relevant issues. This book does not deal extensively with pretrial discovery, but it does discuss this material in connection with examining witnesses.

Legal research early in the litigation provides you with an understanding of the ultimate points that you need to prove. Pretrial investigation and discovery should provide a basis for determining how to prove the important points. You should determine the essential points early in the litigation and use them as a compass in pretrial preparation. This approach helps limit the diversion into detail that often befuddles litigators. Obviously, your vision of the case must change as you uncover facts in discovery, but the essentials usually remain. Focusing on the necessary elements of a favorable decision is a good way to keep the preparation directed.

You should locate and interview witnesses with knowledge of the facts well in advance of the trial. If witnesses are not allied with your side, you generally should depose them to document what they have to say. Use discovery to obtain relevant documents from the adverse side and third parties. You may use other discovery devices to ascertain your opponent's factual contentions and establish uncontested facts.

Pretrial research and investigation provide an understanding of the issues and knowledge of the facts. They do not provide a coherent plan for presenting a favorable version of the facts. This chapter addresses that problem: actual trial preparation. Sections 1-1–1-12 discuss means to best communicate points and a practical approach for planning the trial presentation. Sections 1-13–1-16 address counsel's demeanor during the trial, the best method for preparing arguments, and the preparation of pretrial memoranda.

§ 1-2. The Advocate's Pivotal Role in Trial.

Anyone who tries cases, or intends to try them, has to understand that the trial lawyer makes a huge difference in winning and losing a case. The lawyer is the central figure who communicates his client's story to the jury. Just as the quality of a story depends on the author or the richness of a painting on the artist, the persuasiveness of a case depends on the lawyer. If you take on the challenge of trying cases, you must accept the responsibility of doing it well.

A case presented in a trial is a creation — as much a product of the lawyer's conceptual skill as a recapitulation of evidence. The "facts" exist in jumbled pieces: in the memory of witnesses, buried in documents, or reflected in physical exhibits. The attorney is responsible for making sense of these pieces. He conceptualizes the theme of the case, plans its presentation, narrates his client's story, and documents that it is correct. The jury's acceptance of the attorney's version depends on the vividness and strength of this portrayal.

True, you cannot change the facts. Certain aspects of any case are troublesome. You may have to work with witnesses who are not very articulate and evidence that on the surface seems negative. But you have immense power to influence the impact of the evidence on the jury.

For one thing, the "facts" are not always set in stone. Facts are historic events; reconstructing them often is a difficult chore. The witnesses who know the facts must be located; you then may select which ones to use. Witnesses rarely remember more than portions of events, and their recollection often changes through self-interest or suggestion. Additionally, witnesses are not always articulate or descriptive. If you prepare their testimony to bring out the good "facts" and downplay the rest, you can increase the appeal of your story. Presentation makes a huge difference in the strength of any testimony.

Witnesses

Further, listeners do not always comprehend what they hear. Any teacher, and most students, know there are times in class when people daydream; the same is true in any extensive speech. Trials compound this problem because they last all day — not just the length of a lecture. For jurors to follow your story, you have to dramatize its important points. Making your good facts vivid gives them power and increases the apparent strength of your case.

3

Getting the most out of the facts involves two procedures: selection and emphasis. You must find the good facts and explain them in an impressive way. When a real estate agent tries to sell a house, she shows a photo of the best view; you must make the same portrayal of your case. You must identify the most powerful facts and use them as a basis for your theme. Then, by developing these facts and reinforcing them throughout the trial, you can make them seem more important and compelling than the facts supporting the adverse party.

You — the lawyer — are the person who can portray the facts in their best light. You are the one who explains your story — your version of events — at the beginning of the case. You prepare witnesses so they can describe what they recall and bring out the best points. You paint pictures in cross-examination, drawing out the factors that support your theory. You link the evidence and the facts in closing argument, explaining the logic of your portrayal. You are the architect and the builder of the case; its strength depends on your construction.

The message here is that you can make a difference. As in any contest, he who wins is most often the one who finds a way to win, within the rules. You have to believe in yourself and your ability to affect the outcome. You need to find and come to believe in the strengths of your case. You must conceive a presentation that brings them out.

Making a compelling case requires work. You must know the rules of evidence and the best techniques for bringing out strong points. With a good knowledge of fundamental techniques and a willingness to work, you can and will be effective.

§ 1-3. The Problem of Proving a Case.

The trial process is an exercise in determining and classifying facts. The law sets out the ultimate facts that make a difference to the outcome of a case. In turn, the determination of ultimate facts depends on many underlying facts. Additionally, the facts decide the equities — which party seems most "right" to an objective observer, apart from the law. Evidence is the means used to prove facts. Counsel's job is to marshal the evidence to prove the facts that support the key ultimate findings, while at the same time making the case understandable and convincing to the judge or jury.

In most cases the basic legal principles are settled. The law establishes a rule; the outcome of the case depends on how the facts relate to the rule. Thus, the existence of a contract may depend on whether the facts show, or negate, an intent to be bound; a finding of a tort may depend on whether the facts establish reasonable, or unreasonable, conduct by a defendant; and the validity of a bequest may turn on whether a testator had, or did not have, a sound mental capacity. In many cases, the outcome depends on a number of these ultimate factual conclusions. In any event, the primary focus in the trial is determining the facts. The authorities establish which facts have legal significance.

Even when the legal line is unclear, as when the precise issue is novel or the authorities conflict, the facts are crucial to the outcome. The facts are the basis for citing analogous legal principles, which influence the creation of law. Further, the equities usually affect the determination of a new legal rule, and the equities depend on facts. Thus, marshaling favorable facts is essential even when the law is uncertain.

Additionally, equitable considerations often influence how judges and juries look at the facts. Their view of who is "right" and "wrong" affects how they draw factual conclusions. On any issue the evidence may conflict; equity may influence the jury in determining which party is more correct. Equity also may influence determinations that have a large subjective component: intent, motive, bad faith, fault, and similar points.

You prove facts through the introduction of evidence. If believed, the evidence establishes fact. On any point the evidence may conflict, however, and the trier must decide which version to accept. Moreover, the sources of evidence — witnesses and exhibits — usually provide only parts of the picture. Turning the evidence into fact often involves inferences; in turn, drawing ultimate findings from a jumble of competing facts requires a logical evaluation of the presentations.

In this situation you as the advocate face a substantial challenge. You must convince a judge or jury to draw favorable conclusions on the legally important factual points, while persuading the trier that your position is right. This effort requires framing an overall thematic picture from pieces of evidence that are taken in a jumbled, adversary process.

You must marshal and interweave the evidence in a manner that compels the trier toward the desired factual conclusions. You must explain the meaning of evidence and reconcile facts that appear adverse. You must act as a choreographer, conceiving how to make the presentation, organizing the evidence for the best possible impression, and securing its introduction. Most important, you must portray a coherent factual picture, narrating the story and explaining why it follows from the evidence.

§ 1-4. Need for Preparation.

Preparation is essential to success in litigation, as it is in most aspects of being a lawyer. The effective advocate cannot rely on natural ability and charm to produce a winning case, nor can he expect fate to produce the winning point in an inspired cross-examination. Instead, good litigators depend mostly on hard, painstaking work. This preparation includes identifying the key points of proof, planning the presentation of testimony and exhibits, searching out points for cross-examination, thinking through the likely answers of witnesses and how to deal with these answers, and planning and rehearsing the arguments.

The presentation of a case requires imagination; you must preconceive how evidence might impress the judge and jury, how it will develop during the trial, what pitfalls may arise, and how best to get across the crucial points.[1] Since creative thought is a huge ingredient in crafting a good trial plan, and being creative is hard, you must be willing to work. Preparation can make a powerful, coherent case out of seemingly jumbled facts; without this effort, your presentation may be weak and confusing.

Preparation also is essential to a controlled and smooth presentation. The trial process is difficult to master. The pressure of winning or losing overwhelms many participants, especially those who are inexperienced. The need to "perform" — to speak aloud in front of others and make a good impression, saying and doing the right things in the right order with the right emotional flair — adds to the psychological strain.

Further, the process is adversarial and fraught with uncertainty. An opposing lawyer often tries to trip you up. Favorable witnesses, without advance help, may be unable to communicate their knowledge effectively. Adverse witnesses often attempt to shoot holes in your factual theories. The presence of a judge adds to the pressure, because the court will sustain objections to poorly formed questions and may even chastise you for asking them. Any normal person is likely to feel the strain of performing in these circumstances.

Too often, attorneys respond to the pressures of trial work by failing to confront them. They do not prepare adequately, relying on instinct rather than diligence to carry them through the ordeal. Unfortunately, the lack of preparation usually makes counsel appear befuddled and inept, which only increases the strain. The lawyer may panic, ask foolish questions, miss opportunities, and consequently fail the client. In contrast, an attorney who prepares is far better able to deal with pressure and uncertainty in trial. A well-crafted trial plan permits counsel to keep a steady course, appear in control, and manage adverse events.

A good trial plan, complete with a summary of points for each witness and an outline of questions, serves as an anchor to help you withstand surprises. When the judge makes an adverse ruling, a witness gives an unexpected response, or some other unfavorable surprise occurs, the natural response is to look perplexed and disappointed. Yet the best reaction is to take the event in stride and return to the theme. A trial plan helps you accomplish this goal.

§ 1-5. General Methods to Achieve an Effective Presentation.

The following approaches help make a case understandable and compelling. They are general methods, which are implemented through techniques that are explained later in the text.

---

[1] See generally Robert N. Sayler, *Communicating with Juries*, Keynote Address, The Annenberg Washington Program Conference, Fall 1993, 68 IN. L.J. 1093 (1993).

§ 1-5(a). Theme.

By necessity, speech is the primary means by which attorneys and witnesses communicate with the judge and jury. Yet the content of speech often eludes or confuses listeners. Few people remember the details of an oral presentation even a few hours after hearing it; with the passage of days, a listener usually remembers almost nothing about it. The tendency to forget oral statements is compounded in a trial, where the stories conflict, the witnesses blend together, and the presentations may be boring. In this situation isolated statements generally do not have a big impact.[2]

One way to get your case across in this environment is to use a theme. A listener may miss or forget isolated statements but will remember the points that you hammer home throughout the trial. Indeed, a speaker's overall theme — the general concept that she emphasizes throughout a presentation — is the type of message that often endures with an audience.

You should concentrate on the facts in identifying a theme. You should ask: What is the best general statement I can make about my case? Sometimes there are several general factual points, which can be used as subthemes to contribute to a general theme. Pick out only a few general points, however, as a multiplicity of themes diminishes the impact of them all.

Devise ways to "work" the theme in the trial. Both the opening statement and closing argument should be built on the theme. Emphasize and develop the best factual points — the ones that make up the theme — in direct examination. Employ cross-examination, in part, to gain concessions to portions of the theme. Develop these points by making "mountains out of molehills," building points through specific, related questions.

Generally, the theme should *not* be allegorical or purely conceptual. The use of a conceptual model as a theme usually does not work because the facts rarely fit the model exactly, and an allegorical point sometimes can be turned around. An allegorical theme is a comparative device to illustrate a point about the facts — say a quotation from literature or a reference to a historical event — rather than a thematic description built on facts themselves. The reference is often confusing and at least diverts attention from the actual facts. Further, if the allegory easily can be adjusted to work for the opposing side, it may provide a devastating weapon in your opponent's argument.

Additionally, an attorney taken with his own allegorical concept may concentrate too much on the allegory and not enough on the case, a point that can be made by the opposing party: "My opponent keeps reciting poetry, but doesn't

---

[2] Many studies have stressed the need for the attorney to tie in each piece of evidence to the overall theme. See, e.g., *Jury Comprehension in Complex Cases,* 1989 A.B.A. LITIG. SEC. REP. 34–37, 49; William S. Barley, *Tie Your Case Together with a Good Theme,* 37 Trial 58 (2001).

really address the facts of this case. Perhaps he knows his case is not very convincing." Thus, you usually should use the strongest factual points as the basis for your theme.

This advice is not meant to suggest that you should never use analogies or literary allusions in argument. These tools can be useful in illustrating specific points. But you should not explain your whole case through an allegorical theme because you will divert yourself from the main message.

§ 1-5(b). Story.

The best way to explain a jumble of evidence is through a story — a "word picture" of the events at issue. A story is easy to follow, even for someone unfamiliar with a case. Thus, it leads to quick and easy comprehension. Additionally, a word picture allows you to fill in gaps in the evidence, inserting inferences that arguably flow from the facts. Thus, a story can be a powerful, yet seemingly objective, means of arguing facts.

You should present the story in both the opening statement and the closing argument. Moreover, you should structure your presentations so that pieces of the word picture emerge throughout the trial — in the descriptions provided by favorable witnesses, the facts linked together in cross-examination, the opinions of experts, hypothetical questions, and key exhibits. In this way, the evidentiary presentations reinforce important parts of the story.

Of course, the evidence must fairly support your word picture. You must be confident that your evidence will support your factual assertions directly or circumstantially. Ethical rules require that you have a good faith basis for factual claims. Additionally, your credibility depends on backing up the factual claims with evidence.

§ 1-5(c). Visual Aids.

Visual aids provide another method to overcome the elusiveness of speech. Pictures, diagrams, maps, charts, models, and other demonstrative exhibits can be effective in making an impression on jurors. The real evidence in the case — exhibits such as a murder weapon, bloodstained clothing, a contract, and similar items — also have an impact. Even in questioning a witness, you can aid understanding by having the witness show the listeners "how high," "how big," and other such descriptions that are hard to explain verbally. These techniques help the listeners visualize facts; once visualized the facts will remain in the mind's eye.

§ 1-5(d). Simplicity.

Finding a simple way to explain a case is important to an effective presentation. For some reason, the more you explain a point to someone, the less likely he is to understand it. Unfortunately, attorneys often tend to complicate even simple concepts. Instead, they should do the opposite, finding explanations that persons of average intelligence can easily understand.

Conceiving direct explanations is not easy. You should think through arguments to make sure they are logical, internally consistent, and uncomplicated. Get rid of legalese, translating legal concepts into everyday language. Explain trade jargon and scientific or technical terms. Try out the explanations on third parties, preferably nonlawyers and persons unfamiliar with the facts. Discussing the points may clarify them for you, permitting a better explanation.

A simple explanation usually starts with a brief overview, followed by an orderly description of the underlying material. It requires an easy-to-follow organization — usually chronological or topical. The explanation must be suited to the unfamiliar ear. Too much information — especially complex detail — can easily confuse the jury. You need to consider the listeners and their ability to absorb information, and tailor the presentation for easy understanding.

§ 1-5(e). Consistency.

An essential aspect of a winning case is consistency. Inconsistent arguments establish that counsel is wrong at least on some points; it is not much of a jump to infer she may be wrong on others. Thus, you must find a way to make the facts and arguments work *together*, in a coherent, noncontradictory structure.

A consistent presentation requires an overall explanation of "what happened" that reconciles the facts. Of course, you usually cannot make all the evidence work together, because some of the evidence will conflict in almost any case. A good theory explains most of the evidence, however, and should provide a picture that reconciles the important facts. Often you can show that superficially harmful facts, in context, actually support your overall theory.

You should identify and find a way to deal with the facts that do not fit your picture of the case. Sometimes that accommodation requires adjusting the picture, preferably before the case begins. Avoid falling into a pattern of providing "today's explanation" of harmful facts, because today's explanation often contradicts yesterday's theory. The inconsistencies will be apparent to the jury and great fodder for your opponent's closing argument.

§ 1-6. Need to Plan in Writing for the Trial.

Because the trial requires conceiving a presentation, you need to plan it in advance. The best approach for planning is to prepare a written trial outline. The trial outline should in turn be used as the basis for other outlines — those for opening statement, closing argument, and the interrogation of witnesses. Writing out these plans helps you conceive the best presentation and, later, assists in its implementation.

A good written plan is essential to almost any creation. How does a great artist create a masterpiece? He begins with a rough sketch and improves it until he is ready to paint. How does an architect plan a beautiful building? She sketches, re-sketches and sketches again. How does a writer create a novel? He outlines, fills in the outline, drafts a first effort and improves it until he has a finished product. How do many lawyers prepare for trial? They look over the file for a while and show up to see what happens.

Writing out a plan for the trial raises your intensity level as you engage in planning. For some reason, if you merely think about a problem, the mind deals with it in a passive way. Writing down a point is a small act of creation; it requires an active step in thinking. This step may provoke thoughts about related points and promote the creative process. Generally, when you sit down and write out points and how you intend to prove them, you think of ways to accomplish your goals that you otherwise might not have conceived. Additionally, the process of writing out points may reveal weaknesses, organizational problems, and other defects that you otherwise would not see.

Most lawyers would concede the need to create a written plan for the trial, but many neglect this requirement. The trial outline is much like the outline for a major paper or book; people know they need to have one, but often cannot quite bring themselves to prepare it. As a result, the paper reflects a stream-of-consciousness quality: rambling, disorganized, undirected. A trial is much the same, except the advocate who lacks a plan is much more at the mercy of events than a writer.

The following sections provide a simple, easy-to-follow method for planning the trial. The fact that the method is simple does not mean that planning is easy, but anyone who is willing to work can prepare a good trial plan. You need to have a trial notebook that contains your written material. Preparing a subject matter outline is a good first step in the planning process; this outline can be converted easily into a trial outline. Using the trial outline, you can prepare to interrogate witnesses on both direct and cross-examination. You can also use these outlines to prepare the opening statement and closing argument.

§ 1-7.   Trial Notebook.

You should create a "trial notebook," a binder containing your entire written trial plan. This notebook should contain the trial outline, outlines of arguments, questions or outlines for witnesses, key legal research, and other information.[3] The trial notebook provides ready access to the material necessary for conducting the trial. Additionally, by preparing it, you ensure that you anticipate most problems and make provisions for dealing with them. The trial notebook acts as the road map for the trial, permitting a directed, forceful presentation.

---

[3] James W. McElhaney, *Trial Notebook: Linking*, 19 LITIG. 59 (1993).

You should prepare the trial notebook on loose-leaf pages in a binder. Using a loose-leaf binder permits you to supplement the material as necessary. The notebook should be tabbed by sections: Trial Outline, Opening Statement Outline, Witnesses (each separately tabbed), and Closing Argument Outline. If you expect legal points or admissibility issues to come up during the trial, include a section summarizing applicable authorities.

The following sections might be tabbed in a typical trial notebook:

1. Trial Outline
2. Opening Statement Outline
3. Witnesses on Direct
   a. Louise Brown
   b. Ben Brown
   c. Joe Smith
   [etc.]
4. Witnesses on Cross
   a. Ben Davis
   b. Fred Jones
   c. Mary Ellis
   [etc.]
5. Closing Argument Outline
6. Jury Instructions
7. Evidence/Authorities

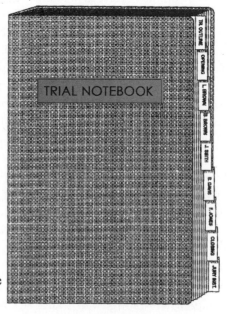

A typical trial notebook, with appropriate tabs, would look like the drawing.

§ 1-8. Trial Outline.

A trial outline provides the basic plan for presenting evidence in the trial. This document should contain a list of witnesses counsel expects to call and those to be called by the adverse party. It should have the points to be proven with each witness and the exhibits that the witness will identify.

Preparing the trial outline helps you identify the facts that you need to prove and conceive the best way to present them. An outline also promotes a thematic presentation by helping you visualize the overall case. Additionally, once you prepare the outline, you can more easily prepare for individual witnesses. Preparing a trial outline involves two steps: First, you should conceive a subject matter outline, identifying the points to prove and how to prove them; second, you should convert this subject matter outline into a plan for presenting the evidence — the trial outline.

§ 1-8(a).   Step 1. Subject Matter Outline.

Preparing a subject matter outline is a good preliminary step to developing the trial outline. A subject matter outline focuses on the issues; you first identify all the major points that *need* to be proven, then determine which witnesses and exhibits can be used to prove them.[4] You should review the legal research and determine the factual elements you require to make out a case. List these points and break them into subpoints, along with any favorable equitable facts and other facts you need for a complete story. Thereafter, list all witnesses who can address each point along with the relevant exhibits they can identify. You should review deposition summaries, witness statements, exhibits, and similar material to determine the facts to which each witness can testify.[5] You should remember that you may prove positive points both with favorable and adverse witnesses. Indeed, a witness called by the opposing side may provide the most compelling evidence for a point if he concedes it during cross-examination. In addition to positive points for adverse witnesses, you should identify points that the opposing party is likely to make. This action enables you to list the relevant counterpoints along with the witnesses and exhibits that support those contentions.

An abbreviated example of a subject matter outline is set forth below. The outline sets out points that might be made in a suit for breach of contract and fraud brought by the owners of a failed franchise, who claim the franchisor promised services and equipment that were never delivered, and failed to disclose material information. The outline is based on a trial advocacy problem script entitled *Danielson v. ComputerCentre Associates*, which is reproduced in Appendix A.[6]

In the problem Jack Danielson and his wife, Margaret Danielson, allege that they were induced to purchase a retail computer franchise in the City of Middletown through the fraud of ComputerCentre Associates. They assert that Dale Atkins, the principal of ComputerCentre Associates, and Jene Nelsen, its sales manager, misrepresented key facts to induce them into the franchise. The Middletown franchise failed after 15 months.

You may wish to review the problem script in Appendix A to gain familiarity with the evidence in *Danielson v. ComputerCentre Associates*, as the problem is used in examples throughout the text. Briefly, the presentation for the Danielsons would encompass all the promises made by representatives of ComputerCentre, Dale Atkins and Jene Nelsen, the inconsistencies between those

---

[4] See generally Edward L. Wolf, *Preparing a Case for Trial,* 2 Prac. Litig. 61 (1991).

[5] See David Schum & Peter Tillers, *Marshaling Evidence for Adversary Litigation,* 13 Cardozo L. Rev. 657, 659 (1991); see also Peter Tilles & David Schum, *A Theory of Preliminary Fact Investigation,* 24 U.C. Davis L. Rev. 931 (1991).

[6] The problem is used and reproduced with the permission of the Practicing Law Institute and the author, Kent Sinclair.

representations and the facts, and the failure to disclose key information. A good thematic focus might make use of documents indicating Atkins thought he could take advantage of the Danielsons because they were "yokels" and "clowns."

For ComputerCentre, counsel would emphasize the overall success of the company's franchises throughout the country, the popularity and profitability of these franchises, and the unavoidability of the temporary problems experienced in fulfilling contractual obligations. A thematic focus might be the Danielsons' unwillingness to follow suggestions of the franchisor, their failure to employ knowledgeable personnel, and their lack of attention to their business.

To identify the evidentiary points to prove for the Danielsons, counsel would be guided by the legal rules. To show fraud the attorney has to prove misrepresentations and/or omissions of material facts. This in turn requires counsel to identify the false statements made by ComputerCentre Associates, the facts that should have been disclosed, and the representations in which material facts were omitted. The "points to prove" would include (1) false representations, (2) omissions, and (3) actual facts.

Additionally, counsel would have to demonstrate the impact of the fraud on the franchise and prove damages. He would have to show that ComputerCentre's actions caused the Danielsons to fail, a likely focus of contention. These categories broadly reflect the areas of proof required under the relevant rules of law. The points of proof within each category depend on facts uncovered in investigation and discovery. These facts may be gleaned from the problem script.

The subject matter outline below covers only the fraud-related issues and does not address additional claims or counterclaims; a full outline would address all the issues that might come up in the trial. The points of proof are necessarily abbreviated, as they would be in any outline prepared by a lawyer already familiar with the facts. For each general point, the outline lists sources of proof. Obviously counsel would bring out many underlying facts in support of general points. The outline refers to certain exhibits repeatedly because they support multiple points.

Subject Matter Outline

POINTS TO PROVE	WITNESS	EXHIBITS
1. Background to seeking franchise	Jack Danielson Margaret Danielson	
2. Representations of ComputerCentre Associates	(J. Nelson can't deny any because can't remember any.)	
a. Profit – San Francisco franchise	J. Danielson M. Danielson D. Atkins	Meeting agenda
b. Training support – Sales and service personnel – Ten day initial session – Technical facility	J. Danielson M. Danielson D. Atkins	Franchise agreement Wall Street Journal ad Meeting agenda
c. Delivery of products – Inventory management – 24-hour shipping	J. Danielson M. Danielson D. Atkins	Meeting agenda Franchise agreement Wall Street Journal ad
d. Advertising support – Institutional ads – Local ad support	J. Danielson M. Danielson D. Atkins	Franchise agreement Meeting agenda
e. Software for office, business use	J. Danielson M. Danielson D. Atkins	
3. Failures to disclose facts		
a. Double markup	J. Danielson M. Danielson D. Atkins	Wall Street Journal ad Meeting agenda Franchise disclosure form
b. Single supplier (Wizard)	J. Danielson M. Danielson D. Atkins	Franchise disclosure form
c. D. Atkins's interest in Wizard	J. Danielson M. Danielson D. Atkins	Franchise disclosure form
d. D. Atkins's relation to Wizard president	J. Danielson M. Danielson D. Atkins	Franchise disclosure form

POINTS TO PROVE	WITNESS	EXHIBITS
e. Delayed shipping of Wizard products	J. Danielson M. Danielson D. Atkins	Franchise disclosure form
f. Lack of technical facility	J. Danielson M. Danielson D. Atkins	Wall Street Journal ad Meeting agenda Franchise agreement
4. Actual facts a. San Francisco franchise had single markup	J. Nelsen	3/2 franchise status report
b. Middletown got double markup	D. Anderson J. Nelsen	3/2 franchise status report
c. D. Atkins's view — Danielsons "clowns"	D. Atkins	3/25 letter
d. D. Atkins had an interest in Wizard — brother was president	D. Atkins T. Johansen	3/25 letter
e. ComputerCentre had no training facility	T. Johansen	
f. Three days' initial training provided rather than two weeks	J. Danielson M. Danielson J. Nelsen	
g. Technical training not provided	J. Danielson M. Danielson D. Atkins T. Johansen	Internal memorandum
h. History of delays in product delivery – Loss of sales	T. Johansen	
i. Middletown product delivery delayed – Initially – Thereafter	J. Danielson M. Danielson T. Johansen L. Walsh D. Anderson	

POINTS TO PROVE	WITNESS	EXHIBITS
j. Software for business/ office use not supplied for a year	J. Danielson M. Danielson D. Atkins	
k. Advertising support curtailed	J. Danielson M. Danielson D. Anderson J. Nelsen	1/17 memorandum
5. Impact and Failure of business		
a. Loss of sales/causes	J. Danielson M. Danielson D. Anderson L. Walsh	
b. Impact of double markup	D. Anderson	12 months income statement Financial statement
c. Losses	D. Anderson M. Danielson	12 months income statement Financial statement
d. Letter of credit loss	J. Danielson D. Anderson	Letter of credit 5/7 letter 6/30 letter
e. Failure	M. Danielson D. Anderson	
6. Damages		
a. Impact of business failure on Danielsons	J. Danielson M. Danielson	
b. Franchise fee	J. Danielson M. Danielson	Franchise agreement Check
c. Business loss	D. Anderson	12 months income statement Financial statement
d. Future profit	D. Anderson	

§ 1-8(b).   Step 2. Trial Outline.

Once you prepare the subject matter outline, you can easily transpose the entries into a trial outline. This process involves determining the order of witnesses and the probable order of subjects and exhibits to be presented with each witness.

In deciding how to order the witnesses, you should seek a presentation that best gets the case across to the jury.[7] The first witness might be one who has the broadest knowledge of the facts and can provide the best overview.[8] Alternatively, you might want to lead with the witness who makes the best impression. You ordinarily should prove the basic facts of a case before calling experts to give opinions on the facts. You must accommodate witnesses' schedules, calling them in a way that minimizes inconvenience and maximizes cooperation.[9] The most important objective, however, is to achieve a coherent, forceful presentation.

As you plan the Trial Outline, you should also begin considering the order in which you will present information to the factfinder. In presenting your opening statement and examining witnesses, you cannot openly argue points, yet you can plan your presentation of information for a persuasive effect. The context in which listeners hear factual points may make a huge difference in their perception of the equities. Thus, you must find the best order in which to introduce these points, both as you describe the case and as you develop the testimony of witnesses.

Your review of the Danielson problem, for example, will reveal that Computer-Centre did not perform timely on all of the promises made to the Danielsons. Counsel for ComputerCentre likely will determine that conceding some of the lapses, but denying that they caused the Danielsons' failure, is the best strategy to deal with these facts. In this connection, the general success of other franchises, even in the face of the same problems, is a key indicator that the failures did not cause the Danielsons' loss. Introducing the information about the success and profitability of other franchises first may make the concessions seem much less significant. If this information were covered after counsel concealed ComputerCentre's lapses, the point might seem defensive and inadequate to defuse the concessions.

If you intend to prove points without calling witnesses — say with a stipulation, through judicial notice, or in an exhibit stipulated as authentic — you should list the means of proof and point to be proven in the outline. This action helps you determine the best time to introduce the evidence and helps you remember to offer it.

For adverse witnesses, you should review discovery and other material to determine the favorable points that the witness should concede. List these points.

---

[7] See generally Richard M. Zielinski, *Prepare Your Witness for Trial*, 35 PRAC. LAW 71 (1989).

[8] *Id.*

[9] *Id.*

Additionally, anticipate the points your opponent is likely to bring out and develop counterpoints, including fact concessions that erode the witness's testimony and matters that undermine the witness's credibility. You also should identify the exhibits that may be useful in the cross-examination.

The trial outline provides an overview of the points you will make with each witness. In preparing for the witness's examination, you may adapt the outline, fill in material for clarity and completeness, and order the points for the best possible effect. An example of a trial outline for a single witness from the *Danielson* case is set forth below. Similar outlines should be prepared for all the witnesses and ordered according to your planned presentation.

Trial Outline

WITNESS	POINTS TO PROVE	EXHIBITS
J. Danielson	1. Background	
	2. Representations of ComputerCentre	
	a. Profit (San Francisco)	Meeting agenda
	b. Training support	Wall St. Journal ad
	– 10-day initial session	Meeting agenda
	– Sales personnel	Franchise agreement
	– Service personnel	
	– Technical facility	
	c. Delivery of products	Wall St. Journal ad
	– Inventory management	Meeting agenda
	– 24-hour shipping	Franchise agreement
	d. Advertising support	Meeting agenda
	– Institutional ads	Franchise agreement
	– Local ad support	
	e. Software for office, business use	
	3. Failures to disclose facts	
	a. Double markup	Meeting agenda
		Franchise disclosure form
	b. Single supplier (Wizard)	Meeting agenda
		Franchise disclosure form
	c. D. Atkins' interest in Wizard	Meeting agenda
		Franchise disclosure form
	d. D. Atkins' relation to Wizard president	Meeting agenda
		Franchise disclosure form
	e. Delayed shipping of Wizard products	Meeting agenda
		Franchise disclosure form
	f. Lack of technical facility	Meeting agenda
		Franchise disclosure form

WITNESS	POINTS TO PROVE	EXHIBITS
	4. Nonperformance	
	a. Only three days' initial training	
	b. Technical training not provided	
	c. Middletown product delivery delayed	
	d. Software for business use not provided	
	e. Advertising support curtailed	
	5. Failure of business	
	a. Loss of sales/causes	
	b. Losses	
	c. Failure	
	6. Damages	
	a. Franchise fee	Franchise agreement
		Check
	b. Impact on Danielsons of business failure	

§ 1-9. Preparation for Questioning Witnesses.

The trial notebook should contain sections, tabbed for easy identification, for counsel's examination notes — those she will use in questioning each witness. The attorney should at least prepare an outline of questions. The general points identified in the trial outline provide a basis for this endeavor, but the outline should be much more detailed. Some attorneys prefer to write out the actual questions, listing with each question the expected points of response.

In complex cases attorneys often prepare separate binders for each witness. These binders include the notes for the witness, a deposition summary, a copy of the deposition, any prior statements, and other relevant information. Counsel should ensure that exhibits to be used with the witness are readily available. Separate binders may be desirable if there are many witnesses, the testimony is lengthy, or the material needed in examining witnesses is voluminous.

The issue of whether to write out questions often arises in advocacy seminars. Many experienced advocates belittle the use of notes, advising that the attorney perform in a more impromptu fashion to enhance eye contact and promote a conversational exchange. This advice often reflects an unjustified focus on form over substance, however; in a seminar, looking good may be more important than winning the case. Further, an instructor need not know much about the problem to deliver a critique that concentrates on delivery.

In a real trial the factfinder is likely to be interested in the facts and evidence, and a well-planned presentation is at least as important as a good style. Additionally, few lawyers have the presence of mind to use a purely impromptu approach and still make all the essential points. Under the pressure of a trial it is often a struggle to direct the witness's testimony without undue leading, elicit the correct testimony, counter objections, offer exhibits, and attend to other tasks; trying to accomplish these goals "off the cuff" often leads to an inept presentation. Thus, you should at least prepare notes for examining witnesses.

The only problem with preparing actual questions is that you may become too tied to the script. When a witness wanders off the point and yet provides pertinent information, you may stick with the script, failing to follow up and pursue the point. Additionally, an attorney with prepared questions often spends too much time looking down for the next question, disrupting eye contact and losing control of the exchange. Yet prepared questions can be a great help if you use them as a resource rather than a crutch and refer to them unobtrusively.

If you write out questions, make a special effort to listen to answers, look at the witness and jurors, and follow up with off-script questions when necessary. If you can do so, the prepared questions will be an advantage, because a script helps ensure that you ask questions correctly. Additionally, prepared questions provide a great safety net when you forget a train of thought, lose an objection, receive a bad answer, or run into other unexpected problems. They allow you to move on as if nothing occurred.

As explained below, whether or not you write out questions, at least prepare notes of the points you wish to elicit from each witness. The notes should be detailed enough to ensure that you have thought through the examination of the witness, anticipated problems, and prepared to deal with them.

§ 1-9(a).   Direct Examination.

The notes for direct examination at least should include a list of the evidentiary points you wish to make with each witness. In effect, you should have a point summary of what the witness is expected to say.[10] These notes give direction to the examination and help ensure that you elicit all the important testimony. With them, an experienced attorney might not need to prepare questions. Alternatively, you can prepare the actual questions and note the points the witness should establish below the questions. The point summary permits you to follow up if the witness misunderstands the question or gives an incomplete response.[11]

To one side of the page, next to the questions, list exhibits where you intend to have them identified. You also may include reminders signaling you to let the jury know when topical transitions occur, to mark and offer exhibits, to make necessary references to demonstrative exhibits, and other matters. Sample outlines for questioning witnesses on direct examination are contained in § 7-8.

---

[10] See Ronald J. Allen, *The Nature of Juridical Proof,* 13 CARDOZO L. REV. 373, 409 (1991).

[11] Newell Edenfield, *Trying a Case to a Jury,* LITIG. 5 (Mar. 1994).

Within the tabbed notebook section for each witness, behind the witness outline, you should include summaries of that witness's deposition testimony, prior statements, and other material you may need during the questioning. Sometimes you must refresh the recollection of a witness on direct examination, even when the testimony has been prepared. Additionally, a witness may surprise you by turning hostile on the stand and it may be necessary to impeach his testimony.[12] For witnesses who have been prepared, these problems should be rare, but you still should be ready for them. A discussion of preparing the witness for direct examination is contained in Chapter 7.

§ 1-9(b). Cross-Examination.

Cross-examination requires even more preparation than direct. Generally, you need to select points that adverse witnesses must concede — based on analysis of their prior statements, litigation position, allegiances, or other material developed for trial — and "paint pictures" by developing these points in cross-examination. You should prepare most of the cross-examination for a typical witness before the witness takes the stand. Unfortunately, many attorneys never realize the power of selection and emphasis in cross-examination and fail to prepare an interrogation that makes positive points; instead, they simply pick at the direct testimony. This approach usually ends up re-emphasizing the adverse party's main points.

Generally, you should prepare precise questions that call for "yes" answers. You may rely on prior statements, such as deposition testimony, in determining what facts the witness will concede. Exact questions based on prior statements make denial difficult, because equivocation or denial opens the witness to impeachment; inexact questions permit equivocation and allow the witness to explain inconsistencies when the impeachment occurs.[13] Thus, you should write out the points you wish to make through your questions, listing deposition references or other citations next to the questions for easy impeachment. Additionally, list exhibits where you intend to use them. Cross-examination is discussed in Chapter 9.

Preparation of points or questions does not mean that you should be bound to the script in cross-examination. You should work on maintaining eye contact and listening to answers.[14] Obviously, the witnesses will not always cooperate, there may be surprises, and you may have to counter unanticipated assertions. You should follow up — leaving the script — to the extent necessary. The outline

---

[12] See FED. R. EVID. 607, permitting the impeachment of any witness.

[13] TERRENCE ANDERSON & WILLIAM TWINING, ANALYSIS OF EVIDENCE (1991); WILLIAM TWINING & DAVID MIERS, HOW TO DO THINGS WITH RULES (3d ed. 1991).

[14] ROBERT V. WELLS, SUCCESSFUL TRIAL TECHNIQUES OF EXPERT PRACTITIONERS 43–44 (1988).

of questions nevertheless supplies a detailed "game plan," keeping you on course and allowing a return to the plan after necessary deviations.

Preparing for cross-examination makes the attorney much more effective at trial. This process requires you to imagine what the witness will say and craft a plan for dealing with those assertions. Often, by conceiving in advance the give and take of the examination, you can prepare approaches that leave the witness no room for escape. Cornering a witness is never easy, but it is much more difficult when you "wing" a cross-examination.

The section of the trial book for each cross-examination should include prior statements, deposition summaries, and other documents that may be needed during the examination. You need easy access to this material for a crisp presentation; a lawyer's search for a missing document, while everyone in the courtroom waits, can detract from factual points and embarrass the advocate. If the witness has been deposed, you should have the deposition readily available. Effective impeachment requires an *immediate* reference to a prior statement. Noting page numbers and page references from the deposition next to questions permits you to refer quickly to the impeachment material.

§ 1-10.   Outlines for Opening Statement and Closing Argument.

You should outline and rehearse the opening statement in advance of the trial. Mark the Opening Statement Outline with a tab in the trial book in its logical place — after the Trial Outline and before the tabs for each witness. You also should at least outline, and preferably rehearse, the key points of the Closing Argument. Include this outline in the Trial Book, after the witness tabs.

Generally, you should be able to look at the jury and speak conversationally as you present both the opening statement and closing argument. Thus, having outlines does not mean that you should rely on them as you deliver the presentations. Preparing the outlines allows you to conceptualize the areas to cover and the best order for reviewing them.

The outlines serve as a basis for rehearsal, which permits the development of a good extemporaneous presentation. Additionally, should you lose your train of thought in the opening statement or closing argument, you can refer to the outline to get back on track. Section 1-14 discusses the preparation and delivery of the opening statement, closing argument, and other arguments. The content of the opening statement is discussed in Chapter 3, and the content of the closing argument in Chapter 12.

§ 1-11.   Authorities.

An effective attorney must anticipate evidentiary and legal issues that may arise during the trial. To the extent you have not briefed key authorities in advance, you should summarize them, or copy them, and include them in the trial notebook. If proposed jury instructions have not been separately briefed, include a section containing copies of the desired instructions (the originals will be given to the judge) and supporting authorities. Once the judge decides on jury instructions, insert a copy in the trial notebook and highlight key instructions for easy reference.

§ 1-12. Exhibit Books.

You should organize the exhibits prior to the trial and ensure that they are easily accessible. In many cases the exhibits are voluminous, and copies must be made for the court and other parties. Thus, you often must deal with a large number of documents. Organizing exhibits in advance eliminates confusion and saves trial time. If the court permits, you may prepare exhibit books in advance for the judge and jurors.

If you do not prepare exhibit books, you should at least have the originals and necessary copies of exhibits organized so that you can find them quickly. One option is to maintain the exhibits and copies in loose-leaf binders, with tabs to identify each exhibit. Another is to keep the exhibits and copies in folders, marked for ready identification and organized in the order of their likely use. Organizing the exhibits in advance allows you to avoid the embarrassment of searching for a lost exhibit during trial. Chapter 8 discusses the introduction and use of exhibits.

§ 1-13. Counsel's Demeanor at Trial.

An issue that perplexes many advocates, especially inexperienced ones, is the appropriate demeanor to use in persuading a jury. The advocate, after all, is the central figure in presenting the client's case. To present it in a good light, he needs to make a good impression. Most lawyers understand that advocates must be performers, actors, bluffers, sympathetic figures, committed believers, and genuine, sincere persons — often simultaneously — but the question remains: How do you achieve and combine these qualities for the best effect?

Psychologists undoubtedly could provide a great deal of advice on the best personal style for persuasion. Experienced advocates often have their own theories, which usually resemble their own styles. Any person can gain insight into the problem, however, by simply placing himself in the position of a juror and asking: What style would I find persuasive? A common sense answer to that question reveals the following traits.

§ 1-13(a). Genuine Self.

In deciding the personal style to present to the jury, the best advice is: "Be yourself." The most effective advocates are those that come across as genuine and sincere; attempting to adopt a new personality can only leave a false impression. Undoubtedly you may need to adapt your personal style for maximum effectiveness, as when the reserved lawyer introduces "oomph" into his voice, but a complete transformation is not advisable. Everyone has aspects of personality that are attractive to others; the best style takes advantage of these qualities, while adjusting them for the special needs of the trial setting.

"Being yourself" does not mean ignoring the need to improve your style. It does mean that you should recognize and value the advantages that you possess. Do not try to be someone else, because you will lose your own attributes. Instead, be yourself, but try to recognize areas that need improvement and alter your style to change them.

The shy, retiring person may believe he has no capacity for success in the courtroom, but this person often comes across as truly sincere and credible. Moreover, a low-key person can easily inject pep into his delivery without appearing too aggressive. A boisterous type can be very successful at capturing attention and dominating the courtroom. He should concentrate on control, modifying his approach to take on a thoughtful component. In both cases counsel uses, but adapts, his own personal style for the best effect.

§ 1-13(b).　Discussion Leader.

The advocate should adopt a role similar to that played by a good discussion leader in a classroom. You should control the presentation, but should treat the jurors as participants in the process of coming to a conclusion. Although the jurors do not speak during the trial, you should realize that they are sifting and evaluating evidence, putting pieces together, evaluating credibility, and searching for a just result. You should try to be a leader in this process. Without lecturing or talking down to the jurors, help them understand the evidence as it is introduced.

The discussion leader in a classroom is different from the students. She has a responsibility to ensure that the subject matter is explored properly and the class learns the lesson. Similarly, an attorney has a responsibility to the client and the justice system to present the case fully and in accord with ethical and legal rules. Thus, you cannot be a friend or confidant to the jurors. This barrier does not prevent you from fostering a shared relationship with the jurors, however, in which all seek to determine the facts and reach the "correct" result. By adopting a discussion leader mentality, you place yourself in a good posture for persuasion.

§ 1-13(c).　Projection.

The advocate must exert control over the proceeding. In presenting a case, he acts as a kind of ringmaster — the person who presents and brings meaning to the evidence. To fill this role, the attorney needs to make an impression that leads the listeners to accept him as director of the presentation. In part, the advocate must exude a "presence" and project it throughout the courtroom.

Obviously, some people have more natural presence than others. Anyone can take steps, however, to project to an audience. The most important element of projection is volume. You must speak loud enough so everyone in the courtroom — not just the jury — can clearly hear. Pitch your voice so that it is audible to those in the last row of the audience, even if they are seated behind you.

If you speak only to the judge or jury, those in the courtroom audience become inattentive. They may whisper to themselves, read, or simply tune out. Unfortunately, the jurors may sense this loss of attention and their own concentration may wane. Few great speakers try to captivate parts of an audience, and speakers who address parts of an audience rarely command attention. Thus, you must try to convince *everyone* that you are right. Projecting throughout the courtroom, will make you more successful with your real targets — the jurors.

Adequate volume also provides an authoritative air to your statements. You appear much more confident, in control, and "right" when you speak loudly. This trait makes it appear that you know what you are doing, even if perhaps you do not. Thus, volume is essential to a strong presentation.

Many attorneys underestimate the attitude adjustment, and volume increase, that are necessary to project oneself in a courtroom. You need to focus on reaching everyone present in court. The advocacy instructor's refrain — "get the voice up" — should encourage you to set the volume a bit higher than you might believe necessary. This action will serve you well in holding the attention of the listeners.

§ 1-13(d). Command and Credibility.

Perhaps the single most important attribute in convincing others is factual command and credibility. As the trial progresses, the jurors should come to regard your assertions as fact. The necessary credibility depends in part on an authoritative manner — discussed above — but it also requires that you deliver evidence to support fact assertions and have a basis for points posed in cross-examination.

A credible presentation requires preparation. You should know the case completely. You should provide accurate descriptions that do not unduly stretch the evidence. You must show direction throughout the trial and appear in control of the facts. These objectives require connecting the evidence to your central theme. A focused and crisp presentation of testimony and exhibits also enhances your credibility.

In cross-examination you must be prepared with material for impeachment, but use it to establish your own accuracy as much as the witness's shortcomings. Thus, for instance, if the witness denies fact X, you should be prepared to immediately counter: "In your deposition, page 42, you said X, is that right?" This approach gives the impression that you have a basis for everything you say.

An alternative approach, "fishing" for favorable concessions, indicates that you are trying to find out the facts, just like everybody else.

As the trial progresses, the jurors should increasingly accept the idea that you knew the facts from the beginning. The only way to give that impression is to prepare so thoroughly that it is true, at least to the extent possible, and bring out the evidence in a way that makes the jurors conclude: "This person really knows her case."

§ 1-13(e). Conviction.

The attorney must show — through his every action — a true belief in the client's cause. Listeners are unlikely to see the merit of any case if its chief advocate does not appear convinced of it. Thus, you must choose a position that you can wholeheartedly endorse and use communication techniques that display this commitment.

Lawyers often are presented with cases in which the client is not right. You nevertheless have a duty to represent the client effectively. One way to do so, with the requisite belief, is to focus on aspects of the case that you can truly endorse. For example, in a criminal defense case, you may have to emphasize the state's failure to carry a burden — essential in the justice system to convict an individual — rather than the client's innocence. In defending a tort suit, you may have to focus on damages if liability cannot in good faith be refuted.

In most instances, however, a good advocate becomes devoted even to a superficially weak case, searching out and promoting strengths until they overcome weaknesses. This trait is a natural aspect of advocacy; you are not paid to be objective, but to believe in, and develop, the best possible case for the client.

§ 1-13(f). Likability.

Although not essential to winning, likability is a great asset. A person who relates well to the jury will have more success in persuasion than one who puts them off. Thus, you should try to show a congenial manner.

What means can be used to relate well with jurors? Changing personalities for the trial is impossible; trying may make you seem insincere. Yet smaller, common sense measures can make a big difference. You should avoid dress that distances you from the jury; professional dress is appropriate, but perhaps not a thousand dollar suit in a country town. A bit of self-deprecation at an appropriate time, showing that you are not totally self-consumed, can go a long way. Raising the eyebrows, keeping the face open rather than pinched, being courteous to others when possible, and smiling occasionally helps you appear non-threatening. Being considerate of the jury — making sure they can see and hear, for instance — is appreciated. You should explain legal and technical terms, but in a way that avoids condescension. These and other actions may make your arguments easier to accept.

Being likable is important, but not as essential as doing the job right. You are still in an adversary setting, which requires that you be contentious. Additionally, you should avoid overdoing the "friendly hometown boy" routine. It may seem obsequious, which can only destroy your overall credibility. Trying to be likable should promote rather than impede the goal of winning.

You should be aware of your appearance and demeanor not only when performing, but at all times during the trial. You and your client are constantly on display and being appraised by the jurors. A rude or offensive action during a break, in a hallway, or even outside the courthouse may be observed and discussed by the jurors. Both you and your client need to be on good behavior.[15]

§ 1-14. Preparation and Rehearsal of the Opening Statement, Closing Argument and Other Arguments.

You should be fully prepared when delivering an oral presentation, but equally important is the ability to look the listeners in the eye, show natural emotion and belief, and speak in a conversational style.[16] These goals apply to the opening statement, closing argument, and any other oral presentation. To achieve these ends, you should outline the presentation and prepare to deliver it using the extemporaneous method. Reliance on a written text, or excessive reliance on notes, impairs your ability to communicate. A poorly prepared presentation — in which you simply deliver an impromptu speech — almost always is undirected and out of focus.

A number of methods are used by attorneys in delivering opening statements and other arguments. Unfortunately, most are ill-suited to effective communication. The types of delivery can be categorized as follows: (1) reading, (2) memorization, (3) impromptu, and (4) extemporaneous. These are discussed below. Of these, you should use the extemporaneous method.

§ 1-14(a). Reading.

You should not read an oral presentation. The reading approach is unsuited to advocacy.[17] It is used by attorneys who wish to prepare fully but are unsure of their ability to maintain control of the presentation without a script. Unfortunately, the written script gets between the attorney and the audience. It may give

---

[15] See Marc Judice, *The Defendant Physician at Trial*, THE LAMMICO LETTER, vol. 12, no. 5 (Sept./Oct. 1994) ("A jury watches a defendant physician's every move.").

[16] See Daniel Linz, Steven Penrod, & Elaine McDonald, *Attorney Communication and Impression Making in the Courtroom*, 10 LAW AND HUM. BEHAV. 281 (1986) (study reflecting the frequent disparity between lawyers' perceptions of their own performance compared to the jury's evaluation of that performance).

[17] ALFRED S. JULIEN, OPENING STATEMENTS (1980).

security to counsel, but it impedes the kind of communication that is essential to persuasion. Indeed, watching a speaker read is often excruciatingly boring.

Anyone who has listened to a speech read from a transcript knows how wooden this delivery can be. No matter how much life the speaker tries to inject into the recital, she never quite connects with the listeners. Ideally, a speaker wants an audience to imagine the events she describes; when she reads, however, the listeners rarely are caught up in the presentation. They dutifully watch the speaker, trying to force concentration on the topic, but soon become tired. Before long the listeners are watching the clock or their minds wander to more pleasant subjects. The difficulty in paying attention is compounded by the fact that most readers have no spontaneity.

The biggest problem with reading is that it reduces eye contact and rapport. When counsel reads the argument, eye contact is forced and spotty, even if the attorney makes an effort to maintain it. Yet eye contact is crucial to communication. As John W. Davis said, "The eye is the window to the mind, and the speaker does not live who can hold the attention of any audience without looking it in the face."[18]

Because it permits an almost subconscious communication, eye contact is a primary means by which a speaker transmits belief, sincerity and commitment. Humans communicated through eye contact, facial expressions, and gestures long before they came upon language; these methods still provide the keys to interpreting speech. In conversation, most people mistrust a person who makes unnatural eye contact or avoids it altogether. They may not mistrust a reader, but they will not extend the trust that accompanies eye-to-eye communication.

Reading also impedes a conversational style. It may make the argument appear wooden and formal. The text impairs counsel's ability to respond to the juror's facial reactions, adapt the presentation to unexpected events, and inject vitality into the delivery. Overall, reading casts a monotonous, heavy blanket on the presentation.

A few attorneys are effective despite preparing a script. Usually, they rehearse so many times that they no longer need to look at the text. Nevertheless, when counsel adopts this approach, the statement does not have as much vitality as an extemporaneous presentation. The delivery instead resembles a memorized speech. Further, with a script, the advocate may not rehearse enough to make the presentation acceptable.

Some advocacy experts recommend that counsel write out a complete opening statement prior to the trial. They do not necessarily recommend reading it; instead, they suggest that the advocate rehearse with the transcript until he no longer needs it. Writing out the text is one way for counsel to focus on the main points of

---

[18] John W. Davis, *The Argument of an Appeal*, 26 A.B.A.J. 895 (1940).

proof, but this focus can be gained just as easily through outlining and rehearsal. Moreover, few attorneys who prepare a complete transcript are likely to discard it. Counsel will use the text as a crutch, telling himself he will maintain eye contact, but progressively sliding into rote reading.

Few people would use a script to ask someone out on a dinner date, plead for a loan, or propose marriage. Nor should you read your client's plea to the jury. Many appellate courts prohibit reading an argument because it is so ineffective. This method is just as inadvisable with a jury.

§ 1-14(b). Memorization.

Memorizing an oral presentation is a variation of the reading method and is also a mistake. A memorized presentation invariably appears monotonous.[19] Counsel focuses not on the listeners, but on remembering a lengthy stream of words. Because of the inner focus, a memorized presentation may bore listeners even more than one read from a text.

Memorization permits eye contact, but the eyes show less life when a speech is memorized. Again, counsel's inner focus takes much of the vigor from eye-to-eye communication. Additionally, a speaker who memorizes often provides emphasis in the wrong places, making the delivery unnatural. The speaker shows forced rather than spontaneous emotion, and listeners can tell the difference. The resulting presentation may seem artificial, reducing counsel's credibility.

Memorization also can be disastrous if the attorney forgets a line in the midst of the presentation. With a different method — one that focuses more on the message than the exact words — the attorney easily can restart the presentation; with a memorized speech, counsel must recapture the precise phrase. If the attorney fails to do so, each passing second of silence will seem an eternity. The embarrassment of drawing a blank may burden counsel throughout the trial.

Memorizing also inhibits flexibility. Often it is necessary to react to points, even in the opening statement. Counsel needs to reorder the presentation to make it most effective in light of developments. A point may be raised in jury voir dire that needs addressing; the judge may make a point that requires comment; opposing counsel's opening statement may require a response. Flexibility is crucial in closing argument, where responses are always necessary. A memorized presentation leaves little room for a natural reply.

Like reading, memorization can be unduly time consuming. The attorney not only has to write out a script, he has to learn it. This effort may divert him from planning a thematic presentation. Further, in preparing for trial the attorney does not need the extra stress of trying to remember thousands of words in order. Time is better spent on other pursuits.

---

[19] See KARLYN K. CAMPBELL, THE RHETORICAL ACT 32 (1982).

To write out an organized presentation, counsel must both prepare an outline and write a script. As compared to the extemporaneous approach, the script is an extra step. Further, this practice forces counsel to focus on correct grammar and exact words — both of which are relatively unimportant in a speech — rather than theme. Thus, memorizing a script is inefficient and unproductive.

§ 1-14(c). Impromptu.

Any formal presentation delivered in court should be well prepared. "Winging it" guarantees that the argument will not be as good as it could be and increases the likelihood that it will be inept. An unprepared presentation is likely to be convoluted and undirected, lacking the theme and organization needed for a good impression.[20] The jury may conclude that listening to the attorney is a waste of time. Thus, you should not use the impromptu method.

"Winging it" also is unprofessional. Judges frequently criticize lawyers as incompetent, but generally the criticisms have their root in counsel's unpreparedness. Even an average lawyer, with preparation and rehearsal, can deliver an effective opening statement or argument. Because this effort requires hard work, however, many attorneys fail to meet the challenge. The best lawyers — those that appear spontaneously inspired — usually depend on preparation and rehearsal. If the best lawyers recognize that preparation is the key to good advocacy, so should less experienced lawyers.

§ 1-14(d). Extemporaneous.

The extemporaneous approach is the best method of delivering virtually any public speech. In this approach, counsel prepares and rehearses the presentation until it becomes fixed in her mind, but without memorizing the words. This approach is particularly well suited to advocacy, because it allows counsel to control the message, while at the same time maintaining eye contact, showing spontaneity, and communicating the belief that is necessary for persuasion.

When an advocate uses the extemporaneous approach, she delivers a well-directed presentation. Although she does not memorize the presentation, she fixes its points in her mind. The attorney does not need notes to remember what to say. Additionally, the extemporaneous approach allows full eye contact, facilitating mind-to-mind communication and permitting both speaker and listener to visualize the subject of the presentation. The extemporaneous approach also fosters flexibility, permitting counsel to expand on points as the need arises.

The extemporaneous method permits the advocate to show belief and spontaneity. Since the words are not memorized, counsel can change them to fit the moment. When inspiration strikes, counsel can make the most of it. At the same time, this life and emotion fits into a well-ordered, controlled presentation, which

---

[20] See ALFRED S. JULIEN, OPENING STATEMENTS (1980).

adds to its power. The same qualities might seem artificial in a wandering monologue.

A step-by-step approach to preparing an extemporaneous presentation is set forth below.[21]

§ 1-14(d)(1). Step 1. Prepare an Outline of the Presentation.

You should first make an outline of the points you intend to cover. Key parts of the presentation — especially the beginning and end — should be more detailed to ensure you get them right. A suggested general outline for the opening statement is contained in § 3-6, and for the closing argument in § 12-13. Within those general approaches, you should outline the points that are basic to the presentation. Ensure that the opening statement is thematic, easy to follow, and to the point.

§ 1-14(d)(2). Step 2. Study the Outline.

After preparing the outline, you should review it, absorbing the points and thinking through how those points would be made to the jury. This process begins putting "meat on the bones" of the presentation.

§ 1-14(d)(3). Step 3. Practice Giving the Presentation without Notes.

After thinking through the topics, you should deliver the entire presentation, start to finish, without looking at your notes. It is essential to complete the presentation without notes, because if you use notes in rehearsal, you will do so in the formal presentation. Stand up and speak aloud in practicing the presentation. This action ensures that the rehearsal is realistic.

Delivering the opening statement adds content to the outline. You will think of things to say and how to say them as you rehearse. Additionally, delivering the presentation implants its content in your mind. It allows you to absorb a basic understanding of the structure and content of the opening statement, without word-for-word memorization. Your control of the presentation will improve with repeated rehearsals.

Your first rehearsal of the presentation is likely to be rough. In effect, you are presenting a "first draft" of the speech. You are likely to repeat points, forget others, stumble over phrases, and otherwise deviate from the plan. You may be strongly inclined to stop, but press ahead to the finish. There is great psychological importance in completing the presentation, start to finish, in the rehearsal. Once you know you can present the entire speech, no matter how rough, fine tuning becomes well within reach.

---

[21] A further explanation of this approach is contained in MICHAEL R. FONTHAM, MICHAEL VITIELLO, and DAVID W. MILLER, PERSUASIVE WRITTEN AND ORAL ADVOCACY: IN TRIAL AND APPELLATE COURTS 168–71 (2002).

The importance of getting through to the end was echoed by a California student after a speech by the author on oral advocacy. The student was a guitar player, but for a long time had difficulty learning tunes. He would practice at length, but found that when he played through an arrangement he would make a mistake, stop, and start over. The next time he would make a different mistake and start over again. Finally someone suggested that he play through to the finish, mistakes and all. Soon he was playing many arrangements without error. The same is true of a speech; if you can get through to the end, it becomes easy to eliminate mistakes.

The mental concentration required to actually deliver an oral presentation has an amazing effect. For some reason, the intensity of this effort helps you conceptualize new arguments and ways of presenting your points. Your concentration may lead to insights and even inspiration, which you can incorporate into the presentation. Additionally, delivering the argument helps you identify points that should be improved or discarded. When you are finished, make these changes.

For the initial rehearsals, find a quiet spot where there are no distractions. Simply stand in an empty room and deliver the presentation. Once the delivery is smooth, you may wish to use a mirror, ensuring that gestures are timely and natural.

§ 1-14(d)(4).   Step 4. Review and Revamp the Outline.

Once you have finished a rehearsal, review and adjust the outline. Add good points discovered during the rehearsal. If necessary, restructure the outline to improve its direction and theme. After adjusting the outline, study it again, but do not waste time in this review. You need to use your time for rehearsal.

§ 1-14(d)(5).   Step 5. Repeat the Rehearsals Until the Presentation is Smooth and Controlled.

You should repeat the rehearsals until the presentation is smooth. For an experienced advocate, one or two rehearsals may be sufficient to deliver a polished product. Inexperienced lawyers may need several practice sessions. Regardless, rehearsal benefits the presentation since it provides direction and control without memorization.

Your exact words will vary with each rehearsal, but you should gain firmer control of your points. Additionally, rehearsals help you spot and correct problems with the presentation. Further, rehearsal allows you to work on gestures, voice pitch, posture, and other aspects of delivery. Since the extemporaneous method does not require memorization, and small changes occur with each new delivery, rehearsal should not make the presentation stale.

§ 1-14(d)(6). Step 6. Rehearse in Front of a Friend or Associate.

One good method of improving any presentation is to rehearse in front of a third party or parties— preferably lay people. After making the presentation, you should discuss the opening statement or argument with the listeners to ensure that they understood it correctly. In addition, you should solicit suggestions for improvement, making it clear that helpful criticism is welcome. You should ask the listeners if they understood the facts, recognized the theme, and found the statement persuasive. This process is likely to be a real eye-opener.

You also may wish to videotape the presentation and review it prior to the trial. A videotape exposes flaws that a speaker may not fully acknowledge, even when they are pointed out by others. Seeing yourself has an immense power to overcome denial and promote improvement. Many law firms and law schools have their own videotape equipment, which may be used for this purpose. If you do not have ready access to this equipment, videotape services exist that provide it for a reasonable fee.

§ 1-15. The Pretrial Memorandum.

You should submit a pretrial memorandum in virtually every case. The pretrial memorandum serves two purposes: (1) to inform the court about the case, and (2) to persuade the court of your position.[22] Some courts require pretrial memoranda and specify the necessary contents; others do not. You should request leave to submit a memorandum unless you feel the memorandum would be ignored. Even in a simple case, a short memorandum may start the court thinking your way.

In most cases, the judge learns about the facts piecemeal by hearing motions and discussing the case during conferences. Given the dockets in most courts, the judge is likely to retain only a vague understanding of the case. Explaining the facts in a pretrial memorandum aids the judge's comprehension. The memorandum provides an overall explanation, which the judge may not obtain from pretrial proceedings. In addition, the memorandum may condition the judge toward viewing the facts and law in a favorable manner.

The pretrial memorandum can be a great means of persuasion. As the first comprehensive presentation of the case, it can make a strong impression. Indeed, the pretrial memorandum is likely to be the only extensive fact and law argument that the judge reviews before she begins making up her mind. The judge is likely to lean one way or the other as the trial proceeds, and most of the time this initial inclination determines the outcome. Thus, the pretrial memorandum can have a huge impact.

---

[22] Donald E. Vinson, Jury Persuasion: Psychological Strategies & Trial Technique (1993).

Additionally, your "delivery" of proof — providing evidence to support factual claims in the memorandum — should enhance your credibility as the trial proceeds. The memorandum sets forth the facts that you expect to prove; when the court later sees that the evidence conforms to this prediction, the court may be more amenable to accepting your arguments.[23]

The pretrial memorandum serves somewhat different functions in judge and jury trials. Opening statements often are not used in judge trials, so the pretrial memorandum is a good means to acquaint the court with the facts. It should identify the legal issues, explain the legal context in which the facts should be analyzed, describe how the facts fit legal principles, and explain *why* the combination of facts and law leads to a particular result. Further, if special evidentiary issues or procedural matters exist, you may address them in the memorandum.

In a jury trial, the judge instructs the jury as to the law, but does not apply the law to the facts. Thus, the pretrial memorandum serves to support favorable jury instructions. At the same time, however, you should strive to persuade the court on the merits. The judge's attitude toward the case — reflected in her demeanor — may strongly influence the jury. Further, the judge still determines evidentiary issues, may be called upon to overrule the jury's verdict, and may play a role in bringing about a settlement. Thus, even in a jury trial, it is important to persuade the judge that your position is correct.[24]

§ 1-16. Contents of the Pretrial Memorandum.

The pretrial memorandum should contain the same basic structure as other briefs. The essentials include: (1) an introductory paragraph or section, (2) a statement of the facts, (3) the argument, and (4) a conclusion. The local rules of court, or the court's pretrial order, may include other requirements.

§ 1-16(a). Introduction.

The introduction should provide an overview of the issue and, if possible, introduce your theme. By presenting an overview, you provide context for understanding the facts. The introduction also should state on whose behalf the memorandum is submitted, identify the parties, and provide other introductory material.

§ 1-16(b). Facts.

The pretrial memorandum should review the facts that you expect to prove during the trial. This expectation ordinarily is based on discovery, witness

---

[23] OTIS M. WALTER, SPEAKING TO INFORM AND PERSUADE 128 (1982).

[24] For a thorough discussion of trial memoranda and brief writing in general, see MICHAEL R. FONTHAM, MICHAEL VITIELLO, and DAVID W. MILLER, PERSUASIVE WRITTEN AND ORAL ADVOCACY: IN TRIAL AND APPELLATE COURTS 168–71 (2002).

interviews, and other information you amass in the pretrial process. You should identify the discovery references on which the factual picture is based, so long as the disclosures do not undermine your trial strategy. References to discovery and other documentation give credibility to your presentation.

You should use the narrative form for fact presentation. Like an opening statement, the facts should provide a "word picture" of the events in controversy; they should bring out a central theme. You should have a theory of the case that accommodates all the facts, both favorable and unfavorable. You should emphasize favorable facts by giving them more extensive treatment.

Present the fact statement in an objective style. Do not engage in obvious argument, but subtly persuade the judge by placing the facts in context and developing favorable material. Make sure the factual claims are accurate, since false predictions undermine your credibility. You may wish to describe some of the facts in broad fashion, rather than with particularity, if you are unsure that the evidence will support the claims. Before making a specific claim, make sure you can provide evidentiary support. In addition, providing citations for important factual claims makes the fact picture more credible.

If you are not sure that the opposing party is aware of certain facts, you may wish to hold them in reserve until the trial. In the modern age of full-blown discovery, however, you cannot easily achieve surprise on major issues. Nevertheless, be careful not to give away trial strategies. Sometimes the promises made in a pretrial memorandum help the opposition prepare its case.

§ 1-16(c). The Argument.

The argument should identify the applicable legal authorities and explain why the holdings control the facts. You should emphasize parallels between the facts and those in favorable holdings. Ordinarily, the argument should contain argumentative headings and should be structured in a manner similar to an appellate brief.

In a judge trial, the argument should persuade the court that your ultimate position is correct. You would have the same purpose in a jury trial but also would make specific arguments for jury instructions. Thus, the argument might address the merits and the jury instructions separately. Alternatively, you might focus on supporting desirable jury instructions, but in the process address the merits.

You also may wish to discuss procedural or evidentiary issues in the pretrial memorandum. Alternatively, you may address these issues in separate motions and supporting memoranda. This second alternative may help the court focus on the issues, but multiple motions could be cumbersome. You may wish to inquire as to the court's wishes on the subject.

§ 1-16(d).   Conclusion.

The conclusion ordinarily should be a single paragraph. It should simply summarize your theme and state the relief you request of the court.

CHAPTER 2

SELECTING THE JURY

---

§ 2-1.   Introduction.

Jury selection provides both a great challenge and an opportunity in the lawyer's effort to win a case. On the one hand, determining which jurors are most likely to accept your arguments usually is beyond human capacity. On the other, jury selection provides your first opportunity to speak with jurors, and thus permits you to begin the process of persuasion; you may or may not succeed in choosing the most receptive jurors, but you can begin persuading them regardless of their predispositions.

This chapter addresses practical, tactical and legal aspects of jury selection. Section 2-2 discusses whether, and under what circumstances, you should seek a jury. Sections 2-3 through 2-9 review methods for conducting jury selection and simultaneously advocating your case. Section 2-10 discusses constitutional limitations on your discretion to challenge jury prospects for reasons based on race or sex.

§ 2-2.   Deciding Whether to Demand a Jury.

In most cases, the initial question in jury selection is whether to request a jury. Lawyers often make this decision based on unverified preconceptions of how a judge or jury might react to a type of case. With this general basis, the decision is little more than a guess. Deciding whether to demand a jury always involves some subjective judgment, but it can also reflect an objective consideration of specific aspects of the case and their likely treatment by a judge or jury.

The United States Constitution guarantees a right of jury trial in serious criminal cases.[1] The Supreme Court has held that the "due process" guarantee of the Fourteenth Amendment applies this protection to state trials involving serious crimes.[2] The United States Constitution also guarantees a right of jury trial in all "suits at common law" involving more than twenty dollars.[3] The

---

[1] U.S. CONST. art. 3, § 2; U.S. CONST. amend. VI. The Sixth Amendment states, in part: "In all criminal prosecutions, the accused shall enjoy the right to a speedy and public trial, by an impartial jury. . . ." The United States Supreme Court has ruled the right applies in "serious criminal cases." Duncan v. State of Louisiana, 391 U.S. 145 (1968), *reh'g denied*, 392 U.S. 947 (1968); Cynthia M. McKnight, *Right to Jury Trial*, 82 GEO. L.J. 1033 (1994).

[2] Duncan v. State of Louisiana, 391 U.S. 145 (1968), *reh'g denied*, 392 U.S. 947 (1968).

[3] U.S. CONST. amend. VII.

Supreme Court has not applied this guarantee to the states,[4] but most states have their own constitutional or statutory requirements guaranteeing the right of jury trials in many civil cases.

In federal civil trials, Rule 38 of the Federal Rules of Civil Procedure reaffirms that the "right of trial by jury as declared by the Seventh Amendment to the Constitution or as given by a statute of the United States shall be preserved to the parties inviolate." Rule 23 of the Federal Rules of Criminal Procedure provides that all cases "required to be tried by a jury shall be so tried unless the defendant waives a jury trial in writing with the approval of the court and the consent of the government."

In federal civil cases either party may file a jury demand within ten days after service of the last pleading directed to the issue on which the jury trial is demanded.[5] In most cases, the plaintiff does not know which judge will get the case until after the complaint is filed and allotted; thus, the plaintiff cannot weigh the advantages of an individual judge against a jury prior to filing suit.

Additionally, under F.R.C.P. 38(d), a party may not withdraw a jury demand without the consent of the other parties, so a plaintiff may be bound by a jury demand once he makes it. Under the rule the plaintiff can hedge, however, omitting the jury demand from the complaint and waiting to file it until ten days after the service of the defendant's answer. By using this approach, the plaintiff can be as fully informed as the defendant in selecting a judge or jury. The potential pitfall is that counsel will forget to make the demand; absent a deadline control reminder, he may forget that a jury demand is due ten days after service of the answer.[6]

Lawyers often choose between judge and jury on superficial grounds. The attorney may not have a solid basis for evaluating an individual judge. Without the benefit of personal experience, counsel must depend on reports that often are vague and allegorical. Even counsel's firsthand experience may consist of isolated instances that provide a poor basis for evaluation. The attorney also can have only a general knowledge of jurors; prior to jury selection counsel must base the evaluation on the general characteristics of the community from which the jury may be drawn.

A few general observations can be made about a "typical" judge versus a "typical" jury. These comments are subject to a huge caveat — no one is typical. Nevertheless, a judge is likely to be better educated than an average juror. He should have a greater familiarity with the law and the manner in which facts and legal rules work together to determine cases. He may have more experience

---

[4] Eilenbecker v. Plymouth County, 134 U.S. 31 (1890).

[5] FED. R. CIV. PRO. 38(b).

[6] See 3 FEDERAL LITIGATION GUIDE ¶ 30.02 (1993).

with witnesses and their tendency to "fudge" in recounting facts. He should be more familiar with attorneys' tactics and less influenced by their theatrics. He should have some sort of decisional record, which provides a basis for predicting his reaction in a specific case.

Citizens often are available for jury duty because they do not have other, more pressing commitments; in other words, they do not have any excuses to get them out of serving. Thus, a typical juror may be jobless — out of work, retired, or intentionally unemployed. Many jurors have limited education. Jurors are likely to be unfamiliar with the judicial process, although they see "snapshots" of it on television. They generally do not understand legal rules or the standards for weighing evidence. Some jurors resent being required to devote the time to service. At the same time, jurors usually bring a fresh and less predictable perspective to determining a case.

The commentators commonly ascribe a number of characteristics to juries. First, some view jurors as likely to favor individuals — especially those who may be personalized as "little guys" — as opposed to large and "powerful" corporations or businesses.[7] This attribute may reflect the fact that the typical juror does not interact socially with rich or powerful people. A judge, in contrast, often mingles with these people and will not necessarily mistrust them. Second, jurors are viewed as more susceptible to emotional appeals than judges, particularly on damage issues in personal injury cases.[8] A judge hears heartrending cases all the time and may become "hardened" to their emotional appeal.[9]

Third, juries are generally viewed as less able to absorb and process information than judges.[10] They have little or no training in hearing evidence, unlike a judge, and no experience in applying legal rules to facts. This factor may explain the increased risk lawyers often associate with jury trials. At the same time, juries are made up of persons with varying backgrounds and the *collective* ability of these people to process information may offset a lack of training.

Both a judge and a juror are likely to seek justice. Most individuals — regardless of their status — take seriously the responsibility to produce the "right" result. A judge is not necessarily more impartial than a juror; he may have different biases, but almost any person has some preconceptions that influence the evaluation of a case. Nor is a judge immune to the emotional considerations that allegedly influence jurors; a judge does not lose his human nature just because he dons a robe.

---

[7] LANE'S GOLDSTEIN TR. TECH. § 9.02 at 4–5 (3d ed. 1993).

[8] See JAMES J. GOBERT & WALTER E. JORDAN, JURY SELECTION: THE LAW, ART AND SCIENCE OF SELECTING A JURY § 3.02, at 82 (2d ed. 1990).

[9] *Id.*

[10] 3 FEDERAL LITIGATION GUIDE ¶ 30.08[2] (1993).

In deciding whether to seek a judge or jury trial, you should consider which decisionmaker gives the best chance for a favorable final result given the particular circumstances of the case. The following factors may affect your decision.

§ 2-2(a). Judge's Predictability.

If you know the judge to whom the case is allotted when it is time for filing the jury demand, you can compare the judge's attributes to those likely in a jury. Judges differ dramatically in their intelligence, attitudes, and biases. You should find out how the judge tends to rule in cases similar to the one you are handling. At least in broad categories — such as criminal cases, constitutional cases, or personal injury cases — most judges quickly acquire reputations for their tendencies. Find out what legal practice the judge engaged in prior to becoming a judge, which should provide insight into the judge's attitudes.

If the judge was elected, determine what segment of the bar contributed the most to the process; if the judge was appointed, the same question may be relevant, although perhaps not as great a concern. In particular, find out if the opposing attorney has any special relationship with the judge, good or bad, that might influence the result. In this same vein, you may wish to determine whether some other attorney might be a good prospect to associate in the case because of a friendly relationship with the judge. You also may glean insights from the judge's opinions in similar cases, which you can determine through computer research.

Most judges acquire a reputation for their damage awards, particularly in personal injury cases. The determination of quantum involves a healthy dose of judgment, since it often requires an evaluation of intangible harm. Attorneys often believe that juries are more generous than judges in awarding damages, but that proposition is not necessarily true. A judge may be more likely to compensate intangible damages simply because he is used to doing so. In any event, a judge of any tenure should be predictable on damage issues.

To the extent possible, you should evaluate the judge's traits in light of the characteristics of the case. The judge's intellect — and the extent to which it exceeds that of a likely juror — is a factor in determining whether he will better understand complex points. The judge's personal biases — racial, social, economic, among others — influence how he will react to particular parties, witnesses, and issues. The judge's personality determines how he might react to an emotional appeal. You must consider the judge's traits along with key aspects of your case to assess his desirability as decisionmaker.

§ 2-2(b). Demographics of Jury Pool.

Although the information is much less specific, you also may draw conclusions by studying the characteristics of the jury pool. Communities often are diverse, but just as often they are composed of people of similar economic status, social class, and ethnic background. Jurors in the community may have a reputation for favoring a side in certain types of disputes, particularly in criminal and personal injury cases. Additionally, in a case large enough to justify the expense, you may gauge the reaction of a potential jury by commissioning an opinion poll.[11]

Be cautious, however, in drawing conclusions about a potential jury from broad information. Individuals have similarities, but they are all different. Particular jurors have their own individual reactions to facts. A juror with a strong personality may have unusual views and exercise a strong influence over other jurors. You cannot count on a jury to follow a community pattern.

§ 2-2(c).　Dependence on Specific Points of Law.

In virtually all cases, you should present a fact-driven theme, in which you develop the facts calling for the application of favorable legal principles. When general legal rules govern the dispute, such as the "reasonable person" standard in negligence cases, judges and juries can easily determine the importance of factual claims. In some cases, however, one side or the other may rely on special legal arguments, which require an understanding of the importance of particular facts. If the existence or non-existence of a legal duty is a point of contention, for instance, you may want to ensure that the decisionmaker understands *which* facts are crucial to the decision. Similarly, if you rely on a special defense such as a limitation period, you must ensure that the decisionmaker focuses on the facts relevant to that point. In these cases a judge may be more desirable because he understands which facts are important in applying the law.

§ 2-2(d).　Complexity of the Issues.

Some cases involve complex questions. Your job is to simplify and translate, but if you cannot easily make the presentation simple, you may prefer a judge trial. The judge is likely to have two advantages: first, she generally is better educated than the average juror; and second, she can study written presentations. The opportunity to brief the issues offers a great advantage to the lawyer whose case is complex. Of course, you should simplify the case even for a judge, but you cannot always eliminate all the complexities.

§ 2-2(e).　Strength of the Case.

Assuming the judge is intelligent and unbiased, a compelling factor favoring a judge trial is a strong case. A strong case tried to a predictable judge generally produces victory. A weak case — perhaps one in which emotional appeal is the only strong point — is usually best tried to a jury. A jury may not give the same

---

[11] Robert D. Meneck, *Using Consultants to Assist Voir Dire*, 497 PLI/LIT 289 (Mar./Apr. 1994).

weight to the important facts and legal standards, and the unpredictability of a jury may enhance the prospect for settlement.

§ 2-2(f).   Relative Briefing Abilities of Counsel.

Judges increasingly rely on written material in resolving cases. Many judges decide most motions — including motions that resolve cases — without even hearing oral argument. Pretrial briefs may strongly influence a judge. Just as the opening statements may make jurors "lean" one way or the other, the initial memoranda may begin the process of persuading the judge. Additionally, preliminary briefs on motions — especially motions that address substantive issues — may influence the judge's outlook. Further, a good post-trial brief may cement the judge's decision and should provide the source material for a solid opinion.

If you have a significant briefing advantage — in other words, you write better than your opponent — this factor is a strong argument for a judge trial. A lawyer with weak briefing skills should favor a jury trial.

§ 2-2(g).   Need for a Fresh Outlook.

Sometimes a jury brings a fresh — and perhaps naive — outlook to a case. An alibi, a sob story, or an improbable version of events may more easily influence jurors, who may not be aware that parties often stretch the facts. If you need a factfinder who has not already "heard it all," you need a jury. Further, jurors often decide criminal cases without access to inadmissible character evidence that is not supposed to, but probably will, influence a judge. Additionally, one legal standard that jurors may apply more forcefully than judges is the "beyond a reasonable doubt" rule. At least the *first* time they hear a criminal case, jurors may stretch their doubts to exonerate the defendant.

§ 2-2(h).   Appealability of the Decision.

Few cases are tried for the appellate court. In extreme circumstances, however, you may have to adopt this approach. If both the judge's record and the jury demographics strongly suggest an adverse verdict, you may have to count on the appellate court for relief. In this situation a judge trial is advisable because the judge's decision is more likely to be reversed than a jury verdict.

Although appellate courts generally are deferential to all decisions from trial courts, they are more respectful of jury verdicts. The right to a jury trial requires that judges be cautious in overturning jury verdicts. Moreover, the secrecy of jury deliberations generally cloaks the jury's rationale, making it difficult to attack the logic of the decision. If a judge does not err in jury instructions, and if some evidence supports the verdict, the jury's decision probably will stand.

A judge's decision receives considerable deference on appeal, but not so much as a jury's. A judge's failure to explain her reasoning is viewed as a flaw rather than a shield. To the extent the judge explains her rationale, the appellate court has a basis for detecting errors. Moreover, if the judge has a reputation for irrational decisions, the appellate judges are likely to scrutinize the judge's rulings.

It seems paradoxical to select a judge trial when the judge is biased for the adverse party. Normally, a lawyer should select a jury and try to win at the trial level. Experience may show, however, that juries in the jurisdiction usually are adverse. Moreover, a biased judge can have a huge and largely unappealable impact on a jury through his comments, facial expressions, and treatment of counsel. Further, the judge's evidentiary rulings may keep vital information from the jury, and it is often difficult to overturn these decisions on appeal. Thus, in extreme cases you may be forced to hedge your bets, try the case to the judge, and hope for relief on appeal.

At the same time, the jury system primarily exists to protect against a biased judiciary. You should not assume too much about individual juries from the larger pattern of jury decisions. With good evidence and the right presentation, you should be able to persuade a jury despite the interventions of a prejudiced judge.

Additionally, a resourceful judge may insulate her decision from appeal by crafting factual findings to support the ruling. If some evidence supports the findings, an appellate court likely will not reverse them. Thus, demanding a jury is usually the best bet when the judge is biased.

§ 2-2(i). Establishing New Law.

In some cases the client may want to establish a principle of law in the jurisdiction. A jury trial may muddy the issues on appeal so that the point is not clearly presented. In a judge's decision the issue should be decided one way or the other, facilitating appellate review. In addition, the application of the law to the facts should be clear. Thus, a lawyer who wishes to establish a principle on appeal probably should select a judge trial.

§ 2-2(j). Relative Success of Counsel in Judge and Jury Trials.

You should consider your own record, and that of your opponent, in judge and jury trials. Some lawyers use tactics that tend to work better with juries than judges. A lawyer's use of dramatics, for instance, may have a more compelling impact on jurors than a judge. Some attorneys' personalities allow them to identify easily with "common folk." Others do better as people get to know them, which makes familiarity with a judge an advantage. Additionally, some lawyers have more clout than others with judges because of professional skill, reputation, background, or special relationships. You must consider these attributes in deciding whether to seek a judge or jury trial.

§ 2-2(k). Delay and Cost.

You should consider how a jury demand affects the time and expense needed to take the case to trial. A jury case may not get to trial as soon as a judge case for a number of reasons: the time allotted for civil jury trials in the district may be limited, the judge's calendar may not permit an early reservation of a significant block of time, the judge may sit infrequently in the county or parish where the jury trial would have to occur, or the jurisdiction may conduct jury trials only at preestablished times. A judge case usually requires a shorter block of time and sometimes can be tried in segments. Thus, greater flexibility exists to obtain an early setting of a judge trial.

In many jurisdictions the party demanding a jury must post a bond to cover the additional costs associated with the jury trial. Usually this expense is not a significant consideration, but in a small case it may be a factor. Costs ordinarily are recovered by the victorious party, but your client may not wish to bear the risk of paying these costs.

§ 2-3. Purposes of Jury Voir Dire.

The jury "voir dire" is the process by which prospective jurors are questioned by the court, counsel, or both, as the basis for determining whether the jurors should be accepted. The theoretical purpose is to develop information about individual jurors; this data allows the court to determine if they should be excused for cause and gives counsel a basis for peremptory challenges.

The obvious goal of voir dire is to select jurors who are favorably disposed to your case. Predicting the reactions of individuals to a specific case based on the information you can develop in voir dire, however, is not always feasible. Thus, you should also focus on the advocacy purpose of voir dire — to begin the process of persuading the jurors that your position is correct. This goal involves two components: (1) developing a relationship with the jurors, and (2) introducing thematic aspects of the case in a manner that invokes a favorable reaction.[12]

Selecting favorable jurors is at best an uncertain process.[13] In the absence of a revelation that a prospect has an interest in or connection with the case, most information developed in voir dire has no provable tendency to suggest a juror's inclination. Many trial lawyers base their decisions to accept or challenge prospective jurors on stereotypes and professional folklore. Most of these precepts — for instance, that women are more generous in injury cases than men, that minorities favor criminal defendants, or that former public servants are prejudiced against plaintiffs — are unproven generalizations. Even if true, they do not

---

[12] David Hittner & Eric J.R. Nichols, *Jury Selection in Federal Civil Litigation: General Procedures, New Rules, and the Arrival of Batson*, 23 TEX. TECH L. REV. 407 (1992).

[13] Gregory M. Perlstein, *Effects of Social Pressures on Jury Decisions*, 50 J. Mo. B. 269 (1994).

necessarily determine an individual's response. Herbert J. Stern, a leading authority on trial advocacy, refers to this type of "stereotype advice" as essentially "worthless."[14] He adds:

> The only way to really know how a person feels about the issues of your case is to ask him about them, or about the kind of related issues that will enable a reliable interpolation. But few judges indeed will allow that kind of direct, on-the-nose questioning of prospective jurors.[15]

The background that you can obtain is usually a poor predictor of a juror's vote.

The unreliability of information obtained in voir dire further complicates the process of predicting juror attitudes. To understand this problem, you should place yourself in the position of a prospective juror. This individual is brought into an unfamiliar setting and process, placed before a judge and a group of strangers, and asked a series of questions that often seem intrusive. Most people feel uncomfortable, even nervous, in this environment. A prospect likely will phrase his answers to make them seem socially acceptable, thereby suppressing the very information that might point to bias. Further, a prospect is often motivated by a personal desire to get *on* the jury, or *avoid* getting on it, and will respond in a manner calculated to achieve the goal. These factors make it difficult to elicit information that might truly predict a juror's attitude.

Additionally, processing the information obtained in voir dire is a daunting task. You must absorb the background of the prospective jurors, listen to prospects' answers and the adversary's questions, exercise and keep track of challenges, and simultaneously try to judge who will be good jurors. With a perfectly programmed computer, you might logically calculate the attitudinal effect of each juror's personal data, but this task is beyond the capabilities of most humans. Instead, lawyers end up relying on "gut instinct," influenced by a few of the juror's attributes.

The difficulty of predicting a jury prospect's predisposition using background information can be illustrated with an example. Suppose counsel learned that a prospect in the *Danielson* case[16] — the suit alleging fraud in the marketing of a computer franchise — was a white male, 38, college educated, married for 15 years with three children, and employed as a residential real estate agent. From this data the attorney might infer that the prospect would be familiar with financial matters, understand contract issues, and have some appreciation of the factors that lead to success in business.

This information could influence counsel's evaluation of the prospect, depending on whether counsel wanted knowledgeable jurors. It probably would not

---

[14] HERBERT J. STERN, TRYING CASES TO WIN 485 (1991).

[15] *Id.*

[16] See Appendix A.

provide a reliable basis, however, for determining how the prospect would react to the specific claims and defenses in the case: the Danielsons' claims that false representations induced them to enter into the franchise contract, versus ComputerCentre's assertions that the Danielsons failed to follow sound advice and neglected their business.

Adding to this base of personal information probably would not make the evaluation easier. If counsel followed the advice of some authorities and developed the prospect's social background, ethnic origin, hobbies, activities, facts about parents, brothers and sisters, wife's education, children's education, residence history, and similar data,[17] the information would not necessarily provide a basis to predict the person's attitude about *Danielson*. One might ask: How would the following alternatives influence a juror's predisposition in *Danielson*?

1. The juror's parents died when he was in his twenties. He has three sisters — two are housewives and one is a social worker. He lived in the city most of his life and attended public schools. He went to college at the State University. He now lives in a middle class residential suburb with his family. He is interested in sports and art. His wife has a college degree, is primarily a housewife, but works part time as a travel consultant. He is a member of a private golf club and an athletic club. He is active in the city's annual art festival. He did not serve in the military.

2. The juror's parents are still alive: His father is retired, and they live in Arizona. He has one brother — an older brother whom he sees frequently. He was brought up in a rural area where he attended a private Catholic school although he is Episcopalian. He went out of state to college, attending a private institution, but dropped out and finished at a local public college. He lives in a residential area of the city with his family. His wife finished two years of college and works full time as a secretary for a large oil company. He is not interested in spectator sports but enjoys fishing and hunting. He is not a member of any clubs but is active in church groups and charitable endeavors. He served in the Army reserves for six months and periodically served summer duty, but is no longer a member.

This history does not provide a reasonable basis to predict a specific reaction to specific issues. Moreover, trying to remember, weigh, and compare all this information for several prospects while conducting voir dire would be next to impossible for any normal person. Counsel's effort to develop this history instead wastes precious time that can best be spent explaining strengths of the case, so counsel can convince the jurors of its fairness *whatever their background.*

---

[17] See, e.g., THOMAS A. MAUET, TRIAL TECHNIQUES 49–50 (5th ed. 2000).

Of course, you can obtain some information in voir dire to use in jury selection. Familiarity with the parties, counsel or the facts, or an interest in the outcome would influence a juror's attitude. Facts tending to identify a juror with a party are also important. An insurance adjuster, for instance, would probably identify with the defendant in an accident case. Information that indicates how jurors will process the facts and interact in deliberations may also be useful. A juror's education and intelligence suggest how well she could comprehend complex issues; her assertiveness and self-confidence indicate whether she may take a lead in deliberations. An attempt to find out everything about the juror's background, however, generally is not profitable.

Given the difficulty of choosing the "right" people, you should concentrate on the other goal of voir dire: to initiate the process of persuasion. Get acquainted with the jurors, introduce the thematic aspects of the case, and begin conditioning the jurors to accept favorable legal principles. The *form* of your questions must indicate you seek information, but their content can be adapted to advocate the case. To be effective, you must ask the questions; those a judge poses normally are too neutral to further the cause. Thus, you should try to get the court to permit some voir dire by counsel. See § 2-4.

In getting acquainted, you may establish a foundation for reasoning with the jury throughout the trial. Since the jurors are new to the case and courtroom, they will appreciate an exchange that relaxes rather than intimidates them. Thus, one objective of voir dire is to get to know each juror in a conversational, relaxed way. You should portray an interest in the prospect, *listen* to her answers, and try to remember some characteristic of the juror.

You should not be overly friendly, because this attitude might seem artificial, but you should nevertheless avoid an interrogating tone. Try to show the same interest that a seminar leader might show in a new group of students: open, friendly, courteous, yet concerned about the task at hand. Avoid questions that pry excessively into jurors' personal histories or put them on the spot. Any reasonable juror would resent these inquiries.

Introducing thematic points requires you to fashion questions that describe what you will contend. As explained in § 2-6, these inquiries must be couched in terms that probe for prospects' preconceptions: for instance, asking the potential jurors if they would have any special reason not to award a verdict if certain facts were proven. Similarly, you can transform a point of persuasion into a legitimate inquiry by explaining it and asking if the juror has any special experience with the facts. These questions begin acclimating the jurors to your version of the dispute. Since it is their first exposure to the case, thematic questions can affect their attitudes.

You should also use voir dire to gain the jurors' acceptance of the key legal principles on which you rely. Some concepts that are uncontroversial to attorneys may seem illogical to jurors. Thus, you should try them out on the jurors in voir dire. As an example, a lay person may not assume that a business should be responsible for the tortious acts of its employees. A reference to this precept — legitimized with the recognition that it will be announced *by the judge* in an instruction — may promote the jurors' acceptance of the principle and expose any latent hostility to it.

Of course, you should only make reference to instructions that actually will be given by the judge. These points are also discussed in § 2-6.

§ 2-4. Voir Dire Process.

The practices for selecting juries vary among jurisdictions, districts, and judges. Generally, the method by which jurors are called to service is established by statute but may be implemented through court rules.[18] Jurors usually are drawn from lists of voters. Statutes or court rules exempt some people from jury service; they include people who are involved in public service occupations, have physical or other infirmities, or are engaged in professions that do not permit their absence.[19] The jury pool may be called to court each day for some period of time and juries selected from its members. Thus, some persons may have recently served as jurors in other cases. Alternatively, the court may notify a certain number of persons to appear on designated days for jury selection.[20]

Depending on the jurisdiction and type of case, the number of persons needed to comprise the jury ranges from six to twelve. Twelve person juries are required in federal criminal trials unless the parties stipulate to a smaller jury with the approval of the court.[21] In federal civil trials the court may seat a jury composed of six to twelve members; many courts have adopted procedures for using six persons.[22] Juries in state court generally also range from six to twelve members.

Varying procedures exist for selecting jurors from the jury pool. Lawyers remove members of the jury panel through two types of challenges: challenges

---

[18] See 28 U.S.C. §§ 1861–63, providing that federal district courts establish jury selection plans to ensure reasonable representation of the population in the jury pool. David Hittner, *Jury Selection in Federal Civil Litigation: General Procedures, New Rules, and the Arrival of Batson*, 23 TEX. TECH L. REV. 407 (1992).

[19] See 3 FEDERAL LITIGATION GUIDE ¶¶ 30.11–30.12 (1993). Examples of persons commonly excused are public servants, persons engaged in professional occupations, individuals whose jobs do not permit their absence, the elderly, those who have recently performed jury service, students, and those who would suffer unusual hardship by serving.

[20] See 3 FEDERAL LITIGATION GUIDE ¶ 30.12 (1993).

[21] FED. R. CRIM. PRO. 23(b). The rule allows the court to accept a verdict from a jury of 11 if one juror must be excused for just cause after the trial commences.

[22] FED. R. CIV. PRO. 48. The parties may stipulate to receive a verdict from a jury of fewer than six persons. The Advisory Committee Note states that local rules in many districts establish "six as the standard size for a civil jury."

for cause and peremptory challenges. Counsel may assert challenges for cause to remove a juror for bias, preexisting familiarity with the case, or some other reason making her unfit to serve; she may exercise peremptory challenges as a matter of right. The jurors may be questioned as a single large panel, after which challenges are exercised and the requisite number of unchallenged persons seated. Alternatively, the jury box may be filled from the panel, those persons questioned and challenges exercised, after which the empty seats are filled and the new potential jurors questioned. Many variations exist to these basic approaches. [23]

Different procedures also exist for questioning potential jurors. In federal courts, the judge almost always conducts general questioning. The judge may permit counsel to follow up with their own questions but usually limits the time allotted for this opportunity. Many judges do not allow counsel to ask questions, but permit them to submit inquiries in writing, to be asked only by the judge. [24] In this situation the advocate has little ability to influence juror attitudes in voir dire. In many state jurisdictions, counsel is provided a greater chance to conduct an oral voir dire; indeed, the opportunity may be established as a right. Even in these courts, the judge usually conducts general questioning, permitting the attorneys to ask their own questions afterward.

Using a questionnaire is one good method of gathering background information on members of the jury pool. Many judges use questionnaires to save the time needed to interrogate individual jurors about personal history. Additionally, orally questioning a prospect about his personal background, in front of other potential jurors and courtroom personnel, may make him uncomfortable. Filling out a form is not usually embarrassing. The prospect's written answer may not be as spontaneous as an oral response, but it should be more considered.

The time saved through the use of questionnaires may be employed in voir dire for persuasion. Moreover, if jurors complete questionnaires in advance, you can organize material on jury prospects before asking oral questions. Your

---

[23] HERBERT J. STERN, TRYING CASES TO WIN 474 (1991): "[T]here are dozens of ways in which various courts around the country conduct the voir dire, and even significant variations among different judges within the same courthouse."

[24] Federal Rule of Civil Procedure 47(a) provides:

> Examination of jurors. The court may permit the parties or their attorneys to conduct the examination of prospective jurors or may itself conduct the examination. In the latter event, the court shall permit the parties or their attorneys to supplement the examination by such further inquiry as it deems proper or shall itself submit to the prospective jurors such additional questions of the parties as it deems proper.

Federal Rule of Criminal Procedure 24 contains a similar provision. See also 3 FEDERAL LITIGATION GUIDE ¶ 30.13 (1993).

The judge should question jury prospects to determine whether they are reasonably calculated to uncover bias. See United States v. Jones, 188 F.3d 773 (7th Cir. 1999).

advance knowledge about individuals — summarized and at hand for easy reference — should make it easier to probe for possible bias.

If the judge does not use a questionnaire, you should ask to submit one. The judge is likely to go along if opposing counsel agrees to the idea. Additionally, even if the judge employs a form questionnaire, you should seek an opportunity to add questions relevant to the particular case. These inquiries may ask the jury prospects whether they know the parties, counsel, or witnesses, are familiar with the facts, or have some identification with a side. In addition, the questions may probe the attitudes of the prospects regarding the cause of action and attendant issues. The responses may establish that follow-up inquiry is necessary.[25]

A good jury questionnaire elicits information in an objective fashion. If you attempt to "load" the questionnaire with slanted inquiries, your opponent is likely to object, and the judge will not submit it. The questions may seek information regarding the jurors' attitudes, however, without pushing a particular point of view. Indeed, an objective question may provoke a more open response than a slanted one. You should work out the phrasing of questions with the opposing attorney in advance, so that a last-minute glitch does not prevent the use of the questionnaire.

In federal civil cases each side is permitted three peremptory challenges regardless of the size of the jury.[26] In criminal cases the number varies according to the nature of the charge.[27] If more than one party is on a side in a civil case, the court may require them to share peremptory challenges but may expand the number of challenges when those parties have adverse interests. The court may exercise discretion to realign parties in allocating peremptory challenges.[28] In state courts the number of challenges for cause generally is prescribed by statute, often modeled after the federal rules. You may assert a peremptory challenge for any reason except the race or sex of the potential juror.[29]

You may assert an unlimited number of challenges for cause, but they are not always successful. Few cause challenges exist that do not allow the judge some discretion in determining bias. Further, a prospective juror rarely admits that she is biased. In most situations, the basis to challenge for cause becomes apparent in voir dire, and the court excuses the prospect without the lawyer having to register a formal challenge. When you base your perception of bias on

---

[25] JAMES J. GOBERT & WALTER E. JORDAN, JURY SELECTION: THE LAW, ART AND SCIENCE OF SELECTING A JURY § 9.01 (2d ed. 1990); HERBERT J. STERN, TRYING CASES TO WIN 496–500 (1991).

[26] 28 U.S.C. § 1870.

[27] FED. R. CRIM. PRO. 24(b).

[28] 3 FEDERAL LITIGATION GUIDE ¶ 30.17 (1993).

[29] See § 2.10.

circumstantial information, however, you may have to persuade the court that there is a serious risk of unfairness.

Generally recognized grounds for cause challenges include the following:

1. Direct or indirect financial or other interest in the case.[30]
2. Strong identification with a party, such as, in a criminal case, a person who works for a prosecutor's office.[31]
3. Prior jury service on a related case that has implanted some bias in the juror.[32]
4. A blood or marriage relationship with a party or counsel, or a close relationship with a party or counsel that likely would bias the juror.[33]
5. Physical or mental incapacity.[34]
6. Familiarity with the facts that might bias the juror.[35]
7. An admission that the juror would develop a bias if certain facts were established.[36]
8. An inability to follow or fundamental disagreement with a controlling principle of law.[37]

The court should remove for cause any juror who admits to a bias toward a party, counsel, or the cause of action. Other grounds, established by statute, rule, or practice, exist in particular jurisdictions.

The manner in which the lawyers exercise challenges may affect jurors' attitudes toward the parties. Counsel risks offending a prospective juror if he challenges the person openly and in the prospect's presence. The prospect may

---

[30] See, e.g., Comm. v. Berrigan, 535 A.2d 91, 98 (1987), *cert. denied,* 493 U.S. 883 (1989); Chestnut v. Ford Motor Co., 445 F.2d 967 (4th Cir. 1971); see 28 U.S.C. § 1870.

[31] See, e.g., Jefferson v. State, 489 So. 2d 211 (Fla. App. 1986); Parks v. State, 343 S.E.2d 134 (1986).

[32] See, e.g., Hancock v. Hobbs, 967 F.2d 462 (11th Cir. 1992); People v. McPeters, 852 P.2d 146 (1992); State v. Loyd, 489 So. 2d 898 (La. 1986), *cert. denied sub nom,* Loyd v. Louisiana, 481 U.S. 1042 (1987). An example of this would be a juror that served as a juror in an earlier trial of the same case. See, e.g., Government of Virgin Islands v. Williams, 476 F.2d 771 (3d Cir. 1973); Griffin v. State, 481 S.W.2d 838 (Tex. Crim. 1972). Also, a person that served as a grand juror in the case. See, e.g., Crosby v. State, 372 S.E.2d 471 (1988); Moya v. State, 691 S.W.2d 63 (Tex. App. 1985). Or a person that sat on an earlier jury that found the defendant guilty of a similar offense. See, e.g., People v. Beirati, 519 N.Y.S.2d 500 (1987); Esterline v. State, 707 S.W.2d 171 (Tex. App. 1986).

[33] 3 FEDERAL LITIGATION GUIDE ¶ 30.16 (1993); Mills v. State, 462 So. 2d 1075 (Fla. 1985); Levy v. State, 749 S.W.2d 176 (Tex. App., Houston, 1988).

[34] 3 FEDERAL LITIGATION GUIDE ¶ 30.16 (1993).

[35] *Id.*

[36] Barnes v. Marshall, 467 S.W.2d 70 (Mo. 1971).

[37] Felder v. State, 758 S.W.2d 760 (Tex. Crim. App. 1988), *cert. denied,* 440 U.S. 950 (1993).

dislike having his objectivity questioned in front of the other potential jurors; additionally, other prospects may resent a challenge to a fellow member of the pool, especially if they have become acquainted. Thus, many judges permit lawyers to make challenges in writing or at sidebar, so the prospective jurors do not hear them.

If the court does not use a procedure to cloak challenges, you should ask the judge to use one. Should the court nevertheless require you to state challenges before the jury, do so in a low-key but businesslike fashion. This approach reinforces the impression that challenges are part of the process, and you are simply doing your job. It also downplays the personal implications of a challenge.

When the court denies a challenge for cause, you generally should use a peremptory challenge to remove the prospective juror. The facts that provoked the cause challenge usually make it prudent to remove the prospect. Additionally, the exercise of a peremptory challenge affirms your sincerity in initially questioning the person's objectivity, which may make further cause challenges more credible to the judge. Further, a prospective juror may become hostile if he knows you attempted to remove him. Thus, you usually should remove the potential juror.

§ 2-5. Preparation for Selecting the Jury.

A good jury voir dire requires preparation. You should prepare questions that communicate thematic points of your case; trial preparation should facilitate this effort. Additionally, you should learn about the judge's voir dire process and the backgrounds of prospective jurors, to permit an organized and effective examination. Your preparation should include the following actions.

§ 2-5(a). Find Out How the Judge Conducts Voir Dire.

As discussed in § 2-4, voir dire practices vary.[38] A statute or rule often establishes the general practice, but variations exist in its implementation. You should find out how the judge intends to conduct the voir dire, how much time — if any — will be allowed the attorneys, how the prospects will be seated and excused, the method by which challenges will be exercised, and whether a jury questionnaire can be submitted.

A good source for this information is the judge herself; indeed, judges often prepare written summaries of their procedures. You can also glean information from the judge's clerk. You should learn the grounds the judge views as appropriate for challenges, areas of inquiry the judge deems off limits, whether the judge is lenient in granting challenges for cause, and similar information. Other lawyers who practice before the court should be a good source of this knowledge.

---

[38] Morris Dees, *The Death of Voir Dire*, 20 Litig. 14 (1993).

If the judge conducts all or part of the voir dire, find out the questions she typically asks the jury prospects. This action permits you to prepare supplemental inquiries. You also should find out the kinds of questions the judge permits attorneys to ask, whether directly or through the court.

§ 2-5(b).   Obtain Background Information on the Jury Prospects.

In jurisdictions where the panel list is available, you usually can obtain basic information about the jury prospects. The data often includes each potential juror's name, address, age, occupation, and marital status. In a small town or rural district, you may already be acquainted with some members of the jury pool. Further discreet inquiries may develop information about other potential jurors.

In a more populated district, you generally can obtain basic information — residence, occupation, marriage partner — from published directories and similar sources. In unusual cases, you may wish to conduct a background investigation of panel members, but you should conduct any such inquiry with extreme caution. If the prospect learns of the investigation and informs the judge, it may provoke an adverse reaction, as the judge may deem the inquiry unduly intrusive. Worse yet, the potential juror may *not* inform the judge, waiting to take out his resentment on you.

A background investigation in most cases involves more trouble and risk than it is worth. The information gained through such an inquiry does not necessarily permit you to predict attitudes. Most of the information could be obtained through a good jury questionnaire or on voir dire. Thus, you usually should obtain information through the traditional methods.

§ 2-5(c).   Prepare Questions in Advance.

You should prepare voir dire inquiries in advance. If the court conducts voir dire, submit questions for the court to ask. If you are permitted to conduct voir dire, you should at least outline the basic content of the questions. Time and thought are required to prepare inquiries that accomplish the twin objectives of discovery and advocacy. In particular, you must plan in order to advocate the theme through questions that — in their form at least — appear to seek information regarding juror attitudes. Of course, you should expect to deviate from the outline in the give-and-take with jury prospects, but you should enter voir dire with a plan tailored to the case.

To prepare questions, you must identify the background facts you need to discover, given the issues, to determine bias. These questions should relate to familiarity with the parties and the facts, matters tending to identify the prospect with one side or the other, and attitudes about the issues.

Additionally, you should identify the factual and legal points that provide the basis for your claims or defenses, including strong equitable points. Use these point statements as the basis for inquiries regarding the prospective jurors' experiences and attitudes. Although couched in a form that seeks information, these inquiries have the primary purpose of beginning persuasion. They expose the prospects to a factual overview of your case and gain acceptance of the legal and fairness principles on which you will rely.

Section 2-6 further discusses the content of questions in voir dire.

§ 2-5(d). Organize Procedures for Recording and Retaining Information.

Voir dire involves questioning a number of people, who usually are strangers. You cannot expect to retain all the background material on these individuals in your head. Additionally, the court often excuses some prospects, then seats others; in some courts, the people in the jury box may also change places as jurors are excused. Often it is difficult to remember who is sitting where. Further, voir dire questions sometimes are directed to the entire jury panel and elicit sporadic responses, which makes it even more difficult to keep the information organized.

During voir dire lawyers often use a chart of the jury box to record information about jury prospects. The chart includes a rectangular space for each seat in the jury box, in which the data can be written. Thus, if there were twelve seats for jurors, the chart would appear as follows:[39]

Alternatively, you can maintain a chart that categorizes jurors according to their positions in the jury box and designates subject areas for recording information. An example[40] follows:

---

[39] See 3 FEDERAL LITIGATION GUIDE ¶ 30.18 (1993).

[40] J. ALEXANDER TANFORD, THE TRIAL PROCESS 238 (1983); HERBERT J. STERN, TRYING CASES TO WIN 494 (1991).

	Juror 1	Juror 2	Juror 3	Juror 4	Juror 5
Name					
Age					
Occupation					
Education					
Marital status					
Spouse's occupation					

These and similar charts can easily be drawn on a yellow pad. You may prefer to use a small poster board or similar device, but make sure that it is not too large or ostentatious. The process of recording information should be subtle, so that it does not make the jury prospects uncomfortable.

You may simplify the recording process by summarizing relevant data in advance. You may obtain this information from the list of jury pool members or — if the court permits — a jury questionnaire. You may wish to prerecord the information on a small sheet with adhesive backing, so you can place it in the relevant box when a juror is seated, and remove it if the juror is excused. Each prospective juror's sheet should have room for recording additional information.

Consider relying on someone else to make notes while you ask questions. Repetitive note taking is likely to bog down the process, intimidate the jury prospects and retard your advocacy. Additionally, a decision to excuse a prospect often is based on observation: the manner in which a prospect looks at a criminal defendant, for instance, may indicate more about her attitude than personal history. You must maintain eye contact to observe these reactions.

You should use procedures in voir dire that maximize your effectiveness at persuasion. While obtaining the kind of information that indicates bias, you need to relate to the jurors and introduce your themes. To accomplish these goals, you should streamline the process of gathering data as much as possible.

§ 2-5(e). Special Methods.

In cases that justify the trouble and expense, attorneys sometimes consult with specialists to determine the likely attitudes of prospects prior to jury selection. An expert in psychology, for example, may help you recognize the implications of body language during the selection process. A sociologist may predict general attitudes of various "types" of persons. Pollsters can develop information regarding community attitudes and differentiate these attitudes by race, sex, age and other attributes. Some advocates even use psychics to advise them at trial concerning prospects' spiritual inclinations.

These methods may be useful in unusual cases, but their value is overblown. General observations are little more help in determining the attitudes of individuals than stereotyped concepts. Counsel is better off trying to improve *the case* — perhaps by trying it out on a mock jury — than trying to develop the profile of a "perfect" juror to hear the case.

§ 2-6. Content of Questions on Voir Dire.

The content of voir dire depends on a number of factors: counsel's appraisal of his own ability to "read" potential jurors, the extent to which the parties' positions are easily identified with prevailing attitudes, limitations placed on counsel's role in voir dire, the thematic facts of the case, and applicable points of law. Counsel must weigh and deal with these considerations in preparing questions.

You should adapt the voir dire inquiries to your case; do not use a "boilerplate" approach. Form questions can do little to expose the jurors' specific attitudes or persuade them that your positions are fair. One goal of voir dire is persuasion; questions need to reflect points about the individual case.[41]

At the same time, you should frame inquiries to expose specific attitudes toward the parties or issues. If you have confidence in your ability to predict juror biases, you may want to spend more time exploring jurors' personal histories, perhaps using questions from other cases, but you should also prepare questions that deal with the issues.

As the first to ask questions, the plaintiff or prosecutor has an advantage in persuading jury prospects. The first spin on a point is often absorbed best by a listener. The attorneys usually take turns asking questions in voir dire, however, so the defense may get to introduce some concepts.

---

[41] DONALD E. VINSON, JURY PERSUASION: PSYCHOLOGICAL STRATEGIES AND TRIAL TECHNIQUES 118–24 (1993).

The defense has a special need to introduce points in voir dire because the plaintiff or prosecutor speaks first in opening statement. Exposing the jury to counterpoints in voir dire should lessen the impact of the opposing side's opening statement. Although taking the second turn in voir dire presents a handicap in persuasion, it may give the defense an advantage in evaluating jury prospects because counsel has time to observe the potential jurors before questioning them. Additionally, he has the information obtained by opposing counsel and may follow up in areas of special interest. Further, once the adverse party initiates personal questioning, defense counsel's questions may seem less intrusive, giving him greater freedom to pursue sensitive information.

Questions that serve the purpose of advocacy stretch the permissible bounds of voir dire. This phase of the trial is supposed to determine the qualifications of potential jurors and whether they might be biased; it is not meant to provide counsel an opportunity for argument. Yet successful trial lawyers use voir dire for advocacy, adopting a form that camouflages the true point.

The trial judge, applying a test of essential fairness, has substantial discretion in permitting inquiries on vior dire.[42] If the advocate poses questions that seem fairly designed to expose bias, courts generally permit them. The fact that the questions also tend to "sell" thematic aspects of the case does not necessarily make them improper. The phrasing of advocacy questions to comply with the requirements of voir dire is discussed below.

You must adjust the voir dire for the extent to which the court permits questioning by attorneys. Usually, the court conducts at least part of the voir dire. Some courts permit the attorneys to participate only by submitting written questions. Courts almost always impose time limits on counsel's questions. Thus, you must make the best use of time.

With these considerations in mind, you can prepare questions to accomplish the twin goals of voir dire: identifying hostile prospects and persuading the panel. The following considerations should influence the form and content of questions.

§ 2-6(a).   Open-Ended vs. Closed-End Questions.

Lawyers typically use two types of questions in questioning prospects, depending on their objectives. Open-ended questions call on the prospect to provide substantive information: "Please explain the duties of your job, Ms. Jones." Closed-end questions are more focused and often suggest the answer: "You wouldn't ignore evidence of self defense if it is presented by the defendant, would you?" Open-ended questions are the kind typically employed in the direct

---

[42] Brown v. United States, 338 F.2d 543 (D.C. Cir. 1964); United States v. Fernandez-Piloto, 426 F.2d 892 (5th Cir. 1970); United States v. Owens, 415 F.2d 1308 (6th Cir. 1969), *cert. denied*, 397 U.S. 997 (1970).

examination of witnesses, while closed-end questions are like those used in cross-examination.

Since open-ended questions require the juror to narrate a response, they are more efficient in eliciting information. Open-ended questions have been compared to a psychological test, in that no answer is right or wrong, yet the answer tends to reveal the prospective juror's makeup and attitudes.[43] In addition, the inquiry may elicit unanticipated comments that guide the lawyer to new areas of inquiry. Moreover, since the open-ended question calls for a narrative answer, it reveals something about the prospect's delivery and assertiveness. This information helps the lawyer estimate "the juror's personality, articulateness, and leadership potential on the jury."[44]

Open-ended questions are effective in revealing biases that the prospect would not disclose in response to a closed-end question. For example, if you ask a potential juror if he is prejudiced against African Americans, the person will likely say no, even if the response is untrue. Few prospects admit such prejudice in front of the court and other panel members. If you ask the same prospect to describe his attitude toward affirmative action, on the other hand, he is forced to choose what words to use, and, on further inquiry, provide examples to illustrate the response. The prospect's answer may reveal enough for the lawyer to determine whether he is biased.[45]

Many lawyers fear that using open-ended questions will reduce their control of the voir dire process. A prospect's response may reflect poorly on the lawyer's client, introduce a subject that the lawyer wishes to avoid, or waste time on unimportant matters. Open-ended questions also may make jury prospects uncomfortable. Some people enjoy the chance to state their views in front of a courtroom audience, but others may think the lawyer's questions put them on the spot. As they speak, the prospects may feel that the attorney is "judging" the responses; this inference may induce a defensive attitude toward counsel generally. Thus, open-ended questions present some risk, so you should employ them selectively. Even so, open-ended questions are much better for obtaining information than closed-end inquiries; some use of these inquiries generally is worth the risk.[46]

You may avoid the potential repercussions of open-ended questions by convincing the court to ask them. Open-ended questions posed by the court do not reflect on counsel. Additionally, a judge may be more effective in getting

---

[43] JAMES J. GOBERT & WALTER E. JORDAN, JURY SELECTION: THE LAW, ART AND SCIENCE OF SELECTING A JURY § 9.15 at 338 (2d ed. 1990). See also ANN FAGAN GINGER, JURY SELECTION IN CIVIL AND CRIMINAL TRIALS § 8.56 (2d ed. 1984).

[44] GOBERT & JORDAN, *supra* note 42.

[45] *Id.* at 338–39.

[46] V. HALE STARR & MARK MCCORMICK, JURY SELECTION § 11.02 at 404 (2d ed. 1993).

prospects to speak freely. The judge may be reluctant to ask open-ended questions because they consume time, but may do so if counsel jointly propose the inquiries. Thus, you should try to secure the opposing attorney's agreement to proposed questions.

If the court exclusively conducts the voir dire, you should make a special effort to promote the use of open-ended questions. Observing the prospects respond to these questions at least provides some basis for evaluating their attitudes. A closed-ended examination by the court is not likely to provide much information that is useful in evaluating the prospects.

Closed-end questions are normally employed for persuasion. Using these inquiries, you can lead the prospect to accept factual points and legal precepts. The content of these inquiries is discussed in the following subsections. Additionally, when you suspect a prospective juror is biased, you can use closed-end inquiries to expose the prejudice; this approach may offend the prospect but can demonstrate to the judge and other jury prospects that a challenge is justified. Further, if you believe a prospect is favorably disposed toward your case, you may use closed-end questions to avoid revealing this predisposition to opposing counsel.

§ 2-6(b).   Introducing Factual Points.

You should use voir dire to expose the jurors to factual points supporting your case — the points that show the fairness of your position or elicit sympathy for your client. These points should reflect the thematic message that you intend to emphasize throughout the trial. The points must be incorporated into questions that *appear* to seek information from the jury prospects, however, and to expose unfavorable bias. Thus, you must give thought to their form.

In fashioning these questions, first identify positive factual points — those supporting the application of a favorable legal rule or showing the fairness of your ultimate position. Often these facts are conclusory. For instance, based on the facts of the *Danielson* case, some of the contentions counsel for the plaintiff might identify are the following:

1.   ComputerCentre Associates made false representations to get the Danielsons to purchase a franchise.
2.   ComputerCentre Associates knew the Danielsons had no business experience and suggested experience was unnecessary.
3.   ComputerCentre Associates' representatives made promises to the Danielsons that they failed to fulfill (including sales training, technical support, business programs, and advertising).
4.   ComputerCentre Associates' president engaged in self-dealing with his brother's company, which charged a double markup to the Danielsons and failed to deliver products on time.

5. The president of ComputerCentre Associates thought he could take advantage of the Danielsons because they were "yokels" who would never know the difference.

Some of the points that might evoke sympathy for the Danielsons are:

1. The Danielsons are lifelong Middletown residents, and Mr. Danielson served in the police department.
2. The Danielsons invested their life savings in the franchise, including the equity in their house, and lost it all when the franchise failed.
3. Mr. Danielson suffered a heart attack during a conversation with ComputerCentre's president, which has left him partially incapacitated.

Counsel might identify a number of other points, but too many may clutter the picture the attorney wants to present.

The initial questions — those that introduce the parties and identify relationships — are a good means of working on jurors' sympathies. The plaintiff in the *Danielson* case might try some of the following questions:

Q. [To the potential jurors] The plaintiffs in this case are Jack and Margaret Danielson, who have lived in Middletown all their lives and reside at 1234 Barstow Avenue. Do any of you know Jack or Margaret?

A. [No response].

Q. The defendant is ComputerCentre Associates, which is run by Dale Atkins. Do any of you have any relationship with this computer company or Mr. Atkins?

A. [No response].

Q. The defendant is represented by Jason Bilbe, Suzanne Ciaccio, and Keith Hall of Smith and Johnson, a Chicago firm of more than 200 lawyers that has an office here in Middletown. Do any of you know Mr. Bilbe, Ms. Ciaccio, Mr. Hall, or any of the other lawyers in that law firm?

A. [No response].

Q. The Danielsons claim they lost their life savings, which they invested in a computer store at the Middletown historic mall, because of fraud and breach of promise by ComputerCentre Associates. Are any of you familiar with the facts of this dispute?

A. [No response].

> Q.   Mr. Danielson suffered a heart attack several months after opening the franchise while registering a complaint with Mr. Atkins of ComputerCentre. Mr. Smith, if Mr. Danielson is unable to attend the trial every day, because of his heart condition, would you hold his absence against him?
>
> A.   No. Of course not.

To use points of argument in voir dire, counsel must transform the points into questions that appear to seek information. These inquiries must at least have a form that seeks to expose adverse bias of potential jurors; otherwise, the questions appear improper. Therefore, counsel must connect the factual point to a plausible concern about jurors' prejudice. One way to accomplish this goal is to ask whether the prospective juror would have any reservation against accepting the point if the evidence supported it. Another is to ask if the prospect has any special experience with facts relevant to the point. Some examples, based on the points identified for the Danielsons, are the following:

> Q.   In this case the Danielsons will contend that they expended their savings to purchase a ComputerCentre franchise because of false representations made by ComputerCentre's president, Dale Atkins, and his assistant, Jene Nelsen, and false representations made in advertisements. Ms. Claypool, are you familiar with the advertising claims of Computer-Centre Associates?
>
> A.   No. I've never seen them.
>
> Q.   Assuming the evidence shows these claims were false, is there any reason why you would be reluctant to accept the evidence on that point?
>
> A.   No.
>
> *   *   *
>
> Q.   Mr. Smith, the Danielsons will contend that computer training is important in running a computer franchise, but ComputerCentre Associates told them that they did not need experience and all necessary training would be provided. Have you ever had any experience in operating a computer franchise?
>
> A.   No. I've been to computer stores, but that's all.

Q. If the proof shows that training really was necessary, is there anything in your experience that would give you difficulty accepting the need for training in operating a computer franchise?

A. No.

* * *

Q. The Danielsons also will contend that Mr. Atkins and Ms. Nelsen made promises of technical support and training that ComputerCentre Associates failed to keep, which caused their business to fail. Ms. Avenson, do you have experience in selling or repairing computer products?

A. No, I don't.

Q. Do any of you have preexisting notions that might prevent you from accepting the need for technical support in operating a computer franchise, assuming the evidence supports this conclusion?

A. [No response].

* * *

Q. Mr. Franklin, do you have experience selling products on order from a warehouse?

A. No.

Q. We contend that the Danielsons' business failed partly because Dale Atkins, the president of ComputerCentre, required the Danielsons to purchase from Wizard Supply — owned by Mr. Atkins's brother. We also contend that Wizard charged a higher than normal markup to the Danielsons and delivered products late. Assuming the evidence shows the products often arrived late, resulting in a loss of sales, is there any reason why you would not be able to accept the conclusion that late delivery could cause customers to cancel their orders?

A. No.

Q. If the evidence shows that Mr. Atkins never revealed to the Danielsons that he had an interest in Wizard, or that the Danielsons were receiving a higher than normal markup, is there anything in your experience that would make you

> assume this type of information should not be revealed to
> a franchisee?
>
> A.   No. I don't see why not.
>
> Q.   The Danielsons contend — based on a letter written by Mr.
> Atkins — that he thought he could take advantage of them
> because they were, in his words, "yokels." Mr. Smith, would
> the fact that the Danielsons were called "yokels" by Mr.
> Atkins lead you to be biased against the Danielsons or to
> conclude that it's all right to lie to them?
>
> A.   No.

Since these questions rather obviously argue the case, counsel should inter-
sperse them with inquiries designed solely to obtain information. Some jurisdictions permit advocacy questions,[47] but others may deem them beyond the proper
scope of voir dire. The attorney may defend the above questions, however, on
the ground that they merely reflect the flip side of inquiries that would reasonably
be asked by the adverse party. In other words, questions that probe the prospects'
attitudes about the *negative* aspects of a case are usually viewed as inoffensive.
For instance, counsel for ComputerCentre Associates would likely be within her
rights to ask:

> Q.   If the evidence shows that ComputerCentre Associates could
> not fulfill certain promises because of unexpected temporary
> problems, but also shows that the temporary failures did not
> cause the Danielsons' business to fail, would you rule for
> the Danielsons simply because of unexpected temporary
> problems?
>
> A.   Not necessarily.

Counsel also can couple questions about factual points with inquiries about
the prospects' ability to accept legal principles, as discussed in the next section.

---

[47] See Dean v. Nunez, 534 So. 2d 1282 (La. App. 4th Cir. 1982), *rev'd on other grounds*, 536
So. 2d 1203 (La. 1989). The court held a valid purpose of voir dire is to:

> [P]romote trial advocacy . . . to pre-conditioning and education on issues in the case,
> neutralizing prejudices which are not grounds for a cause challenge, laying a foundation
> to develop tactics or strategy, exhibiting credibility, introducing the theme or theory for
> the case, setting the stage for opening statements or closing arguments, anticipating
> objections, disclosing weaknesses in the case and becoming acquainted with the jury.

Id. at 1288.

This approach helps legitimize the factual questions because courts generally permit inquiries about the legal rules.

§ 2-6(c). Securing Acceptance of Legal Principles.

You may also use vior dire to introduce and secure the prospective jurors' acceptance of legal propositions. Often these principles are uncontroversial, but lay persons nevertheless may be unfamiliar with them. Thus, for example, the prospects may know that liability can be based on fault, but not that a party may be liable for a defective condition regardless of fault. You may use vior dire to condition the jury prospects to accept the principle. Additionally, voir dire provides you an opportunity to emphasize favorable principles and, in combination with facts, advocate the case.

The legal points you state must be accurate. Additionally, since instructing the jury is a function of the court, you should note that the court will provide legal instructions: "As the court will instruct you at the close of the case, our law provides that a person injured through the fault of another may collect for her damages from the person who caused them." Of course, you may not know all the legal instructions the court will give at the time of voir dire, but you usually know the basic legal claims and defenses. Additionally, the court often has a form that provides most of the jury instructions. When in doubt, you should ask the judge whether a legal point is acceptable.

Applying these principles to the *Danielson* case, the attorney would identify basic legal propositions supporting the theory of liability. Some of these precepts may include:

1.   A party who misrepresents or fails to disclose important facts in selling a franchise commits fraud, which allows the purchasing party to void the transaction and recover his losses.

2.   [If applicable.] A party who has been defrauded may recover punitive damages from the party who committed the fraud, to deter people from engaging in this kind of conduct.

3.   [Assuming failure to perform is alleged.] A party who fails to fulfill his obligations under a contract may be required to pay all the resulting financial losses of the other party to the contract.

You may state these precepts to determine whether jury prospects can accept them. At the same time, if you describe the principles as part of the law to be presented in the judge's instructions, it gives them an aura of validity. You might ask:

> Q.   Ms. Kane, the court will instruct you that under the law of this State, a party that misrepresents or fails to disclose

> important facts in selling a franchise commits fraud, and that a party who purchases a franchise because of fraud is entitled to recover his investment and any other losses. Would you have any difficulty accepting this legal principle in deciding this case?
>
> A.   No. None at all.
>
> Q.   The court will also instruct you that a party who commits fraud in marketing a franchise may be required to pay punitive damages, over and above the actual losses of the defrauded party, to deter fraudulent conduct in the future. Would you have any trouble in accepting this legal instruction and deciding whether an award of punitive damages is appropriate to deter the party who committed fraud from doing it again?
>
> A.   No.

Questions that introduce legal principles take on context, as well as advocacy, if they are combined with factual claims. Additionally, they tend to legitimize inquiries that contain factual claims. Most courts permit questions about the prospective jurors' ability to accept basic legal principles so long as counsel acknowledges the court's role in stating the law.[48] Thus, the plaintiff in the *Danielson* case might fashion inquiries that incorporate fact and law, as follows:

> Q.   Mr. Johnson, the plaintiffs, Jack and Margaret Danielson, contend that ComputerCentre Associates induced them to purchase a ComputerCentre franchise by making false claims that ComputerCentre would provide all the technical training and support they needed and by failing to disclose that the Danielsons would be charged a higher than normal markup for the products they purchased. I believe the judge will instruct you that a party who markets a franchise through false representations or by omitting material facts commits fraud under the law of this state, entitling the other party to damages. Is there any reason why you would not be able to accept this instruction, and find fraud, if the

---

[48] See HERBERT J. STERN, TRYING CASES TO WIN 513 (1991): "[Y]ou must seem to be testing the venire's willingness to follow the instructions of the judge. In this mode you begin your question with, 'If the judge (court) should instruct you that . . .' and finish with a legal instruction, correct on the law, which the venireman is asked whether he would follow. . . ."

> evidence shows that ComputerCentre misrepresented impor-
> tant facts and failed to disclose important facts to the
> Danielsons?
>
> A.   No.
>
> Q.   We will contend that ComputerCentre — through Dale
> Atkins, its president, and Jene Nelsen, his assistant — made
> false representations to take advantage of the Danielsons,
> who Atkins and Nelsen knew were inexperienced, and to
> get them to pay for a franchise. The judge will instruct you
> that if a party commits fraud through false representations,
> a jury may award punitive damages — damages in excess
> of the actual loss — to deter this kind of conduct in the
> future. Would any of you be unwilling to follow this
> instruction if the evidence showed that punitive damages
> are appropriate to deter ComputerCentre from defrauding
> innocent people in the future?
>
> A.   [No response].

Of course, the defendant in *Danielson* also could combine factual contentions
and legal precepts. An example follows:

> A.   Mr. Emerson, ComputerCentre contends that the reason the
> Danielsons failed in their venture was not any failure of
> ComputerCentre, which is successful throughout the coun-
> try, but poor business decisions by the Danielsons, their use
> of untrained salesmen, Mr. Danielson's inability to work at
> the store, and other failures. If the judge instructs you that
> you can award a verdict to the Danielsons only if the
> evidence shows ComputerCentre caused their loss, would
> you follow this instruction, even though you might have
> some sympathy for the Danielsons?
>
> A.   Yes, I would.

Often attorneys spend time in voir dire questioning prospects about their ability
to apply burdens of proof. For example, defense counsel in a civil case might
ask whether prospective jurors will hold the plaintiff to his burden of proving
the elements of his case "by a preponderance of the evidence." Generally, this
focus on the burden of proof is inadvisable. Lay persons may not understand
burdens of proof — which are often described in incomprehensible jargon —
and are more likely to worry about who is right than who has the burden. More

important, a party who makes a big deal of the other side's heavy burden, or his own easy burden, sends a signal that his facts are weak. The attorney is better off pressing his basic theme.

In a criminal case a defendant's emphasis on the burden of proof has more validity. The reasonable doubt standard is well known to lay people, and most have a rough idea of what it means. The standard also has content; it is designed to make convicting the defendant especially difficult. Moreover, a defense attorney sometimes does not present a case; the prosecution's burden may be the primary line of defense. If the attorney does have affirmative points to present, however, she should concentrate on her theory at least as much as the burden.

§ 2-6(d). Disclosing Weaknesses.

As a matter of strategy, you may wish to use voir dire to disclose weaknesses. In disclosing a weakness, you may be able to cast it in a more favorable light than the adverse party would provide. Indeed, in context with other facts, you may be able to portray it as a strength. Additionally, you may reduce the impact of the weak point by getting the prospect to agree it will not be determinative.

Bringing up weak points on voir dire is risky. Undue emphasis of weaknesses may cause the jurors to believe the entire case is weak. Out of context, a weak point may seem more important than it really is, especially if you appear defensive in presenting it. The point of disclosing a weakness is to place it in context, or "draw the sting," by making it less injurious than if first presented by the opposition. You should give careful consideration to whether and how you should bring up a weakness in voir dire. It may be better to present the point in opening statement, where it can be placed in the context of an affirmative case.

An example of disclosing a potential weakness in a way that helps the case, based on *Danielson*, is the following question asked on behalf of the Danielsons:

Q.   The Danielsons will contend that they chose the Computer-Centre franchise because of advertising claims that franchisees did not need experience in marketing computers. As you will learn, the Danielsons did not have any of this experience. Would you hold the Danielsons' lack of experience against them if the evidence shows that Computer-Centre Associates represented that experience was unnecessary?

Counsel for ComputerCentre could combine the disclosure of a weakness with a defense in the manner described in § 2-6(b). The question is repeated here:

> Q. If the evidence shows that ComputerCentre Associates could not fulfill certain promises because of unexpected temporary problems, but also shows that the temporary failures did not cause the Danielsons' business to fail, would you rule for the Danielsons simply because of unexpected temporary problems?

A tougher problem arises when counsel is faced with a really bad fact, such as a prior conviction. Getting a jury prospect to agree that he will limit his use of the conviction, or decide the case on the merits despite the conviction, may be an illusory accomplishment. Yet you eventually must face up to the bad fact, assuming the court will admit it into evidence. One approach may be to discuss the fact as if "everyone knows" it should not be given much weight. An example follows:

> Q. Mr. Treeby, in this case you will hear that Mr. Atkins's assistant, Jene Nelsen, was convicted of fraud a number of years ago, but paid her price to society. Now, of course, you are aware that you are not supposed to allow this event from her past to decide whether she did anything wrong in this case, aren't you?
>
> A. Yes.
>
> Q. You know, of course, that under our law it would be improper to penalize ComputerCentre just because it gave a job opportunity to someone who was once convicted of a crime?
>
> A. Yes.
>
> Q. Do you agree that your evaluation of Ms. Nelsen's conduct in this case should be judged on the facts of this case and not on some event from her past?
>
> A. Yes, I do.

Your statements, of course, must accurately portray the law. If the court has ruled that the prior conviction will be allowed for impeachment only, you validly may state that it cannot be used on the merits — "to decide whether she did anything wrong in this case." If the court finds it admissible for another purpose, you might have to ask different questions.

§ 2-6(e). Securing Juror Explanations for Harmful Evidence.

One effective means of dealing with weaknesses is to involve prospective jurors in conceiving valid explanations for superficially harmful facts. If a juror in *voir dire* suggests an explanation that counsel intends to use in argument, the point may seem more credible than if it were advanced only by the advocate. Additionally, involving the jurors in suggesting explanations may open their minds to the possibility that the bad fact can be explained. Further, this approach may help you identify those jurors who will consider an alternate explanation for a superficially harmful fact.

Involving the jurors in explaining weaknesses requires a two-way substantive dialogue that may not be easy to achieve. If jurors are unwilling to offer substantive suggestions, your questions may backfire, leaving the impression that valid reasons for the harmful fact do not exist. You still may suggest your explanation, but this action may not cure the negative impression left by your failure to secure an explanation from the jurors.

For an example of involving the jurors in conceiving explanations, consider Dale Atkins' use of the terms "yokels" and "clowns" in describing the Danielsons. These condescending descriptions, on first blush, suggest that Atkins is a callous individual who might be inclined to take advantage of unsophisticated franchise applicants. Undoubtedly, counsel for ComputerCentre may expect to hear references to this name-calling throughout the trial and would benefit enormously from an early introduction to an alternative explanation. The example follows:

Q. You will hear from the Danielsons that Mr. Atkins, after attempting to work with the Danielsons for awhile, referred to them in a letter in disparaging terms. Do any of you have any experience with one person calling another by a disparaging name? Mr. Jones?

A. Yes, of course.

Q. Have you ever used a disparaging term to describe someone?

A. I guess so.

Q. Do you believe calling a person a name—say a yokel— always means the speaker would like to hurt or take advantage of that person?

A. Not necessarily.

Q. What other reasons might explain the use of a disparaging term?

> A. Well, the person might be kidding.
>
> Q. Well, right. Surely we all sometimes use terms like that when we're just kidding around. Can anyone think of another explanation for describing someone in uncomplimentary fashion? Ms. Shelton?
>
> A. The person might be mad about something.
>
> Q. In your experience, is that pretty common, a person gets angry or impatient about something, and refers to someone in derogatory fashion?
>
> A. It happens, sure.
>
> Q. Have you ever seen this happen between family members?
>
> A. Oh, yes.
>
> Q. Does that necessarily mean the speaker wants to do any harm to the other person?
>
> A. No.

These questions are often useful in criminal cases, because counsel is often forced to rely on *possible* explanations for evidence—say, possession of stolen goods. If you can involve jurors in suggesting non-criminal explanations for harmful evidence, you lay a foundation for arguing the explanation credibly in the trial.

§ 2-6(f). Contracting with Jurors.

Sometimes attorneys ask a prospective juror to commit that he will grant a favorable verdict if certain facts are proved. Courts frown on these bargains because they may not reflect all the matters that must be weighed in deciding an issue and, to some extent, ask the prospect to predetermine the case before he hears the evidence.

Nevertheless, courts permit some questions that seek bargains. Questions that limit the extent of the prospective juror's commitment — for instance, an agreement to follow a legal instruction — are generally permissible. Broader questions, especially those that commit a juror to an ultimate decision, are objectionable. Since people tend to honor their commitments, you should try for contracts with jurors, but also stay within proper bounds.

You may have most freedom in seeking a commitment that a juror will consider harmful facts only in a manner permitted by law — for instance, a prior conviction on the issue of credibility:

71

> Q.   Can you assure me that you will not consider Ms. Nelsen's past conviction in deciding whether she is the type of person who would misrepresent facts to the Danielsons?
>
> A.   Yes, I can.

Paradoxically, forging a bargain on a weak point may unduly emphasize the point in the prospect's mind. Therefore, be cautious in seeking contracts to limit the impact of bad facts.

A court will be more skeptical of your use of strong points to establish bargains, especially if the questions go to the ultimate decision. The following inquiry, for instance, is probably too close to the ultimate decision:

> Q.   Will you assure me that if the evidence shows Computer-Centre made false claims to the Danielsons, you will find they should pay damages for fraud?
>
> A.   Yes.

A more limited attempt at a bargain — with less of an absolute sound — may be permissible:

> Q.   If the judge instructs you that the Danielsons may recover only for nonperformance that actually caused the failure of the business, and the evidence shows that none of the temporary problems experienced by the Danielsons caused the business to fail, can you assure me that you will put aside any sympathy you have for the Danielsons and apply the law?
>
> A.   Yes.
>
> Q.   And if you find the nonperformance did not cause any harm, you would rule for ComputerCentre on this point?
>
> A.   Yes.

§ 2-7. Demeanor and Tactics on Voir Dire.

Voir dire is counsel's first exposure to the jurors.[49] During this process the prospective jurors draw initial conclusions regarding the attorney's likability, fairness, knowledge, and competence, and these determinations are likely to stick. Thus, you need to make a good impression, which requires common sense and consideration for others. The following methods should help in this effort.

§ 2-7(a). Be Considerate.

You should remember that jury prospects are in an unfamiliar situation. They will appreciate simple consideration for their plight and legitimate needs. People do not like to be embarrassed; they do not like to be left "in the dark"; they do not like others to assume they are stupid, they do not like to be treated with disrespect. You should accord the same treatment to jurors that you would want, if called for jury duty.

Avoid embarrassing prospective jurors. Asking questions they cannot answer, or questions that put them on the spot, is offensive. Usually you can accomplish your objective diplomatically. For instance, if you want to know the extent of the prospect's familiarity with farm machinery, do not ask a question that requires him to admit ignorance. A question that might embarrass the juror is the following:

Q.	Have you ever been on a farm?
A.	No, I haven't.

An inquiry that provides the prospect more room to maneuver — and assumes the likelihood of some knowledge — is more considerate:

Q.	What familiarity do you have with farm operations?
A.	Not much, really — a little, I guess.

If you want to establish a point through an inquiry, help the prospect out by imparting information in the question. The following inquiry would be inappropriate:

---

[49] See Jeffrey T. Frederick, *Effective Voir Dire: From the Mouths of Jurors*, TRIAL 66 (Aug. 1988).

Q.   Do you know when the court gives the legal instructions
      to the jury?

A.   No.

You would accomplish the goal without embarrassing the juror with the
following question:

Q.   Now, you're aware that the court will provide legal instruc-
      tions at the close of the evidence in the case, aren't you?

A.   Yes.

Telling the prospective jurors the general issue in the case, so that they will
see the legitimacy of questions, is also a good idea. Additionally, if you disclose
your point in particular areas of inquiry, potential jurors feel more comfortable
in responding. An approach that "hides the ball," requiring prospects to answer
questions when they do not know where counsel is headed, makes them
uncomfortable and guarded in their answers.

Politeness in phrasing questions also promotes a good relationship. An
occasional "please," "thank you," "I appreciate that," and similar phrases promote
a considerate image. You should not overdo politeness to the point of fawning,
but some graciousness is always appreciated. Additionally, phrase follow-up
questions to avoid any suggestion the prospect was evasive. Rather than "I don't
believe you answered my question," you might say: "I'm afraid my question
wasn't very clear. Let me restate it." Further, adopt the prospect's language. If
the potential juror uses "I think," ask: "What do you think about. . . ."

One of the primary functions of a lawyer in any complex case is translation.
Jurors often are unfamiliar with technical and legal jargon. They appreciate
simple explanations that allow them to follow the conversation. You should
explain special points without talking down to the prospects. By using phrases
such as "You may be aware that . . . ," you can explain technical terms without
taking on a superior air.

You must be considerate of special sensitivities of jury prospects. Avoid
comments that reflect racial, sexual, or ethnic stereotypes. If John Brown and
Louise Smith are jury prospects and you address them as "Mr. Brown" and
"Louise," "Louise" and other women prospects may view the distinction as a
slight. Be aware of your own tendencies that — however unintentionally —
offend others, and try to avoid them. In addition, make sure that you describe

ethnic groups in a manner that *currently* has acceptance in the relevant community.

You should have an open, interested attitude toward potential jurors. Smile occasionally. Your face should be open rather than pinched; raising the eyebrows helps this look. Your overall demeanor should be friendly, but not artificial. An open approach should in turn make the jury prospects more receptive to you.

§ 2-7(b). Be Professional.

Although you should be courteous to the potential jurors, you also should be professional. The prospects know the attorneys are paid to win and therefore have a selfish reason to be friendly. Your role in the trial — that of an advocate and officer of the court — requires that you maintain a respectful distance from the jurors. Thus, you should not be too personal, flattering, or grateful. This type of fawning is counterproductive.

§ 2-7(c). Listen.

A major problem in questioning others is the difficulty of paying attention. Often counsel focuses on what she has to do next — how to phrase the next inquiry — and fails to listen to a prospect's response. This lapse not only deprives the lawyer of information, but interferes with the *dialogue* necessary for true communication. To "click" personally with a jury prospect, you need some two-way conversation, which requires listening to prospects' responses.

§ 2-7(d). Maintain Eye Contact.

You need to maintain comfortable eye contact with jury prospects — a level appropriate to normal conversation. This approach does not require staring, because constant eye contact makes most people uncomfortable. Instead, you should look at a prospect at least part of the time while stating questions and as he responds. The eye contact should suggest that you are fully attentive to what the prospect has to say. For a natural break in eye contact, occasionally look at other members of the jury pool.

Eye contact is essential to true communication. People often communicate without uttering a word, through facial expressions and eye contact. A speaker who communicates through the eyes as well as the ears often provokes the listener's imagination; one who addresses the ears alone may not even hold attention. Moreover, the eyes reveal sincerity, friendliness, and other qualities that forge personal relationships. Eye contact is necessary to observe the jurors; you may learn their attitudes by watching their facial responses, their expressions as they look at the parties, and their body language. Thus, you should maintain good eye contact with the prospects.

§ 2-7(e). Use Time Efficiently.

A listener's opinion of a speaker almost always is influenced by the speaker's use of time. Anyone who is forced to listen to a bland presentation soon begins watching the clock; if a speaker drones on to no apparent purpose, the normal listener usually becomes irritated. In contrast, listeners appreciate a well-directed speaker — one who has an apparent purpose and moves efficiently to achieve it.

In a trial the jurors are a captive audience. They know they must devote their time to hearing the case and most of them do not resent this commitment. At the same time, the jurors do not want to waste time — time that could be spent in more enjoyable pursuits. Moreover, jurors who invest their time want it used in an interesting and purposeful manner. Thus, they appreciate a directed presentation.

Voir dire is your first exposure to the jurors. It also is a phase of the trial in which you may have leeway to wander. The listeners may tolerate some of this exploration because the questions are addressed to different people, but eventually the prospects may form an impression that your questions are aimless. To avoid this image, you need to accomplish the goals of voir dire efficiently.

To appear efficient, you should avoid undue repetition of questions. Asking an advocacy question two or three times is enough.[50] Vary the phrasing of your questions. You should limit the background discovery from jurors, asking about basic personal history and matters that truly relate to the case.[51] Additionally, let jurors know where you are going, so that they are not befuddled by an unfathomable interrogation. The listeners will appreciate being let in on your purpose, will be more interested, and should react more favorably to your theme as the case progresses.

§ 2-8. Deciding to Challenge Jury Prospects.

At some point the attorney must exercise challenges — either challenges for cause or peremptory challenges — to remove prospects from the jury. In making this decision, counsel hopefully will not have to weigh too much information: the pollster's demographic study, the psychologist's body language advice, the psychic's spiritual report, point scores from background checks, and volumes of notes from hours of personal questioning. Drawing reliable conclusions in voir dire is difficult enough without having to process data that would overload a computer. At the same time, the advocate must rely on something in determining which prospects to excuse. Often that "something" is instinct, but it can be

---

[50] *Id.*

[51] HERBERT J. STERN, TRYING CASES TO WIN 488 (1991): "Do not harp on meaningless questions about a juror's background, education, hobbies, and the like."

influenced by a common sense appraisal of the potential jurors in light of the issues.

The difficulty in selecting the "right" jurors is ameliorated somewhat by the mechanics of voir dire. You do not have the right to keep prospects; you only are permitted to challenge them and are limited in the number you may remove through peremptory challenges. Additionally, you do not control the order in which pool members are brought to the jury box. Thus, as a practical matter you can only get rid of the worst prospects and should focus on finding them.[52] In doing so, you should consider the following factors.

§ 2-8(a). Intelligence.

One factor that often makes a difference in challenging prospects is intelligence. In much the same way that you appraise a judge's intelligence in deciding whether you want a jury, you should assess the intelligence of potential jurors in deciding whether to excuse them. If you have a strong case on the facts and the law, you should keep intelligent jurors because they will appreciate a solid argument. If you have a weak case, or depend largely on an appeal to emotion, you should challenge intelligent prospects.

§ 2-8(b). Responsibility.

A corollary consideration is whether the prospect seems responsible. This trait ordinarily is associated with stable family, regular and long-standing employment, community service, and religious devotion. Responsible people perform the jury function properly, seeking the result ordained by the law and facts, because they are used to fulfilling obligations in conformity with societal expectations. They also pay attention. Thus, a responsible person makes a good juror for a lawyer who has a strong case.

§ 2-8(c). Tendency to Identify with a Party.

You should consider the likelihood that prospects will identify with the parties. If your party representative is a business executive and the adverse party is a laborer, you should be suspicious of prospects who are laborers. A significant class difference between your client and a potential juror is a ground for concern because class gaps breed mistrust. You should not excuse a potential juror solely on this ground, but it is a factor to consider.

§ 2-8(d). Potential to Influence Other Jurors.

A prospect with a strong personality or unusual familiarity with a factual area can dilute the impact of your presentation. An engineer, for instance, may lead

---

[52] 3 FEDERAL LITIGATION GUIDE § 30.18[5]: "[Y]ou do not pick a jury; you 'unpick' it. . . . [Y]our task is to identify the panel members who, for whatever reason, may be biased against your client or your case."

jurors away from an engineering conclusion required by the evidence on the basis of her own experience. Excusing prospects who may unduly influence other jurors is often the safest course because it helps you — through your presentation — control the content of deliberations. Of course, if a strong prospect also is a likely ally, you should not excuse her.

§ 2-8(e). Stereotypes.

Stereotypical grounds for judging prospects — blacks will vote for a black, men will vote for a man, etc. — have only a superficial basis. People may identify with others on an ethnic or sexual basis, but that bias may be overpowered by other, more specific biases. Further, even if these biases exist, the evidence often overcomes them. Additionally, excusing a juror for race or sex alone is inconsistent with constitutional limitations on jury selection. See § 2-10. Thus, you should rely on other factors in excusing prospects.

§ 2-8(f). Instinct.

In the end, attorneys rely heavily on instinct in deciding which prospects to excuse.[53] Counsel knows the case, knows his own personality, and is in the best position to know which potential jurors will be responsive to his arguments. When a lawyer appraises a potential juror, he takes account of many factors subconsciously. Eye communication, facial expressions, and body language are evaluated whether the attorney realizes it or not. An instinctive reaction takes account of more information than a point-by-point appraisal and may be more accurate.

§ 2-9. Exercising Challenges.

In exercising challenges, you should openly collaborate with other parties only if you wish to be identified with them. The jurors observe the discussions among the attorneys and naturally view those who consult together as allies. If you want separate consideration for your client, you should not consult with others in the presence of the jury. Additionally, you should avoid terms, such as "my co-counsel," that incorrectly suggest allegiances.[54]

---

[53] One Florida judge states that the following simple formula can be used to decide whether to exercise a peremptory challenge:

  1. You like them? Keep them.

  2. You tolerate them? Keep them.

  3. Your opponent likes them and you like them? Keep them.

  4. Your opponent likes them and you tolerate them? Keep them.

  5. You despise or mistrust them? Challenge them.

Mark R. McGarry, Jr., *Do-It-Yourself Voir Dire*, 10 Litig. 38, 40 (1984); see also Raymond J. Broderick, *Why the Peremptory Challenge Should Be Abolished*, 65 Temp. L. Rev. 369 (1992).

[54] Herbert Stern, Trying Cases to Win 504 (1991).

Avoid stating challenges in front of the jury prospects. You should ask the court to employ a procedure that keeps the potential jurors from knowing the source of a challenge. If the court requires the lawyers to state challenges in front of the prospects, you should do so in a businesslike, low-key fashion.[55]

Your use of peremptory challenges should depend on the method by which the court permits the lawyers to challenge potential jurors. If there is only one chance to challenge a prospect — in other words, if a potential juror is deemed accepted once the parties pass the chance to state a challenge — you should use challenges when a strong reason arises to do so. If you retain the right to go back and challenge prospects who earlier were passed, there is more reason to hold onto challenges.[56]

Since new prospects are seated as others are challenged, the possibility exists that a replacement may be worse than a person who is excused. Thus, you should try to hold at least one peremptory challenge in reserve. Additionally, remember that some prospects — a lawyer's spouse, for instance — are candidates for challenge by both sides. You generally should strike these individuals last, to take advantage of the possibility that the opposing party will challenge them.[57]

§ 2-10. Challenges Based on Race or Sex.

Traditionally lawyers had absolute discretion in exercising peremptory challenges. Counsel could rely on any factor — no matter how arbitrary — in deciding to excuse a prospect.[58] The right to eliminate prospects on the basis of race was constrained by the Supreme Court, however, in *Batson v. Kentucky*.[59] In *Batson*, the Court held that a prosecutor's use of peremptory challenges to eliminate prospects of the same race as the defendant violated the Equal Protection Clause. Several years later, in *Georgia v. McCollum*,[60] the court expanded *Batson* to prevent criminal defense lawyers from using race-based challenges.

A defendant seeking to establish a prima facie case under *Batson* must show that he belongs to a "cognizable racial group" and the prosecutor utilized

---

[55] See § 2-7.

[56] See THOMAS A. MAUET, TRIAL TECHNIQUES 73 (5th ed. 2000): "Some courts allow you to challenge jurors you initially accepted and tendered to the other side."

[57] 3 FEDERAL LITIGATION GUIDE ¶ 30.18 (1993): "By striking in the reverse order of how you would expect your adversary to exercise the same strikes . . . you are maximizing the chances that your adversary will strike one or more of the same jurors that you intend to strike. You will [thus effectively gain additional strikes]."

[58] *See, e.g.*, Photostat Corp. v. Ball, 338 F.2d 783, 786 (10th Cir. 1964).

[59] 476 U.S. 79 (1986); *Leonard L Cavise, The Batson Doctrine, The Supreme Court's Utter Failure to Meet the Challenge of Discrimination in Jury Selection*, 1999 WIS. L. REV. 501; David Hittner, *Jury Selection in Federal Civil Litigation: General Procedures, New Rules, and The Arrival of Batson*, 23 TEX. TECH L. REV. 407 (1992); David Hittner & Eric J.R. Nichols, *The Expansion of Batson in Civil & Criminal Litigation*, 29-OCT HOUS. LAW. 12 (1991).

[60] 505 U.S. 42 (1992).

peremptory challenges to excuse potential jurors who belong to that group. Second, the defendant may rely on the assumption that peremptory challenges permit discrimination.[61] Finally, the defendant must "show that these facts and any other relevant circumstances raise an inference that the prosecutors used that practice to exclude the veniremen from the petit jury on account of their race."[62] Potentially relevant circumstances include a pattern of racial strikes or statements of the prosecutor during voir dire.[63]

If the defendant establishes a prima facie case, the burden shifts to the prosecutor, who must show a neutral justification for the peremptory challenges. This justification "need not rise to the level justifying exercise of a challenge for cause,"[64] but the prosecution must "articulate a neutral explanation related to the particular case to be tried."[65] Under the Court's ruling in *Purkett v. Elem*,[66] so long as the explanation is genuine, it need not be reasonable.

After *Batson*, the Court refined the law of peremptory challenges. In *Powers v. Ohio*,[67] the court held that a defendant of one race could, under *Batson*, challenge the prosecutor's removal of a juror of another race. The Court reasoned that a potential juror has an equal protection right not to be removed from jury service on account of his race.[68] Moreover, the Court held that the defendant had standing to assert the equal protection claim of the potential juror.[69]

The Court in *Campbell v. Louisiana*[70] determined that a white defendant may challenge the exclusion of African-American prospects on account of their race. Further, in *Edmonson v. Leesville Concrete Co., Inc.*,[71] the Court held that *Batson* was applicable to civil as well as criminal cases. The Court stressed that a racial challenge in a civil case infringes on a potential juror's equal protection rights as much as in a criminal trial. As in *Powers,* the Court found that a litigant has standing to raise the equal protection issue.[72]

---

[61] Batson v. Kentucky, 476 U.S. 79, 96 (1986), quoting Avery v. Georgia, 345 U.S. 559, 562 (1953).

[62] *Id.* at 96.

[63] *Id.* at 97.

[64] *Id.*

[65] *Id.* at 98.

[66] 514 U.S. 765 (1991) (per curium).

[67] 499 U.S. 400 (1991).

[68] *Id.* 406–10.

[69] *Id.* at 415.

[70] 523 U.S. 392 (1998).

[71] 500 U.S. 614 (1991); David H. Stacy & Brenda M. Sauro, *Edmonson: Dramatic Change in the Use of Peremptory Challenges*, 21 COLO. LAW. 687 (1992).

[72] See, e.g., United States v. DeGross, 960 F.2d 1433, 1437–39 (9th Cir. 1992) (*en banc*).

The Court subsequently extended the constitutional limitation on peremptory challenges to gender-based strikes. In *J.E.B. v. Alabama ex rel. T.B.*,[73] a paternity action, the state of Alabama used its peremptory challenges to exclude men from a jury. The Supreme Court addressed whether gender discrimination during jury selection "substantially furthers" a litigant's interest in a fair trial. The State struck males because males might be biased in favor of the alleged father. The Court determined that this stereotypical reasoning was insufficient to justify a gender-based challenge.[74] Thus, it held gender-based challenges are impermissible.

The Court limited its opinion to challenges based solely on gender. It held a party may still use a peremptory challenge "based on characteristics that are disproportionately associated with one gender . . . absent a showing of pretext."[75] For example, striking potential jurors with prior military experience would disproportionately eliminate men, yet this challenge "may well not be unconstitutional" since it is not based on race or gender.[76]

One issue that has provoked disagreement in the lower courts is whether *Batson* requires reversal of a verdict rendered after an alternate juror is struck on racial or sexual grounds, but no alternates actually participate in jury deliberations. If alternates do not deliberate, the challenge obviously does not affect the verdict, but a jury prospect nevertheless is denied the right to serve as an alternate. The resolution of this conflict likely will depend on the extent to which the courts are willing to overturn otherwise valid verdicts as a means of discouraging discriminatory practices in jury selection.[77]

The Court's decisions do not eliminate, but restrict, counsel's freedom in using peremptory challenges. The rulings place increased pressure on trial lawyers, who now must be prepared to articulate in neutral terms a reason for excusing a prospect that may be based on instinct.[78] They also may lead parties to increase their objections to peremptory challenges, since this approach can prevent the

---

[73] 511 U.S. 127 (1994).

[74] *Id.* at 138: "We shall not accept as a defense to gender-based peremptory challenges 'the very stereotype the law condemns.' " (Citation omitted.) Patrick J. Guinee, *The Trend Toward the Extension of Batson to Gender-Based Peremptory Challenges*, 32 Duq. L. Rev. 833 (1994).

[75] 511 U.S. 127, 143 (footnote omitted).

[76] *Id.* at 143, n.16; see also *Trial, Peremptory Challenges — Gender-Based — Equal Protection*, 9 No. 5 Fed. Litigator 142 (1994).

[77] *See* Carter v. Kemma, 255 F. 3d 589, 592 (8th Cir. 2001); Ford v. Norris, 67 F.3d 162, 170–71 (8th Cir. 1995); United States v. Canoy, 38 F.3d 893, 899 n.6 (7th Cir. 1994); Nevius v. Sumner, 852 F.2d 463, 468 (8th Cir. 1988).

[78] As one commentator emphasized, "It's one more thing for the trial lawyer to be prepared for in advance: to be ready to explain the unexplainable." Brad Bole, *Trial Lawyers Weigh Impact of Ban on Gender-Based Peremptory Strikes*, 19 Litigation News 7 (August 1994) (quoting William Slusser, Houston, Vice-Chair of the Trial Practice Committee, Section of Litigation, American Bar Association).

opposing party from excusing hostile jurors and divert him from other goals of voir dire. At the same time, the new standards may require courts to permit counsel a greater role in voir dire, to obtain the information necessary to justify challenges. The restrictive limits now applied in many courts, particularly federal courts, may need to be relaxed.

CHAPTER 3

OPENING STATEMENT

---

§ 3-1.   Introduction.

Probably the most important part of any trial is the opening statement. This presentation occurs near the beginning of the trial, when the jurors are alert and expectant. In the opening statement, counsel may present her entire case — both a word picture describing her version of the relevant events and a preview of the evidence that will support this story. The opening statement functions like a picture for a puzzle; it allows the jurors to understand the fit and importance of the evidence that counsel will present. Additionally, the opening statement is the attorney's *last* chance to address the jury directly prior to the closing argument, when most of the jurors have made up their minds. Thus, it is crucial to an effective trial presentation.

Because the opening statement is so important to effective trial advocacy, attorneys must learn to present it well. You must conceive your best presentation and deliver it effectively, using limited time for maximum efficiency. You must begin to persuade the jurors, even though courts generally prohibit argument in opening statement. You must understand how to accomplish your objectives within the bounds of the rules.

Unfortunately, many attorneys fill the opening statement with diversions rather than presenting their points. They offer a civics lesson — "You are the jury, I am a lawyer, she is the judge, we all perform a very important duty under the constitution, you must take your responsibility seriously," and so on — blathering about matters well known to most high school students; or they employ symbolism to describe the case, likening it to some allegorical overlay, rather than explaining the facts; or they openly argue the facts and law, infringing the rules and drawing valid objections from the opposing party.

A good opening statement instead requires a practical, to-the-pont presentation of the facts and evidence. You can make it powerful and persuasive without engaging in objectionable argument. This chapter explains the content and presentation of the opening statement, including its purpose and importance (§§ 3-2–3-3), its content (§§ 3-4–3-13), practical points for its presentation (§ 3-14); and rules and objections applicable to its content (§§ 3-15–3-16). Additionally, § 3-17 provides sample outlines for the opening statement, based on the *Danielson* problem in Appendix A.

In some jurisdictions there are special rules or requirements applicable to opening statement. You should be sure to check whether special rules apply before presenting an opening statement.

§ 3-2. Purpose of the Opening Statement.

The opening statement should provide the judge or jury with a statement of the facts counsel intends to prove. It necessarily includes a brief description of the issues, a description of the party's factual contentions, and a preview of important evidence.

Theoretically, the opening statement should not be used to argue the merits, the credibility of witnesses, or the application of law to facts. Nevertheless, the opening statement provides a great opportunity for persuasion. You can engage in subtle argument by telling a story that implants your version of events in the jurors' minds, including the factual inferences that you want them to draw from the evidence. Additionally, by announcing a theme and presenting the facts in a way that promotes the theme, you can influence the way the jurors assimilate the evidence.

In deciding what to include in opening statement, consider the factual "story" your evidence can credibly support. You may include facts that you will support, directly or circumstantially, with evidence. You generally may rely not only on evidence that you will offer in your own case, but on evidence that you will elicit in cross-examination.[1] You must ensure, however, that your factual conclusions are fairly supported by the evidence, because you will lose credibility if you fail to back up your claims.

In trial advocacy courses instructors often advise young lawyers to use the opening statement for argument. In effect, they counsel students to breach the rules by engaging in open argument whenever they can. This advice not only promotes rule breaking, but is unnecessary. You can "argue" the case through your selection, emphasis, and description of the facts — using an objective style — just as well as you can with overt argument.

Judges often dispense with opening statements in bench trials. A judge may feel the statements would be pointless because she is already familiar with the case from pretrial activities. Even in this situation, you should request the opportunity to make an opening statement. Judges are as human as jurors and may be persuaded by a coherent, thematic fact review. Further, preparing the opening statement orders your thoughts and promotes a thematic presentation of evidence. The methods described in this chapter can be used whether the trier of fact is a judge or jury.

---

[1] See State v. Thompson, 68 S.W. 3d 393 (Mo. 2002), overruling case law in Missouri that precluded any reference in opening statement to facts to be elicited in cross-examination.

§ 3-3. Importance of the Opening Statement.

Although the lawyers usually make some references to the facts in voir dire, the opening statement is the first opportunity for counsel to provide a comprehensive statement of each party's factual claims. Given human nature, the jurors may form an initial impression of who should win by the end of the opening statements.[2] Many jurors draw at least tentative conclusions at this initial stage. Thus, unless there are special reasons not to give an opening statement, you should take advantage of the opportunity to present one.

Opening statements also are important because the evidentiary process provides only piecemeal views of the facts. Absent a clear picture of a party's case, members of the jury may be confused concerning the importance of the testimony and exhibits as this evidence is introduced. With an opening statement that presents the "story" in narrative fashion, the jurors will better understand the pieces of the evidentiary puzzle.[3]

The jurors also are likely to form an initial impression about counsel during the opening statement. If voir dire is conducted by the court, counsel's first interaction with the jury occurs in opening statement. Even if the attorney participates in voir dire, the opening is the first chance for counsel to make a full oral presentation. The attorney's belief, confidence, organization, and manner may influence the way jurors react to him throughout the trial. Thus, the opening statement provides a chance to begin the process of inspiring trust in the jurors.

§ 3-4. Need for an Objective Form.

In theory, the opening statement should be a nonargumentative description of the facts and evidence. In fact, a good opening statement is a great tool of advocacy. You must use an objective *form* in presenting the opening statement, but you may deliver it with great commitment and fill it with hidden argument.

The objective form simply requires that you eliminate obvious argument. You should not argue the credibility of witnesses, openly weigh the competing evidence, or discuss in detail the application of the law to the facts. Generally, you may have a brief reference to the law in describing the issue, but should avoid an argument of ultimate legal issues. You should avoid argumentative language, such as rhetorical questions, discussions of the "reasonableness" or "fairness" of positions, or assertions regarding the believability of witnesses.

---

[2] See ALFRED S. JULIEN, OPENING STATEMENTS § 1.01, at 2 (cum. supp. 1992) ("An opening statement can win the trial of a lawsuit. . . . Jurymen, in cases tried by effectual advocates, have been prone to say that once the opening statements were made there was nothing left to the case.").

[3] Nancy Pennington & Reid Hastie, *A Cognitive Theory of Juror Decision Making: The Story Model,* 13 CARDOZO L. REV. 519 (1991) (explaining theory that jurors actively arrange information presented to them throughout the trial into a structured framework or story); see also E. ALLEN LIND & GINA Y. KE, *Opening and Closing Statements, in* THE PSYCHOLOGY OF EVIDENCE AND TRIAL PROCEDURE 229 (1985).

Even with an objective form, the opening statement can do much to persuade the jury. Indeed, the appearance of objectivity may enhance your credibility as you relate the "story" of the case.[4] In presenting the "word picture," you can fill evidentiary gaps with reasonable inferences, emphasize favorable facts by developing them, and dramatize key points by presenting them with an emphatic delivery. Moreover, through a positive description of key evidence, such as a review of the credentials of an expert or the care taken in preparing a document, you indirectly can argue credibility.

The following examples from the *ComputerCentre* case illustrate the difference between the argumentative and objective forms. Assume counsel for the Danielsons made the following commentary in opening statement:

> ComputerCentre is going to contend that the Danielsons caused their own problems and the failure of their franchise because of inexperience and their own failures. This position is unreasonable. How could they expect the Danielsons to know how to run a franchise when they advertised that experience was unnecessary? Wouldn't any reasonable person expect inexperienced applicants? Of course he would. After evaluating the evidence you will agree that the problems were caused by ComputerCentre.

The conclusory and rhetorical nature of this discussion mark it as argument, beyond the permissible scope of opening statement. The attorney can accomplish the same objective, however, by fashioning a fact-based discussion of the point, phrased in an objective form:

> An issue to be decided is whether ComputerCentre caused the Danielsons' loss through fraud or the Danielsons caused it through their own inexperience. On this point the evidence will show that ComputerCentre advertised that experience was unnecessary. Atkins and Nelsen knew the Danielsons were inexperienced. ComputerCentre failed to train the Danielsons. ComputerCentre failed to perform its promises. ComputerCentre — not the Danielsons — caused the failure of the business.

The fact-based discussion actually is more powerful than the rhetoric and is permissible in opening statement.

Another difference between the argumentative and objective form relates to drawing inferences. Arguing inferences in opening statement is improper; stating them as fact is perfectly permissible. Assume that counsel for the prosecution delivers an opening statement in a murder trial. He has evidence that Smith chased Jones down Maple Street toward Broadway; Smith brandished a knife and

---

[4] See generally *Lawyer Credibility*, TRIAL (July 1984).

shouted threats at Jones. A witness saw the two men turn the corner. Another witness, a few minutes later, found Jones stabbed to death in the street. No one saw the stabbing. Counsel might be tempted to engage in impermissible argument, as follows:

> You will hear that Smith chased Jones down Maple Street. Smith had a knife in his hand and was shouting threats. The men turned the corner. It is only reasonable to believe that Smith knifed Jones after they went around the corner. The defense will contend he didn't, but what other conclusion is reasonable? Smith was the one seen chasing Jones with a knife, not someone else.

The same goal can be accomplished, perhaps with greater force, in an objective description that states the inference as fact:

> [The evidence will show . . .]
>
> . . . Smith confronted Jones. He was enraged and combative and had a knife. Jones began to run down Maple Street. Smith chased him, yelling threats and brandishing the knife. Jones ran all the way to Broadway and turned the corner, toward the river. Smith ran around after him. Exhausted, Jones turned to face Smith. Smith ran up to him and plunged the knife into his chest, piercing his heart. Jones fell to the street and died within seconds. He was found there a few minutes later.

If counsel deems it necessary to address a defense contention, he should do it with a description that centers on evidence and fact, without obvious argument, as in the following example.

> Smith will contend that he was not the person who actually knifed Jones. The evidence will show, however, that the knife was purchased by Smith. Smith — and no one else — threatened Jones for dating Laurie Ann Barcelona. Smith was seen chasing Jones with a knife, shouting threats. Smith was seen running around the corner after Jones. Smith was the only person with the motive and opportunity to kill Jones. Smith, and no one else, is the murderer.

§ 3-5. Need for a Theme in Opening Statement.

Given the elusiveness of the spoken word, a theme is crucial in the opening statement. Most listeners forget the particulars of any oral presentation within a few minutes after they hear it. If the statement is built around a theme, however, the listeners are likely to remember it.[5] A theme is an overall point or points that run throughout the presentation, providing focus to different aspects of the message. It is not simple repetition of the same small point, but a consistent overall message that is built on smaller points. The theme of the opening statement should carry throughout the trial.

A strong, thematic beginning is important because most people have a short attention span. If you can capture their attention in that span, you can hold it, but once the jurors' minds wander, you may have trouble drawing them back. To understand this point, imagine yourself at a cocktail party, trying to decide which group to join for conversation. When you approach to overhear a group, how long do you spend before deciding to join or move on? Most people make up their minds pretty quickly — perhaps a minute or less. Further, once they move on to a more interesting discussion, they rarely come back. Similarly, the jurors are likely to decide pretty quickly whether they should expend the energy required to pay attention to your opening statement. If you lose them, you may have trouble reacquiring their attention.

In most cases, the facts provide the basis for building an appropriate theme. To emphasize the theme, you should call attention to it in the introduction, develop it in presenting the factual "story," reemphasize it when you describe key pieces of evidence, and address it again in the conclusion.[6] For example, a lawyer who expects to build her case around key documents could fashion an introduction that emphasizes the reliability of written evidence, present a narrative built around the preparation and execution of the documents, emphasize the documents in describing the evidence, and close with a reference to the credibility of the written word. This approach implicitly suggests that the adversary's reliance on nondocumentary evidence is less persuasive, without requiring direct argument of the point.

The theme depends on the facts and equities. For example, in a criminal case, the defendant's cruelty, the extensive planning that was part of a premeditated crime, or the reliability of key physical evidence might constitute a theme for the prosecution. The defense might focus on police misconduct, an alibi, the existence of a different suspect, or the lack of direct evidence. The theme usually should be linked to the key points that must be proven under the law. Further, you should ensure that the theme is real: that the facts legitimately support it.

---

[5] See Robin West, *Jurisprudence as Narrative: An Aesthetic Analysis of Modern Legal Theory,* 60 N.Y.U. L. REV. 145 (1985); Gerald P. Lopez, *Lay Lawyering,* 32 UCLA L. REV. 1 (1984).

[6] Daniel G. Linz & Steven Penrod, *Increasing Attorney Persuasiveness in the Courtroom,* 8 LAW AND PSYCHOL. REV. 1, 6 (1984) (stressing the importance of providing jurors with a comprehensible "story," in order to assist jurors' natural reasoning processes in deliberation); see also Richard Lempert, *Telling Tales in Court: Trial Procedure and the Story Model,* 13 CARDOZO L. REV. 559 (1991).

The concept of a theme is often elusive to lawyers, who conceive it as something symbolic or allegorical — such as a Shakespearean play, a popular song, or a historical event. In truth, an accurate overall description of your version of the case should comprise the theme. If someone asked you at a dinner party "Tell me about your case, but don't take too long" — and you had time to think — you would probably present the theme. You probably would not start with a reference to King Lear or the rise and fall of the Roman Empire, and if you did, you might confuse your listener. Competing factual themes can be illustrated using the facts of *Danielson*. For the plaintiffs, counsel might describe the case as follows:

> The Danielsons lost their business and life savings because Computer-Centre Associates made false promises and failed to keep those promises. The president of ComputerCentre thought he could take advantage of the Danielsons because they were — in his words — "yokels." He made them buy products from a family-owned company and gouged them with a double markup, without ever revealing he would do so. As a result the Danielsons' business was ruined.

The key elements of this description — false promises, failure to deliver, deprecation of "yokels," self-dealing, Danielsons' ruin — are the aspects that counsel would emphasize throughout the trial. They are separate points, but work together to form an overall theme.

ComputerCentre also has a factual basis for a positive theme. The key elements in this theme also work together — the Danielsons' inexperience, failure to accept advice, failure to follow directions, and poor business decisions led to their failure — a demise that contrasts with the nationwide success of other franchises. The theme might be expressed as follows:

> The Danielsons did not fail because ComputerCentre did anything wrong. ComputerCentre franchises all over the country were treated just like the Danielsons' and have succeeded. The Danielsons failed to accept the advice and sound practices of ComputerCentre. They chose the wrong location, hired people who didn't know what they were doing, failed to pay attention to their business, and stocked inferior products. Their own poor judgment and inaction led to their failure.

You should present the theme at or near the beginning of the opening statement. This approach gives you a good start because the theme reflects the strength of the case. Additionally, the theme usually provides an overview, making it easier for the jurors to understand the narrative that follows. You should give special attention to the theme in your introduction.

Unfortunately, many lawyers do not begin the opening statement with the theme — or even with a picture of the facts. Instead, these attorneys concentrate on telling the jurors about the trial process, the judicial system, the role of counsel, and other extraneous matters.[7] Sometimes they begin with allegorical references that are unclear to anyone except the speaker. Usually the reason is that counsel is unprepared and cannot present a coherent theme. She takes refuge in the familiar: the civics lessons presented in past opening statements. Alternatively, she presents an imaginary "theme" that does not require confronting and reconciling facts. Neither approach is likely to persuade jurors.

§ 3-6.   Sample Outline of the Opening Statement.

Although each case is different, you may adapt the following sample outline to virtually any case. Section 1-14 reviews the steps you should take in preparing an extemporaneous presentation — the delivery that should be used in the opening statement.

§ 3-6(a).   Introduction.

In your introduction, you should call attention to the issue and provide the first reference to your theme. You should briefly introduce yourself and the parties and describe the points you will cover.[8] The introduction is the most important part of the presentation. It is a chance to grab the jury's attention. It is your opportunity to introduce an appealing them. It provides a road map of the entire statement. It should include:

§ 3-6(a)(1).   Self-Introduction.

Introduce yourself and describe whom you represent. If the jury already knows who you are, reintroduce yourself. "As you know, I am Joe Smith, and I represent Louise Brown, the plaintiff."

§ 3-6(a)(2).   Parties.

Introduce your client: "Ms. Brown is there at counsel table and will be sitting with me at the trial." As plaintiff, you may wish to introduce the defense, as if you were Master of Ceremonies: "The defendant is Smarm Corporation, represented by Mr. Jones. The defendant's manager, Fred Smith, is sitting with Mr. Jones."

§ 3-6(a)(3).   Issue.

Briefly describe the legal issue so that the jury will understand the importance of the facts you will review. Introduce your theme at the very beginning. Try

---

[7] See § 3-9.

[8] THOMAS A. MAUET, TRIAL TECHNIQUES 74–75 (5th ed. 2000); John P. Miller, *Opening and Closing Statements from the Viewpoint of the Plaintiff's Attorney,* 10 PRAC. LAW. 87 (1964).

to describe the issue in a way that grabs attention — and goes to the core of the case — right away. Avoid obvious argument in describing the issue. Example: "This is a case for breach of promise. Smarm Corp. promised to repair Ms. Brown's car, took her money, then failed to provide the necessary repairs. As a result, her engine was destroyed, and she lost her car."

§ 3-6(a)(4). Signposts.

Tell the jury, briefly, the topics you will cover, as noted in § 3-11. This review requires only a sentence: "I will first discuss the facts we will prove, after which I will review the evidence that will support these facts."

§ 3-6(b). Word Picture.

You should provide a narrative description of the facts from the perspective of your client, in "story" form. Begin the discussion with: "We will prove the following facts. . . ." You need not repeat this phrase throughout, although some advocates think occasional repetition of "we will prove" heads off objections that the statement is argumentative. If possible, tell the story without these interruptions. If opposing counsel objects to argument, you always can toss in an occasional "we will prove."

Use selection and emphasis in your story of the case. You should bring out the facts that support key elements by describing them in more detail, and with more animation, than other points.[9] Acknowledge harmful facts, so the statement is accurate, but do not discuss them in the same detail as helpful facts. Employ the theme as you tell the story, describing the facts so they work together to support an overall characterization. The theme gives additional emphasis to favorable facts.

The word picture permits the jury to see — in the mind's eye — the events that transpired. This phenomenon tends to fix a version of the facts in the jurors' imaginations. It also permits start-to-finish comprehension of the facts. In contrast, an approach that focuses on pieces of evidence prompts jurors to visualize witnesses, documents, and evidentiary events, rather than the facts themselves, and provides a jumbled introduction to the case.

The word picture is a great opportunity for permissible argument. Although presented in objective *form*, it necessarily contains inferences, characterizations, and embellishments, and all are permissible. Thus, the word picture should have all the drama that attends any good story. Usually cases turn on facts, and this is a great opportunity to establish a favorable version of the facts. Section 3-7 discusses the importance and content of the word picture.

---

[9] Thomas A. Pyszczynski, Jeff Greenberg, David Mack & Lawrence S. Wrightsman, *Opening Statements in a Jury Trial: The Effect of Promising More Than The Evidence Can Show*, 11 J. APPLIED SOC. PSYCHOLOGY 434–44 (1981).

§ 3-6(c).   References to Key Evidence.

In this part of the opening statement, describe the main items of evidence that support the word picture. Here, you can refer to the most credible witnesses and describe the testimony they will provide. Additionally, you can link your factual portrayal to important items of physical evidence. As you refer to this evidence, you can again present short segments of the word picture, reinforcing these events in the jury's mind. For example, you could tell the jury about a witness, providing a basis for judging his credibility, and then describe the witness's testimony; the description of the testimony allows you to narrate part of the word picture once again.

Focus on the most important evidence in your evidentiary review. Generally, the discussion should not be as long as the word picture. In describing evidence you should stick to the essentials. Droning on about trivia takes the power out of the opening statement.[10]

In this part of the opening statement you should pay special attention to real evidence — the gun, the knife, a key document — and to demonstrative evidence. These items focus listeners' concentration. Show important exhibits to the jurors, but use only a few. Using too many exhibits diminishes the impact of them all and impedes a smooth presentation.

This section of the opening statement also provides an opportunity to address liability and damages as separate topics. In the word picture, the event and its consequences are all part of the same story. In the evidentiary preview you may want to break up the discussion so that the jury understands the two issues and follows the evidence on each in the trial. Thus, you could openly divide the discussion of the evidence into "evidence on liability" and "evidence on damages." As plaintiff, you should review the important evidence on damages because it may evoke sympathy.

§ 3-6(d).   Conclusion.

The conclusion, like the introduction, commands special attention. Listeners usually perk up if they think the speaker is finishing. You should conclude on a high note, using the theme again as your focus. Additionally, explain what verdict you will request at the close of the trial.

§ 3-7.   Importance and Content of the "Word Picture."

The most important advocate's rule in the opening statement is to provide a "word picture" of the facts. Rather than concentrating solely on descriptions of the witnesses and what they will say, you need to deliver a narrative description

---

[10] See ROBERT V. WELLS, SUCCESSFUL TRIAL TECHNIQUES OF EXPERT PRACTITIONERS 232–37 (1988).

of "what happened" — a story. In an accident case, for instance, your word picture would describe the plaintiff and the events that caused his injuries, in story form.

The story follows the introduction and an announcement that "we will prove the following facts." You should avoid unnecessary repetition, however, of the words "we will prove" and "we will show." Say it once, then get on with the story. After delivering the "word picture," when you emphasize key evidence that will support the factual claims, you can reemphasize parts of the story.

Presenting a word picture makes good sense because the "story" of the parties' conflict is the most interesting part of the case. In a dinner conversation, most lawyers would tell what happened, not how they might go about proving what happened. The word picture embodies the drama, emotion, and spontaneity of life; by comparison, the introduction of evidence often is dry and boring. Moreover, in telling the story, you may naturally show belief and emotion, which are important to persuading the jury. An emotional display seems out of place in a description of a witness or exhibit.

The word picture is crucial to advocacy because it allows the advocate to draw inferences from the evidence without engaging in obvious argument. The word picture is a simple, direct factual statement, but since the facts reflect hidden inferences, telling the story permits the lawyer to "objectively" advocate his case. A narrative word picture can include any reasonable inference drawn from the facts. When the advocate thereafter refers to evidence that supports key parts of the word picture, the references buttress the story in the jurors' minds.

As an example, consider the murder case described in § 3-4, in which the defendant was seen brandishing a knife and chasing the victim down a street. The two turned a corner and ran out of sight, where the victim's body was found within a few minutes. If the prosecutor concentrates only on the *evidence*, she must leave a hole for the jury to fill because there is no witness to describe the knifing of the victim. If counsel tells the story, on the other hand, she can describe the stabbing as she believes it occurred. The story describes the event, with no reference to proof, inferences, or gaps, and all the facts seem real. This approach makes it much easier for the jurors to accept inferences.

The word picture also tends to stamp in the jurors' minds a "vision" of the facts — almost as if it were shown on videotape. Once the jurors see the story in the mind's eye, they become more prone to accept it. Additionally, as evidence is admitted, the jurors tend to see the evidence as confirmation of the *entire* word picture, making it easier for counsel to convince the jury that evidentiary gaps have been filled.[11]

---

[11] See generally John Kaplin, *Decision Theory and the Factfinding Process,* 20 STAN. L. REV. 1065 (1968).

The word picture also provides an overview of the facts that helps the jury understand the evidence. With a "story" fixed in his mind, each juror understands its parts as you present them through individual witnesses and exhibits. Without a word picture, the jurors are left to assemble the facts themselves and might not see them in the light counsel hopes to achieve.

Unfortunately, trial lawyers often concentrate on evidence rather than facts in opening statement. They tell the jury about the witnesses and what they will say and the exhibits and what they will prove, in the approximate order of presentation. This approach presents the pieces of a puzzle before the viewer ever sees the picture, forcing him to wait for all the pieces to understand their meaning. The advocate's job is to make sense of the evidence for the jurors, not to force them to put it together.

Talking about evidence is easier than describing facts because the attorney is usually familiar with his proof. Good lawyers take the extra step, however, and reconcile the evidence into a coherent factual theory of the case. This theory in turn should be the core of the opening statement. The evidence should support counsel's version of the facts, but should not replace it.

§ 3-8. Desirability of a Separate Evidentiary Review.

In structuring your opening statement, you should strive to ensure that your word picture and evidentiary review are separate. By separating these parts, you ensure that your story flows freely, without the distractions that may result from evidentiary references. Additionally, separating these components permits you to engage in "non-redundant repetition," emphasizing the strong parts of your case in parts of your statement that serve different purposes. This approach enhances the power of your theme in opening statement.

Your word picture reviews your theory of "what happened"; it need not include the means by which you will prove these facts. Nevertheless, lawyers often mix their means of proof with their stories, perhaps because of their pretrial concentration on the evidence. You need to resist this natural tendency, because it disrupts your story and eliminates your chance to gain a "double bang" with strong points.

In presenting your word picture, you may refer to evidence that formed part of the relevant factual pattern. Thus, for example, counsel in *Danielson* certainly would discuss the ComputerCentre advertisement, the agenda for the Middleton meeting, and Dale Atkins's letter that referred to the Danielsons as "yokels" and "clowns." The advocate might even hold and read from these documents. But he need not discuss how or when they would be introduced into evidence. Similarly, counsel would review the actions of the main figures in the case without predicting the content of their testimony.

In the evidentiary review, in contrast, the advocate would review important parts of the evidentiary presentation. In this section of the opening statement, counsel can reinforce important parts of the word picture, achieving a theme through non-apparent repetition. For example, the attorney could predict that he would introduce and show the jury the advertisement, the agenda and Atkins's letter, referring again to their content as he explains this proof. This separate review allows the attorney to refer twice to key elements of his case.

Your separate reviews of story and evidence need not make the opening statement unduly lengthy. Even though you separate the parts, you cover about the same amount of material as you would in a single, mixed review. Moreover, once your story has been told, you may abbreviate the references to key evidence; this section should buttress, rather than replicate, the story. Further, you can conserve time even in the word-picture by focusing on the most important aspects of your case. You may find that compartmentalizing these parts of your statement actually shortens your overall presentation.

§ 3-9.   Need to Avoid Boilerplate.

In general, you should avoid "boilerplate" in the opening statement. You need not give the jury a "civics lesson" in the operation of the American trial system.[12] This sort of presentation is usually a boring time filler, delivered by the lawyer who is not familiar enough with his own case to get to the point. Unprepared attorneys remember the boilerplate delivered in past openings and use it as a crutch. This approach does nothing to advance the cause, because the jury's understanding of the legal process does not increase their sympathy toward counsel's case.

To understand the silliness of boilerplate, imagine yourself as a potential purchaser of a home. You have consulted two real estate agents, each of whom has identified a house you may want to buy. You meet with the agents to obtain initial descriptions of the houses. You give each the chance to make an oral presentation.

Agent 1 begins by telling you of the importance of the real estate market in America. He then describes the role of the agent, the real estate agency, and buyers and sellers in the marketing of real estate. After that he discusses the presumptions that are often used in valuing real estate. Next he says that you shouldn't believe anything either agent has to say, but should wait to see the houses yourself. Finally he tells you he is sure you will like House No. 1.

Agent 2 starts with an overall description of House No. 2. She emphasizes its strongest points. She then describes the house in detail, illustrating the discussion with pictures. She mentions enough about weak points to give her

---

[12] See ROBERT V. WELLS, SUCCESSFUL TRIAL TECHNIQUES OF EXPERT PRACTITIONERS 177–84 (1988).

presentation an air of credibility. Her manner suggests that she is simply telling you the facts.

Which house would you go to see first? Which agent would you take with you? If you had a question about the houses, which agent's response would you trust? The answer is obvious and undoubtedly guides real estate agents in how they market houses. But for some reason the message has not reached the bar.

In special circumstances, such as when you expect to make many objections, you may need to make some reference to procedure. You may wish to prepare the jury for actions that they might otherwise misunderstand or alert them to special evidentiary rules. If so, you should probably save this discussion until the conclusion of the opening statement, so it does not get in the way of a direct, thematic factual presentation. Additionally, make it brief, getting the necessary points across without describing the entire trial process.

One of the worst forms of boilerplate is the admonition that characterizes your statement as unimportant or meaningless. From start to finish in the trial, you should have the attitude, and give the impression, that everything you tell the jury is correct. The opening statement is the first chance to tell the jury the facts and probably the most important part of the case; you should want the jury to believe every word of the statement. Thus, you should not suggest that the opening statement has little value.

You generally should not tell the jury that the opening statements are "not evidence," that the statements should not be believed absent the introduction of evidence, that they reflect only the words of counsel, or give similar "boilerplate" admonitions, because these comments deprecate *both* lawyers' statements. Your demeanor should reflect the attitude that your opening reflects the truth, and nothing but the truth.[13]

One qualification to these points applies in the defense of criminal cases. Sometimes counsel does not have a positive version of the facts to present and is forced to put the prosecution to its proof, trying to establish holes in the evidence. In that case only the prosecution presents a story to the jury, and the defense tries to undermine it. Thus, counsel generally must emphasize the difference between the prosecution's opening statement and evidence. Additionally, counsel may be forced to focus on burdens and presumptions. Also, in the rare civil case when the defense does not have a story to tell, advising the jury that the opening statements are not evidence is appropriate.

---

[13] See Thomas A. Pyszczynski & Lawrence S. Wrightsman, *The Effects of Opening Statements on Mock Jurors' Verdicts in a Simulated Criminal Trial*, 11 J. APPLIED SOC. PSYCHOL. 301 (1981); Daniel G. Linz & Steven Penrod, *Increasing Attorney Persuasiveness in the Courtroom*, 8 LAW & PSYCHOL. REV. 1, 8–11 (1984).

§ 3-10. Need to Explain Terms of Art.

Because the opening statement is designed to promote the jury's understanding of the evidence, you should explain terms of art and other special information. If the case involves a specialized area, the jury will appreciate this action. You should be careful, however, to avoid patronizing the jury. One way to avoid patronizing is to introduce an explanation of a term of art with "As you know . . . ," "As you probably are aware . . . ," or a similar phrase. [14] By indicating that you are reminding the jury of points, rather than telling them for the first time, you suggest that the jurors already are well informed.

§ 3-11. Use of Signposts and Transitions in the Opening Statement.

It always is easier to follow a speech when the listener knows where the speaker is going. Alerting the jury at the beginning to the main points aids their overall comprehension. This action gives the listener a broad road map of the speech; it also gives the impression that counsel will make a well-directed presentation. The listeners should be more willing to listen, because listening seems a good use of time.

A speaker who does not provide an outline of his major topics often loses the listeners early in the presentation. The speaker knows the case and the relevance of the facts he describes; the listeners, unfamiliar with the facts, may easily get lost. If the attorney provides an overview of major points, the jurors at least have the reference point of structure to aid their understanding.

You also should give signals to communicate transitions. This action helps focus the listeners' attention on major points. It also allows daydreamers — and surely there will be some — to tune back in to the presentation. A short transitional reference will suffice: "This brings me to the major items of evidence we will introduce to prove that ComputerCentre committed fraud." You should also signal your transition to the conclusion. Listeners usually welcome a conclusion and pay increased attention to it. Thus, it makes good sense to let them know it is coming: "And in conclusion. . . ."

The use of signposts and transitional phrases adds to your credibility. If you show that you have a structure, listeners sense that you have thought through what you have to say. They will assume the message itself has substance. Additionally, you must have a structure to announce one, so this technique forces you to organize your presentation.

§ 3-12. Counsel's Positioning for the Opening Statement.

You should be the center of attention during the opening statement. You should place yourself in a position to command the jury's attention. You can best

---

[14] See *Lawyer Credibility*, Trial (July 1984).

accomplish this goal if you stand where you can be seen, rather than behind a podium. You should not stand too close to the jury, however, as this action may invade the jurors' private space. About 8 to 12 feet from the jury box should be a comfortable distance. You should position yourself centrally, to communicate with *all* the jurors.

Sometimes courts require that the lawyers remain at the podium during the trial. If the court insists on this limitation, you obviously should comply, but position yourself so the podium does not totally block the jury's view. The court may permit you to occasionally leave the podium, perhaps to use demonstrative exhibits or demonstrate physical points to the jury.

§ 3-13. Use of Demonstrative Evidence and Exhibits in the Opening Statement.

Demonstrative evidence — such as charts or graphs — may be effective in capturing the jury's attention, emphasizing a theme, and ensuring that the jury remembers a point. Similarly, important documentary exhibits may help you accomplish this objective. You should design the opening statement to get the jurors to *visualize* a version of the facts; a demonstrative exhibit or item of real evidence helps ensure that this goal is accomplished, because it allows the jurors to *see* as well as hear your point. Therefore, you are well advised to use this material in the opening.

Make sure the exhibits are helpful. Overuse of demonstrative evidence and exhibits impedes a smooth presentation; undue concentration on an exhibit may distract the jury from the overall message. Additionally, too many references to exhibits may confuse the jury and distract them from the theme. Thus, you should employ a *few* demonstrative exhibits or charts — those that bring out thematic points. Further, once a chart has been used, put it away so that it does not distract the jurors from the rest of the presentation.

You usually will have a limited time for opening statement. Setting up multiple charts or diagrams may consume much of that valuable time. If you intend to use demonstrative exhibits, plan their presentations so that they occur without undue trouble or delay. Make sure an easel or other equipment to set up the exhibits is readily available. Practice unveiling and putting away demonstrative exhibits. You want to use exhibits as a tool in getting across your message; if they impede this effort, you should not present them.

The use of demonstrative exhibits is discussed further in §§ 8-14 through 8-20.

§ 3-14. Practical Pointers for Opening Statement.

The following practical tips should make the opening statement more effective.[15]

---

[15] See also ALFRED S. JULIEN, OPENING STATEMENTS (1980); LANE'S GOLDSTEIN TR. TECH. (3d ed. 1994).

§ 3-14(a).   Be Direct.

Just about everyone suffers a handicap in giving oral presentations and writing papers. Since third grade we have worried about the question: "How long does it have to be?" The subconscious need to fill time or paper — drilled in since grade school — pushes us to add unnecessary material, especially in the front. Thus, in opening statement speakers often fill up the beginning with boilerplate or review extraneous facts.

You need to use time efficiently. If you are going to capture attention, you have to get to the point immediately; focusing on the theme is the way to do so. In the word picture you need to stick to the important points — those that show you are right in fairness and under the law. You can fill in additional facts as necessary to promote understanding, but do not insert extraneous material. In reviewing the evidence, focus on the most important witnesses or exhibits. Do not describe every matter you intend to present.

Sticking to the essentials helps you hold the jury's attention. A lean, focused portrayal is more effective than a presentation stuffed with detail. Since the opening statement is only an overview, it should not contain trivia.

§ 3-14(b).   Speak with Authority.

You need to project yourself to the entire courtroom during opening statement, so you should speak in a loud, authoritative voice, commanding the attention of everyone in the court. Your comments are directed at the jurors, and you should face them as you speak, but speak as if everyone in the courtroom needs to hear you. The jury will be more inclined to listen if it appears others are listening, including people in the back row. Thus, your voice should be clearly audible to all those in the courtroom. You should vary the tone, using the voice for dramatic effect, but in general employ ample volume. You may need to be a few yards from the jury so that your voice does not seem too boisterous.

§ 3-14(c).   Choose Labels for the Parties.

Figure out in advance how you are going to refer to the parties, then explain it and stick to it throughout the trial. Choose labels that are easy for laymen to understand. Thus, plaintiff's counsel would refer to his client, Louise Brown, as "Mrs. Brown" or "Louise," but not as "the plaintiff." He might refer to the defendant, Widget Corporation, by its corporate name, with the emphasis on "Corporation." Using understandable labels is particularly helpful in multiparty cases, where it is difficult to keep the participants straight, and legal titles complicate the problem. For instance, few jurors could follow the following description:

> Plaintiff asserts that defendant defrauded plaintiff. Defendant contends that the third party defendant really caused the harm to the plaintiff. The

third party defendant denies the defendant's claim and asserts that the plaintiff caused its own loss, in any event.

§ 3-14(d).   Personalize Your Client.

Even if you represent a corporation, emphasize the human beings who are involved the litigation. Call your client by name — not by legal title. If your client is Louise Brown, the plaintiff, introduce her as the plaintiff and refer to the thereafter as "Ms. Brown" or "Louise." You may wish to find an appealing label for your client while depersonalizing the opposing party. If Joe Johnson owns International Can Co., the defendant, you, as defense counsel, might refer to your client as "Mr. Johnson's company," rather than by its corporate name. You may wish, however, to *depersonalize* the opposing party. This is the one instance in which you might refer to an individual by a legal title: "the plaintiff" or "the defendant."

§ 3-14(e).   Avoid Legalese.

Along the lines of the two preceding sections, you should speak in a conversational style. Tell the jury about the case as you would tell a friend. Avoid legal terminology: "The defendant committed a battery with premeditation on the plaintiff/intervenor as the cross-defendant stood by, failing to mitigate the damage." Use instead: "Mr. Jones attacked and beat up Mr. Smith. Mr. Adams, who could have helped, failed to do so."

§ 3-14(f).   Do Not Overstate the Case or Promise What You Cannot Deliver.

The opponent in closing argument will destroy an attorney who promises evidence that he never delivers. You should use the facts that you can prove — not imagined or hoped-for facts — in putting together a forceful opening.[16] Make the best of what you have; faking it may result in disaster. Additionally, promising to prove facts that you cannot prove violates ethical precepts.[17] Try to explain the facts in a way that turns weak points into strong points. Do not try to change the facts.

§ 3-14(g).   Order the Presentation of Information for a Positive Effect.

The order in which you present information in the opening statement may strongly affect its persuasiveness. Particularly with weak points, the context in

---

[16] But see Thomas A. Pyszczynski, Jeff Greenberg, David Mack, & Lawrence S. Wrightsman, *Opening Statements in a Jury Trial: The Effect of Promising More Than the Evidence Can Show,* 11 J. APPLIED SOC. PSYCHOLOGY 434 (1981) (study revealing that when an attorney promised to produce testimony proving the defendant's innocence, the jury became more sympathetic to the defendant regardless of the fact that the promised evidence was never presented).

[17] MODEL RULES OF PROFESSIONAL CONDUCT Rule 3.4(e).

which you review these matters affects their impact. Thus, you should consider the order in which you present information and structure the opening statement for maximum effect.

Generally, starting with positive points provides the best basis for a successful opening statement. Thus, your theme statement at the beginning provides a grounding for a positive overall presentation. On more specific matters, however, you also need to present information in its best light. Counsel for the Danielsons, for instance, would emphasize that ComputerCentre advertised for inexperienced applicants before reviewing the Danielsons' limited experience. This context defuses a potential point for ComputerCentre.

§ 3-14(h).   Subtly Refute Defenses in the Opening Statement.

Although "argument" in opening statement is improper, in the word picture you can anticipate and refute defenses. Emphasis of the facts showing that a defense is invalid is the best way to defeat the defense. Additionally, when you review key pieces of evidence, emphasizing the facts that give credibility to your evidence implicitly refutes that of the opposition. Further, although you cannot openly argue the weakness of opposing contentions, you can raise them and discuss the facts that undermine these assertions.

§ 3-14(i).   Discuss Weaknesses in the Case so as to Draw the Sting.

If you discuss weaknesses, rather than waiting for your opponent to bring them up, you usually lessen their harm. Moreover, superficial weaknesses can be turned to strengths if you show how they comport with an overall fact picture and theme. An affirmative presentation that includes a weakness is much better than a separate discussion of the weakness.

It is surprising how often a fact that looks good for one side can be turned into an advantage for the opposition. Consider, for example, a dispute over the sale of a car. The plaintiff contends the price was $20,000, with $15,000 to be paid at the time of the purchase and $5,000 thereafter. The defendant contends the price was $15,000. If the plaintiff offered the car to several other persons for $20,000, and the court admitted this "collateral" evidence, the plaintiff could argue that the offers showed a pattern supporting the $20,000 price. The defendant could turn the evidence around, however, arguing that the plaintiff's *failure to get* $20,000 led him to reduce the price. The same facts, from different perspectives, lead to different conclusions.

§ 3-14(j).   Do Not Take Too Much Time.

Most people have difficulty following any speaker for more than 20 or 30 minutes. Few openings should consume more than half an hour and many should be 15 minutes or less. If a lengthy opening statement is required — as in a truly complex case —you should use frequent signposts and transitional phrases to rekindle the jury's attention.

§ 3-14(k). Anticipate and Deflect Objections to the Opening Statement.

You may be able to deflect objections by anticipating problem areas. Careful phrasing of factual contentions — and presentation of contentions as objective facts — may avoid interruptions. If you do get caught in argument, start with a phrase like "we will prove" and proceed with a fact-based discussion.

Further, in certain situations, you might avoid an objection by raising a matter with the court in advance. For example, counsel for the plaintiff might mention, in the presence of opposing counsel, how he intends to describe the legal issue in the opening. If no objection is made, counsel can be fairly sure that an objection will not be raised later. You should not be unnecessarily defensive, however. Only those points that are truly questionable need be raised in advance. There is no need to unnecessarily *alert* opposing counsel to problem areas.

§ 3-14(l). See Pointers for Closing Argument.

A number of the pointers that are more germane to the closing argument may also apply to the opening statement. See § 12–12.

§ 3-15. Improper Actions in Opening Statement.

You should avoid the following objectionable actions in opening statement. If the opposing party engages in this conduct, you should not hesitate to object.

§ 3-15(a). Obvious Argument.

You should not argue the credibility of witnesses, the comparative weight of the evidence, or the application of the law to the facts.[18] You may, however, provide your version of events in the word picture. Further, you can state and support conclusions using an objective format. Obvious argument — such as reasoning from evidence to facts — is impermissible.

§ 3-15(b). Reference to Facts or Evidence Known to be Inadmissible.

Referring to inadmissible facts is unethical.[19] You should be careful about discussing "collateral" matters — side disputes that do not directly relate to the

---

[18] Cf. Murphy v. L. & J. Press Corp., 558 F.2d 407 (8th Cir. 1977), *cert. denied*, 434 U.S. 1025 (1978) (the lawyer's opening statement is intended to help the jury understand the evidence and apply the law, but is not to be considered evidence itself).

[19] See Bright v. Coastal Lumber Co., 962 F.2d 365 (4th Cir. 1992); Maxworthy v. Horn Elec. Serv., Inc., 452 F.2d 1141, 1144 (4th Cir. 1972). In *Maxworthy*, the Fourth Circuit emphasized that:

[w]here counsel's references to inadmissible or unprovable facts are so flagrant or

central dispute — as these matters may be deemed inadmissible. When in doubt, file a motion in limine to clarify whether evidence is admissible.

§ 3-15(c).   Inflammatory Rhetoric.

Avoid personal attacks, inflammatory statements, and other actions designed to unfairly prejudice the jury.[20] Often this kind of approach boomerangs, producing a reprimand from the court and retaliation from the opposition. Instead, employ a professional approach.

§ 3-15(d).   Personal Attestation.

An attorney may not express a personal belief in the veracity of her witnesses or the justness of the cause.[21] You may demonstrate your belief through your authoritative speech and manner, but you cannot attest to it. Thus, you may not say "I believe the Danielsons were defrauded," but you can say "the Danielsons were defrauded." See § 12-4.

§ 3-16.   Objections to Opening Statement.

If opposing counsel engages in obvious argument, argues or misstates the law, or engages in another improper action, you generally should object.[22] You should be sure, however, that the matter is important enough to justify an interruption. Further, as with other objections, you may wish to embroider the objection so as to "sell" it to the jury: "Your Honor, opening statement is not the place for argument. Arguing this point is unfair and a waste of the jury's time. I object." You should first consider whether objecting gives undue emphasis to harmful information; in that case, restraint is the best course.

Some advocates believe interrupting an opponent's opening statement or closing argument breaches professional courtesy. This view has merit to a point;

> inflammatory as to affect the fairness of the trial, it is within the sound discretion of the trial judge to take such remedial action as he deems proper, including, if he considers such action appropriate, a mistrial and the exercise of such discretion will not ordinarily be disturbed unless clearly erroneous.

Id. at 1144.

[20] See United States v. Martino, 648 F.2d 367 (5th Cir. 1981) (Generally, a lawyer must refrain from assertions in the opening statement that are intended to inflame the jury. In this case, however, the prosecutor's comment in the opening statement concerning fact that witness was enrolled in the federal witness protection program was not intended to exploit the witness or inflame the jury's passions); U.S. v. Cobleigh, 75 F.3d 242, 247 (6th Cir. 1996) (inflammatory attacks are to be discouraged, but require reversal only when flagrant, subject to timely objection, and not cured by appropriate instruction).

[21] MODEL RULES OF PROFESSIONAL CONDUCT Rule 3.4(e). See United States v. Singer, 660 F.2d 1295 (8th Cir. 1981), *cert. denied*, 454 U.S. 1156 (1982) (distinguishing statements that express a personal belief in defendant's guilt, from those that merely introduce the government's theory of the case).

[22] See LEONARD DECOF, ART OF ADVOCACY: OPENING STATEMENT § 2.03[3] (1995).

objections that have little consequence are not worth bringing up. If your opponent breaches the rules in a way that provides him an advantage, however, you generally need to object. *His* action is discourteous and needs to be corrected; your action is necessary to protect your client's interests.

§ 3-17. Examples of Outlines of the Opening Statement: *Danielson v. ComputerCentre Associates*.

You should present the opening statement extemporaneously, as explained in § 1-14. You should prepare an outline and rehearse until the presentation "sets" in your mind and you can deliver it smoothly. This method permits you to present a directed, coherent statement, while maintaining eye contact, spontaneity and flexibility.

The outline for the opening statement depends on your needs. Some people prefer to start with a detailed outline, while others only need topical points. Usually you should write out the introduction to help you state it clearly, since this part of the opening statement has special importance. You need only outline the body of the statement. You may also wish to write out your conclusion.

The following outlines are examples from the *Danielson v. ComputerCentre* case. They include more detail than necessary, to promote your understanding of the content of the opening statement. Obviously, the outlines reflect only the main points; the attorney would fill in the important details necessary for the "story." The problem script reproduced in Appendix A provides the source material for the outlines.

§ 3-17(a). Outline for the Danielsons.

The following outline could be used by counsel for the Danielsons.

A. Introduction
1. *Introduce self and parties.*
2. *Issue.* This is a suit for fraud brought by the Danielsons against ComputerCentre Associates. The Danielsons lost their business and life savings because ComputerCentre made false promises and failed to keep those promises. The president of Computer-Centre thought he could take advantage of the Danielsons because they were — in his words — yokels. He made them buy products from a family-owned company and gouged them for a double markup without ever revealing he would do so. As a result the Danielsons' business was ruined.
3. *I will cover:*
   (a) the facts we will prove, and

(b)   some of the key evidence.

B.   Word picture.

We will prove the following facts.

1. *Background.*

Jack and Margaret Danielson.

> — Middletown residents.
> — Retired police officer/housewife.
> — Interested in a new business.
> — Looking for opportunities.

2. *ComputerCentre ad — Wall Street Journal.*

> — High profit franchise.
> — Low expertise required.
> — High level of support. [ad blowup]
> — High capital gains.
> — None of the risk — just reap the rewards of our skillful marketing.

3. *Meeting in Middletown.*

   (a)   *ComputerCentre representations.*

Dale Atkins — president.

Jene Nelsen — sales manager.

Representations:

> — No training required. [agenda]
> — Great profits.
> — San Francisco the example.
> — "We train you to make even more."
> — 24 hour supply — little inventory required.
> — Technical facility for repairs.
> — 37 national ads each year.
> — Training for repair personnel.

   (b)   *ComputerCentre failure to disclose.*

> — San Francisco did not have double markup.
> — There was no training facility.
> — Jene Nelsen was a felon, had been convicted of fraud.
> — Computer supplier owned by Atkins' brother.
> — Supplier habitually late.

4. *Danielsons sign up.*

> — Contacted ComputerCentre.

— Met and signed contract. [contract blowup]

— Contract: training; computer selection, technical services, inventory management, shipping, advertising, accounting support.

— Selected Middletown historic mall — ComputerCentre said OK.

— Hired salesmen.

— Planned to open/placed ads.

5. *Nonperformance.*

— Training not provided to Danielsons or their salespeople (only 3 days).

— Technical support not available.

— Shipments from Wizard didn't come on time/sales lost.

— Double markup charged — sapped away profits.

— Ad campaign pulled.

6. *Yokels/clowns.*

— Atkins regarded Danielsons as yokels/clowns. [letter blowup]

— Told his brother — who owned Wizard — to charge double markup.

— "They'll never know difference."

— Atkins profited "both ways" — got dividends.

7. *Failure of business.*

— Sales lost for late shipments.

— Lack of training hurt sales.

— Extra costs to make repairs.

— Danielsons weren't getting any help.

— Jack had heart attack arguing with Atkins.

— Margaret tried to run business.

— Hired Drew Anderson.

— Tried to get by without salesmen.

— Business folded.

8. *ComputerCentre manufactured documents.*

— Atkins had Nelsen prepare after-the-fact addendum.

— Sent copies of signatures.

— Attempt to hold up the Danielsons for more.

C.   **References to key evidence.**

1. *Ad in Wall Street Journal/Meeting agenda.*

Promises:

— No risk — reap rewards.

— High profit.

— San Francisco example.

— Low investment.

— High support.

— Technical facility.

— Advertising.

2. *Jack/Margaret testimony.*

— Promises of ComputerCentre.

— Failure to deliver.

* Little training.

* No technical facility.

* Pulled advertising.

* Harassing approach.

3. *ComputerCentre's own documents.*

— Atkins Letter. [letter blowup]

* Double markup.

* Yokels/clowns.

* "Will never know difference."

— Memo — no tech facility.

— Letter to Nelsen — prepare addenda a year *after the fact.*

— "Do you have to be creative?"

4. *Calculations of damage.*

Drew Anderson and financial statements.

— Lost investment — $52,000.

— Losses — $23,000.

— Lost future profits — $500,000.

— Punitive Damages — the amount you believe will curb this activity.

D.   Conclusion.

The Danielsons lost their business because of the callous fraud of ComputerCentre Associates. Atkins and Nelsen lied to the Danielsons, failed to provide them the support that was promised, and took advantage of their good faith. Atkins had his brother charge a double markup because he thought the "yokels" wouldn't complain.

> They are now complaining. They are here before you asking
> for justice. When you've heard the evidence, you'll agree that
> they are entitled to have this wrong corrected.

§ 3-17(b).   Outline for ComputerCentre.

A sample outline of the opening statement for ComputerCentre Associates is the following:

A.   Introduction.

1. *Introduce self, party, principals.*

2. *Issue:* The Danielsons did not fail because ComputerCentre did anything wrong. ComputerCentre franchises all over the country were treated just like the Danielsons and succeeded. The Danielsons failed to accept the advice and sound practices of ComputerCentre. They chose the wrong location, hired people who didn't know what they were doing, failed to pay attention to their business, and stocked inferior products. Their own poor judgment and inaction led to their failure.

3. *I will cover:*
   (a)   the facts we will prove, and
   (b)   the main items of evidence.

B.   Word picture.

We will prove the following facts.

1. *ComputerCentre's national success.*
   — 84 franchises nationwide.
   — Grown by 43 franchises in two years.
   — Franchises generally lucrative, profitable.
   — ComputerCentre methods have made franchisees successful from Seattle to Miami, Sioux City to Honolulu.
   — Well over 90% of franchises are profitable.
   — People want to be part of ComputerCentre's method of marketing computers and software.
   — Only *one* failure ever — Middletown.
   — Because the Danielsons didn't follow methods.
   — Expected success without necessary effort.

2. *Danielsons sought out ComputerCentre.*
   — They were looking for a business to get into.
   — They called ComputerCentre after seeing ad.

— Mr. Danielson came to meeting.

— He knew Mr. Atkins and Ms. Nelsen were trying to interest people.

— Decided to sign up the very next day.

— Pushed to get an agreement signed.

3. *ComputerCentre's representations were accurate.*

— Based on facts they expected for future.

— Same representations made to all other franchisees. The others are successful.

— Only temporary delays occurred in servicing franchises.

— Atkins/Nelsen never said that success is guaranteed.

— Never said you can make poor judgments and ignore your business and still succeed.

4. *Danielsons failed to seek to follow advice in choosing location.*

— Location very important to new business.

— ComputerCentre success dependent on choice of location.

— ComputerCentre offers study of population area, traffic to help franchisees select location.

— Danielsons chose location before they ever signed agreement.

— Selected Middletown historic mall.

— Less than one-twentieth the annual traffic of Tri-County mall.

— Atkins asked Danielsons to reconsider, but they would not.

— They signed lease before study of the location could even be completed.

5. *Danielsons made poor business decisions.*

(a) *Failed to hire knowledgeable sales reps.*

— Knowledgeable sales reps are essential to success.

— These reps *explain* to customers how the purchased items work.

— This failure ignored advice of ComputerCentre.

— Sales reps could not even explain even the most basic aspects of using computer programs.

(b) *Refused to listen to Jene Nelsen.*

— She tried to provide training.

— They did not show up when she was there and did not listen to her advice.

(c) *Also refused to keep adequate inventory.*

— You have to have some products on hand.

— Danielsons refused to have more than a few computers; very hard to make sales.

(d) *Danielsons ordered inventory late.*

— They knew how long delivery would take when Wizard was having difficulties.

— They neglected to adjust; all they had to do was order a little earlier.

— Ordered computers for opening only *two weeks* ahead of time, although they knew their needs much earlier.

(e) *Ignored pleas of Atkins to correct mismanagement.*

6. *Danielsons failed to participate in business.*

— Jack Danielson — no involvement after heart attack.

— He recovered, but still didn't ever go to the store.

— Losses occurred after he became uninvolved.

— Margaret Danielson couldn't handle decisions.

— She completely withdrew from operation.

— Hired friend of a friend with no sales experience, to take over business.

7. *Danielsons stocked inferior products in violation of agreement.*

— ComputerCentre reputation built on quality, high tech products.

— Drew Anderson — who managed Danielsons' store — stocked cheap, inferior computers.

— Even stocked computer games — like you might find in a discount store.

— Customers couldn't take the store seriously.

8. *Danielsons' allegations incorrect.*

(a) *There is no "double markup."*

— There is a *discount* for high volume franchises — those that purchase in bulk.

— Middletown did not qualify.

— Other stores that get regular price are very successful.

(b) *"Yokels"/"clowns."*

— Atkins did write that.

— He was angry at bullheadedness of Danielsons on location/employees.

— Couldn't understand why they would not listen.

— Had absolutely *no effect* on any treatment of Danielson franchise.

(c) *Jene Nelsen — conviction.*

— Nothing but character assassination.

— She did everything she could to help these people.

— She signed up many other successful franchises.

— Has nothing to do with this case.

(d) *Contract addenda.*

— "Paperwork" was to get the addenda from corporate records.

— The addenda had been mistakenly sent to storage.

— Danielsons knew from the beginning they were supposed to pay royalties.

— It's in the franchise agreement *and* the addendum.

C. References to key evidence.

1. *Evidence of success of ComputerCentre.*

— Atkins/Nelsen franchises nationwide are profitable.

— Use ComputerCentre advice and methods.

2. *Danielsons will admit key facts.*

— No experience.

— Did not seek or follow location advice.

— Did not run business at all last summer.

— Mr. Danielson completely out after six months.

— That's when losses started.

3. *Franchise disclosure statement.*

— Obligations of franchisee established at beginning.

— Maintain adequate inventory as prescribed.

— Don't stock inferior products.

— Maintain quality franchise.

4. *Documents ignored by Danielsons.*

— ComputerCentre location study/never used.

— They went ahead and selected historic mall.

— 1/30 letter Atkins to Danielson.

— Written plea to get experienced sales staff.

— Also to maintain sufficient inventory.

— Atkins will tell you of many other oral pleas.

  5. *Drew Anderson — Danielsons manager — will admit employees were pathetic.*
      — Didn't even have minimal knowledge necessary to sell computers.
      — Couldn't assist customers with products.

D. Conclusion.

   The last thing in the world Dale Atkins wanted was for the Danielsons franchise to fail. If the Danielsons succeeded, they would have paid royalties to ComputerCentre and enhanced its reputation. Atkins and ComputerCentre tried to help the Danielsons but they wouldn't listen. The Danielsons caused their own failure by making bad business decisions and avoiding involvement with their own franchise. They are not entitled to collect for their own failures from ComputerCentre.

These outlines have common traits. Each emphasizes the best parts of the opposing cases through positioning and repetition. In both, the issue statements and conclusions are thematic. The strengths of each case appear in the introduction, the word picture, the evidence review, and the conclusion, although they are described in different ways so that the repetition is not apparent. Both outlines are designed primarily to portray facts rather than preview evidence.

You may wish to see word-for-word examples of opening statements, but presenting them would not be productive. The exact words of any opening statement are unimportant; the theme and overall picture are what people remember. A good outline is sufficient to provide a basis for rehearsal, which allows an extemporaneous delivery. In these rehearsals the attorney would not use the same exact words, but would gain the control necessary to make the right points. Thus, the attorney should use an outline — not a script — to prepare the opening statement.

If you wish to see word pictures in textual form, two examples are presented in the closing argument examples in §§ 12-13 and 12-14. The first is an example for ComputerCentre in the *Danielson* case.

CHAPTER 4

BASIC EVIDENCE AND PROCEDURE

---

§ 4-1. Introduction.

Two evidence rules are so pervasive that they affect the introduction of virtually any evidence: the requirements of a "foundation" and of "relevance." This chapter provides an overview of these rules. (§§ 4-2–4-5; 4-8–4-9). Later chapters discuss the foundation requirements in their specific contexts. This chapter also deals with procedural rules applicable to the introduction of evidence (§§ 4-6–4-7, 4-10–4-11) and rules for evaluating evidence (§§ 4-12–4-13).

§ 4-2. Foundation for the Admission of Evidence — Court's Determination (FRE 104).

The word "foundation" is used in various contexts to describe prerequisites for the admission of evidence. To show that the evidence is admissible, counsel must first "lay a foundation." Unfortunately, there can be no single definition of a required foundation because the prerequisites change with different types of evidence. Nevertheless, certain basic foundation requirements apply to virtually all evidence. Other requirements come up only in special situations.

The basic requirement — that generally associated with "laying a foundation" — is to make a showing of knowledge or genuineness that ensures that evidence will help the factfinder.[1] For example, for a witness to testify about an accident, he has to have personal knowledge of what happened. If he has no personal knowledge, his testimony is no more reliable than any secondhand recapitulation; the witness is not in a position to "help" the jury determine the matter. Similarly, an exhibit must be genuine to be helpful. Further, a person who offers specialized opinions must possess the knowledge necessary to formulate those opinions.

The term "foundation" may also refer to special conditions for admitting evidence in particular situations. These special requirements may ensure that evidence is reliable: for instance, a requirement that the police establish a "chain of custody" before introducing evidence of a crime. Statutory or constitutional requirements for the introduction of evidence also establish foundations. As an example, the prosecution may have to establish that a search was valid before introducing the evidence they discovered in the search.[2] Further, the evidence rules themselves establish foundation requirements, or prerequisites, for admitting certain evidence. To introduce hearsay under a hearsay exception, for example, the proponent must show that the prerequisites for the exception exist.

The court determines whether a requisite foundation exists. FRE 104 provides that "preliminary questions" concerning the admissibility of evidence. It also provides for determining certain preliminary questions outside the presence of the jury, preserves the right against self-incrimination when the accused testifies

---

[1] See, e.g., United States v. Haro-Espinosa, 619 F.2d 789 (9th Cir. 1979).

[2] Cf. Jackson v. Denno, 378 U.S. 368, 377 (1964) (hearing regarding the admissibility of confession should be conducted by the court out of the presence of the jury).

on preliminary matters, and preserves the parties' right to test the weight or sufficiency of evidence that the court admits. FRE 104 states:

Rule 104. Preliminary Questions

(a) Questions of admissibility generally. Preliminary questions concerning the qualification of a person to be a witness, the existence of a privilege, or the admissibility of evidence shall be determined by the court, subject to the provisions of subdivision (b). In making its determination it is not bound by the rules of evidence except those with respect to privileges.

(b) Relevancy conditioned on fact. When the relevancy of evidence depends upon the fulfillment of a condition of fact, the court shall admit it upon, or subject to, the introduction of evidence sufficient to support a finding of the fulfillment of the condition.

(c) Hearing of jury. Hearings on the admissibility of confessions shall in all cases be conducted out of the hearing of the jury. Hearings on other preliminary matters shall be so conducted when the interests of justice require, or when an accused is a witness and so requests.

(d) Testimony by accused. The accused does not, by testifying upon a preliminary matter, become subject to cross-examination as to other issues in the case.

(e) Weight and credibility. This rule does not limit the right of a party to introduce before the jury evidence relevant to weight or credibility.

When the foundation is personal knowledge or authenticity, the barrier to admissibility is a mere "bump" rather than a serious hurdle; the court determines only whether a minimal showing has been made, sufficient to support a finding that the foundation exists.[3] When special conditions must be met to admit evidence, the hurdle is often more substantial.

§ 4-2(a).   Generally Required Foundations (FRE 602, 901(a), 702).

There are three basic foundation requirements: (1) personal knowledge for a fact witness, (2) authenticity for an exhibit and, (3) specialized knowledge for specialized opinion testimony. These requirements ensure that the witness or exhibit can be helpful to the trier of fact.

§ 4-2(a)(i).   Personal Knowledge.

The first prerequisite requires that a fact witness have personal knowledge of any matter to which she testifies. FRE 602 provides:

---

[3] FED. R. EVID. 602, 901.

> A witness may not testify to a matter unless evidence is introduced sufficient to support a finding that the witness has personal knowledge of the matter. Evidence to prove personal knowledge may, but need not, consist of the witness's own testimony. This rule is subject to the provisions of Rule 703, relating to opinion testimony by expert witnesses.

This rule ensures that a witness has a basis to provide helpful information to the trier of fact. Obviously, if a witness speculates concerning facts about which she has no personal knowledge, the testimony would be no better than speculation by the jurors themselves; if a witness offers information obtained from someone else, the information is better received from the source. In the absence of personal knowledge, a fact witness's testimony does not aid the trier.

In determining whether the witness has personal knowledge, the court is supposed to impose a minimal requirement: whether evidence has been introduced "sufficient to support a finding" that the witness has personal knowledge.[4] In other words, the court should admit the evidence if a reasonable person *could* conclude that the foundation exists; if this low hurdle is satisfied, the court should leave it to the jury to evaluate the witness's knowledge along with other aspects of the testimony.[5] The witness himself may establish the foundation by explaining how he has personal knowledge of the fact.

Often a fact witness's testimony is admitted on an implied foundation, without a formal effort to establish personal knowledge. If a witness testifies she was at the corner of Maple and Broadway when an incident occurred at that site and proceeds to describe the event, the court may assume personal knowledge. Attorneys often do not phrase their questions to elicit a preliminary statement that the witness observed the entire incident. On cross-examination, if it comes out that the witness did not actually see what occurred, the court on request may strike her evidence. Thus, foundation is a legitimate subject and a fertile area for cross-examination. Witnesses often testify as if they had personal knowledge, although the evidence is actually based on other sources of information.

§ 4-2(a)(ii). Authenticity.

A second typical foundation requires that exhibits and other evidence be authentic.[6] Under FRE 901, the requirement of authentication, or identification, is satisfied "by evidence sufficient to support a finding that the matter in question is what its proponent claims." Again, the rule establishes a low hurdle for admissibility. The usual way to establish authenticity is to present the testimony

---

[4] Fed. R. Evid. 602.

[5] See Stephen A. Saltzburg, Michael M. Martin & Daniel J. Capra, Federal Rules of Evidence Manual § 6.02 (8th ed. 2002).

[6] See, e.g., Orr v. Bank of America, 285 F.3d 764 (9th Cir. 2002); United States v. Cuesta, 597 F.2d 903 (5th Cir. 1979), *cert. denied*, 444 U.S. 964 (1979).

of a witness with knowledge regarding the subject. In this situation, the witness must have a foundation (knowledge) to lay the foundation for the exhibit (identifying it).

Ordinarily, the attorney establishes the foundation prior to offering the exhibit. The court has discretion to admit the exhibit subject to the condition that it be identified later in the trial, as when several witnesses are needed to fully identify it, but this approach is unusual. Courts generally are reluctant to admit an exhibit that may have to be stricken when its proponent fails to authenticate it.

The requirement that an exhibit be identified as "what its proponent claims" reflects an essential link between foundation and relevance. Any witness would be able to identify a gun as "a gun"; unless a witness identifies it as "the gun" from which the bullets were fired that killed the victim, it is not relevant. Thus, the identification of an exhibit must be specific enough to establish its relevance. See § 8-5. Indeed, you should think of foundation as a basic aspect of relevance.

Rule 901(b) provides an illustrative list of methods to authenticate evidence. The list includes a number of situations in which identification is necessary: handwriting, telephone conversations, voice recordings, and similar instances. It permits various means of authenticating items, including direct testimony, circumstantial proof, and comparison by the trier of specimens with others that have been authenticated. FRE 902 provides for self-authentication of designated evidence, including certain public documents, official publications, and newspapers. FRE 903 provides that the testimony of a subscribing witness is not necessary to authenticate a writing unless specifically required by law.

At common law, a stronger foundation than that prescribed in FRE 901 was required in some circumstances for the admissibility of real evidence — items that played a role in the facts.[7] For example, for evidence seized by the police, some jurisdictions required and still require a showing of a "chain of custody"; this special reliability requirement, which imposes a higher foundation hurdle than the "sufficient to support a finding" standard, apparently has been relaxed by FRE 901.[8]

§ 4-2(a)(iii). Expertise.

A third typical foundation requires that an expert witness be qualified to give opinions on matters requiring scientific, technical or specialized knowledge.[9] FRE 702 provides that, where scientific, technical or specialized knowledge will assist the trier of fact, "a witness qualified as an expert by knowledge, skill, training or education, may testify thereto in the form of an opinion or otherwise."

---

[7] See GLEN WEISSENBERGER, WEISENBERGER'S FEDERAL EVIDENCE 619–21 (2d ed. 1995).

[8] See United States v. Logan, 949 F.2d 1370, 1378 (5th Cir. 1991) (weaknesses in chain of custody go to the weight, not the admissibility, of evidence).

[9] See, e.g., Backes v. Valspar Corp., 783 F.2d 77 (7th Cir. 1986).

This rule also requires that "(1) the testimony is based on sufficient facts or data, (2) the testimony is the product of reliable principles and methods, and (3) the witness has applied the principles and methods reliably to the facts of the case."

The trial court makes the decision as to whether the expert is qualified and appellate courts are supposed to give deference to the ruling. The foundation requirement may be a hurdle rather than a bump, however; appellate courts have indicated that trial judges should scrutinize "expert" opinions to ensure that they reflect reliable analyses and provide the factfinder more than mere advocacy. The exact standard for admitting expert testimony has not been explicitly defined. See § 10-5.

§ 4-2(b).   Special Foundations — Examples.

In addition to the typical foundation requirements, which ensure that evidence is helpful and relevant, there are many situations in which the substantive law requires the fulfillment of conditions before evidence is introduced. Thus, courts require a special showing of some fact as a prerequisite for admitting the evidence. An example is the constitutional foundation for the admissibility of a confession; the government ordinarily must show that *Miranda* warnings were given before the suspect confessed. Additionally, special showings are often required to admit evidence of certain legal transactions, such as a will.

In many situations, the rules of evidence establish conditions to the admission of evidence; counsel must show the required circumstances exist prior to introducing it.[10] Examples of these conditions to admit evidence are:

1. *Conditions for Proving Contents of a Writing, Recording, or Photograph.* For documents, recordings, or photographs, the proponent must provide the original or a duplicate, or satisfy special conditions for the admissibility of other evidence of their contents. FRE 1001-06. See §§ 8-21 — 8-28.

2. *Hearsay Exclusions and Exceptions.* When an out-of-court statement is offered for its truth, and the proponent claims the statement is one defined as "not hearsay" under FRE 801(d) or fits a hearsay exception, the proponent must show the conditions exist for avoiding the hearsay rule. For example, the proponent might have to show that the speaker was an employee or agent of the defendant to qualify his statement as an "admission." FRE 801(d)(2). To use the "excited utterance" exception, the proponent must establish that the statement related to a startling event and was made while the speaker was under the stress of excitement from the event. FRE 803(2).

Often the conditions are evident from the statements themselves, but sometimes the proponent must establish a special foundation. Thus, when the advocate offers

---

[10] See generally David P. Leonard, *Appellate Review of Evidentiary Rulings*, 70 N.C. L. REV. 1155 (1992).

statements in a document as "past recollection recorded," she must first elicit testimony that (1) the witness has insufficient recollection of the facts, (2) the witness once had knowledge of them, (3) the witness prepared a record of the events when the matter was still fresh in his memory, and (4) the record was accurate. FRE 803(5). Special foundations are required for the introduction of business records, public records and for other hearsay exceptions. See FRE 803, 804. See Chapter 6.

3. *Privileged Information.* When a party or witness claims the right to withhold information on the grounds of privilege, the circumstances giving rise to the privilege must be established. See Chapter 11.

4. *Conditions for Impeachment.* To attack credibility with a prior bad act, the proponent must show that the act is probative of truthfulness. FRE 608. To use a prior conviction, the proponent must show that the requirements of FRE 609 are met. In some jurisdictions, extrinsic evidence may be introduced to impeach the witness only after the information has been brought up on cross-examination and the witness has failed to admit it. Thus, counsel would have to satisfy the condition of asking about a prior inconsistent statement before another witness could be called to testify that it was made. The federal rules relax this requirement, but counsel usually may not introduce extrinsic evidence to impeach unless the witness is available to explain or deny the matter. This requirement serves as a condition to admitting the impeaching evidence. See §§ 9-28, 9-31, and 9-32.

Under FRE 104, the court determines whether special conditions exist for the introduction of evidence. Except for preliminary fact conditions for establishing that evidence is relevant, which are governed by the "sufficient to support a finding" standard, the rule does not provide the standard for determining whether conditions are fulfilled. FRE 104(b).

In *Bourjaily v. United States,* [11] the United States Supreme Court gave a strong indication that the "preponderance of the evidence" standard should govern most determinations. It ruled that this standard should govern the determination of whether an out-of-court statement is exempted from the hearsay definitions under the "co-conspirator admission" provision of FRE 801(d)(2)(E). The Court found that the federal rules did not resolve what standard should be applied in resolving preliminary issues under FRE 104(a). Thus, it looked to its prior decisions and found that the "more probable than not" standard should be applied. The Court held:

> We are therefore guided by our prior decisions regarding admissibility determinations that hinge on preliminary factual questions. We have traditionally required that these matters be established by a preponderance of

---

[11] 483 U.S. 171 (1987).

proof. Evidence is placed before the jury when it satisfies the technical requirements of the evidentiary Rules, which embody certain legal and policy determinations. The inquiry made by a court concerned with these matters is not whether the proponent wins or loses his case on the merits, but whether the evidentiary Rules have been satisfied. Thus, the evidentiary standard is unrelated to the burden of proof on the substantive issues, be it a criminal case, or a civil case. The preponderance standard ensures that before admitting evidence, the court will have found it more likely than not that the technical issues and policy concerns addressed by the Federal Rules of Evidence have been afforded due consideration. . . .[12]

Although the decision involved only the co-conspirator admission exemption, the Court's broad language, and its reliance on cases applying the preponderance standard to other preliminary questions, suggests that this standard governs a Rule 104 determination when specific standards are not set out in the rules.[13]

FRE 104 explicitly provides the applicable standard when relevance is dependent on the fulfillment of a condition of fact. The court decides only whether evidence has been introduced "sufficient to support a finding of the fulfillment of the condition." FRE 104(b). In other words, the court should admit the evidence if a reasonable person *could* conclude the condition was fulfilled; the jury decides whether the evidence satisfies the ultimate burden of proof. The judge may require a preliminary showing that the condition is fulfilled or may admit the evidence and strike it thereafter if proponent fails to make the necessary showing.

For an example of conditional relevance, consider testimony from a fingerprint expert identifying the prints on a weapon. The testimony would be relevant only if the weapon were connected to the crime charged. Thus, the testimony would be admitted upon, or subject to, the introduction of evidence sufficient to support a finding that the expert examined the weapon used to commit the crime. Counsel could satisfy the condition by presenting another expert witness to testify that the gun in question fired the killing bullets. See § 4-8.

§ 4-2(c). Voir Dire on Preliminary Issues.

Theoretically, the party opposing the introduction of evidence has a right to cross-examine, or "voir dire," a witness on preliminary questions.[14] Moreover, to protect the jury from being influenced by inadmissible evidence, the opposing party may request that the matter be heard without the jury present. FRE 104(c) provides that hearings on the admissibility of confessions shall be conducted out of the hearing of the jury and hearings on other preliminary questions shall be

---

[12] *Id.* at 175.

[13] *Id.*

[14] EDWARD J. IMWINKELRIED, EVIDENTIARY FOUNDATIONS § 2.05 (5th ed. 2002).

so conducted "when the interests of justice require, or when the accused is a witness and so requests."

The court has discretion to hear most preliminary matters — particularly those that are relatively unimportant or quickly resolved — with the jury present. In practice, the court also may reserve any "voir dire" examination until the witness is cross-examined, admitting the evidence on a prima facie showing that a preliminary requirement is met, but striking it if cross-examination negates the necessary foundation. Counsel may ensure that a preliminary issue is resolved outside the jury's presence by filing a motion in limine prior to the trial.

§ 4-3. Traditional Rule Against Lay Opinions.

Traditionally, lay witnesses could testify only to facts within their personal knowledge; they were barred from giving "opinion" evidence. The justification for the opinion rule is that the trier of fact — the judge or jury — determines the meaning of facts. As to matters that can be interpreted by any lay person, the opinion of the witness provides no help to the trier and may be prejudicial. In a large sense, the opinion rule is a rule of relevance, because the opinion of a lay witness as to the meaning of facts is irrelevant to the jury's determination.

An early American statement of the rule is contained in *Donnell v. Jones*.[15] The court stated:

> The general rule requires, that witnesses should depose only to facts, and such facts too as come within their knowledge. The expression of opinions, the belief of the witness, or deductions from the facts, however honestly made, are not proper evidence as coming from the witness; and when such deductions are made by the witness, the prerogative of the jury is invaded.[16]

The problem with the classic formulation is that many factual accounts contain hidden inferences drawn by witnesses, and many times a witness cannot give a factual account without including some of his own inferences. Thus, a bright line rule between fact and opinion is judicially unmanageable. The following statements contain easily recognizable inferences:

"The man looked badly beaten."

"He walked as if he was drunk."

"The car was going very fast."

Even when a witness testifies to facts, inferences are present. A statement that a person was "six feet tall" or that a car was traveling "40 miles per hour" really reflects the witness's *opinion* as to the meaning of her own visual observation.

---

[15] 13 Ala. 490 (1848).

[16] *Id.* at 511.

In truth, the man may be five foot ten, and the car may have been going 35 m.p.h.

As a result of the difficulty of enforcing the opinion rule and the need for testimony from witnesses who naturally express inferences, the fact-opinion distinction often was relaxed in practice. As McCormick states, good reason exists for this approach:

> If trial judges are given the task of distinguishing on the spur of the moment between "fact" and "opinion," no two judges, acting independently, can be expected to consistently reach the same results on the questions. . . . Thus, good sense demands that the trial judge be accorded a wide range of discretion at least in classifying evidence as "fact" or "opinion," and probably in admitting evidence even where found to constitute opinion. Various courts have expressed this viewpoint. . . .[17]

§ 4-4. Standard Under Federal Rules for Admitting Lay Opinions (FRE 701).

FRE 701 permits the introduction of opinion evidence of lay witnesses. The rule requires, however, that an opinion be rationally based on the witness's perception *and* helpful to a clear understanding of his testimony or the determination of a fact in issue. The rule states:

> If the witness is not testifying as an expert, his testimony in the form of opinions or inferences is limited to those opinions or inferences which are (a) rationally based on the perception of the witness and (b) helpful to a clear understanding of his testimony or the determination of a fact in issue.

This rule is not an all-encompassing mandate to admit opinion evidence, but it does change the basic outlook toward this evidence. In general, the rule opens the door for opinion evidence, eliminating objections based solely on the ground that testimony contains opinion. Nevertheless, the conditions of personal knowledge and a rational basis operate as a foundation requirement, compelling counsel to show that the witness has a sound basis for expressing an opinion. Additionally, the requirement that the opinion be helpful prevents the witness from making jumps from fact to opinion that could just as easily be made by the jury.[18]

The Advisory Committee Note to Rule 701 explains that the primary reason for changing the rule is the practical impossibility of drawing a bright line between facts and opinions. It states:

---

[17] MCCORMICK ON EVIDENCE § 11 (5th ed. 1999). See also Judge Learned Hand's decision in Central R.R. of N.J. v. Monahan, 11 F.2d 212, 214 (2d Cir. 1926) (expressing the view that the exclusion of opinion evidence had been "carried beyond reason in this country").

[18] See Aloe Coal Co. v. Clark Equip. Co., 816 F.2d 110 (3d Cir. 1987), *cert. denied*, 484 U.S. 853 (1987); Denton by Jamison v. United States, 731 F. Supp. 1034 (D. Kan. 1990).

Witnesses often find difficulty in expressing themselves in language which is not that of an opinion or conclusion. While the courts have made concessions in certain recurring situations, necessity as a standard for permitting opinions and conclusions has proved too elusive and too unadaptable to particular situations for purposes of satisfactory judicial administration. Moreover, the practical impossibility of determining by rule what is a "fact," demonstrated by a century of litigation of the question of what is a fact for purposes of pleading under the Field Code extends into evidence also. . . .[19]

The rule leaves it to lawyers to prepare witnesses to give factual testimony so as to "display [the] witness to the best advantage," and to cross-examination to point up the weaknesses in conclusory testimony.[20] Additionally, the committee reaffirms that courts should not permit witnesses to try to do the jury's job. It says: "If, despite these considerations, attempts are made to introduce meaningless assertions which amount to little more than choosing up sides, exclusion for lack of helpfulness is called for by the rule."[21]

Courts are more likely to exclude opinion testimony as it gets closer to the heart of the case. Consequently, a court might allow the observation "he was drunk" if inebriation were not a central issue, but require a more factual description if the subject of the description were charged with driving while intoxicated.

§ 4-5. Need to Emphasize Factual Testimony in Advocacy.

Even under FRE 701, counsel should seek to elicit testimony from lay witnesses that is as factual and concrete as possible. As McCormick states, the tradition of seeking factual detail is a "valuable heritage"; the goal is to "preserve this habit but yet to curb . . . time-wasting quibbles over trivial "opinion" objections . . . ."[22]

Concrete, factual testimony is much more vivid and persuasive to a jury than a conclusory opinion. The observation "he was drunk" may be a rational conclusion based on the witness's observation, but it is not as compelling as a description that leads the jury to the same conclusion:

> The man was staggering around. There was a strong scent of bourbon on his breath. He tried to speak but slurred his words badly. Several times he bumped against the railing. When he looked at me, he cocked his head and squinted his eyes.

---

[19] FED. R. EVID. 701 advisory committee's note (citations omitted).

[20] Id.

[21] Id.

[22] MCCORMICK ON EVIDENCE § 11 (5th ed. 1999).

This description paints a picture of a drunk man, one the jury is likely to remember better than a conclusory description that "he was drunk."

By striving for factual descriptions, counsel helps ensure that a witness is prepared. If the advocate urges the witness to be concrete in preparing, the chances are better that the witness will provide good descriptions on the stand. If counsel accepts vague, conclusory assertions, on the other hand, the witness may not retain a good idea of what he should say. The testimony may turn out ineffective, lacking force and coherence.

The emphasis on concrete descriptions also avoids unnecessary problems. Many judges still resist admitting opinions, despite the more welcoming federal rule. Moreover, some jurisdictions may not be as lenient in allowing opinions as the federal system. Sticking to factual descriptions helps ensure that a court will admit the evidence. You always can argue inferences in closing argument.

On cross-examination, the need for a specific, factual examination is even greater. This approach is essential to secure concessions and limit explanations. If you asks general questions, the witness has an opening to offer gratuitous comments. A specific, detailed cross-examination limits a witness's ability to make points for the opposing side.

§ 4-6. Competence of Witnesses.

Generally, any person is competent to be a witness. The judge and jurors generally may not be witnesses, however, and witnesses are required to swear or affirm they will tell the truth. The rules on witness competency are discussed below.

§ 4-6(a). Competency of "Persons" (FRE 601).

FRE 601 establishes a strong presumption of witness competence, providing that "every person" is competent except as otherwise provided in the federal rules. This rule eliminates traditional objections to witness competence, such as insanity, intoxication, or interest in the outcome of the case.[23] Thus, for example, a person's mental incapacity does not bar him from being a witness, but the factfinder could consider it in assessing the weight and credibility of his testimony. As the Advisory Committee states: "A witness wholly without capacity is difficult to imagine. The question is one particularly suited to the jury as one of weight and credibility, subject to judicial authority to review the sufficiency of the evidence."[24] FRE 601 provides:

> Every person is competent to be a witness except as otherwise provided in these rules. However, in civil actions and proceedings, with respect to an

---

[23] See FED. R. EVID. 601 advisory committee's note.
[24] *Id.*

element of a claim or defense as to which State law supplies the rule of decision, the competency of a witness shall be determined in accordance with State law.

The general rule of competence presumably admits exceptions in extreme cases. A very small child or an obviously deranged, raving lunatic might be deemed incompetent despite the categorical language of the rule. The courts can deal with the issue through other provisions, however, by finding that the witness cannot comprehend the oath or that the testimony would be unhelpful or confusing under FRE 403.

Although any person is competent to be a witness, the person must have personal knowledge to testify to facts and must have expert qualifications to give specialized opinions.[25] These requirements are discussed in § 4-2.

§ 4-6(b). Judge Competence (FRE 605).

The trial judge is not competent to be a witness. FRE 605 contains an absolute prohibition against testimony from the presiding judge. It states: "The judge presiding at the trial may not testify at the trial as a witness. No objection need be made in order to preserve the point."

Few judges would actually take the stand at a trial because this action would require their disqualification.[26] Thus, the provision may be unnecessary. It does serve the purpose, however, of discouraging comment from the bench that effectively amounts to fact testimony or personal opinion regarding the merits. The judge is entitled to instruct the jury on the law and to sum up and comment on the evidence impartially, but not to introduce his own personal observations — gleaned from outside the courtroom — regarding the facts.[27] The judge may take judicial notice of facts, however, and instruct the jury to accept them.[28]

If the judge provides fact testimony, the objection is preserved, whether or not the attorney makes it at the time. The Advisory Committee states:

> To require an actual objection would confront the opponent with a choice between not objecting, with the result of allowing the testimony, and objecting, with the probable result of excluding the testimony but at the price of continuing the trial before a judge likely to feel that his integrity has been attacked by the objection.[29]

---

[25] FED. R. EVID. 602, 702.

[26] 28 U.S.C. § 455.

[27] United States v. Lewis, 833 F.2d 1380 (9th Cir. 1987), *cert. denied sub nom.* Fultz v. Rose, 486 U.S. 1056 (1988); Hersch v. United States, 719 F.2d 873 (6th Cir. 1983).

[28] FED. R. EVID. 201.

[29] FED. R. EVID. 605 advisory committee's note.

Proposed FRE 105 would have codified the prerogative of the judge impartially to comment on and sum up the evidence, so long as he instructs the jury that they are not bound by the summation. The rule was not adopted by Congress, but still reflects the law in the federal system. Nevertheless, the judge's summation should be based on the evidence, not his personal knowledge or experience.

§ 4-6(c).   Juror Competence (FRE 606).

FRE 606 provides that a juror is incompetent to be a witness. Additionally, it severely limits the extent to which a juror may testify or provide other evidence of jury deliberations. The subjects of permissible testimony are (1) whether extraneous prejudicial information was brought to the jury's attention and (2) whether a juror was subjected to an outside influence. The rule states:

Competency of Juror as Witness

    (a) At the Trial. A member of the jury may not testify as a witness before that jury in the trial of the case in which the juror is sitting. If the juror is called so to testify, the opposing party shall be afforded an opportunity to object out of the presence of the jury.

    (b) Inquiry into validity of verdict or indictment. Upon an inquiry into the validity of a verdict or indictment, a juror may not testify as to any matter or statement occurring during the course of the jury's deliberations or to the effect of anything upon that or any other juror's mind or emotions as influencing the juror to assent to or dissent from the verdict or indictment or concerning the juror's mental processes in connection therewith, except that a juror may testify on the question whether extraneous prejudicial information was improperly brought to the jury's attention or whether any outside influence was improperly brought to bear upon any juror. Nor may a juror's affidavit or evidence of any statement by the juror concerning a matter about which the juror would be precluded from testifying be received for these purposes.

In enforcing these provisions, many courts have enacted rules limiting counsel's ability to question jurors after a verdict. The limitations no doubt curb attack on the propriety of jury deliberations, but may also prevent counsel from learning of extraneous information brought to the jury's attention or about outside influence on a juror. Thus, they may prevent the revelation of improprieties.

§ 4-6(d).   Requirement of Oath or Affirmation (FRE 603).

Any witness is required to swear or affirm that she will testify truthfully. The oath or affirmation is supposed to impress the witness with the duty of truthfulness. FRE 603 provides:

Before testifying, every witness shall be required to declare that the witness will testify truthfully, by oath or affirmation administered in a form calculated to awaken the witness' conscience and impress the witness' mind with the duty to do so.

§ 4-6(e). Applicability of Rules to Interpreters (FRE 604).

An interpreter must swear or affirm that the translation she provides is correct. The interpreter must also possess the language skills to make the translation. FRE 604 states:

An interpreter is subject to the provisions of these rules relating to qualification as an expert and the administration of an oath or affirmation to make a true translation.

§ 4-7. Exclusion of Witnesses (FRE 615).

Under FRE 615, a party has a right to have the court exclude the witnesses so that they cannot hear the testimony of other witnesses. If no request is made, the court on its own motion may exclude the witnesses. The exclusion order cannot apply to a party, an officer or employee of a party designated as its representative, a person whose presence is essential to a party's presentation, or a person authorized by statute to be present. FRE 615 provides:

At the request of a party the court shall order witnesses excluded so that they cannot hear the testimony of other witnesses and it may make the order of its own motion. This rule does not authorize exclusion of (1) a party who is a natural person, or (2) an officer or employee of a party which is not a natural person designated as its representative by its attorney, or [sic] (3) a person whose presence is shown by a party to be essential to the presentation of the party's cause, or (4) a person authorized by statute to be present.

This rule gives either side the *right* to require the exclusion of witnesses. It does not specify a particular time for making the request.[30] Thus, the rule might permit a plaintiff to put on a case without requesting the exclusion of witnesses and yet allow the plaintiff to exclude witnesses during the defense's case. To avoid this one-sided outcome, a defendant is wise to require the exclusion of the opposing side's witnesses, or secure an agreement before trial that neither side will request that witnesses be excluded.[31]

Witnesses are exempt from exclusion orders if their "presence is shown by a party to be essential in the presentation of the party's cause." This exception

---

[30] FED. R. EVID. 615 advisory committee's note.

[31] FED. R. EVID. 611(a). See Comer v. Commissioner of Internal Revenue, 958 F.2d 136 (6th Cir. 1992), holding that exclusion request may be made at any time, but an order denying exclusion because the request was untimely would not be reversed absent a showing of prejudice.

contemplates "such persons as an agent who handled the transaction being litigated or an expert needed to advise counsel in the management of the litigation."[32]

When a court issues an exclusion order, you should make sure the terms of the order are clear. Examples of issues that might lead to problems include:

1.　May counsel discuss the evidence admitted in the trial with a witness who has been excluded?

2.　May trial transcripts be reviewed by a witness who has been excluded?

3.　May a witness who has testified discuss the testimony with another witness who has been excluded?

Often during a trial an unforeseen point arises that a sequestered witness easily might clarify. Asking the witness about the point may seem natural and necessary, but may run afoul of the unannounced terms of an exclusion order. Thus, you should determine the exact meaning of the exclusion order in advance.

Penalties for violation of an exclusion order include: (1) a citation for contempt, (2) preventing the witness from testifying, or (3) permitting cross-examination and comment on the violation of the order.[33] In terms of influencing the trial, the first two sanctions reflect the extremes. A simple contempt citation will not cure unfairness resulting from a violation; a refusal to permit the testimony may deprive the trier of fact of valuable evidence. The third option, or a combination of the first and third, provides the most balanced approach to curing a violation. The appropriate sanction depends on whether the violation was intentional and the extent to which it provides an advantage to the witness.

§ 4-8.　Relevance (FRE 401, 402).

The basic standard for the admissibility of evidence requires that it be "relevant."[34] FRE 401 defines "relevant evidence." It states:

> "Relevant evidence" means evidence having any tendency to make the existence of any fact that is of consequence to the determination of the action more probable or less probable than it would be without the evidence.

Rule 402 provides that "[a]ll relevant evidence is admissible," except as provided by law or other evidentiary rules, and "[e]vidence which is not relevant is not admissible."[35]

The determination of relevance necessarily requires logic, and the reasoning process usually involves two steps. First, the evidence must tend to prove a fact.

---

[32] FED. R. EVID. 615 advisory committee's note.

[33] *Emerging Problems Under the Federal Rules of Evidence*, Rule 615 (A.B.A. 1991).

[34] See RICHARD A. GIVENS, MANUAL OF FEDERAL PRACTICE § 7.11, at 59 (3d ed. 1987).

[35] See generally Complaint of Nautilus Motor Tanker Co., Ltd., 85 F.3d 105 (3d Cir. 1996).

This connection often is self-evident, as when a witness testifies directly to the fact, but sometimes is not so clear. For instance, assume that an x-ray, which is offered to prove the condition of a lung, depicts a cloudy area in the lung. Expert testimony would be necessary to connect the x-ray to a specific condition, and opposing experts might disagree on its implications. Second, the fact must be "of consequence" to the determination of the action. In other words, the fact must support an ultimate conclusion that may determine the case under applicable legal standards. Connecting facts and ultimate conclusions often requires logical jumps, or inferences.[36]

A fact need not be the ultimate conclusion to be "of consequence."[37] The difference between direct proof of the ultimate fact, and proof of facts that support an ultimate conclusion through reasoning, can be illustrated with the following example. Assume Smith is accused of murdering Jones with a knife at 2:00 a.m. on July 2, 2002. The elements of this offense — the "ultimate" facts — are probably (1) causing, (2) death, (3) with intent to do so. If Smith's girlfriend, Susan Miller, testifies that she saw the incident and that Jones grabbed the knife from Smith and accidentally fell on it, her testimony would directly tend to disprove an ultimate fact — that Smith "caused" Jones's death. If Miller were the only witness to the incident, her testimony might be the only direct proof of this ultimate conclusion.

Other evidence might *indirectly* — or "circumstantially" — prove that Smith caused Jones's death. Assume a witness, Lisa Powell, testifies she saw Smith chasing Jones down the street, brandishing a knife and shouting threats. Powell says she saw the two turn a corner, where Jones was found a few minutes later with a knife in his chest. This evidence is direct proof that Smith had a knife, chased Jones, and threatened him. It is only circumstantial proof as to the knifing. From this evidence, one would have to make a logical leap to determine that Smith plunged the knife into Jones's chest. To the extent that the evidence requires inference, or reasoning, to make the ultimate fact more or less probable, it is "circumstantial" evidence of the fact. Nevertheless, the evidence is relevant, because it is reasonable to conclude that the person who chased Jones with a knife also attacked him with it.[38]

This example of circumstantial evidence requires only one logical step to reach the ultimate conclusion. Other evidence might require a series of inferences. Suppose, for instance, that a witness identified the knife used in the killing as a type sold at a clearance sale at a sporting goods store several weeks prior to

---

[36] See GLEN WEISSENBERGER, WEISSENBERGER'S FEDERAL EVIDENCE § 401.3, at 68–69 (2d ed. 1995).

[37] See, e.g., Derr v. Safeway Stores, Inc., 404 F.2d 634 (10th Cir. 1968).

[38] See generally RONALD L. CARLSON, EDWARD J. IMWINKELRIED & EDWARD J. KIONKA, MATERIALS FOR THE STUDY OF EVIDENCE 138–42 (1983).

the killing. Testimony that Smith was seen in the store at the time of the sale would lead to the ultimate conclusion through a series of inferences. The evidence would prove a fact — Smith had the opportunity to purchase a knife of the type used in the killing. This fact might justify inferences that he purchased it, it was the same knife, and he used it on Jones. The strength of these logical connections likely would depend on other evidence pointing to Jones as the culprit.

At some point the logical process becomes too tenuous for the proven fact to be "of consequence."[39] Testimony that Smith was an avid sportsman and often took advantage of sporting goods sales would prove a fact several jumps from the conclusion. A factfinder would have to infer from the proven fact — "Smith was a sportsman interested in sales" — that he (1) learned of this sale, (2) purchased a knife, (3) it was the same knife, and (4) he used it to kill Jones. Obviously, to the extent the underlying fact proved anything, it would support the same conclusion concerning thousands of other sportsmen. Thus, absent special circumstances making the connections more compelling, the evidence might be deemed irrelevant.

Facts also may be "of consequence" because they bear on other facts used to prove an ultimate fact.[40] Assume, for instance, that Smith's girlfriend, Miller, presents her alleged eyewitness testimony exonerating him. Thereafter, testimony is elicited — perhaps from Miller herself — that she is deeply in love with Smith. This fact does not directly prove anything about the alleged crime. If Miller never took the stand, it probably would not be relevant. Nevertheless, given the fact that she does testify, it is "of consequence" to assessing her truthfulness. The trier of fact could draw the inference that being in love with Smith might lead Miller to lie for him. Similarly, if another witness testified that Miller was in a bar across town at 2:00 a.m. on July 2, 2002, the evidence by itself would not prove anything about the knifing. It would tend to show that Miller could not have witnessed the incident, however, and would thus be "of consequence" in determining whether her version is correct.

In most cases, facts have meaning only when considered in context with other facts. Further, facts often can be used to support different inferences. Testimony that Jones flirted with Smith's ex-girlfriend might in one context support a conclusion that Smith, in a fit of jealousy, had a reason to kill Jones; in another, it might be read as part of a pattern in which Jones harassed and taunted Smith. Either inference might be argued in a case where different pictures are presented of the motives of the purported "victim" and "perpetrator." Thus, the same fact might be used to support conflicting theories.

Sometimes the relevance of a fact is dependent on an independent fact.[41] The following example of "conditional" relevance is given in the Advisory

---

[39] See *Id.*

[40] See Marsee v. United States Tobacco Co., 866 F.2d 319 (10th Cir. 1989).

[41] See United States v. Ortiz-Rengifo, 832 F.2d 722 (2d Cir. 1987).

Committee's Note to Rule 401: "[I]f evidence of a spoken statement is relied upon to prove notice, probative value is lacking unless the person sought to be charged heard the statement." This example reflects a legal requirement, in specific circumstances, of *actual* notice; the spoken statement proves nothing unless connected to the person entitled to the notice. Presumably the evidence would be admitted, subject to proof that the statement was heard, but could be stricken if the condition were not fulfilled. Although a specific condition for the admission of evidence rarely exists, the example illustrates the manner in which evidence, as a practical matter, may become meaningful only in the context of other evidence.

Evidence is relevant if it has "any tendency" to make a fact of consequence more or less probable than without the evidence.[42] This test suggests that the court should admit evidence if a reasonable person could conclude that it makes a fact of consequence more or less probable.[43] In other words, the court should not substitute its judgment for that of the jury by excluding the evidence, so long as a reasonable juror might conclude that it tends to prove a consequential fact. The court may take a stronger role, however, in balancing relevance against claims of prejudice, confusion, or undue waste of time.[44] See § 4-9.

The need for reasoning to assess relevance points up the importance of a coherent argument. A good attorney usually has a comprehensive factual theory that permits assimilation of as many competing facts as possible. This thematic approach permits the attorney to borrow from the strengths of the case to argue inferences that might alone seem tenuous. When presented in a "word picture," the inferences may seem as real as the facts that have direct evidentiary support.

Moreover, developing a coherent theme lessens the distance between the evidence and the ultimate facts; since all the basic and intermediate facts seem to work together to form the ultimate conclusion, the evidence supporting these facts also may seem directly to support the conclusion. Thus, counsel can rely more on one-step logic, which argues directly from evidence to a conclusion, rather than more complex reasoning to explain the meaning of evidence.

§ 4-9.   Relevance vs. Prejudice, Confusion, Delay (FRE 403).

FRE 403 provides that relevant evidence may be excluded if its probative value is "substantially outweighed by the danger of unfair prejudice, confusion of the issues, or misleading the jury, or by considerations of undue delay, waste of time, or needless presentation of cumulative evidence." This provision requires the

---

[42] FED. R. EVID. 401.

[43] See, e.g., Bettius & Sanderson, P.C. v. National Union Fire Ins. Co., 839 F.2d 1009 (4th Cir. 1988) (emphasizing the generally liberal standard for the admission of evidence).

[44] FED. R. EVID. 403.

court to *balance* relevance versus prejudice, confusion or delay, thus weighing the *degree of relevance* against the countervailing factors.[45]

Since claims of prejudice, confusion, or waste of time often accompany an objection that evidence is irrelevant, the trial court frequently is called on to interpose its judgment of relevance in deciding admissibility, despite the minimal role implied by FRE 401. Presumably the determination can include the court's assessment of credibility. Nevertheless, the court may exclude relevant evidence only if its probative value is *substantially* outweighed by the danger of prejudice, confusion or delay. Thus, the rule still limits the court's discretion to exclude evidence.[46]

A mere reference to the key words usually is not sufficient to win a Rule 403 objection. Counsel must describe why the evidence is prejudicial, confusing or unduly time consuming. At the same time, the attorney should explain its limited probative value. When evidence is prejudicial, counsel should request the right to discuss the matter out of the jury's presence to avoid its harmful impact.

When evidence is highly relevant, FRE 403 generally requires its introduction even when it is also prejudicial or confusing. The court may consider alternatives to limit the prejudice, but only in rare cases should the court exclude the evidence altogether. FRE 403 establishes a strong presumption that the factfinder should hear relevant evidence, even when the evidence may be prejudicial.[47]

§ 4-9(a). Prejudice.

Most evidence that tends to prove a case is harmful to the party against whom it is offered, and in that sense it is prejudicial. The "prejudice" referred to in Rule 403 is a special kind of harm: an effect that might lead the jury to rule

---

[45] See 1 JACK B. WEINSTEIN & MARGARET A. BERGER, WEINSTEIN'S EVIDENCE § 403.04 (2nd ed. 1997).

[46] Regarding the balancing test of Rule 403, see generally Vincent v. Louis Marx & Co., Inc., 874 F.2d 36 (1st Cir. 1989). See generally Edward J. Imwinkelried, *The Meaning of Probative Value and Prejudice in Federal Rule of Evidence 403: Can Rule 403 Be Used to Resurrect the Common Law of Evidence?*, 41 VAND. L. REV. 879 (1988); see also Richard Lempert, *The New Evidence Scholarship: Analyzing the Process of Proof,* 66 B.U. L. REV. 439, 454–62 (1986); Neil B. Cohen, *Confidence in Probability: Burdens of Persuasion in a World of Imperfect Knowledge,* 60 N.Y.U. L. REV. 385 (1985).

[47] In Rubert-Torres v. Hospital San Pablo, Inc., 205 F.3d 472 (1st Cir. 2000), the First Circuit ruled that a district court abused its discretion by banning a plaintiff with cerebral palsy from the courtroom during the trial of her claim that malpractice caused the condition. The plaintiff's experts relied on her physical appearance to support their conclusions, making her presence "highly relevant" in evaluating their testimony. *Id.* at 479. The court said: "When proffered evidence relates to the central issue in the case, it is a difficult matter indeed to show that the prejudicial effect of the evidence substantially outweighs its highly probative nature, as Rule 403 requires." *Id.* The court noted also that a less restrictive means for limiting the prejudice could have been employed. *Id.*

against a party for the wrong reasons.[48] The "right" reasons are those embodied in the legal rules applicable to the case.

For example, in an accident case, a court should not exclude powerful evidence that the defendant was negligent on the ground of unfair prejudice, but it could exclude evidence that he is a drug pusher on this ground. Additionally, evidence likely to produce a disproportionate emotional response in the jurors, such as a grisly photograph of an injury, may be excluded as prejudicial. The Advisory Committee Note to FRE 403 states: " 'Unfair prejudice' . . . means an undue tendency to suggest decision on an improper basis, commonly, though not necessarily, an emotional one."

§ 4-9(b). Confusion.

The grounds of "confusion" and "misleading" are self-explanatory but can only be applied in specific situations.[49] An example of evidence that might mislead the jury is a chart drawn to a particularly narrow scale, which makes the charted results appear more significant than they are in reality. The use of a demonstrative exhibit throughout a trial — for example, a replica of an alleged murder weapon — might lead the jury to subconsciously view the example as the actual weapon. Of course, an instruction may place the evidence in context, but the court's verbal explanation may not fully offset its impact.

§ 4-9(c). Delay.

An objection that evidence will waste time strikes a sympathetic chord with many trial judges. Most judges have limited courtroom time. Proceeding down a "rabbit trail" is not a welcome prospect to a busy judge, particularly if admitting the evidence will necessitate the introduction of answering evidence. Thus, the judge may not hear a controversy that has little importance. Additionally, the court may exclude evidence that is merely cumulative.[50]

§ 4-9(d). Alternatives.

When evidence is relevant, the court should be reluctant to exclude it, even if there is a possibility of prejudice, confusion or delay. One alternative to limit the impact of the evidence is a cautionary instruction. Counsel may wish to suggest the wording of an instruction to secure the right effect and avoid magnifying the harm. Another alternative is to require that the fact be proven with different evidence. The attorney also may consider stipulating a fact so that the evidence is unnecessary.

---

[48] See, e.g., JOSEPH M. MCLAUGHLIN, FEDERAL EVIDENCE PRACTICE GUIDE ¶ 5.04[3], at 21–23 (1991).

[49] See MICHAEL M. MARTIN, BASIC PROBLEMS OF EVIDENCE § 10.02, at 224–26 (6th ed. 1988).

[50] See *Id.*

Courts have considerable discretion in deciding whether to require alternate methods of proof, but the discretion has limits. In Old Chief v. United States,[51] the defendant was charged with possessing a firearm after a prior conviction. He offered to stipulate that the had a prior conviction, thus making it unnecessary to admit the actual judgment of conviction, which disclosed the nature of the offense. The Supreme Court held that a district court abuses its discretion to admit a judgment of prior offense when the defendant concedes this element and the nature of the prior offense is prejudicial. The Court ruled that the district court should have considered the evidentiary alternative offered by the defendant, and balanced any incremental relevance of the actual conviction versus the risk of prejudice.

The primary justification offered for admitting the prior conviction was the prosecutions' right to choose the means of proving its own case. The Court endorsed this concept "as a general matter," recognizing that admissions by a defendant might deprive the prosecution of rich and colorful evidence necessary to carry the heavy burden of proving guilt beyond a reasonable doubt.[52] Nevertheless, because of the inherent danger that a prior conviction may prejudice the jury by leading it to convict for the defendant's character rather than the charged crime, and because the admitted point involved only the defendant's legal status, the Court held "the only reasonable conclusion was that the risk of unfair prejudice did substantially outweigh the discounted probative value of the record of conviction . . . ".[53] It added: "[T]his will be the general rule when proof of convict status is at issue, just as the prosecutor's choice will generally survive a Rule 403 analysis when a defendant seeks to force the substitution of an admission for evidence creating a coherent narrative of his thoughts and actions in perpetrating the offense for which he is being tried.[54]

§ 4-10. Need to Object to Evidence, or Make an Offer of Proof, to Preserve Error (FRE 103(a)).

An error in admitting or excluding evidence must affect a substantial right of a party to be reversible on appeal.[55] To preserve the right to appeal, counsel must make a timely objection or motion to strike, stating the reason for the objection, or an offer of proof, showing the substance of the excluded evidence.

---

[51] 519 U.S. 172 (1997).

[52] *Id.* at 186–88.

[53] *Id* at 191.

[54] *Id.* at 191–92.

[55] Kotteakos v. United States, 328 U.S. 750, 765 (1946) ("But if one cannot say, with fair assurance, after pondering all that happened without stripping the erroneous action from the whole, that the judgment was not substantially swayed by the error, it is impossible to conclude that substantial rights were not affected"); see also United States v. Beasley, 72 F.3d 1518 (11th Cir. 1996).

If the advocate fails to preserve the alleged error, the appellate court may consider it only if the reason for the objection or the substance of excluded evidence is apparent from the record.[56] FRE 103(a) provides:

(a) **Effect of erroneous ruling.** Error may not be predicated upon a ruling which admits or excludes evidence unless a substantial right of the party is affected, and

(1) **Objection.** In case the ruling is one admitting evidence, a timely objection or motion to strike appears of record, stating the specific ground of objection, if the specific ground was not apparent from the context; or

(2) **Offer of proof.** In case the ruling is one excluding evidence, the substance of the evidence was made known to the court by offer or was apparent from the context within which questions were asked.

Once the court makes a definitive ruling on the record admitting or excluding evidence, either at or before trial, a party need not renew an objection or offer of proof to preserve a claim of error for appeal.

These provisions obligate the advocate to provide an explanation of any objection or an adequate description of the evidence excluded by the court's ruling. At the same time, the rule implies a *right* of counsel to explain an objection and, perhaps more important, to make a complete offer of evidence kept out by an adverse ruling.[57] Judges often make snap evidentiary rulings and are impatient with lawyers who attempt to provide explanations. A citation to the rule should convince a hardheaded judge that counsel is permitted to make such a presentation.

The last sentence of FRE 103(a) was added in 2000 to resolve a split among the circuits as to whether a party must renew an objection to evidence when it is offered, in order to preserve the issue for appeal, if the trial court has already ruled on its admissibility. The amendment makes clear that issue is preserved once the court makes a definitive ruling on the record.

The requirement of a "definitive ruling" leaves counsel with the obligation to renew an objection when a trial court's previous evidentiary ruling is only provisional or is based on circumstances that change after the ruling is made. If the relevant circumstances change as the evidence develops, counsel cannot rely on the changed circumstances in an appeal unless they are first brought to the attention of the trial court in a timely objection or proffer.[58] Additionally, if there is any doubt as to whether a ruling is "definitive," counsel has the burden of obtaining a clarification.[59]

---

[56] See, e.g., Morrow v. Greyhound Lines, Inc., 541 F.2d 713, 724 (8th Cir. 1976).

[57] See United States v. Hutcher, 622 F.2d 1083, 1087 (2d Cir. 1980), *cert. denied*, 449 U.S. 875 (1980).

[58] FED. R. EVID. 103(a)(2) advisory committee's note.

[59] *Id.*

§ 4-10(a). Objections.

The rule mandates that you do more than object to inadmissible evidence; you must provide the reason for the objection.[60] You should include a simple explanation supporting the objection and, if possible, a citation to the applicable rule. On important matters you should prepare for objections in advance of trial.[61]

You should avoid legalese in stating objections. You often must object in the presence of the jury; the jurors are more likely to tolerate your interruptions if they have some idea of why the offender's action is improper. Thus, when the objection is not self-explanatory, provide a layman's explanation. Further, you may wish to "sell" the objection to the jury, going beyond its technical basis to a description of why the opposition's action is unfair.[62] Thus, for example, rather than merely objecting that an out-of-court statement is "hearsay," you might state:

> I object, Your Honor. The witness has no knowledge of this matter and is repeating what someone else told him. The testimony violates the hearsay rule and is completely unreliable.

Objections provide a means of accomplishing other objectives, such as distracting the jury from harmful testimony.[63] When a favorable witness gets in trouble on cross-examination, for example, attorneys often interrupt to distract the jury or alert the witness to the danger. This action requires a bit of bravado, but is within permissible bounds of advocacy so long as it is not overdone. You should not interrupt so much that the true purpose is obvious. Excessive interruptions may serve to underscore opposing counsel's success. Moreover, be sure to make evidentiary points in objections. If a witness needs to be alerted to a matter, the point should be folded into the argument. Objections that are nothing more than efforts to coach the witness may cause the court to admonish you.

When the opposing attorney makes a thinly disguised objection to interrupt the flow of testimony, it may be best not to point out counsel's motive. Accusing the attorney of coaching the witness is likely to provoke a flurry of argument that draws everyone's attention from the evidence. You should briefly address the objection and get back to examining the witness. In doing so, however, you may insert a bit of commentary to point up the true purpose of the interruption: "Mr. Jones, now that my opponent has so helpfully reminded us that it was raining

---

[60] See *Id.*

[61] MICHAEL H. GRAHAM, HANDBOOK OF FEDERAL EVIDENCE 11, n.11 (3d ed. 1991).

[62] See JAMES W. MCELHANEY, MCELHANEY'S TRIAL NOTEBOOK 332–34 (3d ed. 1994).

[63] See EDWARD T. WRIGHT, EVIDENCE: HOW AND WHEN TO USE THE RULES TO WIN CASES 195–97 (1990).

that day, perhaps we should follow up on the conditions. . . ." Of course, if opposing counsel repeatedly interrupts with bogus objections, you should seek relief from the court. At that point, halting the objections is more important than avoiding an argument.

Sometimes the grounds for an objection are not clear until after the jury has heard the evidence. In that situation you not only must object, but should ask that the court strike the evidence and instruct the jury to disregard it. The need for an after-the-fact objection arises when the witness volunteers information beyond the scope of a question or testifies to matters not within his knowledge. Additionally, courts sometimes admit evidence on the condition that its relevance will be demonstrated at a later time, or "connected up"; if opposing counsel fails to connect up the evidence, you need to ask that it be stricken. An example of an objection and motion to strike follows.

Q.   Earlier you testified that the car driven by Ms. Brown ran a red light, but you were at home when that happened, is that correct?

A.   What do you mean?

Q.   You were not present when the accident occurred, is that right?

A.   I know about it, though.

Q.   Your basis is what Mr. Green told you, correct?

A.   That's right.

Q.   Counsel: Your Honor, this witness testified to facts outside his personal knowledge that were based on hearsay. I move that the court strike the evidence from the record and instruct the jury to disregard it.

A.   The Court: The motion is granted. Members of the jury, you will disregard what the witness has said about the circumstances of the accident. The witness did not have personal knowledge of those facts and cannot testify to them.

---

§ 4-10(b).   Offers of Proof.

The rule requires that counsel make known to the court the "substance" of the evidence that he wishes to offer. The offer may be made in two ways: (1) providing the actual evidence by eliciting the testimony from the witness, through questions and answers, or offering an exhibit, or (2) offering counsel's oral or written description of the evidence.[64]

---

[64] See STEVEN LUBET, MODERN TRIAL ADVOCACY 241–45 (1993).

When an exclusionary ruling is made, you should request to make an offer of proof. Your right to make the offer is granted implicitly by FRE 103 and you should cite to the rule if necessary.[65] In a judge trial, ask permission to make the offer at the time of the court's ruling.[66] Reasons you might use to support an immediate offer include: (1) the offer will not take extensive time, (2) the witness will not be available later, or (3) a timely offer would help the judge understand the relevance of the evidence. If the judge is naturally curious, she is likely to hear the offer.

In a jury trial, you must make an offer of proof outside the jury's presence. Thus, you must make it in a special hearing before the judge or at a break in the proceeding, depending on whether the court wishes to hear the evidence. Try to get the judge to hear the offer, because you may benefit from any favorable impact of the evidence and provide the judge a timely opportunity to change her ruling.

Opposing counsel should tactfully try to persuade the judge not to hear the offer. He ordinarily should not suggest that the evidence would prejudice the court, since this argument questions the judge's ability to disregard inadmissible evidence (which, paradoxically, is usually the main concern). Counsel might suggest that an offer should be made during a recess or at the end of the day, so as not to consume valuable court time. If the judge agrees, the offer can be made outside her presence. Delaying the offer may keep the evidence out entirely, because attorneys sometimes forget to follow up with an offer.

The best offer of proof consists of the actual evidence. Proffering the evidence itself ensures that an appellate court cannot reject the point on appeal by finding your description of the evidence inadequate. Moreover, if the judge presides as you make the offer, hearing it may cause her to change the exclusionary ruling. Even if the ruling stands, you may gain an advantage from the judge's exposure to the evidence. Thus, in the case of testimony, you should urge that the court permit you to question the witness.

The court may require you to provide a description of proffered testimony rather than eliciting it through questions and answers. If so, make the description as specific as possible. One method is to submit a written description. If you make an oral offer, at least use notes — those prepared for questioning the witness — to describe the evidence.

When you make an offer through actual testimony, opposing counsel has a right to question the witness on the offer.[67] The attorney making the offer should

---

[65] See United States v. Winkle, 587 F.2d 705 (5th Cir. 1979), *cert. denied*, 444 U.S. 827 (1979).

[66] See Myron H. Bright & Ronald L. Carlson, Objections at Trial 299–303 (4th ed. 2001).

[67] See Christopher B. Mueller & Laird C. Kirkpatrick, Federal Evidence § 13 (2nd ed. 1994).

state when the offer begins and ends. If the offer is made while the witness testifies, neglecting to state that the offer is complete may create confusion as to whether other testimony is part of the admitted evidence. At the end of the offer, opposing counsel should question the witness on the offer, and should state when the examination is complete.

§ 4-10(c).   Waiver by "Drawing the Sting" Concerning Prior Conviction.

Even if the trial court makes a definitive pretrial ruling that evidence is admissible, the objecting party may waive his right of appeal if he raises the point first to diminish its impact *Ohler v. United States.*[68]

In *Ohler* the United States Supreme Court ruled that a party who preemptively introduces evidence of a criminal conviction, after the trial court rules the evidence will be admissible, may not complain on appeal that the decision to admit the evidence was erroneous. The ruling presents a serious consequence for a party who "draws the sting" of expected impeachment by disclosure of a criminal conviction in direct testimony and may curtail the use of this trial tactic. The court ruled that any harm resulting from the pretrial ruling necessarily would be speculative since the preemptive disclosure prevented the Government from deciding in the first instance whether to use the conviction.

According to *Ohler*, drawing the sting prevents the Government from deciding whether to impeach the witness with the conviction, even after the court has ruled it admissible.[69] According to the Court, the prosecution might forego the impeachment to avoid the possibility of reversal on appeal. This strategic choice seems highly unlikely when the prosecution already has obtained a ruling permitting the introduction of the evidence. Additionally, the ruling seriously inhibits a time-honored means of tempering prejudice to a criminal defendant from disclosure of his prior crimes.

§ 4-11.   Making and Responding to Objections.

The attorney should address objections and responses to the court. Speaking directly to your opponent on a confrontational point is often seen as impolite. Additionally, the judge may take offense if the attorneys exchange objections and responses without addressing the court. The following exchange illustrates the reaction a judge may have when counsel addresses an objection to his opponent.

---

[68] 529 U.S. 753 (2000).

[69] *Id.* at 758.

> Q.   You were in the house at that time?
>
> Mr. Anderson: Wait a minute, counsel, is that supposed to be a question or what? I don't think I heard a question.
>
> Ms. Hayne: Your Honor, I believe if counsel has an objection he is supposed to address it to the court and state some evidentiary basis for it.
>
> The Court: That's right, Mr. Anderson. I am still here, you know. Objection overruled. Let's proceed.

Michael H. Graham provides a checklist for making objections, quoting advice of Judge Warren Wolfson.[70] Important items on the checklist include:

1.   Make sure the objection is timely.

2.   Make sure you state the specific and correct *evidentiary* grounds for the objection. "That's not fair" is inadequate.

3.   Get a ruling from the judge before your opponent proceeds.

4.   Ask for a "continuing objection" if you are overruled on an objection that will come up repeatedly.

5.   Get the judge to give the reasons for her ruling. (This action may be unnecessary and may irritate the judge unduly, however, if the matter is not important. Follow this advice for important rulings.)

An objection should be made after opposing counsel's question but before the answer. If the witness answers before you object, the damage is done. An instruction may limit the impact of the testimony, but will not erase it. Therefore, you have to *listen to your adversary's questions*, especially when he covers important subjects. Additionally, you must concentrate to recognize improper questions instantly.

Your objection needs to include an evidentiary basis. For simple points — "leading," for example — the objection does not require explanation. Often the objection is grounded in a more complicated basis, however, which requires description. If you can cite a rule of evidence and, better yet, a case, the court usually will pay attention to your point. Objections that really are argument — "He's trying to paint a false picture of the collision" — are improper.

You also need to prepare for responding to objections. Since you prepare the questions, you can anticipate potential evidentiary issues and develop responses. If you think an objection may arise, find the rule or citation that supports your

---

[70] MICHAEL H. GRAHAM, HANDBOOK OF FEDERAL EVIDENCE § 103.1, n.11 (3d ed. 1991).

position and have it handy. Preparing for objections is the best way to defeat them.

Sometimes lawyers decide not to object because they think the objection may highlight harmful evidence. If you think you will lose the objection, keeping quiet is probably a good idea. Jumping up and objecting may wake up jurors who are not listening; it may also suggest that you find the evidence damaging. If the objection goes to an important matter and you have a good basis, however, you usually should object.

§ 4-12. Burdens of Proof.

The party with the "burden of proof" in a trial has the responsibility to produce some amount of evidence to support his claim; absent the introduction of that evidence, the claim fails. The burden to prove the elements of an affirmative case usually rests with the plaintiff or prosecution. A defendant may have the burden to prove the basis for special defenses. Generally, the party who has the responsibility of pleading a claim — fixed by statute or rule of law in the jurisdiction — has the burden of proof to establish the legal elements of the claim.

To understand burdens of proof, you must distinguish facts from evidence. The elements of any claim or defense are the ultimate facts that entitle a party to prevail. These ultimate facts usually encompass many subsidiary facts. A party's factual claims are set forth in pleadings, explained to the jury in opening statements, and reviewed again in closing arguments. The factual contentions are not proof, however; evidence is required to show they are true. Burdens of proof assign responsibility for proving factual claims and establish the degree to which the facts must be established.

The burden of proof usually exists at two levels. At the ultimate level, the party is required to prove his case to a particular degree. One of two degrees of proof is generally required in lawsuits: (1) the "preponderance of the evidence" level that is used in most civil cases, and (2) the "beyond a reasonable doubt" requirement that is imposed on the prosecution in criminal cases. A third burden — proof by "clear and convincing evidence" — is sometimes imposed as an intermediate requirement on particular legal points.

The party with the ultimate burden also has the primary burden of putting on enough evidence to get her case to the jury. This burden — that of "producing evidence" — requires that the party produce *enough* evidence to avoid the dismissal of her claim by the judge. To avoid an adverse directed verdict, a party usually is required to introduce enough evidence that a reasonable person *could* conclude she has satisfied the ultimate burden on the point. Once the judge decides this requirement is satisfied, he permits the jury to determine whether the party has met her ultimate burden.

Burdens of proof are useful tools to assign responsibilities in litigation. Someone has to go first in offering evidence on any particular element of a dispute, and the assignment of the burden determines who must do so. Additionally, the "beyond a reasonable doubt" and "clear and convincing" standards provide substance to legal requirements that a party make a compelling showing to win certain points; often these standards are interposed between an individual's freedom and criminal penalties.[71] The "preponderance of the evidence" burden — usually applied in civil cases — merely requires a party to do better than the opposing side in proving her claims are correct.

The primary burden on a party — the requirement to produce enough evidence to avoid dismissal — is a function of the ultimate burden. To get to the jury, the party generally must introduce sufficient evidence that a reasonable person could conclude that the ultimate burden is satisfied. Thus, in a criminal case the prosecution has the burden of producing sufficient evidence that a reasonable juror *could conclude* beyond a reasonable doubt that the defendant committed the crime. In a civil case, a party must produce sufficient evidence that a reasonable juror could conclude her factual claims are proven by a preponderance of the evidence.

If the party fails to satisfy the production burden on an issue, the judge may dismiss the claim or refuse to submit the issue to the jury, effectively eliminating the claim from the case. If the court submits the issue to the jurors, the party still must persuade them that she has met her ultimate burden.

A simple example can be used to explain these points. Assume Rachel Wendt is injured in a car accident with Randy Smith and sues Smith for her injuries. The elements of her claim include: (1) Smith was negligent, (2) his negligence caused the accident, and (3) she suffered damages caused by the accident. These elements are ultimate facts that she must prove. She has the responsibility to produce evidence — witnesses and exhibits — to establish them.

The burden of production requires that she put on evidence in support of her claims; if she does not, the judge will rule for Smith. It also requires that she produce enough evidence that a reasonable person could conclude by a preponderance of evidence that her claims are correct; again, if she fails, the judge will dismiss her case. The burden of persuasion requires her to introduce enough evidence to persuade *the jurors* that a preponderance of the evidence supports her claims.

---

[71] MCCORMICK ON EVIDENCE § 340 (5th ed. 1999). The clear and convincing standard is used "in a variety of cases involving deprivations of individual rights not rising to the level of criminal prosecution, including commitment to a mental hospital, termination of parental rights, denaturalization and deportation." *See* Crawford-El v. Britton, 523 U.S. 574 (1998), rejecting a rule fashioned by a court of appeals that would have imposed a clear and convincing burden on plaintiffs in proving an improper motive of a public official in a suit brought pursuant to 28 U.S.C. § 1983.

Smith thus far has a defensive posture. He may submit evidence to disprove any of the elements of Wendt's claim. Generally, the judge would focus on Wendt's evidence and view it in a favorable light in determining whether Wendt met the burden of production, since her case could be dismissed only if a reasonable juror could not conclude that she met her burden of persuasion. If the case were not dismissed, the jury would decide whether Wendt met the burden of persuasion.

If Smith raised an affirmative defense — say, contributory negligence — the law likely would assign him the burden of proof on that point. He would have the burden of producing evidence, and the burden of persuasion, to show Wendt's negligence contributed to the accident. If he failed to produce evidence sufficient that a reasonable person could conclude by a preponderance that there was contributory negligence, his claim would not be submitted for a jury determination. If he satisfied that burden, he would still have to persuade the jury of his defense by a preponderance of the evidence.

Regardless of the burden, the determination of whether the proof meets it involves subjective judgment. A "preponderance" does not necessarily mean the most proof; it means the most convincing proof. A party might have a dozen witnesses swear to a fact, but if the jury believes they lied and a single contradictory witness told the truth, the single witness supplies a "preponderance" of evidence. Additionally, all the legal burdens are intangible; the words used to describe them require interpretation, and people understand them in varying ways. Further, since the accepted explanations of the different burdens are legalistic and convoluted, people often do not comprehend them. Thus, the assignment of a burden at best gives the factfinder only a rough idea of how much proof is required.

The judge generally decides whether a party has met the burden of producing evidence at the close of that party's case; alternatively, the judge may decide the matter at the conclusion of the evidentiary phase. Since a party conceivably could make up ground in the adverse party's case, delaying the ruling may change the outcome. If the issues are submitted to the jurors, they rule on the burden of persuasion after considering the evidence submitted by both sides.

Bearing the burden of proof is not necessarily a disadvantage. The party with the burden usually goes first, which is a tremendous advantage. The first impression often launches success in persuasion. Additionally, the party with the burden usually may rebut the adverse party's case and thus gets in the first *and* last words. This combination easily offsets the preponderance burden and largely offsets more difficult burdens. Thus, many attorneys view having the burden as an advantage, at least in civil cases.

In criminal cases the prosecution has the burden of proving each element of the crime beyond a reasonable doubt. The criminal law of the jurisdiction determines the required elements; for instance, in a murder case the prosecution may be required to prove (1) an act, (2) which causes the death of another, (3) committed intentionally, and (4) with premeditation. Often when an accused raises an affirmative defense, however, he is allocated the burden of production or persuasion with respect to that defense. In *Leland v. Oregon*,[72] for instance, the Supreme Court ruled that a defendant may be required to prove his own insanity beyond a reasonable doubt.

When an "affirmative defense" is actually a denial of some element of the crime, however, the government may not constitutionally allocate the burden of persuasion to the accused. For instance, the state may not allocate the defendant the burden of proving a lesser degree of intent than required in the criminal statute.[73] Whether the "defense" actually contradicts an element of the crime depends on the jurisdiction's criminal statute. If the statute does not include a point as an element of the offense, then allocating to the defendant the burden of proving a contrary point to exonerate himself does not violate due process. Thus, the Supreme Court held in *Rivera v. Delaware*[74] that a state may allocate the accused the burden to prove "extreme emotional disturbance" to reduce a second degree murder charge to manslaughter, so long as malice aforethought was not an element of second degree murder.

When the state merely places on the accused the burden of producing evidence of an affirmative defense, the procedure generally is permissible even if the defense contradicts an element of the offense. This procedure does not eliminate the prosecution's burden of proving affirmatively the elements of the crime. Thus, if the defendant wishes to counter an element of the offense — say, by proving sudden provocation, which would counter premeditation — he may be required to produce sufficient evidence to have the issue submitted to the jury.

§ 4-13. Presumptions.

Presumptions perform two functions in trials. First, they conditionally require the jury to accept inferences that flow logically from underlying facts. Second, they often shift the burden of proof from one party to another. Depending on the law, a presumption may shift the burden of production or the burden of persuasion. The intermingling of presumptions and burdens often is confusing, in part because of the legal terminology used to explain their effect.

A presumption is an inference that the law requires the factfinder to draw when a party proves certain underlying facts, absent countervailing proof that the inference is incorrect. In other words, if the factfinder believes an underlying fact, he must also accept the presumed fact unless evidence is introduced to show

---

[72] 343 U.S. 790 (1952).

[73] Mullaney v. Wilbur, 421 U.S. 684, 686 (1975).

[74] 429 U.S. 877 (1976).

the presumed fact did not occur. For example, assume the law contains a presumption that a properly mailed letter is also received. If a party proved that a notice was mailed with proper postage to Stephanie Shuler, the factfinder would be required to presume Shuler received it absent evidence that it did not arrive.

Judges and juries draw inferences in virtually any trial. Often proof on a point is circumstantial, and the factfinder must determine whether it logically supports a conclusion advocated by a party. In the absence of a presumption, however, they are not required to draw inferences even if a logical basis exists to do so. For instance, if Smith is seen chasing Jones with a knife, and Jones is later found stabbed to death, the jury might infer that Smith was the killer even if no one actually saw the murder take place. Other circumstantial evidence — Smith's ownership of the murder weapon, fingerprints on its handle, threats to "get" Jones — would strengthen the inference. The jury would not be required to draw the inference, however, even if no evidence were offered to counter it. The jury could reject the inference as tenuous, illogical, or simply one of multiple inferences that could be drawn from the facts. Thus, the inference would be "permissible" but not required.

A presumption eliminates the factfinder's discretion to reject an inference unless evidence is introduced to counter the presumed fact. Thus, once an underlying fact is proven, a presumption places a burden on the adverse party to introduce evidence contradicting the presumed fact. This shifting of the burden usually reflects two premises: (1) the presumed fact logically follows from the underlying fact; and (2) the party against whom the presumption is drawn is in a superior position to produce evidence regarding the presumed fact.[75] With respect to the "letter mailed was also received" presumption, for instance, the inference has strong logical support, and the alleged recipient is in the best position to prove or disprove receipt.

According to Professor Graham C. Lilly, there are "dozens if not hundreds"[76] of presumptions in jurisdictions throughout the United States. He lists the following examples, among others.[77]

---

[75] MCCORMICK ON EVIDENCE § 343 (5th ed. 1999).

[76] GRAHAM C. LILLY, AN INTRODUCTION TO THE LAW OF EVIDENCE 63 (3d ed. 1996).

[77] Id. at 64.

BASIC FACT	PRESUMED FACT
1. Letter properly addressed and mailed	1. Letter received by addressee
2. Vehicle lawfully stopped is struck from rear	2. Driver of rear car negligent
3. Absence for seven years without explanation or communication	3. Absentee deceased
4. Employee in accident while driving vehicle owned by employer	4. Employee acting within scope of employment
5. Goods damaged while transported by more than one carrier	5. Last carrier caused the damage

In a judge trial applying a presumption is not difficult. The judge makes fact findings based on the evidence, determines if a presumption applies, and decides whether the adverse party introduced sufficient evidence to defeat the presumption. Since the judge, like any factfinder, usually focuses on ultimate determinations, a presumption does little more than buttress the factual conclusions. For a jury trial, however, the judge must instruct the jury as to presumptions. As explained below, this endeavor may be confusing in jurisdictions where presumptions operate to shift the burden of proof.

A presumption generally may fall into one of two categories, depending on the law of the jurisdiction: (1) it may shift to the party opposing the presumption the burden of producing evidence to defeat it, or (2) it may shift to that party the burden of persuasion — the burden to persuade the jury that the fact is not true. The first type of presumption, which shifts the burden of producing evidence, is often referred to as a "bursting bubble" because the presumption disappears if the party opposing it offers evidence sufficient to support a finding that the presumed fact is untrue. The second type of presumption is more substantial, shifting the burden of proof as to the existence of the presumed fact. The two types of presumptions are discussed below.

§ 4-13(a). "Bursting Bubble" Presumptions (FRE 301, 302).

A bursting bubble presumption merely shifts the burden of producing evidence to refute the presumed fact to the party against whom the presumption is drawn. This countervailing evidence must be "sufficient to support a finding" that the fact did not occur but does not have to satisfy the ultimate burden of proof. Once evidence countering the presumption is introduced, the presumption disappears and the jury is free to weigh the evidence directly. The "bursting bubble" theory was advocated by Professor James B. Thayer; it has been accepted in numerous jurisdictions and in FRE 301. Its main advantage is that it is easy to apply.

FRE 301 adopts the "bursting bubble" approach for presumptions in federal civil cases unless a statute or another rule provides otherwise. The bursting bubble rule was substituted for the version prescribed by the Supreme Court, which would have shifted the burden of proof. [78] FRE 301 states:

> In all civil actions and proceedings not otherwise provided for by Act of Congress or by these rules, a presumption imposes on the party against whom it is directed the burden of going forward with evidence to rebut or meet the presumption, but does not shift to such party the burden of proof in the sense of the risk of nonpersuasion, which remains throughout the trial upon the party on whom it was originally cast.

FRE 302 provides that State law shall govern the effect of presumptions in cases where State law supplies the rule of decision. [79] It states:

> In civil actions and proceedings, the effect of a presumption respecting a fact which is an element of a claim or defense as to which State law supplies the rule of decision is determined in accordance with State law.

The advantage of the bursting bubble presumption is that it is easy to administer. The presumption establishes the presumed fact upon proof of the underlying fact if there is no evidence refuting the presumed fact. Thus, for instance, if proof that Mary Coyne owned a car creates a presumption that Coyne was the driver, proof of ownership would establish that Coyne was the driver unless she offered evidence sufficient to support a finding that she was not the driver. The jury would be instructed to accept the presumed fact.

If evidence were offered that Coyne was not the driver — for example, a denial — and the evidence were sufficient to support a finding, the presumption would cease to exist. The judge simply would not mention it in the jury instructions. The underlying fact still might support an inference that the ultimate fact occurred, but the jury would draw the inference on its own.

The problem with this approach is that the judge's failure to say anything about the presumption may leave in place the imbalance that the presumption was

---

[78] Proposed FED. R. EVID. 301 provided: "In all cases not otherwise provided for by Act of Congress or by these rules a presumption imposes on the party against whom it is directed the burden of proving that the non-existence of the presumed fact is more probable than its existence."

[79] The proposed federal rule for criminal proceedings — Proposed FED. R. EVID. 303 — was not adopted by Congress.

created to correct. A presumption often exists to offset a natural advantage of a party in proving a fact. If the party with this advantage defeats the presumption by submitting self-serving evidence — for instance, Coyne's denial that she drove the car — the adverse party's disadvantage is increased. In the face of direct evidence, his circumstantial argument may seem especially tenuous.

Additionally, some presumptions are created to promote public policy — for instance, the presumption that a child born during a marriage is legitimate.[80] The policy cannot be promoted if the presumption is not mentioned. Thus, judges often feel that some discussion of the presumption is required, even if the adverse party satisfies the production burden.[81]

One solution to this problem is for the judge to discuss the logical link between the basic fact and the presumed fact without suggesting that this relationship shifts the burden of proof. A statement that the jury may presume one fact from another may promote the policy supporting the presumption and counterbalance any advantage of the party opposing it. The instruction would have to be carefully worded, however, to avoid suggesting that the presumption is mandatory. The Senate Committee report on FRE 301 emphasized the care needed in describing the presumption's effect. It stated:

> The court may instruct the jury that they may infer the existence of the presumed fact from proof of the basic facts giving rise to the presumption. However, it would be inappropriate under this rule to instruct the jury that the inference they are to draw is conclusive.[82]

§ 4-13(b). Presumptions that Shift the Burden of Persuasion.

A rule that a presumption shifts the burden of persuasion gives greater weight to the logic and policy underlying presumptions than the "bursting bubble" precept. In this situation the jurors must consider the presumption in weighing the evidence. Instructing the jury on the presumption, however, may unduly confuse the issues.

Professor Edmund M. Morgan was a primary advocate of the view that a presumption at least should shift the burden of persuasion.[83] This approach reflects the theory that it is not worth creating a presumption unless it at least requires the adverse party to disprove the presumed fact.[84] The Advisory

---

[80] MCCORMICK ON EVIDENCE § 344 (5th ed. 1999).

[81] *Id.*

[82] S. Rep. No. 1277, 93d Cong., 2d Sess., p. 9 (1974).

[83] Edmund M. Morgan & John M. Maguire, *Looking Backward and Forward at Evidence*, 50 HARV. L. REV. 909, 913 (1937); Edmund M. Morgan, *Instructing the Jury upon Presumptions and Burdens of Proof*, 47 HARV. L. REV. 59, 82 (1933).

[84] MCCORMICK ON EVIDENCE § 344 (5th ed. 1999).

Committee to the federal rules of evidence, which proposed a rule that would shift the burden of persuasion, believed that the "bursting bubble" approach lacked sufficient effect. It said:

> The so-called "bursting bubble" theory, under which a presumption vanishes upon the introduction of evidence which would support a finding of the nonexistence of the presumed fact, even though not believed, is rejected as according presumptions too "slight and evanescent" an effect.[85]

The rule proposed by the Advisory Committee was rejected in Congress, however, in favor of the "bursting bubble" approach.

In a judge trial applying a presumption that shifts the burden of persuasion is not difficult. In a jury trial, on the other hand, the presumption and its effect must be explained in a jury instruction. Lay people may not understand even the clearest explanation, because they are not familiar with burdens and the proof necessary to satisfy them. This problem is complicated because a presumption usually results from a factual determination that the jury may or may not make, requiring the judge to pose hypothetical scenarios in the instruction: "If you find x, then you should presume y."

The following example illustrates the type of instruction required for even a simple presumption that shifts the burden of persuasion.

The plaintiff has the burden of proving, by a preponderance of the evidence, that the driver of the defendant's automobile was acting as his agent with his consent at the time of the collision. As you know, this fact is disputed. The law creates a presumption, however, that a person who is shown to be the owner of a vehicle has given consent or authorized another to act as his agent when that other person operates the owner's car. Thus, if you find the defendant was the owner, you may presume that the driver operated the vehicle as his agent or with his consent. If you do not find the defendant was the owner, you should not make this presumption. Additionally, the presumption is not binding, but simply shifts to the defendant the burden of proving by a preponderance of the evidence that the driver was not acting as his agent or with his consent at the time of the collision. Thus, even if you find that the defendant was the owner, you may determine that the driver was not acting with consent or as his agent if you find that a preponderance of the evidence supports this determination.

When this instruction is read in the midst of other confusing instructions as to legal rules, issues, and burdens, the jury is likely to misunderstand or ignore it. Further, in deliberations the jury is not likely to engage in step-by-step shifting

---

[85] Proposed FED. R. EVID. 301 advisory committee's note.

of burdens between the parties. If multiple issues and presumptions are involved, applying the presumptions would be virtually impossible.

In view of these practical difficulties, the "bursting bubble" approach to presumptions is most workable. In appropriate cases the judge may give substance to a "bursting bubble" presumption by mentioning it as a permissible inference, even when the adverse party produces evidence to counter the presumption.

§ 4-13(c). Presumptions in Criminal Cases.

To the extent a presumption shifts the burden of persuasion to the defendant in a criminal case, it may conflict with the due process requirement that the prosecution prove each element of the crime beyond a reasonable doubt.[86] Thus, presumptions in criminal cases must not only serve public policy but must reflect a logical connection between the underlying fact and the presumed fact. The strength of the logical tie depends on whether the "presumption" is a mere permissible inference, or actually shifts the burden of production or persuasion to the defendant.

In criminal cases permissible inferences are often described as permissive presumptions.[87] A permissive presumption does not shift the burden of production or persuasion; the court instead instructs the jurors that they may, but need not, infer the presumed fact from the basic fact. A permissive presumption is constitutional so long as the trier could rationally make the inference described in the presumption. In *County Court of Ulster County v. Allen*,[88] the Supreme Court ruled that permissive presumptions need only have a rational basis to satisfy due process. It stated:

> Because this permissive presumption leaves the trier of fact free to credit or reject the inference and does not shift the burden of proof, it affects the application of the "beyond a reasonable doubt" standard only if, under the facts of the case, there is no rational way the trier could make the connection permitted by the inference.[89]

This standard requires some logical connection between the underlying and presumed facts, but virtually all presumptions satisfy that requirement.

The Court has suggested a stringent due process requirement for a presumption that shifts the burden of persuasion to a defendant. In *Allen* it determined that this type of presumption is constitutional only if the basic facts by themselves are sufficient to support a finding beyond a reasonable doubt that the presumed

---

[86] In cases in which the accused would have to testify to defeat the presumption, it would also create tension with the privilege against self-incrimination. U.S. CONST. amend. V.

[87] County Court of Ulster County v. Allen, 442 U.S. 140 (1979).

[88] *Id.*

[89] *Id.* at 157.

fact occurred.[90] Few presumptions satisfy this test. Thus, in criminal cases presumptions that shift the burden of persuasion are likely to be unconstitutional.

If a presumption shifts the burden of producing evidence — the "bursting bubble" — it is binding on the defendant only if he fails to produce evidence sufficient to support a finding that the presumed fact is untrue. If he satisfies the burden of production, the presumption disappears and the jury is not informed of it. The presumption presumably would be binding, however, if the defendant offered no evidence on the point. The presumption thus would relieve the prosecution of its burden to prove the presumed fact beyond a reasonable doubt, assuming the logical strength of the presumption itself could not satisfy that standard. Thus, if the court instructed the jury to infer the presumed fact, the instruction theoretically would violate due process.

The Supreme Court in *Francis v. Franklin*[91] expressly reserved decision on whether a presumption that shifts the burden of production requires more than a rational basis. Nevertheless, if the "beyond a reasonable doubt" standard is to have meaning for a defendant who puts the prosecution to its proof, requiring the jury to accept the presumption absent contrary proof would appear to violate due process.

---

[90] *Id.*

[91] 471 U.S. 307 (1985). MCCORMICK ON EVIDENCE § 347 (5th ed. 1999) suggests that the courts would not impose a higher standard for a presumption that merely shifts the burden of producing evidence.

CHAPTER 5

RELEVANCE RULES

---

§ 5-1.   Introduction.

A number of special "relevance rules" were developed at common law to govern the admissibility of evidence in recurring situations. Rules 404 through 411 of the Federal Rules of Evidence codify these principles. The specific areas addressed in these provisions include:

1. Character evidence to prove conduct (FRE 404).

2. Methods of proving character (FRE 405).

3. Evidence of habit or routine practice to prove conduct (FRE 406).

4. Subsequent remedial measures (FRE 407).

5. Settlement offers and negotiations (FRE 408).

6. Offers to pay medical and similar expenses (FRE 409).

7. Pleas in criminal cases and plea negotiations (FRE 410).

8. Evidence of liability insurance (FRE 411).

In addition, FRE 412, which is not based on a traditional rule, governs the relevance of a victim's past behavior in a sex offense case. The rule reflects a modern trend to protect the privacy of sex offense victims. FRE 413–15, enacted in 1995, govern the admissibility of specific acts of sexual assault or child molestation in cases involving sexual assault or child molestation.

Generally, the traditional "relevance rules" are rules of exclusion. The rules prevent the introduction of certain categories of evidence when offered for prohibited purposes.[1] FRE 406, relating to evidence of habit or routine practice, is an exception; it permits the introduction of habit evidence to prove conduct on a particular occasion. Additionally, FRE 413–15 permit the introduction of specified prior acts to prove conduct on a particular occasion.

The fact that a relevance rule excludes evidence for one purpose does not prevent its introduction for another. Indeed, the rules offer illustrative examples of situations in which evidence that is excluded for one purpose otherwise might be admissible. A typical example of a permissible purpose is impeachment; thus, a shrewd examination, which leads the witness to make statements allowing impeachment, may secure the introduction of evidence that otherwise might be barred.

One justification for the relevance rules is that they generally exclude evidence that has little relevance.[2] Additionally, the rules are seen as promoting the reliability of jury verdicts, judicial economy, and social policies.[3] In fact, the "low relevance" justification probably is inaccurate. Some relevance rules exclude evidence that is very probative; for example, if a person accused of assault claims self-defense, evidence that he assaulted others might be very probative of his conduct with the victim. Yet FRE 404 excludes the evidence on the issue of whether he committed the act in question.

The true concern may not be low relevance, but uncertainty that a jury would give appropriate weight to the evidence. The jury in the assault case, for example, might view the prior incident as conclusive proof of the defendant's conduct with the victim, when the jury should give the evidence lesser importance. The difficulty in estimating the importance of evidence appears to be a prime policy supporting many of the relevance rules.

---

[1] See generally MCCORMICK ON EVIDENCE § 184 (5th ed. 1999); JOSEPH M. PELLICCIOTTI, HANDBOOK ON BASIC TRIAL EVIDENCE 39–57 (2d ed. 1988).

[2] See, e.g., RICHARD O. LEMPERT AND STEPHEN A. SALTZBURG, A MODERN APPROACH TO EVIDENCE 187 (2d ed. 1982).

[3] *Id.* at 188–91.

The relevance rules also are a means of conditioning, or limiting, the impact of evidence that the jury might otherwise have difficulty evaluating.[4] For example, the prosecution generally may not introduce evidence of a prior crime to show that the defendant committed the crime charged but often may use it to impeach if the defendant takes the stand. The instruction that the jury may use the evidence only for a limited purpose conditions its impact, avoiding some of the danger that the jury may give the prior crime exaggerated importance. Thus, the purpose-specific rules may reflect historic compromises, in which judges developed means of limiting the impact of specific kinds of evidence.

Evidence excluded by a relevance rule is barred for the cited purpose; the court may not "balance" it into the record under FRE 403. When a rule suggests that a party may offer evidence for a different purpose, however, the court may still apply the balancing test of FRE 403 to exclude it. The court may use the policy reasons supporting the relevance rule as a basis to exclude the evidence if its introduction could prejudice the jury on the issue for which it is inadmissible, even when it is offered for a different purpose.

Sections 5-2–5-15 address the relevance rules. Sections 5-2–5-7 discuss character evidence; § 5-8 discusses the use of prior acts to prove points other than a character-related propensity to act in a particular way and § 5-9 reviews the use of habit evidence to show conduct on a particular occasion. Sections 5-10–5-14 discuss the remaining relevance rules, covering subsequent remedial measures (§ 5-10), compromise discussions (§ 5-11), offers to pay medical expenses (§ 5-12), criminal pleas and plea negotiations (§ 5-13), and liability insurance (§ 5-14). Section 5-15 discusses the use of "similar happenings" to prove an event, an issue not covered by a specific rule.

§ 5-2.   Character Evidence (FRE 404).

The federal rules extensively regulate the admissibility of "character" evidence. Generally, evidence of a person's character is not admissible to prove that the person acted in conformity with that character on a particular occasion; in other words, that a person committed an act because he had a character-driven "propensity" to do so.[5] Propensity evidence on substantive issues is admissible only when it concerns the character of an accused or a victim in a criminal case under the conditions specified in FRE 404(a) and in sexual assault and child molestation cases under FRE 413–15. When a person's character is an "essential

---

[4] See generally GLEN WEISSENBURGER, FEDERAL EVIDENCE § 403–404 (2d ed. 1995).

[5] See Fannon v. Johnston, 88 F. Supp. 2d 753 762 (E.. Mich. 2000) ("Rule 404(a) is designed to prevent the introduction of admittedly relevant character evidence about defendants. The Rule exists to promote the social benefit of limiting juries to convicting individuals only upon the facts demonstrating the occurrence of the specific crimes alleged, rather than upon propensity evidence indicating that the defendant is a bad person.") See also MCCORMICK ON EVIDENCE § 190 (5th ed. 1999).

element" of a claim, the court may admit character evidence to prove or disprove that element.[6] Additionally, character evidence may be admissible to show that a witness has a propensity to lie and thus may be lying on the stand. When character evidence is admissible, the federal rules regulate the methods by which a party may prove character.

The federal rules do not define "character." Essentially, character evidence addresses those general, intangible attributes that make up an individual's personality. A person's character might be described as "honest," "upstanding," "dishonest" or "sleazy." These qualities often are the subject of character evidence. Many other attributes also make up the personality, however, including competence, industriousness, chastity, loyalty, ego, carefulness, klutziness, and violent disposition. Determining character is a matter of subjective judgment. Thus, depending on experience, two individuals may have very different views of a third person's character. Character always is a matter of opinion; when many opinions agree on a person's trait of character and are openly expressed, the person may gain a reputation for that trait.

In some cases a person's character trait is an "essential element" of a claim or defense; in other words, the existence of the trait is an ultimate fact that a party must prove to make out the claim or defense. An example is a libel case in which the defamatory statement addresses a trait of the plaintiff's character. If the plaintiff were branded a "pervert," for example, he would have to prove the statement false and truth would be a defense. Thus, one of the ultimate facts would be whether the plaintiff was indeed a pervert.

This situation — where the character trait itself is an "essential element" of a claim — may be contrasted with one in which a party offers character to imply that a person acted in a certain way on a particular occasion. Assume, for instance, that a defendant is charged with robbery. The defendant's dishonest character is not an element of the charge, since the charge focuses on a single act. Nevertheless, the prosecution might attempt to prove that the defendant is the type of person who would commit robbery, using character to show the defendant's *propensity* to commit the act. In this situation, the character trait would not be an "essential element" of the charge.[7] FRE 404 prohibits this use of character evidence.

Character is an essential element of a claim, charge or defense in relatively few cases. Examples include the following:

1.   A libel or slander case in which character itself is defamed;
2.   A case in which a defendant allegedly caused injury by knowingly placing a person of bad character in a position of trust, such as hiring

---

[6] See generally MICHAEL H. GRAHAM, HANDBOOK OF FEDERAL EVIDENCE § 405.2 (5th ed. 2000).

[7] See THOMAS H. MAUET AND WARREN D. WOLFSON, TRIAL EVIDENCE § 1.2 (2d ed. 2001).

a pedophile at a nursery school, or making an incompetent individual a ferryboat captain;

3.   A criminal case in which entrapment is a defense, making the defendant's predisposition to commit the crime an essential issue;

4.   An employment case in which a defendant validly can assert character as a justification for a termination, as when an alleged philanderer is dismissed as director of the church choir.

When character is an essential element of a claim, charge or defense, evidence of character is admissible.[8] Character evidence offered to prove propensity — that a person acted in conformity with that character on a particular occasion — ordinarily is not admitted. FRE 404 provides exceptions to the propensity rule, applicable only in criminal cases. It provides that a criminal defendant may offer evidence as to his upstanding character, which the prosecution may rebut. The defendant also may offer evidence concerning a pertinent trait of the victim's character — say, violent disposition — and the prosecution may rebut it or offer evidence of the same trait of the defendant's character. Additionally, the prosecution may offer evidence of a victim's peaceful character in a homicide case if the defendant claims the victim was the first aggressor. In 1995, FRE 413–15 were added to permit prior act evidence in sexual assault and child molestation cases, both civil and criminal. The only other propensity exceptions relate to whether a witness is truthful and are governed by FRE 607, 608 and 609. FRE 404(a) provides:

(a) **Character evidence generally.** Evidence of a person's character or a trait of character is not admissible for the purpose of proving action in conformity therewith on a particular occasion, except:

(1) **Character of accused.** Evidence of pertinent trait of character offered by an accused, or by the prosecution to rebut the same; or if evidence of a trait of character of the alleged victim of the crime is offered by an accused and admitted under Rule 404(a)(2), evidence of the same trait of character of the accused offered by the prosecution;

(2) **Character of alleged victim.** Evidence of a pertinent trait of character of the victim of the crime offered by an accused, or by the prosecution to rebut the same, or evidence of a character trait of peacefulness of the alleged victim offered by the prosecution in a homicide case to rebut evidence that the victim was the first aggressor;

---

[8] See Schafer v. Time, Inc., 142 F.3d 1361, 1371 (11th Cir. 1998) ("Our determination of whether character constitutes an essential element requires us to examine the 'authoritative statutory or common law statement of the elements of the prima facie case and defenses.' ").

§ 5-3. Methods of Proving Character (FRE 405).

Three methods exist to prove character.[9] First, a party may offer evidence of a person's prior actions to show what type of person he is. This evidence requires the factfinder to draw an inference as to character based on the prior conduct; for instance, evidence that a person stole things might be offered to show he is a thief. Second, a witness who knows a person may offer an opinion as to the person's character. In this situation the witness draws the inference, presumably based on knowledge of the individual's prior actions and aspects of his personality. Third, a witness may testify as to a person's reputation for a character trait, if a reputation exists and the witness has knowledge of it. The reputation should reflect the consensus of opinions in the community.

When character is an essential element of a claim, charge or defense, a party may use all three methods of proof to prove the pertinent trait. When a party offers character evidence in a criminal case for one of the permissible propensity purposes, he may only offer reputation or opinion evidence. In these situations the party may not use prior acts to prove character on direct examination. In cross-examining a witness who has given reputation or opinion evidence, however, the attorney may inquire into prior acts of the person whose character is being addressed. FRE 405 provides:

Rule 405. Methods of Proving Character

(a) Reputation or opinion. In all cases in which evidence of character or a trait of character of a person is admissible, proof may be made by testimony as to reputation or by testimony in the form of an opinion. On cross-examination, inquiry is allowable into relevant specific instances of conduct.

(b) Specific instances of conduct. In cases in which character or a trait of character of a person is an essential element of a charge, claim, or defense, proof may also be made of specific instances of that person's conduct.

For impeachment, all three methods of proof may be available.[10] FRE 607, 608 and 609 regulate the admissibility of character evidence for impeachment. These rules are discussed in § 9-30 and § 9-32. Generally, evidence bolstering credibility is admissible only if credibility has been attacked.[11] Opinion and reputation evidence are generally admissible to attack the credibility of a witness. Counsel may cross-examine a witness concerning his prior acts to attack his credibility under FRE 608, but only if the court, in its discretion, determines that the evidence is probative of truthfulness.[12] Felony convictions also are

---

[9] See Murl A. Larkin, Federal Evidence Foundations 21–26 (1988).

[10] See generally Kent Sinclair, Trial Handbook 218–34 (2d ed. 1990).

[11] Fed. R. Evid. 607.

[12] Fed. R. Evid. 608.

admissible if they comply with the requirements of FRE 609.[13] Once a party attacks the credibility of a witness, the opposing party may introduce opinion and reputation evidence to support the witness's truthfulness.[14] In any case, a witness who gives reputation or opinion evidence on a witness's truthfulness can be cross-examined concerning prior acts of the person whose truthfulness is being addressed.

The greater leeway to admit opinion and reputation evidence relating to character, as compared to evidence of specific acts, reflects considerations of relevance, prejudice, and judicial economy. First, a witness who gives opinion or reputation evidence must have a sufficient foundation, which means the witness must have knowledge of the person or his reputation. The opinion or reputation reflects the subject's conduct over an extended period. This basis is a more reliable barometer of character than isolated acts, although one might question the reliability of reputation evidence, which reflects secondhand reports.[15]

Second, general testimony regarding a person's character may be less prejudicial than specific acts. A description of intangible qualities often lacks concreteness, as you may see by trying to describe aloud the character of a friend or enemy. The difficulty in describing character with concreteness takes the steam out of this testimony. Additionally, since most individuals impress some people positively and others negatively, a factfinder is not likely to be surprised that someone has a strong opinion about a person one way or the other. Moreover, general testimony does not have the same potential as prior acts to unduly influence the jury. Testimony that a defendant robbed before may push a juror toward the conclusion that he robbed again; testimony that he is "upstanding" or, in rebuttal, "dishonest," is less influential. Further, the need to address prior events places a litigation burden on a party whose character is attacked, and may thus be prejudicial.

Third, and probably most important, prior act evidence may lead to a side trial about events that are not at issue. The presentation of competing cases about a past event may be unduly time consuming. In addition, it may confuse the jurors and distract them from the real issues. Limiting specific act testimony conserves judicial resources and reduces confusion.

§ 5-4. Specific Act Evidence in Sexual Assault and Child Molestation Cases (FRE 413-15).

FRE 413–15 were adopted in 1995 to establish that prior acts of sexual assault may be admitted in sexual assault cases and prior acts of child molestation may

---

[13] See United States v. Howell, 285 F.3d 1263, 1269 (10th Cir. 2002) (highlighting the necessity of using the 403 balancing under FRE 609).

[14] FED. R. EVID. 607, 608.

[15] FED. R. EVID. 405 advisory committee's note.

be admitted in child molestation cases. The rules depart from the principle embodied in FRE 404(a), although some jurisdictions traditionally have permitted this type of evidence as an exception to the propensity rule. The exceptions apply in criminal and civil cases.

FRE 413 provides that evidence of prior sexual assaults is admissible in prosecutions for sexual assault. FRE 414 provides that evidence of prior acts of child molestation is admissible in prosecutions for child molestation. FRE 415 permits the introduction of similar acts in civil cases in which a claim for relief is predicated on a party's alleged sexual assault or child molestation. Each provision requires prior notice of a party's intent to offer the similar act evidence.

The rules were submitted to the Judicial Conference of the United States for comment prior to becoming effective. The Conference recommended that Congress reconsider their adoption. It observed that the new rules: (1) depart from principles embodied in FRE 404 and 405; (2) could lead to wasteful mini-trials within trials; (3) may require courts to admit the similar acts evidence even when there is a great danger of undue prejudice; and (4) arguably could prevent the application of other rules, such as the hearsay rule, to prevent the introduction of similar acts evidence.

Congress did not act on the report of the Judicial Conference. Thus, the rules became effective by operation of law. The rules are set forth below.

Rule 413. Evidence of Similar Crimes in Sexual Assault Cases

(a) In a criminal case in which the defendant is accused of an offense of sexual assault, evidence of the defendant's commission of another offense or offenses of sexual assault is admissible, and may be considered for its bearing on any matter to which it is relevant.

(b) In a case in which the Government intends to offer evidence under this rule, the attorney for the Government shall disclose the evidence to the defendant, including statements of witnesses or a summary of the substance of any testimony that is expected to be offered, at least fifteen days before the scheduled date of trial or at such later time as the court may allow for good cause.

(c) This rule shall not be construed to limit the admission or consideration of evidence under any other rule.

(d) For purposes of this rule and Rule 415, "offense of sexual assault" means a crime under Federal law or the law of a State (as defined in section 513 of title 18, United States Code) that involved —

    (1) any conduct proscribed by chapter 109A of title 18, United States Code;

    (2) contact, without consent, between any part of the defendant's body or an object and the genitals or anus of another person;

(3) contact, without consent, between the genitals or anus of the defendant and any part of another person's body;

(4) deriving sexual pleasure or gratification from the infliction of death, bodily injury, or physical pain on another person; or

(5) an attempt or conspiracy to engage in conduct described in paragraphs (1)–(4).

Rule 414. Evidence of Similar Crimes in Child Molestation Cases

(a) In a criminal case in which the defendant is accused of an offense of child molestation, evidence of the defendant's commission of another offense or offenses of child molestation is admissible, and may be considered for its bearing on any matter to which it is relevant.

(b) In a case in which the Government intends to offer evidence under this rule, the attorney for the Government shall disclose the evidence to the defendant, including statements of witnesses or a summary of the substance of any testimony that is expected to be offered, at least fifteen days before the scheduled date of trial or at such later time as the court may allow for good cause.

(c) This rule shall not be construed to limit the admission or consideration of evidence under any other rule.

(d) For purposes of this rule and Rule 415, "child" means a person below the age of fourteen, and "offense of child molestation" means a crime under Federal law or the law of a State (as defined in section 513 of title 18, United States Code) that involved —

(1) any conduct proscribed by chapter 109A of title 18, United States Code, that was committed in relation to a child;

(2) any conduct proscribed by chapter 110 of title 18, United States Code;

(3) contact between any part of the defendant's body or an object and the genitals or anus of a child;

(4) contact between the genitals or anus of the defendant and any part of the body of a child;

(5) deriving sexual pleasure or gratification from the infliction of death, bodily injury, or physical pain on a child; or

(6) an attempt or conspiracy to engage in conduct described in paragraphs (1)–(5).

Rule 415. Evidence of Similar Acts in Civil Cases Concerning Sexual Assault or Child Molestation

(a) In a civil case in which a claim for damages or other relief is predicated on a party's alleged commission of conduct constituting an offense of sexual assault or child molestation, evidence of that party's commission of another offense or offenses of sexual assault or child molestation is admissible and may be considered as provided in Rule 413 and Rule 414 of these rules.

(b)   A party who intends to offer evidence under this Rule shall disclose the evidence to the party against whom it will be offered, including statements of witnesses or a summary of the substance of any testimony that is expected to be offered, at least fifteen days before the scheduled date of trial or at such later time as the court may allow for good cause.

(c)   This rule shall not be construed to limit the admission or consideration of evidence under any other rule.

Several courts have determined that prior acts admissible under FRE 413 and 414 still may be excluded under the balancing test of FRE 403.[16] These decisions presumably apply by analogy to FRE 415. Thus, concern that the rules would be interpreted as mandating the admission of prior acts of sexual assault or child molestation without any consideration of potential prejudice appears unfounded.

In one of the few federal cases that have applied FRE 415, *Frank v. County of Hudson*,[17] a civil case, a district court ruled that a sexual harassment case involving sexual assault could qualify for application of FRE 415. It also found that evidence of prior sexual acts may be excluded under FRE 403 even if it meets the requirements of the new rules.[18]

§ 5-5. Past Behavior of Victims of Sex Offenses (FRE 412).

FRE 412 governs the admissibility of evidence regarding a victim's past sexual behavior in sex offense cases. Although these cases rarely arise in federal court, the rule was designed as a model for the states. A number of states have enacted similar "rape shield" laws. FRE 412 precludes the introduction of evidence to prove other sexual behavior or sexual predisposition of an alleged victim of sexual misconduct in criminal cases, except in three instances: (1) the accused may offer specific instances of sexual behavior of the alleged victim to prove that someone besides the accused was the source of semen, injury or other physical evidence; (2) the accused may offer specific instances of the alleged victim's sexual behavior with the accused to prove consent and the prosecution generally may offer these specific instances; and (3) the court may admit the evidence when its exclusion would violate the constitutional rights of the defendant. The rule

---

[16] See Doe v. Rudy Glanzer, 232 F.3d 1258, 1270 (9th Cir. 2000); Johnson v. Elk Lake School District, 283 F.3d 138, 144 (3rd Cir. 2002); United States v. Meacham, 115 F.3d 1488, 1494 (10th Cir. 1997); United States v. Guardia, 135 F.3d 1326, 1329 (10th Cir. 1998); United States v. Larson, 112 F.3d 600 (2d Cir. 1997); United States v. Summer, 119 F. 3d 658, 659 (8th Cir. 1997).

[17] 924 F. Supp. 620 (D.N.J. 1996).

[18] *Id.* at 624.

effectively bars the admission of reputation or opinion evidence regarding a victim's past sexual behavior in criminal cases;[19] the constitution rarely will require the admission of this type of evidence.[20]

The rule enacts a balancing test for application in civil cases. It allows the introduction of evidence of sexual predisposition or behavior of an alleged victim when the evidence "is otherwise admissible under these rules and its probative value substantially outweighs the danger of harm to any victim and of unfair prejudice to any party." Additionally, evidence of an alleged victim's reputation for sexual behavior or predisposition is admissible only if the alleged victim raises the issue.

The rule is designed to protect alleged victims of sexual misconduct against unwarranted invasions of their privacy and embarrassment and to encourage them to participate in legal proceedings against alleged offenders. The Advisory Committee states:

> The rule aims to safeguard the alleged victim against the invasion of privacy, potential embarrassment and sexual stereotyping that is associated with public disclosure of intimate sexual details and the infusion of sexual innuendo into the factfinding process. By affording alleged victims protection in most instances, the rule also encourages victims of sexual misconduct to institute and to participate in legal proceedings against alleged offenders.[21]

The rule applies even when the victim is not a party to the litigation;[22] thus, it protects persons who appear in court only as witnesses. Additionally, although the term "alleged victim" is used in the rule, it does not require a formal allegation, stated in pleadings, of sexual misconduct. Nor is there a requirement that the "accused" be subject to a criminal prosecution or even criminal liability.[23]

Subsection (c) of the rule clarifies the procedure for determining admissibility. It requires the offering party to file a motion describing the evidence and the purpose for which it is offered. The court must hold an in camera hearing and afford the parties and the alleged victim a right to be heard. The motion and record of the hearing is to be sealed unless the court orders otherwise. The rule

---

[19] See United States v. White Buffalo, 84 F.3d 1052, 1053 (8th Cir. 1996).

[20] But see United States v. LaJoie, 217 F.3d 663, 670–71 (9th Cir. 2000) (holding that the exclusion of a victim's past sexual history because the defendant failed to meet a notice requirement violated his Sixth Amendment right because the evidence was relevant).

[21] FED. R. EVID. 412, advisory committee's note.

[22] *Id.*

[23] *Id.* "The reference to a person 'accused' is also used in a non-technical sense. There is no requirement that there be a criminal charge pending against the person or even that the misconduct would constitute a criminal offense."

eliminates a provision from its predecessor requiring the court to determine in camera whether a condition of fact is fulfilled for the relevance of evidence offered by the accused. The provision was deemed confusing and possibly an invasion of a criminal defendant's right to a jury trial.[24]

The rule does not govern discovery of evidence of sexual behavior or predisposition. Nevertheless, the principles of the rule should apply to discovery rulings. The Advisory Committee states:

> The procedures set forth in subdivision (c) do not apply to discovery of a victim's past sexual conduct or predisposition in civil cases, which will continue to be governed by Fed. R. Civ. P. 26. In order not to undermine the rationale of Rule 412, however, courts should enter appropriate orders pursuant to Fed. R. Civ. P. 26(c) to protect the victim against unwarranted inquiries and to ensure confidentiality. Courts should presumptively issue protective orders barring discovery unless the party seeking discovery makes a showing that the evidence sought to be discovered would be relevant under the facts and theories of the particular case, and cannot be obtained except through discovery.[25]

FRE 412 provides protection to sex crime victims against forays into their sexual histories. On the other hand, by narrowly circumscribing the purposes for which evidence of sexual history may be offered, imposing procedural requirements, and barring all opinion and reputation evidence, the rule may infringe the rights of defendants. Potential grounds for challenging the rule include: (1) it may unduly limit the right of a defendant to confront and cross-examine his accuser; (2) it may improperly raise the burden of submitting opinion, reputation or other act evidence of consent to the jury; and (3) it may impose undue procedural strictures on the defense case. The rule states:

Rule 412. Sex Offense Cases; Relevance of Alleged Victim's Past Sexual Behavior or Alleged Sexual Predisposition

(a) **Evidence generally inadmissible.** The following evidence is not admissible in any civil or criminal proceeding involving alleged sexual misconduct except as provided in subdivisions (b) and (c):

    (1) Evidence offered to prove that any alleged victim engaged in other sexual behavior.

    (2) Evidence offered to prove any alleged victim's sexual predisposition.

(b) **Exceptions.**

---

[24] Id.

[25] Id.

(1) In a criminal case, the following evidence is admissible, if otherwise admissible under these rules:

(A) evidence of specific instances of sexual behavior by the alleged victim offered to prove that a person other than the accused was the source of semen, injury or other physical evidence;

(B) evidence of specific instances of sexual behavior by the alleged victim with respect to the person accused of the sexual misconduct offered by the accused to prove consent or by the prosecution; and

(C) evidence the exclusion of which would violate the constitutional rights of the defendant.

(2) In a civil case, evidence offered to prove the sexual behavior or sexual predisposition of any alleged victim is admissible if it is otherwise admissible under these rules and its probative value substantially outweighs the danger of harm to any victim and of unfair prejudice to any party. Evidence of an alleged victim's reputation is admissible only if it has been placed in controversy by the alleged victim.

(c) **Procedure to determine admissibility.**

(1) A party intending to offer evidence under subdivision (b) must:

(A) file a written motion at least 14 days before trial specifically describing the evidence and stating the purpose for which it is offered unless the court, for good cause requires a different time for filing or permits filing during trial; and

(B) serve the motion on all parties and notify the alleged victim or, when appropriate, the alleged victim's guardian or representative.

(2) Before admitting evidence under this rule the court must conduct a hearing in camera and afford the victim and parties a right to attend and be heard. The motion, related papers, and the record of the hearing must be sealed and remain under seal unless the court orders otherwise.

§ 5-6. Summary of Character Rules.

The propensity rule still bars the introduction of character evidence for substantive purposes in most cases, subject to the exceptions in FRE 404(a) and 413–15. The impeachment rules permit character evidence on the issue of truthfulness, however, so a party opens the door to character evidence when he takes the stand. See § 9-27.

The rules regulating character evidence, both on substantive issues and for impeachment, may be summarized as follows:

1. When character is an "essential element" of a claim, charge, or defense, character evidence is admissible and may be proven by specific acts, opinion, and reputation evidence.

2. Specific acts of sexual assault may be introduced in a sexual assault case and specific acts of child molestation may be introduced in a child molestation case.

3. Character evidence is inadmissible to show a person's propensity to act in a particular manner in a civil case other than a sexual assault or child molestation case.

4. Apart from sexual assault and child molestation cases, character evidence generally is inadmissible to show a person's propensity to act in a particular manner in a criminal case, except in the circumstances permitted under FRE 404(a):

   a. Pertinent evidence presented by the accused as to his own character, or the prosecution to rebut the same;

   b. Pertinent evidence offered by the accused as to a character trait of the victim, or the prosecution to rebut the same, or evidence as to the same character trait of the defendant, offered by the prosecution in response to character evidence concerning the victim;

   c. Evidence of the victim's peacefulness offered by the prosecution in a homicide case to rebut evidence that the victim was the first aggressor.

   In the instances permitted under FRE 404(a), character may be proven with opinion or reputation evidence, but not with specific acts. Specific acts may, however, be inquired into in the cross-examination of an opinion or reputation witness.

5. Evidence may not be offered to show the sexual propensity of the victim in a criminal sexual assault case, except for specific instances of conduct with the accused to show consent, with another to show the source of semen, injury, or other physical evidence, or when the defendant's constitutional rights require its introduction. In a civil case, the evidence is admissible when its probative value substantially outweighs any harm to the victim or prejudice to a party, but reputation evidence is inadmissible unless the victim places her reputation in issue.

6. The veracity of a witness may be attacked by opinion or reputation evidence. Once attacked, it may be supported by opinion or reputation evidence. A witness who gives opinion or reputation evidence may be

cross-examined concerning prior acts that the court determines, in its discretion, are probative of truthfulness.

7. The veracity of a witness may be attacked through evidence of a prior crime to the extent permitted by FRE 609. The witness may be cross-examined concerning other prior acts that are probative of truthfulness or untruthfulness, subject to the discretion of the court, under FRE 608.

8. A party may present evidence of other prior acts to attack the truthful character of a witness only through the cross-examination of that witness or another witness who presents opinion or reputation testimony concerning his veracity. Extrinsic evidence of other prior acts is not admissible.

§ 5-7. Techniques for Establishing Character.

Planning and preparation are essential to get the most out of character evidence. Opinion and reputation evidence — the means most frequently permitted to establish character — are inherently imprecise; a witness's general description of a person's character usually has a weak impact. Evidence of prior conduct, when admissible, has a stronger effect. In either case, planning is necessary to achieve the best results.

§ 5-7(a). Opinion and Reputation.

A witness who presents opinion or reputation testimony may not on direct examination discuss specific instances of conduct.[26] Thus, the witness must address intangible qualities. The Advisory Committee Note to FRE 405 states:

> The express allowance of inquiry into specific instances of conduct on cross-examination in subdivision (a) and the express allowance of it as part of a case in chief when character is actually in issue in subdivision (b) contemplate that testimony of specific instances is not generally permissible on the direct examination of an ordinary opinion witness to character. Similarly as to witnesses to the character of witnesses under Rule 608(b). Opinion testimony on direct in these situations ought in general to correspond to reputation testimony as now given, *i.e.*, be confined to the nature and extent of observation and acquaintance upon which the opinion is based. See Rule 701.

This limitation intentionally takes some of the punch out of character testimony, at least on direct. Nevertheless, careful preparation can produce a strong presentation. The following techniques help accomplish this result.

§ 5-7(a)(1). Use the Right Witness.

Selecting the right witness is important in presenting character testimony. You need a witness who will make a good impression, but you should give primary

---

[26] See MARK A. DOMBROFF, FEDERAL TRIAL EVIDENCE 57–58.1 (6th ed. 1990).

importance to the witness's knowledge of the subject rather than his own prominence. A friend who knows the subject well will present better character testimony than the bishop who hardly knows him. The witness should be able to discuss the subject's specific acts, good and bad. In cross-examination, a favorable character witness may have to provide exculpatory facts regarding bad acts and may get the opportunity to introduce good acts.

If possible, the witness should have no built-in reason for bias. A favorable character witness ordinarily should not be related by blood or marriage to the subject and should not be a lover; these witnesses are handicapped by a presumed loyalty to the subject. Similarly, a scorned fiancée is not the most credible witness to attack the subject's character. The witness needs to be able to give a clear, specific description, because describing a person's qualities in a compelling manner is difficult.

§ 5-7(a)(2). Develop Context in Establishing Foundation.

A witness who gives an opinion on character must have sufficient personal knowledge to support a rationally based opinion.[27] Generally the witness must have a personal acquaintance with the person that goes beyond isolated meetings. The better the witness's knowledge, the greater the credibility of her opinion. A reputation witness must demonstrate personal knowledge of what others in the community say about the subject. This predicate requires that the witness and the subject have common friends and acquaintances.

A well-developed foundation greatly enhances opinion or reputation evidence. In laying the foundation, you should bring out the *types* of acts with which the witness is familiar without eliciting individual acts. For instance, if honesty is the issue, you might explore the situations in which the witness had the opportunity to observe the subject's honesty; if the witness entrusted funds with the subject or placed him in a position of trust, review the circumstances. The witness's opinion has more impact in this context, as it appears based on repeated and consistent action. Similarly, to the extent a reputation witness can describe how others are familiar with the subject's character, the reputation testimony acquires strength.

Developing the foundation is a way of indirectly introducing specific acts into opinion or reputation testimony. If a witness testifies that Mr. Jones was custodian of the church funds and made all collections, deposits, and reports regarding the funds, his testimony that Mr. Jones is trustworthy gains the persuasive thrust of many honest actions. If the witness explains the opinion in a way that reinforces this context, the opinion has even more impact.

---

[27] See FED. R. EVID. 701.

§ 5-7(a)(3). Differentiate and Present Types of Testimony.

Most character witnesses have a basis for presenting both opinion and reputation evidence concerning the subject. Therefore, you should have a witness present both. This approach produces a double bang, permitting the witness to reinforce his own opinion with the opinions of others. Further, it provides additional contexts for evaluating the opinions; the witness may know the subject in one context, while others in the community have a different basis of evaluation. Thus, the witness can describe multiple areas in which the subject displayed a character trait.

Reputation evidence often is nothing more than opinion. It is human nature to give credence to statements that reinforce one's own opinion and discount those that conflict with it. Indeed, as the Advisory Committee Note to FRE 405 states: "It seems likely that the persistence of reputation evidence [despite its secondhand, gossipy basis] is due to its largely being opinion in disguise." Nonetheless, you should structure the testimony so that you present *both* opinion and reputation. This tactic simply involves breaking the testimony into parts, as most witnesses have a foundation for presenting both.

When evidence of specific acts is admissible to prove character, you should consider combining it with opinion and reputation evidence. Specific acts provide a basis for explaining and developing the witness's opinion. You should take care, however, that the testimony focuses on acts, since they have the most persuasive power. This approach produces an additional "bang" in the testimony. For instance, a witness who knows the subject well might testify to his opinion and the subject's reputation for honesty, then document this general testimony with instances in which the subject displayed that honesty.

§ 5-7(a)(4). Break the Testimony into Parts.

You can give greater substance to conclusionary testimony by breaking it into parts. Thus, for example, counsel could elicit:

1. The witness's familiarity with the subject's business affairs, followed by opinion testimony concerning the subject's honesty in business;

2. The witness's familiarity with others who have business dealings with the subject and knowledge of the subject's reputation in his business dealings, followed by testimony concerning the subject's reputation for honesty among his business associates; and

3. The witness's social interaction with the subject, followed by testimony concerning the subject's honesty in social dealings.

Placing the witness's conclusions in their most specific context tends to strengthen them. Further, this method illustrates the subject's consistent exposition of the character trait. Thus, breaking the testimony into parts tends to give it content. The alternative — presenting the entire foundation first, followed by all the witness's conclusions — separates the opinions from their basis and diminishes their strength.

The following example presents opinion and reputation testimony on honest character, which the prosecution might present in rebuttal to a criminal defendant's character evidence that he is honest and upstanding:

Q.   State your name, please.

A.   Mary Adams.

Q.   Where do you live?

A.   Here in New Orleans.

Q.   Do you know Johnny Reynolds?

A.   Yes. Very well, unfortunately.

Q.   What topic did I ask you to address in your testimony today?

A.   Whether Mr. Reynolds is an honest, law-abiding person.

Q.   How do you know Mr. Reynolds?

A.   I know him through my business and also socially.

Q.   How long have you known him?

A.   About eight years. Since 1994.

Q.   Let's address your business relationship? Could you describe it?

A.   I'm the president of Adams' Florist Shop. Johnny was my manager for three years.

Q.   What responsibilities did he have?

A.   He was responsible for running the shop, dealing with customer complaints, accurately reporting receipts and expenses, keeping expenses under control, and reporting to me on what was going on.

Q.   Did Mr. Reynolds have an opportunity to display his character for honesty in dealing with customers?

A.   Yes.

Q.   How?

A.   He was supposed to deal honestly with the customers and accurately report to me on customer complaints.

Q. Did Mr. Reynolds's character for honesty come into play in dealing with money in the shop?

A. Unfortunately, yes.

Q. In what ways did his honesty come up?

A. He was supposed to keep an honest record of the amounts we received and deposit these funds in our bank account.

Q. How was Mr. Reynolds supposed to be honest in reporting to you?

A. It was his duty to report on problems so that we could take action to correct them. In particular, he needed to let us know if he made any sort of serious mistake.

Q. Why did your business relationship come to an end?

A. We had to fire him.

Q. Based on your business relationship, do you have an opinion of Mr. Reynolds' honesty?

A. Yes, I do.

Q. Tell the court and jury, please, what that opinion is.

A. He is fundamentally dishonest and untrustworthy.

Q. On what do you base that opinion?

A. Three years of dealing with his dishonesty. He is a lying, thieving individual.

Q. Let's turn to your social relationship with Mr. Reynolds. What was that relationship?

A. For a while we were friends. We had a number of mutual friends. We saw each other at parties, dinners, and other social events.

Q. Did you have an opportunity to observe Mr. Reynolds' honesty in your social relationship?

A. Yes.

Q. Do you have an opinion of his honesty in his social life?

A. Yes, I do.

Q. What is your opinion?

A. He is a dishonest, scheming, manipulative person.

Q. Does Mr. Reynolds have a reputation for honesty among those who know him?

173

A.	Oh, yes.
Q.	How are you familiar with his reputation for honesty?
A.	Once anyone gets to know Johnny, that person will soon learn about his deceitfulness. Many people have mentioned their opinions of him to me.
Q.	What is his reputation?
A.	It's terrible. It is very well known that he cannot be trusted.

§ 5-7(a)(5).   Connect the Foundations and Conclusions.

Opinion and reputation testimony naturally reflect conclusions. The perspective from which a witness draws these conclusions is paramount in evaluating their validity. If possible, you should link the foundations for different aspects of the witness's conclusions directly to the different conclusions you present. Thus, to the extent you segment the testimony, present specific foundations in connection with related conclusions.

§ 5-7(b).   Specific Acts.

Evidence of the subject's prior acts may be a powerful means of demonstrating character. People easily empathize with a heartwarming act of charity; they may be inspired by a difficult instance of honesty; they may be revolted by an instance of brutality or greed. Further, people easily generalize the conclusions they draw about a subject from a single act.[28] Thus, prior acts are a potent basis for demonstrating character.

Specific acts are an effective means of illustrating opinion testimony on character. You might ask an opinion witness for an opinion, say as to the subject's honesty, and then question her about examples of that honesty. You may only use this approach, however, when you may offer specific acts to establish character on direct — those cases in which character is an "essential element" of a charge, claim or defense.[29] An opinion or reputation witness nevertheless must respond to questions about specific acts during cross-examination. Thus, counsel should choose a witness who has knowledge to make an effective presentation concerning specific instances. The ability to explain a prior act often is crucial in avoiding the harmful effect of cross-examination on the act.

You most frequently can use specific acts to show character on cross-examination. First, you may cross-examine any witness who provides character testimony in the form of opinion or reputation regarding relevant specific

---

[28] See generally RICHARD D. RIEKE & RANDALL K. STUTMAN, COMMUNICATION IN LEGAL AD-VOCACY 109-32 (1990).

[29] FED. R. EVID. 405.

instances. Second, when character is an essential element of a charge, claim, or defense, you may ask a character witness about relevant specific acts on cross-examination as well as direct. Third, you may use specific instances to attack a witness's veracity during the cross-examination of that witness under FRE 608 and 609.

When prior convictions are used to impeach a witness under FRE 609, courts generally limit inquiry into the circumstances of the crime. You ordinarily are not permitted to go beyond the name of the crime, the date of conviction, and the sentence, unless the witness attempts to exculpate himself. This limitation does not apply to cross-examination concerning other specific instances, however, so you may inquire into the circumstances of those acts.[30] In doing so, you should use the same techniques that are effective in cross-examining on other matters, dramatizing the points by categorizing them, breaking questions down, and constructing "mountains out of molehills." See § 9-15. When you attack a subject's character, it is imperative that you make the assault effective.

One drawback of cross-examining a character witness about specific acts is that it may open the door for the witness to volunteer information regarding different acts. A good character witness may explain away acts that otherwise would undermine his opinion and inject instances that support his view of the subject's character. Whether this testimony is deemed responsive depends largely on counsel's questions. In examining a witness about prior acts, you should be precise; avoid general questions that invite argument. This approach helps prevent the witness from volunteering facts that would not be admissible on direct.

Traditionally, the cross-examination on specific acts had to be phrased in a form appropriate to the type of testimony being presented. Thus, a reputation witness would be asked if he "heard" about specific instances and an opinion witness would be asked if she "knows" about them. FRE 405 eliminates this requirement. The Advisory Committee Note states:

> According to the great majority of cases, on cross-examination inquiry is allowable as to whether the reputation witness has heard of particular instances of conduct pertinent to the trait in question. The theory is that, since the reputation witness relates what he has heard, the inquiry tends to shed light on the accuracy of his hearing and reporting. Accordingly, the opinion witness would be asked whether he knew, as well as whether he had heard. The fact is, of course, that these distinctions are of slight if any practical significance, and the second sentence of [FRE 405(a)] eliminates them as a factor in formulating questions. . . .[31]

---

[30] FED. R. EVID. 608.

[31] FED. R. EVID. 405 advisory committee's note (citations omitted).

Consequently, the "Have you heard? and "Do you know?" formulations are unnecessary under the federal rules. They still may be required in some states.

§ 5-8. Use of Specific Instances of Conduct for Other Purposes (FRE 404(b)).

Although specific instances may not be used to show propensity, they are admissible when offered for other, relevant purposes.[32] FRE 404(b) provides:

> **(b) Other crimes, wrongs or acts.** Evidence of other crimes, wrongs or acts is not admissible to prove the character of a person in order to show action in conformity therewith. It may, however, be admissible for other purposes, such as proof of motive, opportunity, intent, preparation, plan, knowledge, identity, or absence of mistake or accident, provided that upon request by the accused, the prosecution in a criminal case shall provide reasonable notice in advance of trial, or during trial if the court excuses pretrial notice on good cause shown, of the general nature of any such evidence it intends to introduce at trial.

Prior acts evidence often is offered for an assertedly permissible purpose in criminal cases. The prosecution not only offers evidence regarding the act with which the defendant is charged, but seeks to prove that he committed another bad act. This tactic has great potential for prejudice because the jury may conclude from the prior act evidence that the defendant is a "bad person" and convict him for that reason. In this situation the jury would use the evidence for the very purpose barred by FRE 404(b) — to draw a conclusion concerning the defendant's propensity for crime. Thus, courts must exercise care in admitting prior act evidence, even when it is offered under an exception to the propensity rule.

The court uses the balancing test in FRE 403 to determine whether to admit prior crimes evidence for a permissible purpose. As the Advisory Committee Note to FRE 404(b) states:

> No mechanical solution is offered. The determination must be made whether the danger of undue prejudice outweighs the probative value of the evidence in view of the availability of other means of proof and other factors appropriate for making decisions of this kind under Rule 403.

In the balance the court must consider the prejudice from prior acts evidence, the likelihood that the trial of another act will consume time, and the likelihood that it may confuse the jury. The court also must consider the probative value of the prior act on a relevant point and the availability of alternate means of proving that point.

---

[32] See, e.g., United States v. Jones, 248 F.3d 671, 676 (7th Cir. 2001); United States v. Varoudakis, 233 F.3d 113, 118 (1st Cir. 2000).

A fundamental problem is distinguishing between the use of prior act evidence to prove *propensity* and its use for a permissible purpose. Often the road to proving a legitimate point is through reasoning that requires its use for propensity. For example, assume a defendant is accused of robbing a victim at knife point late one evening, but the victim cannot identify her assailant. Assume another victim was robbed earlier the same night and can identify the defendant as the perpetrator. The prosecution might offer the prior crime for "identity" under FRE 404(b), but the prior act does nothing to prove "identity" respecting the charged crime. It proves only that the defendant may have committed the first crime and thus is the type of person who might have committed the second robbery. Thus, the court should exclude it.

More specific facts would be necessary to show a true "identity" purpose. If the victim of the prior crime identified the defendant and also described his clothing, the testimony might prove identity if the victim of the second crime described the same clothing. There would be a direct logical link to identity: a man dressed in specific clothing committed both crimes and could be identified as having committed the first. Similarly, if the victim of the first crime could identify the defendant, and the prosecution showed that a weapon taken from the victim was used in the second crime, the first victim's testimony logically could show the "identity" of the second assailant.

A second issue is whether prior act evidence is offered to prove a relevant point. Counsel may assert that the act is offered to prove identity, motive, or some other permissible matter, but the court should not admit the evidence unless the point is in issue. Assume, for example, that a man is accused of robbery, but contends that the alleged victim gave him the item the victim claims was stolen. In this situation "identity" is not an issue; the parties agree on who the man was, but dispute the circumstances under which the act occurred. Thus, if a prior act were offered to prove "identity," it would be superfluous.

Sometimes it is unclear whether a defendant disputes a point on which prior act evidence is offered. Often a defendant waits for the prosecution to complete its case before showing his hand. Rather than requiring the defendant to concede a point to prevent the introduction of the prior crime, the court may reserve the issue until the prosecution's rebuttal case. At that point it should be clear whether the prior crime is offered on a matter in dispute.

Some jurisdictions permit prior act evidence to show "system" "modus operandi" or "plan." Under this theory, the prior act is presented to prove the accused engaged in a pattern of repeated crimes — almost as part of an overall organized method. This theory comes close to opening the door for all prior act evidence, because the acts of many recidivists have a similar, pattern-like character.

The admission of similar acts may be prejudicial to a defendant. The incidents may merge in the jurors' minds, so that the evidence in each is misused to prove the other. Additionally, because evidence of a similar act portrays the defendant committing that act, it influences the jurors to think of him as a person who would commit crimes. In distinguishing proof of "system" from general propensity, courts have required a detailed showing that the incidents have unique, specific similarities making them nearly identical.[33] Still, it is often difficult to distinguish where "system" or "modus operandi" stops and "character" begins.

An issue in dealing with other act evidence is whether the proponent must satisfy a higher than normal standard of proof for admitting the evidence. Historically, many state courts and some federal courts required that the prosecution present "clear and convincing" evidence that the accused committed the prior act.[34] In *Huddleston v. United States*,[35] the United States Supreme Court rejected this higher standard. It ruled that the prior act evidence may be admitted if a reasonable juror could conclude the prior act was proven by a preponderance of the evidence.[36]

This standard sharply reduces the court's role in scrutinizing the evidence. First, it adopts an ultimate "preponderance" standard for proving the prior act, rather than the more difficult "clear and convincing" test. Second, it requires the introduction of the evidence if a reasonable juror *could* conclude the standard is met, requiring the court generally to submit the issue to the jury.

Lowering the standard for admitting prior act evidence undermines the protection offered defendants by the reasonable doubt standard. In a case in which the "reasonable doubt" standard could be determinative, evidence of another crime may convince the jury to convict. The jurors may see the evidence as additive; if the prosecution almost has enough evidence on the crime charged, some evidence of another crime may be seen as sufficient to carry its burden. This effect is problematic because the jury does not have to conclude the defendant committed the other crime — under any standard — to misuse the evidence. A "clear and convincing" standard at least requires strong evidence that the defendant committed the other crime before it may be presented.

 Evidence of other acts usually is offered in criminal cases. When a civil case involves a nonpropensity issue on which the evidence is relevant, however, it

---

[33] State v. Lee, 340 So. 2d 1339 (La. 1977); see Van Westrienen v. Americontinental Collection Corp., 94 F.Supp.2d 1087, 1109 (D.Oregon 2000) (holding that "[b]ecause plaintiffs intend to use [witness's] affidavit to show that [defendants] operated according to a 'plan' . . . ." and to "show that defendants have a history or plan . . ." admission of the affidavit did not violate either FRE 404(b) or FRE 608(b)).

[34] United States v. Beechum, 582 F.2d 898 (5th Cir. 1978), *cert. denied*, 440 U.S. 920 (1979); State v. Prieur, 277 So. 2d 126 (La. 1973); see FED. R. EVID. 104.

[35] 485 U.S. 681 (1988).

[36] *Id.* at 689.

is also admissible in that context. Evidence of other acts may be used to show a pattern of discrimination by an employer, a defendant's knowledge that an employee was careless, a fraudulent act was not a mistake, and other nonpropensity points. The danger of prejudice usually is less severe in civil than criminal cases. Thus, less reason generally exists to exclude the evidence.

FRE 404(b) requires that, upon request by the accused in a criminal case, the prosecution provide reasonable notice of its intent to introduce evidence of the defendant's other acts. The notice must be provided in advance of trial or during trial if the court finds that good cause excuses the failure to give pretrial notice. The provision does not require a specific form or time limit for the notice, vesting considerable discretion in the court to determine what is "reasonable." The notice provision applies whether the prosecution plans to use the evidence in its case in chief, on rebuttal, or in some other fashion.[37] The requirement limits the potential for unfair surprise and permits an early decision as to the admissibility of the evidence.

§ 5-9. Habit and Routine Practice (FRE 406).

FRE 406 provides that evidence of a person's habit or the routine practice of an organization is admissible to prove action in conformity therewith on a particular occasion.[38] Unlike most of the "relevance rules," the rule provides for the admission rather than the exclusion of evidence. The rule rejects authorities requiring that evidence of habit be corroborated, or admitted only when there were no eyewitnesses to the event at issue. FRE 406 provides:

> Evidence of the habit of a person or of the routine practice of an organization, whether corroborated or not and regardless of the presence of eyewitnesses, is relevant to prove that the conduct of the person or organization on a particular occasion was in conformity with the habit or routine practice.

Since FRE 406 permits the introduction of habit evidence to prove conduct, but FRE 404 generally excludes character evidence to prove conduct, character and habit must be distinguished. Character is a generalized trait that forms part of a person's personality; habit is the specific, near-automatic reaction to particular circumstances, ingrained through repetition. Because a description of a character trait necessarily is conceptual, a person's conduct in particular circumstances might easily be inconsistent with the trait. Habit is considered a more reliable barometer of specific conduct because it represents a near-automatic response to precise circumstances.[39]

Some traits, such as honesty, integrity, and veracity, fall easily into the character category. Particularized, repeated conduct, such as walking several

---

[37] FED. R. EVID. 404, 1991 Amend., advisory committee's note.

[38] See, e.g., United States v. Yazzie, 188 F.3d 1178, 1190 (10th Cir. 1999).

[39] FED. R. EVID. 406 advisory committee's note.

blocks to work each day, or stamping mail "received" upon intake at an office, falls easily into the habit category. Other conduct may fail the habit test although it is oft-repeated; chronic drunkenness, for example, is more character than habit because it occurs under a variety of circumstances. Further, consistent but occasional conduct does not have the particularized repetition that marks habit; a person may have a tendency to get into fights when drunk, but the conduct probably would not constitute a habit.

The identification of habit is somewhat judgmental. As the Advisory Committee states: "While adequacy of sampling and uniformity of response are key factors, precise standards for measuring their sufficiency for evidence purposes cannot be formulated." [40] Habit is marked by specific circumstances that provoke the same response, time after time. Thus, proof of habit requires particularized testimony based on repeated observations. [41]

§ 5-10. Subsequent Remedial Measures (FRE 407).

"Subsequent remedial measures" are actions taken after an event that would have made it less likely to occur: fixing a rickety staircase, replacing a stop sign with a stoplight, carpeting a slippery floor, making inflatable air bags standard equipment on cars, and similar measures. FRE 407 provides that these measures are not admissible to prove negligence, culpable conduct or defectiveness of a product in connection with the event but may be admissible for other purposes. [42] The rule provides:

> When, after an injury or harm allegedly caused by an event, measures are taken that, if taken previously, would have made the injury or harm less likely to occur, evidence of the subsequent measures is not admissible to prove negligence, culpable conduct, a defect in a product, a defect in a product design, or a need for a warning or instruction. This rule does not require the exclusion of evidence of subsequent measures when offered for another purpose, such as proving ownership, control, or feasibility of precautionary measures, if controverted, or impeachment.

The primary justification for this rule is that people should not be discouraged from making improvements by the prospect that their own conduct might be used against them. One might argue whether a person would be discouraged from taking a prudent action by a rule of evidence, but it also seems unfair to use

---

[40] *Id.*

[41] See Mobil v. Cajun Construction Services, Inc., 45 F.3d 96, 99–100 (5th Cir. 1995)("Evidence of the defendant's actions on only a few occasions or only in relation to the plaintiff are not enough; the plaintiff must show regularity over substantially all occasions or with substantially all other parties with whom the defendant has had similar business transactions.").

[42] *See* MICHAEL H. GRAHAM, HANDBOOK OF FEDERAL EVIDENCE § 407.1, at 266–75 (3d ed. 1991).

an improvement against the person who makes it. Additionally, remedial measures arguably have little relevance. To the extent a repair speaks to negligence, it necessarily reflects an opinion, which may not be "helpful" to the trier of fact.[43]

FRE 407 was amended in 1997 "to clarify that the rule applies only to changes made after the occurrence that produced the damages giving rise to the action. Evidence of measures taken by the defendant prior to the 'event' causing 'injury or harm' do not fall within the exclusionary scope of Rule 407 even if they occurred after the manufacture or design of the product."[44] The amendment eliminates the possibility that a court might apply FRE 407 to exclude a design change or improvement made after a product was sold to a purchaser, but before it allegedly caused an injury, or that "event" might be interpreted to include some other pre-injury occurrence.

One justification for excluding subsequent remedial measures is to avoid discouraging people from making safety improvements in products or conditions; after an event causes an injury, the fear that the improvement might be used in court would discourage its implementation. This concern is inapplicable if an injury has not yet taken place. Thus, most courts interpreted the prior rule as applying only to post-injury remedial measures.[45]

The amendment does not address whether a design or plan for an improvement, conceived before an injury but not implemented until after it occurs, is protected by the rule. The implementation of the improvement would be protected, but perhaps not the design. As to the design, the policy supporting the rule would not apply. Nevertheless, a court might reasonably determine that the conception of the improvement is inextricably linked with its implementation. Alternatively, the plan for a change might be excluded under the balancing test of FRE 403.[46]

---

[43] Fed. R. Evid. 701. See also DAVID P. LEONARD, THE NEW WIGMORE: A TREATISE ON EVIDENCE, SELECTED RULES OF LIMITED ADMISSIBILITY § 2.2 135–37 (Revised Edition 2002).

[44] FED. R. EVID. 407, 1997 Amend., advisory committee's note.

[45] See Moulton v. Rival Co., 116 F.3d 22 (1st Cir. 1997); In re Air Crash Disaster, 86 F.3d 498 (6th Cir. 1996); Traylor v. Husqvarna Motor, 988 F.2d 729 (7th Cir. 1993); Cates v. Sears, Roebuck & Co., 928 F.2d 679 (5th Cir. 1991); Huffman v. Caterpillar Tractor Co., 908 F.2d 1470 (10th Cir. 1990); In re Aircrash in Bali, Indonesia, 871 F.2d 812 (9th Cir. 1989), *cert. denied sub nom.* Pan American World Airways, Inc. v. Causey, 493 U.S. 917 (1989); Chase v. General Motors Corp., 856 F.2d 17 (4th Cir. 1988); Ake v. General Motors Corp., 942 F. Supp. 869 (W.D.N.Y. 1996). For the view that the rule applies to exclude pre-injury conduct, see Kelly v. Crown Equipment Co., 970 F.2d 1273 (3rd Cir. 1992).

[46] See Raymond v. Raymond Corp., 938 F.2d 1518, 1524 (lst Cir. 1991). ("[T]he introduction of evidence of pre-accident design modifications not made effective until after the manufacture of the allegedly defective product may reasonably be found unfairly prejudicial to the defendant and misleading to the jury for determining the question whether the product was unreasonably dangerous at the time of manufacture and sale.").

A second 1997 amendment explicitly extended the rule to defectiveness cases, resolving a conflict among courts as to whether it should apply to those matters. A majority of the circuits had determined that subsequent improvements could not be used to prove a defect in a product or its design.[47]

The theory that courts should not discourage litigants from taking measures to prevent injuries applies to defective products as well as fault-based problems. There is reason to question, however, whether an evidence rule would deter a manufacturer from improving a product in the same way it might dissuade an individual from fixing a hazard. Companies that market products have strong motives to improve them for competitive reasons and can ill afford the mass liability that might result from marketing a defective product. Therefore, the possibility that an improvement could affect a single lawsuit probably would not prevent a manufacturer from making it.

The rule also may create practical litigation difficulties because experts who testify in defectiveness cases almost certainly will know of and consider subsequent design improvements in forming their opinions. In many product liability cases, the defendant contends that the product was as safe as possible. An improvement in the product, and the feasibility of making the improvement prior to the event, would be hard to ignore in examining experts on this contention. Moreover, since an expert under FRE 703 may rely on inadmissible evidence if it is reasonably relied on in the expert's field, the improvement might be a basis for his opinion in any event. Given these considerations, preventing other witnesses from discussing the remedial measure has little justification. Since the measure likely will be used in some fashion at the trial, application of the rule does little to serve social policy and may deny important information to the jury.

Presumably the rule would bar an expert from disclosing the design improvement during direct examination, but counsel in cross-examination would have to carefully avoid giving the expert an opportunity to mention it. Moreover, an expert's opinion that a product was completely safe may legitimize the use of a remedial measure for impeachment. For instance, in *Wood v. Morbank Indus., Inc.*,[48] the court held that a manufacturer opened the door for limited rebuttal using subsequent remedial measures by putting on evidence that the design at the time of the accident was the "safest" design, and the design was still being used in the same manner as when the accident occurred. Further, since the "feasibility of precautionary measures" arguably is a controverted issue in many defectiveness cases, and an improvement is admissible on that issue, the rule may be inconsistently applied.

---

[47] FED. R. EVID. 407, 1997 Amend., advisory committee's note.

[48] 70 F.3d 1201 (11th Cir. 1995).

The rule indicates that a party may offer evidence of a remedial measure for a permissible purpose only if the issue is controverted by the opposing side. Thus, a party could not introduce a measure to prove "ownership" unless the adverse party contested the issue.[49]

§ 5-11. Compromise and Offers to Compromise (FRE 408).

Traditionally, settlement offers were inadmissible to prove liability. Statements made in settlement discussions were not protected, however, unless they were "inextricably linked" to the offer, stated hypothetically, or made under a protective agreement. Controversy existed as to the precise scope of the protection and whether the rule adequately promoted settlement. FRE 408 extends the common law rule to protect offers, statements, and conduct in settlement negotiations.[50] The rule provides that this evidence is not admissible to prove liability or damages.[51] It states:

> Evidence of (1) furnishing or offering or promising to furnish, or (2) accepting or offering or promising to accept, a valuable consideration in compromising or attempting to compromise a claim which was disputed as to either validity or amount, is not admissible to prove liability for or invalidity of the claim or its amount. Evidence of conduct or statements made in compromise negotiations is likewise not admissible. This rule does not require the exclusion of any evidence otherwise discoverable merely because it is presented in the course of compromise negotiations. This rule also does not require exclusion when the evidence is offered for another purpose, such as proving bias or prejudice of a witness, negativing a contention of undue delay, or proving an effort to obstruct a criminal investigation or prosecution.

Exception

The rule serves the social purpose of promoting settlement. If a compromise offer could be used at trial, few offers would be made. Protecting statements and conduct in compromise negotiations also facilitates exchanges that clarify the issues and promote agreement.[52] This asserted benefit of the extension is somewhat illusory, however, because lawyers usually puff their cases and avoid concessions even in settlement discussions. Attorneys are aware that a concession

---

[49] See David P. Leonard, the New Wigmore: A Treatise on Evidence, Selected Rules of Limited Admissibility § 2.8.1 239–42 (rev. ed. 2002). See also J.B. Hunt Inc. v. General Motors, Corp., 243 F.3d 441, 445 (8th Cir. 2001) (evidence of a post-accident change deemed inadmissible to prove feasibility of new design because defendant stipulated feasibility).

[50] But see Jane Michaels, *Rule 408: A Litigation Mine Field*, 19 Litig. 34, 34–38 (1992) (discussing potential pitfalls of Rule 408).

[51] See Busse v. Bayerische Motoren Werke, A.G., 1997 WL 106716 (E.D. La. 1997) (granting motion in limine to exclude evidence of prior settlement because such evidence "might create the very inference of liability").

[52] Fed. R. Evid. 408 advisory committee's note.

may undermine a bargaining position, even if it cannot be used at trial. Thus, the rule rarely promotes true frankness.

On the other hand, admitting statements from compromise negotiations would produce little evidence of value. Lawyers would be even more guarded if their statements were admissible. Further, the difficulty in distinguishing "offers" from "statements," and "inextricably linked" statements from others, makes it desirable to have a clear dividing line. Protecting all negotiating statements removes the need for attorneys to use hypotheticals and permits a full exchange when the lawyers perceive that frankness is beneficial. Thus, the policy benefits of extending the rule outweigh any evidentiary loss.

The rule excluding offers is justified by the theory that an offer has little probative value, since it may reflect a desire to resolve differences and avoid litigation cost as much as a concession of liability. Additionally, to the extent an offer speaks to liability, it reflects an opinion on the ultimate issue that may not be helpful. The helpfulness objection usually is unavailing when a party's own opinion is offered against him under the "admissions" hearsay exclusion, on the theory that a party's concessions have special reliability, but a settlement offer is an extreme example of an ultimate conclusion.

An additional reason to exclude settlement offers is their tendency to require explanatory testimony from lawyers. If a court admitted an offer, the attorney who made the offer might seek to explain that it was not based on a fear of liability but on other factors. This mixing of the roles of lawyer and witness might run afoul of ethical rules.[53] Moreover, the attorney's role as an advocate would undermine her credibility as a witness. Thus, courts seek to avoid the need for this testimony.

Concessions of fact in settlement discussions are more reliable. These statements have the credibility of admissions and do not offend the helpfulness rule. Nevertheless, excluding the statements does not deny much valuable evidence to the factfinder. Facts admitted in settlement negotiations may be proven by other means; the rule excludes only the statements and conduct in the negotiations, not the facts themselves. Additionally, parties would rarely make fact concessions in settlement talks if they were admissible.

The rule excludes evidence of civil compromise negotiations when offered "to prove liability for or invalidity of the claim or its amount." The specification of "claim" limits the exclusion to civil proceedings, and suggests that the rule does not exclude statements from civil negotiations in related criminal cases. Additionally, the rule does not bar statements from compromise negotiations if a party offers them to prove a different civil claim. The policy underlying the rule might support the exclusion of these statements pursuant to FRE 403, however.

---

[53] MODEL RULES OF PROFESSIONAL CONDUCT Rule 3.4.

For the rule to apply, the "claim" must be disputed as to validity or amount when the offer is made. Thus, for example, if a party admitted liability for a bill but sought to compromise because of an inability to pay, the offer and concession would be admissible. The limitation to disputed claims has little practical effect because parties usually raise a dispute if they choose not to pay; the dispute may be bogus, but the rule does not suggest an inquiry into its sincerity. Even when a party enters negotiations without formally rejecting the claim, courts are likely to assume a dispute because otherwise negotiations would not have occurred. Thus, most negotiations fall within the rule.

In its illustrative list of permissible uses for statements from compromise negotiations, the rule does not mention impeachment. Nevertheless, since the rule bars the evidence only if offered on liability or amount, the evidence should not automatically be excluded for impeachment. The problem is that a statement from compromise negotiations offered to show the witness is lying almost always can be misused on the forbidden substantive issues. In resolving this conflict, courts should balance the need for impeachment versus the policy of promoting settlement pursuant to FRE 403.

Proving bias is a primary purpose for which evidence of compromise is admissible. Often plaintiffs name multiple defendants and enter settlements with some of them. A court arguably should exclude evidence of the compromise, if offered to show another party's liability for the same claim, because the compromise counters the liability of others. The proponent could argue, however, that a settling party was motivated to testify for another party by an attractive settlement. The "bias" purpose is often a means to secure introduction of the evidence.

§ 5-12.   Paying or Offering to Pay Medical or Similar Expenses (FRE 409).

Evidence that a party paid or offered to pay medical or similar expenses of an injured person is not admissible to prove liability for the injury.[54] FRE 409 provides:

> Evidence of furnishing or offering or promising to pay medical, hospital, or similar expenses occasioned by an injury is not admissible to prove liability for the injury.

The rule does not protect statements made in connection with offers to pay medical expenses. Assume a party stated: "It's my fault. I ran right through that stoplight. I'll take care of your medical expenses." In this case, rule would not require exclusion of the reasons expressed for making the offer. To the extent

---

[54] See, e.g., Waltord v. Evening Star Newspaper Co., 211 F.2d 31 (D.C. Cir. 1954). See also CHRISTOPHER B. MUELLER AND LAIRD C. KIRKPATRICK, MODERN EVIDENCE: DOCTRINE AND PRACTICE § 4.28 402–03 (1995).

that the contemporaneous statement is "inextricably linked" to the offer, however, it might be excluded by analogy to the common law rule regarding statements inextricably linked to compromise offers. See § 5-11. Additionally, statements of remorse made in connection with offers to pay medical expenses may have little evidentiary value. For example, "I am sorry" may not be probative because it does not reveal the reason for the speaker's sorrow. A court probably would exclude this type of statement under FRE 403.

Relevance and policy considerations justify the rule.[55] First, an offer to pay medical expenses may reflect considerations other than a fear of liability; the offeror simply may wish to help the injured party. Second, if the rule did not exist, parties might be discouraged from socially desirable conduct. Third, the rule reflects a disinclination to turn a person's good deed against him.

An offer to pay medical expenses is admissible to show liability for the expenses. Thus, if the offeror later refused to pay, the injured party could use the offer to prove the contract for the expenses, but could not use it to show that the offeror was liable in tort for the injury. Additionally, a party may use the offer for other purposes, such as impeachment. If, for instance, the offeror testified at trial that he felt no responsibility for the accident, the adverse party might use the offer to impeach. Similarly, if inextricably linked statements are excluded under the rule, a party still may use them to impeach if inconsistent positions are asserted at trial.

In some cases, an offer to pay medical expenses might be characterized as a settlement offer. Assume a party stated: "I'll pay your medical expenses if you'll agree not to make any other claims against me." In that situation, FRE 408 probably would apply, and contemporaneous statements and conduct would be protected.

§ 5-13. Pleas, Plea Discussions and Related Statements (FRE 410).

Pleas of guilty and statements made in plea negotiations are inadmissible against the accused in criminal or civil proceedings. FRE 410.[56] The rule protects only the accused; it provides no explicit protection for the prosecution. The protected plea or statement may be admitted to prove perjury. If the court admits a statement of the prosecuting authority, it may also admit a plea or statement of the accused if required for fairness. FRE 410 states:

> Except as otherwise provided in this rule, evidence of the following is not, in any civil or criminal proceeding, admissible against the defendant who made the plea or was a participant in the plea discussions:

---

[55] See CHRISTOPHER B. MUELLER AND LAIRD C. KIRKPATRICK, MODERN EVIDENCE: DOCTRINE AND PRACTICE § 4.28 396–97 (1995).

[56] See, e.g., United States v. Young, 223 F.3d 905, 908 (8th Cir. 2000).

(1) a plea of guilty which was later withdrawn;

(2) a plea of nolo contendere;

(3) any statement made in the course of any proceedings under Rule 11 of the Federal Rules of Criminal Procedure or comparable state procedure regarding either of the foregoing pleas; or

(4) any statement made in the course of plea discussions with an attorney for the prosecuting authority which do not result in a plea of guilty or which result in a plea of guilty later withdrawn.

However, such a statement is admissible (i) in any proceeding wherein another statement made in the course of the same plea or plea discussions has been introduced and the statement ought in fairness be considered contemporaneously with it, or (ii) in a criminal proceeding for perjury or false statement if the statement was made by the defendant under oath, on the record and in the presence of counsel.

The rule excludes pleas of guilty that are later withdrawn. If a plea that is withdrawn could be introduced in a subsequent trial, the withdrawal would do little to help the accused. Thus, as the Supreme Court pointed out in *Kercheval v. United States*,[57] admitting a withdrawn plea would render the decision allowing withdrawal a nullity. Additionally, admitting a withdrawn plea might compel a defendant to explain the reason for entering and withdrawing the plea, which runs counter to the right against self-incrimination. Further, admitting a withdrawn plea might require explanatory testimony from defense counsel, forcing the attorney to mix the roles of advocate and witness.[58]

The plea of *nolo contendere* permits a conviction without a full admission of guilt. It is often used to avoid the admissibility of a criminal plea in a subsequent civil case, such as an antitrust or fraud action. The rule barring introduction of the plea in a subsequent civil or criminal proceeding reflects the compromise nature of the plea.[59] It permits the quick disposition of small-stakes criminal cases — misdemeanor cases, for instance — that carry potentially large civil consequences. If the plea were admissible in the civil case, the defendant would be forced to litigate the criminal charge.

Although FRE 410 prohibits the use of *nolo contendere* pleas against the pleader in any subsequent criminal or civil proceeding, some courts have held that a *conviction* based on a *nolo contendere* plea may be used against the pleader

---

[57] 274 U.S. 220 (1927).

[58] See FED. R. EVID. 410 advisory committee's note; MODEL RULES OF PROFESSIONAL CONDUCT Rule 3.4.

[59] See FED. R. EVID. 410 advisory committee's note.

to impeach.[60] This distinction between the plea and the conviction appears to erode the protection the rule offers to these who plead *nolo contendere*, as it penalizes them for testifying in a subsequent proceeding. On the other hand, there is some question that criminal defendants should be allowed to plead *nolo contendere* at all; protecting certain defendants, often of privileged status, from the effects of criminal judgments in subsequent proceedings may not serve a valid social purpose. Thus, the refusal to protect these defendants from impeachment with convictions based on *nolo contendere* convictions may reflect concerns over the appropriateness of the rule.

The rule protects statements made in proceedings relating to guilty or *nolo contendere* pleas and statements made in the course of plea discussions with an attorney for the prosecuting authority. Thus, it permits frank discussion by an accused, which may promote a just compromise plea. The rule does not protect statements of the prosecuting authority, however. This one-sided approach may reflect the reality that prosecutors are obliged to reveal exculpatory information in any event. Since a prosecutor is not entitled to conceal exculpatory information, the protection is unnecessary to promote free discussion.

The rule explicitly protects only those statements made by the accused to "an attorney for the prosecuting authority." Thus, it suggests that statements to other law enforcement officials are not covered. Suspects often are questioned by police officers and may confess in the hope of securing leniency, although the discussion is not really a plea bargain. Apparently the drafters wished to exclude these discussions from the scope of FRE 410.

Nevertheless, some cases suggest that the rule may extend beyond statements to attorneys. In *United States v. Grant*,[61] the Eighth Circuit interpreted the rule to protect statements made to an FBI agent authorized to negotiate for the prosecution. In *United States v. Robertson*,[62] the Fifth Circuit fashioned a two-tier analysis to determine whether the rule covers statements to law enforcement officials other than lawyers. The inquiry includes (1) whether the accused perceived that he was participating in plea negotiations, and (2) the reasonableness of that perception under the circumstances.[63]

FRE 410 does not specify prohibited purposes for pleas and statements from plea discussions, suggesting the evidence is inadmissible regardless of the reason

---

[60] United States v. Sonny Mitchell Center, 934 F.2d 77 (5th Cir. 1991); Myers v. Secretary of Health & Human Servs., 893 F.2d 840 (6th Cir. 1990).

[61] 622 F.2d 308 (8th Cir. 1980). But see United States v. Marks, 209 F.3d 577, 582 (6th Cir. 2000) ("FBI agents cannot negotiate plea agreements with defendants, so statements that defendants make to them are not 'made in the course of plea agreements.' ").

[62] 582 F.2d 1356 (5th Cir. 1978).

[63] *Id.* at 1366. See also United States v. Jorgensen, 871 F.2d 725 (8th Cir. 1989) ("[W]hen law enforcement officials have express authority from government attorneys to act as their surrogates, statements made to them by a criminal suspect are inadmissible.").

it is offered. This unconditional protection suggests that statements in plea negotiations are not admissible to impeach. Some circumstances may be so extreme, however, that courts fashion exceptions to the rule. For instance, if a defendant called witnesses to testify to a story contradicted by his own statements in plea negotiations, a court might admit the statements to counter the subornation of perjury.[64]

The rule provides that a plea or statement given under oath, on the record, and in the presence of counsel may be introduced in a criminal prosecution for perjury or false statement. The rule apparently is intended to permit a prosecution for falsifying a plea or lying in connection with the plea, which is distinguishable from a prosecution for perjuring trial testimony. Allowing the prosecution to introduce the plea or plea statement in a separate perjury case to show trial testimony was perjured would dilute the protection that the rule provides. The potential use of the plea or plea statement would inhibit the defendant from testifying at trial in much the same way as if the plea evidence could be used in the trial to impeach. Nevertheless, the rule does not explicitly limit the perjury exception to a prosecution for lying in connection with a plea, which may mean that the plea statement can be used in a prosecution for perjuring trial testimony.

If a prosecutor's statement in plea negotiations is admitted against the prosecution, statements of the defendant may be admitted if required for fairness. Often the statements of both sides are needed to give context to each. Thus, a defendant who offers statements of the prosecution may open the door to the use of her own statements.

§ 5-14. Liability Insurance (FRE 411).

Evidence that a person was or was not insured is not admissible to prove or disprove negligence or wrongful conduct.[65] It may be admissible for other purposes. The rule reflects two considerations: (1) the existence or nonexistence of liability insurance has nothing to do with fault; and (2) the information might influence a jury to alter its decision. FRE 411 provides:

> Evidence that a person was or was not insured against liability is not admissible upon the issue whether the person acted negligently or otherwise wrongfully. This rule does not require the exclusion of evidence of insurance against liability when offered for another purpose, such as proof of agency, ownership, or control, or bias or prejudice of a witness.

Plaintiffs have a strong motive to offer evidence of liability insurance for a permissible purpose because of the potential prejudice associated with the

---

[64] United States v. Walder, 347 U.S. 62 (1954); United States v. Havens, 446 U.S. 620 (1980), *reh'g denied*, 448 U.S. 911 (1980).

[65] See, e.g., Reed v. General Motors Corp., 773 F.2d 660 (5th Cir. 1985).

evidence. If jurors know a defendant is insured, they often are more prone to rule for a sympathetic plaintiff. Thus, courts must ensure that an asserted other purpose is relevant and still must weigh relevance versus prejudice in determining whether to admit the evidence under FRE 403.[66] As a last resort, a defendant may prevent the introduction of the evidence by stipulating the fact that the proponent seeks to prove.

The rule only excludes evidence of liability insurance. Other insurance policies, if relevant, may be admissible on the issue of negligence or wrongful conduct. This evidence might have similar potential for prejudice, however, which would be considered under FRE 403.

§ 5-15. Similar Happenings.

There is no federal rule to govern the admissibility of so-called "similar happenings." These happenings are collateral events with arguable relevance to the matters at issue. Because the events are collateral, they have the potential to waste time, confuse the jury and divert attention from the real issues. Their relevance is often circumstantial, which makes it difficult to determine whether the danger of prejudice, confusion or waste of time substantially outweigh the value of the evidence.

The rules regarding similar happenings are sketchy. Many courts appear to apply a test of "substantial similarity" in determining whether evidence of similar events should be admitted.[67] Nevertheless, because of the potential for prejudice and the time that may be expended in examining similar events, courts tend to view the evidence with skepticism.

The "substantial similarity" approach does little to aid the analysis. A better approach is to analyze directly the logical connection between a similar event and the case being litigated. Thus, for example, assume a plaintiff slips and falls on a slick floor on a rainy day. She alleges the floor was not kept in a dry, safe condition. Assume further that another person slipped on the floor several minutes earlier. This prior event should be analyzed not as a "similar happening," but for its probative value to determine whether the floor was slippery when the plaintiff fell.

In the example, the evidence likely would be relevant because it shows the condition of the floor near the time of the accident. If flooring of the exact same type became slippery on numerous occasions under similar conditions, the occurrences might demonstrate a characteristic of the floor in question. If evidence were offered regarding a similar but different floor at a different time,

---

[66] See City of Cleveland v. Peter Kiewit Sons' Co., 624 F.2d 749 (6th Cir. 1980); Hunziker v. Scheidemantle, 543 F.2d 489 (3d Cir. 1976).

[67] See, e.g. Ridge v. Cessna Aircraft Co., 117 F.3d 126 (4th Cir. 1997); Cameron v. Otto Bock Orthopedic Indus., 43 F.3d 14 (1st Cir. 1994).

the potential relevance might be diminished by differences in the condition of the floor and outweighed by the possibilities of confusion and waste of time. In any event, the FRE 403 balancing test provides an adequate method of resolving the issues, without resorting to any special rule.

CHAPTER 6

HEARSAY

Part I. HEARSAY RULE

Part II. ADMISSIBLE HEARSAY: GENERAL PRECEPTS

Part III. HEARSAY EXCLUSIONS

I. HEARSAY RULE

§ 6-1. Introduction (FRE 802).

The rules governing hearsay reflect simple principles, but a complex structure. As the name implies, the rule generally precludes a witness from reporting what he has "heard." It applies, however, only when the hearsay statement is offered for its truth — to prove the fact asserted in the hearsay statement.[1] For example, if a witness reported that someone told him "the light was green for the yellow car," and the statement was offered to prove that fact — the light was green for the yellow car — the statement would be hearsay. The rule also may preclude the introduction of a statement from a document to prove its truth, since the document reports someone's out-of-court statement. Numerous exceptions to the hearsay rule were developed at common law, however, for specified types of hearsay statements. These exceptions generally reflect the view that the specified statements have special reliability.

FRE 801-06 codify the hearsay rules. FRE 802 precludes the admission of hearsay unless its introduction is authorized by the rules or another provision of law. It states:

> Hearsay is not admissible except as provided by these rules or by other rules prescribed by the Supreme Court pursuant to statutory authority or by Act of Congress.

FRE 801 and 803–06 establish four classifications of out-of-court statements: (1) hearsay, (2) statements defined as non-hearsay, although they would otherwise fit the hearsay definition, (3) hearsay exceptions that are applicable whether or not the out-of-court declarant is available to testify, and (4) hearsay exceptions that are applicable only when the declarant is unavailable.

The exemptions and exceptions may not "swallow" the hearsay rule, as some commentators contend, but they certainly chew it up. The federal rules contain two major categories and eight subcategories of statements defined as non-hearsay. These categories are referred to as hearsay "exemptions" in this chapter.

---

[1] See generally GRAHAM C. LILLY, AN INTRODUCTION TO THE LAW OF EVIDENCE 208–386 (3d ed. 1996).

The rules also establish 23 hearsay exceptions that apply regardless of the declarant's availability and five exceptions that apply only when the declarant is unavailable.

This chapter covers the hearsay rule, exclusions to the rule, and the hearsay exceptions. Sections 6-2–6-9 review the hearsay rule, reasons supporting the rule, and its application. Sections 6-10–6-13 discuss considerations applicable to the hearsay exclusions and exceptions. The exclusions are reviewed in §§ 6-14–6-19, exceptions that may be invoked regardless of the declarant's availability to testify are discussed in §§ 6-20–6-34, and exceptions that apply only when the declarant is unavailable and discussed in §§ 6-35–6-42. Section 6-43 reviews the residual exception and Section 6-44 addresses impeachment of a hearsay declarant.

§ 6-2. Policies Supporting the Hearsay Rule.

Hearsay is generally inadmissible because it does not have the safeguards normally present when a witness testifies in court. A hearsay declaration is not (1) given under oath, (2) made in the presence of the trier of fact, or (3) subject to cross-examination. These safeguards exist to ensure a declarant's perception, memory, and description of events are accurate and appropriately tested.[2]

The oath was more important in securing truthful testimony centuries ago, when the average witness perceived the prospect of damnation as a greater threat than he would today, but it is still a powerful incentive to tell the truth. The ritual of taking the oath — or "affirming" that the testimony will be truthful, for those who object to swearing — underscores the need for truth and the potential consequence of a perjurious statement. For the religious, moreover, swearing by God usually has a powerful impact. Witnesses under oath generally are more careful in their descriptions than in everyday conversation. Thus, the oath still promotes accurate testimony.

Observation of demeanor often is cited as a basis to assess credibility. The witness's eye contact, mannerisms, voice strength, emotion, and other characteristics give clues as to whether he is telling the truth. Demeanor may be overvalued, however, because mannerisms often are ambiguous. Some people are accomplished liars and appear completely composed as they falsify facts; other witnesses are naturally nervous and fidget as they tell the truth. A person may *think* she is able to recognize a liar, but that belief may not reflect reality. Thus, demeanor may or may not provide a basis for judging testimony.[3]

Other aspects of the witness's presence promote truthful testimony. The witness usually testifies in the presence of persons who know the facts, which is a powerful impetus for truth. Moreover, the witness may *believe* the jury will

---

[2] FED. R. EVID. 801 advisory committee's introductory note.

[3] See generally CHRISTOPHER B. MUELLER AND LAIRD C. KIRKPATRICK, MODERN EVIDENCE: DOCTRINE AND PRACTICE, 1053–54 (1998).

discern a lie, whether or not they can do so. Further, the solemnity of the occasion may lead the witness to describe events carefully. Finally, to the extent the witness testifies against a party, that party's presence makes lying more difficult. All these aspects of live testimony promote accuracy.

The most important reason to require in-court testimony is the opportunity for cross-examination. This aspect of interrogation is a means to expose the *whole* truth, correct inaccuracies and shift emphasis. Cross-examination was extolled by Wigmore as "the greatest legal engine ever invented for the discovery of truth."[4] It is a vital feature of the Anglo-American judicial system. The procedure is guaranteed in criminal cases by the Confrontation Clause of the United States Constitution and in some civil proceedings by the Due Process Clause.[5] The prospect of cross-examination by a clever, aggressive lawyer dissuades many witnesses from fabrication. Since out-of-court statements are made without fear of cross-examination, and rarely become the subject of cross-examination, they lack this mark of reliability.

The Confrontation Clause provides a related basis for excluding hearsay testimony. The Sixth Amendment provides that in all criminal cases the accused shall enjoy the right "to be confronted with the witnesses against him. . . ."[6] Obviously, the introduction of out-of-court testimony creates tension with this right.

In general, the Confrontation Clause has been interpreted to accommodate the hearsay rule; the historic exceptions to the rule have been upheld under constitutional attack. The Supreme Court has ruled that "firmly rooted" hearsay exceptions do not violate the Confrontation Clause, nor do those that have "particularized guarantees of trustworthiness" equal to those in the "firmly rooted" exceptions.[7] New hearsay exceptions may create constitutional tensions, however.

Despite these reasons to exclude hearsay, the rule is riddled with exemptions and exceptions.[8] One reason to relax the barrier is need. Sometimes hearsay is the only, or at least the best, evidence available to establish a fact. Another justification is the special credibility that attaches to some hearsay statements; an excited utterance, for example, may be so spontaneous as to eliminate the risk of fabrication. Further, the adversary system promotes the introduction of

---

[4] WIGMORE ON EVIDENCE § 1367.

[5] Pointer v. State of Texas, 380 U.S. 400 (1965); see Morrissey v. Brewer, 408 U.S. 471 (1972); Wolff v. McDonnell, 418 U.S. 539 (1974); see § 9.1.

[6] U.S. CONST. amend VI.

[7] See Idaho v. Wright, 497 U.S. 805 (1990); White v. Illinois, 502 U.S. 346 (1992); FED. R. EVID. 801 advisory committee's introductory note.

[8] IRVING YOUNGER, HEARSAY: A PRACTICAL GUIDE THROUGH THE THICKET 107–08 (1988).

some out-of-court statements. If a party's out-of-court pronouncements under-mine his claim, for example, it might not be fair to bar the opposing party from introducing them.

The considerations of necessity, reliability, and adversarial fairness led to the creation of hearsay exceptions. One might imagine the first time a victim's dying identification of his killer produced a "hearsay" objection. No doubt the judge was moved by considerations of fairness to admit the statement, since the murder prevented the victim from testifying, but also ruled that a dying declaration has special reliability. The circumstances occurred enough to spawn a formal exception: in homicide cases, the dying declaration of the victim identifying the killer could be admitted. Specific circumstances led to the creation of other exceptions, reflecting the collective wisdom of common law judges expressed over centuries.

Although the justifications for the hearsay rule — lack of an oath, observation of demeanor, and opportunity to cross-examine — all relate to the witness's absence from court, the declarant's appearance as a witness does not remove his out-of-court statements from the hearsay category. Moreover, there is no general exception for hearsay declarations of those who testify, although the federal rules create certain limited exemptions in this category.[9]

Many attorneys mistakenly believe that the declarant's presence in court removes an out-of-court statement from hearsay. Indeed, Uniform Rule of Evidence 63(1) proposed to admit hearsay if the declarant "is present at the hearing and available for cross-examination." Nevertheless, an out-of-court declaration of a witness generally is hearsay.[10] The *statement* still carries infirmities of hearsay: it was not under oath, was made without observation of demeanor, and was not subject to contemporaneous cross-examination. Further, unless it contradicts the witness's testimony, the hearsay statement is superfluous because the witness can testify to the facts at trial.

In some administrative settings, a witness prepares written testimony, files it prior to a hearing, and adopts it on the stand. This procedure ordinarily is used when an agency, such as the Federal Energy Regulatory Commission, regulates activities requiring complex or technical testimony. Filing the testimony in advance gives the adverse party a better opportunity to prepare an effective cross-examination and otherwise counter the testimony. Thus, the agency's rules effectively waive the hearsay rule for this testimony. No such exception exists, however, in federal court.

The Federal Rules of Evidence accept the basic common law hearsay formula-tion, but create certain exemptions, adjust traditional exceptions, and add

---

[9] See FED. R. EVID. 801(d)(1).

[10] MCCORMICK ON EVIDENCE § 251 (5th ed. 1999).

authority to permit new exceptions. The Advisory Committee Note explains: "This plan is submitted as calculated to encourage growth and development in this area of the law, while conserving the values and experience of the past as a guide to the future."[11]

§ 6-3.　Recognizing Hearsay (FRE 801).

FRE 801(c) sets forth the basic definition of hearsay. It provides:

> "Hearsay" is a statement, other than one made by the declarant while testifying at the trial or hearing, offered in evidence to prove the truth of the matter asserted.

The definition of hearsay thus contains three elements: (1) a "statement," (2) made by someone when not on the witness stand, (3) offered to prove "the truth of the matter asserted." Understanding the meaning of each element — particularly the first and third — is the key to identifying hearsay.

§ 6-3(a).　"Statement."

A statement may be oral or written. It may be nonverbal conduct, if the conduct is intended as an assertion. FRE 801(a) provides that a "statement" is "(1) an oral or written assertion or (2) nonverbal conduct of a person, if it is intended by the person as an assertion."

Oral statements are easy to identify. When a witness reports she "heard" a fact, lawyers usually recognize the statement may be hearsay. Additionally, a written statement may be hearsay. If a writing is offered to prove a fact asserted in the writing, the statement is hearsay. A declarant "tells" the document something out-of-court and the document reports it, as a witness would, to the trier of fact. Further, if a witness reports a statement from a document, the testimony may be hearsay within hearsay. Attorneys often do not recognize that documents may raise hearsay problems.

Nonverbal conduct intended as an assertion is also a "statement." If an assertion is made and a person nods his assent, the "nod" is a statement. If a person points out an assailant, the act of pointing is a statement. If a witness reports this conduct, the testimony may be hearsay. Conduct not intended as an assertion, on the other hand, does not qualify as a statement. Intent must be determined from the circumstances.

A description of a person's conduct, as contrasted with what the person said, may be difficult to recognize as hearsay. The testimony does not report something "heard" or "read" and may appear on the surface to be a firsthand description of events. You must recognize when the firsthand knowledge of the relevant fact really belongs to the out-of-court actor and is communicated through the

---

[11] FED. R. EVID. 801 advisory committee's introductory note.

description of his conduct. If so, the report of the person's conduct, to prove that fact, may be hearsay.

§ 6-3(b). "Other Than" a Statement of the Declarant While "Testifying at the Trial or Hearing."

To be hearsay, the original description of a fact must have been made "other than" by the witness while on the stand; in other words, someone made the statement previously and it is *reported* by the witness or by a document.

This aspect of the rule applies to an *original* statement offered to describe an event. Obviously, when a witness reports a statement, she repeats it while "testifying at the trial or hearing." The declarant who first made the statement, however, spoke out-of-court. The assertion qualifies as hearsay because the person with firsthand knowledge of the fact did not make the statement while testifying.

Even if a witness repeats her own prior statement while on the stand, the original statement usually is hearsay because it was not made when the witness was testifying. The witness could describe the facts from the stand without running afoul of the hearsay rule, but could not quote her own prior description. For example, a witness could not testify: "I told the police I saw Smith chasing Jones down Maple Street," but could state: "I saw Smith chasing Jones down Maple Street."

§ 6-3(c). Offered to Prove the Truth of the Matter Asserted.

The most confusing aspect of the hearsay definition requires that the out-of-court statement be offered to prove "the truth of the matter asserted." This amorphous phrase means that the statement is offered to prove the fact described in the statement. For example, assume a passenger in a car exclaims: "Watch out, the brakes are bad!" If a party offered the statement at trial for its truth — to show that the brakes were bad — the statement would fit the hearsay definition. If he offered it for another purpose, such as to show the driver was warned of the need for caution, it would not be hearsay. In this situation the statement would be offered to show that it was made — thus warning the driver — and not necessarily that it was correct.[12]

Obviously, the *purpose* for which a statement is offered determines whether it may be hearsay. Moreover, some out-of-court statements may be relevant for more than one purpose. In the above example, "Watch out, the brakes are bad!"

---

[12] See United States v. Bowling, 239 F.3d 973, 977 (8th Cir. 2001) (testimony of police officers regarding statements made to them by unavailable informant admissible because statements were offered not for their truth but to establish why they were conducting surveillance); United States v. Calhoon, 97 F.3d 518, 533–34 (11th Cir. 1996) (corporate counsel's out-of-court advice to defendant was admissible not for its truth but to show that defendant was on notice that his actions were improper).

may be relevant to show the brakes were bad *and* that the driver was warned. If so, the court would admit the statement only for the non-hearsay purpose. It would instruct the jury not to consider the statement in determining whether the brakes were bad, but that the jury could use the statement to decide whether the driver was warned. In a bench trial, the judge also would consider the statement only for the permissible purpose.

Since jurors and judges may have difficulty using a statement for one purpose and ignoring it for another, the party offering an out-of-court statement may influence the resolution of both issues by securing its introduction for one. Attorneys often contend that they are offering an out-of-court statement not for its truth, but for some other purpose, when they really want the statement used to prove the fact it describes.

A lawyer may cite a non-hearsay purpose for an out-of-court statement when none exists. Thus, a key aspect of hearsay analysis is determining whether an asserted "other purpose" is relevant. Unless the supposed non-hearsay purpose affects the determination of a relevant fact, the statement should not be admitted. The legal rules in the jurisdiction, coupled with the competing claims and evidence in the case, determine what facts are relevant.

This point can be illustrated with an example. Assume that a yellow car collides with a red vehicle at an intersection. Prior to the collision, a passenger in the yellow car states: "Watch out, the brakes are bad." The driver of the red car sues for damages. If the jurisdiction permits recovery on a theory of strict liability — for instance, a recovery predicated on the ground that a defect in the yellow car caused the accident — the condition of the brakes is relevant for that purpose.[13] The statement is hearsay because it is offered to prove the condition of the brakes.

To avoid the hearsay problem, counsel might assert that the statement is offered only to show the driver was warned. In this situation, counsel offers the statement to show it was made rather than to prove the fact it describes. Thus, the court would have to determine whether the warning itself is relevant. If the plaintiff relies solely on a strict liability theory, the driver's knowledge of a defect is not relevant; the defect alone would support liability. Thus, the only relevant purpose of the statement is to prove its truth, and the statement should be excluded as hearsay.

If the theory is negligence, the driver's knowledge of the defect probably is relevant on whether he exercised proper care; thus, the warning itself is a fact of consequence. The statement could be admitted to show the driver had reason to know of the defect but could not be considered in determining whether the brakes were bad.

---

[13] It may also be relevant to show what caused the accident, whether the theory were strict liability or negligence. The statement would be hearsay if offered for that purpose.

The "relevant fact" analysis is a useful tool in deciding whether statements are offered to prove "the truth of the matter asserted." If the relevant fact is the matter described in the statement, the statement may be hearsay. If evidence reporting the statement proves some other relevant fact, it would not be hearsay.

§ 6-4. Hearsay Theory.

The factors used to evaluate testimony provide the theoretical basis for the hearsay rule. Any time facts are reported by someone else, the listener is dependent on the speaker's capabilities and motivations in determining what occurred. The following factors affect the accuracy of the report:

1. Perception. Did the speaker accurately perceive the event?
2. Memory. Does the speaker accurately remember what he perceived?
3. Narration. Is the speaker's description of the event accurate? This factor in turn breaks down into two elements.
   a. Sincerity. Is the speaker trying to describe the facts accurately?
   b. Description. Does the language chosen by the speaker clearly portray what occurred?[14]

Trial procedures — the oath, the presence of the witness, and cross-examination — encourage witnesses to accurately report events and allow the trier of fact to evaluate the report.[15]

When a witness with firsthand knowledge reports a fact, these factors come into play. The witness may have misperceived the event. He may not remember it accurately or may have developed a false memory through suggestion or imagination. The witness's account may be deliberately skewed to support a litigation position. Even if sincere, the witness may misdescribe the facts. The trier implicitly considers these factors in determining whether an account is correct.

Any time a witness takes the stand, of course, the trier of fact must evaluate the accuracy of his testimony. The four potential pitfalls — perception, memory, sincerity, description — are present whenever the witness reports facts. These risks are offset, however, by the protections of the oath, personal appearance

---

[14] See FED. R. EVID. 801 advisory committee's introductory note:

> The factors to be considered in evaluating the testimony of a witness are perception, memory, and narration. Sometimes a fourth is added, sincerity, but in fact it seems merely to be an aspect of the three already mentioned. (Citations omitted.)

[15] *Id.* The Federal Rules Advisory Committee states:

> In order to encourage the witness to do his best with respect to each of these factors, and to expose any inaccuracies which may enter in, the Anglo-American tradition has evolved three conditions under which witnesses will ideally be required to testify: (1) under oath, (2) in the personal presence of the trier of fact, (3) subject to cross-examination.

and cross-examination. In theory, hearsay problems arise only when the pitfalls all exist *for the out-of-court declarant*. Thus, when a witness reports a statement of another, and all the problems of evaluating the testimony are present for the out-of-court declaration, the statement qualifies as hearsay.

As a device for analysis, some commentators use the so-called "testimonial triangle," conceived by Professor Lawrence Tribe.[16] The triangle permits the classification of hearsay problems as "right leg" or "left leg" issues. The right leg issues are whether the declarant's belief in a fact reflects reality (the perception and memory issues), while the left leg issues are whether the declarant's statement really reflects his belief (the sincerity and "ambiguity," or description, issues). The triangle appears as follows:

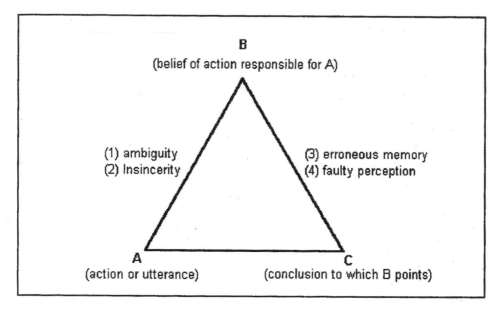

According to Professor Tribe, the trier may conclude that a fact exists ("C") only by eliminating the perception and memory obstacles to the declarant's accurate belief ("B") and the ambiguity and sincerity obstacles to an accurate description of that belief.[17] When all four obstacles exist as to an out-of-court declaration, the statement in theory is hearsay. Professor Stephen Saltzburg has suggested a linear diagram to "straighten out" the triangular analysis. Nevertheless, Professor Saltzburg employs the same left side and right side principles.[18]

---

[16] Lawrence H. Tribe, *Triangulating Hearsay*, 87 HARV. L. REV. 957 (1974); GRAHAM LILLY, AN INTRODUCTION TO THE LAW OF EVIDENCE, 246–247 (3d ed. 1996).

[17] Lawrence H. Tribe, *Triangulating Hearsay*, 87 HARV. L. REV. at 959 (1974).

[18] Stephen A. Saltzburg, *A Special Aspect of Relevance: Countering Negative Inferences Associated with the Absence of Evidence,* 66 CALIF. L. REV. 1011 (1978).

A simpler method of conceptualizing this hearsay theory is to employ a picture. At least two declarants are always involved when a hearsay problem arises — the in-court witness (or document) and the out-of-court speaker (or document). If we assume both are persons, a useful tool to analyze hearsay is the following drawing:

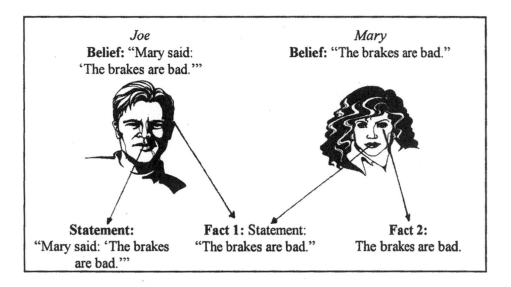

When Joe takes the stand and gives the testimony depicted here — "Mary said: 'The brakes are bad' " — he is describing a fact, that Mary made that statement. As to that fact, Joe has personal knowledge. To conclude that Mary's statement was made, the trier of fact must conclude that Joe accurately reports the fact. The trier must believe Joe heard the statement and remembers it correctly and describes it sincerely and accurately. All the problems inherent in evaluating testimony exist for Joe's description, but since he is on the stand, takes an oath, and is subject to cross-examination, the pitfalls are overcome.

Whether the testimonial problems exist for the out-of-court speaker depends on the relevant fact. If the relevant fact is whether the statement was made at all — perhaps to show the driver was warned — the only problems are those associated with Joe's testimony. The accuracy of Mary's description is not in question.

If the relevant fact is whether Mary *believed* the brakes were bad — say, if she were the driver and the issue was whether she knew of the defect — the left leg problems exist, but not the right leg problems. The accuracy of Mary's description and her sincerity are in question, but not how she acquired her belief. If the relevant fact is whether the brakes were bad — perhaps in a defectiveness case — both the left leg and right leg pitfalls exist. The trier of fact has to consider whether Mary accurately perceived the condition of the brakes and remembered her perception when she stated her belief, as well as the accuracy and sincerity of her description.

Since Mary's statement was made out of court, the trier of fact would have considerable difficulty evaluating its accuracy. Absent hearing the statement and observing her demeanor, the trier could not judge her sincerity or descriptive ability. Without cross-examination, the trier would have little basis for judging her memory or perception. Indeed, the trier probably could not determine whether Mary even had the knowledge to judge the condition of the brakes.

When the out-of-court statement is the relevant fact, the statement is not hearsay. Counsel offers the witness's report of the statement only to show it was made. When the relevant fact is the belief or knowledge of the out-of-court declarant, the statement describing that belief or knowledge should not be hearsay according to some theorists because it involves only "one leg" of hearsay pitfalls. The declarant's sincerity and clarity in describing her belief must be considered, but not her perception and memory. According to two commentators, a statement in this situation should not be classified as hearsay:

> Since the right leg problems are probably the most significant hearsay dangers, and since many hearsay exceptions are justified by only some support [to offset the "dangers" inherent in] one of the legs, it makes sense to classify statements used so as to eliminate right leg dangers as not hearsay.[19]

When a statement is offered to prove the fact it describes — and thus involves both "legs" of hearsay pitfalls — it is hearsay.

Hearsay theory and its definition diverge with respect to one type of statement — that in which the declarant describes her own state of mind and the statement is offered to prove that state of mind. A statement of belief offered to prove that belief fits the hearsay definition, but would not involve the right leg pitfalls of perception and memory. Thus, if Mary said "I am well aware the brakes are bad," and the statement were offered to show her awareness, the statement would fit the hearsay definition because it is offered to prove "the truth of the matter asserted." This conflict of theory and definition is not a problem, however, because a hearsay exception exists for statements describing state of mind.[20]

A statement offered *circumstantially* to prove state of mind does not fit the hearsay definition. For instance, a professor's statement — "I look forward to meeting the eager students in my Saturday morning makeup class" — might be

---

[19] RICHARD O. LEMPERT AND STEPHEN A. SALTZBURG, A MODERN APPROACH TO EVIDENCE 358 (2d ed. 1982).

[20] FED. R. EVID. 803(3).

offered to show the professor had lost all ability to judge student attitudes. The statement would not be hearsay because it was offered not to prove the professor's expectation, but his lack of judgment.

§ 6-5. Examples of Statements Not Offered for Their Truth.

Parties often offer out-of-court statements for purposes other than their truth. These situations usually fall into the following categories.

§ 6-5(a). Statements Having Legal Significance.

Often a central issue in a lawsuit is whether a statement was made. The statement itself tends to prove a fact of consequence, so the statement is offered for its own sake rather than to prove a fact it describes. Examples include the following:

Contracts. In a contract case a binding agreement depends on an offer and acceptance. Thus, statements of the parties may be relevant, whether or not they prove some other fact. If Jones says to Smith, "I will buy your car for $500," and Smith responds, "Sold," the statements form an agreement regardless of the true intent of the parties or their subsequent conduct. Thus, the statements are not hearsay.

Legal declarations. Some communications have special legal significance. For a marriage ceremony, for example, the words of the parties and the celebrant establish the marital relationship. If the fact of marriage were an issue, a party could offer the statements simply to show they were spoken. Similarly, a statement designating a beneficiary, disowning an heir, or donating property may carry legal consequences.

Further, statements may modify the legal effect of parties' actions. Thus, if Mary transfers $20,000 to her fiancé, Bill, stating, "This is a loan," the statement would show the transfer was not a gift. In this case, the statement itself has legal consequences and is not hearsay if offered to prove the legal act.

Defamatory statements. In libel and slander cases, the defamatory statement is an element of the claim. If Dodd tells others that Wittmann is "a scoundrel and a thief," Wittmann may later offer the statement to prove defamation. Wittmann would offer the statement not for its truth, but to show it was made; indeed, Wittmann would also try to prove the statement was false.

Fraud. In a fraud case the defendant's representations (or omissions) are an element of the claim. Thus, Cunningham might offer Louiselle's statement, "The engine in this car is 100 percent new," not for its truth, but to show the statement was made to induce a purchase. Cunningham also would seek to prove the engine was *not* new.

§ 6-5(b). Notice or Awareness.

In some cases whether a person had notice of a fact, or was aware of it, affects liability. Thus, for example, if Judice fell on a staircase after Zimmering told him "Watch out, that staircase is slippery," the owner might offer the statement to show that Judice knew of the risk and assumed it, or that he was contributorily negligent. Similarly, if Judice said "I'm going to be careful on these stairs," the statement might be offered to show he was aware of the risk. For these purposes, the statements would not be hearsay. Of course, a party might also offer the statements for their truth, but for that purpose they would be hearsay.

§ 6-5(c). Impeachment.

In many cases a party offers a witness's prior inconsistent statement to show she is lying. Assume the issue is whether Becker's car entered the intersection when the light was red. Johnson, a witness, told an investigator shortly after the accident that Becker "ran a red light." At the trial Johnson testifies for Becker that "the light was green when Becker's car entered the intersection." In this situation Johnson's prior out-of-court statement can be used to show she is lying, even if it is hearsay as to the color of the light.

§ 6-5(d). Statements Circumstantially Showing State of Mind.

In cases where a person's state of mind is relevant, statements that circumstantially show that state of mind are not hearsay. The statement is offered not for its truth, but as the basis for an inference concerning the person's mental state. Thus, if the mental capacity of the declarant were in issue, his statement — "I am surrounded by alien beings from Jupiter" — might be offered to show he lacked a grip on reality. The declaration, "Jack is a no-good s.o.b." might be offered in a testamentary case to show the decedent did not like Jack. In neither case would the statements be offered — nor even have relevance — for their truth.

A statement that circumstantially proves state of mind is not hearsay because the statement is not offered to prove the fact it describes. Nevertheless, the trier must conclude that the statement reflects the declarant's mental state. In making this inference, the trier encounters the "left side" hearsay pitfalls — the statement may be insincere or ambiguous. One can easily imagine the term "no good s.o.b." used in fun or as a term of endearment. The trier does not encounter the "right leg" problems, however, because the declarant does not perceive and remember an extraneous fact when he implicitly reveals his own state of mind.

If the declarant makes a statement that directly describes her state of mind — "I am in love with John" — and it is offered to show that state of mind, the statement fits the hearsay definition. The statement is offered to prove the fact it describes, even though it does not involve the "right leg" hearsay pitfalls.

Paradoxically, this direct evidence of state of mind is more trustworthy than a statement used circumstantially, because there is less risk of misinterpretation. Nevertheless, a hearsay exception exists for statements that directly describe states of mind, so the fact that the statement may be hearsay is unimportant in practice. [21]

§ 6-5(e). The "Thing Done," or "Res Gestae."

Occasionally, spontaneous declarations occur as part of an event. Witnesses may report these statements because they occurred and explain other events, rather than for their truth. Assume for example that a policeman describes his pursuit of a bank robber. The policeman testifies:

> A bystander said, "A man with a gun ran down the street." I then ran down Green Street and found the defendant hiding under a house. I ordered him to throw down the gun and arrested him.

The policeman's description of the bystander's statement is helpful to understand the event — how the officer apprehended the defendant. In that sense, it is offered to show the statement occurred and not necessarily for its truth. For the intended purpose it is not hearsay.

Statements uttered during an occurrence traditionally were referred to as "res gestae," which means they are part of "the thing done." [22] This term was often misused, however, to admit statements that were really offered for their truth. [23] Thus, its use fell into disfavor with legal scholars. The federal rules do not employ the term. [24]

A statement that is relevant in itself is not hearsay because it is not offered for its truth. Thus, labeling the statement "res gestae" is unnecessary. To the extent the statement is offered to prove a fact it describes, it is hearsay and must fit an exclusion or exception. Calling the statement "res gestae" does not remove it from hearsay.

Many statements made during events can be used both to show they occurred and to prove facts they describe. Thus, the statements could have a hearsay and

---

[21] FED. R. EVID. 803(3).

[22] GRAHAM C. LILLY, AN INTRODUCTION TO THE LAW OF EVIDENCE 279 (3d ed. 1996).

[23] Id.

[24] A hearsay exclusion for "things said or done" is created by the Louisiana Code of Evidence. Article 801(D)(4) provides:

> **Things said or done.** The statements are events speaking for themselves under the immediate pressure of the occurrence, through the instructive, impulsive and spontaneous words and acts of the participants, and not the words of the participants when narrating the events, and which are necessary incidents of the criminal act, or immediate concomitants of it, or form in conjunction with it one continuous transaction.

non-hearsay purpose. In the above example, for instance, the bystander's statement might be relevant both to show that the defendant ran down Green Street and why the officer did so. In this situation, the court must ensure that the statement is relevant for a non-hearsay purpose and, if the court admits the statement, instruct the jury to consider it only for that point. Of course, many spontaneous declarations fit hearsay exceptions, such as the exceptions for present sense impressions and excited utterances,[25] and are admissible in any event.

§ 6-6. Hearsay Distinguished from Lack of Personal Knowledge.

Generally, a witness must have personal knowledge to testify to facts. FRE 602 establishes this "foundation" requirement, providing that a "witness may not testify to a matter unless evidence is introduced sufficient to support a finding that the witness has personal knowledge of the matter."[26] The personal knowledge requirement often overlaps the rule against hearsay. The rules are conceptually different, however, and do not serve identical purposes.[27]

When a fact witness has no personal knowledge, the testimony is objectionable for lack of foundation. The witness may simply make up, or surmise, what occurred. Alternatively, the witness may rely on hearsay. If the witness does not report the hearsay, the foundation objection is appropriate because personal knowledge is lacking as to the facts he relates. If the witness repeats the hearsay, he *does have* personal knowledge of the fact he reports — the statement — but the statement is objectionable as hearsay.

For example, assume a witness testifies that "The traffic light was red when the yellow car entered the intersection." The witness states he was standing near the intersection when the accident occurred. On cross-examination, the witness admits he was looking the other way and did not really see the accident. The witness further states that he "heard" from another bystander that the light was red when the yellow car entered the intersection.

As to the first statement, that the light was red, the witness lacks personal knowledge. The witness has a hearsay basis for the statement, but until he testifies to the hearsay, the appropriate objection is lack of personal knowledge. When the witness reports the out-of-court *statement*, which is offered to prove the light was red, the basis for an objection shifts to the rule against hearsay. The witness now has personal knowledge of the statement he reports — "Someone told me the light was red when the yellow car entered the intersection" — but that

---

[25] FED. R. EVID. 803(1), (2).

[26] The rule is modified in FED. R. EVID. 703, which permits experts to rely on information beyond their personal knowledge, if it is reasonably relied on in the expert's field, in providing opinion testimony.

[27] See United States v. Nieto, 60 F.3d 1464, 1467 (10th Cir. 1995). See DAVID F. BINDER, HEARSAY HANDBOOK §§ 6.01–6.02, at 95–97 (3d ed. 1991).

statement is hearsay. Of course, the witness still lacks personal knowledge of the relevant fact — the color of the light — and both objections are meritorious as to that fact. Thus, after bringing out the witness's hearsay basis, counsel should argue that the witness lacks personal knowledge of the relevant fact *and* is relying on hearsay.

§ 6-7. Hearsay Within Hearsay (FRE 805).

A hearsay statement may itself contain hearsay. Assume, for instance, a witness testifies: "John told me that Mary told him 'The traffic light was red when the yellow car entered the intersection.' " The witness is reporting a statement made by John, which incorporates a statement made by Mary, which is offered to prove the fact Mary's statement describes. The hearsay pitfalls exist not only for Mary's statement, but for John's report to the witness. Thus, the statement in court is "hearsay within hearsay."

The federal rules implicitly exclude hearsay within hearsay unless an exception exists for each hearsay component of the statement.[28] FRE 805 provides:

> Hearsay included within hearsay is not excluded under the hearsay rule if each part of the combined statements conforms with an exception to the hearsay rule provided in these rules.

The Advisory Committee notes: "On principle it scarcely seems open to doubt that the hearsay rule should not call for exclusion of a hearsay statement which includes a further hearsay statement when both conform to the requirements of a hearsay exception."[29] The rule and comment implicitly endorse the corollary: hearsay within hearsay should be excluded unless an exception exists for each level of hearsay.

Hearsay within hearsay can be difficult to recognize. Assume a witness testifies: "I read in a report that the traffic light was red when the yellow car entered the intersection." Counsel may identify the witness's statement as hearsay, but might not realize that the report, if offered, also would be hearsay. Thus, the testimony contains hearsay within hearsay. Someone told the report, which told the witness, who testifies to the statement in court. The report also may contain multiple hearsay layers, since the author may have relied on information passed on by others.

Documents often contain hearsay within hearsay. Just because an exception exists for the hearsay document does not necessarily mean that the hearsay it contains is admissible. In the case of regularly kept records, hearsay within hearsay may be admitted so long as the information in the document was communicated in the course of a "regularly conducted business activity"; FRE

---

[28] See, e.g., Wilkerson v. Columbus Separate School Dist., 985 F.2d 815 (5th Cir. 1993).

[29] FED. R. EVID. 805 advisory committee's note.

803(6) implicitly requires that the communicators have a business *duty* to be accurate. See § 6-26. In most other cases, each level of hearsay within hearsay must satisfy a hearsay exception.[30]

Since FRE 805 literally applies only to "hearsay within hearsay," it arguably does not require a separate exception for hearsay incorporated in statements defined as "non-hearsay" under FRE 801(d). The analysis nevertheless is the same, requiring a hearsay exclusion or exception for each level of hearsay. A "non-hearsay" statement that contains hearsay is like other evidence that reports hearsay. In each case, the hearsay is inadmissible unless it satisfies a hearsay exclusion or exception. The fact that an out-of-court statement is defined as "not hearsay"[31] does not authorize the introduction of hearsay within the statement.

§ 6-8.　Special Hearsay-Related Problems.

The hearsay rule raises a number of practical and theoretical issues. These special problems are discussed below.

§ 6-8(a).　Documents.

When a document is offered to prove a fact it describes — as opposed to being offered to prove its existence — the statement in the document fits the hearsay definition. The document contains an out-of-court statement that is offered for its truth. Put another way, the statement is hearsay because someone told the document the relevant fact and the document reports that fact to the trier.

Statements in documents often do not draw hearsay objections. Lawyers sometimes miss the objection because there is no oral report of hearsay. Moreover, attorneys often focus on the authenticity of documents, ignoring other potential objections. Further, the tangible nature of documents gives them apparent credibility. Nevertheless, all the hearsay pitfalls exist when a party offers a statement in a document for its truth: the author's perception or memory may be faulty, and her narration may be insincere or inaccurate. Further, the declarant does not take the oath, does not appear in court, and is not cross-examined. Nor can the opposing party cross-examine the document itself. Thus, strong reasons support applying the hearsay rule.[32]

Of course, many documents are offered for non-hearsay reasons. Documents may be relevant themselves — to prove a contract, the course of negotiations,

---

[30] See Bonder v. Bic Corp., 947 F.2d 1531, 1533–34 (6th Cir. 1991) (social worker's written report that child stated that she had started fire with matches was admissible because social worker's report fit the business record exception and child's statement was the statement of a party opponent).

[31] FED. R. EVID. 801(d).

[32] Paradoxically, the testimonial pitfalls do not exist for the document itself. Whatever narration, memory or perception problems exist for the author, the document reports faithfully what it is told. This point is unavailing, however, because the hearsay rule is concerned with the statement of the out-of-court declarant.

notice, necessary recordation, or other matters. When a party offers a document to prove a fact described in the document, however, it fits the hearsay definition. Documents always involve a potential hearsay objection because they report the author's out-of-court statements. Counsel should use the "relevant fact" analysis to determine whether a statement is offered for its truth.

§ 6-8(b). Omissions.

An interesting hearsay issue is whether an omission from a statement can be hearsay. Since hearsay is defined as a "statement," and a "statement" is defined as an "assertion," one might argue that the absence of an assertion does not qualify.[33] The better analysis treats an omission as hearsay, however, if it is used like a statement offered for its truth.

Assume a register at a doctor's office, showing that Dan Smith is not listed, is offered to prove that Dan Smith never appeared for treatment. If the register were offered to prove that others did sign, it would include written assertions offered for their truth, which would be hearsay. Since the register is offered to prove a name was *not* entered, however, the question arises whether the omission fits the hearsay definition.

Although the register is offered to prove an omission, the evidence is meaningful only if the trier of fact considers the names that *are* listed. In effect, the register shows all the people who *did* register on the day in question, so the factfinder may draw the inference that Dan Smith did not. Each name on the list is offered for the implicit assertion, "I register as John Doe." To the extent affirmative statements must be considered to give the omission meaning, the register is classic hearsay, because the testimonial pitfalls exist for each out-of-court declarant.

This analysis applies to most omissions. A blank piece of paper, or a description of a silent man, would be "omissions" that could be considered non-hearsay, but they would prove nothing. Only in the context of affirmative statements do non-statements typically take on meaning. To the extent that context is required, and hearsay statements provide it, the omission should be considered hearsay.

The federal rules do not necessarily adopt this view; nevertheless, the framers deemed it necessary to create a hearsay exception for the "[a]bsence of an entry" in a business record.[34] The Advisory Committee notes without explanation that the omission is "probably not hearsay as defined in Rule 801."[35] It states, however, that "decisions may be found which class the evidence not only as

---

[33] See FED. R. EVID. 801(a), (c).

[34] FED. R. EVID. 803(7).

[35] FED. R. EVID. 803(7) advisory committee's note.

hearsay but also as not within any exception."**36** Thus, the exception is created "to set the question at rest in favor of admissibility. . . ."**37**

§ 6-8(c). Facts Implicit in Intended Assertions.

Occasionally, a statement is offered to prove a fact implicit, but not described, in the statement. Thus, the statement is not literally offered to prove "the truth of the matter asserted." Assume, for example, a child is hurt in a playground incident, badly spraining his shoulder. When he sees the teacher, he states: "Johnny broke my shoulder." A party would offer this statement not for its literal truth, but to prove that Johnny caused the sprain; in effect, the factfinder would interpret the statement in light of facts unknown to the speaker when it was made. In this situation the statement is hearsay. To the extent it is offered to prove a fact — here that Johnny caused the injury — it is offered for its truth. All of the hearsay pitfalls exist as to that fact, because the out-of-court speaker must accurately perceive, remember and describe the fact for it to be correct.

Many statements take on meaning in a particular context. Law enforcement agencies often use code words in radio transmissions. The statement, "The bird is on the way to the nest, and he has the worm," properly interpreted might mean, "The suspect is on the way home with the cocaine." Because people often use jargon, an explanation may be necessary to understand the meaning of the terms. "He's a really bad dude" might mean "He's a neat guy." When statements like these are offered to prove the facts they implicitly describe, in context, they should be treated as hearsay.

§ 6-8(d). Nonverbal Conduct as Hearsay.

Often a person intends to communicate information without speaking. A victim viewing a lineup may point to the person who assaulted him. Individuals in an audience may raise their hands when asked to indicate whether they fit a certain category. Persons who are mute, or communicating with the deaf, may employ sign language. To the extent conduct is intended as an assertion, it is a "statement" within the hearsay definition. FRE 801(a), which defines the term "statement," includes "nonverbal conduct of a person, if it is intended by the person as an assertion." Of course, to be hearsay, the conduct also must be offered to prove the truth of the intended assertion.

§ 6-8(e). Nonassertive Conduct.

Under FRE 801(a), conduct not intended as an assertion is not a "statement" and cannot fit the hearsay definition. Commentators have argued that some nonassertive conduct is used by the trier of fact in the same manner as an assertion

---

36 *Id.*

37 *Id.*

and should be classified as hearsay. An example that emerged from a hypothetical discussion in the early case of *Wright v. Doe dem Tatham*[38] is that of a sea captain observed checking his ship before embarking on a voyage with his family. Theoretically, if his conduct were offered to prove the ship was seaworthy, the trier of fact might infer that the sea captain formed a belief it was seaworthy, since he took the boat to sea, and would assert that belief if asked. Thus, the trier's logic might involve the same hearsay pitfalls as it would for an actual assertion.

Although this analysis has theoretical appeal, it does not justify extending the rule to nonassertive conduct. First, conduct may be relevant even if the trier does not infer what the actor believed. In the ship captain example, the mere fact that he checked the boat may be a fact of consequence in determining seaworthiness. Certainly if no one checked the boat, that fact would be relevant and not hearsay; allowing proof that someone did check it seems equally appropriate. Additionally, the captain's departure on the voyage is relevant to show how the ship was lost. Thus, the evidence might well be used for a non-hearsay purpose.

Second, even if interpreting conduct requires logic similar to that for a statement, the conduct still is not an assertion. Hearsay is objectionable in part because people filter and color communications with their own experiences, biases and imagination. The information gleaned from conduct does not depend on the actor's communication skills. As the Advisory Committee states:

> Admittedly evidence of this character is untested with respect to the perception, memory, and narration (or their equivalents) of the actor, but the Advisory Committee is of the view that these dangers are minimal in the absence of an intent to assert and do not justify the loss of the evidence on hearsay grounds. . . . [T]he likelihood [of fabrication] is less with the nonverbal than with the assertive verbal conduct.[39]

Third, classifying the circumstances in which conduct should be treated as hearsay would be difficult. Hearsay objections at trial must be instantaneous; trial lawyers do not have the luxury of analyzing how jurors might infer facts from a person's conduct. A hearsay rule applicable to nonassertive conduct would be difficult to apply in practice and would lead to haphazard results. Therefore, the approach in the federal rules is reasonable.

§ 6-8(f). Facts Determined by Mechanical Process.

Some real evidence provides information in a manner analogous to hearsay. An x-ray or photograph, for example, reflects information "perceived" in a mechanical process and "reported" visually to the observer. A radar gun

---

[38] 7 AD. & E. 313 (Ex. 1837), *aff'd* 5 Cl. & Fin. 670 (H.L. 1838).

[39] FED. R. EVID. 801 advisory committee's note.

"perceives" the speed of a car and "reports" that speed to a traffic officer. This information is not hearsay because it does not involve human perception, memory and narration. When human assertions are involved, as when an analyst inputs information into a computer, the human aspects of the communications may constitute hearsay. Thus, the attorney should focus on whether mechanical processes include information provided by humans.

§ 6-9.   Hearsay in Electronic Communications and Data Compilations.

The increasing use of computers makes it more and more likely that parties will rely on computer-generated material to prove facts in court. In addition to authenticity and original writing issues, this material often raises hearsay issues. To the extent a party offers messages or information from the Internet, computer-generated material or other electronic evidence to prove facts described in the electronic statements, the material may be hearsay.

Assuming a party can establish the authenticity of electronic information and there are no original writing issues, the hearsay analysis should be much like that accorded documentary evidence. An e-mail message, for instance, would not be hearsay if offered for its independent legal significance — say to prove a contract — but would constitute hearsay if offered to prove facts it described. Computer-generated records or data compilations would also be hearsay if a party offered them for their truth. The information nevertheless might be admissible under a hearsay exclusion or exception.

Parties in litigation often obtain information from Internet web sites and offer it to prove facts described on the web site. Assuming a party can establish authenticity, traditional hearsay analysis should apply. Statements from the Internet offered for their truth constitute hearsay. A party's statement on its own web site should be admissible against him as an "admission," however, and many Internet publications may be admissible under hearsay exceptions. The exceptions for public records and reports (FRE 803(8)), market reports and commercial publications (FRE 803(17)), and learned treatises and periodicals (FRE 803(18)) may permit the introduction of this information.

As noted in § 8-10, material from the Internet may present special reliability problems because of the potential for alteration of electronic messages and publications. Courts should deal with these potential problems as authenticity and original writing issues, however, rather than hearsay issues. If the material can be authenticated as "what its proponent claims" under FRE 901(a), the traditional hearsay analysis should apply.

II.   ADMISSIBLE HEARSAY: GENERAL PRECEPTS

§ 6-10.   Structure of Hearsay Exclusions and Exceptions.

Under the federal rules, three types of out-of-court statements may be admitted although they fit the basic hearsay definition. They include:

1. Statements excluded from the hearsay definition [FRE 801(d)];
2. Hearsay exceptions that apply whether or not the out-of-court declarant is "available" to testify in court [FRE 803];
3. Hearsay exceptions that apply only if the out-of-court declarant is "unavailable" to testify [FRE 804].

The Advisory Committee Notes do not explain why they draw a distinction between statements defined as "not hearsay" and hearsay "exceptions." The distinction does not appear to have evidentiary consequences in the federal system; a factfinder may rely on a statement admissible under an exception to the same extent as a statement defined as non-hearsay. The drafters may have expected the rules to be adopted in the states, where the classification could have evidentiary consequences, such as a requirement of corroboration for a hearsay as opposed to a non-hearsay statement.[40]

§ 6-11. Foundation Required for Out-of-Court Declaration.

Even if an out-of-court declaration is admissible under an exemption or exception to the hearsay rule, the declarant generally must have firsthand knowledge for a fact description or the specialized knowledge required for a technical opinion. Thus, counsel may be able to exclude the statement for lack of a foundation.

The out-of-court statement itself, or the circumstances described by the witness who reports it, may contain facts establishing the declarant's personal knowledge. If not, the proponent must demonstrate a foundation. A showing that an out-of-court declarant possesses specialized knowledge ordinarily requires testimony, but might be inferred from circumstances. If a declarant wore a doctor's hospital coat and an insignia with an "M.D.," for instance, her observation that a patient was "in shock" might be presumed to have a foundation.

For certain out-of-court statements, the foundation requirement is waived or relaxed. For some "admissions" — statements of a party that are offered against that party — no showing of firsthand knowledge or expertise is required. The foundation requirements also are relaxed for statements in business and public records. Generally, however, a showing of foundation is required to admit an out-of-court declaration.

---

[40] See RICHARD O. LEMPERT AND STEPHEN A. SALTZBURG, A MODERN APPROACH TO EVIDENCE 422 (2d ed. 1982). The authors state:

> The distinction between a statement which is considered not hearsay and a statement which is considered hearsay but admitted under some exception is not always a meaningless one. In some jurisdictions one might be entitled to an instruction that hearsay evidence merits less weight than non-hearsay evidence, and occasionally one will be in a jurisdiction where the substantive law in certain areas requires corroboration of admissible hearsay. . . .

§ 6-12.   Standard of Proof for Determining Fulfillment of Conditions for Admitting Statements Under Hearsay Exclusions and Exceptions.

Although it dealt only with the admissibility of statements of coconspirators, *Bourjaily v. United States*[41] provides guidance concerning the standards for admitting statements as non-hearsay or under hearsay exceptions. *Bourjaily* indicates that a court should apply the preponderance of the evidence standard in determining whether conditions of admissibility are fulfilled. Additionally, it suggests that the federal rules supersede the prior rule against "bootstrapping" out-of-court statements into evidence.

In *Bourjaily*, the United States Supreme Court ruled that the conditions for the introduction of a coconspirator's statement pursuant to FRE 801(d)(2)(E) need only be proven by a preponderance of evidence. In doing so, it said:

> We are . . . guided by our prior decisions regarding admissibility determinations that hinge on preliminary factual questions. We have traditionally required that these matters be established by a preponderance of proof. . . . [T]he evidentiary standard is unrelated to the burden of proof on the substantive issues, be it a criminal case, or a civil case.[42]

Since *Bourjaily* was a criminal case, and dealt with an especially controversial category of admission, the adoption of the relaxed "preponderance" standard suggests that the same test would apply to other out-of-court statements.

Bourjaily also held that the court can consider the statement itself in determining whether the conditions for its admissibility are fulfilled, thus overruling decisions requiring independent proof of the conditions. Prior decisions prohibited a court from "bootstrapping" a statement into evidence — permitting hearsay to "lift itself by its own bootstraps to the level of competent evidence."[43] The Court held that FRE 104, which provides that courts are *not* bound by the rules of evidence in deciding most preliminary questions of admissibility, overruled the "bootstrapping" rule. The Court stated:

> [In enacting FRE 104] Congress has decided that courts may consider hearsay in making these factual determinations. Out-of-court statements made by anyone, including putative conspirators, are often hearsay. Even if they are, they may be considered, *Glasser* and the bootstrapping rule notwithstanding. . . .[44]

---

[41] 483 U.S. 171 (1987).

[42] *Id.* at 175 (citations omitted).

[43] Glasser v. United States, 315 U.S. 60, 75 (1942).

[44] 483 U.S. at 178.

This broad language, and the Court's reliance on FRE 104, implies that other out-of-court statements may "bootstrap" themselves into evidence. The statements may require corroboration, but courts can use them in determining whether conditions for their own admissibility are fulfilled. Thus, for example, an agent's statement — "I am the driver for Quicky Cleaners" — could be considered in determining whether an agency relationship existed.

FRE 801(d)(2) was amended in 1997 to add language regulating the extent to which a statement may be considered in determining the existence of an agency relationship or a conspiracy. The amendment adopts the holding of *Bourjaily* for coconspirator's statement and extends it to agency statements. Additionally, the amendment addresses an issue left open by *Bourjaily* — whether the statement alone is sufficient to establish the conspiracy — by providing that the statement alone cannot establish the conspiracy or agency relationship. The amendment states:

> The contents of the statement shall be considered but are not alone sufficient to establish the declarant's authority under subdivision (C), the agency or employment relationship and scope thereof under subdivision (D), or the existence of the conspiracy and the participation therein of the declarant and the party against whom the statement is offered under subdivision (E).

The Advisory Committee note explains that the amendment "codifies the holding in *Bourjaily*" by stating that a court shall "consider the contents of a coconspirator's statement in determining 'the existence of the conspiracy and the participation therein of the declarant and the party against whom the statement is offered.' "[45] Additionally, the amendment provides that the statement alone will not suffice to establish the prerequisites for its introduction, but the court must consider in addition the circumstances surrounding the statement, such as the identity of the speaker, the context in which the statement was made, or evidence corroborating the contents of the statement in making its determination as to each preliminary question.[46] Finally, the amendment "extends the reasoning of *Bourjaily*" to statements offered under subdivisions (C) and (D) of Rule 801(d)(2).[47]

§ 6-13. Confrontation Clause Implications of Hearsay Exceptions.

The Sixth Amendment to the United States Constitution provides that a criminal defendant has a right to be confronted with the witnesses against him. This provision serves the same purposes as the hearsay rule: requiring the

---

[45] Fed. R. Evid. 801(d)(2), 1997 Amend., advisory committee's note (quoting Bourjaily).

[46] *Id.*

[47] Fed. R. Evid. 801(d)(2), 1997 Amend., advisory committee's note

appearance of witnesses in court, under oath, and subject to cross-examination.[48] The Supreme Court has extended the Sixth Amendment guarantee to the states.[49]

Since hearsay exemptions and exceptions admit testimony that is not subject to confrontation and cross-examination, they may conflict with the principles underlying the Confrontation Clause. Nevertheless, while the United States Supreme Court has not equated the hearsay rule and the Confrontation Clause, it has interpreted the Confrontation Clause to permit the introduction of out-of-court statements that fit within "firmly rooted" exceptions to the hearsay rule or have equivalent guarantees of trustworthiness.[50]

There is no constitutional requirement, in most cases, that the prosecution prove the declarant is unavailable before admitting testimony under a hearsay exception. In a 1980 decision, *Ohio v. Roberts*,[51] the Court suggested that the Confrontation Clause normally requires the prosecution to show that the declarant is unavailable when it attempts to introduce his out-of-court statement.[52] Later cases restrict that ruling, however, so that it now appears to apply only when prior testimony is introduced.[53] This interpretation is consistent with the federal hearsay rules, because FRE 804 requires unavailability for the introduction of prior testimony.

In *White v. Illinois*,[54] the Court held that the Confrontation Clause generally does not require the prosecution to show the unavailability of the declarant before admitting statements that fall into "firmly rooted" hearsay exceptions. The Court held that the "unavailability analysis is a necessary part of the Confrontation Clause inquiry only when the challenged out-of-court statements were made in the course of a prior judicial proceeding."[55] In the case of prior testimony, the prosecution may have a heavier constitutional burden to show the defendant's unavailability than it would under the hearsay exception.[56] See § 6-37.

A plurality of the Court in *Lilly v. Virginia*[57] held that the Confrontation Clause bars the introduction against a criminal defendant of an accomplice's confession that inculpates the defendant. Justice Stevens and three other members of the Court determined that accomplices' confessions, even though against the penal interest of the declarant, lack the reliability to be considered within a "firmly

---

[48] Pointer v. State of Texas, 380 U.S. 400, 406 (1965).

[49] Morrissey v. Brewer, 408 U.S. 471 (1972); Wolff v. McDonnell, 418 U.S. 539 (1974); Greene v. McElroy, 360 U.S. 474 (1959).

[50] White v. Illinois, 502 U.S. 346 (1992); Idaho v. Wright, 497 U.S. 805 (1990).

[51] 448 U.S. 56 (1980).

[52] *Id.* at 65.

[53] United States v. Inadi, 475 U.S. 387 (1986); White v. Illinois, 502 U.S. 346 (1992).

[54] 502 U.S. 346 (1992).

[55] *Id.* at 354.

[56] Idaho v. Wright, 497 U.S. 805, 823 (1990).

[57] 527 U.S. 116 (1999).

noted" hearsay exception. The plurality determined that these statements are untrustworthy because they are not necessarily against the declarant's interest — they may attempt to shift blame or minimize the declarant's role in the crime. They held: "The decisive fact, which we make explicit today, is that accomplices' confessions that inculpate a criminal defendant are not within a firmly rooted exception to the hearsay rule as that concept has been defined in our Confrontation Clause jurisprudence."[58]

The Chief Justice and two other members of the Court concurred in the judgment, finding that the accomplice's statements incriminating the defendant were separable from the statements against the accomplice's own penal interest and therefore were not truly against interest. According to these justices, the Court should not have reached the broader issue of whether a truly self-inculpatory statement falls within the "firmly rooted" classification. Justices Scalia and Thomas also concurred in the judgment.[59]

The Confrontation Clause also may exclude hearsay that otherwise would be admissible under the "residual" hearsay exception — FRE 807 — if the statement does not have marks of reliability equivalent to those in the firmly rooted exceptions. In deciding whether statements are reliable, the Supreme Court has ruled that corroborating evidence may not be considered; thus, the statement itself and the circumstances in which it was made must have the requisite trustworthiness.[60]

III. HEARSAY EXCLUSIONS

§ 6-14. Non-Hearsay: Admissions (FRE 801(d)(2)).

An "admission" is an out-of-court statement of a party litigant in the lawsuit that an opponent offers against that party. The admissions category is the most important of the hearsay exclusions and exceptions. Parties in civil lawsuits almost always obtain discovery from the opposing side, which can be used at trial; discovery from the parties is obtained in many criminal cases as well. Thus, the admissions exclusion provides the opportunity to introduce a large class of out-of-court statements. Additionally, a statement of a party often is a powerful means of proving a fact against him. Thus, admissions are a strong weapon in litigation.

---

[58] *Id.* at 134.

[59] In United States v. Torrez-Ortega, 184 F.3d 1128 (10th Cir. 1999), the Tenth Circuit held that a defendant's Confrontation Clause rights were violated when the Grand Jury testimony of a witness was read into the record after the witness improperly refused to testify. Although the witness was present in court, his refusal to testify made cross-examination impractical. The court determined that the introduction of the prior testimony violated the Confrontation Clause and was improper under FRE 801(d)(1).

[60] Barber v. Page, 390 U.S. 719 (1968); see MCCORMICK ON EVIDENCE § 252 (5th ed. 1999).

The adversary system supplies the primary justification for introducing admissions.[61] In a lawsuit, parties typically seek to prove very different versions of the facts. If one of them has made a statement that tends to undermine his litigating position, it seems only fair to permit its introduction. A party hardly can deny the trustworthiness of his own statement and can explain it if it is introduced out of context. Excluding the statement, on the other hand, would permit the party to "get away" with adopting a stance for trial that is inconsistent with his own prior assertions.

The admissions exclusion also is justified by other factors. Since an admission usually is made by a party or his representative, the declarant is likely to appear as a witness. Thus, in most cases he will be cross-examined. Further, although admissions need not conflict with the declarant's interest when made, they often do. In making the statement, the declarant may be aware that it could be used against him. Since he likely would not concede a fact unless it were true, the statement has special reliability.

Hearsay "admissions" often are confused with statements against interest and judicial admissions. A hearsay admission is *any* out-of-court statement of a party. The declarant need not expect it to be used in court. The statement need not be against the declarant's interest; indeed, a party often makes a statement in discovery that he believes will *help* his case, only to have it turned against him at the trial. The statement need not be a concession of liability, fault or any other legal point. In short, the declarant need not have any idea that he is "admitting" anything.

 Statements against interest fall into a hearsay exception that requires the declarant's unavailability.[62] This exception applies to a statement against interest of any unavailable declarant, not just a party. The statement must conflict with the declarant's interest when it is made. See § 6-40. Of course, an admission often is against the interest of the party, but that is not a condition for its admissibility.

 Judicial admissions are concessions of factual or legal points in litigation, usually in pleadings. These concessions may also be hearsay admissions, but the hearsay admissions category is much broader. Again, the declarant need not believe he is conceding anything when making a statement later offered as a hearsay admission. Further, a party may be precluded from contesting her own judicial admission, but is not prevented from disputing or explaining a hearsay admission.[63]

---

[61] FED. R. EVID. 801(d)(2) advisory committee's note: "Admissions by a party-opponent are excluded from the category of hearsay on the theory that their admissibility in evidence is the result of the adversary system rather than satisfaction of the conditions of the hearsay rule."

[62] FED. R. EVID. 804(3).

[63] See RICHARD O. LEMPERT AND STEPHEN A. SALTZBURG, A MODERN APPROACH TO EVIDENCE 385 (2d ed. 1982).

Although an admission of a party may be offered against her, it may not be offered by the party to support her case. When offered by the party, her own statements are hearsay and may not be introduced unless they fall into another hearsay exclusion or exception. Thus, admissions have a true adversarial character; they only are admissible against the party who made them.

Only statements of the parties, or their representatives or agents identified in the rule, are admissions. A statement of a non-party witness does not fit this category. A witness's prior statement may be treated as non-hearsay under FRE 801(d)(1), but only if the witness testifies and certain conditions apply. See § 6-19. A party's admission may be introduced even if she does not testify.

§ 6-15.   Types of Admissions.

FRE 801(d)(2) defines admissions to include not only the statements of the party, but certain statements of agents, representatives and coconspirators. It provides:

(d) **Statements which are not hearsay.** A statement is not hearsay if—

*   *   *

(2) **Admission by party-opponent.** The statement is offered against a party and is (A) the party's own statement in either an individual or a representative capacity or (B) a statement of which the party has manifested an adoption or belief in its truth, or (C) a statement by a person authorized by the party to make a statement concerning the subject, or (D) a statement by the party's agent or servant concerning a matter within the scope of the agency or employment, made during the existence of the relationship, or (E) a statement by a coconspirator of a party during the course and in furtherance of the conspiracy. The contents of the statement shall be considered but are not alone sufficient to establish the declarant's authority under subdivision (C), the agency or employment relationship and scope thereof under subdivision (D), or the existence of the conspiracy and the participation therein of the declarant and the party against whom the statements is offered under subdivision (E).

The types of admissions are discussed below.

§ 6-15(a).   Personal Admissions.

FRE 801(d)(2)(A) defines an admission a "party's own statement, in either an individual or representative capacity," which is offered against that party at trial. In this category the "party" is an individual. In the words of the Advisory Committee, this type of statement "is a classic example of an admission."[64] The adversarial justifications for introducing admissions are most persuasive when an individual's own statement is introduced against him.

---

[64] FED. R. EVID. 801(d)(2)(A) advisory committee's note.

Sometimes individuals sue others, or are sued, in a representative capacity. For example, a person may act as the trustee of a bankruptcy estate. In that capacity he may sue or be sued individually, but as the representative of the estate. If the person makes a statement relevant to the suit, the personal admission may be offered against him in the representative capacity. According to the Advisory Committee, the proponent need not show that the declarant was acting in the representative capacity when the statement was made; the statement need only be relevant to the affairs in which he acts as a representative.[65]

§ 6-15(b).   Adoptive Admissions.

An adoptive admission is a statement that a party adopted, by accepting it or otherwise indicating she believes it is true. FRE 801(d)(2) excludes from hearsay a "statement of which the party has manifested an adoption or belief in its truth," when the statement is offered against that party. The party may adopt the statement through words or conduct. Even silence may adopt a statement when circumstances call for a denial.

For an example of an adoptive admission, assume a mechanic points out a defect in a car's tire to the driver: "You've got a bad tire there; better change it." The driver responds, "You're right, but I think I can make it home." The statement "You're right" is an adoption of the mechanic's observation. Since both statements made up the admission, both could be introduced against the driver if he were later sued.

A person's response to another's statement, unfortunately, is often ambiguous. A nod or a smile may be read as assent but may constitute nothing more than politeness. Silence may be acceptance; it also may be sullen denial. Even responsive statements can be interpreted in different ways. Assume in the bad tire example the mechanic says "You've got a bad tire there; better change it," and the driver responds: "Sure." The word "Sure" could mean "You're right," or it could mean "You don't know what you're talking about." Moreover, after the fact, when litigating positions influence memory, a witness may be inclined to read more into a responsive comment than the speaker originally intended.

In civil cases, the introduction of ambiguous statements or conduct as adoptive admissions is not unfair because the party can explain her true intent. In criminal cases, the need to explain creates tension with the privilege against self-incrimination. Nevertheless, a defendant's adoptive admissions are admissible in criminal cases. Silence in the face of accusations generally is not admissible

---

[65] FED. R. EVID. 801(d)(2) advisory committee's note: "[N]o inquiry whether he was acting in the representative capacity in making the statement is required; the statement need only be relevant to representative affairs." As the Advisory Committee notes, the Uniform Rules of Evidence would require the statement "to be made in a representative capacity" before it would be admissible against the representative. *Id.*, citing UNIF. R. EVID. 63(7).

when an accused is in custody and *Miranda* warnings have been given; silence in other circumstances may be admissible.[66]

§ 6-15(c). Authorized Admissions of Agents.

Under FRE 801(d)(2)(C), a statement made by a person "authorized by the party to make a statement concerning the subject" can be introduced against the party as an admission. This provision permits the introduction of an agent's statement against the principal when the agent was authorized to speak — for instance, when the agent was authorized to issue a press release, conduct a negotiation, or disseminate information. It presumably includes statements that are implicitly authorized, such as the statement of a corporation president concerning corporate affairs. Even if implicitly authorized statements were not covered, however, they would be admissible under FRE 801(d)(2)(D), which includes statements of agents concerning matters in the course and scope of the agency or employment.

Defining agents' statements as admissions provides a means of introducing statements of corporations and other legal entities, which speak through their representatives. Additionally, the "authorized agent" rule includes the statements of agents authorized to speak by individuals.

Under the authorized agent provision, a statement of a partner conducting partnership affairs can be introduced against the partnership.[67] As a person with an interest in the business, the partner has implicit authority to speak for the partnership. The partner's statements could not be introduced, however, in a suit against his partner individually, unless the claim were based on a liability of the partnership.[68]

A major issue at common law was whether the statement of an agent to his own principal was an admission. Some jurisdictions restricted the authorized admissions category to statements made to third parties. The federal rules treat both statements to the principal and to third parties as admissions. As the

---

[66] See Doyle v. Ohio, 426 U.S. 610 (1976); MCCORMICK ON EVIDENCE § 132 (5th ed. 1999). McCormick states that courts have developed safeguards against the misuse of silence as an adoptive admission. They require that (1) the party actually heard the statement; (2) she must have understood it; (3) the subject of the statement must have been within her knowledge; (4) there must have been no physical or emotional impediments to a response; (5) the party must have the type of character and relationship to the person making the statement that would make it reasonable to expect a denial; and most important, (6) the statement must be the type that would call for a denial if it were untrue.

[67] See MCCORMICK ON EVIDENCE § 259 (5th ed. 1999): "[W]hen the existence and scope of the partnership have been proved, the statement of a partner made in the conduct of the business of the firm is receivable as the admission of the partnership."

[68] *Id.*

Advisory Committee states: "The rule is phrased broadly so as to encompass both."[69]

§ 6-15(d).　Agents' "Scope of Employment" Admissions.

FRE 801(d)(2)(D) treats as an admission any statement made by an agent or employee concerning matters within the scope of the agency relationship. It includes "a statement by the party's agent or servant concerning a matter within the scope of the agency or employment, made during the existence of the relationship."

The rule adopts a liberal view of agency admissions. Prior to the federal rules, many jurisdictions did not treat agents' statements as admissions unless the agent was authorized to speak for the principal; a trend had developed, however, to include any statement relating to the agency relationship. The Advisory Committee supports the adoption of the broader rule by noting, in part, that it avoids the "'loss of valuable and helpful evidence."[70]

Most frequently, FRE 801(d)(2)(D) is used for the introduction of statements of employees relating to matters within their employment[71]. For these admissions the rule requires that the statements be a) made during the existence of the relationship and b) concern matters within the scope of employment. These limitations help to ensure the reliability of the admissions. An employee is not likely to make a statement that might be used against his current employer unless the statement is true. Additionally, an employee is likely to have knowledge of matters within the scope of his employment. A statement of an ex-employee, or one made concerning matters outside the employee's duties, would not have these marks of reliability.[72]

Applying these limitations depends on the facts of particular cases. Assume, for instance, that a truck driver involved in an accident states: "Our mechanic didn't repair the brakes properly." If this statement were offered against the employer, its admissibility would turn on whether the statement concerned a matter "within the scope of . . . employment." In a broad sense, since the driver operates the truck, the condition of the brakes relates to his employment. On the other hand, it might not be within his duties to determine the adequacy of mechanics' repairs. A good basis to resolve the issue is whether the driver's duties required him to be informed of the brakes' condition, thus fulfilling a basis on which agents' "scope" statements are deemed reliable.

---

[69] FED. R. EVID. 801(d)(2)(C) advisory committee's note.

[70] See FED. R. EVID. 801(d)(2)(D) advisory committee's note.

[71] See, e.g., United States v. Photogrammetric Data Services, Inc., 259 F.3d 229, 242–43 (4th Cir. 2001).

[72] See e.g., In Re Air Crash Disaster, 86 F.3d 498, 536 (6th Cir. 1996).

§ 6-15(e). Coconspirators' Statements.

A statement of a coconspirator may be offered against a fellow coconspirator if the statement was made during, and in furtherance of, the conspiracy. FRE 801(d)(2)(E) includes as an admission "a statement by a coconspirator of a party during the course and in furtherance of the conspiracy."

To introduce the statement of a coconspirator against a party, the proponent must prove that (1) there was a conspiracy, (2) the statement was made during its course, and (3) the statement was made in furtherance of the conspiracy. Under FRE 104, the court determines whether these preliminary facts are proven.[73] One way to do so is to take evidence in a "mini-hearing" outside the presence of the jury.[74] A second is for the prosecution to prove the conspiracy during the trial prior to offering the coconspirator's statement.

The third method is to admit the statement conditionally, subject to proof of the conspiracy later in the trial. This approach has the most potential for prejudice because the jury hears a statement that may turn out to be inadmissible. If the government fails to fulfill the conditions for introducing the statement, the court instructs the jury to disregard it, but an instruction cannot erase it from their minds. On the other hand, the conditional admission of a coconspirator's statement saves time. Additionally, judges usually have a good idea of the government's proof and can inquire as to how the government will fulfill the conditions. When a judge is satisfied the proof will be forthcoming, the decision usually turns out correct.

In *Bourjaily v. United States*,[75] the United States Supreme Court determined the standard for deciding whether the conditions are fulfilled to admit coconspirators' statements. The Court ruled that the proponent need only prove their satisfaction by a preponderance of the evidence.[76] It also discarded the historic rule against using the out-of-court statement to establish the conditions for its own admissibility.

§ 6-16. Privity and Relational Admissions.

One generally recognized category of admission not adopted in FRE 801(d)(2) is the so-called "privity" or "relational" admission. It applies when a party effectively stands in the shoes of the declarant in bringing or defending the suit; the declarant's statement is admissible against the person who succeeds to the declarant's interest. Assume, for example, a roof is damaged on a house, and the owner has a claim against his insurance company. The owner makes the

---

[73] See United States v. Irorere, 228 F.3d 816, 823 n.1 (7th Cir. 2000) (ordinarily the court decides whether co-conspirator statements are admissible through pretrial proffer).

[74] United States v. Vinson, 606 F.2d 149 (6th Cir. 1979), *cert. denied*, 444 U.S. 1074 (1980).

[75] 483 U.S. 171 (1987).

[76] *Id.* at 175.

statement, "The roof was in pretty bad shape anyway." Subsequently, the owner transfers the house and claim to a purchaser, who brings suit against the insurer. In that situation, some jurisdictions allow the former owner's statement to be admitted against the purchaser.

The rule is grounded in the theory that the purchaser derives his claim from the declarant and should be bound by his statement. Additionally, the statement usually has the reliability associated with admissions; the owner probably would not have made a statement that could be used against him unless he had knowledge of the facts and the statement were true.[77]

Additional examples of situations in which the privity or relational admissions doctrine would apply are the following:

1.   A decedent's statement is offered against a successor who sues for the decedent's wrongful death;

2.   A child's statement is offered against the child's parent or guardian in a suit for damages caused by the child;

3.   A statement by a person who allegedly caused injuries through his negligence is offered in a direct action suit against the person's insurer to recover damages for the injuries.[78]

The federal rules did not adopt privity or relational admissions. Apparently, it was believed that these statements might be admissible under other provisions, such as the "declaration against interest" exception. Further, the omission reflects a reluctance to use substantive legal concepts to define admissions, since these concepts do not ensure statements are reliable. The approach follows the admonition of Professor Morgan: "Joint ownership, joint obligation, priority of title, each and all furnish no criterion of credibility, no aid in the evaluation of testimony."[79]

On the other hand, it seems only fair to bind a successor to statements made by the person through whom the successor brings or defends a claim. The transfer of the claim or liability, or the requirement to bring suit through a representative party, is a formalistic basis for denying admissibility. Thus, some jurisdictions

---

[77] RICHARD O. LEMPERT AND STEPHEN A. SALTZBURG, A MODERN APPROACH TO EVIDENCE 399 (2d ed. 1982); MCCORMICK ON EVIDENCE § 269 (5th ed. 1999).

[78] See, e.g., LSA-C.E. art. 801(D)(3)(c)-(f). A description of the "privity" admission can be convoluted. LSA-C.E. art. 801(D)(3)(c) describes one such admission as follows:

> (c) In a civil case, a statement by a declarant when the liability, obligation, or duty of the party against whom it is offered is derivatively based in whole or in part upon a liability, obligation, or duty of the declarant, or when the claim or right asserted by that party is barred or diminished by a breach of duty by the declarant, and when the statement would be admissible if offered against the declarant as a party in an action involving that liability, obligation, or breach of duty.

[79] Edmund M. Morgan, *Admissions*, 12 WASH. L. REV. 181, 202 (1937).

recognize this category of admissions, despite its omission from the federal rules.[80]

§ 6-17. Use of Admissions at Trial.

A lawyer typically uses a witness's prior statement as a basis to prepare for cross-examination. If the witness denies the fact described in a prior statement, you may use the statement to impeach. See § 9-28. When the witness is a party or an agent or coconspirator of a party, the out-of-court statement is also an admission, which gives you greater flexibility to use the statement.

Since admissions are non-hearsay, their use is not subject to the same limitations that apply to other witness statements.[81] First, you can offer an admission even if the declarant does not testify. Second, you may introduce an admission even if it is not inconsistent with the witness's trial testimony. Third, in jurisdictions that admit prior inconsistent statements only for impeachment, you may use a prior inconsistent statement that also is an admission to establish relevant facts. Thus, you can do more with admissions than other statements.

Since an admission is not hearsay, you may introduce it at any time. You can authenticate and offer the relevant pages of a transcript, deposition or statement, or call a witness to testify to the statement. The declarant need not be a witness, nor even be available to testify, for the statement to be introduced.

If the party or agent will testify, you have the option of saving the statement for cross-examination. This approach saves time, since the subject matter may be covered at one time. It also permits you to introduce facts in a context developed through cross-examination. Additionally, if the party departs from the prior statement in his testimony, you may use it to attack his credibility.

The normal method of using a prior statement to impeach is to first ask the witness to concede the fact, then read the prior statement if he denies the fact. See § 9-28. Since the admission is independently admissible, you could ask the witness about the admission first — establishing the fact first through the admission. This approach is cumbersome, however, since counsel and the witness focus more on the prior statement rather than fact. Thus, you usually should follow the traditional method.

Impeachment is a common use of out-of-court statements. Traditionally, if a prior statement was not admissible under a hearsay exclusion or exception, it could come in only to impeach. Thus, the witness would have to take the stand and testify inconsistently with the prior statement before an attorney could use it. Further, it could come in only to show that the trial testimony was false — not to prove the fact described in the statement. This traditional rule was altered

---

[80] E.g., LSA-C.E. art. 801(d)(3).

[81] See IRVING YOUNGER, HEARSAY: A PRACTICAL GUIDE THROUGH THE THICKET 71-106 (1988).

by FRE 801(d)(1)(A) for prior inconsistent statements given under oath, but still prevails in some jurisdictions and still applies in the federal jurisdiction to prior inconsistent statements that are not sworn.

A prior inconsistent statement that also qualifies as an admission may be used both to impeach and establish a fact. Thus, if counsel chooses to save the admission until she examines the witness, and offers it to counter inconsistent trial testimony, it may be used for both purposes. Under the expanded non-hearsay definitions in the federal rules, the court may receive other prior inconsistent statements given under oath as non-hearsay. See § 6-19. The admissions category is broader, however, since it includes any statement of a party or its agent, whether or not given under oath.

§ 6-18. Absence of Foundation Requirement for Admissions.

Although most out-of-court statements are subject to the personal knowledge requirement of FRE 602 for factual assertions and the expertise requirement of FRE 702 for specialized opinions, these prerequisites generally do not apply to admissions. Additionally, opinions that are not helpful — in the sense that they invade the jury's province — may be admissible. The same adversarial considerations that justify treating admissions as non-hearsay support eliminating the foundation requirements. Fairness requires that a party's statement be considered when it undercuts his litigation stance. Additionally, a party would not make a statement that could be used against him unless it had a reliable basis.

Assume a corporation denied liability for a traffic accident. The president, who was not at the scene, tells a police investigator: "Our own driver was negligent in operating our truck." This out-of-court statement likely is based on reports of others and reflects an opinion on an ultimate issue. Thus, it does not have the foundation of personal knowledge, nor does it meet the requirement that testimony be helpful to the jury's decision making. Nevertheless, since the president is a spokesman for the corporation, the statement likely is admissible.

The corporation cannot avoid consideration of its own damaging statements. The fact that the corporation adopted a legal stance inconsistent with its president's statement makes it fair to admit the assertion, and this adversarial consideration has more weight than the evidentiary shortcomings of the statement. Although the corporation could not offer a hearsay-based opinion of its president, his hearsay-based opinion may be received against it.

The federal rules do not expressly authorize eliminating the foundation and helpfulness requirements for admissions. The Advisory Committee Note makes it clear, however, that they are waived. It states:

> No guarantee of trustworthiness is required in the case of an admission. The freedom which admissions have enjoyed from technical demands of

searching for an assurance of trustworthiness in some against-interest circumstances, and from the restrictive influences of the opinion rule and the rule requiring firsthand knowledge, when taken with the apparently prevalent satisfaction with the results, calls for generous treatment of this avenue to admissibility.[82]

The extent to which the foundation and helpfulness requirements are waived depends on the type of admission being offered. If the admission is personal, adoptive or authorized, these prerequisites generally do not apply. To the extent a legally-implied relationship renders a statement an admission, however, a court may impose the foundation and helpfulness requirements. The adversarial considerations justifying their elimination are not so strong when a party is being held to the statements of an unauthorized "spokesman," even if an agency relationship exists. Thus, depending on the circumstances, courts may be reluctant to admit agents' or coconspirators' statements if they do not have the traditional indicia of reliability and helpfulness.[83]

Although some legal scholars advocate a firsthand knowledge requirement for admissions of agents,[84] the federal courts have not adopted this suggestion.[85] Nevertheless, in determining the admissibility of agents' or coconspirators' statements, the courts in effect may require a foundation. For employee statements to be admitted against the employer, the statements must concern matters "within the scope of the agency or employment." FRE 801(d)(2)(D). This limiting language provides a means of excluding admissions that have no foundation; to the extent the statement concerns a matter on which the employee has no personal knowledge, the court may deem it outside the "scope" of employment. The limitations on the admissibility of coconspirators' statements — that they be made "during the course" and "in furtherance of" the conspiracy — also are a means of requiring assurance of a foundation. A requirement that the statement be trustworthy is especially important when its introduction creates tension with the Confrontation Clause.

§ 6-19. Non-Hearsay: Certain Prior Statements of Witnesses Who Testify at Trial (FRE 801(d)(1)).

Even if a witness testifies at the trial, her own prior statements ordinarily are hearsay. Although the testimony is subject to the courtroom safeguards of appearance, oath, and cross-examination, the out-of-court statement is not, and

---

[82] FED. R. EVID. 801 advisory committee's note.

[83] RICHARD O. LEMPERT AND STEPHEN A. SALTZBURG, A MODERN APPROACH TO EVIDENCE 285 (2d ed. 1982): "When a statement is by an agent or coconspirator of a party, courts may reimpose the firsthand knowledge requirement and be more reluctant to admit opinion."

[84] 4 WEINSTEIN AND BERGER, WEINSTEIN'S EVIDENCE ¶ 801(2)(2)(c)[01] at 277–80 (1990).

[85] MCCORMICK ON EVIDENCE § 255 (5th ed. 1999).

the statement fits the classic hearsay definition. The opportunity to cross-examine the witness concerning the statement, however, eliminates much of the difficulty the trier might have in evaluating its credibility. Moreover, to the extent a witness adopts a prior statement at the trial, the adoption transforms the statement into non-hearsay evidence: "Yes, I said it, and it's still true." Thus, many commentators argue that prior statements of testifying witnesses should not be treated as hearsay.[86]

Although hearsay, prior statements traditionally could be admitted on the issue of credibility. Prior inconsistent statements were admissible to impeach; prior consistent statements could be introduced to rebut a claim that the witness fabricated testimony; a prior identification often came in to show the trustworthiness of a courtroom identification. Jurors could not reasonably be expected, however, to consider a prior statement only for credibility and ignore its tendency to prove a fact. To the extent these statements are admissible for credibility, then, it is realistic to permit their consideration to establish facts.

The federal rules continue to define most out-of-court statements of testifying witnesses as hearsay. Nevertheless, FRE 801(d)(1) defines three categories of statements as non-hearsay. For these categories, the rule requires that the out-of-court declarant testify and undergo cross-examination concerning the statement at the trial before the factfinder can consider it for substantive purposes. FRE 801(d)(1) provides that a statement is not hearsay if:

> **(1) Prior statement by witness.** The declarant testifies at the trial or hearing and is subject to cross-examination concerning the statement, and the statement is (A) inconsistent with the declarant's testimony, and was given under oath subject to the penalty of perjury at a trial, hearing or other proceeding, or in a deposition, or (B) consistent with the declarant's testimony, and is offered to rebut an express or implied charge of recent fabrication or improper influence or motive, or (C) one of identification of a person made after perceiving the person. . . .

The limited exclusions reflect an "unwillingness" of the Advisory Committee "to countenance the general use of prior prepared statements as substantive evidence, but with a recognition that particular circumstances call for a contrary result."[87]

The Model Code of Evidence permitted the introduction of any prior statement of a witness when the declarant "is present and subject to cross-examination."[88] The federal rules reject this blanket position, primarily because the rule would implicitly countenance introducing a prepared statement through a witness and

---

[86] See FED. R. EVID. 801(d)(1) advisory committee's note; see UNIF. R. EVID. 63(1).

[87] FED. R. EVID. 801(d)(1) advisory committee's note.

[88] MODEL CODE OF EVIDENCE RULE 503(b).

tendering him for cross-examination.[89] This method of examination, if permitted, would be detrimental to the factfinding process. It would allow attorneys to draft a witness's testimony, circumventing the prohibition against leading. Moreover, it would reduce the jury's opportunity to observe demeanor. Further, a prepared statement would take much of the life out of the presentation. Additionally, the rule might encourage lawyers to introduce deposition rather than live testimony, which also would reduce spontaneity. Thus, retaining the general precept that a witness's prior statements are hearsay makes good sense.

The requirement that the witness be "subject to cross-examination concerning the prior statement" creates some confusion. When a witness testifies that she cannot remember the prior statement, the statement in one sense cannot be cross-examined, raising the issue of whether the requirement is satisfied. Yet the introduction of the prior statement may do more to advance the cross-examiner's cause than if the witness admitted and explained it. Thus, the opportunity to cross-examine regarding the witness's inability to remember the statement satisfies the rule. In *United v. Owens*,[90] the United States Supreme Court held that the opportunity to cross-examine regarding lack of memory satisfies the requirement that the statement be subject to cross-examination.

An example illustrates that cross-examination is effective even when a witness denies any memory of a prior statement. Assume a witness testifies that she saw Smith, the defendant, chasing Jones with a knife. She previously testified in a deposition that she saw no knife. The questioning might occur as follows:

Q. You now say you saw a knife in Mr. Smith's hand as he chased Mr. Jones?

A. Yes.

Q. Do you remember giving a deposition at my office on July 2?

A. I'm not sure.

Q. On July 2, in that deposition, at page 12, you said: "I saw no knife or other weapon in the possession of Mr. Smith," is that right?

A. I can't remember.

Q. May I approach, Your Honor? Perhaps this will help you. I show you a deposition dated July 2, 1993. Is that your signature on the last page?

---

[89] FED. R. EVID. 801(d)(1) advisory committee's note.
[90] 484 U.S. 554 (1988).

> A.   It looks like it.
>
> Q.   Please read page 12, line 16.
>
> A.   "I saw no knife or other weapon in the possession of Mr. Smith."
>
> Q.   Can you tell us if you made that statement?
>
> A.   I still don't remember it.
>
> Q.   Your Honor, I would like to offer page 12 of this deposition. It is certified by the court reporter.
>
> The Court: Any objection to authenticity? Let it be admitted.
>
> Counsel: I have copies, Your Honor. May I distribute them to the jurors, calling their attention to line 16?
>
> The Court: Please do so.
>
> [Each juror reads: "I saw no knife or other weapon in the possession of Mr. Smith."]

In this situation, if the witness admitted and explained her statement, her credibility would seem stronger than her claim of no memory. Additionally, the repeated reference to the statement, when the witness denies remembering it, has a stronger tendency to establish facts in the jurors' minds than if the witness explained it. Thus, cross-examination can be effective even when a witness testifies to a lack of memory.

Additionally, since the prior statement conflicts with trial testimony, the cross-examiner *wants* the prior statement to be treated as substantive evidence. The cross-examiner should not be penalized because the witness denies remembering the prior statement. Therefore, fairness supports treating any cross-examination concerning the prior statement as sufficient to make the statement non-hearsay.

When a prior consistent statement or a prior identification is offered to *bolster* a witness's credibility, the witness's denial of memory would diminish the impact of the statement. If the witness denies remembering a prior consistent statement, the jury is likely to give it little weight. Again, a cross-examination that dramatizes the lack of memory is more effective than one in which the witness defends and reiterates the statement. Thus, the interests of the cross-examiner are adequately protected through the opportunity to bring out the lack of memory.

When the witness testifies to a lack of memory of both the underlying fact and the prior statement, the opportunity to cross-examine concerning memory generally should be sufficient. In this context, a prior statement supporting the party who sponsors the witness would be admissible only if it were a prior identification. If the witness denies remembering the event and the identification, the testimony would have little persuasive impact, and cross-examination on the lack of memory would diminish it further. Thus, the cross-examiner's interests are not impinged by the rule.

Occasionally, counsel chooses to introduce a prior inconsistent statement after the witness leaves the stand. The impeachment rules require that the witness still be available to explain the statement.[91] If the witness is available, but does not take the stand to explain, the statement is not literally subject to cross-examination. Again, however, the party introducing the statement ordinarily prefers that the witness not explain it. Thus, the absence of cross-examination does not hurt that party's interest and the statement should be treated as non-hearsay. The party sponsoring the witness should not be able to avoid this result by declining to recall the witness.

The three types of prior statements excluded from hearsay are discussed below.

§ 6-19(a). Prior Inconsistent Statements Made Under Oath.

Prior inconsistent statements generally are admissible to impeach a witness's credibility, although they traditionally have been regarded as hearsay if offered for their truth. The federal rule retains this approach for many prior statements. If a prior inconsistent statement was given under oath, however, the rule admits it as substantive evidence.

The witness must first state or deny a fact on the stand. If he previously made an inconsistent statement, the prior statement may be used to show the testimony is false. Ordinarily, lawyers ask the witness to admit the prior inconsistent statement during cross-examination — thus proving the statement "intrinsically." The attorney may, however, offer another witness or a document — "extrinsic" evidence — to prove the inconsistent statement, so long as the witness is still available to explain or deny it. If the witness denies the prior inconsistent statement during the cross-examination, the attorney must prove it extrinsically. The rules regarding impeachment with prior inconsistent statements are discussed in § 9-28.

When a prior inconsistent statement is admitted solely to impeach, it theoretically may not be used as evidence of a fact in dispute, but only as a basis for assessing the witness's truthfulness.[92] Consider the following example, in which a witness testifies at trial that she saw a yellow car enter an intersection against a red light, although she earlier told an investigator the light was green:

---

[91] FED. R. EVID. 613(b).

[92] See Carson Harbor Village, LTD. v. Unocal Corp., 270 F.3d 863, 874 (9th Cir. 2001) *cert. denied* 122 S. Ct. 1437 (2002).

[Cross-examination]

> Q.   Ms. Coyne, you testified on direct examination that the yellow car had a red light at the intersection, is that correct?
>
> A.   Yes.
>
> Q.   In truth, however, the light was green for the yellow car, is that correct?
>
> A.   No. It was red.
>
> Q.   Do you remember speaking to Marcus Brown, an investigator, in your home last Monday?
>
> A.   Yes.
>
> Q.   You told Mr. Brown: "The yellow car had a green light when it went into the intersection," is that right?
>
> A.   I guess I might have said that.
>
> Q.   You did tell him the light was green, correct?
>
> A.   Yes.

In this example, the witness admits the prior statement, in which she stated the light was green. Nevertheless, since the inconsistent statement is hearsay if offered for its truth, it can be admitted only to impeach. Thus, the statement *cannot* be used to establish that the light was green but *can* be used to determine the witness is lying when she says the light was red. Obviously, if the jurors believed the prior statement, they would have difficulty ignoring it in determining whether the car had a green light.

An instruction to consider a prior inconsistent statement in evaluating credibility, but not to establish facts, is difficult for jurors to follow. Nevertheless, it may cause jurors subconsciously to adjust the weight they accord the statement, thus accomplishing a rough equivalent of using the statement for a limited purpose. Additionally, jurors' inability to follow the instruction may not make much difference. If other evidence supports the fact described in the prior statement, the determination that the courtroom testimony is incredible simply leads the jury to accept the other evidence.

A problem arises, however, when no other evidence establishes the fact described in the prior statement. Even if the jury disbelieves the courtroom testimony, the jury may have no basis for a contrary determination. A verdict based only on the prior statement — if it is hearsay — might have to be set aside.

One reason to limit the use of prior inconsistent statements is that these statements often are disputed. If the witness's testimony conflicts with the statement, she may deny the prior assertion, claim it was changed, or explain it in a different context. These points often are valid; the spoken word is elusive and listeners often misinterpret a speaker's intent, particularly if they want to hear a predetermined message. Thus, prior statements may be unreliable.

FRE 801(d)(1) exempts from hearsay those prior inconsistent statements made under oath — in a prior hearing, trial, or deposition. Other prior inconsistent statements may be admitted only to impeach. The exemption of inconsistent sworn assertions is based on two rationales: first, the prior statement was transcribed, so the witness cannot dispute that it was made; second, the prior statement was given under oath, and subject to the opportunity for cross-examination, giving it special reliability.[93] Indeed, when a lawyer introduces a prior inconsistent statement, the safeguards of the oath and the opportunity for cross-examination apply twice; the witness may be examined about the fact described in the statement both in the prior proceeding and at the trial.

A witness's prior sworn statement is excluded from hearsay only if it is inconsistent with his trial testimony. Thus, the witness must testify inconsistently with the prior statement before it can be used as substantive evidence. A lawyer's attempt to offer a prior statement without first eliciting the witness's testimony is impermissible unless the prior statement fits another hearsay exemption or exception.

Attorneys often ask about a prior statement before asking the witness to concede the fact it describes, presumably because they feel that the witness will admit prior testimony more easily than a fact. This approach generally is objectionable, however, and may allow a witness a greater opportunity to explain away a damaging statement. The use of prior statements in cross-examination is discussed in § 9-8.

The hearsay exemption for prior inconsistent testimony is not the same as the "former testimony" exception of FRE 804(b)(1). The former testimony exemption applies only when a witness is unavailable. Obviously, since the witness cannot testify, the "former testimony" need not be inconsistent with trial testimony. The former testimony exception is discussed in § 6-38.

§ 6-19(b). Prior Consistent Statements Offered to Rebut Contentions of Fabrication.

Prior statements consistent with trial testimony traditionally were hearsay. A prior consistent statement could be introduced, however, to support credibility if a party alleged that the witness fabricated testimony or changed it under an

---

[93] FED. R. EVID. 801(d)(1) advisory committee's note.

improper influence.[94] FRE 801(d)(1)(B) exempts from hearsay prior consistent statements that are offered "to rebut an express or implied charge against the declarant of recent fabrication or improper influence or motive."

The federal rule applies only when the witness expressly or implicitly is accused of lying. The accusation may take the form of an express suggestion during cross-examination, the introduction of evidence suggesting undue influence, or a cross-examination that attacks the witness's character as well as his testimony. A cross-examination that focuses more on the facts than the witness's character would imply only that the witness misremembered — not that he fabricated testimony.

Allowing use of prior consistent statements to establish facts is justified by adversarial considerations. The statements often are used to counter prior inconsistent statements that, when sworn, can be considered as substantive evidence; the rebutting evidence should receive the same treatment. Further, the statements can be introduced only if the opposing party "opens the door" by attacking the witness's truthfulness. As the Advisory Committee states: "If the opposite party wishes to open the door for its admission in evidence, no sound reason is apparent why it should not be received generally."[95] Additionally, the rule recognizes the difficulty of separating credibility from proof of facts, particularly when the statements offered for credibility support those made on the stand, which can be used to determine facts.

The exemption for prior consistent statements is not limited to those made under oath. The greater breadth of the exemption, as compared to that for prior inconsistent statements, reflects the adversarial consideration mentioned above — the adverse party opened the door by attacking the witness's truthfulness. This consideration is more important than the loss of reliability associated with an unsworn statement.

At common law a prior consistent statement could be introduced to rehabilitate a witness only if made prior to the occasion of any motive to fabricate. In *Tome v. United States*,[96] the United States Supreme Court held that this requirement still applies under the federal rules. A prior consistent statement made after the motive arose is not admissible to prove substantive facts or even to counter the

---

[94] In United States v. Ruiz, 249 F.3d 643, 647–648 (7th Cir. 2001), the 7th Circuit uses a four-part test to determine if a person's prior consistent statement is admissible for the purpose of rehabilitating his credibility: "1) the declarant testifies at trial and is subject to cross-examination, 2) his prior statement is indeed consistent with this trial testimony, 3) the statement is offered to rebut an explicit or implicit accusation of recent fabrication, and 4) the statement was made before the declarant had a motive to fabricate." See also MCCORMICK ON EVIDENCE § 251 (5th ed. 1999).

[95] FED. R. EVID. 801(d)(1)(B) advisory committee's note.

[96] 513 U.S. 150 (1995).

impeachment, although it may be admissible if necessary to give context to the impeaching statement. See § 9-37.

§ 6-19(c).   Prior Statements of Identification.

Prior statements identifying persons, the third category of prior statements exempted from hearsay, need not be inconsistent with trial testimony or offered to rebut a charge of fabrication. Nor must a prior identification be made under oath. So long as the declarant testifies and the statement is subject to cross-examination, it is exempt from hearsay under FRE 801(d)(1)(C).

Many prior identifications affect the credibility of a courtroom identification. If the witness previously identified a different person, the prior identification undoubtedly would be introduced on cross-examination to attack the testimony. Paradoxically, a prior consistent identification also may be used to attack credibility; if the circumstances were suggestive, both identifications may be tainted. Further, the defense in a criminal case normally attacks a courtroom identification and a prior identification can be used in response to bolster the witness's credibility. In each instance jurors would be hard pressed to separate a credibility purpose from proof of facts.

Although they fit the traditional hearsay definition, prior statements of identification traditionally were admissible even if not offered on credibility. According to the Advisory Committee, the "basis is the generally unsatisfactory and inconclusive nature of courtroom identifications as compared with those made at an earlier time under less suggestive conditions."[97] As a practical matter, it would be difficult to exclude most prior identifications in the give and take of cross-examination. A witness asked to explain the basis for the courtroom identification could not be expected to avoid discussing a prior identification. Moreover, a prior identification may be related to an arrest or other relevant event. Thus, treating the identification as hearsay would be impractical.

IV.   HEARSAY EXCEPTIONS: AVAILABILITY IMMATERIAL

§ 6-20.   Introduction (FRE 803).

The second major category of admissible out-of-court statements is the class of hearsay exceptions that apply whether or not the declarant is available. The exceptions are grounded on reliability — the prescribed circumstances provide assurances of trustworthiness. Thus, live testimony would not necessarily provide more trustworthy evidence and the court may admit the statement even if the witness is available. This category differs from exceptions requiring the declarant's unavailability, where need primarily justifies the exceptions; under those exceptions the statements would not be admissible if the witness could be called to the stand.

---

[97] FED. R. EVID. 801(d)(1)(C) advisory committee's note.

FRE 803 sets out 23 hearsay exceptions that apply "even though the declarant is available as a witness." The rule synthesizes exceptions developed at common law, but revises the common law exceptions "where modern developments and conditions are believed to make that course appropriate."[98]

§ 6-21. Present Sense Impression (FRE 803(1)).

FRE 803(1) permits the introduction of present sense impressions.[99] It defines a present sense impression as follows:

> **(1) Present sense impression.** A statement describing or explaining an event or condition made while the declarant was perceiving the event or condition, or immediately thereafter.

Present sense impressions are trustworthy because the declarant is unlikely to fabricate a concurrent description of facts. The contemporaneous nature of the description leaves no time for reflection, which ordinarily is required for fabrication. Additionally, a contemporaneous description avoids any chance of faulty memory.

The exception has three key components. First, the statement must describe an event or condition. Statements that merely relate to the event or condition do not fit. Second, the declarant must actually perceive the event or condition. Third, the description must be made while, or immediately after, the declarant perceived the event or condition. The elements of the exception may be established by the witness who heard the statement or by the statement itself. If the declarant testifies, her testimony also may establish the conditions.

The exception for present sense impressions is closely related to, and overlaps with, that for excited utterances. Both types of statements are reliable because of their spontaneity. The speaker does not have to be excited, however, for her declaration to be a present sense impression. Nor must the statement describe a startling event.

One issue in applying the exception relates to the scope of the phrase "immediately thereafter." The Advisory Committee Note emphasizes that spontaneity is crucial to the exception, but recognizes that "in many, if not most, instances precise contemporaneity is not possible, and hence a slight lapse is allowable."[100] A delay normal for a contemporaneous description should be allowed, but not one that would permit the interference of a motive to fabricate.

Assume a driver is operating a car and observes another car in the next lane. The driver states "That car is weaving into our lane" seconds after observing

---

[98] FED. R. EVID. 803 advisory committee's note.

[99] See, e.g., U.S. v. Campbell, 782 F.Supp. 1258, 1259–61 (N.D. Ill. 1991); People of Territory of Guam v. Ignacio, 10 F.3d 608 (9th Cir. 1993).

[100] FED. R. EVID. 803(1) and (2) advisory committee's note.

the car do so. In that situation the delay reflects the normal time associated with processing facts and the statement should be allowed. If, on the other hand, the cars collided, and the driver immediately after the collision stated, "That car weaved into our lane," the statement should not be allowed. The driver's statement uses the past tense — a sign of a non-contemporaneous description — and may be influenced by a motive to avoid fault.

§ 6-22.   Excited Utterances (FRE 803(2)).

FRE 803(2) excepts from hearsay any "statement relating to a startling event or condition made while the declarant was under the stress of excitement caused by the event or condition." To qualify for the exception, then, (1) a statement must relate to a startling event or condition, (2) it must be made while the declarant was excited, and (3) the excitement must be caused by the startling event or condition.[101]

§ 6-22(a).   Theory.

The exception reflects on the theory that statements made when a declarant is emotionally agitated are reliable. As the Advisory Committee states, "[t]he theory . . . is simply that circumstances may produce a condition of excitement which temporarily stills the capacity of reflection and produces utterances free of conscious fabrication."[102] In other words, if a person is emotionally upset from a startling event, his statement regarding the event is unlikely to be influenced by extraneous motives.

The argument that excited statements are not likely to be fabricated is reasonable, but does not guarantee their reliability. A person may misperceive or misdescribe facts precisely because he is agitated.[103] Additionally, emotional distress may interfere with a person's memory. An emotionally upset person may exaggerate a startling incident because of a temporary inability to place it in perspective.

Despite the conflicting arguments on excited statements, courts often use the exception to admit hearsay. Litigation, especially criminal and tort cases, frequently involves stressful events. Persons who were on the scene sometimes cannot be located to testify. Yet their excited statements relating to the event may be admitted.

The exception is broader than that for present sense impressions in that the excited statement need only relate to, rather than describe, the startling event

---

[101] See e.g., United States v. Brown, 254 F.3d 454 (3rd Cir. 2001) *cert. denied* 122 S.Ct. 1332 (2002); Morgan v. Foretich, 846 F.2d 941 (4th Cir. 1988).

[102] FED. R. EVID. 803 (1) and (2) advisory committee's note.

[103] *Id.*; Robert M. Hutchins and Donald Slesinger, *Some Observations on the Law of Evidence: Spontaneous Exclamations*, 28 COLUM. L. REV. 432 (1928).

or condition. Additionally, the statement does not have to be contemporaneous with the event. On the other hand, the event or condition must excite the declarant and he must still be excited when he makes the statement.

Time is an important factor in determining whether a person is still excited from a startling event.[104] As time passes, the stress of the event ordinarily wanes. The spontaneity of the statement is also a determinant; exclamations are more spontaneous, and reliable, than responses to questions.[105] The most important factor, however, is the declarant's emotional state. If the party offering the statement can show that the speaker was still excited from an event, the statement regarding that event should be admitted.

§ 6-22(b).   Establishing Conditions for Admitting an Excited Utterance.

To introduce an excited statement, the attorney must establish that a startling event or condition occurred, the statement was made under the stress of the exciting event or condition, and the statement related to the startling event or condition. If the declarant testifies, she may establish these conditions. Alternatively, another witness may establish them. The statement itself may be considered in determining the basis for its admission.[106]

Establishing that a declarant was excited through another witness requires inference. Theoretically, a witness could not have personal knowledge of another's emotional state. The witness could describe facts from which the trier could infer, however, that the declarant was excited. Additionally, FRE 701 permits a lay witness to give opinions that are (1) rationally based on the witness's perception and (2) helpful to the trier of fact. Thus, the witness may offer an opinion regarding the declarant's emotional state. Indeed, some opinion may be necessary for the witness to describe the subject's excitement.

Generally, you should elicit testimony that is as factual as possible in establishing excitement. A broad question that openly calls for a conclusion — such as, "Was the woman excited?" — may unduly invade the factfinder's province. Thus, you should ask specific questions that bring out the physical manifestations of excitement. If the witness offers some opinions in the course of responding, the court likely will view them as necessary to an accurate description. An appropriate examination is set forth in the following example:

---

[104] See United States v. Joy, 192 F.3d 761, 766 (7th Cir. 1999) ("An excited utterance need not be contemporaneous with the startling event to be admissible [but] must be contemporaneous with the excitement engendered by the startling event.") See also RICHARD O. LEMPERT AND STEPHEN A. SALTZBURG, A MODERN APPROACH TO EVIDENCE 418 (2d ed. 1982).

[105] *Id.*

[106] See Bourjaily v. United States, 483 U.S. 171 (1987), holding that courts under FED. R. EVID. 104(a) need not limit themselves to independent evidence in determining the admissibility of coconspirators' statements; the statements themselves may be used.

Q.   After you saw the men run from the store, what did you see?

A.   A woman came out.

Q.   What did she do?

A.   She looked around and then ran over to a man, standing on the sidewalk, and grabbed his arm.

Q.   Describe her physical appearance.

A.   She was quite flushed. She was holding her chest with her left hand. Her movements were quick, jerky.

Q.   Could you describe her breathing?

A.   Yes. She was taking deep, gulping breaths. As I said, her hand was on her chest. She was extremely agitated.

Q.   Did you hear her say anything?

A.   Yes.

Opposing
Counsel: Objection, Your Honor. Hearsay.

Counsel: Your Honor, I'm still laying the foundation for the excited utterance exception.

The Court: Proceed.

Q.   Before you tell us what she said, how did she say it?

A.   She said it in a high-pitched, squeaky voice — almost yelling. She was quite upset.

Q.   What did she say?

Opposing
Counsel: Objection. Hearsay.

The Court: Please approach the bench. [The Court determines that counsel expects the statement to relate to a robbery that occurred moments earlier in the store].

The Court: I'll allow the statement under the excited utterance exception.

Q.   Again, Ms. Jones, what did the woman say?

A.   She said: "Johnny Thomas just robbed Mr. Dorbey's store. Get the police!"

In the example, opinion enters the witness's description. Some of it — "looked scared," "agitated," "quite upset" — may go beyond what some judges would permit. In the context of specific questions, however, the comments should not draw an objection, and in any event seem necessary to describe the subject's emotional state.

§ 6-23. Statements Describing Contemporaneous Mental, Emotional, or Physical Condition (FRE 803(3)).

FRE 803(3) creates a hearsay exception for statements that describe a declarant's state of mind, emotion, sensation or physical condition.[107] It does not except assertions describing a past condition, except for statements relating to wills. The rule provides:

> **(3) Then existing mental, emotional or physical condition.** A statement of the declarant's then existing state of mind, emotion, sensation, or physical condition (such as intent, plan, motive, design, mental feeling, pain, and bodily health), but not including a statement of memory or belief to prove the fact remembered or believed unless it relates to the execution, revocation, identification, or terms of declarant's will.

The exception is closely related to that for present sense impressions. The Advisory Committee states the exception "is essentially a specialized application of Exception (1), presented separately to enhance its usefulness and accessibility."[108] Statements within the exception are descriptions of what the declarant thinks, believes or feels. Thus, "I feel great," "I plan to go to Chicago," "I'm depressed," "This chicken tastes great," and "My tummy hurts" all fit.

The rule codifies the common law exception for "state of mind." There are no memory and perception pitfalls when a declarant describes his own mental, emotional or physical state. The statements may be deceptive, since people sometimes exaggerate physical or mental distress or misdescribe their own intent, but the requirement that the statements be contemporaneous eliminates some of this concern. The exception generally does not include statements describing a past state of mind, emotion or condition. Obviously, the memory pitfall exists when a declarant describes his past state of mind.

The exception does not permit the introduction of a declarant's belief in a fact to prove the fact. The exclusion of statements of memory or belief to prove facts remembered or believed codifies rulings against an undue expansion of the state of mind exception. When a party uses a declarant's belief to prove an external fact, it is the fact rather than the state of mind that is relevant. Thus, the state of mind exception is inapplicable. Further, using the "state of mind" exception

---

[107] See ROGER C. PARK, DAVID P. LEONARD, AND STEVEN H. GOLDBERG, EVIDENCE LAW 272 (1998).

[108] FED. R. EVID. 803(3) advisory committee's note.

to prove facts reflected in the state of mind would open the door to virtually all hearsay, because a hearsay statement almost always describes a fact that the declarant remembers or believes. The rule specifically prohibits this result to ensure against a mistaken application of the exception.[109] The provision is unnecessary, however, since a relevance analysis should exclude a statement of memory or belief to prove "state of mind" when that state of mind is not itself a fact of consequence.

A contemporaneous description of state of mind may be introduced to prove intent, which can be used to infer subsequent conduct. Assume, for example, a declarant states: "I intend to kill myself next Wednesday." The declarant's then-existing state of mind is relevant as circumstantial evidence that his death the following Wednesday was self-inflicted. The declarant's contemporaneous statement of intent does not have memory or perception problems, and, if the intent can be used as a basis for inferring a fact, should be admitted. The rule was established in *Mutual Life Insurance. Co. v. Hillmon*,[110] where the United States Supreme Court held that letters expressing an intent to take action in the future could be introduced to show the declarant later took that action.

An exception to the rule against using statements of memory to prove past facts is a statement of a testator relating to his will. Since the testator is unavailable, a special need exists for his hearsay statements. Moreover, the testator's statements usually are reliable. *McCormick* explains the reasons for carving out the exception as follows:

> Impetus to recognize such an exception is furnished by the unavailability of the person who best knew the facts and often was the only person with that knowledge, *viz.*, the testator. Special reliability is suggested by the undeniable firsthand knowledge and lack of motive to deceive, though the possibility may exist that the testator wished to deceive his or her relatives. . . .[111]

The federal rule codifies decisions adopting the special exception. This action rests "on practical grounds of necessity and expediency rather than logic."[112]

---

[109] *Id.* The Advisory Committee states: "The exclusion of 'statements of memory or belief to prove the fact remembered or believed' is necessary to avoid the virtual destruction of the hearsay rule which would otherwise result from allowing state of mind, provable by a hearsay statement, to serve as the basis for an inference of the happening of the event which produced the state of mind." See Shepard v. United States, 290 U.S. 96 (1933).

[110] 145 U.S. 285 (1892).

[111] MCCORMICK ON EVIDENCE § 276 (5th ed. 1999).

[112] FED. R. EVID. 803(3) advisory committee's note.

§ 6-24. Statements for Medical Diagnosis or Treatment (FRE 803(4)).

FRE 803(4) excepts from hearsay those statements made for medical diagnosis or treatment that are reasonably pertinent for those purposes.[113] It provides:

> **(4) Statements for purposes of medical diagnosis or treatment.** Statements made for purposes of medical diagnosis or treatment and describing medical history, or past or present symptoms, pain, or sensations, or the inception or general character of the cause or external source thereof insofar as reasonably pertinent to diagnosis or treatment.

This rule overlaps with FRE 803(1) and (3), but also allows statements of past facts if made for medical diagnosis or treatment.

The theory supporting the exception is that statements for diagnosis or treatment are reliable; a patient seeking medical treatment generally has a strong motivation to be truthful. This incentive for truthfulness justifies the inclusion of descriptions of past conditions, even though their accuracy depends on memory.[114] The statements need not be made to physicians. The Advisory Committee states that "[s]tatements to hospital attendants, ambulance drivers, or even members of the family might be included."[115] Additionally, the patient need not make the statement so long as the factors suggesting reliability are present. Thus, for instance, a mother's statement to a physician regarding an injury to her child would be covered.

While statements for medical treatment logically are reliable, some statements for diagnosis may be self-serving — those made to a physician who will testify. Many jurisdictions excluded these statements because they were not trustworthy.[116] The Advisory Committee rejected this approach because, under FRE 703, an expert could rely on the statements and could refer to them in explaining his opinion. The Committee believed that jurors would have difficulty considering the statements to evaluate opinion but not in determining facts.[117] Under the current version of FRE 703, however, an expert generally cannot refer to inadmissible evidence in explaining his opinion. Nevertheless, the hearsay exception has not been modified.

---

[113] See, e.g., O'Gee v. Dobbs Houses, Inc., 570 F.2d 1084 (2d Cir. 1978).

[114] FED. R. EVID. 803(4) advisory committee's note.

[115] *Id.*

[116] *Id.*

[117] *Id.* The Advisory Committee noted that under conventional doctrine, "these statements were not admissible as substantive evidence, [but] the expert was allowed to state the basis of his opinion, including statements of this kind. The distinction thus called for was one most unlikely to be made by juries. The rule accordingly rejects the limitation."

One issue in applying the exception is the scope of the "reasonably pertinent" limitation.[118] Statements describing the cause of an injury or sickness may not be especially reliable. Although courts generally exclude statements of causation, some decisions admit them when they actually are a factor in diagnosis or treatment. If not, or if the statement might unduly influence the determination of liability, the court should exclude the statement.[119]

§ 6-25. Recorded Recollection (FRE 803(5)).

FRE 803(5) provides an exception for "recorded recollection" — a record of a matter made when the witness remembered it, but as to which the witness no longer has complete recollection.[120] The exception states:

> **(5) Recorded recollection.** A memorandum or record concerning a matter about which a witness once had knowledge but now has insufficient recollection to enable the witness to testify fully and accurately, shown to have been made or adopted by the witness when the matter was fresh in the witness' memory and to reflect that knowledge correctly. If admitted, the memorandum or record may be read into evidence but may not itself be received as an exhibit unless offered by an adverse party.

§ 6-25(a). Theory.

The exception reflects a natural evolution from the practice of showing a document to a witness to refresh recollection. At common law, if the witness's recollection was not refreshed, she was permitted to read from the record if she recognized the writing and testified it was accurate when made.[121] This procedure is only a small step from having the witness testify from a refreshed recollection, because a fine line separates a revitalized memory from mere recitation of the record.

The exception for recorded recollection is justified by the opportunity for cross-examination regarding the accuracy of the record. This safeguard limits the problems that might be associated with ambiguous language or a writer's insincere motives. Additionally, since the witness must testify that her recollection was fresh when the record was made, memory problems are minimized. Further, if the exception did not exist, some witnesses might falsely claim a refreshed recollection in order to regurgitate the contents of a record.

[118] See United States v. Gabe, 56 F.3d 954, 958–59 (8th Cir. 2001) (victim's statement to physician identifying abuser was inadmissible because physician did not explain to victim that identifying her abuser was pertinent to diagnosis and treatment.).

[119] See *Emerging Problems Under the Federal Rules of Evidence*, Rule 803(4) (1991), indicating that courts will not admit a statement of causation that "enters the realm of fault."

[120] See, e.g., In Re Corrugated Container Antitrust Litigation, 756 F.2d 411 (5th Cir. 1985).

[121] MCCORMICK ON EVIDENCE § 279 (5th ed. 1999).

Although the preparer testifies regarding the record, she is in a sense "unavailable" to testify about the underlying facts. Because she lacks a complete recollection of the event, she cannot be fully cross-examined regarding it. FRE 803(5) does not require a total lack of memory; the witness must have "insufficient recollection to enable him to testify fully and accurately." Nevertheless, the witness must lack memory as to some of the facts, which impairs the protection afforded by cross-examination.

The rule permits the introduction of a record when the preparer's memory is impaired, but not if the memory is clear. Paradoxically, if the witness has a full memory, the opportunity for cross-examination provides greater assurance of the record's reliability than if her memory is inadequate. Nevertheless, permitting the introduction of recorded recollection when the witness does not have an impaired memory would encourage the introduction of prepared statements in lieu of live testimony. This action would diminish the spontaneity of trials and open the door for the introduction of selective factual accounts. As the Advisory Committee states, eliminating the impaired memory requirement would "encourage the use of statements carefully prepared for purposes of litigation under the supervision of attorneys, investigators and claims adjusters."[122]

The exception permits the proponent to have the record read, but allows its introduction as an exhibit only by the adverse party. This approach reflects a determination that recorded recollection should not carry more weight than oral testimony.[123] If memory were refreshed, and the witness testified to an event, her record would not be admissible. The rule also prevents any undue influence that might result if the exhibit were taken into deliberations.

The rule does not require that the record be made by the witness. So long as the witness adopted it when her memory was fresh, the memorandum can be prepared by another party. As the Advisory Committee states: "Multiple person involvement in the process of observing and recording, as in Rathburn v. Brancatella, 93 N.J.L. 222, 107 A. 279 (1919), is entirely consistent with the exception."[124] The witness generally must have read and adopted the record, however; if the witness simply gave an oral account to another, who later transcribed it, the document would be hearsay within hearsay and would not fit the exception.

The courts have extended the exception to include a memorandum dictated by a person with knowledge and simultaneously transcribed by another, even if the memorandum was not then checked by the person recounting the event. The person with knowledge must testify that the account was accurate and the person who made the record must testify that it was transcribed accurately. The

---

[122] FED. R. EVID. 803(5) advisory committee's note.

[123] ROGER C. PARK, DAVID P. LEONARD, STEVEN H. GOLDBERG, EVIDENCE LAW 280 (1998).

[124] FED. R. EVID. 803(5) Advisory Committee's note.

transcription must be simultaneous; if the recorder testifies that he accurately wrote out an oral account subsequent to hearing it, the exception does not apply.[125]

§ 6-25(b). Establishing Conditions for the Introduction of Past Recollection Recorded.

Four conditions must be established to introduce a writing under FRE 803(5). They are: (1) the witness must have had knowledge of the matter when the record was made, (2) the witness must have insufficient recollection to enable him to testify "fully and accurately," (3) the record must have been made or adopted when it was fresh in the witness's memory, and (4) the memorandum must accurately reflect the witness's knowledge. The testimony of the person who prepared or adopted the memorandum is necessary to establish these conditions.[126]

Since the memorandum is a document, it must be properly authenticated. Moreover, since the document is offered to prove its contents, it must comply with the original writing rule.

Usually a record is shown to a witness first to refresh recollection. If the witness testifies that his recollection is refreshed, he can orally recount the event. Sometimes the testimony is little more than a recitation of the memorandum; thus, opposing counsel may wish to have the writing taken back from the witness to prevent a regurgitation of its contents. If the witness testifies that his memory is not completely refreshed, counsel should establish the requirements for introducing the writing. The witness need not testify to a total lack of memory. So long as his recollection is insufficient for a full and accurate description, and the other conditions are met, the writing may be read to the jury.

For the well-prepared witness, it usually is not necessary to introduce past recollection recorded. If the witness reviews his own memorandum before testifying, and has the opportunity to reflect, his memory usually is refreshed. The witness can then provide live testimony. Presumably the exception is used most often with witnesses who are not well prepared. If the witness does not review the memorandum in advance it reasonably might not refresh his recollection, especially if he is someone who makes numerous reports.

---

[125] RICHARD O. LEMPERT AND STEPHEN A. SALTZBURG, A MODERN APPROACH TO EVIDENCE 438 (2d ed. 1982). The authors state:

> The simultaneous transcription is crucial to this extension of the past recollection recorded exception, since an important justification for this exception is the fact that there is little danger that the witness's words will be reported incorrectly.

[126] See generally United States v. Ryder Transportation Servs., Inc., 206 F.3d 772, 774–75 (8th Cir. 2000).

In establishing the conditions for the exception, counsel may be tempted to lead the witness. When legalistic conditions must be established, attorneys often form questions that recite the conditions, calling for a simple "Yes" from the witness: "Mr. Jones, was this record made by you when you had knowledge of the accident and the matter was fresh in your recollection and did you accurately record what you knew?" Judges usually are tolerant of this form, knowing the difficulty of establishing the conditions without suggesting answers. A better approach, however, is to frame nonleading questions that refer to the conditions, but ask the extent of compliance. The following questions are examples:

Q.   What knowledge did you have of the accident when this document was prepared?

Q.   How accurate was your memory of the facts when you prepared this document?

Q.   How accurate was the narrative you prepared?

These questions focus the testimony on the conditions, while permitting the witness to supply the pertinent information.

The following is an example of an examination establishing the basis for the exception.

Q.   What was your involvement in the accident that occurred on June 3, 1990?

A.   I was a witness.

Q.   Where were you standing?

A.   I believe I was on the street corner at Hurst and Joseph. It's a little hazy.

Q.   What cars were involved in the accident?

A.   There was a green car, but I really can't remember. . . . I can't remember the other, and I can't remember which was green.

Q.   Do you recall what occurred?

A.   Not very well. I certainly couldn't swear to it.

Q.   Your Honor, may I approach? [Court nods.] [Counsel hands copy of document to opposing counsel.] Let me show you a document. Can you tell the Court and jury what it is?

A.   That's a statement I wrote out and signed after the accident. An investigator asked me for it.

Q.   Read it over if you will. [Witness reads]. Does that refresh your recollection as to what happened in the accident?

A.   I can't really say that it does. This is correct, I know that, but I still don't really remember this stuff.

Q.   When you wrote that statement, how accurate was your memory of the accident?

A.   Oh, it was accurate. That was only a few days after it occurred.

Q.   How accurately did you describe what you knew in the statement?

A.   It was completely accurate.

Counsel: I ask that the witness be permitted to read the document as past recollection recorded.

The Court: Any objection? Please do so.

On cross-examination, you may use a record prepared by the witness to refresh recollection or introduce it as past recollection recorded if it does not refresh the witness's memory. Nevertheless, you generally will be most effective if you do not first show the document to the witness. Presumably, if the document has not been introduced, the witness testified from memory on direct. The memorandum can be used as a basis to establish facts on cross-examination. See § 9-16.

To the extent the prior statements are inconsistent with the witness's testimony, you may ask the witness about them without showing him the document.[127] Allowing the witness to review the document may shift the advantage from you to the witness, giving the witness time to anticipate your questions.[128] Nevertheless, many lawyers do not follow this rule of advocacy; they gratuitously hand a document to the witness to "refresh recollection" when they should be framing questions to establish facts and impeach testimony.

If the witness denies recollection of a fact described in a prior statement, the "I don't recall" is not inconsistent with the statement and impeachment theoretically is improper. In the rat-tat-tat of cross-examination, however, the denial of memory may seem inconsistent. Thus, there may be no objection if you use the document as if you were impeaching. The following exchange, involving both denials of facts and a claimed lack of memory, illustrates this point.

---

[127] FED. R. EVID. 613(a); see § 9-16(b).

[128] See § 9-16(b).

Q.   Mrs. Jones, you said you saw the accident at the corner of Joseph and Hurst, is that correct?

A.   Yes.

Q.   You were about half a block from the corner, is that true?

A.   No. I was closer.

Q.   You wrote out and signed a statement concerning the accident and gave it to an investigator named Dan Smelting about three days after the accident occurred. Do you remember that?

A.   Yes.

       [Counsel is holding the document. On request, it must be shown to opposing counsel, but not necessarily to the witness].

Q.   In that statement, you said: "I was about half a block away." Is that right?

A.   I guess so.

Q.   There also were several cars in the way, impeding your view, is that right?

A.   I don't think so.

Q.   In your statement you said: "There were about four or five cars in the way that made it hard to see." Is that correct?

A.   Oh, yes. That's right. There were some cars.

Q.   There also were some bushes in the way, is that true?

A.   I don't remember.

Q.   In your statement you said: "There were bushes in the way also, so I could not see too well." Is that right?

A.   I guess I said that.

In this example the prior statement regarding the bushes does not directly contradict the claim of no memory, yet the use of the statement in the impeachment format does not seem improper. Technically, counsel should be required to show the document to the witness to refresh recollection when the witness claims lack of memory, before following up with questions. An effective cross-examiner usually succeeds, however, in skipping this step.

§ 6-25(c). Use of Other Material to Refresh Recollection.

You are not limited to refreshing a witness's recollection with his prior writings. You can show virtually any pertinent document to a witness to refresh recollection. The document need not have been prepared, or ever reviewed, by the witness, and it need not be an exhibit.

Assume, for example, John Decker and Joe Trammel attend a meeting. Trammel prepares a memorandum of the meeting and sends it to a file. Decker later testifies. If Decker states that he cannot remember the meeting, counsel could show Trammel's memorandum to him to refresh his memory. Since refreshing recollection does not require the introduction of the exhibit, and opposing counsel can examine the witness concerning his reliance on the document, courts generally permit wide latitude in the material used for this purpose. You cannot use a document that a witness has not prepared or adopted, however, as prior recollection recorded.

§ 6-26. Regularly Kept Records (FRE 803(6) and (7)).

One of the broadest exceptions to the hearsay rule applies to "records of regularly conducted activity." The rule excepts business and similar records that are regularly kept, opening the door to many forms of written hearsay. Additionally, the rule excepts hearsay within hearsay if it conforms to certain requirements. Further, the rule allows the introduction of many opinions. Lawyers often invoke it to introduce documentary hearsay, especially when witnesses with firsthand factual knowledge cannot be presented.

FRE 803(6) sets forth the exception for regularly kept records. FRE 803(7) creates a separate exception for the *absence of an entry* in regularly kept records. FRE 803(6) and FRE 803(7) except the following from hearsay:

> **(6) Records of regularly conducted activity.** A memorandum, report, record, or data compilation, in any form, of acts, events, conditions, opinions, or diagnoses, made at or near the time by, or from information transmitted by, a person with knowledge, if kept in the course of a regularly conducted business activity, and if it was the regular practice of that business activity to make the memorandum, report, record, or data compilation, all as shown by the testimony of the custodian or other qualified witness, or by certification that complies with Rule 902(11), Rule 902(12), or a statute permitting certification, unless the source of information or the method or circumstances of preparation indicate lack of trustworthiness. The term "business" as used in this paragraph includes business, institution, association, profession, occupation, and calling of every kind, whether or not conducted for profit.

> **(7) Absence of entry in records kept in accordance with the provisions of paragraph (6).** Evidence that a matter is not included in the memoranda, reports, records, or data compilations, in any form, kept in accordance with

the provisions of paragraph (6), to prove the nonoccurrence or nonexistence of the matter, if the matter was of a kind of which a memorandum, report, record, or data compilation was regularly made and preserved, unless the sources of information or other circumstances indicate lack of trustworthiness.

§ 6-26(a).   Basis for the Exception.

The exception is justified by the theory that a business or similar organization, which maintains records in the course of a regularly conducted activity, has a strong interest in ensuring their accuracy. Those who work for the organization presumably are required to make correct recordings. The regularity of the record keeping tends to ensure that knowledgeable, trained persons make the entries. The records often are checked and sometimes verified by outside audit. The business or organization would not regularly keep the records unless they were important to its function. A business bases decisions on its regularly kept records; if the business deems the records reliable, they are a trustworthy source of information in court.

The rule originated at common law as a means for tradesmen to prove debts for goods and services sold. It permitted the introduction of their "shop books" into evidence. The "shop book" exception was a necessary accommodation to the common law rule prohibiting a party from appearing as his own witness; it provided an alternate means of proving transactions. Subsequently, the rule was expanded to include entries made in the regular course of business by persons who since had died. The rule evolved to its modern form largely because of need, to cover the many situations in which the persons who make entries in business records were unavailable at trial.[129] In the modern version there is no requirement of unavailability.

§ 6-26(b).   Elements of the Exception.

The exception is a basis for introducing information recorded in a regularly conducted business activity. The information may be hearsay within hearsay, so long as all persons contributing to the report had a "business duty" of accuracy. The records may also include opinions if they are normally recorded in the business activity. "Business" is broadly defined to include "business, institution, association, profession, occupation, and calling of every kind. . . ." The elements of the exception are discussed below.

§ 6-26(b)(1).   Documents.

The regularly kept records exception is broadly phrased to include many types of documents. The rule permits the admission of a "memorandum, report, record, or data compilation, in any form. . . ." Since oral reports could not be "kept"

---

[129] See generally MCCORMICK ON EVIDENCE § 286 (5th ed. 1999).

by a business, they are not captured by the exception.[130] The Advisory Committee Note explains that the exception covers computer records and information stored in new ways through developing technology. It states:

> The form which the "record" may assume under the rule is described broadly as a "memorandum, report, record, or data compilation, in any form." The expression "data compilation" is used as broadly descriptive of any means of storing information other than the conventional words and figures in written or documentary form. It includes, but is by no means limited to, electronic computer storage. . . .[131]

With the advent of voice message systems, oral reports captured and "kept" as part of a regular business activity presumably can be included if the other requirements of the exception are met.

§ 6-26(b)(2). Knowledgeable Informant.

The source of the information in the record must be a person with personal knowledge. If the person who makes the record has personal knowledge, the rule is satisfied. If the information is relayed among individuals within the business, the source must have personal knowledge, and each person in the chain, including the source, must have a "business duty" of accuracy. The "business duty" requirement is discussed below.

The informant's knowledge may be established by testimony or by the report itself. Even if the report does not state the basis of the source's knowledge, it may describe facts permitting the court to infer knowledge. Additionally, if the witness testifies that the business made it a practice to observe the matter, this evidence may circumstantially establish knowledge, absent countervailing proof.[132]

§ 6-26(b)(3). Business Duty of Those Transmitting Information.

Business records often contain reports transmitted through several persons. The exception expressly includes reports made "from information transmitted by a person with knowledge;" thus, it authorizes the introduction of some hearsay within hearsay. The rule requires, however, that the report be made as a "regular practice" of the business. Although the rule does not explicitly require that all informants report the information as part of a regular practice, the Advisory Committee Note makes clear that it envisions "an informant with knowledge acting in the course of the regularly conducted activity."[133] The committee explains the basis for the rule as follows:

---

[130] MCCORMICK at § 287: "[T]he provision that the report be 'kept' negates the idea that oral reports are within the rule."

[131] FED. R. EVID. 803(6) advisory committee's note.

[132] MCCORMICK ON EVIDENCE § 290 (5th ed. 1999).

[133] FED. R. EVID. 803(6) advisory committee's note.

Sources of information presented no substantial problem with ordinary business records. All participants, including the observer or participant furnishing the information to be recorded, were acting routinely, under a duty of accuracy, with employer reliance on the result, or in short "in the regular course of business." If, however, the supplier of the information does not act in the regular course, an essential link is broken; the assurance of accuracy does not extend to the information itself, and the fact that it may be recorded with scrupulous accuracy is of no avail. . . .[134]

As part of the "regular practice" condition, the courts require that each person in the information chain have a "business duty" to report accurately. This requirement predates the federal rules and emanates from *Johnson v. Lutz,*[135] which determined that information supplied by a bystander with no business duty to the organization was inadmissible. The requirement that all informants have a business duty is consistent with the rationale for the exception — that the information will be accurate because those reporting it are obliged to provide correct reports and their performance is subject to review.

An employee easily fulfills the "business duty" requirement. So long as the employee provides the information as part of a regular practice, he reports it under a business duty. The issue is fuzzier when the informant is not employed by the organization but has some other affiliation with it — perhaps a volunteer in a charity. In that case the informant does not have a "duty" in the sense of an employee who is subject to sanction, and may not have the same motivation to be accurate. Nevertheless, the strength of the affiliation and regularity of the practice may supply equivalent guarantees of reliability.[136] The admissibility of the record depends on circumstances, but some kind of obligation to the organization is required to admit the informant's report.

If the chain of information includes someone with no business duty, the information still may be admissible if that transmittal fits another hearsay exception or exclusion. Typically, the problem arises when the source is outside the organization, as when a bystander reports information to an employee, who relays it as part of a regular report. If the source's statement would otherwise be admissible — perhaps as an excited utterance — the record still could be introduced.

---

[134] *Id.*

[135] 253 N.Y. 124, 170 N.E. 517 (1930).

[136] See FED. R. EVID. 803(6), Sen. Comm. Report. The committee suggests that records of schools, churches and hospitals, even though not strictly those of a "business," are of "equivalent trustworthiness and should be admitted into evidence." Sen. Comm. on Judiciary, FED. RULES OF EVID., S. Rep. No. 1277, 3d Cong., 2d Sess., p. 16 (1974).

§ 6-26(b)(4). Regular Activity and Practice.

The report must be "kept in the course of a regularly conducted business activity," and it must be the "regular practice of that business activity to make the . . . report." In addition to requiring a business duty, these provisions mandate that the organization have a recurring, normal practice of making and keeping the report. Regularity is essential because it is a reason to assume the report is reliable.

The federal rule stops short of requiring that the record keeping be "routine." Mandating a "routine" practice would unduly emphasize the frequency and sameness of the procedure as compared to other attributes establishing reliability, and could result in the exclusion of helpful evidence.[137] The regularity requirement does suggest, however, that the record be part of a recurring practice undertaken for business rather than litigation purposes. An isolated memorandum, particularly one prepared to defend a lawsuit, would not qualify.[138]

The prime mark of reliability of a business record is an organizational need for accurate information. If good information promotes the organization's objectives — usually profit — it is reasonable to assume the organization would ensure its reliability. The assumption is weakened if the reports are infrequent, because the organization might not enforce its requirements for isolated reports. If misleading information could promote the organization's interests — for example, a self-serving accident report — it would not be reasonable to assume the report is accurate.

§ 6-26(b)(5). Timeliness.

The rule requires that the record be made "at or near the time" of the event or matter being reported. Thus, the report should be prepared soon enough to allow an inference that the matter was fresh in the informant's memory. The allowable time lapse depends on circumstances. For a major event, a report prepared after several days might be timely; for small transactions, a virtually simultaneous record might be required.

§ 6-26(b)(6). No Lack of Trustworthiness.

The exception calls for exclusion of a report if the source of information, the method of preparation, or the attendant circumstances indicate it is not trustworthy. The provision is deliberately imprecise, but emanates from decisions excluding records when the preparer had a special motive to present the facts in a self-serving way.

---

[137] Cf. FED. R. EVID. 803(6) advisory committee's note criticizing "a tendency unduly to emphasize a requirement of routineness and repetitiveness. . . ."

[138] See Certain Underwriters at Lloyd's, London v. Sinkovich, 232 F.3d. 200, 205 (4th Cir. 2000); Jones v. Board of Trustees Community College, 75 F.Supp.2d 885, 889 (N.D. Ill. 1999).

The leading case, *Palmer v. Hoffman*, [139] excluded an accident report prepared by an engineer who was involved in a grade crossing collision. The court determined that the report was not admissible because it did not have the reliability of routine, systematic reports. The court did not specifically rely on the engineer's self-serving motive, but the requirement of routineness appears designed to exclude reports prepared to support a litigation interest. As the Advisory Committee states:

> The report was prepared for use in litigating, not railroading. While the opinion mentions the motivation of the engineers only obliquely, the emphasis on records of routine operations is significant only by virtue of impact on motivation to be accurate. The opinion of the Court of Appeals had gone beyond mere lack of motive to be accurate; the engineer's statement was "dripping with motivations to misrepresent." Hoffman v. Palmer, 129 F.2d 976, 991 (2d Cir. 1942). . . . [140]

A motive to falsify records is not, by itself, a reason to exclude them. Fabrication of business records frequently would promote self-serving interests. When a statement is issued for a sale, for instance, the seller arguably has a self-serving motive to overstate the bill. Nevertheless, a seller's accounts made in the regular course of business generally are admitted. The seller's need for an honest reputation and accurate internal accounting presumably outweighs the short-run motive to fabricate. Additionally, the fact that the records are prepared as part of a recurring process lessens the likelihood that individual statements may be falsified.

Circumstances sometimes arise, however, in which the preparer's self-serving motive is strong enough to counterbalance the presumption of accuracy. When an employee might be blamed for an erroneous action, for instance, her motivation to avoid a penalty might render her report suspect despite the business need for accurate records. Additionally, when an accident might subject the business to liability, the business's desire for a strong litigating position may outweigh its motivation to maintain correct records. The determination of untrustworthiness depends on circumstances. As the Advisory Committee states: "The formulation of specific terms that would assure satisfactory results in all cases is not possible." [141]

FRE 803(6) does not adopt the "routineness" test of *Palmer v. Hoffman* to guarantee trustworthiness. A routineness requirement would exclude many reliable records prepared as part of a regular — but not routine — practice. Moreover, some routinely prepared records may nevertheless be untrustworthy,

---

[139] 318 U.S. 109 (1943).

[140] FED. R. EVID. 803(6) advisory committee's note.

[141] *Id.*

such as accident reports prepared by drivers for transit companies. The routine-ness requirement does not substitute for an analysis of whether the organization has reason to require accurate reports.

§ 6-24(b)(7). Qualified Witness, or Certification

The rule requires "the testimony of the custodian or other qualified witness" or a certification authorized by the rules or by statutes to establish the elements of the exception. A witness is "qualified" if she has knowledge of the record keeping practices of the organization. The witness need not have personal knowledge of the events described in the record, nor the exact manner in which the information was acquired and conveyed. She must describe the organization's "regular" practice sufficiently to support an inference that the record satisfies the exception.

The rule and FRE 902 were amended in 2000 to permit the introduction of certified regularly kept records. Although FRE 902(11) and (12) require notice to adverse parties of a party's intent to offer a certified copy of a business record, and a fair opportunity for inspection, the elimination of the requirement of a live witness to lay the foundation for regularly kept records has questionable basis. The exception permits the introduction of hearsay within hearsay, when a "business duty" exists for all the declarants in a chain, and opinions that are recorded as part of a regular activity. Given the liberal scope of the exception, the proponent properly should be allocated the burden of proving an adequate foundation. The provision permitting the introduction of certified records inappropriately shifts this burden to the adverse party and may lead to the introduction of evidence that would not be admitted if a witness were required to appear and were cross-examined on the foundation.

§ 6-26(c). Hearsay Within Hearsay in the Record.

Unlike most other hearsay exceptions, the regularly kept records exception permits the introduction of hearsay within hearsay. So long as each participant in the communications chain has a "business duty" to the organization, the information he transmits is admissible. The business duty requirement is discussed in § 6-26(b)(3). If a participant does not have a business duty, the information he transmits is admissible only if another hearsay exclusion or exception applies.

§ 6-26(d). Opinions in Regularly Kept Records.

FRE 803(6) permits the introduction of "opinions, or diagnoses" in regularly kept records. The rule appears to do more than merely except opinions from hearsay, since it also may relax the foundation requirement of FRE 702 for expert opinions. The Advisory Committee Note makes clear that the "rule specifically includes both diagnoses and opinions . . . as proper subjects of admissible

259

entries,"[142] but does not clarify whether it requires a showing that the person rendering the opinion was qualified.

The rule permits the introduction of many opinions in business records without a special showing of a foundation. The extent to which it waives the normal foundation requirement, however, is unclear. *McCormick* asserts the opinions "will still be subject to requirements governing proper subjects for expert opinions and qualification of experts,"[143] but suggests the requisite foundation may be inferred if the institution is reputable and there are no special circumstances suggesting unreliability.[144] Lempert and Saltzburg contend that "standard" expert judgments based on objective evidence are admissible, but more conjectural opinions are not.[145] The ABA's Trial Evidence Committee concludes that the rule permits the introduction of opinions requiring conjecture, but generally would not allow the admission of those addressing causation or fault.[146]

The rule requires that opinions in business records be recorded as part of a "regular" practice. This provision supplies a basis for establishing that opinions are reliable, even without a special foundation. Opinions that go beyond those necessary for the institution's regular functions would not have the reliability stemming from the institution's need for accuracy. A hospital diagnosis ascribing fault for an automobile accident, for instance, would usually fall outside the hospital's "regular" diagnostic practice. Additionally, an institution would not regularly use opinions given by unqualified employees. Thus, even if the rule relaxes the foundation requirement for expert opinions, the need for regularity imposes analogous conditions.

The exception also provides for the exclusion of information in business records if the "source of the information or other circumstances indicate lack of trustworthiness." Under this provision, an opinion submitted by an unqualified informant should be excluded. Additionally, speculative and untrustworthy opinions may be excluded. If the opinion merely rephrased the claims of a litigant, for instance, it could be excluded as untrustworthy.

FRE 803(6) appears to allow the admission of lay opinions. Under FRE 701, lay opinions are admissible if rationally based on the perception of the witness and helpful to the trier of fact. Since FRE 803(6) requires that the original source of the information have "knowledge" of the facts, it appears to incorporate the rational basis requirement. The rule probably waives the traditional preference for concrete over conclusory descriptions, however, since a record does not have

---

[142] *Id.*

[143] MCCORMICK ON EVIDENCE § 287 (5th ed. 1999).

[144] *Id.* § 293.

[145] RICHARD O. LEMPERT AND STEPHEN A. SALTZBURG, A MODERN APPROACH TO EVIDENCE 443 (2d ed. 1982).

[146] *Emerging Problems Under the Federal Rules of Evidence*, Rule 803(6) (1991).

the live witness's ability to rephrase a description. Nevertheless, an opinion that states an ultimate conclusion, which the jury could reach itself, should be excluded as unhelpful.

§ 6-26(e). Absence of Entry in Regularly Kept Records.

FRE 803(7) allows a showing that a matter is not included in a business record to prove the nonoccurrence or nonexistence of the matter, if the matter would have been recorded as part of the business's regular practice. The Advisory Committee suggested that the evidence is "probably not hearsay as defined in Rule 801" but adopted the exception to "set the question at rest in favor of admissibility."[147] Proving the absence of an entry usually requires consideration of the entries in the record, which may explain why some courts have treated omissions in records as hearsay.[148] The business record exception would permit the introduction of the record, however, so an additional exception for the omission appears redundant. In any event, the record must satisfy the requirements of FRE 803(6).

§ 6-26(f). Admissibility of Public Records Under FRE 803(6).

The business records exception on its face appears to permit the introduction of regularly kept public records, such as reports made by law enforcement officers. FRE 803(8) specifically deals with public records, however, and precludes their admission against criminal defendants under certain circumstances. The question arises whether a report that would be inadmissible under FRE 803(8) could be introduced pursuant to FRE 803(6).

The courts generally have refused to allow the use of the business records exception for this purpose.[149] The exclusions in FRE 803(8) reflect a policy determination that certain law enforcement reports should not be introduced in criminal cases; the policy would be frustrated if the courts allowed the introduction of these reports under FRE 803(6). Public reports may be introduced under FRE 803(6), however, when they do not run afoul of the concerns that led to the exclusions in FRE 803(8). Thus, a party could introduce a report that merely documents unambiguous facts unrelated to the criminal investigation.[150]

---

[147] FED. R. EVID. 803(7) advisory committee's note.

[148] *Id.*

[149] United States v. Oates, 560 F.2d 45, 78 (2d Cir. 1977); United States v. Orozco, 590 F.2d 789, 793 (9th Cir. 1979), *cert. denied*, 442 U.S. 920 (1979).

[150] United States v. Brown, 9 F.3d 907, 911 (11th Cir. 1993) ("Many courts . . .have drawn a distinction between police records prepared in a routine, non-adversarial setting and those resulting from a more subjective investigation and evaluation of a crime."); United States v. Darcy, 861 F.2d 77 (5th Cir. 1988).

§ 6-26(g). Establishing Conditions to Admit Regularly Kept Records.

A "qualified witness" must establish the requirements of FRE 803(6). The witness must have knowledge regarding the institution's record keeping practices. He must be able to testify that a person with knowledge regularly reported the information in the records and the records are regularly kept. An example of testimony that provides the foundation for business records is set forth below:

Q.	State your name, please.
A.	Mary Adams.
Q.	What is your occupation?
A.	Firm administrator for Ivy Distributors, Inc.
Q.	What is your familiarity with the record keeping practices of the firm?
A.	I am in charge of supervising our record keeping. The records are maintained by employees whom I supervise.
Counsel:	Your Honor, may I approach the witness?
The Court:	You may.
Q.	I show you a document previously marked for identification as Plaintiff's Exhibit 3. Can you tell me what it is?
A.	It is a delivery report from our records.
Q.	What is your firm's practice concerning the preparation of delivery reports?
A.	They are prepared by our truck drivers immediately after the delivery of merchandise.
Q.	How regularly are they prepared?
A.	Our drivers are required to prepare them after each delivery.
Q.	What is done with these reports?
A.	They are used to calculate the bills we send customers. They are organized by customer and maintained in our files for ready reference.
Q.	Your Honor, I offer Plaintiff's Exhibit 3 as a regularly kept record of Ivy Distributors, Inc.
The Court:	Any objection? Let it be admitted.
Counsel:	May I distribute copies to the jury?
The Court:	Please do.

For computer and other electronic records, you may have to provide more information regarding the inputting of data and the program under which the data is sorted and presented. In general, however, computer records are admissible without the need to call a computer expert.[151] Problems may arise when data is accumulated in a regular practice, but presented through a program used specially for the litigation. In that case the underlying data may be admissible under the business records exception, but the special presentation of the data may require expert testimony.

§ 6-27. Public Records (FRE 803(8)).

FRE 803(8) creates a broad exception for records and reports of public agencies. The exception does not contain all the conditions for admitting business records, so it provides a special avenue for introducing many public records. FRE 803(8) permits the introduction of public records setting forth (1) the agency's activities, (2) "matters observed" pursuant to a legal duty, on which there was a duty to report, except law enforcement reports in criminal cases, and (3) "factual findings" made pursuant to a legally authorized investigation, except in criminal cases against the defendant and unless the report is untrustworthy.

The exception broadens the traditional common law rule by making it clear that reports containing factual conclusions are admissible. Although the exception does not require that the records be "kept," and thus might be construed to include oral reports, it was not intended to do so. Thus, the rule has been construed to require written or equivalent reports.[152]

The exception reflects the assumption that reports prepared pursuant to a legal duty are accurate. Moreover, since public records are open to inspection and criticism, officials have a special motivation to make them accurate and inaccuracies are likely to be discovered. Further, the rule reflects a policy determination that public officials should not be required to leave their jobs to appear in court.[153] Additionally, many public records are "regularly" made and subject to government audit and review, so they have some of the guarantees of reliability attributed to business records.

Factual findings in government reports may substantially affect litigation. The government often issues reports dealing with public health and safety, which have relevance in products liability, tort, environmental, and other litigation. The government has resources to compile information beyond the reach of many civil litigants. Additionally, government findings may be persuasive because an

---

[151] McCormick on Evidence § 294 (5th ed. 1999).

[152] Richard O. Lempert and Stephen A. Saltzburg, A Modern Approach to Evidence 448 (2d ed. 1982): "[N]owhere in the legislative history of the rule is there any suggestion that it will not require a writing. . . ."

[153] McCormick on Evidence § 295 (5th ed. 1999).

apparently neutral arbiter issues them. Thus, the exception provides a powerful weapon to civil litigants.[154]

The exception authorizes the introduction of determinations based on hearsay. Thus, a record of agency activities would be admissible even if it reflected information distilled from reports; an accident report would be admissible even if based on information transmitted by others, so long as those in the chain of information had a legal duty to report the information; factual findings made under legal authority would be admissible even if based on information from others.[155] Double hearsay may be a basis, however, for excluding investigative findings as untrustworthy.[156] Additionally, the court may strike double hearsay reiterated in a public record if the underlying statement could not otherwise be admitted.[157]

FRE 803(8) excepts from hearsay the following public records:

(8) Public records and reports. Records, reports, statements, or data compilations, in any form, of public offices or agencies, setting forth (A) the activities of the office or agency, or (B) matters observed pursuant to duty imposed by law as to which matters there was a duty to report, excluding, however, in criminal cases matters observed by police officers and other law enforcement personnel, or (C) in civil actions and proceedings and against the Government in criminal cases, factual findings resulting from an investigation made pursuant to authority granted by law, unless the sources of information or other circumstances indicate lack of trustworthiness.

The three categories included in the rule are discussed below.

§ 6-27(a). Activities of the Office or Agency.

Subpart A excepts records reflecting the agency's functions and activities. These records are analogous to business records in that they are usually made as part of a "regular" practice. The exception would authorize the introduction of meter readings made by an electric department, inspection reports of a health department, citations issued by a parking violations bureau, and similar records. The Advisory Committee provides as an example "[t]reasury records of miscellaneous receipts and disbursements."[158] The records are admissible to show that the agency inspections, citations, and other activities occurred — not necessarily

---

[154] RICHARD O. LEMPERT AND STEPHEN A. SALTZBURG, A MODERN APPROACH TO EVIDENCE 447 (2d ed. 1982).

[155] See FED. R. EVID. 803(8) advisory committee's note, cited example of "map prepared by government engineer from information furnished by men working under his supervision."

[156] McKinnon v. Skil Corp., 638 F.2d 270, 278–79 (1st Cir. 1981).

[157] CHRISTOPHER B. MUELLER AND LAIRD C. KIRKPATRICK, MODERN EVIDENCE: DOCTRINE AND PRACTICE 1297–98 (1995).

[158] FED. R. EVID. 803(8) advisory committee's note.

to prove the correctness of matters described in the reports.[159] To prove activities occurred, these records generally are reliable and uncontroversial.

§ 6-27(b).   Reports Made Pursuant to Legal Duty.

Subpart B permits the introduction of reports of matters observed when there was a duty to observe the matter *and* make the report. The provision permits the introduction of inspection reports, accident reports, and similar records to prove the matters observed. The Advisory Committee lists weather bureau rainfall reports, army induction reports, and similar records as examples of records admissible under the provision.[160]

Subpart B allows the introduction of police and law enforcement reports in civil cases but precludes their admission to prove facts observed in criminal cases. Read literally, the rule would exclude the reports whether offered by the government or the defense. It was intended, however, to protect the criminal defendant from the introduction of law enforcement officers' reports when there is no opportunity for cross-examination.[161] Thus, the courts have interpreted the provision to permit the introduction of police reports against the government in criminal cases.[162] Additionally, routine, nonadversarial reports may be introduced by either the prosecution or the defense.[163]

§ 6-27(c).   Factual Findings Made Pursuant to Legal Authority.

Subpart C excepts factual findings resulting from an investigation made under legal authority. The findings may be introduced in civil actions, and against the government in criminal cases, except where the circumstances indicate lack of trustworthiness. Initially, the question arose whether factual conclusions fell within the meaning of "findings." In *Beech Aircraft v. Rainey*,[164] the Supreme Court held that the exception includes fact-based opinions and conclusions. A court may exclude the conclusions, however, if they are untrustworthy.[165]

In deciding whether factual findings are untrustworthy, the courts rely primarily on four factors suggested in the Advisory Committee Note: (1) the timeliness of the investigation, (2) the skill or experience of the person making

---

[159] RICHARD O. LEMPERT AND STEPHEN A. SALTZBURG, A MODERN APPROACH TO EVIDENCE 448 (2d ed. 1982).

[160] FED. R. EVID. 803(8) advisory committee's note.

[161] 120 Cong. Rec. 2387 (Feb. 6, 1974). The rule was amended in the House of Representatives to protect the accused's right of cross-examination.

[162] MCCORMICK ON EVIDENCE § 296 (5th ed. 1999).

[163] *Id.*

[164] 488 U.S. 153 (1988).

[165] *Id.*

the findings, (3) whether a hearing was held, and (4) potential motives of the official to present the facts in a biased manner.[166]

A court may also consider the source of the information and the nature of the factfinding process in assessing trustworthiness. If the agency merely adopts the subjective views of private parties, as when a document submitted by regulated companies is accepted as an agency position without adversarial hearings, a court reasonably could view the "findings" untrustworthy.[167] Similarly, if an investigator's report summarizes the subjective views of witnesses, a court may deem it untrustworthy.[168]

Factual findings of government officials may strongly influence litigation. Once the government makes and documents findings, a subsequent factfinder may be reluctant to reach different conclusions. Moreover, exposure to the factual characterizations of an agency may lead the jury to view the facts in a similar way. *Beech Aircraft* suggests that the conclusions are admissible even if they are "unhelpful," where the trier could draw the necessary inferences without considering another's opinion. Thus, the exception provides a weapon for litigants whose positions are supported by official conclusions.

Given the potential impact of agency reports, the courts have a special obligation to ensure the reliability of the fact finding process. In an analogous circumstance involving expert opinions, the Supreme Court determined that the courts must make a "preliminary assessment" of the reliability of the expert's methods.[169] A similar assessment of agency or investigators' procedures may be required when a claim is raised that findings are not trustworthy. Assessing reliability could require significant resources when the findings deal with complex issues.[170] In most cases, however, the determination focuses on the fact-finding process or the qualifications and motives of the investigator, which should be a straightforward inquiry.

§ 6-27(d). Admission of Public Records Under Other Exceptions.

FRE 803(8)(B) and (C) preclude the introduction against criminal defendants of "matters observed" by police or law enforcement personnel and "factual findings" made pursuant to legally authorized investigations. These provisions preclude the introduction of the excluded material under other hearsay exceptions, as they reflect a policy that criminal defendants should not be denied the right

---

[166] See FED. R. EVID. 803(8) advisory committee's note; Beech Aircraft Corp. v. Rainey, 488 U.S. 153 (1988), refers to the list as "noncxclusive."

[167] See *Emerging Problems Under the Federal Rules of Evidence*, Rule 803(8) (1991).

[168] McKinnon v. Skil Corp., 638 F.2d 270, 296 (1st Cir. 1981); John McShain, Inc. v. Cessna Aircraft Co., 563 F.2d 632, 635–36 (3d Cir. 1977).

[169] Daubert v. Merrell Dow Pharmaceuticals, Inc., 509 U.S. 579 (1993).

[170] *Emerging Problems Under the Federal Rules of Evidence*, Rule 803(8) (1991).

to cross-examine the persons who authored the records.[171] When the author testifies, however, a court may admit the report if another exception — for instance, that for past recollection recorded or for business records — permits its introduction.[172] In that circumstance the accused is not denied the right to confront and cross-examine the witness.

§ 6-28. Public Records of Vital Statistics (FRE 803(9)).

FRE 803(9) creates an exception for a special category of public records — those reflecting reports of vital statistics made to a public office pursuant to legal requirements. Even though the person making the report typically is not a public official, the records are reliable because they involve events — births, deaths and marriages — that routinely are reported. The reports may be required by local, state or federal law. The federal rule governs admissibility in federal court even if a state or local law requiring the report contains different provisions for its introduction.[173] FRE 803(9) excepts:

> **(9) Records of vital statistics.** Records or data compilations, in any form, of births, fetal deaths, deaths, or marriages, if the report thereof was made to a public office pursuant to requirements of law.

§ 6-29. Absence of Public Record or Entry (FRE 803(10)).

FRE 803(10) allows the introduction of a certificate or testimony that there is no public record of an event, to prove its absence or that the event did not occur, if a record of the event ordinarily would have been made and preserved in the public record. The rule excepts:

> **(10) Absence of public record or entry.** To prove the absence of a record, report, statement, or data compilation, in any form, or the nonoccurrence or nonexistence of a matter of which a record, report, statement, or data compilation, in any form, was regularly made and preserved by a public office or agency, evidence in the form of a certification in accordance with rule 902, or testimony, that diligent search failed to disclose the record, report, statement, or data compilation, or entry.

FRE 803(10) is an extension of FRE 803(7), governing the absence of an entry in business records. It applies to "public records of the kind mentioned in Exceptions (8) and (9)."[174] A party may use the rule whether the existence of the record, or the occurrence of the event that would be reported in the record, is the issue.

---

[171] United States v. Oates, 560 F.2d 45, 77–84 (2d Cir. 1977).

[172] United States v. Hayes, 861 F.2d 1225, 1230 (10th Cir. 1988).

[173] MCCORMICK ON EVIDENCE § 297 (5th ed. 1999).

[174] FED. R. EVID. 803 (10) advisory committee's note.

Under the rule a party may introduce a certified copy of a record to show that it does not include an entry. Testimony that an entry is not present would be sufficient if the witness testified she made a "diligent search" for the entry. The rule apparently permits a certificate from a public official stating that a record does not include a matter but implies that the official must attest to a "diligent search." If a certificate stated that the entry did not exist, however, a court likely would infer that a search had been conducted.

§ 6-30. Other Public Records.

FRE 803 excepts from hearsay several other categories of public records. They are discussed below.

§ 6-30(a). Public Records of Documents Showing Property Interest (FRE 803(14)).

FRE 803(14) excepts public records of documents establishing or affecting an interest in property where a statute authorizes the recording of the document in the public office. The record may be used to prove the content of an original document. It also may be used to show execution and delivery of the document for "each person by whom it purports to have been executed." The exception provides:

> **(14) Records of documents affecting an interest in property.** The record of a document purporting to establish or affect an interest in property, as proof of the content of the original recorded document and its execution and delivery by each person by whom it purports to have been executed, if the record is a record of a public office and an applicable statute authorizes the recording of documents of that kind in that office.

§ 6-30(b). Judgment of Previous Conviction (FRE 803(22)).

FRE 803(22) establishes an exception for final judgments entered after a trial or on a plea of guilty, adjudging a person guilty of a felony, to prove any fact essential to sustain the judgment. The exception does not permit the government in a criminal case to offer a judgment entered against someone other than the accused, except for impeachment. The rule does not except misdemeanor convictions or civil judgments from hearsay. It provides:

> **(22) Judgment of previous conviction.** Evidence of a final judgment, entered after a trial or upon a plea of guilty (but not upon a plea of nolo contendere), adjudging a person guilty of a crime punishable by death or imprisonment in excess of one year, to prove any fact essential to sustain the judgment, but not including, when offered by the Government in a criminal prosecution for purposes other than impeachment, judgments against persons other than the accused. The pendency of an appeal may be shown but does not affect admissibility.

This exception removes any hearsay impediment to the introduction of felony convictions for impeachment. Additionally, it removes hearsay as a bar to the use of a felony conviction to establish facts essential to the conviction in subsequent civil cases and in criminal cases where the accused was the person previously found guilty. The rule permits the use of convictions in a manner similar to factual findings in investigative reports. Although the conviction rests on hearsay — evidence submitted in a different proceeding — it can be used to prove the facts on which the judgment is based.

The rule does not include misdemeanor convictions because the motivation to defend against misdemeanor charges often is minimal.[175] Judgments based on pleas of *nolo contendere*, which do not necessarily concede underlying facts, are not included.[176] Nor can judgments of acquittal be used to establish facts, since they do not necessarily reflect a finding of innocence.[177]

Civil judgments are not included because the facts underlying civil judgments are not always clear, and the standard of proof is lower than in criminal proceedings. Additionally, a party is not always motivated to defend a civil suit. The restriction may reflect a concern that civil judgments would unduly invade the jury's province, but this concern also applies to criminal convictions used in subsequent cases.

Admitting convictions of third parties to prove facts against the accused likely would violate the right of confrontation. Thus, a third party conviction may be used only to impeach the third party if he appears as a witness.

§ 6-30(c).   Judgment Proving History or Boundaries (FRE 803(23)).

This exception removes the hearsay bar for judgments establishing matters of personal, family or general history if reputation evidence could be admitted to prove the fact under FRE 803(18) or (19). The exception allows the use of judgments to prove property boundaries, citizenship, ancestry, and general history.[178] It states:

> **(23) Judgment as to personal, family, or general history, or boundaries.** Judgments as proof of matters of personal, family or general history, or boundaries, essential to the judgment, if the same would be provable by evidence of reputation.

---

[175] MCCORMICK ON EVIDENCE § 298 (5th ed. 1999).

[176] See Powers v. Bayliner Marine Corp., 855 F. Supp. 199, 205 (W.D. Mich. 1994 (conviction of negligent homicide after plea of nolo contendre inadmissible in civil action; to admit conviction as evidence of negligence would create risk of unfair prejudice).

[177] See United States v. De La Rosa, 171 F.3d 215 (5th Cir. 1999); United States v. Marrero-Ortiz, 160 F.3d 768, 775 (1st Cir. 1998).

[178] FED. R. EVID. 803(23) advisory committee's note. The note lists manorial rights, public rights of way, immemorial custom, disputed boundary, pedigree, alienage and citizenship among the facts provable with judgments.

§ 6-31. Learned Treatises and Articles (FRE 803(18)).

Traditionally an attorney could use a learned treatise or scholarly article in the cross-examination of an expert, at least to the extent the expert relied on the publication or recognized it as authoritative.[179] The publication could only be used in evaluating the expert's opinion, however; if offered to prove the truth of matters it described, the treatise would be hearsay. As in the case of other statements offered to impeach, it is unrealistic to expect the jury to consider a statement for one purpose but disregard it for another. Thus, FRE 803(18) creates an exception for statements in scholarly publications used to examine an expert.[180] The publication must be established as reliable by the witness's admission, other expert testimony, or judicial notice. It may be read to the jury, but may not be received as an exhibit. FRE 803(18) provides:

> **(18) Learned treatises.** To the extent called to the attention of an expert witness upon cross-examination or relied upon by the expert witness in direct examination, statements contained in published treatises, periodicals, or pamphlets on a subject of history, medicine, or other science or art, established as a reliable authority by the testimony or admission of the witness or by other expert testimony or by judicial notice. If admitted, the statements may be read into evidence but may not be received as exhibits.

The rule does not require that the witness concede the publication is authoritative, if its stature can be established by another expert or judicial notice. Thus, the expert cannot avoid cross-examination on the publication by denying that it is authoritative. The rule requires that the scholarly material be presented in the examination of an expert; this provision helps ensure that it is explained. The concern that the jury might misunderstand the publication supports the restriction against introducing it as an exhibit.[181]

§ 6-32. Quasi-Official and Ancient Private Documents.

FRE 803 excepts statements in five categories of private documents having special indicia of reliability. They include the following:

---

[179] See FED. R. EVID. 803(18) advisory committee's note.

[180] According to the Second Circuit, a medical videotape may qualify as a "learned treatise" for purposes of FRE 803(18) even though it is not a published treatise, periodical or pamphlet. Constantino v. Herzog., 203 F.3d 164 (2d Cir. 2000). The court recognized that its ruling made new law at the federal level. It determined: "[W]e agree with [the district court] that it is just 'overly artificial' to say that information that is sufficiently trustworthy to overcome the hearsay law when presented in a printed learned treatise loses the badge of trustworthiness when presented in a videotape," *Id.* at 171.

[181] FED. R. EVID. 803(18) advisory committee's note.

§ 6-32(a). Records of Religious Organizations (FRE 803(11)).

FRE 808(11) excepts records of religious organizations when a party offers them to prove a subject's personal or family history. The records ordinarily reflect births, deaths, marriages and similar events. They are considered reliable because religious organizations are unlikely to receive or record false data concerning these events. FRE 803(11) excepts:

> **(11) Records of religious organizations.** Statements of births, marriages, divorces, deaths, legitimacy, ancestry, relationship by blood or marriage, or other similar facts of personal or family history, contained in a regularly kept record of a religious organization.

§ 6-32(b). Marriage and Sacramental Certificates (FRE 803(12)).

FRE 803(12) creates an exception for statements of fact in certificates of ceremonies by public officials, religious officials and others authorized by law or religious organizations to perform them. The certificate must have an issuance date at or reasonably near the time of the ceremony. The rule includes:

> **(12) Marriage, baptismal, and similar certificates.** Statements of fact contained in a certificate that the maker performed a marriage or other ceremony or administered a sacrament, made by a clergyman, public official, or other person authorized by the rules or practices of a religious organization or by law to perform the act certified, and purporting to have been issued at the time of the act or within a reasonable time thereafter.

When a certificate is issued by a private rather than public official, it is not self-authenticating under FRE 902. Thus, "proof is required that the person was authorized and did make the certificate."[182] Once authenticated, the certificate may be used as proof of the date of execution, however, since there is a presumption that "a document was executed on the date it bears."[183]

§ 6-32(c). Family Records (FRE 803(13)).

Statements of fact regarding family history are excepted if contained in family Bibles, memorials, and similar records likely to be reliable. FRE 803(13) describes the exception:

> **(13) Family records.** Statements of fact concerning personal or family history contained in family Bibles, genealogies, charts, engravings on rings, inscriptions on family portraits, engravings on urns, crypts, or tombstones, or the like.

---

[182] FED. R. EVID. 803(12) advisory committee's note.
[183] Id.

§ 6-32(d). Statements in Documents Affecting Property Interests (FRE 803(15)).

Documents that dispose of property interests often contain fact recitals. Given the seriousness of these transactions, the fact statements generally are reliable. Thus, FRE 803(15) excepts these statements from hearsay unless they are inconsistent with the property disposition or subsequent dealings with the property. FRE 803(15) excepts:

(15) Statements in documents affecting an interest in property. A statement contained in a document purporting to establish or affect an interest in property if the matter stated was relevant to the purpose of the document, unless dealings with the property since the document was made have been inconsistent with the truth of the statement or the purport of the document.

§ 6-32(e). Statements in Ancient Documents (FRE 803(16)).

FRE 803(16) excepts statements in documents that are more than 20 years old and established as authentic. It provides:

(16) Statements in ancient documents. Statements in a document in existence twenty years or more the authenticity of which is established.

The rule emanates from the common law doctrine authenticating ancient documents; even if the document was authentic, statements in the document could only be admitted for their truth if they also were excepted from hearsay.[184] The age of these documents give them credibility, since they usually were prepared long before the controversy arose. The need to authenticate the document offers some opportunity for testing its reliability.

§ 6-33. Market Reports and Commercial Compilations (FRE 803(17)).

FRE 803(17) creates an exception for market reports, tabulations, and compilations generally relied on by the public or professionals. It states:

(17) Market reports, commercial publications. Market quotations, tabulations, lists, directories, or other published compilations, generally used and relied upon by the public or by persons in particular occupations.

The provision does not provide a clear definition of its scope. It is intended, however, to authorize the admission of market reports, city and telephone directories, professional tabulations, and other publications that report objective, straightforward facts.[185] The reports are reliable because accuracy is essential

---

[184] See FED. R. EVID. 803(16) advisory committee's note.

[185] See White Indus., Inc. v. Cessna Aircraft Co., 611 F. Supp. 1049 (W.D. Mo. 1985); JACK B. WEINSTEIN AND MARGARET A. BERGER, WEINSTEIN'S EVIDENCE ¶ 803(9)[01] at 317–21 (1993).

to the publisher's success. When a commercial report contains a subjective evaluation of facts, which could reasonably be disputed, it should not be admitted.

§ 6-34. Reputation.

FRE 803(19), (20) and (21) except various types of reputation evidence from hearsay. This type of evidence is viewed as trustworthy when persons in the community are likely to have discussed the topic, leading to the disclosure of facts from persons with knowledge and sufficient credibility to lead to general acceptance of the facts in the community.[186] The exceptions are discussed below.

§ 6-34(a). Reputation Concerning a Person's Personal or Family History (FRE 803(19)).

FRE 803(19) excepts a person's reputation in his family, among associates, and in the community as to his personal or family history. It provides:

(19) **Reputation concerning personal or family history.** Reputation among members of a person's family by blood, adoption, or marriage, or among a person's associates, or in the community, concerning a person's birth, adoption, marriage, divorce, death, legitimacy, relationship by blood, adoption, or marriage, ancestry, or other similar fact of his personal or family history.

§ 6-34(b). Reputation Concerning Property Boundaries and Historic Events (FRE 803(20)).

FRE 803(20) applies to reputation in the community, arising before the controversy, as to property boundaries, and reputation as to important historic events. The requirement that the reputation predate the controversy applies only to property boundaries, although reputation of historic events generally also would satisfy that requirement. The rule provides:

(20) **Reputation concerning boundaries or general history.** Reputation in a community, arising before the controversy, as to boundaries of or customs affecting lands in the community, and reputation as to events of general history important to the community or State or nation in which located.

§ 6-34(c). Reputation as to a Person's Character (FRE 803(21)).

Reputation evidence is a traditional means of proving a person's character. FRE 808(21) removes any hearsay bar to the introduction of the evidence. Its admissibility also is governed by FRE 404 and 405, which relate to the relevance and proof of character, and FRE 608, which governs impeachment of witnesses with character evidence. FRE 803(21) excepts:

(21) **Reputation as to character.** Reputation of a person's character among associates or in the community.

---

[186] FED. R. EVID. 803(19), (20), (21) advisory committee's notes.

V.　HEARSAY EXCEPTIONS: UNAVAILABILITY REQUIRED

§ 6-35.　Introduction (FRE 804).

FRE 804 excepts five types of statements from hearsay if the declarant is unavailable to testify. The requirement of unavailability apparently rests on the assumption that the statements excepted by FRE 804 are less reliable than those listed in FRE 803.[187] The Advisory Committee implies that the statements covered by FRE 804 do not possess the same "qualities" that make availability of a witness irrelevant under FRE 803.[188]

If reduced reliability is the rationale for limiting the admissibility of the statements covered by FRE 804, the distinction does not withstand scrutiny. Two of the statements excepted by the rule — statements against interest and dying declarations — are made under circumstances strongly suggesting they are trustworthy. Former testimony, which is admissible only if subject to examination, also has marks of reliability. Statements of personal or family history arguably are as trustworthy as many of the statements excepted by FRE 803. Thus, a difference in trustworthiness does not explain the more limited scope of FRE 804.

The exceptions in FRE 804 are justified in part by need. The unavailability requirement establishes preferences: live testimony is preferred over hearsay; hearsay meeting one of the specified standards "is preferred over complete loss of the evidence of the declarant."[189] Thus, the exceptions permit the introduction of hearsay when a party cannot produce the declarant as a witness and her testimony would otherwise be lost to the trier of fact.

The exceptions are based on the common law. Different unavailability requirements were attached at common law to different statements; for instance, the "dying declaration" could be admitted only if the declarant was dead. The federal rules discard these variations, enacting a common unavailability test for all the statements excepted by FRE 804.

§ 6-36.　Definition of Unavailability (FRE 804(a)).

FRE 804(a) specifies five circumstances in which a hearsay declarant is deemed "unavailable" to testify. It provides:

(a) Definition of unavailability. "Unavailability as a witness" includes situations in which the declarant—

(1) is exempted by ruling of the court on the ground of privilege from testifying concerning the subject matter of the declarant's statement; or

---

[187] ROGER C. PARK, DAVID P. LEONARD, STEVEN H. GOLDBERG, EVIDENCE LAW 280 (1998); FED. R. EVID. 804(b) advisory committee's note.

[188] FED. R. EVID. 804(b) advisory committee's note.

[189] Id.

(2) persists in refusing to testify concerning the subject matter of the declarant's statement despite an order of the court to do so; or

(3) testifies to a lack of memory of the subject matter of the declarant's statement; or

(4) is unable to be present or to testify at the hearing because of death or then existing physical or mental illness or infirmity; or

(5) is absent from the hearing and the proponent of statement has been unable to procure the declarant's attendance (or in the case of a hearsay exception under subdivision (b)(2), (3), or (4), the declarant's attendance or testimony) by process or other reasonable means.

A declarant is not unavailable as a witness if exemption, refusal, claim of lack of memory, inability, or absence is due to the procurement or wrongdoing of the proponent of a statement for the purpose of preventing the witness from attending or testifying.

These situations are discussed below, along with the provision preventing the proponent of a hearsay statement from securing its admission by bringing about the declarant's unavailability.

§ 6-36(a). Exercise of Privilege.

When a witness claims a privilege and the court exempts the witness from testifying, FRE 804 deems the witness unavailable. The court must actually rule on the claim of privilege. The ruling must exempt the witness from testifying on the same subject matter as that addressed in the hearsay statement.

§ 6-36(b). Refusal to Testify.

If the witness refuses to testify concerning the subject matter of the hearsay statement, she is considered unavailable. The court must first order the witness to testify and she must "persis[t]" in refusing to do so.

§ 6-36(c). Lack of Memory.

A witness is unavailable if he "testifies to a lack of memory on the subject matter" of the hearsay statement. Since the witness must testify to the lack of memory, the rule contemplates that he is available for cross-examination regarding the statement, his memory, and the subject matter.[190] Thus, a claimed lack of memory does not fully shield the witness from cross-examination. If the witness claims a partial lack of memory, the hearsay statement should be admissible to the extent necessary to fill a gap.[191] In many cases, however, the statement should refresh the recollection of the witness, making resort to the exception unnecessary.

---

[190] FED. R. EVID. 804(a) advisory committee's note.

[191] MCCORMICK ON EVIDENCE § 253(3) (5th ed. 1999).

§ 6-36(d). Death or Infirmity.

Death renders a witness irrevocably unavailable. Physical or mental illness or infirmity qualifies if it prevents the witness from testifying. If the illness is temporary, however, the judge may delay the trial to obtain the witness's live testimony. The importance of the testimony and the type of proceeding would affect a decision on whether to grant a continuance. The court may be more inclined to grant a delay in a criminal case, where the Confrontation Clause gives added strength to a claim of need.

§ 6-36(e). Absence.

The absence requirement provides that the declarant be "absent from the hearing" and that the proponent of the statement be unable to procure his attendance by a) process, or b) other reasonable means. The rule impliedly requires some additional effort to obtain the declarant's attendance when service of process is unsuccessful. If the witness cannot be located by the official assigned to make service, it may require a showing that an effort was made to find the witnes. If the witness is outside the jurisdiction, the proponent may have to prove he attempted to induce the witness's voluntary appearance, perhaps by offering to pay the witness's expenses.

With respect to FRE 804(b)(2), (3) and (4) — dying declarations, statements against interest and statements of personal or family history — the proponent of the statement must show that the attendance *or testimony* of the witness could not be obtained through process or other reasonable means. This requirement was added in the House of Representatives and adopted in the Senate-House Conference report to require an effort to obtain testimony, "such as by deposition or interrogatories."[192] This requirement does not apply to the "former testimony" exception of FRE 804(b)(1), since former testimony may be a deposition or its equivalent.

§ 6-36(f). Procurement of Unavailability.

The declarant will not be considered unavailable under FRE 803(a) if the proponent of the statement procures or wrongfully causes the unavailability. The rule suggests that the procurement of the witness's unavailability blocks the admission of a statement only if done "for the purpose of preventing the witness from attending or testifying." This wording raises an issue: what if the proponent killed, maimed or silenced the declarant for another purpose? The focus on "purpose" suggests that the declarant would be considered unavailable, but the courts likely would presume that the action was intended to prevent the witness from testifying and require a strong showing that it occurred for another reason.

---

[192] H.R. FED. RULES OF EVIDENCE, Conf. Rep. No. 1597, 93d Cong., 2d Sess., p. 12 (1974).

§ 6-37. Special Confrontation Clause Requirement for Unavailability.

The Confrontation Clause requires that the accused in a criminal case be confronted with the witnesses against him. A number of Supreme Court cases decided prior to 1986 suggested that the Confrontation Clause required the prosecution to show the unavailability of a witness before introducing any hearsay. In *Ohio v. Roberts*,[193] the Court suggested that in the "usual case" involving an offer of hearsay, "the prosecution must either produce, or demonstrate the unavailability of, the declarant whose statement it wishes to use against the defendant."[194] Additionally, the cases suggested that the prosecution would be required to show a good faith effort to secure the testimony of a witness before introducing his hearsay statement,[195] or that the witness was beyond the reach of process, and his former testimony was thoroughly cross-examined.[196]

The Court's opinion was not limited to cases in which the applicable hearsay exception mandated unavailability. Instead, it appeared to apply to all hearsay. This interpretation is logical, since there would be less justification for waiving a requirement of confrontation if the witness could be produced than if he were unavailable. The cases involved prior testimony, however, for which the traditional hearsay rule required unavailability.[197] Thus, they could be interpreted to apply only to prior testimony or to hearsay exceptions conditioned on unavailability.

In more recent decisions the Court retreated from the broad pronouncement of *Ohio v. Roberts*. It now limits the constitutional unavailability requirement to cases involving former testimony. In *United States v. Inadi*,[198] the Court determined that the constitutional unavailability requirement does not apply to statements of co-conspirators that are introduced against the accused as admissions.[199] In 1992, in *White v. Illinois*,[200] the Court interpreted *Roberts* to apply only in former testimony cases. It reviewed *Roberts* and *Inadi* and said:

> So understood, *Roberts* stands for the proposition that unavailability analysis is a necessary part of the Confrontation Clause inquiry only when the

---

[193] 448 U.S. 56 (1980).

[194] *Id.* at 65.

[195] See United States v. Ochoa, 229 F.3d 631, 637–38 (7th Cir. 2000) (witness properly deemed unavailable after the government made good faith, reasonable effort to find him). See also Barber v. Page, 390 U.S. 719 (1968).

[196] Mancusi v. Stubbs, 408 U.S. 204 (1972).

[197] Barber v. Page, 390 U.S. 719 (1968); Mancusi v. Stubbs, 408 U.S. 204 (1972); California v. Green, 399 U.S. 149 (1970).

[198] 475 U.S. 387 (1986).

[199] *Id.* at 394–96.

[200] 502 U.S. 346 (1992).

challenged out-of-court statements were made in the course of a prior judicial proceeding. [201]

The Court declined to apply an unavailability requirement to the "spontaneous statement" and "statements for medical examination" exceptions to the hearsay rule. [202] It determined that "where proffered hearsay has sufficient guarantees of trustworthiness to come within a firmly rooted exception to the hearsay rule, the Confrontation Clause is satisfied." [203]

White eliminates any constitutional requirement that the prosecution establish unavailability as a precondition to introducing out-of-court declarations under the hearsay exclusions of FRE 801(d) and the exceptions in FRE 803. It apparently does not disturb the rulings requiring a special showing of unavailability in the former testimony cases. The decision leaves open the issue of whether the Confrontation Clause imposes an unavailability requirement and a special effort to produce the witness for other exceptions that traditionally required unavailability.

§ 6-38. Former Testimony (FRE 804(b)(1)).

FRE 804(b)(1) applies to testimony given in a prior hearing or deposition, whether or not conducted in the same proceeding. It requires that the party against whom the testimony is offered or, in a civil matter, the party's "predecessor in interest," must have had an (1) opportunity and (2) similar motive to develop the testimony when it was given. FRE 804(b)(1) excepts:

> **(1) Former testimony.** Testimony given as a witness at another hearing of the same or a different proceeding, or in a deposition taken in compliance with law in the course of the same or another proceeding, if the party against whom the testimony is now offered, or, in a civil action or proceeding, a predecessor in interest, had an opportunity and similar motive to develop the testimony by direct, cross, or redirect examination.

Former testimony has two strong marks of reliability: It is given under oath and is subject to cross-examination. A major difference between live and former testimony, however, is the opportunity for the jury to observe demeanor. The facial expressions, voice tenor, and physical behavior of the witness often give a special meaning to testimony that cannot be gleaned from a transcript. Thus, FRE 804(b)(1) reflects a preference for live over former testimony. As the Supreme Court stated in *United States v. Inadi*: [204]

---

[201] *Id.* at 354.

[202] *Id.* at 357.

[203] *Id.* at 356.

[204] 475 U.S. 387, 394-95 (1986).

If the declarant is available and the same information can be presented to the trier of fact in the form of live testimony, with full cross-examination and the opportunity to view the demeanor of the declarant, there is little justification for relying on the weaker version. When two versions of the same evidence are available, longstanding principles of the law of hearsay, applicable as well to Confrontation Clause analysis, favor the better evidence. But if the declarant is unavailable, no "better" version of the evidence exists, and the former testimony may be admitted as a substitute for live testimony on the same point.

Former testimony also may bear a special mark of unreliability: it often reflects a one-sided and lawyer-driven version of events. In some preliminary proceedings, a party may present testimony to establish a prima facie basis for an action. Counsel and the witness may carefully prepare this testimony, but for strategic reasons the adverse party may not subject it to probing cross-examination. Even more often, deposition testimony reflects a one-sided examination. A lawyer often counsels a witness not to volunteer information in a deposition, to avoid alerting the opposing counsel to key facts. Further, a lawyer representing a witness rarely develops his deposition testimony. Thus, the testimony may be much different from the version that might come out at trial.

The requirements of the former testimony rule are discussed below.

§ 6-38(a). Party or Predecessor in Interest.

In a criminal case the party against whom former testimony is offered must have been a party in the proceeding in which the prior testimony was taken. In a civil case, the party or a "predecessor in interest" must have been a party. The rule does not specify the circumstances in which a different party qualifies as a "predecessor in interest." Thus, while the provision opens the door for the introduction of former testimony in civil cases against parties who did not participate in the prior hearing or deposition, it leaves unclear the circumstances in which this relaxed requirement may be used.

One approach to interpreting the provision is to require privity, agency, or some other legal relation between the party and the "predecessor." This approach incorporates substantive law strictures, however, that the federal rules generally attempt to avoid. Nevertheless, the requirement of some legal relationship is consistent with the intent of the House Committee. The provision submitted to Congress by the Supreme Court permitted the introduction of former testimony if the party against whom it is offered, or any other party with a similar motive and interest, had the opportunity to examine the witness. The House Committee introduced the "predecessor in interest" requirement, asserting:

[I]t is generally unfair to impose upon the party against whom the hearsay evidence is being offered responsibility for the manner in which the witness was previously handled by another party. The sole exception to this, in the Committee's view, is when a party's predecessor in interest in a civil action or proceeding had opportunity and a similar motive to examine the witness. . . .[205]

Unfortunately, the House Committee provided no further guidance on how the provision should be interpreted.

A second interpretation would require only that the party in the prior proceeding have a similar interest to that of the party against whom the testimony is offered. This interpretation would render the predecessor in interest language redundant, since a similar interest is the same thing as a similar motive. Thus, it would be unfaithful to Congress' intent in adding the provision.

One method of addressing the issue would require that similarity of interests be demonstrated by the predecessor in the prior examination. If the party is the same, binding him with his prior examination — even if it is ineffective — is not unfair so long as he had a similar reason to develop the testimony. If the party is different, an ineffective examination should not bind him, regardless of a similar "motive."

The courts could require an actual examination similar to what might be expected if the witness appeared. If there was no examination or it was ineffective, a court could find the previous party did not perform as a true "predecessor in interest" and it is not fair to hold his examination against another party. This approach would give meaning to "predecessor in interest" beyond "similar motive," allow the courts to promote fairness, and avoid undue emphasis on fictional legal relations.

§ 6-38(b).　Similar Motive.

The "similar motive" requirement evolves from common law decisions requiring an "identity of issues" in the proceeding in which the former testimony was taken and that in which it is offered. Identity of issues was required "as a means of insuring that the former handling of the witness was the equivalent of what would now be done if the opportunity were presented."[206] Subsequent decisions relaxed the requirement, allowing the introduction of former testimony when there was a "substantial" identity of issues.[207] The Advisory Committee determined that the similar motive language better expressed the concept underlying the "identity" requirement: "Since identity of issues is significant only in that it bears on motive and interest in developing fully the testimony of the witness, expressing the matter in the latter terms is preferable."[208]

---

[205] House Comm. on Judiciary, FED. RULES OF EVID., H.R. Rep. No. 650, 93d Cong., 1st Sess., p. 15 (1973).

[206] FED. R. EVID. 804(b)(1) advisory committee's note.

[207] Id.

[208] Id.

Under the formulation of FRE 804(b)(1), identity or substantial identity of issues is sufficient to satisfy the "similar motive" provision. Even if the issues are not similar, the testimony may be admissible if the party or predecessor had a good reason to test its credibility. Thus, for example, if the accused at a suppression hearing offered a witness's testimony that police officers beat the accused to force a confession, that testimony likely would satisfy the "similar motive" requirement in a subsequent tort suit against one of the officers, because the state had a reason to examine the testimony in the prior hearing. There would still be an issue of whether the state could qualify as a predecessor in interest.

The focus on issues as the means of determining motive has longstanding precedential support, but it ignores the practical realities of modern litigation. Preliminary hearings and depositions often are used to discover facts known to the adverse party. A primary motive of counsel opposing these efforts may be to save key facts for the trial. Attorneys frequently forgo examining witnesses — particularly those who are friendly — for this reason. Additionally, even the lawyer conducting an examination may save important points. Thus, lawyers often do not thoroughly develop testimony in these preliminary examinations.

The traditional focus on issues, developed when former testimony usually came from a prior trial, does not take account of tactical motives in preliminary proceedings. Although perhaps not intended, the "similar motive" formulation of FRE 804(b)(1) may allow courts to consider these litigating strategies in deciding whether former testimony has truly been developed.[209]

§ 6-38(c). Opportunity to Examine.

The party against whom prior testimony is offered need not have actually examined the witness in the prior proceeding. The opportunity to examine is sufficient, at least when the former testimony is offered against a party who was represented in the prior proceeding. As suggested above, the courts should require an actual, competent examination in cases where it was conducted by a "predecessor in interest."

The opportunity to develop testimony may take the form of cross, direct or redirect examination. Thus, testimony may be offered against a party who

---

[209] An argument that litigants did not have the same tactical motive for testing and cross-examining an adverse expert in a deposition as they would at trial was rejected as a basis for excluding former testimony in Battle v. Memorial Hospital at Gulfport., 228 F.3d 544 (5th Cir. 2000). The Fifth Circuit found that the defendants were on the same side and had the same interest in prevailing on the issues in both the deposition and at trial. Because the defendants did not suggest that the different tactical motive — exploring rather than cross-examining the testimony — affected its reliability, the court ruled the deposition was properly admitted. *Id.* at 553. It did suggest, however, that if a party could identify cross-examination areas foregone because of a different tactical motive, the foregone opportunities could be considered as a factor in assessing admissibility. *Id.* at 552–53. See also United States v. Geiger, 263 F.3d 1034, 1038–39 (5th Cir. 2001).

previously sponsored it. The Advisory Committee determined that a party has an adequate opportunity to develop harmful testimony on direct or redirect. It said:

> Allowable techniques for dealing with hostile, double-crossing, forgetful, and mentally deficient witnesses leave no substance to a claim that one could not adequately develop his own witness at the former hearing. An even less appealing argument is presented when failure to develop fully was the result of a deliberate choice.[210]

This argument may not ring true to litigators, who might excuse a witness who surprisingly turns adverse as soon as possible. It nevertheless may be justified by adversarial considerations. If a party chooses to call a witness, the party fairly may be bound by his own handling of the witness, even in a subsequent proceeding. The adversarial rationale does not produce the same sense of fairness, however, when the prior testimony was presented by a "predecessor in interest."

§ 6-39. Dying Declaration (FRE 804(b)2)).

FRE 804(b)(2) enacts a modern form of the hearsay exception for dying declarations. It includes:

(2) Statement under belief of impending death. In a prosecution for homicide or in a civil action or proceeding, a statement made by a declarant while believing that the declarant's death was imminent, concerning the cause or circumstances of what the declarant believed to be impending death.

The exception applies only to those statements made when the declarant believed her death was imminent. It must concern the cause or circumstances of the perceived impending death. Statements made under these circumstances are admissible in (a) civil cases and (b) criminal prosecutions for homicide, but not other criminal proceedings.

The exception is based on the theory that a person who believes her death is imminent is likely to be truthful. If the declarant is religious, she would not lie for fear that God would punish her after death. Additionally, a person facing imminent death has no motive to fabricate facts for personal gain. Further, the person likely would view her last statements as having special importance and take care to make them accurate. Thus, dying declarations have special marks of reliability.

Fairness and need also support the exception. In a homicide case in which the declarant is the victim, excluding as hearsay a statement that might help convict the killer seems unjust. Indeed, the homicide makes live testimony impossible. Moreover, the victim's statement often is essential to determining

---

[210] FED. R. EVID. 804(b)(1) advisory committee's note.

how the homicide occurred; excluding it would impede the search for truth. These factors were justifications for the rule at common law and led to rulings limiting its application to homicide cases.[211]

Although the trustworthiness of dying declarations is generally accepted,[212] valid arguments exist against their reliability. First, a person whose death is imminent may be disoriented, upset or mentally infirm, and prone to make factual errors. Second, the speaker would not fear the worldly consequences of being found out in a lie. Third, a person facing death may have a last motivation to harm an enemy. These factors undermine the contention that dying declarations are especially trustworthy, and support the view that fairness and need — not reliability — justify their admissibility.

As originally formulated, FRE 804(b)(2) would have excepted dying declarations in civil and all criminal proceedings — not just homicide cases. The rule was amended in the House of Representatives to limit the exception. The House Committee report stated:

> The Committee did not consider dying declarations as among the most reliable forms of hearsay. Consequently, it amended the provision to limit their admissibility in criminal cases to homicide prosecutions, where exceptional need for the evidence is present. . . .[213]

The committee approved the extension of the exception to civil actions, "where the stakes do not involve possible imprisonment."[214]

The exception applies only to those statements that relate to the "cause or circumstances of what the declarant believed to be impending death." Thus, statements describing other facts are not admissible as dying declarations.[215] The Advisory Committee believed that the motivation to be truthful resulting from the impending death is attenuated when the speaker discusses other matters.[216]

FRE 804(b)(2) does not require that the declarant be dead, so long as he is unavailable. If the statement was made under a belief of impending death, the fact that the declarant recovered does not preclude using the exception. The statement itself may establish the declarant's belief, or the proponent may offer other evidence, known to the declarant, that would lead a rational person to conclude his death was imminent.

---

[211] MCCORMICK ON EVIDENCE § 311 (5th ed. 1999).

[212] See Idaho v. Wright, 497 U.S. 805 (1990); Mattox v. United States, 156 U.S. 237, 244 (1895).

[213] House Comm. on Judiciary, FED. RULES OF EVIDENCE, H.R. Rep. No. 650, 93d Cong., 1st Sess., p. 15 (1973).

[214] Id.

[215] United States v. Fernandez, 892 F.2d 976 (11th Cir. 1989, amended 1990), cert. denied, 495 U.S. 944 (1990).

[216] FED. R. EVID. 804(b)(2) advisory committee's note.

Even if they are not dying declarations, statements made near death often fit other exceptions. If the speaker was injured or attacked, his statement may qualify as an excited utterance. Many statements made near death fit the exceptions for present sense impressions, statements of then existing condition, and statements for medical diagnosis or treatment. Thus, there may be other avenues for introducing them.

§ 6-40. Statements Against Interest (FRE 804(b)(3)).

FRE 804(b)(3) establishes an exception for statements that are against the declarant's interest when made. It provides:

> **(3) Statement against interest.** A statement which was at the time of its making so far contrary to the declarant's pecuniary or proprietary interest, or so far tended to subject the declarant to civil or criminal liability, or to render invalid a claim by the declarant against another, that a reasonable person in the declarant's position would not have made the statement unless believing it to be true. A statement tending to expose the declarant to criminal liability and offered to exculpate the accused is not admissible unless corroborating circumstances clearly indicate the trustworthiness of the statement.

The exception incorporates its own rationale: a reasonable person ordinarily would not make a statement that harms her own interest unless she believed it to be true. Put another way, a reasonable person would not make up a story that harmed herself. Additionally, a person is likely to be sure that harmful facts are correct before conceding them to others.[217]

You should not confuse statements against interest with admissions. In particular, there is no exception for an "admission against interest," despite the contrary belief of many lawyers. An admission is a statement of a party, whether or not it was against interest when made, offered against that party at the trial. If a party makes an out-of-court statement, it may be admitted against the party without resorting to FRE 804(b)(3). A statement against interest is a statement of any declarant that was against his interest at the time it was made. For the exception to apply, the declarant must be unavailable.

The rule is phrased to include only those statements that affect material interests, civil claims, or criminal liability. It does not cover statements against less tangible interests, such as reputation. The original rule proposed to Congress would have included statements making the declarant "an object of hatred, ridicule, or disgrace. . . ."[218] This language was deleted in the House of Representatives. The House report states: "The Committee eliminated [this] category from the subdivision as lacking sufficient guarantees of reliability."[219]

---

[217] See United States v. Gallegos, 191 F.3d 156, 167 (2nd Cir. 1999).

[218] House Comm. on Judiciary, FED. RULES OF EVIDENCE, H.R. Rep. No. 650, 93d Cong., 1st Sess., p. 16 (1973).

[219] *Id.*

The rule requires corroborating circumstances that clearly indicate trustworthiness for a statement tending to expose the declarant to criminal liability and offered to exonerate a criminal defendant. The exposure to criminal liability is a strong reason to avoid an untrue confession, but competing considerations may motivate a person to confess falsely and exculpate another. Bribery, threats, love, loyalty or other motives may bring about a false confession. Further, the declarant's unavailability makes it difficult to determine whether the confession was influenced by these motives.

The rule does not require corroboration for a statement that exposes the declarant *and* the accused to criminal liability. When an unavailable declarant's statement against interest is offered against an accused, however, a Confrontation Clause issue arises. Moreover, since defendants often inculpate others to gain favor with the authorities, the statements are not necessarily reliable. Thus, the courts have read into the rule a requirement that the statement have special "indicia of reliability."[220] Courts are especially skeptical of a confession that inculpates another when it is made while the declarant is in custody.[221]

§ 6-41. Statements of Personal or Family History (FRE 804(b)(4)).

FRE 804(b)(4) excepts statements of fact concerning a declarant's personal history or the history of her family members or persons in another family with which she is intimately associated. It includes:

(4) Statement of personal or family history. (A) A statement concerning the declarant's own birth, adoption, marriage, divorce, legitimacy, relationship by blood, adoption, or marriage, ancestry, or other similar fact of personal or family history, even though declarant had no means of acquiring personal knowledge of the matter stated; or (B) a statement concerning the foregoing matters, and death also, of another person, if the declarant was related to the other by blood, adoption, or marriage or was so intimately associated with the other's family as to be likely to have accurate information concerning the matter declared.

The rule does away with any requirement that the declarant have personal knowledge of the facts, apparently presuming that the declarant would have reliable information regarding her own history or that of her family.[222] It adopts a liberal view of "family," covering statements made about family history when the declarant "was so intimately associated" with the other family "as to be likely to have accurate information concerning the matter declared."

---

[220] United States v. Riley, 657 F.2d 1377, 1383 (8th Cir. 1981), *cert. denied*, 459 U.S. 1111 (1983); United States v. Oliver, 626 F.2d 254, 260 (2d Cir. 1980).

[221] United States v. Sarmiento-Perez, 633 F.2d 1092, 1104 (5th Cir. 1981), *cert. denied*, 459 U.S. 834 (1982).

[222] See United States v. Hernandez, 105 F.3d 1330, 1332 (9th Cir. 1997) *cert. denied* 522 U.S. 890 (1997).

Unlike FRE 803(19), which excepts reputation concerning personal or family history, FRE 804(4) requires that the declarant be unavailable. Thus, if a witness testified to reputation concerning personal or family history, the sources on which he relied would not have to be unavailable; if the witness testified to a statement of fact by an out-of-court declarant regarding her personal or family history, the declarant would have to be unavailable.

§ 6-42. Forfeiture by Wrongdoing (FRE 804(b)(6)).

FRE 804(b)(6) excepts a statement by a person whose unavailability is procured by a party, when the statement is offered against the party. The rule, which applies in civil as well as criminal cases, excepts:

> **(6) Forfeiture by wrongdoing**. A statement offered against a party that has engaged or acquiesced in wrongdoing that was intended to, and did, procure the unavailability of the declarant as a witness.

The declarant is not considered unavailable under FRE 803(a) if the proponent of the statement procures or wrongfully causes the unavailability; this rule prevents a party from introducing a statement through wrongdoing. The new provision addresses the opposite situation, permitting the introduction of a statement against a party who procured the unavailability of the declarant as a witness. The Advisory Committee states:

> Rule 804(b)(6) has been added to provide that a party forfeits the right to object on hearsay grounds to the admission of a declarant's prior statement when the party's deliberate wrongdoing or acquiescence therein procured the unavailability of the declarant as a witness. This recognizes the need for a prophylactic rule to deal with abhorrent behavior "which strikes at the heart of the system of justice itself." United States v. Mastrangelo, 693 F.2d 269, 273 (2d Cir. 1982), *cert. denied*, 467 U.S. 1204 (1984). The wrongdoing need not consist of a criminal act. The rule applies to all parties, including the government.[223]

The rule requires a showing that the party alleged to have procured unavailability must have acted with intent to procure the unavailability of the declarant. Thus, unless the defendant in a murder case killed the victim to prevent him from testifying, the exception would not permit the introduction of the victim's hearsay statements against the defendant.[224]

Although every circuit that had addressed the situation interpreted the wrongful procurement of unavailability to bar a hearsay objection, the circuits applied different tests to establish when this misconduct took place. The Advisory

---

[223] FED. R. EVID. 804(b)(6) advisory committee's note.

[224] Daniel J. Capra, *New Amendments to the Federal Rules of Evidence*, NY LAW JOURNAL, January 9, 1998, p. 3.

Committee notes that "[t]he usual Rule 104(a) preponderance of the evidence standard has been adopted in light of the behavior the new Rule 804(b)(6) seeks to discourage."[225] The Fifth Circuit had previously imposed a clear and convincing evidence standard for determining whether the requisite misconduct had occurred, while other circuits applied a preponderance of the evidence standard.[226]

A split has developed as to whether a court must hold an evidentiary hearing outside the presence of the jury before determining that a defendant waived his Confrontation Clause objection to the introduction of hearsay by procuring through wrongdoing the absence of the declarant. In *United States v. Dhinsa,*[227] the Second Circuit held that a district court must conduct an evidentiary hearing outside the presence of the jury, in which the Government must prove by a preponderance of the evidence that the defendant directly or indirectly procured the unavailability of the declarant and acted, at least in part, with the intent to prevent the declarant's appearance as a witness.[228] In *United States v. Emery,*[229] the Eighth Circuit held that a separate hearing outside the presence of the jury is not required; instead, it held the evidence establishing the preconditions for admitting the evidence under FRE 804(b)(6) may be admitted during the trial.

VI. RESIDUAL EXCEPTION AND IMPEACHING HEARSAY

§ 6-43. Residual Exception (FRE 807).

FRE 807 permits a court to except other statements from hearsay even if they do not fit a hearsay exception. It sets out certain requirements, the most important of which are: (1) the statement have "equivalent guaranties of trustworthiness" to those supporting specific exceptions, and (2) the statement be the most probative evidence available to prove the point. The rule also requires that the statement be relevant and that its admission serve the purpose of the rules and interests of justice. The proponent of the statement must provide advance notice of his intent to use the exception. Until 1997 both FRE 803 and 804 contained residual exceptions, but they were transferred to a single, separate rule in 1997. FRE 807 provides the following exception:

---

[225] FED. R. EVID. 804(b)(6) advisory committee's note.

[226] Compare United States v. Thevis, 665 F.2d 616, 631 (5th Cir.), *cert. denied*, 459 U.S. 825 (1982), with United States v. Aguiar, 975 F.2d 45, 47 (2d Cir. 1992); United States v. Potamitis, 739 F.2d 784, 789 (2d Cir.), *cert. denied sub nom.* Argitakos v. United States, 469 U.S. 918 (1984); Steele v. Taylor, 684 F.2d 1193, 1199 (6th Cir. 1982), *cert. denied sub nom.* Kilbane v. Marshall, 460 U.S. 1053 (1983); United States v. Balano, 618 F.2d 624, 629 (10th Cir. 1979), *cert. denied*, 449 U.S. 840 (1980); United States v. Carlson, 547 F.2d 1346, 1358–59 (8th Cir.), *cert. denied sub nom.* Hofstad v. United States, 431 U.S. 914 (1977).

[227] 243 F.3d 635 (2d Cir. 2001).

[228] *Id.* at 653–54.

[229] 186 F.3d 921 (8th Cir. 1999), *cert. denied*, 528 U.S. 1130 (2000).

A statement not specifically covered by Rule 803 or 804 but having equivalent circumstantial guarantees of trustworthiness, is not excluded by the hearsay rule, if the court determines that (A) the statement is offered as evidence of a material fact; (B) the statement is more probative on the point for which it is offered than any other evidence which the proponent can procure through reasonable efforts; and (C) the general purposes of these rules and the interests of justice will best be served by admission of the statement into evidence. However, a statement may not be admitted under this exception unless the proponent of it makes known to the adverse party sufficiently in advance of the trial or hearing to provide the adverse party with a fair opportunity to prepare to meet it, the proponent's intention to offer the statement and the particulars of it, including the name and address of the declarant.

The exception was adopted because it would "be presumptuous to assume that all possible desirable exceptions to the hearsay rule have been catalogued and to pass the hearsay rule to oncoming generations as a closed system."[230] The Advisory Committee explained the predecessors to FRE 807 as follows:

[FRE 24 and FRE 804(5)] do not contemplate an unfettered exercise of judicial discretion, but they do provide for treating new and presently unanticipated situations which demonstrate a trustworthiness within the spirit of the specifically stated exceptions. Within this framework, room is left for the growth and development of the law of evidence in the hearsay area. . . .[231]

Residual exceptions initially proposed to Congress were deleted in the House of Representatives on the grounds that they would interject uncertainty in the law of evidence and make trial preparation difficult. The Senate Judiciary Committee adopted the more narrow residual exceptions, but without a notice requirement. The provision for notice was added in conference.[232] In explaining its reasons for reinserting the residual exceptions, the Senate Committee expressed an intent that they be used rarely. It said: "It is intended that the residual hearsay exceptions will be used very rarely, and only in exceptional circumstances."[233]

The primary considerations in applying the residual exceptions is whether a statement has "equivalent circumstantial guarantees of trustworthiness" to the listed exceptions and is "more probative" on the point for which it is offered than other available evidence. These factors are discussed below.

---

[230] FED. R. EVID. 803(24) advisory committee's note.

[231] *Id.*

[232] H.R. FED. RULES OF EVID., Conf. Rep. No. 1597, 93d Cong., 2d Sess., p. 11 (1974).

[233] Sen. Comm. on Judiciary, FED. RULES OF EVID., S. Rep. No. 1277, 93d Cong., 2d Sess., p. 18 (1974).

§ 6-43(a).   Equivalent Guarantees of Trustworthiness.

In deciding whether a statement has "equivalent" guarantees of trustworthiness, the courts often consider the reasons statements falling within the listed exceptions are deemed reliable. Courts also may compare statements to those falling within closely analogous exceptions; this approach usually leads to a comparison of reliability guarantees. The following factors support multiple exceptions and would provide evidence of trustworthiness:

1. *Strong motive to be accurate.* This factor supports FRE 803(4) (statements for medical treatment), (6) and (7) (regularly kept records), (17) (market reports), and (18) (scholarly publications), and perhaps others. It applies when inaccuracy could result in personal, professional or other harm to the declarant.

2. *Timeliness.* A statement made at or near the time of an event is likely to describe it accurately because there is little opportunity for memory to become distorted. Additionally, the declarant does not have an extended time to consider whether his personal interests might be served by fabrication. Timeliness is a mark of reliability reflected in FRE 803(1) (present sense impression), (2) (excited utterance), (3) (then existing condition), (5) (recollection recorded when fresh), and (6) (timely report in business record).

3. *Testing and verification.* If a person knows her statement is likely to be scrutinized or checked, she is likely to ensure that it is accurate. This factor forms part of the justification for FRE 803(6) and (7) (business records), (8) and (10) (public records), (17) (market reports), and (18) (scholarly publications). In addition, to the extent reputation evidence reflects community verification of facts, it supports FRE 803(19), (20) and (21).

4. *Reliable process.* If a fact is reported or determined in a reliable process, the process may provide credibility to the determination. This circumstance supports FRE 803(6) and (7) (facts collected under business duty), (8) (facts observed or found in public records), and (22) and (23) (felony judgments).

5. *Solemnity or importance of declaration.* Some statements have such personal or financial importance that affected persons can be expected to ensure their accuracy. This consideration supports FRE 803(9) (vital statistics), (11), (12) and (13) (personal and family events in religious records, certificates and family records), and (14) and (15) (records and documents affecting property interests). It also supports the admissibility of prior inconsistent statements made under oath (FRE 801(d)(1)(A) and certain prior testimony (FRE 804(b)(1)).

6.   *Objectivity of facts reported.* Data that is straightforward and unambiguous is not likely to be altered. A person who falsifies this type of information can easily be discovered, as the facts usually can be verified. This consideration supports FRE 803(17) (market reports) and (9) (vital statistics).

Of course, other marks of trustworthiness undoubtedly exist, and other factors may offset the indicia of reliability in particular circumstances.[234]

All of the above factors relate to the circumstances under which a statement is made. Additionally, some courts considered the extent of corroboration in evaluating the trustworthiness of a statement. The validity of this approach was thrown into question, however, by the Supreme Court's 1990 decision in *Idaho v. Wright.*[235] In that case the Court determined that corroboration could not be considered one of the "particularized guarantees of trustworthiness" legitimating the admission of hearsay that does not fit a "firmly rooted" exception in a criminal case under the Confrontation Clause.[236] The constitutional ruling is likely to guide interpretations of the federal hearsay rules because the rules apply in both criminal and civil cases and divergent interpretations would be unwieldy.

Additionally, the decision strongly suggests that corroboration does not make the statement itself reliable: "[T]he use of corroborating evidence to support a hearsay statement's 'particularized guarantees of trustworthiness' would permit admission of a presumptively unreliable statement by bootstrapping on the trustworthiness of other evidence at trial. . . ."[237] The Court found that the statement itself must "be so trustworthy that cross-examination of the declarant would be of marginal utility."[238]

Some courts also have relied on the availability of the declarant for cross-examination as a guarantee of trustworthiness. This factor generally should not be considered under FRE 807, however, because live testimony is preferable to a hearsay report. Thus, if the witness were available, the hearsay would not be "more probative . . . than any other [available] evidence," and its introduction would not be permitted. If the declarant had completely lost a memory of the facts, the hearsay might be preferable, but in that case cross-examination would do little to guarantee reliability.

---

[234] McCormick on Evidence § 324 (5th ed. 1999) lists the following as "among" the factors suggesting reliability: "Whether the declarant had a motivation to speak truthfully or otherwise, whether the statement was under oath, the duration of time lapse between event and statement, whether the declarant had firsthand knowledge, and other factors going to the declarant's credibility."

[235] 497 U.S. 805 (1990).

[236] *Id.* at 822.

[237] *Id.*

[238] *Id.*

One issue that arises under FRE 807 is whether a statement that nearly fits an exception should be admitted. For instance, if a declarant made a statement under the stress of excitement, but the statement did not relate to the exciting event, A court might view the utterance as reliable. In this situation, however, the wording of an exception may show an intent to limit its scope. Thus, admitting statements that nearly fall within exceptions may run counter to policies embodied in the rules.

A good example is the "statement against interest." This exception is based on the trustworthiness of the statement, but its incorporation in FRE 804 reflects a policy choice to require that the declarant be unavailable. If the exception were extended to statements against interest of available declarants under FRE 807, the extension would frustrate this policy.

§ 6-43(b). More Probative than Other Available Evidence.

This requirement mandates that the hearsay evidence be reasonably necessary to prove the point. It involves consideration of the credibility and force of the hearsay evidence versus alternatives. Further, the court must consider the difficulty of proving the point through alternative means, which may include the effectiveness of process, the diligence of the proponent in obtaining other evidence, and the cost of using alternatives.[239]

§ 6-43(c). Requirement of Notice.

The rule requires that the proponent give notice of the intent to offer the evidence to the adverse party. It does not prescribe a specific time limit, but requires enough notice that the party has a fair opportunity to respond to the evidence. The notice must include the declarant's name and address and the particulars of the statement. This requirement is one means of assuring that the declarant is not reasonably available; it gives opposing counsel a chance to check. Additionally, it may induce the proponent to seek alternate proof prior to giving the notice, which may reduce the occasions for use of the residual exception.

§ 6-44. Impeaching a Hearsay Declarant (FRE 806).

A party is entitled to attack the credibility of a witness who appears at the trial and the opposing party may support the witness's credibility once it is attacked. See § 9-27. FRE 607–609 and 613 govern the circumstances in which a witness's testimony may be impeached or bolstered. Additionally, FRE 613 provides a "foundation" requirement for introducing extrinsic evidence of a witness's prior inconsistent statement: the witness must still be available and have an "opportunity" to explain or deny the statement.

---

[239] McCormick on Evidence § 324 (5th ed. 1999).

When an out-of-court statement is introduced under a hearsay exclusion or exception, it too is subject to impeachment and, once impeached, bolstering. FRE 806 provides:

> When a hearsay statement, or a statement defined in Rule 801(d)(2)(C), (D), or (E), has been admitted in evidence, the credibility of the declarant may be attacked, and if attacked may be supported, by any evidence which would be admissible for those purposes if declarant had testified as a witness. Evidence of a statement or conduct by the declarant at any time, inconsistent with the declarant's hearsay statement, is not subject to any requirement that the declarant may have been afforded an opportunity to deny or explain. If the party against whom a hearsay statement has been admitted calls the declarant as a witness, the party is entitled to examine the declarant on the statement as if under cross-examination.

FRE 806 permits the same methods to attack or support credibility as would be available for a witness. It maintains the requirement that a witness's credibility may be supported only if it is first attacked.[240] The rule applies to statements defined as hearsay and three kinds of statements excluded from the hearsay definition. It does not apply to prior statements defined as non-hearsay under FRE 801(d)(1), since the declarant actually is on the stand when those statements are introduced. The normal rules of impeachment are sufficient. Additionally, it does not permit a party to impeach his own admissions defined as non-hearsay by FRE 801(d)(2), (A) and (B).

The rule permits the introduction of an inconsistent statement of the declarant, even if it occurred subsequent to the hearsay declaration. Although a party as a practical matter could not examine a live witness on inconsistent statements the witness makes after the trial, no sound reason exists to apply a parallel treatment to hearsay declarations. Whether made before or after a hearsay declaration, an inconsistent statement undercuts credibility. Additionally, if the declarant presented live testimony, all inconsistent statements could be used to impeach, whether or nor they preceded a prior consistent declaration that might be admitted to bolster.

The rule dispenses with the rule that extrinsic evidence of an inconsistent statement may not be admitted unless the witness has the opportunity to explain or deny it. A hearsay declarant often is not available and cannot be afforded this opportunity. Even if the declarant is available, the failure to explain is more the choice of the proponent of the hearsay, who chose not to call the declarant, than the impeaching party.

The rule also permits a party against whom hearsay has been admitted to call the declarant and examine him about the statement "as if under

---

[240] FED. R. EVID. 608(a).

cross-examination." The examination thus would be the same as if the hearsay were presented as live testimony. Generally, the rule would permit leading questions, unless the declarant were closely aligned with the party that introduced his statement.

When a hearsay declarant is not available to testify, the declarant cannot be impeached with prior bad acts under the procedure established under FRE 608(b) because she cannot be cross-examined and the rule prohibits the introduction of extrinsic evidence. In *United States v. Saada*, [241] the Government argued that extrinsic evidence of bad acts should be admissible since the declarant was not available for questioning about his prior conduct. The court ruled, however, that the ban on extrinsic evidence applies to hearsay declarants, even those who are unavailable.

---

[241] 212 F.3d 210 (3d Cir. 2000).

CHAPTER 7

DIRECT EXAMINATION

---

§ 7-1. Introduction.

In "direct examination," the advocate calls a witness for interrogation as part of his own case. Usually the witness is friendly, but occasionally an adverse or hostile witness must be called to prove important facts. "Cross-examination" is conducted by counsel for the opposing party or parties, usually right after the completion of direct.

A good direct examination permits the witness to tell her story in a fashion that is interesting and easy to follow. The "story" should emphasize factual points known to the witness that provide the basis for a favorable result. The witness, rather than the attorney, should dominate the jury's attention, but the lawyer should control the discussion and bring out key parts of the portrayal. The most important prerequisite for a good direct examination is preparation.

An important aspect of direct examination — often lost on lawyers — is that the advocate should know the answers when she asks questions. The attorney is not truly an interrogator, seeking to discover facts. Instead, counsel acts as a director, guiding the witness to describe facts that the lawyer needs to prove to the jury. In this process, the questions identify subjects on which the witness should testify.[1] The attorney must select the points to be made, prepare the witness to testify effectively, and plan an examination that vividly communicates important facts.

The attorney needs to be in control in direct examination but should not divert attention from the witness. Jurors believe a story more quickly if it comes from the witness rather than the lawyer. Additionally, jurors are more interested in hearing from the witness, since he is a fresh face, with his own personality and a unique perspective. Jurors identify with witnesses more easily than with a lawyer. Therefore, counsel should not try to dominate the discussion, but should act as a guide through the witness's story.

This chapter discusses the presentation of an effective direct examination. Sections 7-2 and 7-3 address the goals of direct-examination and techniques to

---

[1] See PETER MURRAY, BASIC TRIAL ADVOCACY 108–09 (1995).

accomplish them. Sections 7-4–7-6 discuss the form of questions in direct examination. Sections 7-7–7-9 discuss preparing for and ordering a direct examination and §§ 7-10–7-15 review suggestions for an effective presentation. Sections 7-16–7-17 discuss techniques to refresh recollection, § 7-18 addresses redirect examination, and §§ 7-19 and 7-20 provide examples of direct examinations.

Section 7-21 discusses preparing a witness for cross-examination.

§ 7-2. Goals of Direct Examination.

Direct examination provides your basic opportunity to make a case. Generally, witnesses on direct are friendly and want to be helpful. Usually they look on the lawyer as a protector who will aid them through the ordeal of testifying; thus, they are happy to cooperate in preparing. Witnesses you call for direct examination often identify with your client, which enhances their willingness to be helpful. Thus, these witnesses present the best opportunity to prove essential facts.

Although witnesses you call on direct usually want to cooperate, they often do not know what is important in the case. Lay people generally do not understand the legal principles that determine lawsuits or the facts that make a difference in applying them. Thus, you must find out what the witness knows, determine what is important, and figure out how to bring it out. Additionally, you need to work with the witness to ensure that descriptions are understandable and persuasive.

Many lawyers' direct examinations fail to focus on important points. The attorney allows the witness to tell his story, perhaps comprehensively, but without developing important matters and eliminating needless detail. The important testimony cannot impress the jurors because it has equal status with less crucial fact descriptions. In adopting this passive approach, the attorney fails to take advantage of his opportunity to emphasize important matters. Additionally, because spoken words are elusive and difficult to remember, the attorney's failure to emphasize essential facts may cause the jurors to forget them.

Two goals — the *selection* and *emphasis* of favorable facts — should shape any direct examination. You need to identify facts within the witness's knowledge that (1) support the application of favorable legal principles, (2) show your position is equitable, and (3) refute the relevant claims of the opposing party. By positioning these points for maximum impact and using methods that permit unobjectionable repetition, you can highlight favorable points. You should permit the witness to fill in the facts necessary for a coherent story, but not to wander into unimportant detail.

Another goal of direct examination is understandability. For a listener to follow any oral discourse, the presentation needs to be simple. You should use an easy-to-follow structure, which usually means reviewing the story chronologically.

The jurors do not already know all the facts and may not easily understand an oral discourse; they need help in achieving comprehension.

An example of the importance of counsel's direction can be provided from the *Danielson v. ComputerCentre* material in Appendix A. Jack Danielson, a former police officer, and his wife claim that they were defrauded by Computer-Centre Associates when they purchased a computer franchise. In an affidavit previously filed in support of a motion for summary judgment, Mr. Danielson describes a marketing presentation of ComputerCentre, conducted by Dale Atkins and Jene Nelsen, as follows:[2]

I attended the presentation on February 12 at the Holiday Inn in Middletown. There were perhaps 12 or 13 other people present, some married couples and some individuals. It was at this meeting that I first made the acquaintance of Dale Atkins, the head of ComputerCentre. There were other people at the meeting from ComputerCentre. One I remember was named Jene Nelsen, an incredibly pushy and insistent salesperson. Nelsen was in attendance throughout the presentation and was constantly asking us personal questions and insisting on our agreement with every tiny fact which was mentioned about the nature of the computer revolution, the amount of money that people were making in marketing computers, the wisdom of the concept of franchise sales, the need for expert assistance in the marketing of a complex technological device like a computer, and virtually every other statement which was made. If we did not nod our head or indicate our assent verbally, Nelsen would specifically ask us if we did not agree with the observation which had been made in the sales presentation. I found Nelsen's presence quite eerie and after a while it became nerve-wracking to do anything other than agree with the fact that Nelsen wanted us to accept. Particularly in the group setting with others present we felt that to deny these facts, most of which seemed to be correct, would have been disruptive on our part and might have been embarrassing.

I felt quite relieved when the day was over. It was a very long presentation and by the end of it, constant reinforcement of the statements of Atkins had left me quite drained. I felt I had no opportunity to reflect on the presentation because the moment a statement was made we had been asked to assent to it. Before I was allowed to leave the conference room at the Holiday Inn, around 4:00 p.m. Nelsen came around to get our agreement to meet

---

[2] Appendix A.

> on a further occasion to take further steps to sign up to become owners of a franchise for a ComputerCentre. . . .

Another part of Danielson's affidavit shows that Atkins and Nelsen made representations at the meeting. These include the statements that ComputerCentre would make technical decisions for the Danielsons, provide training for a computer technician, ship products immediately so that the Danielsons could maintain a small inventory, and provide accounting software for use in handling books and inventory. The affidavit states[3]

> Over coffee, my wife and I discussed the seeming completeness of the plans which ComputerCentre Associates had made for the management of the franchises. It seemed like all of the difficult technical decisions in figuring out which computers to stock would be handled by Atkins and his experienced assistant Nelsen. Since the shipping arrangements would be very fast from the ComputerCentre Associates depot in Boston, we would not be required to maintain a huge inventory locally. Thus, we thought that we would not have to take out too large a mortgage on our house, which we felt had an equity value of approximately $90,000. The presentation the prior day had also promised training for a technician to be our repair person, and complete "accounting software" for operating our business; we would get all of the computer programs necessary to set up our own books of account to handle invoices and inventory without creating an entire set of books and paperwork on our own.

The file confirms the representations at the meeting. An agenda establishes that Atkins and Nelsen described "How the Profits Mount" and used the San Francisco franchise as an example of 19 percent profitability.[4] Moreover, it shows the presentation suggested prospective franchises would be trained to do even better. Further, the agenda indicates that Atkins and Nelsen promised there would be little need to maintain inventory, described the technical facilities available to franchisees, and promoted national and local advertising support — including 37 national ads a year.[5]

Danielson, a lay person, might not have a good idea of what to emphasize about the meeting. The tone of his affidavit suggests a personal resentment toward the "pushy" and "insistent" tactics of Jene Nelsen. Left to tell his story, Danielson probably would describe these tactics in detail and his own adverse reaction to them. The description would focus more on the intimidating style of Nelsen than the representations made in soliciting prospects.

---

[3] Appendix A.

[4] Appendix A.

[5] Appendix A.

From the attorney's perspective Danielson's emphasis would be inadvisable. First, pushiness and insistence are not elements of fraud; the Danielsons need to prove that Atkins and Nelsen made false representations and omitted important facts. Second, Danielson is a former police officer with twenty years experience. His own description of cowering at the pushy sales pitch of Jene Nelsen, a woman, is not likely to evoke sympathy from reasonable jurors. This description sounds like after-the-fact whining. Third, Danielson's affidavit suggests that the meeting should have put him on guard, not that it should have induced him to believe the false representations. Yet the Danielsons called and asked for a franchise the next day.

As director and theme master, the attorney should guide Mr. Danielson to emphasize the representations at the meeting that turned out to be false. The circumstances in which they were made — including the pushiness of Jene Nelsen — might be mentioned but not emphasized. An extensive review of the circumstances only diverts attention from counsel's theme: Nelsen and Atkins made false statements. Counsel should focus on the representations, setting the stage for further testimony that ComputerCentre did not fulfill its promises. The attorney would achieve this goal by guiding Mr. Danielson to the right points and asking questions to develop them for the jury.

 One way to test the content of the direct examination is to ask yourself how the opposing side is likely to react to it. If the material is "filler" that will not bother opposing counsel, it should be de-emphasized. You should also consider whether the witness's description might actually play into the hands of the opposing attorney, allowing him to turn around the facts to support his own theory. This testimony needs to be eliminated or reduced. If a description will hurt the opposing party, forcing him to contest it, you should find ways to develop it.

§ 7-3. Techniques for an Effective Presentation.

You should plan the direct examination to achieve the goals of understandability and advocacy. You need to make the presentation simple, while emphasizing the strong points that the witness can describe. To achieve these goals you should employ the following techniques.

§ 7-3(a). Preparation.

The only way to present an effective direct examination is through preparation. You must plan the examination and meet with the witness to review and practice it. The presentation can be effective only if you and the witness both know what you are trying to accomplish. Preparation for the direct examination is discussed in §§ 7-7 and 7-8.

§ 7-3(b). Simple Structure.

You need to employ an understandable structure. Usually a chronological approach is the easiest to understand. You can *stop* the story to develop and emphasize helpful details — which often involves developing the latest topic — but avoid major back-and-forth leaps in time. Alternatively, you may select a topical presentation, but this approach generally should be reserved for technical witnesses and others who do not have a "story" to tell. In any event, you need to organize the examination for simplicity. See § 7-9 for a suggested sequence of direct examination.

§ 7-3(c). Positioning.

You should emphasize important points by positioning them for maximum impact in your presentation. Placing the thematic points at the beginning and end of a portrayal provides an overview of the testimony and highlights your main points. Thus, you should try to touch on main points at the beginning and end of the examination. Additionally, during the examination you should focus on important points by signaling your transitions, breaking down favorable material, and following up to develop key facts. For important events, you may ask to relate a short narrative that describes the event, and follow up to develop facts mentioned by the witness. See § 7-13 for a discussion of the "step-step-step — whirr! — replay-replay-replay" approach.

§ 7-3(d). Persuasive Ordering of Information.

Choosing the right order in which to present information is a key requirement for a persuasive presentation. You must cover both good and bad facts to ensure that you do not leave the witness unduly vulnerable on cross-examination. The order in which you present the topics can make a great difference in their impact. For example, in examining Dale Atkins in the *Danielson* case, you might want to review ComputerCentre's general success and that of its franchisees before addressing the problems encountered by the Danielsons. Placing Computer-Centre's lapses in context — other franchisees succeeded in spite of the temporary problems — would lend credibility to Atkins's explanation of his conduct. You perhaps should review alternative presentations with the witness, however, before deciding on the best order of presentation.

§ 7-3(e). Selection of Words.

Your choice of words in forming questions may influence the character and vividness of direct examination. If you use the verb "smashed" in describing a collision, the witness is likely to describe a more violent occurrence than if you used "bumped." Additionally, the suggestive power of your description makes the listener imagine a more violent collision. You need to avoid leading on direct, but you retain considerable discretion to choose terminology.

301

§ 7-3(f). Repetition.

A good way to develop and emphasize strong points is through repetition. You cannot just repeat points, however; restating the witness's testimony is improper. What you can do is follow up, taking important elements of a witness's story and developing them. In doing so you legitimately can repeat points by folding them into questions. This method is explained further in § 7-13.

§ 7-3(g). Control.

Although you want the witness to dominate a direct examination, you need to be in control. You do not want the witness — who may be eager to get out a point — jumping ahead in the presentation. You not only must plan the examination and practice it with the witness, but choose questions that direct the witness *specifically* to the topics you want her to address. These specific "cues" help the witness remember your plan. If you use inquiries that are too broad, a witness easily can lose her place and address points out of context, when they do not have maximum impact. See § 7-11.

Some witnesses, eager to tell a story, may jump ahead without waiting for your cues. To maintain control you may need to interrupt. You should not be afraid to stop the witness when she exceeds the bounds of a question. This action avoids a lengthy narrative, which would be objectionable, and helps the jury focus on your point. Try to find a breaking point in the witness's account and step in politely to stop her: "Ms. Jones, let me stop you for a minute because I'd like to follow up on the point you just made."

§ 7-3(h). Visual Aids.

One way to enhance any listener's comprehension is to show him what the witness describes. If you and a witness need to describe an important scene, you can guarantee success by showing the jury a picture. Making sure the jurors see items of real evidence — the gun, knife, key document or other item — also enhances understanding. Additionally, you can promote comprehension by having the witness *show* the jurors the distance, length, width, or other measure he is trying to estimate. This approach illustrates the witness's estimate:

> Q.   How far away was the man?
>
> A.   I'd say about twenty feet.
>
> Q.   Can you identify something in the courtroom that is about the same distance from where you're sitting?
>
> A.   Yes. About from you to me.

§ 7-3(i). Agreeable Storytelling Flow.

You should try to arrange a dance-like "flow" to the questions and answers. You should control the presentation; the witness should follow. Vary the length of answers. Find ways to give the story life. Watch out for long-winded narratives on unimportant material. Details should only be covered when helpful in emphasizing important points. You should cover unimportant material with a broad brush.

§ 7-3(j). Drawing the Sting.

You should have the witness address unfavorable points in the direct examination. Bringing them out in direct — in the context of an affirmative presentation — is much less damaging than if they are raised for the first time in cross-examination. Additionally, once your witness admits an unfavorable point, the jurors may find it offensive for opposing counsel to dramatize it in cross-examination. Find a way to bring the matter out in context and with any necessary explanation.

§ 7-3(k). Listening to Answers.

Attorneys, who must phrase questions in nonleading form, often think of the next question while witnesses respond. This natural effort to think ahead often causes lawyers to *miss* the answer. If the witness omits an important point, the attorney may never realize it. Thus, you need to hear the witness's answer *before* you formulate the next question.

§ 7-4. Use of Nonleading Questions (FRE 611(c)).

Ordinarily, a lawyer on direct examination must conduct a direct examination with nonleading questions, while the cross-examiner may use leading questions. "Leading" questions are those that suggest the answer to the witness. In some instances, however, the use of leading questions is permitted on direct examination and denied on cross-examination.

FRE 611(c) provides:

> **(c) Leading questions.** Leading questions should not be used on the direct examination of a witness except as may be necessary to develop his testimony. Ordinarily leading questions should be permitted on cross-examination. When a party calls a hostile witness, an adverse party, or a witness identified with an adverse party, interrogation may be by leading questions.

Under this rule, interrogation by leading questions usually is permitted on direct examination:

1. When the witness is hostile, an adverse party or identified with an adverse party.[6] The "direct examination" of an adverse party or adverse witness is discussed in §§ 9-23 and 9-25.

2. When necessary to develop the testimony of a witness, as when a small child is a witness.[7]

In addition, the trial judge may permit leading questions on unimportant matters or to quicken the pace of the trial. Rule 611(a) permits the court to control the mode of interrogating witnesses to "avoid needless consumption of time."[8]

A "leading" question is one that suggests the answer. In other words, the question itself provides substantive information. It makes no difference that the witness can answer the question "yes" or "no," or even that the attorney expects a "no." For example, "were you holding a knife?" is leading, regardless of whether counsel expects a "yes" or "no;" the role of the witness in responding is only to endorse or deny the attorney's premise.

A nonleading question asks the witness to supply the information. Generally, questions that elicit information through the "Five Ws and H" — Who, What, Where, When, Why and How — are nonleading. Thus, "What happened next?", "Where were you standing?", "What were the lighting conditions?", "How were you dressed?" are nonleading questions.[9]

A cousin of the leading question is one that assumes a fact: "How were you holding the knife?" In this question counsel again injects information into the record, although the question appears to seek information. This type of question is permissible if the witness has *already* testified that he held a knife, but not if the inquiry introduces the knife.

Allowing the witness to select one of two or more options does not cure a leading question. Assume the following question:

---

[6] Stahl v. Sun Microsys., 775 F. Supp. 1397, 1398 (D. Colo. 1991) (allowing the use of leading questions on direct examination of adverse witness, even though witness was no longer employed by the defendant, when witness continued to have a post-employment business relationship with defendant).

[7] See Idaho v. Wright, 497 U.S. 805, 818-19 (use of leading questions with children does not necessarily render responses untrustworthy). Many courts allow leading questions in the direct examination of a child witness in a molestation case. *See e.g.,* United States v. Archdale, 229 F.3d 861, 865-66 (9th Cir. 2000).

[8] Stine v. Marathon Oil Co., 976 F.2d 254 (5th Cir. 1992) (allowing both sides to use leading questions to speed the examination of witnesses).

[9] See MCCORMICK ON EVIDENCE § 6 (5th ed. 1999).

> Q. Did you leave and go to your car or stay in the house after the shooting?
>
> A. I went to my car.

In this exchange counsel's question suggests the relevant information; the witness merely adopts one of the options. A sufficient answer would be "The former." Since the attorney suggests the substantive testimony, the question is leading. The inquiry is also objectionable on a separate ground — it is compound. If the witness answers "yes," the answer may be accurate, but the listeners will not know which option was correct.

When the possible answers are limited, a question that suggests them is not so objectionable. Thus, if the witness describes seeing a man, and the attorney asks "Was he tall or short?" the question usually does not provoke an objection. Still, the inquiry technically is inappropriate. "Describe his height" or "How tall was he?" would be more appropriate. The latter question, though suggestive, is acceptable because people commonly ask a person's height by reference to the word "tall."

You cannot completely avoid leading questions. Some leading is required to steer a witness to a subject area, time of day, event, and similar matters. Leading permits you to cover ground quickly, which may actually be appreciated by the court and the adverse party. Nevertheless, you generally should avoid leading, especially on important points.

Nonleading questions focus attention on the witness — where you want it — rather than the lawyer. Additionally, nonleading questions minimize the likelihood that opposing counsel will disrupt the presentation with objections. Since you may have difficulty rephrasing to a nonleading question in the heat of the moment, using a correct form may also save you some embarrassment.[10]

An objection that a question is leading, or assumes facts, may easily befuddle a novice attorney. It is not easy to rephrase an inquiry in a nonleading form in a few seconds when you are thinking about the answer you want. The best approach is to begin the next question with a "W" word — Who, What, When, Where, Why — or with "How." Usually the inquiry that follows can be phrased in a nonleading manner.

Although you do not lead a witness, at the same time you need to control the testimony and help the witness understand your questions. Thus, the nonleading form must be combined with substantive terms that direct the witness

---

[10] *Id.*

specifically to a subject area. You generally should use specific, close-end questions rather than general inquiries. These questions sometimes contain some suggestion — "what did he say?" assumes the subject said something — but courts usually permit this type of direction. Almost any inquiry assumes the existence of some fact and providing the witness specific cues focuses and speeds the testimony. You should avoid questions that assume facts in controversy, however, and maintain a nonleading form.

If you do provoke an objection and an unfavorable ruling, you might try adding "if anything" to the question: "What, if anything, did he say?" Lawyers traditionally have employed this formalism to avoid the "assumes facts" objection, although it should not be necessary. Specific, closed-end questions are discussed further in § 7-11.

§ 7-5. Questions That Call for Narratives.

Although the witness should tell the story in a direct examination, it should not come in the form of a lengthy narrative. Narratives — and questions that obviously call for them — are objectionable because they permit the witness to introduce inadmissible material before the opposing lawyer has an opportunity to object.[11] Additionally, long-winded answers may burden the presentation. These answers often tend to lose their focus, which may bore and confuse the jury.

Moreover, if you give up control of the examination, the witness may jump ahead, blurt out points not called for by the question, and generally confuse the presentation. Thus, you need to retain control, using the question and answer format but permitting the witness to provide the relevant information. You generally should seek short answers, but mix in questions that allow an occasional longer response. One approach to achieve this objective is set forth in § 7-13.

Questions that are too open-ended often lead to narratives. If you ask "What happened next?" the witness may well understand that he is supposed to relate everything that happened next. In doing so the witness may emphasize the wrong points and fail to mention important facts. Thus, employ questions that are as specific as possible. See § 7-11. Additionally, by rehearsing with the witness prior to the examination and stopping him in narratives, you can train the witness to provide more limited answers.

§ 7-6. Objections to the Form of the Question in Direct Examination.

Some "form" objections are common during direct examination. You should prepare so as to avoid these objections. If the opposing party offends these rules in direct examination, and the matter is important, you should object.

---

[11] *Id.* § 5.

§ 7-6(a). Leading.

A leading question suggests the answer. See § 7-4. In special circumstances, such as an examination of the adverse party on direct, counsel may lead.[12]

§ 7-6(b). Calls for a Narrative.

A question phrased so as to call for a long, story-like response is objectionable because it eliminates the opportunity for timely objections. See § 7-5 An example: "Tell the jury what you know about the runway job."[13]

§ 7-6(c). Assumes Facts.

When counsel asks a question that assumes a fact, the inquiry is objectionable. This approach is the cousin of leading because it allows the lawyer to articulate the facts. For example, if the witness has not testified to seeing a gun, the question "where was he holding the gun?" would be improper. The classic "assumes a fact" question, of course, is "When did you stop beating your wife?"[14]

§ 7-6(d). Repeating Testimony.

In an effort to emphasize testimony, lawyers often repeat the statements of the witness. This effort to underscore the witness's words is objectionable. Counsel is not supposed to testify, even as repetition.[15] A way around the problem is to ask follow-up questions *about* a point made by the witness. Fold the point into the following questions: "Where was he holding this foot-long knife?"

§ 7-6(e). Compound.

Often questions give the witness alternatives: "Were you in your car or on the sidewalk?" The compound form is improper because the answer may be confusing — what if the witness says "yes"? This approach is also a variation of leading, as counsel is still suggesting the answer.[16]

---

[12] See § 7-4 *supra*.

[13] But see United States v. Silva, 748 F.2d 262, 264 (5th Cir. 1984) (narrative testimony allowed in order to get "some of the background out," when the narrative testimony did not preclude objections, and when a question and answer format immediately followed the background information); United States v. Young, 745 F.2d 733 (2d Cir. 1984) (narrative testimony allowed to accompany videotape).

[14] See LANE'S GOLDSTEIN TR. TECH. § 13.40 (3d ed. 1994); see also United States v. Sanchez-Lopez, 879 F.2d 541 (9th Cir. 1989).

[15] See Blissett v. Lefevre, 924 F.2d 434 (2d Cir. 1991).

[16] See LANE'S GOLDSTEIN TR. TECH. § 13.46 (3d ed. 1992).

§ 7-6(f).   Asked and Answered.

If the attorney repeats a question that has been answered, the question is objectionable as cumulative and wasteful of time.[17]

§ 7-6(g).   Calls for Speculation.

"What if" questions are no help to the jury because they call for speculation as to what might have happened: "If he had provided the material, what would you have done?" If speculation really is necessary, the jury can speculate as well as the witness.[18] Additionally, questions that are phrased in the subjunctive literally call for speculation, even though they are not intended to do so. "What would you have been doing at that time?" is phrased as a hypothetical, but probably is intended to mean "What were you doing at that time?" You should stick with the past tense unless the question is truly hypothetical.

§ 7-7.   Preparing a Direct Examination.

Preparation is essential to a good direct examination. Both lawyer and witness must be aware of the goals of the testimony. The examination should flow naturally, with the lawyer and the witness combined in a storytelling partnership. The witness's responses should be clear and direct. The witness should be well prepared for cross-examination. To accomplish these objectives, both lawyer and witness must prepare.

To prepare the witness, you should first identify the evidentiary "points" that the witness can prove and any exhibits that the witness should authenticate. Then, outline the order in which you will elicit those points — more or less in story form. Prepare an outline of points or a list of questions. In connection with each point or question, make notes of each significant matter you want the witness to describe.[19] See § 7-8.

Often lawyers fail to prepare witnesses adequately to give direct testimony. The attorney either puts the witness on the stand with no preparation or briefly reviews for the witness the matters counsel wants the witness to describe. In either case, the trial testimony is likely to wander and confuse the listeners. The witness may misunderstand questions, omit facts, present thoughts in a garbled fashion, and make other mistakes that accompany any first draft. If the attorney tries to help by leading, opposing counsel may further disrupt the testimony with objections.

You should meet with the witness before he testifies and discuss the points you will cover. This undertaking should not be an effort to put words in the

---

[17] *Id.* § 13.109.

[18] *Id.* § 13.47.

[19] See generally Clark D. Cunningham, *A Tale of Two Clients: Thinking About Law as Language,* 87 MICH. L. REV. 2459 (1989).

witness's mouth, but to bring out the witness's knowledge in a clear, focused way.[20] In this connection, you actually should ask questions and hear the responses. It is amazing how often witnesses miss points during preparation sessions; a run-through often eliminates misunderstandings. Additionally, a practice session allows you to suggest ways to clarify and focus the testimony and may alert you to problems.

A run-through also permits the witness to think through the testimony, organize it properly, and find the best way to present it. Rehearsing tends to fix points in the witness's mind, which focuses the presentation. Practicing also should bolster the confidence of the witness; once she has presented the testimony, it is much easier to deliver it in court.

In preparing a witness, you should explain that you will be unable to lead. You should prepare questions that direct the witness specifically to your points, but the witness should provide the relevant information concerning each topic. Explain the point you want the witness to cover in response to each question. Ask the witness to answer each question and, if necessary, suggest the areas that require more or less emphasis.

You should require the witness to rehearse explanations of charts, diagrams, and other demonstrative exhibits. Practicing promotes a clear, understandable presentation. It also brings out unforeseen difficulties in handling the exhibits. If an exhibit is unwieldy, difficulties in setting it up can easily detract from its content.

You should not ask the witness to deliver pat responses or memorize answers. Instead, you should encourage her to choose her own words and emphasize the need to tell the truth. There is nothing improper, however, with ensuring that the witness is aware of the points you are trying to make and presents them clearly. In this connection, the witness should not hesitate to concede, if asked, that she discussed the testimony with you. This preparation is normal and appropriate. Further, you should talk over this point so that the witness is not unduly defensive. You might say: "If he asks whether we discussed your testimony, don't worry about telling him 'yes.' Preparation is normal. We're just trying to bring out the truth."

§ 7-8. Mechanics of Preparation.

You should prepare the outline of the direct examination on loose-leaf pages in your trial notebook. List the outline or questions on the right side of each page. On the left side you should note when exhibits must be introduced. Make prominent notes of when to announce transitions in the testimony, refer to demonstrative exhibits, or take other special action. The outline should reflect the "points to prove" from the trial outline but should be organized for a simple

---

[20] See THOMAS A. MAUET, TRIAL TECHNIQUES 114–15 (5th ed. 2000).

and effective presentation. You may either prepare questions or outline the points you want to prove.

§ 7-8(a). The Question Approach.

An abbreviated example of a question list and outline for Jack Danielson in the *ComputerCentre Associates* case follows. The example contains complete questions, but they do not need to be that elaborate; entries sufficient to permit the framing of nonleading questions are sufficient. You should expect to follow up with additional questions — to ensure completeness and spontaneity in the actual interrogation — regardless of the prepared list. An example of a direct examination of Jack Danielson is presented in § 7-19.

	J. Danielson
	State your name.
	Where do you live?
	What role do you have in this case?
	— Plaintiff
	— Owned franchise
[Space to list exhibits or other notes]	Why did you sue the defendant, ComputerCentre Associates?
	— Misrepresentations
	— Failure to deliver on promises
	— Franchise failed
	— Lost all savings
	[Turning to background]
	How long have you lived in Middletown?
	What is your marital status?
	What is your professional background?
	— Retired police officer
	— With wife, sought franchise
	How did you become aware of the ComputerCentre franchise offer?
	— Ad in Wall Street Journal
P. Ex. 1	[Mark exhibit]
[Wall Street Journal ad]	I show you an exhibit marked for identification Plaintiff's Exhibit 1. Can you identify it?
	— Wall Street Journal ad
	[Offer exhibit]
	What interested you in a ComputerCentre franchise?
	— Opportunity for low-cost enterprise
	— Experience not needed
	— Support from franchisor
	What did you do after seeing this ad?
	— Called listed 800 number
	— Was told about local seminar
	How did you respond to this information?

	— Attended seminar
	When was the seminar conducted?
	Where?
	— Holiday Inn
	— Meeting room
	What interested persons were in attendance?
	— J. Danielson
	— About 13 local residents
	Who represented ComputerCentre?
	— D. Atkins, President of ComputerCentre
	— J. Nelsen, Sales Manager
	Who led the discussion?
	— D. Atkins
	What general areas did he cover?
	— Profits
	— Support to be provided
	— Low overhead
	— Advertising
P. Ex. 2	Can you tell the jury what this is for?
Agenda	
	— Agenda for meeting
[Using agenda items.]	What did Mr. Atkins say about the likely profitability of a franchise?
	— San Francisco example
	— 19% profit
	What did Mr. Atkins say about the support to be provided?
	— Training
	— Delivery of products
	What type of training did he promise?
	— Technical facility
	— Sales representatives
	— Service personnel
	To what extent did he discuss the need to maintain inventory?
	What did he say?
	— Quick delivery promised
	— Little inventory needed
	What training did he say would be provided for the sales personnel?
	— Three-week course
	— On-job support
	— Follow up
	To what extent did Atkins discuss technical training?
	Where was this training to be provided?
	— Technical facility
	How much training did he promise?
	— As needed by technical personnel

311

> [The outline would include other areas, including the failure to fulfill promises, ensuing problems, loss of the business and damages.]

§ 7-8(b). The Outline of Expected Testimony.

Another approach to preparing direct examination is simply to make notes of what you expect the witness to say — without framing questions. This method requires that you make up the questions as the examination proceeds. It permits you to remember the points that need to be covered, however, and promotes eye contact when you state questions.

One of the pitfalls of this approach is that it may induce you to ask leading questions. Turning a note into a nonleading question in the courtroom, under pressure, is not easy. The fact that the note itself is the answer makes it difficult to use it in a nonleading way. For inexperienced attorneys, it may be easier to plan questions in advance. Additionally, preparing some of the questions may help you pace the testimony, mixing one-line answers with short narratives.

An abbreviated example of the outline approach — again for Jack Danielson in the *ComputerCentre Associates* case — follows.

J. Danielson

Name — Jack Danielson
Address — 1234 Barstow Avenue
Middletown
Plaintiff
Suing because:
    1. ComputerCentre Associates made misrepresentations
    2. Failed to perform promises
    3. Franchise failed
    4. Lost life savings
[Background]
Retired police officer
With wife, sought franchise
Interested in ComputerCentre because of ads
    No need for experience
    Training provided
    Inventory support
    Low investment
    Advertising

P. Ex. 1   I.D. Wall Street Journal ad [etc.]
Wall Street Journal ad

Followed up by calling listed numbers
    Attended seminar
P. Ex. 2   Seminar at Holiday Inn
Agenda

[Using agenda items.]

March 13, 1993
Meeting room
Agenda distributed - i.d.
Present - J. Danielson
      13 other residents
      Atkins and Nelsen
Discussion - Atkins
Representations
    Profits
      — San Francisco example
    Support/training
      — Technical facility
      — Sales training
      — Service training
    Inventory support
      — 24-hour delivery
      — Inventory management
    Advertising support
      — Institutional ads
      — Local ad support
    Software for office and business use
[Again, the outline would include all the areas to be covered in the testimony.]

You need not rely on either of these extremes. A good compromise is to make shorthand notes of questions, sufficient for framing nonleading questions. List the points to be made with the witness, however, to protect against omissions.

§ 7-9. Suggested Sequence for Direct Examination.

You should plan the direct examination to make it understandable, yet powerful. The order of presentation depends on the witness and the subject. The following sample outline may be used with a typical witness, but you should adapt it for special circumstances.

§ 7-9(a). Introduction and Overview.

You need to elicit the witness's name and the reason for his involvement in the case. Additionally, you should set a thematic tone, show the witness is in a special position to relate facts, or otherwise grab the juror's attention. See § 7-10. This action helps hold the jury's attention for the next phase of the testimony.

§ 7-9(b). Review of Background or Qualifications.

Generally you should review some of the personal history or qualifications of important witnesses. The more important the witness is to the case, the more the jurors need to know her. Reviewing personal background of a party in the case may lead the jurors to like and believe her. The information is not really

313

relevant, but courts usually permit a modest review. For an expert or technical witness, the person's qualifications provide the basis for credibility, but some personal history make the witness appealing. Do not overdo the background, however, as it can easily become boring.

§ 7-9(c). Review of Main Points.

The main points of the testimony should follow the background. You should take a witness through fact testimony in chronological order or with another simple organization. Within the story, be sure to focus on important points. Signal your transitions to help the listeners follow the structure. With technical witnesses, you can often break the testimonies into topics, using transitional signposts to help the jurors follow the exchange. For topical witnesses you must take extra care to communicate your transitions.

When you have a witness who addresses more than one main topic — such as a witness who knows several aspects of the facts or an expert who addresses different subjects — you should couple specific foundations with specific subjects. Thus, review a fact witness's vantage point on scene one, then have him discuss scene one; review the vantage point on scene two, then discuss scene two. With an expert who addresses separable topics, link your review of specific qualifications for each subject with the testimony on that matter.

For subject areas within the main points, a good sequence would be the following.

1.   *Signal the transition to a new topic.* "Now, Ms. Jones, I'd like to address what you saw on Maple Street."
2.   *Review the witness's basis for testifying on the particular topic.*
3.   *Bring out the testimony.*
4.   *Follow up for emphasis.*

The "step-step-step — whirr! — replay-replay-replay" approach is a good method to cover the basis, bring out the testimony and follow up. See § 7-13.

§ 7-9(d). Conclusion.

You should also try to end on a high note. Let the jurors know you are closing because it will make them perk up. Ask a question or short series that recaptures the theme, summarizes the testimony, or sounds a final note.

§ 7-10. Strong Start and Finish.

A crucial element of a good direct examination is a strong beginning. Within the first minute, you and witness should bring out the essential theme of the testimony or some other attention-grabbing point. You can then present any necessary background and the overall story. Additionally, you should find a way to close the examination on a memorable note.

A striking beginning grabs the interest of the jurors and makes them more attentive. The average person has a short attention span; for example; most people decide whether they are interested in a conversation at a cocktail party soon after joining it. Moreover, the trial process makes the telling of a story cumbersome. If you waste time getting to the point, the jurors' interest may wane. Thus, you need to make a strong impression at the start.

A thematic beginning also sets the stage for testimony that follows. A thematic point captures the overall impact of a group of related facts. Thus, a beginning that includes the general point provides context — like a picture frame — for the facts that will be "painted in" on the canvas. This context promotes the jurors' comprehension of the testimony.

An example of a strong beginning, which focuses attention on the theme, is the following:

Q. State your name, please.

A. Margaret Danielson.

Q. Ms. Danielson, what is your role in this case?

A. My husband and I are the plaintiffs.

Q. Why have you sued the defendant, ComputerCentre Associates?

A. Because they lied to us to get us to sign up for a franchise and then failed to deliver the training and products we needed to survive.

Q. What were the consequences of their actions?

A. We lost everything — our entire life savings, our home, and our means of support.

Q. Now, Ms. Danielson, I'd like to review your background. Please tell the jury

---

This short series of questions and answers brings out the core of what the witness will tell the jury, and at the same time grabs their attention. With this beginning, the factual background seems all the more meaningful and interesting. Without this beginning, the background might seem dull, and the jury may not understand its importance.

The witness's vantage point is another topic that can provide a good beginning, especially for witnesses who have no particular interest in the case. Letting the jury know that the witness was in a position to observe crucial facts enhances interest and makes the testimony credible. An example follows:

Q.   State your name, please.

A.   Oscar Smith.

Q.   What is your occupation?

A.   Construction supervisor.

Q.   Were you involved in the runway renovation project at the New Orleans International Airport?

A.   Indeed I was.

Q.   What was your day-to-day involvement?

A.   I was the construction supervisor on that job. I was there every day. I supervised or participated in laying the asphalt on the entire runway.

Just as a strong opening is important to a good direct examination, so is a strong ending. The ending is the second most memorable part, after the beginning, of any oral presentation. Since audiences always welcome endings, you should provide a signpost that it has arrived: "Finally, Mr. Smith, ..." This transition may wake up a few dreamers. Additionally, the closing should reemphasize the theme or bring out a final, poignant point:

Q.   Finally, Mr. Smith, I'll ask you: To what extent did you see anything about the construction job that was defective?

A.   There was nothing defective. That was one of the most careful, well-constructed jobs I've ever seen. The workmen were extremely attentive to good standards. It was just in general a well-done job.

Paying attention to the beginning and end of the testimony helps both you and the witness focus on important points. Additionally, it often gives a thematic aspect to the presentation, since key facts come out at the beginning, in the body, and at the end. Further, this approach comes across as crisp and directed, giving the listeners a sense that their time is being used efficiently. Thus, counsel should find ways to achieve strong starts and finishes.

§ 7-11. Use of Specific, Closed-End Questions.

Although you should promote the witness's role in direct examination, you should also retain control. To achieve this goal, you should employ specific, closed-end questions, which direct the witness as much as possible to particular parts of the topic. These narrow questions should compose much — but not necessarily all — of the examination.

Preparation alone does not ensure that the witness will follow counsel's directions on direct examination. Witnesses often become confused, wander off the subject, jump ahead, and omit important points. Because leading is prohibited, advocates often find it difficult to control witnesses without drawing objections. Using questions that direct the witness to a topic, and limit its scope, helps you avoid these problems.

A question may be specific and closed-end without being leading. You still should permit the witness to provide the evidence, but should direct the testimony to confined subjects. Examples of open versus closed-end questions are set forth below:

OPEN-END	CLOSED-END
Describe the man's appearance.	How tall was the man?
	Describe his build.
	What clothes was he wearing?
	What color was his hair?
	Did you notice his eyes? What color were they?
	What type of shoes was he wearing?
What did you see at the intersection?	What streets cross at the intersection?
	How many lanes is Maple Street?
	How many lanes is Broadway?
	What traffic control devices were present?
	Describe the shrubbery near the streets.
What happened next?	[Assume the witness described a man running with a knife].
	In what direction did he run?
	How was he holding the knife?
	What did he do with the knife as he ran?

What, if anything, did he say?

Closed-end questions create tension with the rule against leading because they often contain assumptions about facts. "Describe the shrubbery at the corner" assumes that there was shrubbery, unless the shrubbery was previously mentioned by the witness. If the existence of shrubbery is not disputed, however, and the question does not suggest how to describe the shrubbery, the court probably will not deem it leading. On a matter in dispute, a question that assumes a fact generally is objectionable. For instance, if a witness said she saw a man, and counsel said, "Describe the knife he was holding" before the witness mentioned a knife, the question would be objectionable for assuming a fact not already in evidence.

Referring specifically to a subject area generally is permissible so long as counsel does not suggest facts about matters in dispute. If your opponent objects to a question because it suggests an introductory fact — say a conversation — and the court upholds the objection, one remedy is to add the phrase "if anything" to the question: "What, if anything, did he say?" This formalism does not really cure the suggestiveness of the question, but traditionally has been viewed as removing its susceptibility to an objection. Another way of phrasing a question that introduces a topic is to use the words "To what extent": "To what extent did he discuss advertising?" The witness should describe the amount of discussion, after which you can ask: "What did he say?"

Another method to avoid the "assumes facts" objection is to get the witness to introduce the topics, after which you follow up with the specific questions. Thus, if you asked Mr. Danielson "What topics did Mr. Atkins discuss," and the witness named the topics, you could follow up on each without provoking an objection. Or you could use an exhibit — say the agenda of the Middletown meeting — as the basis for developmental questions.

Closed-ended questions provide a great means of emphasizing important points. You want to develop your strong factual points and breaking them into component parts is a great tool for development. If you cover unimportant material generally, with overview questions, but break down and develop your strong points, the strong material takes in more significance. For example, in the *Danielson* case counsel for the Danielsons should find ways to develop the alleged misrepresentations of ComputerCentre. Rather than forcing the witness to remember and describe everything, counsel should break down the material into parts. An example of the two approaches follows:

OPEN-END	CLOSED-END
What did Mr. Atkins tell you about the franchise?	What training did Mr. Atkins promise for your salesmen?
	What training did he promise for your technicians?
	What training did he say ComputerCentre would provide for running the store?
	To what extent did he suggest advertising would be provided?
	What type of advertising?
	How much advertising?
	What did Mr. Atkins suggest about the delivery of products?
	How much inventory did he suggest you would need to maintain?
	What did Mr. Atkins suggest about the profitability you could expect?
	[Etc.]

Not all your questions should be closed-end. Occasionally you may first set the stage for a short narrative, then ask the witness to describe what happened next. Even in that situation, you may wish to limit the scope of the question: "What happened in the next few minutes?" You may ask the witness to describe a scene or topic, mentioning the notable aspects or main points, after which you can follow up with specific questions. In the follow-up approach, closed-end questions do not assume facts, because you merely seek greater description of facts already stated by the witness.

§ 7-12. Importance of Signposts.

An important tool for directing an examination is the transition signal. This signal alerts the listeners to changes in topics and transitions in the story. Announcing transitions helps the jury follow the testimony and provides emphasis to upcoming subjects. You can accomplish these goals through the technique of telling the witness what you are about to cover (which the witness already knows). Examples follow:

> Q. Now, Ms. Danielson, I'd like to review your background. Please. . . .
>
> Q. This takes us to a very important subject: the representations ComputerCentre made to you. When did you. . . .
>
> Q. I'd like to turn now to the subject of what happened after your business failed. What . . . .
>
> Q. Now, Mr. Smith, I'd like to cover the actual laying of the asphalt on the North-South runway in July. Please describe. . . .

The transition signal serves a number of purposes. It gives the appropriate emphasis to each part of the witness's testimony. It breaks the overall testimony into parts, which makes it easier to understand. It alerts everyone to changes in subjects and to what is coming next. Perhaps most important, it allows daydreamers — who assuredly exist — to tune back in to the testimony easily. All of these consequences enhance communication.

§ 7-13. Flow and Emphasis: Step-Step-Step — Whirr! — Replay-Replay-Replay.

One of the most important aspects of direct examination is achieving an appropriate balance between short and long answers. As discussed in § 7-5, full-blown narratives are objectionable. Eliciting a lengthy narrative also is unwise because it may bore the jury. Nevertheless, for the witness to truly communicate some descriptions, particularly, a description of an event, some narrative is necessary. This aspect of "telling the story" also helps establish rapport between the witness and the jury. Further, by using a narrative, the witness can get the jury to visualize events. If the jurors visualize one side's version, they are more likely to accept that version as reality.

One method of balancing these considerations is to lead to key material with short answer questions, then let the witness tell a short story, and then follow up with additional short answer questions — the "step-step-step — whirr! — replay-replay-replay" approach. The "whirr!" in this description is the rolling of the videotape. This approach focuses attention on the best part of the testimony and permits the attorney, without leading, to emphasize its key elements. The following exchange provides an example of leading to, and calling for, a short narrative:

Step

Q.   Where were you on the night of July 29?

A.   At the corner of Washington and Prytania.

Q.   What were you doing?

Step

A.   I had just left the Still Perkin' coffee shop and was walking home.

Q.   What time was it?

Step

A.   About 11:15 p.m.

Q.   How was the lighting?

Step

A.   Pretty good. There were several street lights nearby.

Q.   What did you see?

Step

A.   I saw a man with a knife chasing another man.

Q.   How far were you from the man when you saw them?

A.   Across Prytania. I'd say 50 feet.

Q.   Can you show the jury how far by comparison to something in the courtroom?

A.   Yeah. From here to the courtroom doors.

Whirr!

Q.   Thank you. Tell the jury what happened.

(The "video" runs.)

A.   These two men came running down Washington from the direction of St. Charles. One was chasing the other, yelling "I'll get you, Jonesy." He had a large knife in his hand. They were both running and the guy running away looked really scared. They ran toward Magazine. The man with the knife was catching up. I started after them. I saw them turn the corner at Magazine. When I got there, I found a man on the street, bleeding. He was dead.

With this approach, the "storytelling" does not seem objectionable at all. The rat-tat-tat of question and answer leads the witness to the storytelling phase, and "Tell the jury what happened" seems the most natural statement in the world. The question, though it obviously calls for a narrative, is so focused by the earlier questions that it does not *seem* to elicit a narrative. Perhaps more important, the step-step-step process invites attention, giving prime billing to the short story that follows. The witness has a great opportunity to communicate with the jury.

This technique is even better if the advocate uses short answer questions to follow up the narrative. In framing the questions, counsel can bring the important aspects of the story into stark focus. Thus, for instance, an attorney who wants to emphasize the fact that the defendant carried a knife might follow up as follows:

Q. Let me ask some follow-up questions. Which man had the knife?

Replay

A. The one who was chasing the other.

Q. Where was he holding this knife?

Replay

A. In his right hand at about shoulder level.

Q. How big was this knife?

Replay

A. It was really long, like a hunting knife. About a foot I'd say.

Q. How fast was the man with the knife running?

Replay

A. Real fast. He was trying to catch the other guy.

Q. When he yelled, "I'll get you, Jonesy," how was he holding the knife?

Replay

A. A little higher. Above his head.

Q. Do you see the man who held the knife in this courtroom?

A. Yeah. He's the defendant, sitting at that table.

This technique allows you to reemphasize key points, but in the form of nonleading questions. Since the witness already has testified to the crucial events, and the questions merely seek *more* information about them, the repeated references to matters in evidence are permissible. They would not be permissible, however, if offered as gratuitous repetition of the witness's statements. Thus, the follow-up approach permits nonobjectionable repetition — and emphasis — of key facts.

§ 7-14. Setting Scenes.

One use of the "step-step-step" approach is to set the scene for action. Before a witness describes the key event — the chase, the wreck, the murder —you should ensure that everyone understands the scene at which the action occurred. This approach avoids confusion and helps the jurors visualize events. Often a map or diagram may aid this process. It is inadvisable, however, to bring out every conceivable detail regarding the scene. Over-description easily becomes monotonous.

An example of setting a scene follows:

Q. Where were you on the night of July 29?

A. Beno's Bar on Maple Street.

Q. What occurred that night?

A. I saw a shoving and yelling match between Johnny Smith and Joe Jones.

Q. What were you doing at Beno's?

A. I had a few beers with friends.

Q. What time were you there?

A. About 10:00 p.m. to midnight.

Q. [Referring to a demonstrative exhibit]. I show you an exhibit previously marked State Ex. 10. Do you recognize it?

A. Yes. That's a sketch of the inside of Beno's Bar.

Q. Where were you that night?

A. I was sitting at the table, near the door [gesturing].

Counsel: May the witness approach the exhibit, Your Honor?

The Court: Yes.

Q. Would you please point out the table?

A. Right there. I was sitting here, on the door side.

Q. Would you mark the spot with your initials?

A.   Yes. [Marking the exhibit].

Q.   Who was sitting at this table, near the bar?

A.   Joe Jones — we call him "Jonesy" — was sitting there with Brenda Joseph and some other people I didn't know.

Q.   Would you mark that table with a "J.J." for Joe Jones and an "B.J." for Brenda Joseph?

A.   Yes. [Complies].

Q.   Did you know anyone else in the bar?

A.   I knew Johnny Morris, who was sitting at another table by himself. I knew the bartender and a few other people.

Q.   Where was Johnny Morris sitting?

A.   Right there [pointing], at the table in the corner.

Q.   Would you mark that spot with a "J.M."?

A.   Yes. [Witness complies].

Q.   I direct your attention to the shoving match you mentioned. When did that occur?

A.   Shortly before midnight.

Q.   How did you know the time?

A.   I was planning to leave at midnight. I was watching the clock, and remember noting it was almost 10 'til.

Q.   Please tell the court and jury what occurred at that time.

A.   [Witness describes]. Johnny was looking over at Jonesy and Brenda Joseph. She started kissing and hugging Jonesy. Johnny jumped up and ran over there [Whirr!] and pushed her away. He was yelling at both of them. Then Jonesy and Johnny started shoving each other and wrestling. Johnny got pushed down on the floor, but the bartender came around and broke it up. The bartender told Johnny he had to leave, and he did. He and Jonesy were still yelling at each other when he left. Johnny was pointing at Jonesy and saying: "I've had it with you chasing after Brenda. You haven't seen the last of me." He was cursing and yelling other stuff, too. (Counsel follows up.)

§ 7-15. Counsel's Position and Movement During Direct Examination.

You should position yourself to allow the jurors full view of the witness. Thus, avoid standing at or near the witness box, where you might block the jurors' view of the witness. In many courts attorneys are required to stand at a podium in questioning witnesses; this positioning is usually mandated when a microphone at the podium amplifies the sound or transmits it into chambers. If there is no such requirement, you should stand where the jury can see both you and the witness without excessive head-turning. This may simply mean standing at counsel table. Usually, you should have notes for the examination and a podium or table facilitates their use.

If you wish to approach the witness — usually to show her an exhibit — ask the court's permission: "Your Honor, may I approach the witness?" This open acknowledgment that the judge controls the proceedings should win you points and enhance your freedom to move about. Moreover, some judges feel it is improper for counsel to approach a witness without permission. You should ask permission for other, similar actions, such as unveiling a demonstrative exhibit or using a chalkboard.

§ 7-16. Refreshing a Witness's Recollection With a Writing on Direct Examination; Requirement to Disclose Writing (FRE 612).

Although no federal rule directly addresses the circumstances under which you may refresh recollection, the traditional practice permits you to show virtually any document to a witness to refresh his recollection. A lawyer often shows documents to a witness as the witness prepares to testify; the witness may review a file, pleadings, important papers, or any number of other documents. With good preparation, most witnesses do not need to refresh their recollection during direct examination. If the witness forgets a point, however, you are entitled to show the witness a document to refresh his memory. The document need not have been prepared by the witness; for instance, you may use a memorandum of a meeting prepared by another participant to refresh recollection.

Refreshing recollection is permissible only if the witness testifies to a lack of memory. An example follows:

Q. Do you remember who was at the meeting?

A. No, I really don't. I know I was there.

Q. Let me show you a memorandum prepared by Ms. Mann. Does that refresh your recollection?

A. Oh, yes. I remember now. Ms. Mann and Ms. Hayne were there with me.

Once her recollection is refreshed, the witness is supposed to testify from memory. Repeating the content of a document without a truly refreshed recollection is improper. Opposing counsel may want to ask that a document be returned to counsel to ensure that the witness does not read from it. Otherwise, the witness almost surely will refer to the document while testifying.

If you show a writing to a witness to refresh recollection while the witness is on the stand, the adverse party is entitled to have the writing produced, to inspect it, cross-examine the witness on it, and introduce portions relating to the testimony. FRE 612 establishes these points and implicitly authorizes the use of documents to refresh recollection. Theoretically, a lawyer could write out a note and show it to the witness to refresh recollection; he is not likely to do so, however, since his opponent can obtain the note and examine the witness about the special "cue."

When a document is used to refresh recollection prior to the witness taking the stand, opposing counsel has these rights "if the court in its discretion determines it is necessary in the interests of justice."[21] If a claim is made that the writing contains matters unrelated to the testimony, the court should examine the document in camera and delete the unrelated material. FRE 612 provides:

> Except as otherwise provided in criminal proceedings by section 3500 of title 18, United States Code, if a witness uses a writing to refresh memory for the purpose of testifying, either —
>
> (1) while testifying, or
>
> (2) before testifying, if the court in its discretion determines it is necessary in the interests of justice,
>
> an adverse party is entitled to have the writing produced at the hearing, to inspect it, to cross-examine the witness thereon, and to introduce in evidence those portions which relate to the testimony of the witness. If it is claimed that the writing contains matters not related to the subject matter of the testimony the court shall examine the writing in camera, excise any portions not so related, and order delivery of the remainder to the party entitled thereto. Any portion withheld over objections shall be preserved and made available to the appellate court in the event of an appeal. If a writing is not produced or delivered pursuant to order under this rule, the court shall make any order justice requires, except that in criminal cases when the prosecution elects not to comply, the order shall be one striking the testimony or, if the court in its discretion determines that the interests of justice so require, declaring a mistrial.

To obtain a document an adverse witness used to prepare for trial, you must show that production would serve the interests of justice. Ordinarily you may satisfy this requirement by showing that the witness relied on the document. Paradoxically, examining the document may be the only way to determine how

---

[21] FED. R. EVID. 612; see also John S. Applegate, *Preparing for Rule 612*, 19 LITIG. 17 (1993).

it influenced the testimony; thus, if doubt exists on the issue, the court at least should inspect the document. The witness may have reviewed many documents, however, and may not specifically tie his recollection to any of them. To obtain production, you should at least demonstrate that the witness relied on a particular document or documents.[22]

If the writing contains work product or privileged attorney-client communications, the courts must balance the need for the document against the policy supporting the privilege. Again, assuming the witness's present recollection can be tied to a particular document or documents, strong reasons exist to require their production. The attorney who refreshed recollection chose to put the document "in play" — whether or not this action is a formal waiver — by using it to prepare testimony. Unless there are alternative means to test the witness's knowledge and memory, the court should require that the writing be produced, absent a strong showing of hardship on the producing party.

The requirement to produce a writing used to refresh recollection applies to documents used in preparing for a deposition.[23] The courts may require a stronger showing to obtain production, however, because any determination of need may be premature prior to the trial.[24]

§ 7-17. Refreshing Recollection With Questions.

When a witness testifies to a lack of memory, you have some leeway to refresh recollection with leading questions. This is one instance when the court may allow leading to "develop the witness' testimony."[25] The court may sustain an objection, however, if you attempt to lead on a matter in serious dispute.

To refresh recollection by leading, you must establish that the witness lacks a memory of some fact. An example follows:

> Q. Do you remember who was at the meeting?
>
> A. No, I really don't. I know I was there.
>
> Q. Was Mr. Holton there?
>
> A. Oh, yes. He was. I remember now.
>
> Q. Anyone else?
>
> A. Yes. Ms. Hayne was there, too.

---

[22] See, e.g., Sporck v. Peil, 759 F.2d 312 (3d Cir.), *cert. denied*, 474 U.S. 903 (1985).

[23] *Id.*

[24] Desderian v. Polaroid Corp., 121 F.R.D. 13 (D. Mass. 1988).

[25] FED. R. EVID. 611(c). See also advisory committee's note to FRE 611(c), which notes an exception to the rule against leading for "the witness whose recollection is exhausted."

If no one disputes the attendees at the meeting, this approach is uncontroversial. If the matter is disputed, opposing counsel may object to your leading question. You may have to show a good faith basis for believing that the witness once had a memory of the facts, as follows:

Q.	Do you remember who was at the meeting?
A.	No, I really don't.
Q.	Was Mr. Holton there?
Mr. Carver:	Objection. Leading. She's putting words in the witness's mouth.
Ms. Hobgood:	Your Honor, I'm trying to refresh recollection. Perhaps I could back up and demonstrate my basis for doing so.
The Court:	All right.
Q.	Do you remember discussing the meeting with me several months ago?
A.	Yes.
Q.	At that time you remembered who was there, didn't you?
A.	Yes.
Q.	You told me who was there?
A.	Yes. We went over that.
Q.	Do you remember whether Mr. Holton was at the meeting?
A.	I remember it now. He was, and so was Ms. Hayne.

With a well-prepared witness this problem should rarely arise on direct. You should refresh the witness's recollection *before* you put her on the stand.

§ 7-18. Redirect Examination.

An effective redirect examination requires that you consider the goals of direct, the actual damage done on cross-examination, and the likelihood that matters can be improved on redirect. Just as cross-examination too often recapitulates the direct, redirect too often emphasizes the damaging points from the cross. You should have two primary goals: (1) correct errors and explain important damaging testimony from the cross-examination, and (2) strike a thematic note.

Too often attorneys on redirect go over points made in the cross-examination, asking questions from their notes. This method works to counsel's disadvantage. Many points that seem important at the moment lose their impact within a few minutes. By the end of the day few listeners remember most of the points. Going over matters in redirect only emphasizes them. <u>Moreover, if your witness is defensive or tentative about a point, the redirect may damage your case.</u>

Of course, some matters from cross-examination need explanation. To decide which matters to cover, you should identify (1) mistakes that the witness should correct, and (2) matters important enough to need further discussion. Generally, a point is important if opposing counsel might use it in closing argument or if it could contribute to an adverse verdict.

You should ask the court to grant a recess before conducting redirect. If you do not plan the redirect testimony with the witness, his answers may be defensive and confused. In a few minutes of consultation you can explain the points you wish to cover and help the witness organize his responses. If possible, try to get the witness to actually articulate answers before he goes back on the stand.

A thematic or poignant focus is essential in a redirect examination. Try to organize the questions to reestablish the points made on direct. In redirect, you may be able to ask more conclusionary questions than on direct, which allows thematic summations. Examples follow:

Q. Ms. Barrasso, counsel asked you a number of questions on cross-examination concerning the lighting in the area. After considering those questions do you have any doubt about your testimony that Mr. Usdin — the defendant — was the man with the knife?

A. No. None at all.

Q. Why not?

A. As I said, I got a very good look at him. I could see him clearly even though there was no street light.

* * * * * *

Q. Mr. Jones, counsel made a number of references to steam coming from the asphalt. Does that affect your testimony that the construction practices were proper?

A. Not at all.

Q. Why not?

A. You always have steam on humid days. We made absolutely sure the water content was within limits, however.

The following suggestions should guide you in conducting redirect:

1.   *Stick to the essentials.* Don't go over every point made by your opponent. Find the matters that really make a difference and address them.

2.   *Signal your reference points.* You need to make references to your opponent's questions on the matter you want to cover. This action helps prevent an objection that your questions exceed the permissible scope of redirect. Thus, signal the prior reference point: "Ms. Danielson, counsel for ComputerCentre asked you about the products you stocked from unapproved sources. Can you tell me whether Wizard Supply was able to deliver that type of product?"

3.   *Organize your points.* Try not to wander through the examination, skipping back and forth among subjects. If the cross-examination wanders, and you don't reorganize, you'll wander too. Put questions on the same subjects together.

4.   *End on a high note.* You need to end on a strong note because redirect is often defensive. A good technique is to find a reference point in the cross-examination that allows you to ask the witness about a conclusion from the direct examination.

§ 7-19. Example of a Direct Examination: *Danielson v. ComputerCentre Associates.*

The following is an example of a direct examination of Jack Danielson in *Danielson v. ComputerCentre Associates.* The testimony is fairly extensive. Note that the examiner selects the important events and focuses on the elements of the claim: promises, representations, and nonperformance. If you review the *Danielson* material, you will find that the examination de-emphasizes a significant amount of information that is unimportant to proving the case. Note the transitions among topic areas, even in a chronological review, and the follow-up questions that develop important evidence.

Mr. Bilbe: The plaintiff calls Jack Danielson.

(The witness was duly sworn.)

Q.   Please state your name.

A.   Jack Danielson.

Q.   What is your age?

A.   Forty-four.

Q.   You are the plaintiff in this case?

A.   Yes. My wife and I are the plaintiffs.

Q.   Why did you sue ComputerCentre Associates?

A. We sued because they made false promises to get us to buy a franchise. We invested our entire life savings based on what they told us. It turned out that ComputerCentre never delivered on its promises. Our business failed, and we lost our life savings.

Q. All right, Mr. Danielson. I'd like to review a bit of your background. First, where are you from?

A. I'm from here in Middletown.

Q. How long have you lived here?

A. All my life.

Q. What is your address?

A. 1234 Barstow Avenue.

Q. What is your occupation?

A. I am retired. I do some part-time security work.

Q. What did you do before you retired?

A. I was a police officer with the Middletown Police Department.

Q. How long were you with the police department?

A. Twenty years. After twenty years you are eligible to retire.

Q. What did you do in the police department?

A. For several years I was a patrolman. After that I began working in the department's youth programs. I was involved in the youth programs for about ten years. Then I became a detective, investigating major crimes. For the last three years with the department I was with the rackets and fraud division.

Q. How many fraud cases did you investigate?

A. Not really very many. Most of the time we helped out other law enforcement agencies. We exchanged a lot of information with these agencies and provided them information when they needed it.

Q. What were your interests upon your retirement?

A. My wife and I had always planned to get involved in a business of our own. As soon as I retired we began looking around to try to find the right business.

Q. What type of business were you interested in?

A.   We wanted something that would not require a lot of expertise. My wife was a housewife and my experience in the police department was not really very good training for going into a new field. Therefore, we knew we would need a lot of help.

Q.   Mr. Danielson, I'd like now to turn to your involvement with ComputerCentre Associates. Can you tell us how you became interested in a computer franchise?

A.   Well, I had dealt with computers a bit in the rackets and fraud division. I learned how to use a computer terminal and knew that computers were being used more and more in businesses. I was also aware that they are used increasingly in daily life. I thought it would be a good business to get into.

Q.   Did you have any special experience with computers?

A.   No, not really. As I said, I knew how to operate a computer terminal and knew a little bit about inputting data and obtaining results, but I really didn't learn anything about computer programming or the detailed operation of computers.

Q.   How did you learn about ComputerCentre Associates?

A.   We saw an ad in the Wall Street Journal.

Q.   What attracted you to ComputerCentre Associates?

A.   The possibility of starting a franchise where you would not need expertise, you would not have to invest a lot of capital, and the franchisor would provide a completely packaged product.

Mr. Bilbe: Your Honor, may I approach the witness?

The Court: Yes.

Q.   Mr. Danielson, I show you a document I have marked for identification as Plaintiffs' Exhibit 1. Your Honor, I believe counsel has a copy. Mr. Danielson, can you identify this?

A.   Yes. That's the ad in the Wall Street Journal.

Mr. Bilbe: Your Honor, I would like to offer this document as Plaintiff's Exhibit 1.

The Court: Any objection? Let it be admitted.

Mr. Bilbe: May I have copies distributed to the jurors?

The Court: Yes, go ahead.

(Pause.)

Mr. Bilbe: Your Honor, I have some follow up questions about the ad.

Q.   What about this ad interested you, Mr. Danielson?

A.   The statement that the franchise was a high-profit computer store. The fact that it was a completely packaged concept. The statements that there would be low levels of expertise and capital investment required. Also, because we did not have much to invest, the statement that a low inventory was required. Obviously, we were also interested in the high profits that were advertised.

Q.   How did you respond to the ad?

A.   I called the telephone number that was listed below the advertisement. I was told there would be a meeting in Middletown on February 12, 1993.

Q.   What was your next involvement with ComputerCentre Associates?

A.   I went to the meeting.

Q.   Let's focus on that meeting for a minute. Where was the meeting held?

A.   At the Holiday Inn in Middletown.

Q.   Who attended the meeting?

A.   I went by myself. My wife had something else to do. There were twelve or thirteen other people at the meeting who were interested in a franchise.

Q.   Who represented ComputerCentre Associates?

A.   Dale Atkins and Jene Nelsen.

Q.   Who are they?

A.   Dale Atkins is the president of ComputerCentre, and Jene Nelsen is his assistant.

Q.   How long did the meeting last?

A.   It lasted most of the day.

Q.   What occurred at the meeting?

A.   They told us about what they could offer in a computer franchise. They made a very strong presentation.

Q.   Can you describe the subject areas that were covered?

A.   Yes. They talked about how profitable a franchise would be. They provided an example — the San Francisco franchise. They discussed the fact that franchisees did not need a lot of training. They talked about the low inventory concept. They also talked about the help they could provide for the business, by supplying accounting software. They also discussed their advertising program.

Q. All right, let's focus on those matters. What did they say about profitability?

A. They made a presentation using the San Francisco franchise as an example. They said that San Francisco made a 19% profit. They said the profits were high for all the Computer-Centre franchises. They said we could do just as well, and they could train us to do even better.

Q. Did they say what markup on computer products is charged to the San Francisco store?

A. No. They didn't say anything about markups at all.

Q. What did they tell you about the computer expertise required for a franchise?

A. They said that no expertise was required. They said that ComputerCentre would supply the complete package. Ms. Nelsen said she would provide a 10-day training session for the business managers and salespeople.

Q. What did they say about inventory?

A. They made a big point that maintaining inventory is expensive. They said a ComputerCentre franchise is not required to maintain a big inventory because of their quick delivery. They said they could obtain products from a supplier who could deliver almost immediately, most of the time within 24 hours. Therefore, they said it was not necessary to make a big investment in inventory.

Q. What did they tell you about the training of technicians?

A. They said that ComputerCentre Associates had a facility for technician training. We could hire someone to be a technician and send that person to the center, where he would be fully trained to work on our products. They said they would do this at no expense to us.

Q. What about advertising — what did they tell you?

A. They told us there was a national advertising program paid for by the franchisor. They said they would provide support for local advertising.

Q. What type of national advertising did they promise?

A. They said there would be newspaper ads and television ads.

Q. What help did the promise for local advertising?

A. They said they would give us samples and formats for print advertising and they would provide videos advertising their products. They said they would help us place any TV or radio ads.

Q. What was your overall understanding of the Computer-Centre franchise concept?

A. My understanding was that they would take care of all the technical and business aspects of getting us ready to run a franchise. They would provide the complete package, and they would support us after we went in business.

Q. What was your reaction to this presentation?

A. Well, I was very tired at the end of the day. I thought it was a very strong sales pitch. I was also very excited about the idea of a franchise that required low expertise and capital requirements. I thought this concept was exactly what we were looking for.

Q. What did you do after leaving the meeting?

A. I discussed the presentation with my wife.

Q. What did you all decide to do?

A. We decided that we would go forward. We needed to take advantage of the franchise while it was available. We believed that Atkins and Nelsen would help us with our important decisions. Also, we thought we could count on them to support our business.

Q. What plan did you have for financing the franchise?

A. We decided we could do it by placing a mortgage on our home. We knew we could get about $55,000 for the equity in our property. Since we would not need an extensive inventory, we believed this would be sufficient.

Q. What action did you take to proceed?

A. I called the 800 number for ComputerCentre Associates. I spoke directly with Mr. Atkins. We arranged to meet in Middletown on March 10.

Q. What did you and Mr. Atkins discuss in that conversation?

A.   We talked about the terms for the franchise.

Q.   What were those terms?

A.   He told me that it would cost $50,000 for a franchise and $2,000 for the training they would provide.

Q.   Did he say what training that would cover?

A.   Yes. That was for the training of us and our sales people. He said that the training of our technicians would be free.

Q.   Did you discuss a location for your franchise?

A.   Yes, we did. I told him we were thinking about locating the franchise in the Middletown Historic Mall. We thought that would be a good location because lots of businesses had been opening there. We thought we could take advantage of an emerging area in the city.

Q.   Why did you like that location?

A.   We thought that would be a good location because lots of businesses had been opening there. We thought we could take advantage of an emerging area in the city.

Q.   What did he say about that location?

A.   He said he would check it out and make sure it was all right.

Q.   When did you plan to meet to sign up for a franchise?

A.   We agreed to meet on March 10, in Middletown.

Q.   What did you and your wife do after that discussion?

A.   We got our finances in order. We took out a mortgage on our house and received $55,000 from the bank. We got a check for $52,000 to pay for the franchise and the training. The rest we put in the bank to cover our initial expenses.

Q.   Now, Mr. Danielson, I'd like to focus on the meeting conducted March 10. Tell the jury where that meeting was conducted.

A.   At the Holiday Inn here in Middletown.

Q.   What time did the meeting occur?

A.   At about 10:00 a.m.

Q.   Who was present at the meeting?

A.   My wife and myself, and Atkins and Nelsen.

Q.   What topics were discussed at that meeting?

A. We discussed a number of matters about the franchise. We also discussed the terms of the agreement.

Q. What discussion did you have about the franchise?

A. We discussed the location. We also talked about advertising support. They also told us about how profitable we would be.

Q. What did you discuss about location?

A. We asked Atkins about our plan to locate in the Middletown Historic Mall. He said that ComputerCentre had not been able to conduct the study he was supposed to provide. He asked us a few questions about the location. For one thing, he asked whether we had any interest in the Tri County Mall. We told him our reasons for wanting to open in the Middletown Mall, and he said that it sounded like we were probably right. He told us to go ahead with that location.

Q. Did Mr. Atkins suggest to you that the Tri County Mall was a better location?

A. No. Not at all.

Q. Did he show you any charts or diagrams regarding the best location?

A. No. He said go ahead with our plan.

Q. What was discussed about advertising?

A. We were concerned about the cost of advertising. All our money was tied up in the franchise fee. Atkins told us not to worry about the cost. He said they would contribute half the cost of all our local advertising. He also said they would supply the material for local ads. He also said they would provide national advertising.

Q. Did Mr. Atkins say how much national advertising would be provided?

A. No, but Jene Nelsen did.

Q. What did she say?

A. She told us that there was no limit to the cooperative advertising program. She said that all the franchises would have to do thousands of dollars of advertising for it to be limited. She said she didn't foresee any such problem.

Q. What action did you take with respect to acquiring the franchise?

A.   We signed the documents. We gave them our check for $52,000.

Q.   What discussion occurred with respect to royalties?

A.   Atkins told us not to worry about royalties. He said we could agree on royalties once our business was successful.

Q.   I'd like to ask you some questions, focusing on the time you signed up. At the time you signed the document, did anyone from ComputerCentre ever tell you that you would receive a different markup on products than other franchises received?

A.   No.

Q.   Did anyone ever tell you that the computer supplier — Wizard Computer Supply — was a family-owned business and that Mr. Atkins owned a part of it?.

Ms. Hayes: Objection. Compound.

Mr. Bilbe: I'll rephrase.

Q.   Did anyone ever tell you Wizard was owned by the Atkins family?

A.   No.

Q.   Did anyone tell you Mr. Atkins owned a share of it?

A.   No.

Q.   Did anyone tell you that ComputerCentre Associates had no technical facility to train technicians?

A.   No. They said they could provide training.

Q.   Did anyone tell you that Wizard had been habitually delayed in shipping products to ComputerCentre franchises?

Ms. Hayes: Objection, Your Honor. These facts are not in evidence. Counsel is assuming facts in his questions.

Mr. Bilbe: Your Honor, I believe evidence as to these facts will be introduced. I am trying to save the court time so that I do not have to recall Mr. Danielson.

The Court: I am going to allow it. The testimony will be stricken, however, if you fail to connect it up later.

Q.   Did anyone tell you that Wizard Supply habitually had been delayed in supplying computers to franchises?

A.   No.

Q. Did Mr. Atkins tell you that he regarded you as a "yokel" and a "clown"?

A. No.

Q. Did Mr. Atkins tell you that Wizard would charge you a higher markup because you were a yokel and a clown?

A. No.

Q. All right. I would like to turn to the next matter — your efforts to open the franchise. What did you and your wife do with respect to finding a location?

A. We went to the Middletown Historic Mall and looked for a suitable site. We found some space that we thought would be good. We signed a lease and arranged to make the necessary improvements to the site.

Q. How did you pay for the improvements?

A. With a line of credit from the bank.

Mr. Bilbe: I have here a document that I have marked Plaintiffs' Exhibit 2 for identification. Your Honor, may I approach the witness?

The Court: Yes.

Q. Do you recognize this document?

A. Yes.

Q. Tell the jury what it is.

A. It is a letter of credit issued to us by the bank. We could show that to suppliers to establish that we had a line of credit.

Mr. Bilbe: I offer this as Plaintiffs' Exhibit 2.

The Court: Any objection? Let it be admitted.

Mr. Bilbe: May I distribute it to the jury?

The Court: Yes.

(Pause.)

Q. What did you and Mrs. Danielson do about obtaining a staff?

A. We hired two salespeople.

Q. What training did you require?

A. We wanted people who were experienced in sales. We didn't worry about computer training because Computer-Centre promised to provide our salespeople training.

Q.   When did you intend to open?

A.   We picked a date in May. May 15.

Q.   What other actions did you take for the opening?

A.   We placed ads in the local papers. We made fliers and distributed them to businesses in the area. We told our friends and asked them to get the word out as well as they could. We planned to have free refreshments on the opening day.

Q.   What training did ComputerCentre Associates provide you prior to your opening?

A.   They didn't provide any.

Q.   Why not?

A.   Jene Nelsen was supposed to provide the training, but they told us she was not available. We were told she was busy selling franchises in other parts of the country and would get to us later for the training.

Q.   What training did your salespeople receive?

A.   They didn't get any. Jene Nelsen was supposed to provide it.

Q.   I'd like to focus on the opening of your store. What occurred?

A.   It was a nightmare.

Ms. Hayes: Objection. The witness is characterizing facts.

The Court: Sustained. Mr. Danielson, please try to stick to the facts.

A.   I'm sorry, Your Honor.

Q.   What problems did you encounter?

A.   We hardly had any products to sell.

Q.   Why not?

A.   First, we had no help in ordering the products because Jene Nelsen never showed up. We sat down with the brochures and decided what products we thought we should have to display. We ordered the products about two weeks before the opening, but most of them never showed up.

Q.   What did you do when the products didn't come?

A.   We called ComputerCentre and asked what the problem was. We were told that Wizard was having difficulty in supplying products on time. They said they would try to hurry it up, but nothing changed.

Q. What was the effect of the delay?

A. We opened with very few products to sell. The store was almost bare. People came in and looked around and generally left after a few minutes. The money we spent on refreshments and advertising was wasted.

Q. What sales did you make in the grand opening?

A. We made only one sale. Given the circumstances we were happy about that, but we should have had a bunch of sales.

Q. I want to talk about the ensuing months and the representations that ComputerCentre had made to you. First, after you opened, what happened with respect to ComputerCentre's promise to provide training?

A. Well, Jene Nelsen finally got around to coming to Middletown several weeks after we opened. She stayed only three days, however, rather than ten. She said that was all she could afford because she was too busy in the marketing effort.

Q. What training did she provide?

A. She helped me a bit in learning how to set up our business forms, daily sales and expense sheets, and so on. But that was about all. She did not train the salespeople at all.

Q. What conversations did you have about training the salespeople?

A. I asked her to do it. She said she would get back to us when she had more time. I said our salespeople needed training to help us make sales, and she said she understood, but she just didn't have time to help out right away.

Q. What about ComputerCentre's program for supplying you with products?

A. Everything came late. Our experience on the first day kept repeating itself. ComputerCentre kept saying that the products would come within a few days, but it often took several weeks and even months.

Q. What was the effect of the delays?

A. Usually a customer would give up and go buy the product somewhere else. It was very embarrassing to tell customers that their orders had not arrived. Customers would come in on several occasions, looking for the product, and then just cancel their orders.

Q. How many people canceled their orders?

A. During the summer, about 15. It involved a bunch of computer products. We would have received more than $10,000 just for those sales.

Q. Did ComputerCentre supply the technical training it promised?

A. They didn't provide any technical training. They told us they didn't have a facility, but they intended to get one in the future. Therefore, they told us we would have to find local service companies to provide technical services at our own expense.

Q. What did you do?

A. We had to get an RCA facility to do the service on our products at our own expense. It wound up costing several thousand dollars.

Q. What happened with respect to the accounting and business software that ComputerCentre promised?

A. It never came. We had to do everything by hand.

Q. What was the effect of doing your books by hand?

A. Basically, it took me out of the business. I had to spend most of my time taking care of the books. It was very time-consuming, and I did not get involved in selling the computers and promoting the business.

Q. How competitive were you in your pricing of computer products?

A. Not very competitive. It was very hard to compete with the computer store in the Tri County Mall.

Q. Why was it hard to compete?

A. Our product costs were very high, sometimes higher than the prices offered by ComputerLand. I asked why Wizard's prices to us were so high, and I was told that it was the same price charged to everyone else. ComputerCentre said it could not control Wizard's pricing.

Q. I'd like to focus on September of 1993. What occurred to you personally at that time?

A.   I had a very serious heart attack.

Q.   What was the effect of that heart attack?

A.   I was totally incapacitated. I was hospitalized for about six weeks. I had to go through a long recuperation period.

Q.   What is the current state of your health?

A.   I am still under doctor's orders to take it easy. I'm not allowed to have any stress at all. Basically, I'm partially recovered from the heart attack, but not fully recovered.

Q.   Tell the jury how your heart attack happened.

A.   I was talking with Dale Atkins on the telephone. I was calling about the accounting software, which they promised to supply but never did. I was extremely unhappy because all of my time was being consumed in keeping the books. When I complained about the failure to deliver the software, Atkins began yelling at me. He said that we should know how to do things for ourselves. He acted like we were at fault because the software was never supplied.

Q.   What happened?

A.   All of a sudden I had a tremendous pain in my chest. I felt it running through my left arm. I knew something was seriously wrong.

Q.   What did you do?

A.   I began yelling to Margaret for help. I lay down and she came in and took me to the hospital.

Q.   What happened then?

A.   I was in the hospital for about six weeks. The first couple of weeks were spent in intensive care while they tried to find out what the problem was. Eventually, they told me I would need major bypass surgery because of a blockage. They said I had been under too much stress.

Ms. Hayes: Objection, Your Honor. The witness is testifying to hearsay — what someone at the hospital told him.

Mr. Bilbe: Your Honor, I believe we're just trying to establish what happened at the hospital.

The Court: The objection is sustained. The jury will disregard the statement about the reason for the blockage.

Ms. Hayes: Thank you, Your Honor.

Q.   Mr. Danielson, what was your involvement in the ComputerCentre franchise after your heart attack?

A.   I haven't been involved in the actual operation of the franchise. Every time I try to get involved I can feel the stress. A couple of times I've had pains in my chest. Therefore, I've tried to stay away from major decisions.

Q.   Who has run the franchise in your absence?

A.   My wife tried to do it for a while. She doesn't have a business background, however, and she never got any help from ComputerCentre. Last spring she hired Drew Anderson to take over as manager.

Q.   Are you aware of the circumstances of the closing of the franchise?

A.   Yes.

Q.   How do you know?

A.   I was still involved in reviewing the financial material. Additionally, I was the one who received the letters from the bank.

Q.   What happened to the business?

A.   Basically we went broke. Our debts piled up, and we didn't have revenues to pay them. We lost our line of credit, and we lost our savings.

Mr. Bilbe: May I approach the witness, Your Honor?

The Court: Yes.

Q.   I show you a document I have marked Plaintiffs' Exhibit 3 for identification. Can you identify it?

A.   Yes. This is a letter from the bank telling us they were reducing our line of credit. We received it last May.

Mr. Bilbe: May it please the Court, I offer Plaintiffs' Exhibit 3.

The Court: Any objection? Let it be admitted.

Mr. Bilbe: May I distribute it?

The Court: Yes, you may.

[Pause.]

Q.   What was the effect of the reduction in the line of credit?

A.   We had very little money to operate the business. It reduced the flexibility to get new products.

Q. What happened to your line of credit after you received that letter?

A. After that the bank told us we were overdrawn and that they could not carry us anymore. The line of credit was withdrawn.

Mr. Bilbe: May I approach the witness?

The Court: Yes.

Q. Mr. Danielson, I show you a letter marked Plaintiffs' Exhibit 4. Can you tell the jury what that is?

A. That's a letter from the bank, telling us to reduce our balance from $44,000 to $25,000.

Q. What happened?

A. We couldn't reduce the balance, and the bank withdrew the entire letter of credit. After that the bank sued us.

Mr. Bilbe: I offer Plaintiffs' Exhibit 4.

The Court: Objection? Let it be admitted.

Q. What happened to the business?

A. Without money, we could no longer operate. Drew Anderson made the decision to close the franchise.

Q. Mr. Danielson, what losses have you and Mrs. Danielson sustained as a result of losing your business?

A. We lost all of our savings. Our house is mortgaged to the hilt. We owe about $50,000 to the bank, which we can't pay. We owe several thousand dollars to other vendors.

Q. Have you made a calculation of your losses?

A. Not the exact amount. I believe Drew Anderson has the actual numbers.

Q. What have you done since the business failed?

A. I'm working part-time as a security consultant. I'm making enough to supplement my pension so that we can pay our current bills. We still don't know what we're going to do about our debts.

Q. Mr. Danielson, I have one final question. Of the major reasons you signed with ComputerCentre — the training, the quick delivery, the accounting software, the other support — what did ComputerCentre actually wind up providing?

> A.   None of it. They left us on our own. They didn't come through on any of their promises.
>
> Mr. Bilbe: Your Honor, that completes the direct examination.

§ 7-20.   Example of a Direct Examination of a Fact/Expert Witness.

The following example of a direct examination is taken from a trial advocacy demonstration involving the mock case of *Paves v. Johnstone*. The case involves a claim by Paves that Johnstone defamed him by criticizing his fee and drawings for a city contract, resulting in Paves's loss of the contract. Robinson is called to testify for Johnstone. His witness script is reproduced in Appendix B.

Through the witness counsel tries to make three points: (1) Paves did not have the experience to draw a public building, (2) the drawings Paves submitted were inadequate; and (3) Paves's services were not worth his fee. An example of a direct examination of the same witness, but for the opposing side, is presented in § 10-21. Comparing the two illustrates how selection and emphasis can change the witness's portrayal. Obviously, a short script allows greater flexibility to fill in facts than you would have with a real witness, but there is always some room to develop favorable material.

Note that counsel never officially qualifies the witness. Counsel links the qualifications in each area with the testimony in that area without ever asking the court to certify the witness as an expert. This technique may be appropriate with this testimony, but some courts might insist on cross-examination on qualifications and certification of the witness before he testifies. Indeed, this approach may be necessary under *Daubert v. Merrill Pharmaceuticals, Inc.,*[26] discussed in § 10-5. Nevertheless, the examination is a good example of linking the basis and substance of testimony by topics.

> Q.   Your Honor, the defense calls Aubrey Robinson.
>
> A.   Would you proceed, please.
>
> Q.   Will you state your name, please?
>
> A.   Aubrey Robinson.
>
> Q.   Where are you from, Mr. Robinson?
>
> A.   I'm from Fredericksburg.
>
> Q.   How long have you lived here in Fredericksburg?
>
> A.   All my life.

---

[26] 509 U.S. 579 (1993).

Q. What is your occupation?

A. I'm an architect.

Q. And where do you practice?

A. I practice in Fredericksburg.

Q. In what capacity? Are you with a firm?

A. No, I have my own practice.

Q. How long have you practiced architecture here in Fredericksburg?

A. More than ten years.

Q. Mr. Robinson, I asked you to appear here in court today to give testimony, did I not?

A. That's correct.

Q. What are the areas that I asked you to address in that testimony?

A. The standards and requirements for public office buildings, the adequacy of schematic drawings by John Paves, and the reasonableness of the fee charged by John Paves for the schematic drawings.

Q. Do you know the two parties in this case, Mr. Paves and Mr. Johnstone?

A. Yes, I do.

Q. What is your basis for knowing them?

A. I know them as architects in the Fredericksburg area; it's a fairly close-knit community of architects, and I know them that way.

Q. Were you personally involved in the Fredericksburg municipal project?

A. Yes, I was.

Q. Would you tell the jury how you were involved?

A. I was invited by the City Manager as one of four architects to tour the Post Office Building, and I was also asked about submitting a proposal for a new City Hall, and one of the considerations that the City wanted to know about was a renovation of the Post Office Building.

Q. Did you submit a bid on that project?

A. No, I did not.

Q. What was your understanding of the approximate price range that the City wanted with respect to this project?

A. My understanding was that the City was looking for a proposal in the range of approximately two hundred fifty thousand dollars.

Q. Now, Mr. Robinson, I would like to turn to the area of architectural practices for public office buildings. Can you tell the jury first, do you have any educational degrees?

A. Yes, I do. I have a bachelor of science in architecture from the University of Virginia.

Q. When did you get that degree?

A. I got that degree eleven years ago.

Q. Now in the course of pursuing that degree, did you have any special education respecting architecture for public office buildings?

A. Yes, at UVA I concentrated in courses that dealt with public office buildings.

Q. And what sort of courses did you take?

A. Well, they were courses that dealt with the design of public office buildings, courses that dealt with design of municipal buildings, state and local government projects, those are the types of courses. I don't recall the exact names.

Q. Where did you finish in your class, Mr. Robinson?

A. I finished at the top of my class.

Q. Have you had occasions since the time of your graduation to pursue other educational opportunities in the area of architecture for public office buildings?

A. Yes, I have.

Q. Would you tell the jury what those opportunities were?

A. I attended a course at the Harvard School of Architecture. It was approximately a four-to six-week course in designing public office buildings. I have also attended a four-to six-week course given by the American Institute of Architects that dealt with the design of municipal office buildings.

Q. Have you ever done any teaching that concentrated in the area of architectural standards for public office buildings?

A. Yes, I have.

Q.   Would you tell us what that experience is?

A.   I am currently an adjunct professor of architecture at the University of Richmond.

Q.   Have you had any publications in the area of architectural design of public office buildings?

A.   Yes, I have.

Q.   And what were those publications?

A.   I have been published in the University of Virginia School of Architecture Journal and the Harvard School of Architecture Journal.

Q.   Would you tell the jury about your professional background to the extent that it concentrates in the area of the architectural design of public office buildings?

A.   All right. Since my graduation and licensing as an architect in the Commonwealth of Virginia, my practice has been both extensive and primarily in the area of design of public office buildings. I've designed buildings for state, local and the federal government. I would say that at least 80 percent of my practice is developed and has been devoted to the design of those types of buildings.

Q.   Can you give the jury some recent examples of public office buildings that you have been involved in preparing the architectural drawings for?

A.   Yes. I did the renovation of the state capitol in Richmond. I've also done the renovation of the governor's office in New Jersey. I've also done the office, county administration office, in Hanover County, as some recent examples, but there's many others if you want me to continue.

Q.   Have you ever won any awards for the design of a public office building?

A.   Yes, I have.

Q.   Would you tell the jury what that award was, please?

A.   I've won the Frank Lloyd Wright Memorial Award for innovation and excellence with respect to the state capitol building.

Q.   And that's the project you described just a few moments ago?

A.   Yes, in Richmond.

Q.   Now, Mr. Robinson, I'd like to focus on the preparation of plans for public office buildings. Are there any special considerations that an architect must take into account in preparing plans for a public office building as opposed to other kinds of buildings?

A.   Yes, there are.

Q.   What are some of the areas in which there are special considerations?

A.   Just to summarize, one of the primary considerations has to do with space relationships in a public building.

Q.   Well, let's take that. Would you describe what sort of differences that there are in architecture for the space requirements of a public office building versus some other kind of building?

A.   Well, I think the starting point is the understanding that a public office building is intended to be used by many, many people who are going to be coming down there for specific needs, and there might be a need to travel from one department to another. So what we're talking about is a circulation issue. We're talking about a spacing issue for the adequacy of certain departments, and we're also talking in consideration that the people that are using these facilities quite often have special needs.

Q.   What do you mean by special needs? Does that have implications for the architect?

A.   Yes, it does. We're talking about people who might have disabilities or any other type of special need.

Q.   And what does the architect have to do to provide for that?

A.   Well, they have to do a number of things. They have to make sure that there is sufficient access to the building, they have to make sure that there are certain facilities in the building by way of, for example, restrooms. They also have to have appropriate waiting areas. They have to also have areas that can direct people, such as a bulletin board type of area.

Q.   Well, how are these requirements different from any other type of building?

A.   Well, they're different from the standpoint that other types of buildings are not viewed as having these special needs of people coming in, being directed to one department and then having to be shifted to another department in the same building, and also the need to get information from one department to another department within the same building.

Q. Are there special legal requirements that the architect must comply with respect to public office buildings as opposed to other kinds of buildings?

A. Yes, there are.

Q. And what are those?

A. Well, there are specific requirements, in the form of codes, dealing with health, safety, access, that all have to be complied with.

Q. Can you give an example?

A. For example, this auditorium. There are specific requirements needed for exits.

Q. And why is that?

A. Well, in case there's a fire in the building, to make sure that everyone can get out and there's not a hazard posed.

Q. Now, we've been discussing special requirements with respect to the area of public office buildings. What implication does that have for the architectural profession?

A. Well, what that, the implication is that you typically find that the type of people that do this sort of work are, at least in the Fredericksburg area, relatively few because there're relatively few people who have, by training and education and experience, what I perceive are the appropriate qualifications to do this sort of work.

Q. What are the necessary qualifications?

A. You preferably need special education or training in the architecture of public office buildings. You need experience working on these buildings before you try to do one yourself.

Q. Have you reviewed John Paves's qualifications?

A. Yes.

Q. Does he have the experience to do these type of drawings?

A. No. He has no experience in this area. He may know how to do it, but not from experience.

Q. What qualifications does he lack?

A. He has no special education or training in designing public office buildings. He lacks any significant experience in that specialized area.

Q. I'd like to turn, Mr. Robinson, to the schematic drawings that were prepared by Mr. Paves and submitted to the city. Now you've had an opportunity to review those drawings, is that right?

A. That's correct.

Q. I'd like to ask you, do you have any special experience in developing professional standards for architectural drawings and, in particular, schematic drawings.

A. Yes, I do.

Q. And, can you describe what that experience is?

A. Yes. I'm a member of the American Institute of Architects, and there is a committee called Public Office Buildings, and I am the chair of that committee, and as part of the work of that committee we have developed standards with respect to the design of public office buildings.

Q. And those standards, do they address the issue of schematic drawings?

A. Yes, they do.

Q. Now, what about with respect to Virginia? Do you have any special experience in, or knowledge concerning, the standards for architectural drawings and particularly schematic drawings in Virginia?

A. Yes, I do.

Q. Can you describe what that is?

A. Yes. I'm a member of the Tri-County Architectural Board, and in the last couple of years, that board has essentially adopted the work that the American Institute of Architects has performed, but they have adopted it on a local basis. So we essentially use the same standards that have been developed to be used nationally.

Q. And do these standards also address the issue of schematic drawings?

A. Yes, they do.

Q. Now, I believe you mentioned earlier that you've taught at the University of Richmond. Does your course address the issue of appropriate requirements for schematic drawings?

A. As part of the course that I teach on the design of public office buildings, one section of course is devoted to design requirements of drawings.

Q. To what extent have you yourself prepared schematic drawings that have been used in public office building projects?

A. Well, as I indicated, since a majority of my practice is devoted to it, I've done many such schematic drawings myself. In addition, in my role as a consultant or an expert, I have also had occasion to review schematic drawings. And finally, I also serve in the capacity as a fee mediator, and I have been requested to review schematic drawings in that role.

Q. Have you, in this case, in connection with the municipal office building for Fredericksburg, have you looked at the preliminary drawings that were prepared by Mr. Paves?

A. Yes, I have.

Q. And those were the schematic drawings that we referred to earlier?

A. That's correct.

Q. Have you looked at any other information?

A. Yes, I have. I've looked at Mr. Paves' cost estimate. In addition, I've also looked at the space analysis that he performed.

Q. The schematic drawings that were prepared by Mr. Paves and submitted to the city — did they comport with the applicable professional standard that would apply to schematic drawings?

A. No, they did not.

Q. Can you briefly state the manner in which they were out of compliance?

A. Well, yes. Just by way of summary, they in my opinion were skimpy and incomplete. They were not sufficient on which to perform a cost estimate. They did not comply with various laws, in that they did not convey the real sense of what the building was going to look like upon completion.

Q.   Would you tell the jury, please, what schematic drawings are supposed to accomplish?

A.   Well, schematic drawings are supposed to tell the person what the project is going to be upon completion. It's to give — the only thing that it's not supposed to do is give the detail. It's supposed to give everything else, I think is the best way to describe it.

Q.   And what would be required of schematic drawings to accomplish that goal?

A.   Well, what's supposed to, you're going to have to have adequate space allocations, you're going to have to have, exhibit compliance with code for fire and safety, for example, for access; they're going to have to be of such quality that you can develop an accurate cost estimate upon which the construction cost can be estimated.

Q.   Now, let's turn again to the schematic drawings that were submitted by Mr. Paves. I believe you mentioned that they were skimpy and incomplete. What do you mean by that?

A.   Well, I mean exactly that. They were sloppy, they weren't detailed, they did not show in the drawings exactly how things were going to be done. For example, there were exit doors that were missing from an auditorium. He missed an exit in an area where there were supposed to be two exits. He didn't put in certain other things in the drawings that I would have expected to be there.

Q.   Can you explain whether these schematic drawings were adequate to prepare a reasonable cost estimate for this project?

A.   In my opinion, they weren't close to being sufficient for that purpose.

Q.   And why not?

A.   Well, I think the best explanation is that they were completely contrary to even Mr. Paves' own space analysis, that the drawings didn't even comply with the space analysis that he performed.

Q.   Well, what do you mean by that? To what extent did it not comply with the space analysis?

A.   Well, the space analysis showed that, I believe, a need for approximately twenty thousand square feet; in that, the drawings that were prepared by Mr. Paves showed square footage of approximately twenty-nine thousand square feet. So his drawings had approximately nine thousand square feet more than the space analysis that he prepared showing what the municipality needed.

Q. Well, to what extent did the space analysis with respect to individual departments comport with the drawings that he submitted?

A. They — in particular I recall that there were two departments that were grossly exaggerated or in which he was just plainly erroneous. One was the welfare department. My recollection was that in his drawings, he indicated that the welfare department was in excess of five thousand square feet, when in his space analysis it was like in the neighborhood of three thousand square feet. The city council chambers were another department that he had significantly overestimated the amount of space that was needed.

Q. What is the effect of an overestimate of the amount of space that would be needed, as compared to the actual space analysis?

A. What it does, it has a cumulative effect. The cumulative effect is that it results in an increase in the projected construction cost, which in turn results in an increased fee for the architect.

Q. What about compliance with code requirements and safety requirements? To what extent did these schematic drawings submitted by Mr. Paves comply with the law?

A. They didn't.

Q. And in what phase did they not comply?

A. Well, in particular with fire safety and emergency exits.

Q. Can you explain that?

A. Yes.

Q. I think you mentioned the auditorium earlier.

A. Right. Well, for example, in addition to that there were a number of doors that he had indicated on the drawings that opened in as opposed to out. In another example is that in one instance on the drawing, he had a corridor leading into a room as opposed to there being an exit.

Q. What about the auditorium? What was the safety problem with that?

A. He didn't have sufficient exits.

Q. And what are the implications of that?

A. Well, the implications are that in the event of some sort of an emergency, if people needed to leave they could be trapped in the building.

Q. Now, Mr. Robinson, I'd like to turn to the issue of the fee that was charged by Mr. Paves for these schematic drawings in this case. Are you familiar with prevailing fees in the Fredericksburg area?

A. Yes, I am.

Q. What is your basis for being familiar with the fees that are charged by architects in Fredericksburg?

A. There are essentially three bases. One is based on my own personal experience, having worked in the Fredericksburg area for the last ten years or so. A second way is, as I think I mentioned earlier, I am a fee mediator, and consequently I have in front of me from time to time disputes regarding fees, and therefore I see what is at issue on the dispute. The third way is I'm familiar with the texts and treatises that are used, and in fact I forgot there is a fourth way. Because I submit projects on public buildings that are typically through bids, I have the occasion after the bids are awarded to find out what the amount of the fee is, and that way I keep current, and I need to because I have to take that information into consideration when I submit my next bid on a project.

Q. Well, Mr. Robinson, let me ask you this. A ten percent fee for a completed competent project, such as the municipal project here, is that an unreasonable fee in your personal opinion?

A. Assuming, as part of your question, that it was competent, my opinion would be it would be reasonable.

Q. Okay. But I want to ask you now about this particular case, and I want to refer you to the issue of the fee charged for the schematic drawings. Do you know what the fee that was charged by Mr. Paves for the schematic drawings in this case was?

A. My recollection was that it's ten and a half percent, I believe.

Q. Well, what was the amount that he charged?

A. Oh, I'm sorry, I misunderstood. I believe that he billed the City of Fredericksburg in excess of ten thousand dollars for the schematic drawings that he had prepared.

Q. Is that fee, ten thousand dollars for schematic drawings of the quality you described, is that consistent with the prevailing standard for fees for architectural services in the Fredericksburg area?

A. No, it is not.

Q. And why not?

A. Well, because of all the reasons that I previously gave. These were just not properly prepared in accordance with prevailing standards and consequently the fee that was charged, in my opinion, was excessive.

Q. Was this fee reasonable for the quality of schematic drawings that were submitted by Mr. Paves?

A. No, it was not.

Q. And why not?

A. For all of those same reasons that I previously gave. I mean, you're talking about work that was inaccurate, you're talking about work that was incomplete, that was skimpy, from which you couldn't determine what the real sense of the building was. There wasn't compliance with various laws. And for all those reasons, I believe the fee was excessive.

Q. Mr. Robinson, I'd like to ask you a couple of questions in ending your testimony here. The schematic drawings that were submitted by Mr. Paves to the City of Fredericksburg just before the project was terminated and he was terminated — were those schematic drawings adequate to proceed with a project of this nature?

A. No, it was not.

Q. Did the city pay a fair price for the schematic drawings that it received?

A. My understanding is that although Mr. Paves charged ten thousand dollars, the city only paid something more than

> seven thousand, but in my opinion, even that amount that
> the city paid was excessive.
>
> Q.   I have no further questions.

One means by which counsel might improve this examination is to *show* the
jurors the inadequacies in the drawings, using a blowup of what Mr. Paves
prepared. Counsel could ask the witness to describe the inadequacies first, then
unveil the exhibit and ask the witness to point them out. This approach produces
a "double bang," emphasizing a crucial part of the witness's testimony. Moreover,
it would ensure that the jurors understand the deficiencies the witness describes.

§ 7-21. Preparing a Witness for Cross-Examination.

You not only must prepare your witness for direct examination, but for cross-
examination. You must anticipate and discuss the areas of inquiry that you would
bring up if you were cross-examining. Help the witness determine how to address
these points. Additionally, review with the witness the best approach to answering
questions on cross-examination.

You want your witness to appear credible and persuasive. Credibility requires
that the witness fairly respond to your opponent's questions, because evasions
and off-the-point answers suggest that the witness will not admit difficult facts.
Persuasiveness, on the other hand, requires that the witness limit the impact of
damaging points and, hopefully, make points for you. Blending these objectives
requires the witness to give responsive answers, but take advantage of openings
that your opponent provides in framing questions.

A good witness performance in cross-examination requires symmetry. Specific,
tight factual questions naturally call for short responses — often "yes" or "no."
The witness has a right to explain, but a long-winded explanation for a limited
fact question usually seems out of place. Broad questions naturally call for longer
answers. Conclusory questions invite disagreement, explanations and sometimes
commentary. Complex questions — these loaded with premises or multiple points
— similarly call for explanations. To the extent your opponent strays from
specific factual questions, your witness has opportunities to make points for you.

The witness generally should maintain a reserved, calm demeanor. Too much
emotion may make the witness appear partisan or insincere. If your opponent
tries to bait or provoke, the witness generally should resist. An angry witness
sometimes makes crucial mistakes. Staying calm permits thoughtful responses.

The following rules are good basic guidelines for your witness in responding
to questions on cross-examination.

1.   *Listen to the questions.* To appear responsive, the witness must listen
      to counsel's questions. Focusing on preconceived points, rather than the
      questions, produces non-responsive answers that may appear evasive.

2. *Answer directly.* The witness ordinarily should provide a direct response to a question. Any necessary explanation should follow. The backwards approach — explaining the answer before providing it — always appears defensive and weak. Providing a frank answer followed by a decent explanation appears more forthright and indicates confidence.

3. *Explain as necessary.* The witness should provide any explanation required to fairly portray his answer. He has a right to explain and should not waste it. But every answer does not require explanation and the witness should not inject them unnecessarily,

4. *Take advantage of openings.* Complex, conclusionary, and argumentative questions fairly call for in-kind responses. In answering these types of questions, your witness often can use points supporting your side without losing credibility. Unlike a deposition, when you ordinarily would not want the witness to reveal your good points, you want to put your best points forward in the trial. Your witness should be able to sense his opportunities, but should use them carefully. Going overboard can hurt the witness's credibility, which is usually more important than making a few counterpoints.

Sometimes your opponent may provide direct opportunities to the witness, asking inadvertently for damaging information. Questions such as "Why?", "How can that be true?", and similar inquiries legitimately require explanations that should help you. Your witness should use these opportunities, but again should stay within the fair bounds of the question. An overly lengthy answer may destroy the symmetry of the question and response.

CHAPTER 8

EXHIBITS

---

§ 8-1. Introduction.

Exhibits provide a powerful means of persuasion. Exhibits capture attention, give substance to a presentation, and promote understanding. Exhibits give staying power to oral descriptions, which otherwise are transitory. Thus, you should use exhibits to make your presentation powerful and persuasive. To do so, you must understand the rules governing their use.

Exhibits fall into two general categories. "Real" exhibits are items of evidence from the case: a gun used in a crime, a contract, a fingerprint, a letter, and similar items. "Demonstrative" exhibits — sometimes called "illustrative" exhibits — are prepared for the trial to illustrate facts for the jury. A chart, photograph, or model used to explain testimony is a demonstrative exhibit.

The federal rules of evidence establish the necessary foundation for the admissibility of real exhibits: authentication.[1] Additionally, the rules establish a preference for the original to prove the contents of a writing, recording, or photograph and set forth standards for receiving other proof of contents.[2] Documents offered to prove facts described in the documents also raise hearsay issues, covered by the hearsay rules.[3]

The federal rules do not specifically deal with the admissibility of demonstrative exhibits. Generally, courts may receive these exhibits if they depict relevant information in a helpful and reasonably accurate manner. Courts must balance relevance with the chance of prejudice, confusion, or delay in determining the admissibility and use of demonstrative exhibits.[4]

Advances in computer technology now make it possible to introduce and display various types of electronic data during trial. People now correspond via e-mail, store information electronically, obtain information from the Internet, and use computers to simulate or illustrate events. The evidence rules governing exhibits must be flexible enough to accommodate these advances and lawyers must take advantage of computer advances in trial.

This chapter addresses the admissibility and use of exhibits. Section 8-2 discusses the importance of exhibits in proving a case. Section 8-3 reviews developments in the use of electronic data and computer-generated material in court. Sections 8-4–8-13 discuss the authentication and use of real exhibits and §§ 8-14–8-20 review the admissibility and use of demonstrative exhibits. The requirements of the Original Writing Rule are reviewed in §§ 8-21–8-28.

§ 8-2. Importance of Exhibits in Proving a Case.

Exhibits provide a tangible basis for factual assertions that cannot be provided solely through testimony. Oral testimony is the primary means of proving facts, but oral descriptions are often unclear. Additionally, listeners often misinterpret oral statements. Further, the spoken word is impermanent; most listeners forget

---

[1] FED. R. EVID. 901–03.

[2] FED. R. EVID. 1001–08.

[3] FED. R. EVID. 801–06.

[4] FED. R. EVID. 403.

the details of an oral description shortly after they hear it. Verbal accounts therefore may not, by themselves, stick with the jurors.

Exhibits compensate for these problems. First, the jury can see and often touch an exhibit. The "real" thing is presented rather than someone's attempt to describe the thing, eliminating any problems in communicating the facts. Second, the combination of sensual impressions — visual, oral, and perhaps touch — tends to fix the image in the jurors' minds. Once they have seen an exhibit, they will not quickly forget important details.

Using exhibits adds power to a presentation. Exhibits make facts seem more real and tangible. If the prosecution shows the jury a blood-stained knife found in the defendant's house, it has more impact than if a witness tries to describe the knife. Indeed, the combined parts of the presentation — the description and exhibition of the knife — have a "double whammy" effect.

Additionally, exhibits are great attention getters. When you pull out an exhibit, people naturally look at it. An exhibit brings a focus to an oral description that heightens interest. Displaying an exhibit can recapture the attention of a juror whose mind wanders. Indeed, exhibits are so powerful that they often hold the attention of jurors even after the lawyer and witness go on to new subjects.

Because exhibits have the power to hold attention, you must use them carefully to avoid distractions from your testimonial proof. But used tactically, they offer a proven means to persuade jurors. Thus, you must find ways to use them not only as a means of proof, but to emphasize your thematic points.

§ 8-3. Increasing Use of Electronic Information and Courtroom Technological Capabilities.

The expanding use of computers to analyze, store and display information and the explosive use of the Internet have changed the manner in which people communicate and conduct business. These developments in turn affect the evidence available to prove facts at trial and the methods for introducing and displaying this material. A correspondence that in 1992 would have occurred by mail, for example, now might well occur by e-mail over the Internet. Introducing this correspondence into evidence requires a flexible application of the federal rules and an effective means to display the evidence to jurors.

Advances in courtroom technology make courts more and more receptive to electronically-generated or stored evidence. A growing trend toward "e-courtrooms" permits the introduction and use of material in electronic form. Additionally, the installation of advanced equipment permits lawyers easily to display information to jurors, present video depositions, introduce testimony from remote locations, and present electronic depictions of events.[5] Attorneys must

---

[5] Frederic I. Lederer, *The Road to the Virtual Courtroom? A Consideration of Today's and Tomorrow's High Technology Courtrooms*, 50 S.C. L. Rev. 799 (1999); Francis S. Burke, *The Lawyer's New Presentation Tools of the Trade — Practical Tips*, SG007 AL1-ABA 113 (2001).

adapt to this trend and take advantage of the opportunities it provides for persuasion.

Many courts already have or permit the use of equipment that allows the display of electronic information, animations, remote appearances of witnesses, and similar advances. One basic device is the portable document camera, which converts anything placed below it into a computer image, displaying the image on a monitor. When necessary, counsel utilizes an electronic pointer to aid in the presentation. Experiments suggest that the use of electronic devices increases the liveliness of a presentation and promotes comprehension.[6] Judges in high-tech courtrooms boast that electronic presentations increase efficiency and provide better justice because of jury comprehension.[7]

Computer equipment also creates opportunities in the presentation of demonstrative evidence, frequently used by experts to illustrate their testimony. The electronic evidence presentation may vary from a mere illustration to a changing illustration based on varying assumptions that the witness inputs to a computer. These displays carry a significant risk of prejudice, but courts can deal with the problems by fashioning rules for the presentation and issuing cautionary instructions.

Although high-tech evidence may seem foreign to many lawyers, courts can determine the admissibility of this evidence using the traditional rules. Of course, all evidence must be relevant and not unduly prejudicial or time-consuming. Electronic communications, data compilations and similar items of real evidence must meet the authenticity and original writing requirements ordinarily applied to exhibits. Just as factual assertions in documents raise hearsay issues, these statements in electronic material also raise them. This chapter addresses the authenticity, original writing and potential prejudice issues for electronic exhibits as well as hard-copy exhibits.

I. REAL EXHIBITS

§ 8-4. Real Evidence.

Exhibits that actually played a part in the facts of the case are referred to as "real" evidence. Real evidence might include a weapon used in a crime, a contract that forms the basis for a dispute, correspondence containing terms of an agreement, a canceled check used to pay a bill, or any other tangible item that is part of the underlying facts.[8] "Real" evidence can be distinguished from demonstrative evidence, which a party creates or obtains for the trial to illustrate the facts.

---

[6] *See* Lederer, *The Road to a Virtual Courtroom? A Consideration of Today's and Tomorrow's High Technology Courtrooms*, 50 S.C.L. REV, 799, 814–15 (1999).

[7] *Id.*

[8] See FED. R. EVID. 901–03.

Real evidence can have a substantial impact on jurors because it is *tangible*. The written words of a contract, for instance, seem more weighty to the average person than an after-the-fact description of the parties' intent. Similarly, jurors are more impressed if they see the gun used in a robbery than if a victim simply describes it. Jurors can see real evidence, which gives reality to counsel's "word picture" of the facts. As explained in § 8-5, to lay a foundation for introducing real evidence, you must make a showing sufficient to support a finding that it is what you claim.

Since real evidence is tangible, it has a special potential for prejudice. Physical evidence may seem more important than oral testimony, causing the jurors to give it undue weight. Further, if the evidence evokes an emotional response — blood on a pair of underpants, for instance — its presentation in tangible form enhances the prejudicial impact. Therefore, courts often must weigh relevance versus prejudice in deciding whether to admit physical evidence.

Discovery in many cases involves the production of thousands of documents. The advent of modern equipment for document creation — word processors, computers, and copy machines — means that parties often have files full of documents that relate to a dispute. Lawyers often spend hundreds of hours looking through reams of documents for relevant material. Unfortunately, a lawyer lost in a blizzard of documents sometimes has difficulty determining which are important.

The production of numerous documents in discovery carries over to trials; the parties sometimes offer hundreds or thousands of documentary exhibits. The avalanche of documents creates a special problem, because a case overburdened with documents is worse than one with no documents at all. Rather than focusing attention, the ritual identification, offer, receipt, and publication of hundreds of documents puts everyone to sleep. None of the exhibits seems important because there are so many. Therefore, you usually should focus on a few documents. Even if you must introduce many documents to complete the record, find ways to magnify those that are important. Introduce the others in a way that consumes little time.

You should focus on the important parts of documents. Often it is unnecessary and impractical to read an entire document to the jury. Highlighting the relevant material — perhaps by having the witness read a passage — prevents a tedious publication of the exhibit. Additionally, it avoids confusion as to why the document is important. In any event, you need to ensure that introducing exhibits does not detract from the presentation.

§ 8-5. Foundation for Introduction of Real Exhibits (FRE 901(a)).

The foundation required to introduce a "real" exhibit is a showing sufficient to support a finding that it is what its proponent claims — that it is "authentic." FRE 901(a) provides:

(a). **General provision.** The requirement of authentication or identification as a condition precedent to admissibility is satisfied by evidence sufficient to support a finding that the matter in question is what its proponent claims.[9]

This provision establishes a low threshold for identifying an exhibit. The court needs to find only that a *reasonable person could conclude* the exhibit is what its proponent claims. If a juror reasonably could find the evidence sufficient, the court is not supposed to interpose its own view as to whether the exhibit is authentic. By the same token, the introduction of the exhibit is not binding on the jury; opposing counsel can still argue that the jury should not believe the witness who identified the exhibit.

A showing of authenticity does not necessarily mean that the exhibit is admissible. It still must be relevant, and, if there is a claim that the exhibit is prejudicial, confusing, or will waste time, it must pass the balancing test of FRE 403. Additionally, the exhibit may be objectionable on other grounds. See § 8-21.

Showing that an exhibit is "authentic" simply means explaining what it is. Usually a witness can identify the exhibit, which provides the basis for finding it authentic. Thus, for instance, if counsel showed a gold band to a witness, the witness might explain it is "the gold ring given to me by my boyfriend on my twenty-first birthday, which was stolen in the robbery." This testimony gives meaning to the gold band in relation to the issues in the case. See § 8-6.

If no single witness can identify an exhibit, counsel may use other means of proof. The testimony of several witnesses together may supply the basis for identification, circumstances may support its authentication, or the jurors may identify an exhibit by examining it themselves in light of other evidence that permits its identification. Various methods of identification are discussed in §§ 8-7–8-10.

When a party offers an exhibit, the opposing party theoretically has a right to cross-examine the witness on the identification. This examination — traditionally called a "voir dire" on foundation — occurs before the exhibit is introduced. If the cross-examination shows the witness cannot identify the exhibit, it is not received and has no potential to prejudice the jury. Many courts require the attorney to wait for cross-examination to inquire about the foundation, however, in the interest of conserving time and avoiding interruptions in the opposing party's examination. If the cross-examination shows the foundation is inadequate, the court strikes the exhibit and instructs the jury to disregard it.

Obviously, the more damaging the exhibit and the weaker the foundation, the greater the need to conduct a voir dire before it is admitted. For unimportant

---

[9] See United States v. Cardenas, 864 F.2d 1528, 1531 (10th Cir. 1989), *cert. denied*, 401 U.S. 909 (1989) (the rationale for Rule 901(a) is that "in the absence of showing that the evidence is what its proponent alleges, the evidence is simply irrelevant"); see also United States v. Hernandez-Herrera, 952 F.2d 342 (10th Cir. 1991).

exhibits, asking to cross-examine on foundation is unnecessary. If the matter is important, you should explain the purpose of cross-examining and the prejudice that may be caused by the exhibit. With a solid basis you should win the right to cross-examine on the foundation. Alternatively, ask that the court refrain from admitting the exhibit or showing it to the jury until after you address it in cross-examination.

§ 8-6. Relationship of Authenticity and Relevance.

The fact that a witness can identify an exhibit does not make it relevant. To establish its relevance, you must provide an identification sufficient to show the logical connection of the exhibit to the case. For instance, assume that a person wearing a red sweater is kidnapped, and at the trial of the alleged kidnapper a red fiber is marked as an exhibit. Assume further the following different statements of identification of the fiber by a police officer with personal knowledge:

1.   "This is a red fiber."
2.   "This is a red fiber found in the defendant's car."
3.   "This is a red fiber found in the defendant's car, of the same type used in the manufacture of the kidnap victim's sweater."
4.   "This is a red fiber found in the defendant's car, which has been matched by spectrographic analysis to the fibers in the sweater worn by the kidnap victim when she was kidnapped."

In all of these cases, the testimony provides an identification of the fibers, but not necessarily an identification sufficient to establish relevance.[10] The testimony in the first example would not establish that the fiber is relevant in the kidnapping; a red fiber, without a connection to the case, proves nothing. The second identifying statement provides some connection, but it may be too tenuous to justify the fiber's introduction and may mislead the jury. The third statement provides a logical but general connection to the case; it probably satisfies the minimal hurdle for establishing relevance, but the relevance could be outweighed by prejudice or confusion. The fourth statement specifically connects the red thread to the kidnap victim *and* the defendant and certainly shows relevance.

These examples illustrate that foundation is closely related to relevance. An attorney can always establish that an exhibit is *something*, but a showing of relevance usually requires a specific identification of the exhibit. For this reason, foundation is often viewed as an aspect of relevance. To determine whether an

---

[10] See United States v. Miller, 994 F.2d 441, 443 (8th Cir. 1993) (explaining when a "real or physical object is offered as evidence in a criminal prosecution, an adequate foundation for the admission of that object requires testimony first, that such object is the same object which was involved in the alleged incident, and that the condition of that object is substantially unchanged").

identification is sufficient to admit an exhibit, you should ask: "What is the relevant fact?" The authentication must be adequate to show that the exhibit logically tends to prove that fact.

§ 8-7. Normal Procedure for Admitting an Exhibit.

To establish the foundation for an exhibit, counsel needs to identify the exhibit as "what its proponent claims." For example, if the prosecution claims a wristwatch was stolen in a robbery, the victim would identify the wristwatch as the stolen item. The exhibit, as identified, must be relevant. To establish foundation, the attorney normally would take the following steps.

§ 8-7(a). Mark the Exhibit.

You should mark the exhibit, giving it an appropriate number, such as "Plaintiff's Exhibit 1." Mark the exhibit yourself, or ask that the clerk mark the exhibit, depending on the practice in the court. In many courts, exhibits are marked prior to the trial. The marking of the exhibit identifies it for the record, even if it is not received. Describe the marking aloud so that it will be in the record: "I mark this document as 'Plaintiff's Exhibit 1,' for identification."

Generally, an attorney states that he is marking an exhibit "for identification," signifying that it has not yet been introduced. You must provide the identifying number or letter since you will refer to it in attempting to establish authenticity; this action keeps the record clear even if the court excludes the exhibit. You are not required to state the words "for identification," however, since identification is the only purpose of marking an exhibit in any event. You may nevertheless prefer to use this terminology to show your awareness that the court still must rule on the exhibit.

§ 8-7(b). Show It to Opposing Counsel.

Before showing the exhibit to the witness, show it to opposing counsel or provide a copy to counsel. If the opposing party already has a copy, this action is not necessary. Instead, you should identify the exhibit so that opposing counsel can find it. Examples: "The exhibit is premarked as Plaintiff's Exhibit 6"; "The exhibit is a letter dated January 13, 1992 on the stationary of Widget Corp."

§ 8-7(c). Ask Permission to Approach the Witness.

You should ask the court's permission to approach the witness to show him the exhibit. In approaching, make sure you do not block the jury's view of the witness. Additionally, back off before you begin asking questions about the exhibit. The witness needs to speak to the jury, not to you. If you stand right next to the witness, your exchange may develop into a private conference, impeding the witness's communication with the jurors.

§ 8-7(d). Ask the Witness to Identify the Exhibit.

In identifying the exhibit, the witness should tell the jury what it is and, preferably, how he recognizes it. A typical question: "Can you tell us what this exhibit is?" Often attorneys provide the description for the witness: "Can you identify this document as a letter written by you to John C. Jones on June 23, 1994?" Since the document usually reveals key information about itself, which is restated in the question, this approach may not produce an objection. Nevertheless, since the form of the question is leading, it is better to ask a question that lets the witness provide the description.

§ 8-7(e). Offer the Exhibit.

You should offer the exhibit, describing it with the assigned exhibit number. Many attorneys make the offer in a stilted, legalistic fashion: "May it please the court, I offer, file and introduce the exhibit marked Plaintiff's Exhibit 1." This overly formal offer is unnecessary. Use words that describe what you are doing. Examples: "I offer the exhibit as Plaintiff's Exhibit 1"; "I ask that the court receive this letter as Plaintiff's Exhibit 1." The court at this point ordinarily asks if there is an objection. If not, it admits the exhibit. If your opponent objects, you will need to argue the admissibility of your exhibit.

§ 8-7(f). Make Sure the Exhibit is Shown to the Jury.

You need to show the exhibit to the jury, or "publish" it. Often an attorney secures the introduction of an exhibit and simply hands it to the clerk or court reporter. The jurors, who have to decide the case, are left in the dark as to what the exhibit contains. Jurors are as curious as anyone else, and they may not appreciate being denied access to the exhibit.

Since you want to *include* the jurors in the presentation, you need to ensure that they see the evidence. Methods of showing exhibits to the jury are discussed in § 8-11. If the exhibit is not important — offered perhaps as a precaution to complete the record — state aloud the reason for not showing it to the jury: "I don't think we need to spend any time reading through that exhibit. Let's go on to. . .."

An example of how an identification might occur is set forth below:

Mr. Lee:	Your Honor, I request permission to mark an exhibit for identification and to approach the witness.
The Court:	All right.
[Counsel hands a copy to the opposing attorney.]	

> Q. Mr. Baron, I show you a three-page document that I have marked for identification "Plaintiff's Exhibit 3." Do you know what this document is?
>
> A. Yes.
>
> Q. Please describe it.
>
> A. This is a letter I wrote to Lane Kollen describing the terms of my offer to buy his house.
>
> Q. Whose signature is on the letter?
>
> A. That's my signature.
>
> Counsel: I offer this letter as "Plaintiff's Exhibit 3."
>
> The Court: Any objections? All right, it will be admitted.
>
> Counsel: May I distribute copies to the jury?
>
> The Court: Yes.

Often judges require that exhibits be marked prior to the trial and that the parties stipulate authenticity if no one disputes it. When the parties stipulate the authenticity of an exhibit, a witness need not identify it as a precondition to admissibility. You still need to show that the exhibit is relevant and meets other evidentiary requirements. Even if authenticity is stipulated, you may wish to have a witness describe the exhibit to aid the jury's understanding.

An example of how counsel might offer records when authenticity is stipulated is set forth below.

> Counsel: [questioning an accountant] May it please the Court, in connection with the testimony of this witness, I would like to offer into evidence at this time Plaintiff's Exhibit 37, which is stipulated to be a packet of 18 canceled payroll checks from Widget Corp. to John C. Raymond.
>
> The Court: Any objection? Plaintiff's Exhibit 37 is admitted.
>
> Counsel: Your Honor, may I ask Mr. Jones to hold the checks up so the jury can see?
>
> The Court: Go ahead.
>
> Q. Mr. Jones, just hold the checks up so the jurors can see them, all right?
>
> A. [Showing checks to jury.] Sure.

Q.	Mr. Jones, did you have occasion to review these checks to determine their total?
A.	Yes.
Q.	What was the total?
A.	One hundred sixteen thousand four hundred seventy-one dollars and 22 cents.

§ 8-8. Positioning Description, Offer and Follow-Up for Multiple Impact.

When you wish to give special emphasis to an exhibit, you can do so by having the witness describe the exhibit or the event involving the exhibit first, after which you introduce the exhibit and follow up for emphasis or development. The advance discussion raises the jurors' expectations and heightens the impact of the exhibit. Additionally, the positioning of description, offer and follow-up achieves repetition that does not seem redundant. The different reviews enhance the impact of the exhibit and increase the jurors' understanding of your points. An example follows.

Q.	What happened in the store?
A.	A man came in holding a gun.
Q.	What did the gun look like?
A.	It was a strange-looking gun. It had a long barrel with stones on it. It also had a pearl handle.
Q.	To what extent are your familiar with guns?
A.	I've seen hundreds, I collect guns and have been to many gun shows.
Q.	In your experience how distinctive was this gun?
A.	I've never seen one like it.
Q.	Would you recognize this gun if you saw it again?
A.	Yes.
Counsel:	Your Honor, I'd like to mark an exhibit as State's Exhibit 15 for identification.
The Court:	Okay.
Counsel:	May I approach the witness?
The Court:	Go ahead.
Q.	Do you recognize this?

A.	Yes.	
Q.	What is it?	
A.	It's the gun the man was holding.	
Counsel:	May it please the Court, I offer this gun as State's Exhibit 15.	
The Court:	Objection? Let it be received.	

[Handing gun to witness].

Q.	Can you show us the stones in the barrel that you previously referred to?	
A.	[Gesturing]. These are the stones I was talking about, here on the barrel. They sort of shine.	
Q.	Can you show the jury the handle?	
A.	Yes, Notice the pearly exterior. It covers the entire gun handle.	
Counsel:	Your Honor, may I show it to the jurors and let them pass it around?	
The Court:	Yes.	

This method of emphasis also works well with demonstrative exhibits. When introducing documents, however, avoid asking the witness directly to describe the contents of a document before you offer it. The original writing rule generally prohibits offering secondary evidence of the contents of a document. You usually can have the witness describe the fact that an agreement was entered, correspondence exchanged, or other events that led to the creation of the document, and the general subject matter it addressed. Then introduce and publish the document, after which you can follow up with inquiries concerning its contents. See § 8-21.

§ 8-9. Illustrations of Other Means to Identify Exhibits (FRE 901(b)).

Identification by a witness is the typical, but not the only, means to authenticate an exhibit. In most civil cases, and many criminal cases, the parties establish the authenticity of exhibits prior to the trial, allowing the introduction of the exhibits without identifying testimony. Additionally, exhibits may be identified by circumstances, their own unique characteristics, comparison by the jurors themselves to an identified sample, and other methods. FRE 901(b) sets forth a list of illustrative methods to identify exhibits.

In civil cases, parties often establish the authenticity of documents and other exhibits prior to trial. Through the use of pre-trial discovery, including interrogatories and requests for admission, parties can secure concessions that exhibits are authentic. Moreover, many courts require the parties to stipulate to the authenticity of exhibits unless genuine doubt exists on the point. Thus, lawyers usually do not encounter major authenticity issues in civil trials. These issues still may arise, however, in criminal cases where discovery is limited, in civil proceedings involving summary procedure, and when parties have genuine grounds to dispute the genuineness of exhibits.

FRE 901(b) provides "examples of authentication or identification conforming with the requirements of this rule." The examples illustrate some acceptable methods of authentication; they are not intended to limit the methods of identifying exhibits. The rule deals primarily with writings, but also addresses more unusual matters, such as identifying the speaker in a telephone conversation. It also permits the identification of physical objects from their distinctive characteristics or by comparison to other specimens that are already identified.

According to the Advisory Committee, the examples are drawn largely from "the experience embodied in the common law and statutes. . . ." The examples taken from these sources, however, do not always conform to the spirit of FRE 901(a) and the requirements of other rules. For instance, the requirement of FRE 901(b)(2) that nonexpert opinions on handwriting be based on "familiarity not acquired for purposes of the litigation" implicitly prevents a lay witness who becomes familiar with handwriting for the litigation from identifying the handwriting, although his identification could satisfy the "sufficient to support a finding" standard.[11]

Conversely, the example in FRE 901(b)(9) for authenticating a "process or system" presumably incorporates the low threshold for admissibility from FRE 901(a). It cannot apply to novel scientific processes, however, because a low threshold for admissibility of scientific evidence is not consistent with FRE 701–05, as interpreted by the Supreme Court in *Daubert v. Merrell Dow Pharmaceuticals, Inc.*[12] See § 10-5. Thus, the illustrations may conflict with FRE 901(a) and other rules.

Each of the illustrations is discussed below.

§ 8-9(a).   Testimony of a Witness with Knowledge.

The classic method of identifying an exhibit is to present the testimony of a person who has knowledge to identify it. FRE 901(b)(1) states that "[t]estimony that a matter is what it is claimed to be" is sufficient to identify an exhibit. Usually, familiarity with the exhibit supplies the necessary knowledge. If specialized knowledge is necessary to describe the exhibit or show its relevance, an expert must identify the exhibit.

---

[11] FED. R. EVID. 901(b)(2).

[12] 509 U.S. 579 (1993).

§ 8-9(b). Nonexpert Opinion on Handwriting.

FRE 901(b)(2) permits a witness who is not an expert to identify handwriting, so long as the witness's familiarity with the handwriting was not acquired for the litigation. It gives the following example of a permissible identification:

Nonexpert opinion as to the genuineness of handwriting, based upon familiarity not acquired for purposes of the litigation.

The illustration implicitly excludes evidence that would otherwise be admissible under FRE 901(a) — nonexpert opinion based on familiarity that *is* acquired for the litigation. Indeed, the Advisory Committee Note states that "[t]estimony based on familiarity acquired for purposes of the litigation is reserved to the expert. . . ."[13]

The exclusion of nonexpert testimony based on a comparison made for the litigation departs from the minimal standard of FRE 901(a), but is not important in practice. This type of nonexpert comparison can easily be made by the trier of fact; thus, it may not be "helpful." A party might justify the nonexpert testimony on the theory that the comparison requires analysis that could not easily be made by jurors, but that argument suggests the need for special expertise. Thus, nonexpert testimony based on a comparison made for the litigation has little value.

A nonexpert with independent knowledge often has a greater familiarity with handwriting than the knowledge acquired for litigation. Additionally, a witness with independent knowledge is less likely to be biased than someone who makes a comparison specially for the case. Further, a witness with independent knowledge can base her identification on that knowledge, permitting an identification even when samples for comparison are unavailable. Thus, this kind of nonexpert testimony is generally more reliable than nonexpert testimony prepared for the litigation.

§ 8-9(c). Comparison by Trier or Expert.

FRE 901(b)(3) permits an unusual method of identifying an exhibit: comparison by the trier of fact. It also permits an expert to make a comparison. The example allows "[c]omparison by the trier of fact or by expert witnesses with specimens which have been authenticated." Thus, to use this method counsel would have to first identify a specimen for comparison — perhaps handwriting, a distinctive earring, a shoe, or some other item that permits a match. A jury could compare items familiar to lay people — shoes, for instance — and reach a conclusion without expert help. Expert testimony could be used whenever it would help the trier. If specialized knowledge were required for an identification

---

[13] FED. R. EVID. 901(b)(2) advisory committee's note.

- for instance, a comparison of DNA in blood samples — counsel would have to present expert testimony.

Permitting the authentication of a specimen based on the jury's comparison appears to conflict with FRE 104(a), which reserves preliminary questions of admissibility to the court. A literal reading of the illustration suggests that the jurors would determine authenticity. The illustration is probably intended only to eliminate the need for testimony to identify the exhibit, however. The court would determine whether the specimens are comparable enough that a reasonable person could conclude the exhibit in question is authentic;[14] the jurors in turn would decide whether the exhibit is genuine, based on their own comparisons.

§ 8-9(d). Distinctive Characteristics and the Like.

Sometimes authentication can be based on circumstances. FRE 901(b)(4) permits identification of an exhibit based on "[a]ppearance, contents, substance, internal patterns, or other distinctive characteristics, taken in conjunction with circumstances." For further illustration, the Advisory Committee states that "a letter may be authenticated by content and circumstances indicating it was in reply to a duly authenticated one."[15] In other words, if the contents of a letter and the circumstances of its receipt showed that it was a reply to a letter already admitted, the letter itself in combination with circumstances would establish authenticity. Similarly, a witness might identify an e-mail correspondent by statements disclosing facts known only to the witness and that person.[16] The "circumstances," of course, must be established with testimony or other evidence.

§ 8-9(e). Voice Identification.

FRE 901(b)(5) deals with identification of voices. The need to identify voices arises when a party introduces recordings, since the jurors cannot see the alleged speakers. Additionally, witnesses sometimes overhear statements without actually seeing the speakers. The example makes clear that a witness can make a voice identification in these circumstances. It permits:

> Identification of a voice, whether heard firsthand or through mechanical or electronic transmission or recording, by opinion based upon hearing the voice at any time under circumstances connecting it with the alleged speaker.

When a recording is offered, the proponent may establish the identity of the speakers by lay opinion based on familiarity acquired at any time. The rule treats

---

[14] See FED. R. EVID. 901(b)(3) advisory committee's note, which rejects precedent requiring the judge to make a finding of genuineness based on a high standard of persuasion and appears to approve the use of the standard set forth in FED. R. EVID. 104(b).

[15] FED. R. EVID. 901(b)(4) advisory committee's note.

[16] See generally United States v. Siddiqui, 235 F.3d 1318 (11th Cir. 2000), cert. denied, 533 U.S. 940 (2001).

voice identification like visual identification — not a matter that requires expert testimony.[17] Unlike the identification of handwriting, the witness does not need independent familiarity with the voice.

§ 8-9(f). Telephone Conversations.

FRE 901(b)(6) permits the identification of a participant in a telephone conversation by evidence showing that a call was made to the number assigned to the person or business, but also requires other corroborating circumstances, such as self-identification by the recipient of the call. It permits identification as follows:

> Telephone conversations, by evidence that a call was made to the number assigned at the time by the telephone company to a particular person or business, if (A) in the case of a person, circumstances, including self-identification, show the person answering to be the one called, or (B) in the case of a business, the call was made to a place of business and the conversation related to business reasonably transacted over the telephone.

The rule thus permits a witness to identify the speaker in a telephone conversation by testifying that he called the number listed for the person and the individual who answered gave his name or made statements showing his identity.

In requiring corroboration, this illustration demands more than the minimal showing permitted in FRE 901(a). Preexisting authorities required more to authenticate a telephone conversation than the mere dialing of an assigned number, by itself, or a mere assertion of identity by the answering party.[18] Indeed, there was a division in the authorities on whether these factors in combination were sufficient. The illustration recognizes that the combination will suffice.[19]

§ 8-9(g). Public Records or Reports.

FRE 901(b)(7) provides a simple method to identify public records and documents filed in public offices. It permits a party to identify these records by supplying:

> Evidence that a writing authorized by law to be recorded or filed and in fact recorded or filed in a public office, or a purported public record, report, statement, or data compilation, in any form, is from the public office where items of this nature are kept.

---

[17] FED. R. EVID. 901(b)(5) advisory committee's note: "[A]ural voice identification is not a subject of expert testimony. . . ."; see Millender v. Adams, 187 F.Supp.2d 852, 869 (E.D. Mich. 2002) (minimal familiarity with voice sufficient for identification).

[18] FED. R. EVID. 901(b)(6) advisory committee's note.

[19] Id: "Example (6) answers in the affirmative on the assumption that usual conduct respecting telephone calls furnish adequate assurances of regularity. . . ."

Anyone who has knowledge that the report came from a public office can identify it. The rule authorizes authentication of public records and reports by showing that a report or record is from the public office and that a writing required to be recorded or filed in a public office was recorded or filed there. The rule includes data stored electronically. As the Advisory Committee states, "[t]he example extends the principle to include data stored in computers and similar methods, of which increasing use in the public records area may be expected."[20]

Authentication by showing that a document is from a public office, without more, shows only that the document is a record from the office. It does not necessarily prove other attributes of the document.

§ 8-9(h). Ancient Documents and Data Compilations.

FRE 901(b)(8) adopts the common law rule for authenticating ancient documents. It provides for identification as follows:

> Evidence that a document or data compilation, in any form, (A) is in such condition as to create no suspicion concerning its authenticity, (B) was in a place where it, if authentic, would likely be, and (C) has been in existence 20 years or more at the time it is offered.

The rule selects 20 years as the time for establishing a document is "ancient," rather than the 30-year period imposed at common law; either would provide a strong guarantee that the document was not created for the litigation.

The ancient document rule is based partially on necessity, as witnesses often are unavailable to authenticate these documents. Additionally, ancient documents are viewed as reliable because they usually preexist the controversy. This factor, coupled with the requirement that a party show that the document appears genuine and was where it was supposed to be, provides a good basis for finding the document authentic.

§ 8-9(i). Process or System.

FRE 901(b)(9) illustrates the authentication of a "process" or "system." It allows:

> Evidence describing a process or system used to produce a result and showing that the process or system produces an accurate result.

The illustration permits a witness to describe a process or system and explain that it produces a correct result. The witness would have to possess satisfactory knowledge to give this testimony. For most "processes" and "systems," expert testimony may be required. For some processes that are used frequently as proof of facts — such as an x-ray or a radar gun — the court may not require an expert.

---

[20] FED. R. EVID. 901(b)(7) advisory committee's note.

The illustration leaves open the issue of whether an expert may authenticate a novel scientific process under the "sufficient to support a finding" standard. Placing the example in FRE 901 suggests that it incorporates this minimal standard. The Supreme Court's decision in *Daubert v. Merrell Dow Pharmaceuticals, Inc.*,[21] however, suggests that more exacting court scrutiny is required for novel scientific processes and tests. Thus, the hurdle for admissibility is probably higher than that implied by FRE 901. See § 10-5.

§ 8-9(j). Methods Prescribed by Statute or Rule.

FRE 901(b)(10) permits the use of any authentication method prescribed by Congress or the Supreme Court. It allows:

> Any method of authentication or identification provided by Act of Congress or by other rules prescribed by the Supreme Court pursuant to statutory authority.

The Advisory Committee states: "The example makes clear that methods of authentication provided by Act of Congress and by the Rules of Civil and Criminal Procedure or by Bankruptcy Rules are not intended to be superseded."[22]

§ 8-10. Authenticating Electronic Exhibits.

The ever-increasing use of computers to transmit, process and store information makes it increasingly necessary to prove facts in trial with electronic evidence. Electronic evidence raises special identification issues, however, along with original writing and reliability concerns. Because of these issues, you may need to provide more information to authenticate electronic evidence than you would in offering documents.

Unlike documents, electronic evidence easily may be edited to change its original form. A party against whom the evidence is offered might have difficulty showing that the original was altered. Thus, there may be special concerns regarding the authenticity and reliability of electronic exhibits.

Assume, for example, that John claims an e-mail exchange produced a contract. Assume John contends that Mary agreed to buy his souped-up convertible for $10,000. Mary agrees she agreed to buy the convertible, but contends the price was $9,000.

If John produces an electronic image on a computer terminal or printout in which Mary offers $10,000, Mary will claim it is not the authentic e-mail offer. She will be able to show that electronic messages may be edited and that tracing the edit is virtually impossible. Further, the cost of proving the alteration might

---

[21] 509 U.S. 579 (1993).

[22] FED. R. EVID. 901(b)(10) advisory committee's note.

be prohibitive. By the same token, it likely would be difficult and expensive for John to prove conclusively that the e-mail was not altered.

Despite the possibility of alteration of the e-mail, Mary should have means to contest its accuracy. If she deemed her offer important, she likely would have kept her own electronic copy of the e-mail. Indeed, as electronic commerce increases, parties will establish procedures to preserve important correspondence. If necessary, she may seek a copy from her own Internet service or the service used by John. A different version of the e-mail provides a basis for contesting its authenticity and its compliance with the original writing rule.

If Mary raises no serious dispute about the authenticity or reliability of the e-mail, John should easily satisfy the authenticity requirements of FRE 901. The standard for admissibility presents a low hurdle; John need only provide evidence sufficient to support a finding that it is what he claims: an e-mail received from Mary.[23] To do this, he would describe the circumstances of the correspondence, identify the return address as Mary's e-mail address, and relate any special facts indicating that it must have come from Mary. Even if Mary raises serious issues as to the accuracy of the e-mail, they likely will not prevent its introduction given the welcoming standard for admissibility.

The federal courts generally have held that e-mail transmissions are admissible, leaving it to the parties to argue accuracy and reliability. Thus, in *United States v. Siddiqui*,[24] the Eleventh Circuit held that adequate evidence supported the identification of e-mails as authored by Siddiqui, the appellant. It relied on the following circumstances: a) the e-mails bore Siddiqui's e-mail address, b) the e-mails contained information relative to Siddiqui's actions, c) the e-mails were signed with Siddiqui's nickname, and d) Siddiqui by telephone made requests similar to those contained in the e-mails.

The Tenth Circuit has upheld the introduction of a computer printout of a chat room discussion allegedly involving the defendant. *United States v. Simpson.*[25] The court relied on information, including an e-mail address, tying the chat room messages to Simpson.[26] The Ninth Circuit has also affirmed the introduction of chat room log printouts based on evidence tying the defendant to the chat room name used in transmitting the messages. *United States v. Tank.*[27]

The same analysis applies to electronic data stored or processed by computer. A party would have to establish the circumstances under which the material was prepared and show that the images or printouts presented in court are accurate.

---

[23] FED. R. EVID. 901(a).

[24] 235 F.3d 1318 (11th Cir. 2000), *cert. denied*, 533 U.S. 940 (2001).

[25] 152 F.3d 1241 (10th Cir. 1998).

[26] *Id.* at 1251.

[27] 200 F.3d 627 (9th Cir. 2000).

A *prima facie* showing on these points would establish authenticity. Hearsay issues may enhance the burden, however; § 6-9 deals with this point.

An example of an identification of a computer printout of an e-mail transmission follows:

Ms. Joseph:	Your Honor, I have marked an exhibit for identification as "Plaintiff's Exhibit 4." I have a copy for opposing counsel (tendering). I ask permission to approach the witness
The Court:	Proceed.
Q.	Mr. Pipes, can you tell this jury what this document is?
A.	It's an e-mail transmission I received from Celeste Coco-Ewing.
Q.	Where did you receive it?
A.	On my computer terminal at the office.
Q.	How do you know it is an e-mail from Ms. Coco-Ewing?
A.	It bears her e-mail address. Also it responds to an offer I made by e-mail to sell her my car.
Q.	How did you make this printout?
A.	The computer has a printer. I simply clicked on "print," which instructed the computer to make this printout.
Q.	How accurately does this printout reflect the electronic version you received on the computer?
A.	It's exactly the same except it's a hard copy.
Ms. Joseph:	Your Honor, I offer Plaintiff's Exhibit 4.
The Court:	Any objection?
Ms. Weinstein:	Yes, Your Honor. This product reflects an electronic message that can easily be altered. There is no way to really tell that the e-mail is authentic.
The Court:	That objection goes to weight, not admissibility. Ms. Joseph has established a *prima facie* identification of the exhibit. Let it be admitted.

---

§ 8-11. Showing Exhibits to the Trier.

Introducing an exhibit does not ensure that the judge or jury actually examines it. You not only must make sure that the court admits the exhibit, but that it has its intended impact. To achieve this objective, you should "publish" the exhibit in a way that promotes easy comprehension and brings out the important information.

You need to make sure that you take advantage of the persuasive potential of an exhibit, if you do not show the exhibit to the jurors, it cannot have any effect. Additionally, publishing exhibits is necessary to make jurors feel included in your presentation. You need to choose a method that does not unduly delay the presentation, however, and you must find ways to focus the jurors' attention on key material. Otherwise the jurors may get lost in information that makes little difference to the case.

In most courts the judge has a preferred means of publishing exhibits. Inquire in advance as to the court's practice. If you wish to depart from the court's procedure to achieve a point of advocacy, bring up the matter in advance. If your suggestion saves time or work, the court is likely to grant a dispensation.

Methods of publication include the following:

§ 8-11(a). Examination by Trier.

Once the court admits an exhibit, you may ask permission to give it to the jury so they can pass it from person to person. This method works well with unique pieces of evidence that cannot be copied or replicated, such as a knife, gun, or bloodstain. It may be acceptable with photographs and documents that do not contain substantial writing. For more lengthy documents, however, one-after-the-other reading by the jurors becomes tedious. Additionally, using this approach gives up much of your ability to emphasize important passages. Thus, if documents are lengthy or there are many documents, do not use this method to publish them.

§ 8-11(b). Exhibition.

A quicker method of showing a unique exhibit to the jurors is simply to hold it where they can see it. You should ask the court's permission to show the exhibit and then do so. Alternatively, you might have the witness hold up an object for the jury to see. You need to make sure the exhibit is large enough that the jurors will recognize its characteristics from several feet away.

§ 8-11(c). Providing Copies to Jurors.

One way to quicken the examination of documentary evidence is to provide copies to jurors. This approach saves time because each juror can read the exhibit simultaneously. Unless you find a way to emphasize key passages, however, the document may not have its intended effect. To address this problem, you should ask permission to highlight key portions — subject to counter-highlighting by the opposing side [28] — so you direct the jurors' attention to important passages.

---

[28] See FED. R. EVID. 106.

You may also ask the witness to read key passages as the jurors read along, as explained in § 8-11(e). Alternatively, you might simply call the jurors' attention to part of the document: "I direct the jury's attention to paragraph 3."

The problem with giving jurors exhibits is that they may peruse them after you go on to other subjects. Thus, if you use this method you should allow the jurors time to read important passages, then get the copies back before moving on.

§ 8-11(d). Exhibit Books.

When the documents are voluminous, or you must refer to them frequently, you may suggest that the jurors be provided exhibit books. The parties can make copies of the exhibits for each juror and, once the court admits each exhibit, give them to the jurors to place them in the exhibit books. Alternatively, the exhibits can first be placed in the exhibit books and their admissibility determined prior to the trial, or the jurors can be instructed not to refer to exhibits until they are admitted. This approach permits the jurors to refer to exhibits without having them handed out repeatedly.

One pitfall of this approach is the likelihood that the jurors will peruse exhibits during oral testimony. In doing so the jurors may focus on extraneous information and reach erroneous conclusions about the exhibits. To avoid this problem, you might ask the court to advise the jurors to keep the exhibit books closed unless exhibits are being reviewed. Additionally, you should allow jurors time to read documents and provide a signal when you are ready to proceed. "Now, Mr. Jones, I'm finished with that letter [looking to make sure jurors have read it]. Let's discuss what happened after you read it." This action gives the jurors a cue to close the books and listen.

§ 8-11(e). Reading the Contents.

An easy method of publishing exhibits is to read them to the jury. If the judge allows it — and she likely will — important passages designated by each side may be read. A problem arises, however, in deciding who does the reading. A clerk can perform the task, but perhaps without emotion; the witness can be asked to do it, but may not perform very well; counsel can request to read it, but the opposing party may object that an advocate will emphasize the wrong parts. The best approach is to prepare the witness to read the document, since you may not be permitted to do the reading.

Reading alone is not a very effective means of publishing exhibits. The jurors are likely to forget quickly an oral review of the contents. This approach is a means, however, of emphasizing key parts of a document that you have introduced. You can call the witness's attention to the important paragraph and ask the witness to read it; if the jurors have copies, they can read along.

If the opposing party objects to reading on the ground that the document "speaks for itself," you should explain that you are trying to save time by focusing on the important part. Alternatively, if you intend to ask the witness about the passage, you can suggest that it should be in the transcript for completeness. Usually the court will permit this approach if you really have additional questions. Thus, you might state: "Your Honor, I intend to ask the witness about the investigation he performed prior to writing paragraph three. I would like the witness to read that paragraph for the record." Alternatively, you might address the same message to the witness, alerting the court to your intent: "Mr. Adams, I intend to ask you about your investigation prior to writing paragraph three. Would you read that paragraph so that it will be in the transcript?"

Merely asking the witness to repeat a passage already shown to the jury may be deemed improper repetition. Additionally, asking the witness to interpret a document may be deemed not helpful — the document speaks for itself, and usually the trier can interpret it. Thus, you should formulate questions that do not directly elicit interpretations. Instead, ask for background leading to the document or events that occurred because it was written.

§ 8-11(f).   Replication in Demonstrative Exhibits.

Many attorneys blow up key passages in documents for use during testimony and argument. If the court allows it, this practice is a good way to emphasize a favorable passage. To use the blowup, you must ensure that the court admits the source document. If you use the exhibit with a witness, you should formulate permissible questions — those that elicit facts leading to or resulting from the document, rather than obvious requests for repetition or interpretation of language.

When a part of a writing or recording is introduced, FRE 106 allows the opposing party to introduce any other part required for fairness. The rule implicitly authorizes exhibiting a *portion* of a writing in a demonstrative exhibit. Opposing counsel presumably could require the simultaneous exhibition of another portion of the writing. In practice, opposing attorneys usually wait to present their exhibits during their own examinations.

If you use a blown-up version of a document, you should make sure the writing is visible from a reasonable distance. Attorneys often blow up documents on demonstrative exhibits, but the original print is often too small to enhance to a size discernable from even several feet away. For proper emphasis you need to limit the material on the exhibit and reproduce it in a size fit for viewing. If you display too much, the crucial portion loses its impact.

An overhead projector or projection on computer terminals provide other methods of exhibiting writings. These methods capture attention, but setting up the projector or document camera, finding the right slide or document, and showing it on the screen is often cumbersome. Additionally, since the projections usually present photographic images of documents, they do not emphasize key passages. You need to plan the exhibitions and find ways to highlight important material.

§ 8-12.   Self-Authentication (FRE 902).

FRE 902 establishes 12 categories of documents that authenticate themselves; in other words, no showing external to the document is required to identify it. In general, the categories include documents that would be difficult to forge: documents that bear official seals or certificates, certified copies of public records, newspapers, official publications, and similar documents. According to the Advisory Committee, the rule "collects and incorporates" the situations in which self-authentication previously had been permitted, "in some instances expanding them to occupy a larger area which their underlying considerations justify."[29]

FRE 902 was amended in 2000 to add two new provisions to permit the certification of business records so that they may be introduced without the testimony of a live witness. Together with a change to FRE 803(b), the amendments permit the introduction of regularly-kept records without the presentation of a live witness familiar with the manner in which they were recorded. The provisions provide for notice to the adverse party and an opportunity to review the declaration and the record sufficiently in advance of the offer to fairly permit a challenge.

Even if a document is self-authenticating under FRE 902, the opposing party has the right to dispute its authenticity.[30] The issue rarely arises because most self-authenticating documents are genuine. Further, authenticity usually can be checked prior to trial.

FRE 902 provides:

Self-Authentication

Extrinsic evidence of authenticity as a condition precedent to admissibility is not required with respect to the following:

(1) **Domestic public documents under seal.** A document bearing a seal purporting to be that of the United States, or of any State, district, Commonwealth, territory, or insular possession thereof, or the Panama Canal Zone, or the Trust Territory of the Pacific Islands, or of a political subdivision, department, officer, or agency thereof, and a signature purporting to be an attestation or execution.

---

[29] FED. R. EVID. 902 advisory committee's note.

[30] Id.

(2) Domestic public documents not under seal. A document purporting to bear the signature in the official capacity of an officer or employee of any entity included in paragraph (1) hereof, having no seal, if a public officer having a seal and having official duties in the district or political subdivision of the officer or employee certifies under seal that the signer has the official capacity and that the signature is genuine.

(3) Foreign public documents. A document purporting to be executed or attested in an official capacity by a person authorized by the laws of a foreign country to make the execution or attestation, and accompanied by a final certification as to the genuineness of the signature and official position (A) of the executing or attesting person, or (B) of any foreign official whose certificate of genuineness of signature and official position relates to the execution or attestation or is in a chain of certificates of genuineness of signature and official position relating to the execution or attestation. A final certification may be made by a secretary of embassy or legation, consul general, consul, vice consul, or consular agent of the United States, or a diplomatic or consular official of the foreign country assigned or accredited to the United States. If reasonable opportunity has been given to all parties to investigate the authenticity and accuracy of official documents, the court may, for good cause shown, order that they be treated as presumptively authentic without final certification or permit them to be evidenced by an attested summary with or without final certification.

(4) Certified copies of public records. A copy of an official record or report or entry therein, or of a document authorized by law to be recorded or filed and actually recorded or filed in a public office, including data compilations in any form, certified as correct by the custodian, or other person authorized to make the certification, by certificate complying with paragraph (1), (2), or (3) of this rule or complying with any Act of Congress or rule prescribed by the Supreme Court pursuant to statutory authority.

(5) Official publications. Books, pamphlets, or other publications purporting to be issued by public authority.

(6) Newspapers and periodicals. Printed materials purporting to be newspapers or periodicals.

(7) Trade inscriptions and the like. Inscriptions, signs, tags, or labels purporting to have been affixed in the course of business and indicating ownership, control, or origin.

(8) Acknowledged documents. Documents accompanied by a certificate of acknowledgment executed in the manner provided by law by a notary public or other officer authorized by law to take acknowledgments.

(9) Commercial paper and related documents. Commercial paper, signatures thereon, and documents relating thereto to the extent provided by general commercial law.

(10) Presumptions under Acts of Congress. Any signature, document, or other matter declared by Act of Congress to be presumptively or prima facie genuine or authentic.

(11) Certified domestic records of regularly conducted activity. The original or a duplicate of a domestic record of regularly conducted activity that would be admissible under Rule 803(6) if accompanied by a written declaration of its custodian or other qualified person, in a manner complying with any Act of Congress or rule prescribed by the Supreme Court pursuant to statutory authority, certifying that record —

(A)   was made at or near the time of the occurrence of the matters set forth by, or from information transmitted by, a person with knowledge of those matters;

(B)   was kept in the course of the regularly conducted activity; and

(C)   was made by the regularly conducted activity as a regular practice.

A party intending to offer a record into evidence under this paragraph must provide written notice of that intention to all adverse parties, and must make the record and declaration available for inspection sufficiently in advance of their offer into evidence to provide an adverse party with a fair opportunity to challenge them.

(12) Certified foreign records of regularly conducted activity. In a civil case, the original or a duplicate of a foreign record of regularly conducted activity that would be admissible under Rule 803(6) if accompanied by a written declaration by its custodian or other qualified person certifying that the record —

(A)   was made at or near the time of the occurrence of the matters set forth by, or from information transmitted by, a person with knowledge of those matters;

(B)   was kept in the course of the regularly conducted activity; and

(C)   was made by the regularly conducted activity as a regular practice.

The declaration must be signed in a manner that, if falsely made, would subject the maker to criminal penalty under the laws of the country where the declaration is signed. A party intending to offer a record into evidence under this paragraph must provide written notice of that intention to all adverse parties, and must make the record and declaration available for inspection sufficiently in advance of their offer into evidence to provide an adverse party with a fair opportunity to challenge them.

§ 8-13. Authentication Without Subscribing Witness (FRE 903).

FRE 903 establishes that the testimony of a person who signed or witnessed a document is not necessary to authenticate it unless the laws of the governing jurisdiction require that the witness testifies. At common law, the proponent of a document had to produce or account for attesting witnesses.[31] This requirement was done away with over time, except when mandated by statute. The rule provides:

> The testimony of a subscribing witness is not necessary to authenticate a writing unless required by the laws of the jurisdiction whose laws govern the validity of the writing.

II. DEMONSTRATIVE EXHIBITS

§ 8-14. Demonstrative Exhibits in Trial.

Often you can aid the jury's understanding of evidence through exhibits that compile or illustrate facts. Models, maps, diagrams, charts, and similar exhibits are examples of "demonstrative" evidence; these exhibits are extremely helpful in getting factual points across. Unlike a "real" item of evidence, such as a murder weapon, a "demonstrative" exhibit would be a model of the weapon, a diagram of its working parts, or a similar device. A demonstrative exhibit typically is used by a witness to explain matters to the jury.

Demonstrative exhibits have gained a large role in advocacy because they are successful in illuminating facts. "A picture is worth a thousand words" precisely because there is often a gap between a speaker's intent and a listener's understanding. Listeners often conceptualize a verbal description different from the picture the speaker intends to communicate.

Pitfalls in oral communication beset both speaker and listener. The speaker's description may be inaccurate; the listener may misunderstand or fail to pay attention. A picture of the scene virtually eliminates these problems. It allows the listener to visualize what the witness describes without relying solely on the speaker's words. Additionally, the illustration captures attention, avoiding the problem of the wandering mind.

Demonstrative evidence also helps a witness present facts. With the aid of a chart or diagram, a witness usually provides a more organized and complete description, because the exhibit serves as an outline. Additionally, by allowing the witness to explain an exhibit, counsel focuses attention on the witness and increases his status. A chart, model, or diagram gives substance to the witness's account. Additionally, it allows him to assume the role of teacher, which increases the jurors' willingness to listen.

---

[31] FED. R. EVID. 903 advisory committee's note.

The foundation requirement for demonstrative evidence is that the evidence accurately portray what the witness is attempting to describe. As with other "fact" evidence, the trial judge generally should admit the evidence on the basis of testimony sufficient to support a finding that it represents what the proponent claims.[32] McCormick states:

> Models, maps, sketches, and diagrams (as distinguished from duplicates) are by their nature generally not easily confused with real evidence, and are admissible simply on the basis of testimony that they are substantially accurate representations of what the witness is endeavoring to describe. Some discretionary control in the trial court is generally deemed appropriate, however, since exhibits of this kind, due to inaccuracies, variations of scale, etc., may on occasion be more misleading than helpful. Nevertheless, when the trial court has exercised its discretion to admit, it will only rarely be found in error, at least if potentially misleading inaccuracies have been pointed out by witnesses for the proponent, or could have been exposed upon cross-examination.[33]

To be relevant, the evidence must help the jury understand or interpret facts of consequence to the resolution of the case. You must show that the exhibit is a reasonably accurate portrayal of information that relates to the issues. To use an illustrative exhibit, such as a photograph of a scene or a model of the human body, you need not present the person who took the photo, created the model, or made the illustration. You need only present testimony that the illustration is accurate from a person with knowledge *of the matter being depicted.* Thus, a person who observed the scene of an accident could identify an illustrative photograph even if he never before saw it.

For an exhibit that summarizes or depicts information in the record, the witness must possess knowledge that the illustration is accurate. For example, if the exhibit were a chart of concrete deliveries to a construction project, the witness would have to at least check the accuracy of the chart. Often experts leave it to others to prepare demonstrative exhibits. If the expert does not personally know an exhibit is accurate, the court may stop him from using it. Some courts are lenient in allowing the use of exhibits prepared under an expert's "supervision," leaving it to the opposing party to bring out errors, but a "supervisory" foundation in theory is not sufficient.

The court may exclude demonstrative evidence if it is misleading. Thus, a chart drawn to a scale that unduly exaggerates underlying data could be deemed unduly prejudicial. Nevertheless, courts usually allow some room for advocacy in these

---

[32] FED. R. EVID. 901; Nachtsheim v. Beech Aircraft Corp., 847 F.2d 1261, 1277 (7th Cir. 1991) (in airplane crash case, court admitted manufacturer's videotape regarding ice accumulation and de-icing, combined with expert's testimony).

[33] MCCORMICK ON EVIDENCE § 214 (5th ed. 1999).

exhibits, leaving it to opposing counsel to bring the matter into perspective. Generally, you should present exhibits that favorably depict the facts but do not distort them.

Technologic advances make it increasingly practical to use demonstrative exhibits in court.[34] You can use computer software to prepare charts and diagrams, and blow them up for the trial. Additionally, you can use computers to simulate and display animated reenactments of events. Specialty firms produce graphic exhibits for lawyers; the artists often give helpful advice on how to depict technical material. Some large law firms have this capability in-house. Thus, there is no reason to miss this opportunity to influence the jury.

The effective use of demonstrative exhibits requires preparation and thought. You must identify matters that can be clarified with illustrations and conceptualize the best ways to present them. The exhibits must be simple, so that they clarify rather than complicate the points. They must fairly present the facts or they will be excluded as prejudicial. Often experimentation is required to find the best illustrations.

To achieve success with demonstrative exhibits, you should begin preparing them well in advance of trial. Try them out on colleagues to make sure they are understandable. Solicit suggestions for improvement. Work with witnesses to achieve the best illustrations of their testimony. Remember that a confusing exhibit only detracts from your presentation.

§ 8-15. Procedure for Introducing Demonstrative Exhibits.

The procedure for using a demonstrative exhibit is similar to that for a real exhibit. The showing is different, however; you need to establish that the exhibit is a reasonably accurate depiction and that it will help the trier understand relevant facts. The courts have considerable discretion to balance the helpfulness of an exhibit versus the potential for prejudice, confusion, or delay.

Some courts do not formally admit demonstrative exhibits because they are not really evidence from the case; these courts allow their use only as illustrations. The distinction makes little difference, however, since the exhibits need to be part of the record for appeal. Thus, you must mark and identify them and the court must decide if they can be used.

Since a demonstrative exhibit usually is large enough for the jurors to see, the opposing party may object if you unveil the exhibit before it is identified. To eliminate problems in using demonstrative exhibits, you may wish to exchange these exhibits with your opponent prior to the trial. Many courts require this procedure, which allows the parties to resolve disputes by agreement or through

---

[34] See Robert D. Brain & Daniel J. Broderick, *Demonstrative Evidence: The Next Generation*, 17 LITIG. 21 (1991).

motions in limine. If your opponent has seen your exhibit and wishes to avoid its exposition, he can ask that the court rule on its admissibility outside the presence of the jury. In any event, to smooth the presentation of a demonstrative exhibit, you can have the witness state what it is before you unveil it.

§ 8-15(a). Maps, Sketches, Photos, Diagrams, and Similar Illustrations Not Created by the Witness.

An exhibit that illustrates facts, rather than compiling or explaining them, need not be created by the witness. If the witness did not create the exhibit, a good way to introduce it is to use the steps for a real exhibit, adapting them for the identification of the demonstrative exhibit. The steps are explained below.

1. *Mark the exhibit.* You should mark the exhibit and describe the marking for the record, as explained in § 8-7. State it is demonstrative and if necessary, mark it to show it is a demonstrative exhibit; "I have marked this exhibit for identification as Plaintiff's Exhibit 3, and I have marked it as demonstrative."

2. *Show it to opposing counsel.* If opposing counsel has not seen the exhibit, show it to her. If you have exchanged copies, inform her of the one you are using. Even if your demonstrative exhibit is blown up for exhibition, you usually can make smaller copies. This action permits you the option of including the smaller version in the record. If you only have a blowup, show it to your opponent prior to the testimony. Otherwise she may ask to review it when it is unveiled, disrupting the presentation.

3. *Ask permission to approach the witness or to unveil the exhibit.* If the exhibit is small, you need to approach the witness to show it to him. If it is large, it needs to be displayed on an easel or other device. Have the exhibit ready for a smooth unveiling. Make sure the exhibit is displayed where the witness, the judge and the jurors can all see it.

4. *Ask the witness if the exhibit is an accurate depiction.* You must establish that the exhibit is a reasonably accurate depiction of the scene, area, or other matter you are illustrating. Attorneys often use a leading form for this identification: "Does this exhibit accurately portray the corner of Poydras and Carondelet as you saw it on July 15, 2002?" The form is objectionable, but courts often tolerate leading to identify exhibits. A better form: "How does this photograph compare to the scene you observed at the corner of Poydras and Carondelet on July 15, 2002?" The answer: "It looks the same."

5. *Offer the exhibit.* Make your offer: "Your Honor, I would like to offer this as an accurate illustration of the scene at Poydras and Carondelet on the day in question." Stating that the exhibit is illustrative should smooth its introduction. Since the exhibit is only illustrative, you may

not need to offer it in some courts. Indeed, the court may not formally receive it as an exhibit. You need to find out the court's practice in advance so the presentation goes smoothly.

6. *Show the exhibit to the jury.* Usually the exhibit is introduced in front of the jury, so they can look at it as it is identified. You still need to make sure the jurors have a chance to study it for a few seconds. If the exhibit is admitted before you address it — for instance, after a dispute as to its admissibility is heard outside their presence — unveil it where they can see it.

7. *Use the exhibit.* Put the exhibit to its intended use. Have the witness explain the facts, pointing to the exhibit as necessary. If having the witness approach the exhibit will help the explanation, ask the court to permit him to do so.

An example of the introduction of an illustrative exhibit — a photograph — is set forth below.

Counsel:	Your Honor, I have here a blown-up photograph of the corner of Poydras and Carondelet that I'd like to use for illustrative purposes. My opponent has seen it. May I set it up on this easel?
The Court:	Go ahead.
Counsel:	I will mark this exhibit as Plaintiff's Exhibit 16 for identification.
Q.	Mr. Jones, please take a look at this photograph. Can you tell me how this scene compares with the scene you observed at Poydras and Carondelet on July 15, 2002?
A.	Yes. It looks just the same.
Q.	Are there any differences?
A.	Not that I can think of.
Q.	Can you tell me the vantage point of this photograph?
A.	The same as the one I had. I was standing just up Carondelet, on the side of Poydras away from downtown.
Counsel:	I'd like to offer this exhibit for illustrative purposes as Plaintiff's Exhibit 17.
The Court:	Any objection? Let it be admitted. [The court may instruct the jury on the illustrative nature of the exhibit.]

Counsel:	May I ask the witness to approach the exhibit to explain what happened on the day of the accident?
The Court:	Yes.

One way to secure a "double bang" in presenting a demonstrative exhibit is to have the witness describe a scene or other matter first, after which you unveil the exhibit and have the witness explain it. When a matter is important, this method provides emphasis without seeming repetitive.

§ 8-15(b). Illustrative Exhibits Prepared by the Witness.

If a witness prepares an exhibit for use with testimony, you may want to take a slightly different approach. One good method is to have the witness explain his conclusions before referring to the illustrative exhibit. You can then ask the witness if he has prepared an exhibit to illustrate his findings. Besides achieving a "double bang," this approach defuses potential objections and heightens the jury's interest. Again, you need to lay the foundation for a demonstrative exhibit, as explained below.

1. *Ask the witness about the exhibit.* When you reach the point when you wish to use the exhibit, ask the witness if he brought a chart, model, or other aid to illustrate his testimony. An example follows:

Q. Doctor, do you have a model of the human spine that illustrates the points you are making?

A. Yes.

Q. Did you bring that model with you today?

A. Yes.

Q. Would it help you explain your diagnosis?

A. I think it would be very helpful.

---

2. *Ask the court's permission to unveil the exhibit.* Once the witness says the exhibit would be helpful, ask the court if you can unveil it: "Your Honor, may I show the model to the witness?"

3. *Mark the exhibit.* Mark the exhibit for identification and state the marking for the record.

4. *Have the witness identify the exhibit and explain why it would be helpful.* Have the witness explain what the exhibit illustrates. Often its helpfulness in explaining facts is obvious. To ensure that you can use it, you may want to have the witness explain why it would be helpful in understanding the testimony. An example follows:

Q. Doctor, what is this model?

A. That's a model of the human spine that I made for this testimony.

Q. Would it help you explain what happened to Ms. Miller's back?

A. Yes, it would.

Q. Why?

A. I need a model to show the jury how a ruptured disc looks and why it causes the problems she is experiencing.

---

5. *Use the exhibit.* Usually you can display and use the exhibit before offering it. This action enhances the foundation for the exhibit. You may want to ask the court's permission to proceed: "Your Honor, may we proceed to use this model in explaining the injury?" If the court wishes to rule on an offer first, make the offer and use the exhibit after court admits it.

Have the witness use the exhibit to explain her points. Make sure the jury can see the exhibit. Stay out of the way. You want the witness to speak to the jury. Keep control of the examination through your questions so that the witness does not lecture, but let the witness make the presentation. If helpful, have the witness approach the exhibit to explain her points. Ask the court's permission for this action.

6. *Offer the exhibit.* If you do not offer the exhibit prior to the testimony, offer it afterwards, assuming the court receives demonstrative exhibits in evidence. With a model, perhaps one used by an expert in multiple cases, you may want to substitute a photograph or other replica. Opposing counsel should agree unless the actual model is necessary to preserve points for appeal. In any event, you want the model or a replica in the record.

The following example illustrates the introduction of an illustrative chart.

Q. Mr. Finn, with respect to your analysis of the air content reports on the asphalt, what did you do?

A. I reviewed the reports to determine how many samples complied with the specifications.

Q. What did you find?

A. I determined that many of the reports — a majority — were outside the permissible bounds for air content.

Q. Did I ask you to prepare an illustrative chart on this point?

A. Yes, you did.

Q. What did you do?

A. I illustrated the air content test samples from the job, showing those that were in and out of the boundaries specified.

Counsel: Your Honor, may I place a chart on the easel here? Counsel has a copy. It was premarked Plaintiff's Exhibit 18.

The Court: You may.

Q. Mr. Finn, what is this?

A. It's the chart of test reports on air content that I prepared.

Q. Who actually reviewed the reports and plotted the results on this chart?

A. I did.

Q. Are they all accurate to your knowledge?

A. Yes.

Counsel: Your Honor, may I ask that the witness be permitted to approach the chart to explain it?

The Court: Mr. Finn, if you want to approach the chart, please do.

Q. Mr. Finn, please explain what the chart represents.

A. [The witness explains the chart, describing what it represents and drawing his conclusions in response to questions from counsel. The attorney needs to make sure that the witness identifies for the record matters he points and refers to. If necessary, counsel should have references noted on the chart.]

[At conclusion of the explanation:]

Counsel: Your Honor, we offer this exhibit as Plaintiff's Exhibit 18.

The Court: Any objection? It will be admitted.

These approaches are suggestions. You may want to vary them as circumstances and your personal style require. Just remember to establish why the exhibit is helpful, that it is accurate, and remember to offer it. Additionally, use the exhibit to emphasize important aspects of the witness's testimony.

§ 8-16.   Using Demonstrative Exhibits.

Demonstrative exhibits are a great means to explain complicated testimony. These exhibits grab attention and provide a means for emphasis. You need to make sure that the exhibits enhance rather than clutter the presentation, however, and that the record accurately reflects their use. Otherwise, the exhibits may be counterproductive.

As helpful as demonstrative exhibits can be, you should not force them into the presentation. Use these exhibits when they can aid understanding or emphasize points. If you use too many demonstrative exhibits, the most important ones lose their impact. Additionally, numerous exhibits may make the presentation cumbersome. A sparing use of demonstrative exhibits keeps the presentation smooth.

When used for emphasis, demonstrative exhibits are like italics in a brief. If the author inserts emphasis throughout the document, the reader is not likely to take special note of any of it. Emphasis on truly important passages, on the other hand, has its desired effect. Similarly, picking the best points for emphasis, and limiting the number of exhibits, are important in bringing out key points.

Generally, the witness should explain the exhibit. Direct examination is supposed to focus on the witness; having him explain an exhibit is a great way to provide this focus. If possible, have the witness approach the exhibit so that he can "teach" the jury what it means. Keep control of the presentation by using specific questions, but let the witness do the explaining. Stay a good distance from the witness and exhibit so that he can speak to the jurors freely; if you approach the exhibit, your exchange with the witness may seem to leave the jurors out. Do not get between the jurors and the exhibit.

You should prepare testimony with every witness you call on direct, but this action is especially important with a witness who sponsors demonstrative exhibits. The presentation should be planned and rehearsed to ensure that key points are clear. Both you and the witness should have the same understanding of the plan for developing points. In the testimony, address the mechanics of the exhibit first. Then, the witness can explain the meaning of the exhibit, without the need for explanatory digressions.

Additionally, you should plan the physical use of the exhibit. Keep it hidden until the time for its presentation. You should ensure that you can set up the exhibit quickly and efficiently. If you have additional points to cover once the exhibit is presented, put it away. If time is needed to set up the exhibit, do it during a break.

One of the biggest problems in using an exhibit is making sure the record captures the witness's explanations. Frequently, references to the exhibit are not recorded because no one bothers noting them. The people in the courtroom can see what happens, but a panel of appellate judges cannot. An example illustrates this point:

Counsel:	[Questioning witness with a map] Now that you've identified the map, can you tell us where you were standing?
A.	Right here.
Q.	Where were the two men you saw running?
A.	About there.
Q.	Which way were they headed?
A.	This way.
Q.	Which way did they turn?
A.	Like this.
Q.	Thank you. I'd now like to discuss . . . .

Obviously, the appellate judges would not have the faintest idea what the witness described. Thus, you need to have the witness make his references on the exhibit, explain his testimony by reference to the exhibit, or otherwise make a record of his explanation. An example follows.

Q.	Where were you that evening?
A.	About right here, on Maple.
Q.	You're pointing to the corner of Maple and Lowerline?
A.	Yes.
Q.	Would you mark a T for Thompson at that point, using the marker?
A.	Sure [marking].
Q.	Where were the two men?
A.	Here.
Q.	For the record, you're pointing to a spot across Maple, still near Lowerline?
A.	Right.

> Q.   Mark that with two Ms, please, for two men.
>
> A.   Okay [marking].
>
> Q.   Which way did they go?
>
> A.   This way.
>
> Q.   Which way is that on the map?
>
> A.   Toward Broadway.
>
> Q.   Put a little arrow pointing in that direction, please.
>
> A.   Sure [marking].

This approach permits the appellate judges to reconstruct the witness's testimony. In making sure the record is complete, some leading is usually permitted. Alternatively, you can describe what the witness is doing "for the record," so long as your description is accurate.

A more difficult problem arises when the witness draws on a blackboard. This kind of illustration is sometimes necessary when a point is more difficult to explain than you anticipated. An impromptu drawing can make it simple. The only problem is that the blackboard is not part of the record; the drawing may "disappear" for purposes of appellate review. Therefore, you should copy the drawing for the record, perhaps during a break, so you can offer it. Alternatively, you could take an instant photograph and offer the picture.

In cross-examination, your opposing counsel can use your exhibit and may try to mark on it. You can object, but your effort to stop the marking may seem unfair, and the judge may allow it. Thus, you may want to have a clear overlay available to permit your opponent to make markings without changing your exhibit. Similarly, if *you* want to mark on your opponent's exhibits in cross-examination, have an overlay available. You can use the overlay if direct marking is not allowed.

You also can use demonstrative exhibits to illustrate matters in cross-examination. Most judges allow counsel to have an expert create an exhibit in cross-examination, assuming this approach does not consume too much time. A better approach is to prepare an exhibit in advance and lead the witness through it. If you use an exhibit for cross-examination, plan your questions and use of the exhibit carefully. As long as the presentation is crisp, the judge should allow it.

§ 8-17.   Videotapes, Computer Recreations, and Similar Exhibits.

A higher than normal foundation may be required for videotapes, motion pictures, tape recordings, computer animations, and similar exhibits, because of the heightened opportunity to fabricate or distort events and the enhanced potential for prejudice.[35] Generally, the photographer, the recording engineer, or a witness must testify to the circumstances of the filming or recording, so that the opposing party has the opportunity to uncover any attempts at distortion. If the evidence does not accurately represent what its proponent claims, the court should exclude it.[36]

Two types of videotapes or films are commonly used in trials. One is the surveillance film, often used to show that a purportedly injured plaintiff is capable of normal activities. Those films have the potential to distort events because they usually show brief intervals of activity. Periods of rest typically are not included, and the film may not reflect the plaintiff's discomfort. Courts thus are wary of surveillance films. Nevertheless, the evidence is highly probative as to damages and should be admitted unless there is a special reason for concern. The court may require that you provide the evidence to the opposing party before the trial so there is an opportunity to respond to perceived distortions.

A second typical film is one depicting a "day in the life" of a plaintiff, to dramatize the person's injury. These films are easily staged and may provide the jurors with little information beyond what they can see in court. The films also may create excessive sympathy. On the other hand, a day-in-the-life film is sometimes the only reasonable method to provide a full understanding of the plaintiff's discomfort.

Courts are wary of films that are geared more to create sympathy than provide information. They often apply procedural safeguards to the filming. Normally, notice of the intent to use a "day in the life" film must be given the opposing party and that party must be allowed to review the film. The opposing side also is entitled to conduct discovery regarding the filming process.

Computer simulations and mechanical recreations are great means of persuasion, but they also have special potential for prejudice. People tend to give added credence to simulations and recreations. Some jurors may confuse an animation with the real event. In deciding whether to admit the evidence, the court must determine whether it really will help the jury's understanding; it must weigh that benefit against the potential for prejudice.

One test of an illustrative animation is its consistency with the facts that are known about an event. The input assumptions must "fit" the facts or the exhibit should be deemed irrelevant and unduly prejudicial. The sponsoring witness must have knowledge of the basis for the animation and the process by which it was created, or the opposing party cannot effectively cross-examine the accuracy of the animation. If the simulation is not offered to illustrate the event itself, but

---

[35] See Robert D. Brain & Daniel J. Broderick, *Demonstrative Evidence: The Next Generation*, 17 LITIG. 21 (1991).

[36] MCCORMICK ON EVIDENCE § 214 (5th ed. 1999).

to illustrate more general principles, a cautionary instruction may be necessary to ensure the jury understands the difference.

When a computer simulation is not merely illustrative, but provides the basis for an expert's opinion, the expert must establish the reliability and fit of the model used to derive his results. Section 10-5 discusses these requirements.

§ 8-18.　Pointers for Creating Demonstrative Exhibits.

Demonstrative exhibits should serve two purposes: (1) they should aid the trier of fact in understanding the evidence, and (2) they should further the goal of persuasion. The following techniques should help you accomplish these objectives.

§ 8-18(a).　Make Sure the Exhibit is Large Enough to See.

To be effective, an exhibit has to be large enough for the audience to see it. Not only the overall chart, but its content — including the numbers and the print — should be visible. This concept seems obvious, but attorneys routinely present demonstrative exhibits that are not visible to all the members of the audience.

Often attorneys present blowups of printed or typed material. The blowup may be a key paragraph from a contract, a construction specification, a damaging admission in a letter, or other written material that counsel wishes to emphasize. Unfortunately, the original written material is often so tiny that an enlargement is still too small to read from several yards away. Further, counsel sometimes neglects to delete extraneous material, so that the key passage seems to be lost in gray. As a result, the blowup may fail to bring out the important information.

A better way to dramatize a written passage is to have it printed or drawn in clearly visible letters. Delete unimportant portions of the passage. You should not unfairly edit the passage to present a one-sided picture, since it may be objectionable as incomplete.[37] Include the essential complete passage that you wish to emphasize.

Use the same approach with other demonstrative exhibits. You should make sure that information necessary to understand exhibits is visible, including any legend or numerical range that gives meaning to bar charts and graphs. Similarly, you may wish to use enlarged models. For instance, rather than using a life-size skeleton to illustrate a spinal injury, you might employ an enlarged version of the spinal column. This approach makes it easier for viewers to see the presentation.

---

[37] See FED. R. EVID. 106.

§ 8-18(b). Set Up the Ranges of a Chart or Graph to Dramatize its Points.

The numerical range on a chart or graph can have a huge effect on its demonstrative success. Without distorting the data unfairly, you should select a range that brings out the importance of the values displayed on the exhibit. Generally, the range should be smaller, to make the differences or trend on the chart appear larger.

As an example, assume a party wishes to emphasize the excessive profits earned by a corporation in a three-year period. If an annual profit of 10 percent were "normal," based perhaps on an historic average, profits of 13, 14 and 15 percent would represent substantial increases. Assuming counsel presented a bar chart reflecting these results, depicted over a range of zero to 50 percent, the differences would appear very small. This approach is depicted in Figure 1. If the advocate chose a range of 10 to 15 percent, on the other hand, the differences would appear substantial. This strategy is reflected in Figure 2.

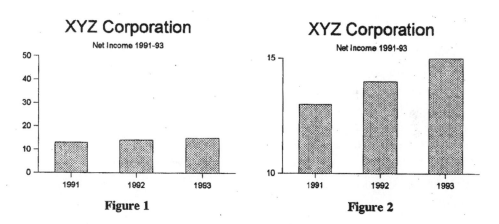

Figure 1   Figure 2

This form of advocacy rarely produces an objection so long as the method of emphasis is defensible.[38] In the presentation of profits, for instance, you might argue that the range of 10 to 15 percent is more consistent with the earnings experience of most companies than a greater range. You should have a reason ready for the choice of range, but it is usually unnecessary to present it. You also should make sure that the witness sponsoring the chart — usually an expert — is able to testify that the range is reasonable.

---

[38] See Roland v. Langlois, 945 F.2d 956, 963 (7th Cir. 1991) (demonstrative evidence does not have to be completely accurate to be admitted, provided that the jury is alerted to any perceived inaccuracies).

§ 8-18(c).   Use Colors to Dramatize the Message.

Color is another method of emphasizing the point of a chart or graph. Different colors bring out different aspects of a chart in a dramatic way.

In the charts set forth in the preceding paragraph, you could use blue to color the portions of each bar below the "normal" line, while employing red to represent the earnings above the norm. The different colors dramatize the impact of the "over" earnings. Similarly, if you presented a chart of construction test samples, you might choose red for the entries that were outside specifications and another color for the rest. This approach makes it easy to see the point of the exhibit.

The colors on any chart should be consistent. If red is "bad," all the bad should be red. The colors should be consistent with common expectations; red is an expected choice for "bad," blue a color that might be "good," and green a color associated with "money." Illustrate different concepts with different colors; if you use the same color to illustrate different points, the exhibit may confuse the viewers. You should experiment with colors to see which combinations have the best impact.

§ 8-18(d).   Make the Exhibits Simple.

Demonstrative exhibits often are used to illustrate complex processes. Unfortunately, the exhibit sometimes turns out as complex as the process, serving only to compound any confusion. Thus, you should conceive exhibits that demonstrate points in a simple, while accurate, way.

Spend time thinking about the point and how it could be illustrated graphically. Make rough drawings of various ideas, trying to see which works the best. As you make these attempts, new ideas may occur that improve the illustration. Seeking advice from others — especially disinterested persons who are not caught up in the case — also can be effective to simplify an exhibit.

You should employ the following tests to determine if an exhibit is unduly complex:

1. *Does the exhibit seek to accomplish too much?* Do not try to make too many points with a single exhibit. Generally, limit the exhibit to a single concept.

2. *Is the exhibit too busy?* On the best exhibits, the theme stands out. Usually the way to make it stand out is to surround it with white, black or other blank space. If the observers have to pick out the key concept from a maze of arrows, lines, bars or other symbols, the chances are they will be confused.

3. *Does the exhibit contain too much writing?* Except for those that are designed solely to depict writings, the best exhibits emphasize graphics. The point of an exhibit is to illustrate a matter the witness will explain.

Thus, explanatory writing may be unnecessary and may clutter the illustration. Some descriptive writing obviously may be helpful — to label the parts of a machine, for instance — but lengthy written explanations are inadvisable.

§ 8-18(e). Limit the Use of Textual Exhibits.

Simply to have demonstrative exhibits, many attorneys blow up pages of text. Often they include too much writing, so that the important passages receive no emphasis. Moreover, the print is often so small — even on a blown-up poster — that the material is difficult to read. You need to make sparing use of textual exhibits and make sure they are really helpful.

Lawyers often use exhibits that merely list points for testimony or argument. These are "lazy lawyer" exhibits. They provide something to look at, but add nothing to the presentation. The only true benefit of a point list is to illustrate your structure, but good transitional techniques accomplish the same purpose. Additionally, point lists sometimes deaden a presentation because the listeners focus on the list rather than the testimony. Thus, you should use exhibits to illustrate, rather than list, your points.

§ 8-18(f). Make Sure the Exhibit Is Accurate and the Witness Has Knowledge to Sponsor It.

Just as a good illustration can bring a point home, an error in an exhibit may undercut its impact and call into question the sponsoring witness's credibility. People naturally assume that something committed to writing — particularly an exhibit to be used at trial — will be prepared correctly. Unfortunately, counsel and the witness too often delegate the task of preparing exhibits and fail to check them. If the error is brought out in cross-examination, the jury may give it undue importance. Additionally, the discovery of an error in the depiction of data may unnerve the witness and facilitate cross-examination.

The easy solution is to ensure that the sponsoring witness actually prepares the exhibit or at least checks it against source data. You should also check the exhibit. This approach avoids unnecessary embarrassment.

§ 8-18(g). Watch Out for Boomerangs.

One of the biggest killers in a trial is an exhibit turned against its proponent. Witnesses unwittingly may prepare exhibits that contain points for the opposing side. You should scrutinize the exhibit to avoid this problem.

III. OBJECTIONS AND SUBMISSIONS OF EXHIBITS TO JURY

§ 8-19. Potential Objections to Exhibits.

Exhibits, like other evidence, are always objectionable for lack of foundation or relevance. Both requirements are mere "bumps," rather than hurdles, however. The necessary foundation is evidence sufficient to support a finding the exhibit is what its proponent claims.[39] An exhibit having any tendency to make a fact of consequence more or less probable satisfies the relevance requirement.[40] Exhibits offered for their contents must satisfy the original writing rule. Other common objections include the following:

§ 8-19(a). Prejudice.

Some exhibits are so stark as to present a danger of inflaming the jury. Depending on whether the exhibits are needed to present the case, the court may exclude them or limit the number that may be introduced.[41] As an example, the court might admit one photograph of a bloody wound, but exclude others. The ruling would reflect the "balancing" test of FRE 403: Is relevance substantially outweighed by prejudice?

§ 8-19(b). Misleading or Confusing.

Under the Rule 403 balancing test, the court may exclude an exhibit if its relevance is substantially outweighed by the likelihood that it would mislead or confuse the jury. A chart drawn to an extremely biased scale or a photograph of only part of a scene might be deemed inadmissible for this reason.

§ 8-19(c). Hearsay.

Documents containing statements and offered to prove facts the statements describe raise the hearsay issue. Someone made the written statement out of court; thus, it is an "out-of-court statement offered for the truth of the matter asserted." The hearsay rules apply to written statements as much as oral statements. Of course, a party often offers a document for other purposes than to show the truth of the document's contents. For example, a contract might be offered to show its existence; a written warning might be offered to show notice. Additionally, the rule might define the statement as non-hearsay or provide a hearsay exception to permit its introduction.[42] Nevertheless, you must consider the hearsay problem whenever you offer an exhibit containing written statements.

---

[39] FED. R. EVID. 901.

[40] FED. R. EVID. 401.

[41] See Nachtsheim v. Beech Aircraft Corp., 847 F.2d 1261, 1276–77 (7th Cir. 1991).

[42] See generally United States v. Merida, 985 F.2d 198 (5th Cir. 1993).

§ 8-20. Submitting Exhibits to Jury During Deliberations.

Conflicting practices exist on whether jurors may take exhibits into deliberations. Explicit rules on the subject do not exist in many jurisdictions; the court instead balances the need for review of the exhibit against the potential for prejudice. An attorney whose case depends heavily on exhibits — or feels she has won the "exhibit war" — may gain an advantage by convincing the judge to submit exhibits for deliberation. Conversely, opposing counsel should try to keep them out of the jurors' hands.

§ 8-20(a). "Real" Exhibits.

Courts are more likely to provide real exhibits for jury deliberations than demonstrative exhibits. These exhibits are not prepared especially for the trial and are less likely to be prejudicial. Thus, they often are allowed in deliberations. Even so, the court must balance need versus prejudice in deciding whether to submit real exhibits. A tangible object, such as a gun, knife, or bloody underpants, does not require close reexamination to remember it; at the same time, an undue focus on such an object might inflame the jurors' passions.

Unlike an object that can be remembered after observation — such as a knife — the jury may need a contract or similar writing to remember its contents. So long as they receive the entire writing, the likelihood of prejudice is small. Writings generally should be submitted to the jury absent a special reason for concern that they may be blown out of proportion.

§ 8-20(b). Demonstrative Exhibits.

The courts are less likely to submit demonstrative exhibits for jury deliberations. First, it may be impossible to provide the exhibits. A live, in-court demonstration or reenactment could not be submitted to the jury. Second, submitting models and exhibits used for demonstrations may tempt the jurors to conduct their own experiments. This extra-record experimentation could prejudice their deliberations. Third, the jurors' lack of expertise may preclude them from operating the equipment used in many demonstrative exhibits. Fourth, these exhibits often reflect advocacy, as they are created for the trial. The court may fear that the exhibits will unduly influence the jurors.[43]

Some courts hold it improper to submit demonstrative exhibits to the jury, some allow the practice, and some place the matter within the judge's discretion.[44] Obviously, if you have strong demonstrative exhibits, you should try to

---

[43] See generally Robert D. Brain & Daniel J. Broderick, *The Derivative Relevance of Demonstrative Evidence: Charting Its Proper Evidentiary Status*, 25 U.C. DAVIS L. REV. 957, 1022–23 (1992).

[44] The Ninth Circuit has held that a chart that is used only as a pedagogical device and an aid to understanding should not be admitted into evidence and should not be taken into the jury room. United States v. Wood, 943 F.2d 1048, 1053 (9th Cir. 1991); United States v. Abbas, 504 F.2d

convince the court to submit them. The strongest argument emphasizes why the jury needs the exhibit to understand the evidence. An exhibit that has an objective appearance and accurately reflects underlying evidence has the best chance of being given to the jury.

IV.   ORIGINAL WRITING RULE

§ 8-21.   Original Writing Rule (FRE 1002).

Historically, the law preferred the original to prove the contents of a writing.[45] Other evidence of its contents could be submitted only if the proponent showed that the original was unavailable and that unavailability was not due to his own procurement or serious fault.[46] The rule is often referred to as the "best evidence" rule, but that term often leads to misunderstandings. The rule applies only when counsel chooses, or is required, to prove a fact by offering the contents of a writing.

The federal rules adopt the original writing rule as a rule of preference. The rules generally permit the introduction of duplicates and relax the standard to admit other proof of a writing's contents. The rules extend the original writing requirements to the contents of photographs and recordings. The rule and related provisions are set out in FRE 1001-08. The basic rule requiring an original writing, recording, or photograph to prove its contents is FRE 1002. It provides:

> To prove the content of a writing, recording, or photograph, the original writing, recording, or photograph is required, except as otherwise provided in these rules or by Act of Congress.

The original writing rule is designed to ensure that the actual contents of a writing are provided the trier of fact. It requires that the actual language in a document be provided the trier rather than a witness's description, which might

---

123, 125 (9th Cir. 1974) (court stated that in general it was "better practice" not to allow the jury to take demonstrative exhibits to the jury room during deliberations), *cert. denied*, 421 U.S. 988 (1975); see also In re Guam Asbestos Litig. v. Owens-Corning Fiberglass Corp., No. 92-00064A, 1993 U.S. Dist.LEXIS 21131 (D. Guam 1993).

The Sixth Circuit has held that when a demonstrative exhibit has been properly admitted into evidence, the court may allow that exhibit to be submitted to the jury during deliberations. United States v. Scales, 594 F.2d 558, 564 (6th Cir. 1979), *cert. denied*, 441 U.S. 946 (1976).

Other federal circuit courts state that this issue is within the trial court's discretion. See, e.g., United States v. Pinto, 850 F.2d 927 (2d Cir. 1988), *cert. denied*, 488 U.S. 932 (1988) (trial court has discretion to allow properly admitted summary charts to be taken into the jury room during deliberations); United States v. Hofer, 995 F.2d 746 (7th Cir. 1993) (provided that district court is evenhanded in its evidentiary rulings, district court has wide discretion over whether an exhibit may be taken into jury room).

[45] MCCORMICK ON EVIDENCE § 229 (5th ed. 1999).

[46] *Id.*

have self-serving or even unintentional distortion. Thus, the rule serves as the basis for the objection that "the document speaks for itself," an objection often raised when a witness begins describing the contents of a document.

Additionally, the rule provides some protection against the fraudulent creation of documents and the selective copying of parts of writings; if the original must be produced, an adverse party may more easily discover errors and omissions.[47] Further, prior to the development of modern techniques for exactly replicating documents, the methods for making copies had the potential for errors. The requirement to produce the original protected against receipt of erroneous copies.

The use of the term "best evidence" suggests a broader application than that contained in the rule, one that is often misunderstood. The rule simply requires the original — subject to exceptions — when counsel seeks to prove the contents of a writing, recording, or photograph. The rule has no application to other kinds of real evidence.

Sometimes the writing is an ultimate fact that counsel needs to prove — the terms of a contract, the boundaries contained in a deed, the defamatory statement in a letter, and similar facts. In that situation, counsel would need to prove the contents of the writing and would have to introduce the writing to do so. Thus, the rule necessarily would apply.

In other cases, a writing is merely a means of proving independent facts: a receipt may be evidence of a sale, a memorandum may describe an event, or a recording may reflect a conversation. In proving that independent fact — the sale, the event, or the conversation — counsel would have to use the original only if he chose to use the writing, photograph or recording to prove the fact; if he chose to present testimony the rule would not apply.

The Advisory Committee Note explains the focus on proof of contents as follows:

> Application of the rule requires a resolution of the question whether contents are sought to be proved. Thus an event may be proved by non-documentary evidence, even though a written record of it was made. If, however, the event is sought to be proved by the written record, the rule applies. For example, payment may be proved without producing the written receipt which was given. Earnings may be proved without producing books of accounts in which they are entered. . . .[48]

In the example of a sale, a witness could testify that he paid the vendor for merchandise even if a receipt was provided as part of the transaction. Additionally, the witness could testify that a receipt was provided at the time of the sale,

---

[47] *Id.* § 231.

[48] FED. R. EVID. 1002 advisory committee's note.

assuming the mere existence of the receipt, rather than its contents, was relevant.[49] He could not testify, however, as to the content of the receipt — for instance, that it was marked "Paid." This original writing would be required to prove its content.

The rule rarely comes into play when testimony is presented concerning a scene that is also captured in a photograph. A witness who testifies concerning the scene does not describe what he saw in the photograph but describes the scene itself. If a photograph is used with the testimony, its purpose usually is illustrative: the witness adopts the photograph to illustrate his own description of the scene. According to the Advisory Committee, this method of illustrating the witness's testimony is not the same as proving the contents of the photograph, and the original photograph is not required. It states:

> The usual course is for a witness on the stand to identify the photograph or motion picture as a correct representation of events which he saw or of a scene with which he is familiar. In fact he adopts the picture as his testimony, or, in common parlance, uses the picture to illustrate his testimony. Under these circumstances, no effort is made to prove the contents of the picture, and the rule is inapplicable.[50]

Similarly, the witness could use a large drawing made from a picture to illustrate a description without violating the rule. Even though the drawing is based on the contents of the photograph, its use is permissible because it is only illustrative. If the content of the photograph were the subject of proof — perhaps in a copyright case — the rule would apply.

In civil litigation, most original writing issues are resolved in pretrial proceedings. The parties usually establish that the original writing rule is satisfied when they agree on the authenticity of documents. Problems may arise, however, in criminal cases and civil proceedings in which discovery and pretrial identification of evidence is restricted. In those situations the attorney needs to ensure compliance with the rule.

§ 8-22. Applicable Definitions: Original Writing Rule (FRE 1001).

FRE 1001 sets out the definitions used in interpreting the original writing rule. This provision contains an expansive definition of "writings and recordings." It also defines photographs. It makes clear that photographic prints, as well as negatives and printouts of computer data, are "originals." Similarly, the rule provides a printout or other readable output of electronic data stored in a computer

---

[49] MCCORMICK ON EVIDENCE § 233 (5th ed. 1999): "[E]vidence that a certain document is in existence or as to its execution or delivery is not within the rule and may be given without producing the document."

[50] FED. R. EVID. 1002 advisory committee's note.

is an original. Additionally, it defines electronic, chemical, and mechanical reproductions of originals as "duplicates." The rule states:

For purposes of this article the following definitions are applicable:

(1) Writings and recordings. "Writings" and "recordings" consist of letters, words, or numbers, or their equivalent, set down by handwriting, typewriting, printing, photostating, photographing, magnetic impulse, mechanical or electronic recording, or other form of data compilation.

(2) Photographs. "Photographs" include still photographs, X-ray films, video tapes, and motion pictures.

(3) Original. An "original" of a writing or recording is the writing or recording itself or any counterpart intended to have the same effect by a person executing or issuing it. An "original" of a photograph includes the negative or any print therefrom. If data are stored in a computer or similar device, any printout or other output readable by sight, shown to reflect the data accurately, is an "original."

(4) Duplicate. A "duplicate" is a counterpart produced by the same impression as the original, or from the same matrix, or by means of photography, including enlargements and miniatures, or by mechanical or electronic re-recording, or by chemical reproduction, or by other equivalent technique which accurately reproduces the original.

The definition of "writing" is broad enough to include inscriptions on objects, such as vehicle identification numbers and serial numbers. Obviously, counsel would have difficulty producing in court the "original" vehicle identification number on a car. As a practical matter, however, the provision does not present a problem because a photograph may be offered under FRE 1002 as a "duplicate." Further, under FRE 1004, other evidence of the writing may be offered if the matter is collateral.

§ 8-23. Admissibility of Duplicates (FRE 1003).

Modern techniques to produce exact copies of documents by mechanical or similar processes limit the need for an original writing rule. These duplicates are treated as reliable in the ordinary course of commerce and no reason exists to reject them in court absent a genuine question of authenticity. Thus, FRE 1003 permits the introduction of duplicates unless a genuine issue is raised as to the authenticity of the original or it would be unfair to admit the duplicate. The rule states:

A duplicate is admissible to the same extent as an original unless (1) a genuine question is raised as to the authenticity of the original or (2) in the circumstances it would be unfair to admit the duplicate in lieu of the original.

The original may still be required when a party offers a copy of part of an original, depending on whether the remainder of the document would change its meaning.[51]

§ 8-24. Other Evidence of Contents of a Writing, Recording, or Photograph (FRE 1004).

FRE 1004 permits the introduction of other evidence when the original is lost or destroyed, so long as the proponent did not lose or destroy it in bad faith. It also allows other evidence when a party cannot obtain the original by judicial process, the opposing party has the original and should have known it would be the subject of proof, or the evidence is collateral. The allowance of "other evidence" goes beyond duplicates to other types of copies and testimony. The rule states:

> The original is not required, and other evidence of the contents of a writing, recording, or photograph is admissible if —
>
> > **(1) Originals lost or destroyed.** All originals are lost or have been destroyed, unless the proponent lost or destroyed them in bad faith; or
> >
> > **(2) Original not obtainable.** No original can be obtained by any available judicial process or procedure; or
> >
> > **(3) Original in possession of opponent.** At a time when an original was under the control of the party against whom offered, that party was put on notice, by the pleadings or otherwise, that the contents would be a subject of proof at the hearing, and that party does not produce the original at the hearing; or
> >
> > **(4) Collateral matters.** The writing, recording, or photograph is not closely related to a controlling issue.

Although Section 2 of the rule is phrased in absolute terms — requiring that the original cannot be obtained by "any available judicial process or procedure" — it probably requires only that the proponent make reasonable efforts to produce the original.[52] Additionally, a party is not required to engage in a pointless effort when judicial process obviously will be unavailing.

---

[51] FED. R. EVID. 1003 advisory committee's note.

[52] 6 JACK B. WEINSTEIN & MARGARET A. BERGER, WEINSTEIN'S EVIDENCE § 1004.02 (2nd ed. 1997).

When the proponent has lost or destroyed an original, he has the burden of proving the absence of bad faith. If he fails to provide a satisfactory explanation, the court may exclude the secondary evidence.[53]

§ 8-25.   Certified or Compared Copies of Public Records (FRE 1005).

FRE 1005 creates a special hierarchy for proof of official records and documents recorded in public offices. It provides:

> The contents of an official record, or of a document authorized to be recorded or filed and actually recorded or filed, including data compilations in any form, if otherwise admissible, may be proved by copy, certified as correct in accordance with rule 902 or testified to be correct by a witness who has compared it with the original. If a copy which complies with the foregoing cannot be obtained by the exercise of reasonable diligence, then other evidence of the contents may be given.

The rule, designed to avoid the production of original public records in court, is more restrictive than FRE 1003, which permits the introduction of duplicates of other documents. FRE 1005 requires that copies of public records be certified or that a witness testify the copy is correct after comparing it with the original, unless complying with these requirements is not feasible. Thus, it creates a "preference . . . for certified or compared copies," in order to avoid opening the door "to the introduction of every kind of secondary evidence of contents of public records. . . ."[54]

§ 8-26.   Charts, Summaries, and Calculations (FRE 1006).

FRE 1006 permits the introduction of summaries, charts, and calculations depicting voluminous original material. It requires that the proponent make the originals or duplicates available for inspection and copying and permits the court to order their production in court. The rule states:

> The contents of voluminous writings, recordings, or photographs which cannot conveniently be examined in court may be presented in the form of a chart, summary, or calculation. The originals, or duplicates, shall be made available for examination or copying, or both, by other parties at reasonable time and place. The court may order that they be produced in court.

This provision allows the use of charts, summaries, and calculations in lieu of the original documents.

The rule does not limit the use of charts and other demonstrative evidence to circumstances where records are voluminous. Charts or summaries may be

---

[53] See Seiler v. Lucasfilm, Ltd., 613 F. Supp. 1253 (N.D. Cal. 1984), *aff'd*, 797 F.2d 1504 (9th Cir. 1986).

[54] FED. R. EVID. 1005 advisory committee's note.

presented simply to illustrate complex material. See § 8-14. Any chart or summary would have to fairly reflect evidence admitted into the record, however, so the original writing rule would already be satisfied as to that evidence. If the original material were voluminous, FRE 1006 would permit the introduction of the summary so long as the originals were made available.

§ 8-27. Adverse Party's Written or Testimonial Admission as to Contents (FRE 1007).

FRE 1007 permits proof of the contents of a writing, recording, or photograph by the testimony or deposition of the party against whom it is offered or by his written admission. This proof may be accepted in lieu of the original. The evidence must be offered against the party making the admission. The rule requires that the party make the admission in trial testimony, a deposition, or in writing. It does not allow proof of contents through a party's ordinary statements because of the risk of misunderstanding. The rule provides:

> Contents of writings, recordings, or photographs may be proved by the testimony or deposition of the party against whom offered or by the party's written admission, without accounting for the nonproduction of the original.

Presumably the definition of "party" would be determined consistently with FRE 801(d)(2), governing non-hearsay admissions. Obviously, the substantive scope of FRE 1007 is more restrictive, however, because it requires a written or testimonial admission; ordinary oral statements would be excluded. FRE 801(d)(2) treats any statement of a party offered against that party as an admission.

Read literally, the rule permits the examination of the adverse party on the contents of a document even if the original is available. The original writing rule would prevent this examination for anyone else. If the original already is in the record, however, this inquiry might nevertheless be circumscribed since the document "speaks for itself" and the testimony would be cumulative.

§ 8-28. Role of Judge and Jury Concerning Proof of Contents (FRE 1008).

FRE 1008 establishes the role of judge and jury with respect to the original writing rule. Essentially, it delegates to the court the function of determining whether factual conditions for admissibility are fulfilled: for instance, whether an original is lost or destroyed. It preserves to the jury issues relating to the existence or contents of the original if the matter is disputed. Thus, even if the court determined that a copy could be admitted, the jury still could decide if the copy was a forgery.[55] The rule provides:

---

[55] FED. R. EVID. 104.

When the admissibility of other evidence of contents of writings, recordings, or photographs under these rules depends upon the fulfillment of a condition of fact, the question whether the condition has been fulfilled is ordinarily for the court to determine in accordance with the provisions of rule 104. However, when an issue is raised (a) whether the asserted writing ever existed, or (b) whether another writing, recording, or photograph produced at the trial is the original, or (c) whether other evidence of contents correctly reflects the contents, the issue is for the trier of fact to determine as in the case of other issues of fact.

CHAPTER 9

CROSS-EXAMINATION AND IMPEACHMENT

---

§ 9-1.   Introduction.

In cross-examination, the attorney questions witnesses called as part of her opponent's case. The witnesses typically are highly to mildly adverse, so the rules permit counsel to lead them — suggesting facts and asking the witnesses to concede that they are correct. Cross-examination permits the lawyer to bring out the "other side" of the story the witness relates. At the same time, counsel often can prove facts central to her own case through cross-examination. These facts become highly credible building blocks for argument, because they come from witness called by the adverse side.

Cross-examination presents a special opportunity for advocates. Listeners, sensing a coming conflict, often heighten their attention for cross-examination. The attorney takes the stage in cross-examination, leading the discussion, ordering the topics and choosing the terminology to describe facts. With a powerful cross-examination, a lawyer can establish huge momentum in her effort to persuade jurors that she is right.

To cross-examine witnesses effectively, you must know the rules governing the examination, including the rules for impeachment. You must understand the psychology of cross-examination, prepare thoroughly, and apply the best techniques. This chapter addresses these matters. Sections 9-2 and 9-3 discuss the constitutional stature and importance of cross-examination. Sections 9-4 and 9-5 review rules governing the examination. Section 9-6 addresses the goals of cross-examination and §§ 9-7–9-23 address methods to achieve an effective cross-examination. Examples of cross-examination are set forth in §§ 9-24 and 9-25. Sections 9-26–9-37 discuss the rules governing impeachment and effective impeachment techniques.

I. CROSS-EXAMINATION

§ 9-2. Constitutional Guarantee of Cross-Examination.

The right of cross-examination is basic to the American judicial process. Legal scholars, judges, and lawyers endorse it as the most effective procedural tool for determining the truth. Cross-examination is essential to securing accurate testimony in view of witnesses' tendencies to make mistakes, selectively recall and emphasize facts and, in some instances, perjure themselves.[1]

The right has constitutional status. In criminal cases it is guaranteed as part of the right of confrontation, provided in the Sixth Amendment. As Justice Hugo Black stated in *Pointer v. State of Texas*,[2] "There are few subjects, perhaps, upon which this Court and other courts have been unanimous than in their expressions of belief that the right of confrontation and cross-examination is an essential and fundamental requirement for the kind of fair trial which is the country's constitutional goal." The Supreme Court also has held that the due process clause

---

[1] See generally United States v. McClintock, 748 F.2d 1278 (9th Cir. 1984), *cert. denied*, 474 U.S. 822 (1985); United States v. Williamson, 202 F.3d 974, 977 (7th Cir. 2000); Boggs v. Collins, 226 F.3d 728 (6th Cir. 2000).

[2] 380 U.S. 400, 405 (1965).

requires confrontation in some noncriminal proceedings, although the scope of the due process right is more restricted than the Sixth Amendment right.[3]

The premise that cross-examination is essential to determining the truth is the principal justification for the rule excluding hearsay. The premise also explains why prior testimony, taken when the adverse party had the opportunity for cross-examination, traditionally has been admitted under an exception to the hearsay rule when the declarant is unavailable.[4]

§ 9-3. Importance of Cross-Examination.

In a trial each party portrays a picture of the facts that favors his side. Generally, a witness on direct examination testifies to facts supporting the party who calls him. Cross-examination is the means by which the adverse party brings out facts that support his case, limits the impact of the witness's damaging testimony, or demonstrates that the witness is not believable.

Cross-examination often is a time of drama. The listeners realize that this event is a contest, pitting the lawyer against the witness. They expect to see confrontation and fireworks. Thus, they perk up and listen, at least until their expectations prove erroneous. Cross-examination therefore is a great opportunity to get points across.

Facts proven through cross-examination provide a powerful basis for persuasion. The jurors expect witnesses on direct examination to support the party who calls them. If a witness supports the adverse party's contentions, the concessions take on special weight. The attorney can argue that his claims are supported by witnesses for *both* sides, which removes much of the jury's difficulty in resolving conflicts. Thus, a major goal of cross-examination is to secure favorable concessions.

Cross-examination is also a great advocacy tool because it puts the lawyer on display. The attorney — not the witness — generally states the facts that become evidence; the witness accepts or denies them. By posing facts with an authoritative air, the attorney reinforces the impression that his claims are credible.

In a good cross-examination the witness must agree to counsel's points. A well-planned cross-examination establishes that the attorney knows the facts, making his "word picture" seem more credible. Further, by breaking down the facts within individual topics and linking questions for emphasis, counsel can "paint pictures" that support his portrayal. The momentum established in a good cross-examination can devastate the opposing side.

---

[3] See, e.g., Morrissey v. Brewer, 408 U.S. 471 (1972); Wolff v. McDonnell, 418 U.S. 539 (1974); Hannah v. Larche, 363 U.S. 420 (1960); Greene v. McElroy, 360 U.S. 474 (1960); *Confrontation and Cross-Examination in Executive Investigations*, 56 VA. L. REV. 487 (1970).

[4] FED. R. EVID. 804(b)(1).

Unfortunately, the typical cross-examination does not accomplish these objectives. Usually attorneys do not plan their cross-examinations well enough to have a powerful impact. Instead, they wait to hear a witness's direct testimony and repeat it, picking at isolated facts, arguing, and scoffing at explanations, without preplanned goals or backup material to establish that counsel is correct. This approach generally reemphasizes the points made on direct examination. It does not permit an offensive presentation because it replicates the structure chosen by the opposing party. Further, it suggests that counsel does *not* have a good basis for questions. Argument or scorn cannot substitute for a *demonstration* that the attorney's questions are fair.

The elements of a good cross-examination are those that govern the overall presentation: selection and emphasis. You should not go over everything the witness said but should *choose* subjects for discussion. By selecting topics in which the witness must concede points, you ensure that the examination advances the case. Additionally, you should develop and emphasize favorable points through the organization and form of questions. The combined effect of choosing the topics, organizing their presentation and breaking down the points into related, specific assertions — making "mountains out of molehills" — makes your points seem important and compelling.

A good cross-examination requires preparation. Contrary to the views of many lawyers, substance is more important than style. Attorneys may think their fulminations carry weight with jurors, but facts and backup evidence are more persuasive. You do need a strong, authoritative, credible style, but you also need a plan. Selecting the topics, breaking the points into specific parts, organizing a powerful presentation, and obtaining the backup material to secure concessions provides the basis for an authoritative air.

§ 9-4. Scope of Interrogation and Form of Questions (FRE 611(b)(c)).

Cross-examination usually is limited to (1) subjects covered during the direct examination, and (2) matters affecting the credibility of the witness.[5] Of course, the cross-examining attorney may pursue matters in greater depth than they were covered by the direct examiner and may cross-examine on subjects fairly connected with the subject of direct.[6] Thus, if the witness on direct mentioned that he observed an accident, counsel could probe the relevant details respecting

---

[5] See United States v. Ellis, 156 F.3d 493, 497–98 (3rd Cir. 1998) (affirming trial court's decision sustaining government's objection to [cross-examination] that exceeded scope of direct examination and did not involve matters of credibility).

[6] See United States v. Lara, 181 F.3d 183, 199 (1st Cir. 1999) (stating that "it is standard fare" for cross-examiners to inquire into matters not mentioned on direct examination, but related to that examination). See also United States v. Walker, 613 F.2d 1349 (5th Cir. 1980), *cert. denied*, 446 U.S. 944 (1980); United States v. Wolfson, 573 F.2d 216 (5th Cir. 1978).

that event, or could try to show that the witness was really in another city at the time.

The limit on the scope of cross-examination is designed to promote an orderly presentation of the case.[7] The rule generally permits the party presenting a case to choose the topics of discussion. Additionally, the rule historically was justified on the ground that a party vouched for her own witness; permitting an attorney to cover new areas on cross, rather than recalling the witness to present the new matter on direct, would allow her to escape that requirement. The concept of vouching for a witness is now rejected in FRE 607 and could not support the scope limitation.[8]

Finally, the rule was defended on the ground that a party should not be allowed to lead on direct examination. Since covering new areas on cross examination is the same as conducting direct examination, the leading usually allowed on cross would be inappropriate. This problem is best dealt with, however, by requiring counsel to change the form of her questions.[9] Thus, only the first reason truly supports the restriction.

Despite the "orderly presentation" rationale, permitting counsel to cover new areas on cross-examination — but with nonleading questions — may expedite the trial, promote the convenience of witnesses, and permit the most logical presentation of the facts. In many cases it may be inconvenient to terminate an examination and require a witness to be recalled. Further, "new" areas often are interrelated with matters already covered; determining the exact scope of the direct examination may be difficult. Thus, the rule is "phrased in terms of a suggestion rather than a mandate to the trial judge"[10] and gives him discretion to permit inquiry into new areas "as if on direct examination." Rule 611(b) states:

> (b) Scope of cross-examination — Cross-examination should be limited to the subject matter of the direct examination and matters affecting the credibility of the witness. The court may, in the exercise of discretion, permit inquiry into additional matters as if on direct examination.

The Advisory Committee states that a lawyer covering new issues "cannot ask leading questions but must act as if he were undertaking to present the witness' direct examination."[11] Presumably, the party could lead a hostile or adverse witness on new points, since this practice would be permitted on direct.[12]

---

[7] FED. R. EVID. 611(b) advisory committee's note.

[8] *Id.*

[9] *Id.*

[10] FED. R. EVID. 611(b) advisory committee's note.

[11] *Id.*

[12] See § 7-4.

Some jurisdictions depart from the traditional common law approach and allow "wide open" cross-examination — questioning on any relevant issue.[13] This approach also can be justified under the "orderly presentation" rationale, since it promotes a complete examination of each witness and avoids the repetition that might occur if a witness were recalled. Additionally, the rule permits the defendant to present his evidence during the case of the prosecution or plaintiff, which may keep the jury from jumping to unwarranted conclusions.

In permitting the trial judge to allow inquiry into new matters on cross-examination, the federal rule recognizes that the more restrictive approach does not have compelling support. The judge generally should restrict the scope of cross-examination but has discretion to dispense with the rule when he deems it appropriate.

FRE 611(c) generally permits the lawyer to interrogate the witness with leading questions. Leading questions are those that suggest the answer; the lawyer, rather than the witness, provides the substantive assertion in a question form: "You were wearing a plaid jacket, is that correct?" FRE 611(c) states that "[o]rdinarily leading questions should be permitted on cross-examination." This rule is designed to make the use of leading questions on cross-examination a matter of right, except when the "cross-examination" is really so friendly that leading questions should not be permitted.[14] The rule contains no explicit exception, but the term "[o]rdinarily" suggests that leading questions are improper in some circumstances, such as when an advocate "cross-examines" his own client.[15] The Advisory Committee note to Rule 611(c) states:

> The purpose of the qualification "ordinarily" is to furnish a basis for denying the use of leading questions when the cross-examination is cross-examination in form only and not in fact, as for example the "cross-examination" of a party by his own counsel after being called by the opponent (savoring more of redirect) or of an insured defendant who proves to be friendly to the plaintiff.

Court rulings indicate that the trial judge has discretion to deny the use of leading questions in this situation.[16]

---

[13] LSA-C.E. art. 611.

[14] FED. R. EVID. 611(c) advisory committee's note.

[15] There is not an absolute right to ask leading questions on cross-examination. See Harris v. Steelweld Equip. Co., 869 F.2d 396 (8th Cir. 1989); Oberlin v. Marlin American Corp., 596 F.2d 1322 (7th Cir. 1979).

[16] See United States v. Koskerides, 877 F.2d 1129 (2nd Cir. 1989) (holding that determining the scope of cross-examination is a proper exercise of the district court's discretion). See also United States v. Wellman, 830 F.2d 1453 (7th Cir. 1987); Morvant v. Construction Aggregates Corp., 570 F.2d 626, 635 (1978); United States v. Hansen, 583 F.2d 325 (7th Cir. 1978).

§ 9-5. Common Objections to Cross-Examination.

The attorney should prepare the cross-examination to avoid running afoul of objections. The following objections are typical.

§ 9-5(a). Outside the Scope of Direct.

Generally, cross-examination is limited to the subject matter of the direct examination and matters affecting credibility. The court has discretion to permit inquiries on other relevant matters, but if the witness is not a party or identified with a party, may require that the additional examination be conducted with nonleading questions. The scope limitation does not prevent a detailed inquiry regarding subjects covered on direct, nor does it preclude an examination on matters logically connected to the direct.[17]

§ 9-5(b). Argumentative.

Often a poorly prepared cross-examination deteriorates into an argument. The witness makes an assertion unsatisfactory to counsel, and the attorney responds with a question that incorporates some perceived reason the witness is wrong: "But you couldn't have seen a knife if the street light was a block away, could you?" One or two questions of this type might be permitted as legitimate follow up, but once it is apparent counsel and witness are simply jousting, the court should not permit the continuation of the line of inquiry.[18]

§ 9-5(c). Rephrasing or Paraphrasing.

Attorneys often restate the witness's testimony or paraphrase the testimony of others during cross-examination. An example:

Q.	Earlier you said you weren't paying much attention as you approached the traffic light. How far away were you when you noticed the light?

This gratuitous "testifying" by counsel is improper. A sharp witness may intervene and correct an inaccurate predicate, but generally the opposing attorney must object.

---

[17] See Roberts v. Hollocher, 664 F.2d 200, 203 (8th Cir. 1981) ("cross-examination may embrace any matter germane to direct examination, qualifying or destroying it, or tending to elucidate, modify, explain, contradict, or rebut testimony given by the witness"). But see Chesire Medical Center v. W.R. Grace, 853 F. Supp. 564 (D.NH 1994) (holding that Rule 611(b) does not confer upon a federal judge the right to permit inquiring beyond the scope of direct in every case. Rather, the general prescription is precisely the opposite.).

[18] See United States v. Medina, 992 F.2d 573, 578 (6th Cir. 1993), *cert. denied*, 510 U.S. 1109 (1994).

§ 9-5(d).   Compound.

A compound question is objectionable on cross-examination as well as on direct. Additionally, since this form allows the witness greater flexibility in answering, it may work to counsel's disadvantage. Indeed, the witness may respond to the part that can be denied, without addressing the rest of the inquiry; this tactic may leave the impression that the witness refuted the entire question. Additionally, a clever witness can make an attorney look silly in answering a compound question. Consider the following exchange:

> Q.   Were you in the car or in the house when you first realized your keys were missing?
>
> A.   Yes.

The witness's answer forces the attorney to clarify his own question and illustrates for all that it was compound.

§ 9-5(e).   Assumes Facts Not in Evidence, or "Misleading."

Counsel has the right to lead a witness in cross-examination, which permits putting words in the witness's mouth. If the attorney forms questions around a premise that has not been established, however, the inquiry may unfairly confuse the witness and mislead the jury.[19] Assume the following exchange:

> Q.   Why didn't your workmen provide timely construction reports to the engineer?
>
> A.   I can't imagine why not.

The answer may signify only that the witness is unaware of the fact asserted as the premise, yet suggests that the premise is true. The witness — who may not be quick enough to refute both question and premise — needs protection in this situation. Counsel should provide the protection, objecting to the assumption of a fact in the question. The attorney should describe the unfairness of the question in a way that both witness and jurors understand.

---

[19] See United States v. Oshatz, 912 F.2d 534, 537 (2d Cir. 1990), *cert. denied*, 500 U.S. 910 (1991) (court emphasized that, regarding non-expert character witness, a hypothetical question that assumes the defendant's guilt should not be allowed); United States v. Luffred, 911 F.2d 1011, 1016 (5th Cir. 1990) ("[a]n alleged bad act must have both a basis in fact and be relevant to character traits at issue before it may be used in cross-examination of a character witness"). See also United States v. O'Keefe, 128 F.3d 885 (5th Cir. 1997).

§ 9-5(f).   Asked and Answered.

If the witness fairly responds to a question, the attorney is not supposed to repeat it.[20] Repeating questions is a cousin of arguing with the witness, and happens more often in cross-examination than in direct. Counsel *is* entitled to a legitimate answer, however; thus, if the answer is not responsive, the attorney should be allowed to ask it again.[21] If you are forced to repeat a question, give some signal that the answer was not satisfactory: "Perhaps you misunderstood the question. Let me try again. . . ." Otherwise, the repetition may seem awkward and opposing counsel will be more prone to object.

§ 9-5(g).   Admonishing the Witness.

Often attorneys on cross-examination try to tell the witness how to answer a question and, in particular, not to explain: "Mr. Jones, I want you to answer this question 'yes' or 'no.' " This action is objectionable because the court, not counsel, has the job of admonishing the witness. Moreover, a witness is entitled to offer a fair explanation, even if the answer is "yes" or "no."

The advocate has a right to have the court require the witness to be responsive. Counsel should only ask for this instruction when the witness is obviously nonresponsive, however; the court is not likely to take sides unless the evasiveness is apparent. A better technique may be to subtly refer to the nonresponsiveness or ask the witness's cooperation in a personal way. See § 9-20. A request for cooperation is still technically outside counsel's role, but will not seem overreaching, may expedite the examination, and probably will not produce an objection.

§ 9-5(h).   Calls for Speculation.

As in direct examination, asking a hypothetical to a fact witness is objectionable as calling for speculation.

§ 9-6.   Goals of Cross-Examination.

Most lawyers fail to take advantage of the opportunity of cross-examination. They approach it defensively and off-the-cuff, sniping at the witness's direct testimony and relying on inspiration to provide the right questions. Cross-examination can be much more effective if used offensively, to establish points that support your version of the facts. Additionally, it has two defensive uses:

---

[20] This issue is within the court's discretion. See, e.g., United States v. Robinson, 832 F.2d 366 (7th Cir. 1987), *cert. denied*, 486 U.S. 1010 (1988).

[21] See United States v. Rubin, 733 F.2d 837, 841 (11th Cir. 1984) (district court correctly restricted cross-examination questions on matters that the witness already had responded to, because further evidence on these matters would have been merely cumulative); see also United States v. Coven, 662 F.2d 162, 170 (2d Cir. 1981), *cert. denied*, 456 U.S. 916 (1982).

(1) to limit or discredit the witness's factual account, or (2) to show that the witness is an untruthful person. To achieve any of these purposes you need to prepare, but preparation is especially important to an offensive presentation. The purposes are discussed below.

§ 9-6(a).   Offensive Cross-Examination.

In offensive cross-examination, you obtain the witness's agreement to facts that support your case. Often a witness called by the adverse party can support many of your assertions. If you gain her agreement on those matters, you eliminate reasonable dispute that those facts are correct. When a fact is supported both by your witness *and* the adverse party's witness, there is nothing for the jury to decide. Further, even if some adverse witnesses dispute your point, the fact that others support it gives you an edge in argument. Additionally, if you link and develop the concessions so that the witness appears to endorse part of your word picture, you reinforce that picture with the jury. Thus, offensive cross-examination can have great persuasive impact.

§ 9-6(b).   Defensive Cross-Examination.

There are two kinds of defensive cross-examination. Both are designed to counter the witness's testimony. The more typical examination focuses on the witness's factual portrayal, limiting its scope, undermining its basis, or showing it is mistaken. The second approach attacks the witness himself, showing that the person is likely to lie. These approaches are discussed below.

§ 9-6(b)(1).   Limiting and Discrediting Testimony.

You can attack the witness's testimony in cross-examination without necessarily impugning the witness's integrity. You may show that the witness does not have a good basis to testify — for instance, that he was not in a good position to observe the facts. You might attack the witness's certainty. You may ask the witness to concede facts that are logically inconsistent with his conclusions. While these methods imply that the witness's assertions are inaccurate, they are consistent with a failure of memory and descriptive errors as well as overt fabrication. Thus, they do not force the jury to judge the witness's character.

Cross-examination that limits or discredits testimony is consistent with, and can supplement, offensive cross-examination. Both approaches seek concessions that support your position. In offensive cross-examination, the witness is led to directly support your factual claims; in a fact-based, defensive cross-examination, his concessions indirectly support you by undercutting his adverse testimony. Therefore, the two approaches may be used together.

§ 9-6(b)(2).   Destroying the Witness's Credibility.

The second type of defensive cross-examination attacks the witness's credibility; in other words, it impugns his capacity to be truthful. Adopting this approach raises the stakes for both lawyer and witness. The cross-examination may destroy the witness's credibility, but it may not. Jurors typically do not want to conclude that a witness is a bad person. If you fail in your attack, the jurors may draw an adverse conclusion about you.

When you attack the witness's character for truthfulness, you attack him as a person. You may use his prior crimes or prior bad acts to show he has an untruthful character. You may show that he has a reason to testify falsely: bias, interest, or motive to fabricate. These grounds necessarily assume the witness would lie for loyalty or personal gain. You may adopt an attitude so scornful that it implies the witness cannot be believed. All of these approaches suggest that the witness is a liar, not that he is mistaken.

An attack on the witness's character can be combined with a defensive cross-examination that limits or discredits the testimony. It is harder to attack character while you simultaneously conduct an offensive cross-examination. The witness cannot establish points for you if he is a liar. Therefore, absent special circumstances, you generally would not combine an attempt to establish facts with an attack on the witness's integrity.

§ 9-7. Balance of Advantages in Cross-Examination: Lawyer vs. Witness.

In the contest of cross-examination, the witness and the lawyer each have advantages. Understanding these competing strengths should help you be effective. On balance, you have the upper hand in cross-examination, but only if you prepare thoroughly and use the right techniques.

The witness's primary advantage is the jury's sympathy. People generally identify with a lay person called as a witness; at the same time, they may not hold lawyers in the highest esteem. Additionally, they assume lawyers are trained for cross-examination and that the contest between lawyer and witness is an unfair fight. Since most people side with the underdog, particularly a sympathetic one, the jurors are likely to pull for the witness in cross-examination.

You can counter this advantage by focusing on facts rather than the witness's character; if the witness endorses the facts, you accomplish your objective without forcing the jurors to choose between you and the witness. You face an uphill battle, however, if you expect the jurors to accept your sarcasm and argument over the witness's factual descriptions. When the witness's testimony is obviously incredible you may succeed in doing so, but these situations are unusual.

Another advantage of the witness is his personal knowledge. The witness knows what he saw; your factual knowledge is secondhand. Thus, the witness has a better *basis* for portraying facts within his knowledge than you. Additionally, the witness may know facts that you have not discovered. These witness advantages provide the reason to be cautious in cross-examination; the wrong question may elicit credible, damaging evidence. To compensate for this advantage, you need to stick to selected topics and use the right questions.

Despite these witness strengths, you posses more powerful advantages. First, you get to choose the topics. You do not have to address subjects where the witness can hurt you. You decide the order in which the topics are addressed; since the witness has already told his story, you do not need to use a chronological structure. Further, you get to state the factual points, phrasing the questions so that the witness is forced to agree. In short, you *control* the discussion. If you use this control effectively, you can force the witness to support you, at least on selected matters. If the witness tries to change the subject or evade your questions, the jury's sympathies should shift toward you.

Second, you can develop good points. So long as you do not repeat yourself, you have considerable freedom to explore details. You can break points into smaller parts, each established through individual questions, and link them thematically to make them seem important. You can organize questions to build toward conclusions that counter the witness's general descriptions. You can even "paint pictures" by linking related facts and developing them through bit-by-bit enhancement.

Third, you should have a much better understanding of the overall fact picture than most witnesses. You know what other witnesses have said and will say. You know how the facts fit within the legal rules. You can use facts in ways that most witnesses cannot anticipate. Unless a witness has been prepared extensively, he is usually defenseless against a novel use of his testimony.

Fourth, you get to articulate the fact descriptions. You state the facts; if you can back them up, the witness must agree. In questions, you get to emphasize the words. In impeaching, you get to trumpet the key words from prior statements. The ability to choose and emphasize language allows you to dramatize the witness's concessions.

Fifth, although a reasonable lawyer approaches cross-examination with trepidation, the witness generally is more scared than the attorney. You at least know your plan and can prepare to make it work; the witness is not sure what to expect. More important, the witness may not be sure what material you have for impeachment. Because of their uncertainty, many witnesses — particularly inexperienced ones — give up concessions easily. You may be able to train a nervous witness to concede your assertions by "punishing" him — through impeachment — when he fails to agree.

These factors give you an advantage in cross-examination, but only if you employ them effectively. You need to be more prepared than the witness, have a plan for developing concessions, and use techniques that force the witness to agree to your assertions. Methods to accomplish these objectives are discussed in the following sections.

§ 9-8. Means to Obtain Factual Concessions.

The point of most cross-examinations is to get the witness to agree with your assertions. That said, the question remains: how do you do it? You generally cannot accomplish this objective with volume, argument, scorn, or disdain. You need to consider the witness's perspective. What would make him agree with your facts? Once you understand the witness's perspective, you can plan an examination that elicits concessions.

A witness usually wants to tell the truth. The oath — and the specter of a perjury prosecution — strengthen this commitment. At the same time, a witness generally has some relationship with the party who calls him. Typically he wants to help that party. Most witnesses meet with counsel before they testify and gain at least a general understanding of the attorney's objectives. Thus, the typical witness knows what the party wants to prove and tries to help, so long as he does not have to lie.

A witness may help your opponent's case during your cross-examination by injecting into responses information that helps your opponent. The response may deny your assertion, "explain" in a way that benefits your opponent, or depart from the question to address a different topic. To be effective, you need to formulate questions that the witness must answer correctly and that limit his ability to introduce harmful information.

Although loyal to your opponent, the typical witness has a stronger loyalty to himself. No one likes to look bad in front of an audience. Given a choice between supporting the party's case and appearing reasonable or truthful, virtually any witness chooses himself. Thus, a witness will try to avoid looking bad even if it hurts the party's case. Given these circumstances, you can develop a strong cross-examination using the witness's prior statements, rules of common sense, and propositions that have good general acceptance.

1. *Prior Statements.* Witnesses hate to appear untruthful. They do not like to be caught in inconsistencies. Most witnesses are aware of their prior testimony and feel compelled to repeat it. They also tend to conform their testimony to their other prior statements. They do not like to contradict documents that they prepared, reviewed, or otherwise adopted. Thus, prior testimony and other written material provide a good basis to determine what they will concede.

When a witness contradicts his own prior statement and is confronted with the inconsistency in trial, he pays a personal price. The fact that the witness made conflicting statements implies that he lied at least once. Being caught in the inconsistency is embarrassing. A witness who feels the pain of being exposed in a contradiction usually tries to avoid it happening again. Once he is convinced that the lawyer has prior statements or other documentation to support the facts posed in the examination, he tends to concede those facts. See § 9-13.

2. *Reason.* Witnesses also do not like to appear unreasonable. They tend to concede facts that flow logically from other, established facts. They do not like to defend positions that appear untenable. Therefore, their testimony often can be driven by logic and common sense. See § 9-13.

3. *"Motherhood" precepts.* Because witness do not wish to appear unreasonable, they readily accept propositions that they believe the factfinder would endorse. Thus, witnesses readily accept that "you must work to be successful," "a mother always loves her children," "preparation is important to success in school," and similar precepts. If the witness denies these points, usually he will undermine his legitimacy with jurors. Thus, these precepts provide a means to secure concessions. See § 9-14.

These factors provide the basis to prepare cross-examination. The witness can be counted on to protect himself. He generally will not defy common sense. He will try to avoid looking unreasonable or unfair. He will accept the correctness of facts asserted in his prior statements and other documents he endorsed or adopted. With these precepts in mind, you can predict with reasonable certainty what the witness will say.

The type of questions you ask also determines whether the witness will concede facts. Assuming you are prepared to back up your inquiries, the more specific your question, the more the witness is forced to concede it. General and conclusionary questions *invite* the witness to argue or explain. Argumentative questions invite argument. Specific, fact-based questions leave little room for explanation.

Additionally, a witness who attempts to evade or explain in response to a specific question appears unresponsive. Most witnesses are uncomfortable with this appearance and do not add explanations when they have no place. Even if a witness does so, the jurors can see when the answer goes beyond the scope of the question; they may conclude that the witness is advocating a position rather than telling the truth. In contrast, it seems appropriate for a witness to explain a response to a conclusionary or argumentative question.

§ 9-9. Taking Discovery for Cross-Examination.

To prepare a good cross-examination you need information to use in securing favorable responses. For important witnesses you need to take a comprehensive deposition. Additionally, you should organize documents that the witness has authored, adopted or must accept. For less important witnesses, you at least need a witness statement or report of an interview.

To conduct a useful deposition you need to understand its purpose. Most depositions are conducted for discovery. In this context, deposing a witness is like mining for gold; you have to sift through a lot of material to find the nuggets. Sometimes they are not apparent until you place them in context. Therefore, you should use a deposition for exploration. You need to find out what the witness has to say, whether it seems to hurt you in the deposition or not.

If the witness will be called by your adversary, the adversary generally can not use the deposition because it is hearsay. You can use it for impeachment, and you get to select what you use. Thus, getting "hurt" in a deposition makes no difference at the trial. At the same time, once alerted to problems in the deposition, you can prepare for them at trial.

Generally, you should not go into a deposition to make points. If you "destroy" the witness in a deposition, he will better prepare for meeting you at the trial. You need to find out everything the witness has to say, not just what the documentary discovery suggests he should say. Of course, you need to follow up on subjects and pin things down, but the overall tone should be exploratory.

Go into a deposition with an outline, not a list of questions. Make the outline comprehensive, but do not incorporate many preconceptions. Use open-ended questions that invite explanation. Keep the witness talking. Do so even if he seems to be hurting your case. Remember, enduring a little pain — which does not matter in the long run — gives you a great basis to prepare.

A comprehensive deposition allows a solid cross-examination. At trial, you get to select the nuggets, link them together by topic, and use them to establish your points. Frequently, assertions that appear damaging in a deposition can be used to support the questioner's position at trial. If material truly is harmful, you can omit it from your offensive presentation and prepare to counter it defensively.

In special situations, you may want to limit your exploration in a deposition. If you take a deposition to preserve testimony for trial — perhaps when the witness will be unavailable — you need to approach it as you would a trial examination. When you do not want to alert your opponent to certain points, you may wish to avoid them in a deposition. But generally you should assume your opponent will prepare adequately. Thus, you must explore to prepare yourself.

You also need to find and use other documents. In the modern era, most lawyers quickly become expert at document discovery, so it is not necessary to cover that topic here. Lawyers are not so good, however, at selecting documents for usc at trial. You need to find a few important documents — those that support the key points — and plan your cross-examination with them.

Usually an important document can be used for multiple purposes, eliminating the need to repeatedly lay foundations. If you use too many documents your cross-examination may become tedious, particularly if each supports a minor point. You should not spend most of your time identifying and referring to papers.

§ 9-10. Preparing for Cross-Examination.

Just about every advocate has his own idea of how to conduct a good cross-examination. Unfortunately, attorneys often seem to believe that their inherent talent produces an effective examination; thus, they conduct the questioning impromptu. Other attorneys give some thought to the points they want to make but fail to plot out precise strategies to accomplish their goals.

Many times, a generalized preconception of how the testimony will develop turns out to be off the mark. Counsel may wander through a lengthy recapitulation of the direct examination, making an occasional point, but leaving the jury with little to remember. The failure in this approach is lack of preparation. As with other aspects of advocacy, there are proven techniques for an effective, thematic cross-examination, and *preparation* is the key to using these techniques.[22]

Generally, in cross-examination you should try to establish points: those that favor your own case, undermine the opposing case, or discredit the witness. The examination should develop these points so they seem consequential. The more concessions are magnified though related questions asked in a series, the more important they seem to be. Further, you should control the examination, phrasing questions as assertions to which the witness must agree. To achieve these goals, preparation is essential.

To prepare for cross-examination, you should review and abstract prior statements of the witness, including any deposition or other prior testimony. The "abstract" should contain the content of the witness's testimony — in point form — and the page on which each point appears. You also should review documents that reflect the witness's prior actions, commitments, and positions, and abstract the relevant points from these documents. If the witness is a party, the pleadings and memoranda may reflect his positions.

Once you review all the relevant material, organize the prior statements and positions by subject matter. The categories should reflect the thematic "points" you hope to make with the witness. You should have identified most of these points in the trial outline, but in preparing to cross-examine, you may see others. This topical approach permits a topical cross-examination, in which you select the subjects and develop facts within them. As you review and organize this information, you naturally conceptualize strategies for employing the prior concessions in cross-examination.

Each "point" category, once this process is complete, should reflect the many little points the witness must agree to within each category, and the source document and page number that you rely on for each conclusion. The documents containing this information serve as the basis for preparing the cross-examination. You also should make notes of points the witness logically must agree to, points

---

[22] Scott Baldwin, *Cross-Examination*, 23 TRIAL 76 (1987).

on which you "can't lose," and other fruitful areas for cross. See §§ 9-13 and 9-14. You then can mix all of this information into an effective outline or list of questions.

An abbreviated example of an abstract of a deposition — an initial step in planning for cross-examination — is set forth below. You should make notes even of seemingly unimportant points. Mark the important points with asterisks or otherwise highlight them. You also should leave enough room in the margin for notes.

Joe Smith
Deposition Abstract

Page	*Testimony*
1	Age 52
	Current employer — Ace Construction
2	General workman
	32 years
	Primary experience is asphalt
3	Prior employment
	1960-71 Jones Construction
4	1972-83 Smith Construction
	Served as foreman of jobs
	Mostly asphalt
5	1983-92 Ace Construction
	Served as foreman of jobs
	All asphalt jobs
6	Recent jobs
	US 52 Highway Project
	July–Nov. 1991
	Foreman
	Asphalt overlay
7	St. Charles Avenue Overlay
	Feb.–June 1991
	Asphalt project
	Foreman
8	Duties as foreman — general
	Oversee laborers
	Plan laydown

9	Inspect laydown
	[etc.]

An example of a by-category organization of the witness's testimony, again quite abbreviated, follows:

Cross-exam preparation
Joe Smith

	Experience		*Job oversight*
D1	Age — 52	D59	Was not on job every day
D1	Works at Ace Construction	D72	Relied on others to oversee job
D7	10 years at Ace	D29	Only out to job about twice a week
D12	Concentration asphalt	D37	Oversight by telephone
D14	No prior experience on runways	D45	Top assistant no prior experience
D22	Was boss of runway job	D71	Does not know frequency laydown was stopped
D3	1960-71 Jones Construction	D62	Company rule — at least must have assistant supervisor in job
D8	No asphalt Jones Construction	D26	Assistant was in office half day usually
	[etc.]		[etc.]
Spec. Review			
D62	Did not check specs before job		
D71	Did not check reports for compliance		
D91	Relied on testing lab to check		
D107	"No responsibility" to check spec. compliance [etc.]		

To this material, add categories and underlying assertions that are based on other material in the case, or logically flow from facts you can establish. If the witness worked on an asphalt runway, for instance, the job plans, reports and related material would provide a basis for factual points. Your own inspection would reveal facts about the job that the witness presumably would concede. Break this material into subpoints within categories.

Once you break down the points, you should prepare a list or outline of questions. In this process you can break down prior statements into smaller points, reflecting matters implicit in the statements. You may see points that flow logically from the witness's statements, which you may incorporate into the list.

As you plan your questions, stick with factual assertions and make them specific. Break down facts into subparts so you can elicit multiple concessions in making a point. Avoid conclusory assertions — judgmental or ultimate factual contentions; these questions invite argument and may be objectionable. Allow the jury to draw the ultimate conclusion as you demonstrate, using the facts, that it is true.

In determining your organization, you generally should group questions by topic. Choose a subject and stick with it until you finish. This approach makes your points on cross-examination more understandable and gives momentum to the examination. Some advocates recommend misdirection and "hiding the ball," but these tactics often confuse and bore the listeners. If you lay a foundation to make a point, follow through and make it. Some fishing may be required at times, but do not overdo it.

Once you have organized your questions within topics, choose a sequence that tends to support the overall picture you want to present. Some topics naturally follow from, or build on, others. Make sure the sequence permits an orderly, logical presentation. Try to imagine how the examination will sound and adjust it to promote comprehension.

Think about the order in which you will introduce topics and elicit facts from the witness. If your witness is strongly adverse and you have a strong point to make with him, you may want to make it first to put the witness on the defensive. When you need certain foundational facts to make a point, and you are not sure the witness will concede them, you should consider eliciting them before the witness or jury can see where you are going, so a denial will not hurt you. Additionally, when points are built on other points, establish them in logical sequence so you can use their combined force. Go over your examination after you plan it and assess the order in which you present your points.

Be realistic in assessing how the witness must answer your questions. Just because you believe an assertion is true does not mean the witness must accept it. If the correct answer would not be apparent to an objective observer, make sure you have backup ammunition — say a prior statement — to support it. When you rely on reason, make sure your logic is solid and easily understood.

You should be prepared with your outline or list prior to the direct examination. Obviously, you may need to address matters from the direct examination; if so, try to incorporate additional points into your plan. This approach usually gives your assertions more power. If your plan cannot easily accommodate a point about the direct examination, address it at the beginning or end of cross-examination. To ensure you remember it, you may want to do it first.

The fact that you have an outline or list of questions should not deter you from following up in the actual examination. You need to be flexible and spontaneous, able to catch a witness in evasions. Good preparation should help you in this effort, so long as you are not tied to a script. Use your prepared material, but be ready to depart from it. *Listen* to the answers rather than focusing on the next question. If you need to pursue a point with the witness, do so; you can always go back to your outline.

§ 9-11.   Need to Have a Purpose on Cross-Examination.

You should not ask questions solely to hear yourself speak. You must determine whether it is helpful to cross-examine, which primarily depends on whether the witness must concede helpful facts. It may also depend on whether the direct testimony hurts the case and needs to be countered. If you cross-examine, have a goal. "Fishing" at trial results in more damage than gain. The time to explore is in discovery.

You should know prior to the direct examination whether cross-examination can establish points supporting your case, from the trial outline and the notes you prepared in advance for the witness. In most cases, with adequate discovery you at least can identify positive or limiting points for cross-examination. Additionally, you must determine the impact of the direct examination. If the witness makes a dramatic, forceful presentation, you may need to defuse the testimony.

One downside of cross-examination is the opportunity it gives opposing counsel to conduct redirect examination. Lawyers sometimes forget to ask about key matters in direct examination. A clever lawyer can repair the damage during redirect, even though the questions do not strictly address matters brought out on cross. If you do not conduct cross-examination, your opponent has no opportunity to correct the omission.

§ 9-12.   Formulating Questions for Cross-Examination.

For most cross-examination, the witness is at least mildly adverse. Your purpose is to gain the assent of the witness to facts. Thus, you generally should employ leading questions. The best form is a statement of fact, followed by the inquiring phrase: "is that right?", "is that correct?", "is that true?", "do you agree?" Thus, a typical question might be: "The light was red when you entered the intersection; is that right?"

The technique of stating the fact first, followed by the phrase that transforms it to a question, makes the facts as clear and prominent as possible. If the fact comes first, rather than the questioning phrase, the fact comes across with more power. Further, you appear more authoritative, which lends credibility to your factual presentation. Consider the following alternatives:

Q.	The title of your presentation was "How the Profits Mount;" is that correct?
A.	Yes.
Q.	Isn't it true that the title of your presentation was "How the Profits Mount"?
A.	Yes.

Although the difference is subtle, positioning the fact at the front gives the first question more authority. The introductory phrase ending with "that" gets in the way of the fact in the second question.

When the fact drives the question, you are the person establishing facts. Often with a compliant witness the questioning phrases are not even necessary to produce agreement, as in two "questions" in the following example:

Q.	You were standing at Maple and Lowerline; is that correct?
A.	Yes.
Q.	You saw two men; is that right?
A.	Yes.
Q.	These men were running; right?
A.	Yes.
Q.	And one of them was holding a knife?
A.	That's right.
Q.	The one with the knife was chasing the other man; is that correct?
A.	Yes.
Q.	They were running toward Broadway, right?

> A. Yes.
>
> Q. You saw them only for a few seconds?
>
> A. Correct.

You should frame and state the questions so that they establish the key facts in the story as assent is gained from the witness. In this connection, accuracy is important. The jury, over the course of the trial, should come to view you as knowledgeable and reliable. If your credibility is established on fact points, your arguments also gain persuasive power. The cross-examination is an opportunity for you to testify, indirectly, through the process of propounding questions, and to establish that your view of the facts is correct.

Generally, you should avoid negatives in framing questions. State the fact in a positive fashion and call for a "yes" answer. The negatively phrased question — starting with "Isn't it correct that" or ending with "isn't that correct?" — can cause unnecessary confusion. Consider the following example:

> Q. Isn't it correct that you never saw the man when he was holding the knife?

It would be hard to determine what a "yes" answer to this question really means; indeed, a "no" might signify assent. The answer will be much clearer if the question is phrased as follows:

> Q. You never saw the man when he was holding the knife; is that right?

A "yes" here means "yes, you're right, I never saw the man when he was holding the knife." Usually, the witness understands that a "yes" signifies agreement, and the listener should correctly interpret the exchange. If the witness misunderstands and answers "no," meaning "I never saw him," counsel can easily correct the confusion:

> Q. You mean I am right, you never saw the man when he was holding the knife?
>
> A. Right.

Although you generally want to pose the facts in cross-examination, it can be effective to shift the focus to the witness for a damaging admission. Forcing the witness to articulate a concession can add to its dramatic impact. Thus, you may want to ask a more open-ended question if there is only one answer. An example follows:

    Q.   As sales manager, did you give the luncheon talk?

    A.   Yes.

    Q.   This talk was made to Mr. Danielson and the other prospects; is that correct?

    A.   Yes.

    Q.   What was the first main topic of that speech?

    A.   Profitability.

    Q.   What aspect of profitability did you list as the subject?

    A.   How the profits mount.

    Q.   What other main subject did you address?

    A.   Training them to make even more.

This approach is especially effective if you build to a single conclusion, then force the witness to hang herself with the crucial answer.

Asking an occasional question that requires the witness to provide information also gives variety to your presentation. Too much of the same form can be tedious. If the answer is obvious — or a surprise answer really will not hurt — let the witness provide it. Additionally, you need to vary your own words and structure. Shift from "is that correct?" to "do you agree?" to "is this true?" to "right?" and other forms of inquiry.

One other caveat to stating facts in cross-examination: When you present a statement of the witness that you do not endorse, differentiate yourself from it. You do not want to appear as if you believe the point is true. If you do not differentiate yourself from the position, you may seem to endorse it:

    Q.   You did not mislead the Danielsons; is that correct?

    A.   That's absolutely correct.

Thus, you should use a phrase such as "Your position is . . . ." or "You contend . . . ," as in the following example:

> Q.   You contend you did not mislead the Danielsons; is that right?
>
> A.   Yes.

§ 9-13. Being Right on Cross-Examination: "Knowing" the Answers.

The asserted "golden rule" of cross-examination is that you should never ask a question unless you "know" the answer. The rule is a bit absurd, because you can never "know" what a witness might say in response to a question, but you can know what a witness reasonably should say. You should have a solid basis — in reason, prior statements or other material — for expecting the witness to concede your factual assertions. If the answer to your question is obvious to the listeners or you can back up your assertions with impeachment material, the witness will lose credibility by denying your assertion.

Nor is it always necessary to "know" what the witness should say. You can take some chances with questions when they are innocuous. Additionally, when the overall importance of the answer will not be clear to the jury, as when an expert is asked preliminary questions on technical matters, you may fish to see what the witness says in uncertain areas. In general, however, you need a basis for your questions.

To reasonably predict the witness's answers, you must prepare. This effort requires a review of what the witness has said and the positions she must endorse, and conceptualization of what the witness will say as the trap closes. Witnesses usually are loath to deny facts to which they previously testified and often are acutely aware of their prior statements. Thus, prior testimony and other statements are a fruitful basis for preparing cross-examination. You can present these statements in the context *you* prefer, so that they support your position. Additionally, points that are implicit in the witness's statements and her position in the case are fruitful sources for cross-examination. The means for identifying likely answers include:

§ 9-13(a). Discovery.

The answer is in the witness's deposition, a transcript, a letter, or some other document. If the witness said it before, she is likely to say it again, or at least pay the price of impeachment. Additionally, the witness generally must agree with statements of a party with which she is identified. An employee of a company, for instance, would probably accept a company policy statement on matters relating to the employee's duties.

§ 9-13(b).   Witness Interviews.

The witness has given a statement containing one answer. If a witness is not deposed, you should try to obtain a written statement signed by the witness. If not, another person who interviewed the witness needs to be available to testify if impeachment becomes necessary. You should depose any important witness who is likely to be adverse if possible. You need to thoroughly explore the witness's knowledge to plan cross-examination.

§ 9-13(c).   Direct Testimony.

The witness said it, or implied it, on direct examination.

§ 9-13(d).   Facts Applicable to the Witness's Testimony.

The answer is established by, or logically follows from, facts about the case. For instance, if the witness is a construction supervisor, and his listed duties include "inspection of the job," he surely will admit that this was one of his duties. If the witness works for a company, and its annual statement discloses a fact, the witness is likely to endorse it.

§ 9-13(e).   Uncontested Facts.

The fact is not reasonably subject to dispute, as with the position of a traffic light at an intersection.

§ 9-13(f).   Litigation Positions.

If the witness is a party or identified with a party, the fact necessarily follows from the party's litigation position. Aspects of a litigating position, placed in a different context, can produce surprising results on cross-examination.

"Knowing" the answer to a question really means counsel *can demonstrate the correctness of the question* if the witness denies it. The demonstration requires impeaching with a prior statement or adopted document, refreshing the witness's recollection with an uncontested document, and relying on obvious logical connections. When you stray into areas where you think you are "right," but cannot back it up, the witness can inflict damage without paying a price. Thus, "knowing" the answer really means having a solid basis for the fact that the question seeks to establish.

§ 9-14.   "Can't Lose" Questions: Motherhood and Apple Pie.

Questions that are build on "apple pie" propositions — generally accepted tenets of morality, duty, responsibility, love of family — will work for you regardless of the witness's answer. If the witness gives an unexpected answer, denying, for instance, that she "loves her children very much," the answer undercuts the witness's credibility. Additionally, it gives the jurors a strong reason not to identify or sympathize with the witness. If the witness concedes the point, you achieve your objective and can use the premise for further cross-examination.

Can't lose questions often are used to lay the groundwork for a point. An attorney might establish with the witness the need for hard work to succeed in business, for instance, only to use the point later in reviewing the witness's failure to work hard. When the content is not apparent, the witness usually concedes the point, and it can be juxtaposed later against the witness's actual performance.

Examples of possible "can't lose" questions include:

Q.   A franchisor should be truthful with people who inquire about a franchise; is that right?

Q.   As an engineer, you believe that those in your profession should abide by accepted safety standards; is that correct?

Q.   A surgeon ordinarily should review the chart thoroughly to ensure that he fully understands the nature of the problem and the recommended surgery; is that right?

Q.   A lawyer charged with the responsibility of ensuring her client a fair trial should update her research to make sure it is current; is that correct?

Any of these questions might be good tools to lay the groundwork to establish that the adverse party failed in the relevant obligation. If the witness says "Yes," the point is won, and the concession can be used in argument or brought up again in cross-examination when the wrongful conduct is discussed. Indeed, the question may implicitly ask the witness to condemn his own conduct. If the witness says "No" to a question that seems eminently reasonable, he loses the appearance of reason with the jury.

Although "can't lose" questions generally reflect accepted tenets, and witnesses almost always concede them, witnesses do not necessarily put the tenets to practice. If a law student were asked, "A responsible law student should prepare diligently for class, correct?," the student likely would say "Yes" even if he never prepared for class. Indeed, many students do not prepare for class, yet they would be embarrassed to express disagreement with the question. Thus, because "can't lose" questions refer to practices that a person *should* endorse, even if he behaves in a contrary manner, they allow you to force him to condemn his own conduct. You should establish the tenet first, however, so the witness will not see how it can be used against him.

§ 9-15. Breaking Down Points and Painting Pictures on Cross-Examination: the "Mountain Out of a Molehill" Approach.

A key ingredient of a good cross-examination is the "mountain out of a molehill" approach.[23] You should take any good overall factual point, break it into as many subpoints, or facts, as possible, and gain assent to each little point. This approach creates the impression that you are gaining a lot of ground. Further, since accurate, specific questions make it difficult for the witness to equivocate, this method usually produces concessions. If the witness does try to equivocate regarding precise questions, he usually appears evasive.

Breaking a point into subpoints requires thought. You should not merely repeat points, as repetition is objectionable. The questions must be different. Usually you do not have prior statements documenting each aspect of a point. Thus, you must develop assertions that are implicit in prior statements, logically follow from prior statements, or are based on other sources of questions. You should then conceive questions that identify and link the facts within overall points.

When you have an extensive deposition of the witness, or other prior testimony, one method of making a mountain out of a molehill is to identify each different way that the witness has described a key point. You then can use the different versions in questions, without exact repetition. Ordinarily, you should begin with more precise versions of the facts and proceed to the more conclusory questions. This approach makes the questions seem different and enhances the perception that you are making headway, as in the following examples:

Q.	You observed water crystals on the asphalt; is that correct?
Q.	Sometimes you saw water running out of the asphalt; is that right?
Q.	Water occasionally ran out of the back of the asphalt trucks; is that correct?
Q.	You often saw steam rising out of the hot asphalt; is that true?
Q.	You were concerned that there was too much water in the asphalt mixture; is that correct?

When you have only a statement or summary from the witness, another method of creating the "mountain" is to take a prior statement and determine the specific facts that logically are implicit in it. You then can turn these facts into points,

---

[23] See LANE'S GOLDSTEIN TRIAL TECHNIQUE § 19.33 (1992): "The successful trial lawyer takes [a] fact [and] builds up that fact until it assumes unusual importance through the medium of a series of questions that lead the witness into a trap from which he is unable to extricate himself."

to be asserted in the form of questions. For instance, assume a witness saw one man chasing another down the street; the person being chased was later found dead. Assume the witness previously testified that she was standing at an intersection, the man "whizzed by," and "it was dark." You know the nearest street light was half a block away. The following points might follow from these two statements:

"Whizzed by"	"It was dark"
Men were running	Night
Running very fast	Not much light
Passed by very quickly	Streetlight down street
Saw for short time	Half block away
	Streetlight provided little illumination
	Observed man in dark

You can turn each point into a *series* of questions. Generally, you should proceed *first* with the facts flowing logically from the prior statement, then with the fact in the statement. This tactic keeps the prior statement in reserve to bail you out of trouble — through questioning and impeachment — if the witness denies the preliminary questions. Thus, you should prepare a cross-examination like the following:

	Whizzed by
	You saw two men, correct?
	These men were running, right?
	They were moving very fast, correct?
	You saw them only a short time, right?
	They were past you very quickly, true?
Statement p. 3	Indeed, they whizzed by you, right?
	Dark
	It was night, correct?
	There was only artificial light, right?
	There was not much of this artificial light, right?
	The nearest light was half a block away, correct?
	It did not provide much illumination, right?
Statement p. 1	You thought it was dark, right?
Statement pp. 1, 3	You observed the two men whiz by in the dark, correct?

By asking the "logically implicit" questions first, you take little risk, because you always can move to the question for which the backup material is available. This action removes the negative impact of any prior equivocation and establishes your fairness in asking the prior question. Consider the following example, in which the witness equivocates in answering the preliminary questions, but has to admit the core fact:

Q.	The men were running; is that correct?
A.	I wouldn't say so.
Q.	They were moving very fast; is that right?
A.	I'm not sure I agree with you.
Q.	To get it exactly right, they whizzed by you; is that true?
A.	Yes.

If the witness tries to deny the core fact, she is subject to impeachment. Effective impeachment quickly trains the witness to respond affirmatively. See § 9-28.

Compare the above example to one in which counsel establishes the core fact first, then tries to make the "mountain" by following up. In that case, there is no "ace" in reserve, and counsel may well be stuck with an equivocal answer. Consider the following:

Q.	The two men whizzed by you; is that correct?
A.	I guess so.
Q.	That means they were running; is that right?
A.	No. They could have been walking fast.
Q.	They were moving very fast; is that true?
A.	Well, I'm not sure. They weren't going that fast. I got a good look at them.

In this case, counsel does not have impeachment to fall back on, because the witness has admitted the fact contained in the prior statement. He can try to go back to "whizzed by," but that question would be met with the objection "Asked and answered." Counsel may be forced to leave the subject in a muddled state.

Painting pictures in cross-examination can be illustrated with the testimony of a utility witness in a case involving an electric power-sharing contract. A regulatory agency claimed that the utility should not have treated certain electric generating units that were in mothballs, or "extended reserve shutdown," as "available" to provide service. The utility had counted the units as "available" under the power contract because they could be refurbished and placed back in active status. The questioner wanted to dramatize the extent to which the units were in disrepair. The witness, who was experienced and able, tried to avoid outright concessions. The illustration follows:

Q. Now, I would like to ask you some questions about putting a unit into extended reserve shutdown status or mothball status. Would you agree that to put a unit into this condition it is necessary to remove moisture from the air to the extent possible?

A. Yes, it is better to try to dehumidify the air in certain part of the equipment.

Q. You need, if possible, to use dehumidifying equipment in order to remove that moisture from the air at the facility; is that correct?

A. Well, you could use dehumidifying equipment, or you could put certain gases in the unit that prevent moisture from entering.

Q. I believe, if I am not mistaken — and you can help me — Entergy has used this technique of putting certain gases into the areas where it wants to maintain a low humidity condition; is that right?

A. Such as — yes, such as nitrogen in the boiler.

Q. And this is what is referred to as a "nitrogen blanket"; is that right?

A. Yes.

Q. Now, a nitrogen blanket consists of enclosing the machinery in some way or placing nitrogen into an enclosed area so that it will displace oxygen; is that right?

A. That's correct.

Q. And would you agree that a human being could not survive for long in that environment?

A. Yes.

Q. Now, when you put a unit into this extended cold shutdown status, the fuel tanks on the equipment are empty; is that right?

A.   If it had — if it was a single unit plant, and there were places to store oil, then we would remove that oil.

Q.   And water is put into the fuel tanks instead of fuel to keep them from floating away in the event of flooding; is that right?

A.   Yes, that is true whenever you might empty a tank, whether it is associated with a unit on extended reserve shutdown or not.

Q.   Now, with regard to one of these extended cold shutdown units, the plan that you all devised called for allowing the smaller equipment that could easily be replaced to simply corrode, or go ahead and rust, and not worry about it; is that right?

A.   There were not steps taken to prevent corrosion on all of the equipment, that is true.

Q.   And the idea was that it would be easier to replace this corroding equipment than it would be to try to maintain it constantly while the unit was in extended cold shutdown; is that correct?

A.   Well, the thinking really — it would be more economic not to take the preventative measures than it would be to replace it if necessary.

Q.   Okay. Now, in addition to that, the plan was that you all would put concrete partitions in front of the traveling screens on the intake water lines and the circulating water lines; is that right?

A.   I don't recall that, [counsel]. I would have to look at the report in detail to refresh my memory. If you could point to me where it states that.

Q.   Yes, perhaps I can show it to you. [Pause.] If you take a look at page 17, down at the bottom it says, "It is recommended that a concrete partition be placed in front of the traveling screens" — this is on the intake and circulating water lines — "to keep out mud and debris." Is that right?

A.   Yes, that is what it says.

Q.   Now, in addition, at one of these extended cold shutdown units the staff is transferred elsewhere or terminated, so that the staffing can be reduced, and savings can be achieved; is that correct?

A.   In virtually all instances staffing was reduced, yes.

*   *   *

Q.   I would like to turn, if you will, to a few of the units that are in extended reserve shutdown, for illustrative purposes.

I would like first to take the Paterson unit. Paterson — which one is the one with the cracked casing? Paterson 3?

A.   Paterson 4 is the one that has some casing problems.

Q.   And which is the one that requires repairs in the boiler?

A.   That is Paterson 4 as well.

Q.   Okay. When put into ERS, Paterson 4 had problems in the boiler; is that right?

A.   That is correct.

Q.   And . . . a cracked casing was another problem?

A.   Well, the problems that Paterson 4 had at the time that we decided to put it in extended reserve shutdown were there were some real problems in the boiler, and there were signs of excessive rust in the structure. There was a casing problem, and the high pressure rotor had a bow in it.

Q.   Now that unit was last operated in 1985; is that right?

A.   That is correct.

Q.   And it could not run at the rated level safely; is that correct?

A.   At the state of repair that it was in, it could not be run. It could have been fixed and run at its demonstrated capacity.

Q.   But it was not fixed?

A.   It was not fixed.

Q.   It was placed in storage in the unrepaired state; is that right?

A.   That is correct.

Q.   To bring it on line would require repairs and removal of the preservation material that exists there and staffing it up; is that right?

A.   That is correct.

Q.   Now with respect to Paterson 4, in addition to the fact that it has problems in the boiler, it has a cracked casing, it had a bow in the pressure rotor, it has signs of extensive rust, it has a nitrogen blanket; is that right?

447

A.   To the best of my recollection, it does, [counsel].

Q.   And it would require, in your estimation, eight to ten months to get that unit into service; is that correct?

A.   I am of the opinion that we could probably return that unit somewhat more quickly than that. I think we could probably get it back within six months.

Q.   At page 82 of your deposition, I asked you "How long would it take to fix all the rusting and so on at Paterson 4?"

"If they were to decide today to bring Paterson 4 back into service, we think we probably could do it within eight to ten months."

Q.   Did you say that, sir?

A.   I probably did, and if that is the case, I would accept that as well.

Q.   I asked you again — "eight to ten months?" Answer, "yes." Did you say that?

A.   I assume I did. I don't have it in front of me.

Q.   Okay. Now at the time that Paterson 4, with the rusting and the cracked casing and the problems in the boiler, was put into extended reserve shutdown, you all thought that you were going to need a new high pressure rotor; is that right?

A.   I think there was some concern that that would be the case, yes.

Q.   And as a matter of fact, you thought that if you needed a high pressure rotor, it would take a year lead time to even order it; is that correct?

A.   If we were to have to replace the high pressure rotor, we would need about a year lead time to get it ordered, yes.

Q.   And what you wound up doing was taking that high pressure rotor and loading it on a truck and sending it back to the manufacturer to get it straightened out; is that true?

A.   That is correct.

Q.   Now can you tell me this — do you all have concrete partitions in front of the screens on the intake and circulating water lines at Paterson 4?

A.   I do not know.

Q.   Have you put water in the fuel tanks at Paterson 4 to avoid flotation if there is a flood?

A.   Again, I can't specifically say that we have done so, [counsel]. My recollection is that we probably haven't, but like during Hurricane Andrew, we did put the water in — whenever we expect an event, then we put water in those tanks to keep them from flooding.

Q.   Well, you have transferred or terminated and otherwise reduced staffing there; is that right?

A.   That is correct.

Q.   In the extended reserve shutdown study, Mr. Gallaher, it was recommended — if I can find it, it might take a second — it was recommended that one person be in the plant at all times. This person's job will be to act as a watchman and to monitor any operating equipment. Do you have a watchman out at Paterson 4?

A.   No, we do not.

Q.   I would like to turn to Lake Catherine. Lake Catherine is a multi-unit plant up in Arkansas; is that true?

A.   Yes.

Q.   Now, you've got two of the Lake Catherine units in extended reserve shutdown; is that right?

A.   That is correct.

Q.   Last time Lake Catherine operated was back in 1984; is that true?

A.   That is correct.

                         *   *   *

Q.   And Lake Catherine, one of the units there, requires extensive repairs to the boiler; is that right?

A.   I would not call it extensive repairs. There are repairs needed to the boiler.

Q.   Well, is it true that there are several expansion joints that will need to be replaced on the boiler?

A.   Yes, that's correct.

Q.   Is it true that a major inspection in the turbine generator is required?

A.   Yes, that's correct.

Q.   Is it true that it's required that ducts be repaired on Lake Catherine?

A. Yes, there is some duct work that will have to be done.

Q. Lake Catherine has a nitrogen blanket; is that right?

A. That is correct.

Q. And you expect that it would take six months for you all to get Lake Catherine back on line if you needed it; is that right?

A. Yes.

Q. And it would cost one-and-a-half million bucks; is that true?

A. Per unit.

Q. Let's talk about Lynch 3. Lynch 3 is another unit that's in extended reserve shutdown; is that right?

A. Yes, it is.

Q. It last operated back in 1986; is that correct?

A. Yes, that's correct.

Q. Now, in Lynch 3, the insulation needs replacing; is that right?

A. There is probably some insulation that needs work. . ..

* * *

Q. Is Lynch 2 in need of total replacement of the insulation?

A. No, there is work that needs to be done on Lynch 2 in both the refractory and the insulation, but it is not a complete replacement.

Q. Let me ask you this: Is it true that Lynch 3 has boiler problems?

A. There are some problems with the boiler on Lynch 3, yes.

Q. Is it true that the refractory needs replacing in a lot of places?

A. On Lynch 2, that is the matter. And on Lynch 3, there is some refractory, but not to the extent as required on Lynch 2.

* * *

Q. Is it true that the furnace floor needs repairs?

A. On Lynch 2, that is correct.

Q. Is it true that casing on the boiler needs to be replaced?

A. Not all of it has to be replaced. There is some boiler casing work that needs to be done.

Q. Expansion joints on the boiler need repair; is that right?

A. I don't believe that either one of the Lynch units has problems with expansion joints.

Q. At page 97, you said, "we are going to have to replace the casing and some of the expansion joints need attention on the boiler." Did you say that?

A. Well, needing attention and replacing are different. I think we could repair the expansion joints.

Q. I said — I asked, do expansion joints on the boiler need repair?

A. I thought that you had said extensive repair. They need repair.

Q. Okay. The air preheater needs retubing; is that right?

A. On Lynch Unit 3, that is true. Part of the air preheater, not the entire air preheater, but part of it needs retubing.

Q. Well, with respect to Lynch 3, is this true: You all removed the low pressure rotor.

A. That's true.

Q. You took the low-pressure rotor out of Lynch 3, and you used it in another unit; is that right?

A. That is correct.

Q. So, basically because you needed a low-pressure rotor in a different unit, you basically salvaged it from Lynch 3 and used it in that other unit; is that correct?

A. What we did, we — it was used in the Couch unit, and rather than repair the low-pressure turbine in the Couch unit, we just removed it to be used at Lynch and deferred repairing the LP turbine. And since we could use the one at Lynch, we just took it down to Couch and installed it, thereby deferring maintenance dollars.

Q. Where is the broken low-pressure rotor that used to be at Couch?

A. It's probably — well, I don't know. I don't know whether it's at Couch or we moved it up to Lynch. I don't know. But we still have it.

> Q.   Do you even have a low-pressure rotor at Lynch right now?
>
> A.   I am not sure that we have got one physically located at Lynch. However, we have got an LP turbine that needs repairs that we will put at Lynch.
>
> Q.   All right.
>
> A.   I just don't know where we have it stored at the present time, [counsel].
>
> Q.   Does Lynch 3 have a nitrogen blanket on it?
>
> A.   I can't say for sure that Lynch 3 has a nitrogen blanket. We did — we do have dehumidified air circulating through the equipment.
>
> Q.   Does Lynch 3 have water in the fuel tanks to avoid their floating away in the event of a flood?
>
> A.   I do not know.
>
> Q.   It does have significantly reduced staffing, does it not?
>
> A.   At Lynch, yes, it does.
>
> Q.   Is there a watchman out there?
>
> A.   No, but Lynch has people at the plant so that it is manned.
>
> Q.   It would take approximately 10 months to get Lynch out of extended reserve shutdown; is that right?
>
> A.   Lynch 3 would take approximately 8 to 10 months.
>
> Q.   And it would cost about $4.2 million; is that correct?
>
> A.   For Lynch Unit 3, that is correct.
>
> [Counsel pursues further illustrations].

In the example the cross-examiner's intent was to paint a picture of dilapidated, run-down, stored units that could not provide service. The technique of breaking down the facts and asking about them individually brings out the desired picture. A few conclusionary questions would not have the same effect.

§ 9-16. Using Documents in Cross-Examination.

Documents provide a fertile basis for preparing a cross-examination. Correspondence, contracts, memoranda, and other documents often contain factual assertions; a witness involved in their preparation usually is forced to agree with these statements. You should be careful, however, to avoid letting the documents control the examination. Too often attorneys organize their cross-examinations around documents. Instead, you should conceive and organize the cross-examination to promote the theory of the case; documents should be used to support this effort.

§ 9-16(a). Questioning About Facts First.

A lawyer who uses a document other than prior testimony in cross-examination often intends to make it an exhibit. If the content of the document supports your theory, introducing it into the record should provide tangible support for your case. In the questioning process, however, you should consider using the document as a basis *first* for securing oral concessions, and *second* as an exhibit to be introduced. This approach produces the maximum impact because it has a double bang.

For instance, consider a situation in which a construction supervisor on an asphalt job prepared a memorandum recording observations at the site. Counsel wants to show that the job was faulty, in part because the asphalt had excess water in the mix. Among other entries, a paragraph in the memorandum states:

> The asphalt at laydown, about 10 a.m., gave off a large amount of steam. There may have been too much water in the mix. I asked Tommy Jones to check the plant to make sure the aggregate was being allowed to dry enough before mixing.

This entry provides a great basis for preparing questions. To get a "double bang," counsel should prepare an examination that first secures fact concessions based on the document, knowing the document is available for impeachment; he then may introduce the document if it is not barred by the hearsay rule. In this case, the memorandum likely is an agent's admission if the supervisor worked for a party, so it would not be hearsay. See § 6-15(d). If there were no need for impeachment, the questioning might proceed as follows:

Q. Steam is an indication of water in the mix; is that right?

A. Yes.

Q. On July 27, you noticed steam coming off the asphalt mix; is that correct?

A. Right.

Q. Indeed, you noticed a large amount of steam coming off the asphalt mix; is that right?

A. I guess so.

Q. The asphalt was being laid on the runway when you noticed this steam; is that true?

A.   Yes.

Q.   This laydown, when you noticed the steam, occurred about 10 a.m.; is that right?

A.   I think that's right.

Q.   Is this a true statement: Based on observing a large amount of steam coming off the asphalt, you concluded there may have been too much water in the mix?

A.   Well . . . yes.

Q.   You were concerned enough about water in the mix to ask that the drying process be checked; is that right?

A.   True.

Q.   You were concerned that water was not being removed from the aggregate prior to drying; is that correct?

A.   I think that's probably true.

Q.   Now, Mr. Jones, you recorded your observations and concerns that day; is that right?

A.   Yes.

Q.   May I approach the witness, your Honor? I show you an exhibit marked for identification as Plaintiff's Exhibit 57. This is a memorandum you prepared on July 28; is that true?

A.   Yes, it is.

Counsel: Your Honor, I'd like to offer this as Exhibit 57.

The Court: Any objection? It is admitted.

Counsel: May I ask the witness to read the third paragraph to the jury?

The Court: All right. Please read it.

The Witness: "The asphalt at laydown, about 10 a.m., gave off a large amount of steam. There may have been too much water in the mix. I asked Tommy Jones to check the plant to make sure the aggregate was being allowed to dry enough before mixing."

Having the witness read this paragraph is one alternative of informing the jury of its content. Counsel could have the document, or copies, shown to the jury, could ask permission to read it himself, or could ask that it be read by the clerk.

Since most witnesses know the contents of their prior statements, this line of questions is likely to produce "yes" responses. If not, counsel has the document in reserve, can impeach with it, and can prove the points by introducing it. Even if the witness waffles in answering the questions, counsel should ask them, confident that each expresses a fact. Counsel might should show disappointment in the witness's failure to be candid. When the content of the document comes out, the jury will understand that the advocate, not the witness, was forthright in presenting the facts. Indeed, if the witness denies a fact, counsel can make the point three times, by asserting the fact in the question, asserting it again in impeachment, and confirming it by introducing the document.

The line of inquiry in the above example might go as follows if the document is held in reserve, then used to make the point through impeachment if the witness denies the facts:

Q. Steam is an indication of water in the mix; is that right?

A. Sure.

Q. On July 27, you noticed steam coming off the asphalt mix; is that correct?

A. I'm not sure I recall that.

Q. You noticed a large amount of steam coming off the mix when asphalt was being laid on the runway; is that true?

A. I don't think there was any steam.

Q. Is this true: On July 27, at about 10 a.m., you observed that the asphalt at laydown gave off a large amount of steam. There may have been too much water in the mix.

A. I told you that isn't true.

Q. You prepared a memorandum reporting your daily observations at the site; is that correct?

A. Yes.

Q. On July 28, you reported:

[Counsel hands copy to opposing counsel and reads from document]

"The asphalt at laydown, about 10 a.m., gave off a large amount of steam. There may have been too much water in the mix."

Q. Did you report that?

A. I guess so.

Q. You concluded that the aggregate might not be dried enough prior to the mixing; is that right?

A.   No.

Q.   You asked an assistant to check the plant to make sure the aggregate was being allowed to dry enough before mixing; is that correct?

A.   I don't think so.

Q.   In your report of July 28, you said:

"I asked Tommy Jones to check the plant to make sure the aggregate was being allowed to dry enough before mixing."

Did you report that?

A.   Yes, I recall that now.

With prior testimony, the examination ends when the impeachment is completed. See § 9-28. Since the memorandum is real evidence, however, and probably would be classified as a non-hearsay as an "admission," counsel also can introduce the memorandum as an exhibit:

Q.   Let me show you this memorandum. May I approach the witness, your Honor? [Court nods.] I show you a document marked for identification Plaintiff's Exhibit 57. Is this the memorandum you prepared July 28?

A.   Yes.

Counsel: Your Honor, I offer this memorandum as Plaintiff's Exhibit 57 and ask permission to show copies to the jury, directing their attention to the third paragraph. [Counsel could, alternatively, ask that the third paragraph be read to the jury].

When you conduct the cross-examination in this manner, you keep control of the fact presentation. You are able to focus attention on the key facts and emphasize them through legitimate repetition. The exercise shows that you know the facts; it also trains the witness to concede facts as the examination continues, because few witnesses enjoy being impeached with documentary evidence.

The hold-in-reserve approach can be used with other kinds of documents. If fact recitals are contained in a contract, for instance, you can ask about the facts before identifying the contract and calling attention to the recitals; if safety standards are contained in a manual, you can ask about individual standards before identifying the manual. You can use the same techniques whenever the witness is likely to concede facts in a document. Ask about the underlying facts, however; asking about the contents of the document directly, before impeachment, violates the original writing rule and may violate the hearsay rule. See §§ 8-21, 6-3(b).

Often when a lawyer uses a document as a basis for questions, opposing counsel asks that the document be shown to the witness. This action is intended to help and protect the witness; if he looks over the document, he can find explanations, think about responses, and prepare himself for new questions. The request, however, has no valid basis; the fact that a question is *based on* a document is not the same as an *actual reference* to a document. The question is just that: a question. Thus, the attorney need not comply with the request. An example follows:

Q.	On July 27, you noticed steam coming off the asphalt mix; is that correct?
Opposing Counsel:	May I ask if counsel is referring to a document? Perhaps he could show it to the witness so he'll be able to refer to it.
Cross-Examiner:	Your Honor, I merely asked a question about a fact. If the witness denies it, I may then get to a document, but I haven't referred to one yet.
The Court:	Proceed.

Additionally, in questioning a witness about a prior statement in a document, you are *not* required to show it to him. This point is explained in the next section. Thus, even if you do refer to the document it need not be shown to the witness. Opposing counsel, however, has a right to see it.

§ 9-16(b). Withholding Document From the Witness: Rule in The Queen's Case Overruled (FRE 613(a)).

Traditionally, in some jurisdictions, if the advocate questioned a witness about the witness's prior statement contained in a writing, she was required to show the writing to the witness before inquiring about it. This rule was first established in England in *The Queen's Case*,[24] and gained some acceptance in the United States.[25] The Federal Rules of Evidence abolished this requirement, which is referred to by the Advisory Committee as a "useless impediment to cross-examination."[26] FRE 613(a) provides:

---

[24] 2 Br. & B. 284, 129 Eng. Rep. 976 (1820).

[25] McCormick on Evidence § 28 (5th ed. 1999).

[26] Fed. R. Evid. 613 advisory committee's note.

(a) Examining witness concerning prior statement. In examining a witness concerning a prior statement made by the witness, whether written or not, the statement need not be shown nor its contents disclosed to the witness at that time, but on request the same shall be shown to opposing counsel.

Federal Rule 613(a) thus clarifies that a statement need not be shown to the witness before he is questioned about it. A written statement must be shown to opposing counsel upon request, to "protect against unwarranted insinuations that a statement has been made when the fact is to the contrary."[27]

Even in jurisdictions where *The Queen's Case* is still applicable, this rule does not preclude you from asking a witness fact questions based on a prior statement, without showing the prior statement to the witness. Thus, if the witness previously wrote the memorandum concerning the asphalt mix, you could ask the fact questions developed from the memorandum without showing it to the witness. Only when you referred to the prior statement itself would the rule come into play. Thus, assume counsel asked the following fact question based on a prior memorandum prepared by the witness:

> Q.   On July 27, you noticed steam coming off the asphalt mix; is that right?

Even if the advocate were holding the memorandum — and to secure a favorable response counsel might do so — there would be no requirement to show it to the witness, because the attorney merely asked a question about a fact. Only if the advocate referred to the memorandum *in the question* could she be required to show it to the witness. Thus, a jurisdiction that enforced the rule would apply it if counsel asked:

> Q.   You wrote a memorandum on July 27 in which you stated that steam was coming off the asphalt mix; is that right?

The Queen's Case rule is viewed as an impediment to cross-examination because it hinders the strategy of getting the witness to deny the contents of the prior statement, after which counsel produces the statement to impeach. Once the prior statement is shown to the witness, he is less likely to deny it, and this method of attacking credibility is defeated. This strategy is primarily an attack on veracity and is relatively unimportant if counsel's primary aim is to establish facts. See § 9-27.

---

[27] FED. R. EVID. 613 advisory committee's note.

The Queen's Case rule apparently was invoked infrequently even before the passage of the Federal Rules. It was abrogated in England by Parliament in 1854.[28] In the United States, most judges and practitioners were unaware of it. *McCormick* states:

> It is believed, however, that actual invocation of the [*Queen's Case*] rule in trials is relatively infrequent in most states in which the rule has not been changed, and that the generality of judges and practitioners in these jurisdictions are unaware of this possible hidden rock in the path of the cross-examiner.[29]

Thus, even in jurisdictions where the Federal Rules have not been adopted, attorneys generally may impeach with a prior statement without showing it to the witness.

§ 9-16(c). Use of the Document First.

Many lawyers cannot resist the temptation to go directly to the document in cross-examination. Often young lawyers, who spend much of their time reviewing documents, get too attached to a documentary fact trail and let the documents run the case. Moreover, for many lawyers the "document first" approach seems the safest course. The attorneys may not be comfortable with the risk that the witness will quibble with a fact question and do not realize the value of a double "bang."

Unfortunately, the "document first" approach often diffuses rather than focuses attention on the crucial facts. The process of identifying and introducing each document, and allowing the witness to review and explain it, softens the impact of the facts. Moreover, to some extent this exercise transfers control to the witness and opposing counsel. Further, unless you are adept at following up, the examination provides only a single "bang."

When the attorney uses the document first, the questioning often proceeds like this:

Q.   Did you prepare a memorandum on July 28, 1989?

A.   I may have. May I see it?

Q.   Sure. I show you a document that has been marked for identification Plaintiff's Exhibit 57.

A.   May I read it?

---

[28] McCORMICK ON EVIDENCE § 28 (5th ed. 1999).

[29] *Id.*

Q.   Sure

[All wait as the witness reviews the memorandum. The witness *thinks* as he reads, preparing for any questions about the document.]

A.   Yes, I prepared this.

Q.   In that memorandum, you said. . ..

Opposing
Counsel: Your Honor, excuse me, but I believe the memorandum will speak for itself. Can't it simply be shown to the jury?

Counsel: That's fine. Your Honor, I move the introduction of the document and ask permission to show copies to the jury, directing their attention to paragraph 3.

Counsel may be able to increase the impact by following up, asking questions to *develop* the facts in the memorandum, but questions that merely repeat its contents may not be allowed. Additionally, the witness may be able to explain away the memorandum in the follow-up process. Further, you have the ability to follow up in both the "fact first" and "document first" approaches. Thus, the examination is less effective when the document is used first.

§ 9-16(d).   Documents Not Prepared or Adopted by the Witness.

Different considerations exist when you want to use a document that the witness did not prepare, adopt, or implicitly endorse. Any document can be shown to a witness if fairly calculated to refresh recollection, once the witness testifies that his recollection is inadequate. The witness need not have knowledge regarding the creation of the document. Obviously, in this situation, the witness cannot lay a foundation for introducing the document but may be able to testify about the facts after reviewing it. Once an unfriendly witness has testified to a faulty recollection, however, he may contend that the document does *not* refresh his memory.

When you are unsure whether a witness will concede points reflected in a document prepared by someone else, you might consider showing the document to the witness before asking the questions. Assume a record of a meeting was prepared by someone other than the witness and was never shown to the witness. Theoretically, you could show the document to the witness for the purpose of identification, although in this case identification is unlikely. You can also show it to him to refresh recollection, assuming the witness testifies that he does not remember something about the event. Showing the document to the witness *before* establishing a faulty memory is technically improper, but may not produce an objection. You can always explain: "I intend to ask about this meeting and thought it only fair to show this record to the witness."

If you ask the witness to review the document, it may tend to "fix" a fact scenario in the witness's mind. Once the witness testifies that she did not prepare the document, you need not refer to it further. You can proceed to ask questions about the event, hoping the witness's review of the document will promote concessions. In this situation, however, the document cannot be used for impeachment because the witness did not prepare or adopt it.

§ 9-17. Applying Cross-Examination Strategies.

Cross-examination precepts can be illustrated with examples from the *Danielson v. ComputerCentre Associates* file, using the material available to cross-examine Jene Nelsen. As the sales manager of ComputerCentre and one of the persons accused of fraud, Ms. Nelsen likely would be contentious on cross-examination. At the same time, she would want to make a good impression on the jury. She would not want to contradict her own prior statements and those of ComputerCentre, nor would she want to appear unreasonable. Additionally, she would be less inclined to argue with specific fact assertions than conclusionary statements.

Ms. Nelsen would be forced to agree with "motherhood" statements. Examples are the following:

Q. In marketing a franchise, you agree it is only fair to be truthful; is that right?

A. Yes.

Q. It is only right to be candid about the important facts?

A. True.

Q. Would you agree you have a responsibility to tell the whole story?

A. Yes.

If she denies these statements Ms. Nelsen does herself more harm than if she agrees, although the questions obviously set her up for a confrontation on the adequacy of ComputerCentre's disclosures.

Ms. Nelsen's affidavit in the ComputerCentre file is not extensive. One potentially relevant statement is the following:

> I thought that Jack Danielson in particular overrated the utility of his experience at the police department as a means of being prepared for sales of microcomputers.[30]

---

[30] Appendix A, Jene Nelsen.

Implicit in this statement are the following facts: Ms. Nelsen knew Danielson had been in the police department, knew he was inexperienced with computers, and thought he was overrating his experience with computers when he purchased a franchise. Logically, then, she knew that he needed training. Questions would thus be developed from this prior statement:

Q.   You were aware Mr. Danielson had been a career police officer; is that correct?

A.   Yes.

Q.   You knew he did not have prior experience in the sale of microcomputers, right?

A.   Yes.

Q.   You knew he had not been involved in other aspects of marketing computers; is that true?

A.   Yes.

Q.   You thought he overrated his experience in the police department as a means of being prepared for the sale of microcomputers; is that correct?

A.   Right.

If Ms. Nelsen denies these questions, you can use the prior statement to impeach her and show you had a basis to ask the question. You are allowed to read it back to her, right after she disagrees with your assertion. See § 9-28. You need to make a reference to the circumstances in which the prior statement was given, but the reference can be brief. Thus, you are able to quickly juxtapose the prior statement against the witness's denial of your question, which was based on the prior statement.

Q.   You knew he did not have experience in the sale of microcomputers, right?

A.   I don't believe so.

Q.   Well, you knew his only experience with computers was from using them in police work?

A.   I don't think so.

Q.   Ms. Nelsen, is this true: You thought he overrated his experience in the police department as a means of being prepared for the sale of microcomputers.

> A.   No, not really.
>
> Q.   Do you remember signing an affidavit in this case?
>
> A.   Yes.
>
> Q.   In that affidavit, you said: "I thought that Jack Danielson in particular overrated the utility of his experience at the police department as a means of being prepared for sales of microcomputers." Did you say that?
>
> A.   Yes, I guess so.

This rat-tat-tat presentation of backup serves several purposes. It establishes counsel was fair. It punishes the witness for changing her story. Further, *it tends to establish the asserted fact*. The jury actually hears the assertion twice and learns there is a solid basis for it. Under the hearsay rules, a prior inconsistent statement does not always serve as substantive proof, but as a practical matter it has this impact. Thus, it is important to quickly juxtapose the prior statement against the denial.

From the witness's perspective, being caught in an inconsistency hurts, especially when it is apparent that counsel fairly relied on the prior statement. If the witness becomes convinced that the lawyer has backup for the entire examination, she will become averse to disagreeing with counsel's assertions. Additionally, producing the backup material shows that counsel had a fair basis to expect a favorable answer.

You do not need an extensive review of all the circumstances of the prior statement: the oath, the intent to tell the truth, the witness's good memory at the time, and other matters. These facts get in the way of a quick, understandable demonstration that the question was fair. Nor do you want to ask the witness to explain the inconsistency. She has a right to inject an explanation, but you should not ask for it. If you do, the witness may provide one that counters or defuses your point:

> Q.   How do you explain the discrepancy in your affidavit, Ms. Nelsen?
>
> A.   I'd say the affidavit was incomplete. Mr. Danielson turned out to be much more bullheaded than I thought. He acted like he knew everything, not just from his police department experience. But we found that out when we tried to train him.

From the base established by the prior statement — she knew Danielson "overrated" his experience — it logically follows that she knew he would need training. If she denies that precept, she risks her credibility. Thus, the following questions should produce affirmative responses.

Q. You thought that Jack Danielson in particular overrated the utility of his experience at the police department as a means of being prepared for sales of microcomputers; is that right?

A. Yes.

Q. Thus, you knew training would be necessary for him to succeed?

A. Yes.

Q. You knew that he would have to depend on Computer-Centre's expertise; is that true?

A. Yes.

To the extent the attorney employs conclusionary rather than fact-based questions, he invites argument and explanation. Consider the following exchange:

Q. You did not disclose all the material facts to the Danielsons, did you?

A. Yes we did. We always make full disclosure. Our disclosure forms have to comply with securities laws. We are very careful to disclose all material facts.

The answer here appears fair because the question is broad and judgmental. The witness thus has freedom to expound in responding.

Even a question dealing with facts fairly calls for explanation if it is too general. An example:

Q. At the seminar in Middletown on February 12, you promised big profits to the people attending; is that correct?

A. I'm sure we told them they could be profitable if they worked hard and followed our advice.

Questions that contain multiple points also give the witness room to maneuver. An example follows:

Q.   Knowing the Danielsons were not experienced and in a seminar where you were supposed to explain about franchises, you emphasized the high profits that could be received without much experience; is that correct?

A.   I wouldn't put it like that. We tried to explain exactly what they needed to know.

Because there is so much built into counsel's question, it sounds like it contains opinion. Thus, the witness may fairly inject opinion into the response. Moreover, it would be hard to demonstrate through impeachment that the witness overreached because there are too many points to cover. Simpler questions make it easier to control the witness.

Based on the seminar agenda, counsel can be much more specific with Ms. Nelsen, making her explanations seem gratuitous.

Q.   The title of your talk was "How the Profits Mount," correct?

A.   Yes, but we also discussed a lot of other topics.

Q.   Your talk used the San Francisco franchise as an example of profitability; is that true?

A.   We told them they'd have to work hard.

Q.   Did you hear my question?

A.   What was it?

Q.   You used the San Francisco franchise as an example of profitability, right?

A.   Maybe so, but they knew that profits aren't automatic.

When questions are specific, the explanations seem out of line. Further, counsel can employ subtle methods to point out the witness's unresponsiveness and can even ask that unresponsive answers be stricken. See § 9-20.

You can also use other documents to support your questions. If a document is in evidence and the witness is familiar with it, you can ask her to read it. If it is not in evidence and she knows what it is, you can introduce it through her testimony and have a crucial part read. You can also show a document to a witness to "refresh recollection," which usually produces agreement with your assertion and shows you have a basis for your question, even if the document is not introduced. An example of using a document as backup follows:

Q.		Ms. Nelsen, the title of your talk at the February 12 meeting was "How the Profits Mount," correct?
A.		I don't believe so.
Counsel:		May I approach?
The Court:		Yes.
Q.		I show you Plaintiff's Exhibit 2. Is that the agenda for your meeting?
A.		Yes.
Q.		What's the title of your talk, Ms. Nelsen?
A.		I see it now.
Q.		Read it to the jury, Ms. Nelsen.
A.		"How the Profits Mount."

Of course, if you have documents as backup, you may not have to use them. When the witness sees that your questions have a basis — and perhaps sees you holding a document — she will generally agree to your assertions.

Impeachment with prior statements is addressed in § 9-28.

§ 9-18. Need to Start and End Well.

Opening the cross-examination with a strong point may partially offset the favorable impact of a good direct examination. It may also unnerve the witness, paving the way for a successful cross. Further, it should help attract the jury's attention to the cross-examination. There is no need to be guided by your opponent's organization. Choose a subject that allows a strong start. Additionally, you generally want to find a way to end with a flourish.

A good way to start cross-examination is to ask thematic questions. These inquiries may reflect the theme of your case or the ensuing examination. Often you can use "can't lose" questions to make a thematic point. In the *Danielson v. ComputerCentre Associates* case, counsel might use the following questions with Jene Nelsen, who is accused of misrepresenting facts to the Danielsons:

Q.	You are in charge of providing information to prospects interested in franchises; is that correct?
A.	Yes.

Q. Would you agree it is only fair to be truthful with your prospects?

A. Yes.

Q. Would you agree that a franchiser should be candid with prospects in disclosing facts?

A. I think so.

Q. How about this: it's only fair to tell the whole story to prospects?

A. I guess so.

Q. It's only right to disclose the failures as well as the successes, would you agree?

A. Yes, but we don't have any failures.

Q. Would you agree it's only fair to reveal the problems you are having in fulfilling your obligations?

A. I guess so, if they're important.

Another possible focus with Jene Nelsen would be her prior conviction for mail fraud. In all likelihood, the court would determine the extent of permissible inquiry on the issue prior to the trial. The attorney at least would be allowed to impeach with the conviction, which would permit references to the name of the crime, date of conviction, and sentence. Additionally, if the conviction were deemed a fact that should have been disclosed by ComputerCentre, counsel could explore its basis in greater depth. An example of a brief examination follows:

Q. Ms. Nelsen, you were the main person at ComputerCentre who was responsible for making disclosures to prospects interested in franchises, correct?

A. Yes.

Q. And you are a convicted felon, right?

A. I had a conviction, but I served my time, and the charges were bogus.

Q. To be more precise, you were convicted of defrauding people; is that true?

A. Mail fraud.

Q. You were convicted of using the mail to defraud people, correct?

A.   I suppose you could put it that way. But the charges were bogus.

Q.   You were convicted of defrauding people you solicited for a weight-loss preparation; is that right?

A.   Yes. But it was a trumped-up charge.

Q.   A jury heard the evidence and convicted you of fraud in those solicitations; is that true?

A.   Yes.

Q.   A judge sentenced you to two years in jail for that fraud, right?

A.   Yes.

This approach throws Nelsen on the defensive and establishes the context for an examination about fraud in the *Danielson* case.

Early in cross-examination you should consider asking a number of simple questions that will elicit "yes" answers. The questions might review points about the witness's background, job, duties on the job, or similar matters on which there is no dispute. They should be precise enough so as not to invite explanations. This technique gets the witness used to saying "yes." Once a pattern of agreement is established, the witness may be less inclined to volunteer explanations. An example follows.

Q.   I'd like to cover a few additional points about your background. You indicated you were construction supervisor; is that right?

A.   Yes.

Q.   You held that job for two years; is that correct?

A.   Yes.

Q.   You started in that job in December, 1992, right?

A.   Yes.

Q.   You were an assistant superintendent before that; is that correct?

A.   Yes.

Q.   You held that job for three years, right?

A.   Yes.

You should not overdo the background, because you may lose the jury's attention, but this method establishes a pattern of nonequivocation. Once the pattern is established, explanations may appear gratuitous.

You need not restrict yourself to a single technique. A strong start with a bombshell, followed by a bit of witness training, is an effective combination. After a strong overall point the background will have more context, which makes it easier to hold attention. In any event, the choice of how to start depends on your ammunition.

If possible, you should also plan a final question or series that allows ending the examination on a high note. A closing that ties points together or captures the theme is a great way to complete testimony. More important, however, is making sure the witness has to agree with your points. Since the beginning and end are the parts that usually last with listeners, you need to devote extra effort to planning these parts of the examination.

§ 9-19.   Using Signposts.

Just as signposts are important on direct examination, they are an effective aid in cross-examination. By calling attention to transitions, you focus the jury's attention on new subjects and enhance understanding. This action also reinforces the impression that you are in control of the case. An example might be: "First, I'd like to discuss your criminal record."

One of your advantages in cross-examination is the ability to select topics. You get to choose what to discuss, when, and how much. The only problem is that the jury may not follow your examination; without a chronological or other obvious organization, you may lose your listeners. Giving a signal that shows you are moving to a new topic allows them to follow the questioning.

In some cases, you may not want to reveal to the witness where you are going before you have established some points. Thus, you would not want to provide a signal that identifies your topic. Nevertheless, you generally should indicate that you are moving to a new area. An example: "I'd like to move on to something else. First, let me ask you. . . ."

§ 9-20.   Dealing with the Difficult Witness on Cross-Examination.

No matter how well you prepare for cross-examination, you undoubtedly will encounter witnesses who refuse or simply fail to answer your questions. Often these witnesses are intent on replaying the themes of the direct examination; they restate points they have already made, without acknowledging or addressing the new points introduced through your questions. Sometimes witnesses offer elaborate explanations, wandering far from the original point of a question to introduce information helpful to their positions. Some witnesses — particularly expert witnesses — may ask questions about your questions to reverse the roles of questioner and witness. Some witnesses may try to bait you, to provoke an angry reaction. In dealing with these difficulties, you must keep your focus on the goals of the examination and compel the witness to respond to your inquiries.

Using narrow, specific questions that focus on factual points is the best technique to limit the witness's ability to wander from your points. The more narrow the question, the more it calls for a "yes" or "no," making an out-of-context explanation appear superfluous. Questions that embody broad conclusions or make multiple points tend to invite explanation. Additionally, choosing understandable language in your questions will help make it obvious to jurors that a recalcitrant witness is avoiding, rather than misunderstanding, your point.

Even if you use well-crafted questions, some witnesses will insist on recalcitrance. The difficulties you may encounter in cross-examining witnesses, and some suggestions for dealing with the problems, include the following.

§ 9-20(a).   Witness "Explains" to Introduce Counter-Points.

Frequently witnesses who have a stake in the outcome of a case look for ways to introduce points helpful to their side in responding to your cross-examination questions. They may not include legitimate answers to your questions with their explanations. Witnesses may launch into long narratives, introducing topics that relate not at all to your questions.

How do you control a witness who offers gratuitous statements? First, make your questions specific. Explanations seem out of place when you ask specific, fact-based questions. Second, you can use subtle techniques to remind everyone that the witness's answer is unresponsive. "Getting back to my question," for instance, is an introductory phrase that performs this function. Another example: "Well, that's interesting, but I'd like to return to the subject of my question. What did you. . .?" Third, you can politely *ask* the witness for help. You fairly may request, for instance, that the witness answer your questions *before* explaining, or that the witness listen carefully to a question. This approach is inoffensive, so your opponent is not likely to object:

Q.   Ms. Nelsen, I'd like to ask you to try to answer the following question yes or no if you can, and then provide any necessary explanation. . . .

Q.   Mr. Danielson, I'd appreciate it if you listen carefully to my next question. . . .

Fourth, you can ask the court to instruct the witness to answer your questions and strike unresponsive answers. The judge may not want to admonish the witness, however, so you generally should try other approaches before seeking the court's intervention.

When the garrulous "explainer" appears on the stand, he may subject you and the jurors to long narratives. Experts often fall into this category, answering every question with a lecture. Since these discussions often go on for several minutes, you are forced to choose between interrupting to object and enduring the lecture. One method to deal with the problem is to pointedly ignore the response once it exceeds a reasonable length. You might return to counsel table, sit down and go through papers, or begin a whispered conversation with a colleague. This action sends a strong signal to everyone — including the witness — that the answer exceeds a proper bound. At the same time, you should not *actually* stop listening, because the witness may say something improper of introduce a point that requires you to follow up. If a witness repeatedly answers your questions with lectures, you should ask the court to instruct the witness to limit himself to answering your questions.

§ 9-20(b). Witness Answers a Question Different From the One You Pose.

Witnesses sometimes use a more egregious tactic to avoid an attorney's question: simply ignoring the question and addressing a different point. A lawyer who fails to listen to the answer may miss the disconnect, allowing the witness to succeed in avoiding the inquiry. You must listen to the answers and ensure that the witness concedes your points, or follow up to compel appropriate answers.

You can use the same methods as those described in § 9-20(a) to deal with a witness who refuses to answer your questions and addresses different topics. Phrase your follow-up inquiries to signal that the witness was unresponsive, as follows:

Q. Getting back to my question, ...

Q. Perhaps you didn't understand my question. . . .

Q. I don't believe my question addressed moisture in the mix. Returning to what I asked, would you agree. . . .

If the witness remains unresponsive despite repeated efforts to compel legitimate answers, ask the court to direct the witness to respond appropriately.

§ 9-20(c). Witness Tries to Interrogate You.

Some witnesses, particularly experts, try to throw attorneys off track by asking them questions about the cross-examination questions. Typical ploys include asking the lawyer to define technical terms and asking for more specific information about questions. Giving in to these tactics cedes control of the examination to the witness and destroys the momentum of a cross-examination.

If a witness asks you to define a term, you can turn the request around and ask him how *he* would define it. You can then decide whether to continue questioning based on the witness's definition. You should always understand the meaning of technical terms used in your questions, however, and be ready to offer a definition that furthers your point. You then have the option of posing the definition in the witness and asking if he agrees. Be sure to request the agreement, so you keep control of the interrogation. If the witness asks for more information, ask him what he needs to permit accepting the definition. This approach keeps the witness in the role of the respondent.

When a witness asks for more information about a question, rephrase with a more specific inquiry. If you believe the witness posed an insincere inquiry to buy time, you might ask a question that points up the absurdity of the inquiry: "You don't know which contract my question refers to?" In any event, hold on to your role as interrogator as you move the process forward. Since the witness wants to confuse the listeners and destroy your momentum, rephrase as necessary to regain a focus on *your* point.

§ 9-20(d).   Witness Baits or Insults You.

An experienced witness who senses an attorney gaining momentum in a cross-examination may try to make her angry. Suggesting the attorney does not understand an issue, or that the attorney is trying to mislead the court or jury, often is really designed to make the attorney angry. If the lawyer allows the witness to succeed, she may lose focus on the subject and control of the interrogation. Descending into an argument or shouting match with the witness is not the way to maintain control.

If the witness baits you, keep your composure. Direct the witness back to the question as you deflect any commentary: "Your opinion on my understanding is interesting, but let's get back to my question. . . ." Your control will impress the listeners. The witness, frustrated himself, may concede points he otherwise would have avoided. In any event, you need to maintain the momentum of your interrogation.

Even if you are not fully successful in dealing with a difficult witness, you should keep in mind that you may win the interrogation anyway. A witness who avoids your questions, launches into lecturers, or offers gratuitous insults is not likely to impress the listeners favorably. Your control in the face of these tactics will reinforce your stature and credibility. Further, to the extent you compel an evasive witness finally to answer your questions, the jurors are bound to conclude that you "win" the point. Thus, a difficult witness may offer you a greater opportunity for success than one who answers your questions helpfully.

§ 9-21. Dealing with Damaging Information Revealed in Cross-Examination.

Sometimes a witness on cross-examination delivers a right cross directly to counsel's chin. An ill-conceived question may elicit the damaging point or the witness may include it in a non-responsive answer. Often an attorney shows the effect of the damage through his physical or verbal reaction — perhaps by appearing befuddled or pausing as if startled. Worse yet, lawyers sometimes follow up with inept questions, permitting the witness to expand the damaging testimony.

You should avoid appearing injured by a damaging answer in cross-examination. Hold a poker face. Remember that listeners may not understand the damage and they are likely to forget it soon in any event if you can reestablish your momentum. Move on to a safe question. Do not compound the damage by following up unless you can impeach the witness or contradict the damaging point.

If you are confident you can deal effectively with a damaging point, you must consider whether to address it when the witness brings it up. Assuming it is important and relates to the topic you are addressing, you may wish to pursue it before you forget the matter. You must remember, however, that a digression takes you away from the point you are pursuing. You must evaluate whether the matter is worth a possible loss of momentum. Be particularly careful when the follow-up is likely to lead you off your point.

Unless you are sure you can refute or neutralize a damaging point, leave it alone. Further inquiry may well subject you to further damage. If you move on as if the point were never made, many of the jurors may miss it altogether.

One method of distracting the listeners from damage inflicted in an answer is to suggest that a question needs rephrasing. As you rephrase, you can switch to a somewhat different question. The implication that you misstated the question or the witness misunderstood it may take some punch out of the answer. This approach is illustrated below:

Q. In your estimation the cracking in the concrete walls was thermal in nature, is that correct?

A. No, counsel, quite the opposite. The cracking as was caused by hydration shrinkage because there was too much water in the mix.

Q. Well, perhaps I misstated the question. Let me try it this way. Thermal conditions can cause concrete to crack, is that right?

> A. Yes.
>
> Q. And in your report you listed thermal cracking as one possible cause of the cracks in the wall, true?
>
> A. Yes. But we did not conclude they were thermal.
>
> Q. You did list thermal cracking?
>
> A. Yes.

This approach requires that you adjust quickly to a "safe" question on a topic close to the damaging point. Thus, it may be difficult to carry off without further damage. Moreover, you do not want to suggest falsely that the witness was unresponsive, particularly since some listeners may realize you changed the question. You may be wise to move on to safer questions.

§ 9-22. Counsel's Demeanor and Positioning.

Jurors usually pull for a witness rather than a lawyer, believing the witness is overmatched when confronted by a trained attorney. Therefore, you usually will fare better if you discredit the *testimony* and secure *factual concessions* rather than attack the witness as a person. Bullying the witness may backfire, causing the jury to resent your attitude.[31] If the witness scores points under these circumstances, they may have an exaggerated impact. Additionally, often you should use the witness to prove your points. Concessions you secure from a witness for the other side add credibility to your word picture. In conducting the examination, consider the following pointers.

1. *Emotion.* During the cross-examination, feel free to show controlled emotion. Thus, in the right circumstances, reactions such as surprise, disgust, and dismay may validate your position. The key is to keep them in their proper place — where the reaction is appropriate to the testimony. The last thing you want is for the jury to conclude that your emotional response is faked or overdone. Further, you should always be aware that people expect you to be professional, which requires emotional control. Your reaction should be less apparent than might be expected from a layman.

2. *Conviction.* In examining the witness you should have an air of conviction and certainty. Speak in a loud, authoritative voice. You should give the impression that you know the facts and have material to back them

---

[31] See generally Robert A. Sayler, *Rambo Litigation: Why Hardball Tactics Don't Work,* A.B.A.J. at 78 (1988) ("It defies all common experience to believe that meanspiritedness is persuasive. Try to find some other field of endeavor — from politics to public relations — where this is the case." *Id.* at 79); see also Marvin W. Mindes and Alan C. Acock, *Trickster, Hero, Helper: A Report on the Lawyer Image,* 177 Am. B. Found. Res. J. (1982).

up. This attitude makes you the storyteller and lends credibility to your contentions. Additionally, it should make the witness reluctant to dispute your statements.

3.   *Position.* Stand when you conduct the examination. Sitting generally sends a passive, submissive signal. Moreover, it cedes prominence to the witness, as his chair is usually positioned higher than yours. Additionally, it is hard to exude a "presence" from a sitting position. By standing, you assume the dominant role and help yourself control the exchange.

Since you do not necessarily want attention focused on the witness in cross-examination, you should stand where the jurors can see you as well as the witness. Try to stand in front of the jury box so that they do not have to look back and forth. If the court makes you stand at a podium, try to position it so that the jurors can observe both you and the witness.

4.   *Eye contact.* You should look at the witness during the examination. Eye contact makes it harder for the witness to dispute your assertions. If you are looking at the witness, and he looks down, you appear to be the one who is right. Additionally, if you show emotion it seems more real if you look at the witness. You obviously need to check your notes periodically, but do so unobtrusively. You also must listen to what the witness has to say. You cannot impeach if you do not know what the witness says. Looking and listening are essential to controlling the examination.

5.   *Courtesy.* Although many attorneys try to admonish and instruct witnesses in cross-examination, they are not entitled to do so. The court, not the examiner, is empowered to instruct witnesses how to respond. Additionally, the lawyer is not entitled to limit the witness to "yes" or "no"; a witness generally may explain a response. Indeed, if a question cannot fairly be answered with a "yes" or "no," the witness is entitled to respond in a different manner. The attorney does have a right to an answer that responds to the question, however; if the witness addresses a different matter, the court may strike the answer as unresponsive.

Bullying a witness generally is counterproductive. If you interrupt, admonish, and instruct the witness to answer "yes" or "no," you will provoke an objection. Some judges have unusual rules for cross-examination, but most tend to protect the witness — giving him the right to explain without interruption. Further, most judges do not permit counsel to instruct or admonish a witness. Thus, your action may produce a rebuke. Additionally, even if the judge allows you to cut off and bully a witness, this action may make the jurors pull for the witness. Thus, you must find more agreeable ways to control the witness and force a response, as discussed in § 9-20.

§ 9-23. Calling a Hostile Witness or a Witness Identified with the Adverse Party (FRE 611(c)).

Sometimes you must call the adverse party, someone identified with that party, or a hostile witness to support your case. When you do so, you call the witness on direct examination. Nevertheless, because the witness is likely to resist providing information that helps you, you have a right to lead. FRE 611(c) provides: "When a party calls a hostile witness, an adverse party, or a witness identified with an adverse party, interrogation may be by leading questions."

In calling the adverse party, you do not have to make a special showing before being permitted to lead. You may simply begin questioning the witness as if on cross-examination. If the opposing party objects, cite FRE 611(c). Before you lead other witnesses under this rule, however, you may have to show that the witness is "identified" with the adverse party or is hostile.

Usually an employee, business partner, relative, or person in privity with the adverse party is "identified" with that party. Thus, in an accident case an insured probably would be "identified" with the insurer, even if only one of them were named as the defendant. To lead, you may first have to ask questions showing the relationship between the witness and the party.

Establishing that a witness is hostile involves showing he has interests antagonistic to your case or resents being a witness. Often the witness's manner demonstrates his hostility; once recalcitrance is evident, the court will permit leading. In other situations you may have to demonstrate the witness's motive for hostility before you can lead. The court has considerable discretion to determine whether you have made an adequate showing of hostility.

The need to call an adverse or hostile witness arises frequently in trial. Often a party has to prove facts within the knowledge of his opponent. Although these facts often are disclosed in discovery, calling a witness is often the best way to prove them. In the *Danielson v. ComputerCentre Associates*[32] case, for instance, the plaintiffs likely would call an executive or employee of Computer-Centre to establish facts about the company's operation that were inconsistent with representations made to the Danielsons. For instance, a ComputerCentre executive might be the best witness to show that there was no technical facility to train technicians at the time ComputerCentre promised technical training. If Dale Atkins or another ComputerCentre executive were called for this purpose, the court would permit leading.

When you call your adverse party or a person identified with him, your opponent ordinarily should *not* be allowed to lead in the "cross-examination." The qualification in FRE 611(c), which provides that leading "[o]rdinarily" should be permitted on cross-examination, permits the court to preclude leading

---

[32] See Appendix A.

when the examination is really more like direct.[33] For example, a lawyer generally should not be permitted to lead her own client in a so-called "cross-examination."

When you call an adverse witness on direct, your strategy should be similar to that used for cross-examination. Since the witness has not already told a story, you should pay greater attention to structure, using a chronological or topical approach that ensures your presentation is understandable. You have the same right to impeach as you would on cross-examination.

You often gain the advantage of surprise in calling the adverse party. Often a plaintiff catches a defendant unprepared if she calls the defendant in her own case. This action may force the party to undergo an examination without adequate preparation. Attorneys often wait to prepare witnesses until shortly before they call them, which makes this strategy surprisingly successful.

If your client is called to testify by the adverse party, you must decide whether to cross-examine immediately or wait until your own case. If the witness is prepared, you generally should proceed with those points that respond to the direct. Clearing up damaging points immediately is usually the best strategy. If the witness is unprepared, you may want to wait. The judge is not likely to allow you to go over the same territory twice. You should also consider asking permission to cover new matters while the witness is on the stand. This action allows you to make affirmative points for your side in the adverse party's case. The court has discretion to allow inquiry into new areas under FRE 611(b).

§ 9-24.   Example of a Cross-Examination: Jack Danielson in Danielson v. ComputerCentre Associates.

The following cross-examination of Jack Danielson is based on the *Danielson v. ComputerCentre Associates* material.[34] The examination was developed based not only on the affidavit of Jack Danielson, but those of Margaret Danielson and Drew Anderson. Since these affidavits were filed on behalf of the Danielsons in connection with a motion for summary judgment, Jack Danielson probably reviewed and approved them. If so, you can use them to impeach. Additionally, the examination is developed from other documents in the case with which Mr. Danielson should be familiar. Before reviewing the example, you may benefit from looking over Mr. Danielson's affidavit in Appendix A.

> Q.   Good afternoon, Mr. Danielson.
>
> A.   Good afternoon.

---

[33] FED. R. EVID. 611(c) advisory committee's note.

[34] See Appendix A.

Q. Mr. Danielson, when you obtained your ComputerCentre franchise, you never had operated a business before; is that true?

A. Yes.

Q. As a reasonable person, you knew there was some risk in starting a new business; is that right?

A. I guess so.

Q. You knew that part of the risk was the possibility of financial failure; would you agree with that?

A. I guess I would.

Q. You were entering a new area for you; is that true?

A. Yes.

Q. You were venturing into the competitive world; is that right?

A. That's right.

Q. When a person enters a new business in the competitive world, what would you say ordinarily makes the difference between financial success and failure?

A. I'm not really sure what you mean.

Q. Well, would you agree that one of the elements of success when a person enters a new business in the competitive world is hard work?

A. I suppose I would agree.

Q. Would you agree that one of the determinants of success in a competitive business venture is making intelligent business decisions?

A. I'd have to accept that.

Q. Would you agree that dedication to the business is necessary to make a competitive business venture successful?

A. I suppose so.

Q. How about this: An element of success in a new business venture is getting the right people to work for the business — would you agree?

A. That's probably true.

Q. And would you agree that finding the right location is often an ingredient of success for a new business venture, particularly a sales location?

A.   I suppose.

Q.   One other question in this area, Mr. Danielson: Would you agree that typically it's not easy to be a success with a new business venture?

A.   What do you mean?

Q.   Success isn't handed to you on a silver platter — do you agree?

A.   Yes.

Q.   I want to review your entry into the computer business. When you decided to start looking for a franchise, you were retired from the Middletown Police Department; is that correct?

A.   Yes.

Q.   You're in your 40s; is that true, Mr. Danielson?

A.   Yes.

Q.   You wanted to supplement your retirement income; is that right?

A.   That's right.

Q.   You were looking to find a franchise of some type; is that correct?

A.   Yes.

Q.   You had never operated a business before; is that true?

A.   That's correct.

Q.   Your wife had never operated a business before; is that correct?

A.   Yes.

Q.   You thought the micro and mini computer business was a timely business; is that correct?

A.   Yes, my wife and I did.

Q.   You did not want to go back to school for training; is that right?

A.   I don't know what you mean.

Q.   You did not want to go back to school for extensive retraining in order to enter a new business; is that right?

A.   That's not really true.

479

Q.   Mr. Danielson, you gave an affidavit in this case in connection with a motion for summary judgment. Do you remember that?

A.   Yes.

Q.   In that affidavit, in paragraph 3, you said: "We thought that was a timely business, with a rapidly expanding market, and that we could be part of the so-called 'high tech' revolution without having to go back to school for extensive retraining, by means of purchasing a franchise." Did you say that?

A.   Oh, yeah. I guess that's correct.

Q.   Let's turn to the meeting at the Holiday Inn. You attended that meeting alone; is that correct?

A.   Yes.

Q.   Your wife did not go to the meeting; is that correct?

A.   That's right.

Q.   There were twelve to thirteen other people there; is that right?

A.   Yes, that's correct.

Q.   There was a presentation by Dale Atkins and Jene Nelsen; is that right?

A.   Yes.

Q.   It was a very long presentation, correct?

A.   It lasted all day, yes.

Q.   They went over the success of other ComputerCentre franchises; is that true?

A.   Yes. They went over that in great detail.

Q.   And you were well aware that they were marketing a product?

A.   Yes. I knew that.

Q.   You knew it was a sales pitch for computer franchises, didn't you?

A.   That became very evident.

Q.   You were quite put off by the presentation; is that correct?

A.   I don't know what you mean.

Q.   You found it eerie and nerve-wracking; is that true?

A. Oh, yes, I did.

Q. You were actually relieved when it was over; is that correct?

A. Yes.

Q. And yet you decided to sign up for a franchise within 24 hours; is that true?

A. We decided the next day.

Q. The next morning?

A. Yes.

Q. That was within 24 hours; is that correct?

A. Yes.

Q. In fact, by the next day you and your wife had already made an initial decision on a location; is that true?

A. We had talked about it.

Q. Well, you had already identified the Middletown Historic Mall as a potential location; is that correct?

A. Yes, we thought it would be a good location.

Q. And you called ComputerCentre; is that right?

A. Yes.

Q. You called ComputerCentre at 10:00 a.m. the next morning without any further communication from ComputerCentre; is that true?

A. Yes, I guess so.

Q. And at that time you had already decided to sign up for a franchise?

A. Yes. I told him we wanted to purchase the franchise if the fee was not exorbitant.

Q. He told you the standard fee was $50,000 plus $2,000 training; is that right?

A. Yes.

Q. That was satisfactory to you; is that correct?

A. Yes, it was, for what we thought we were getting.

Q. In retrospect, you believe it sounds silly to have made the decision so quickly; is that correct?

A. I'm not sure what you mean.

Q.   In your affidavit, in paragraph 8, you said: "I know it sounds silly to have decided so quickly, but right after breakfast we decided to go ahead with the venture." Did you say that?

A.   I guess so.

Q.   I want to focus on the question of your involvement in the franchise's operation. You knew when you signed up that owning a business required personal involvement; would you agree with that?

A.   Yes.

Q.   You went into the business expecting to be personally involved on a full-time basis?

A.   Yes, I did.

Q.   You expected that your wife would be involved full-time also; is that true?

A.   Well, at least most of the time.

Q.   You were involved for the first three months of operation; is that correct, Mr. Danielson?

A.   Yes.

Q.   And in those first three months, the franchise was profitable, was it not?

A.   I'm not so sure about that.

Q.   You don't know if it was profitable?

A.   No, I don't.

Q.   You were in charge of the franchise, weren't you?

A.   Yes.

Q.   You were in charge, but you don't know if it was profitable?

A.   I said I wasn't sure.

Q.   In September of 1993, you suffered a heart attack; is that right?

A.   Yes.

Q.   The doctors discovered you had blockages in your arteries; is that correct?

A.   That's right.

Q.   Because of these blockages, bypass surgery was required?

A.   Right.

Q.   You had surgery in October 1993, correct?

A.   Yes.

Q.   It required four months for you to recuperate; is that right?

A.   That's about right.

Q.   Your recovery was complete in February of 1994. Is that a fair statement?

A.   I don't know what you mean by recovery.

Q.   Let's try it this way: You underwent open-heart surgery October 2, 1993, and began a successful four month recuperation. Is that right?

A.   I wouldn't call it completely successful.

Q.   Mr. Danielson, you and your wife filed a Complaint against my client in this case. Do you recall that?

A.   Yes.

Q.   In that Complaint at paragraph 25, you said: "After consultation with cardiovascular experts, plaintiff Jack Danielson underwent open-heart surgery October 2, two years ago, and began a successful four-month recuperative period." Did you say that?

A.   If you say so. Perhaps my attorney was optimistic.

Q.   Mr. Danielson, your attorney got his information from you, did he not?

A.   And my wife.

Q.   You swore out a verification of the statements in that Complaint, didn't you?

A.   I guess I did.

Q.   Mr. Danielson, you were not involved in the business when you were recuperating from your heart attack; is that right?

A.   Yes. I couldn't be involved, counsel.

Q.   After February 1994, when you had recovered, you were not involved in the day-to-day operation of the franchise; is that true?

A.   Yes.

Q.   Your wife had to manage the store by herself?

A.   She did.

Q.   Your wife asked for your assistance, did she not?

A.   Once in a while.

Q.   She asked for your advice?

A.   Sometimes.

Q.   You knew she was having difficulty running the store; is that correct?

A.   She said that.

Q.   She told you she felt overwhelmed, didn't she?

A.   She may have said that.

Q.   The store's profits were eroding at that time; is that correct?

A.   If we ever had any profits.

Q.   She was frustrated; is that correct?

A.   Perhaps.

Q.   She was distraught?

A.   At times she acted that way.

Q.   Yet you did not go into the store to help; is that correct?

A.   It was too stressful.

Q.   You didn't go in to help; is that right?

A.   No.

Q.   I am right, you did not go in?

A.   Yes, that's right.

Q.   Your wife felt you wouldn't focus on the problems you were having; is that right?

Opposing
Counsel: Objection. He can't know how his wife felt.

Q.   I'll rephrase. Your wife told you that she felt you wouldn't focus on the problems at the store; is that correct?

A.   What are you referring to?

Q.   I am asking you a question. Your wife told you she felt you wouldn't focus on the problems you were having at the store?

A.   She may have said that.

Q.   You gave her no concrete suggestions of how to improve your sales; is that correct?

A.   That's not true.

Q.   Your wife gave an affidavit in this case; is that correct?

A.   Yes.

Q.   You looked at it at the time; is that true?

A.   Yes.

Q.   You thought her statements were true, did you not?

A.   Yes.

Q.   In her affidavit, she said: "Whatever the reason, I had difficulty last spring in getting Jack to focus on the problems we were having, and he was, frankly, not much help in coming up with concrete suggestions of how to improve our sales or find a way to improve our profit margin on the sales we were making." Did you see and agree with that?

A.   Probably.

Q.   Was it true?

A.   I guess so.

Q.   She complained that you were unwilling to help her manage the store; is that correct?

A.   She might have said that.

Q.   By the summer of 1994, you knew there were serious difficulties with the franchise; is that true?

A.   I knew it before then.

Q.   You knew the hours had been shortened?

A.   Yes.

Q.   The reason was because there were no employees to greet customers; is that correct?

A.   Yes.

Q.   You knew your wife was too drained to be there every day, correct?

A.   I knew that.

Q.   You left it to someone else to make the decisions; is that true?

A.   It was too stressful.

Q.   Getting back to the question, you left it to someone else to run the store, right?

A.   Yes.

485

Q. That someone was Mr. Drew Anderson; is that right?

A. Yes, it was Mr. Anderson.

Q. Mr. Anderson had been in the Navy; is that right?

A. Yes.

Q. You knew he had no prior experience selling computers at retail, true?

A. I knew that.

Q. You knew he had no experience with your store or your customers; is that right?

A. Yes.

Q. You knew he dismissed your employees; is that correct?

A. My wife told me that.

Q. And you knew your wife was not able to go in every day because she was emotionally drained?

A. Yes.

Q. You knew Mr. Anderson had to shorten the hours, correct?

A. Yes. The evening hours.

Q. He was not even open in the evening; is that right?

A. That's true.

Q. Is this a fair statement: In the three-month period when you had a new manager, who had no experience with your business or your customers, who had no staff, and at a time when losses were mounting and the store couldn't be open normal hours, and after your successful recuperation, you never once even set foot into your store?

A. I told you it was too stressful to go there.

Q. I want to back up and talk about your sales personnel. Mr. Danielson, you were aware of the need for trained personnel to sell your computers; is that true?

A. When are you talking about?

Q. You were aware at the very beginning of the need for trained personnel to sell your computers; is that correct?

A. I don't think anyone told me that.

Q. Jene Nelsen told you in February 1993 that you need expert assistants in the marketing of a complex technological device like a computer, did she not?

A.   Oh. Yes, she did.

Q.   You knew computers were technical machines; is that right?

A.   I guess.

Q.   Your wife had no prior experience in programming?

A.   No, she didn't.

Q.   You had no prior experience operating computers?

A.   That's correct.

Q.   You had no prior experience in selling computers?

A.   That's true.

Q.   You knew your customers would have questions about these computers, didn't you?

A.   Sure.

Q.   You knew they might ask how to operate the computers, true?

A.   I guess I knew that.

Q.   You were aware they might ask how to program the computers, weren't you?

A.   Yes.

Q.   Customers usually expect salespeople to answer these questions, don't they?

A.   I guess so.

Q.   So you knew it would be helpful to have knowledgeable people to sell your computers; is that true?

A.   I thought we would get help from ComputerCentre.

Q.   But that's not my question. You knew it would be helpful to have knowledgeable salespeople, correct?

A.   I guess.

Q.   The two people you hired had no prior experience in marketing mini or micro computers, did they?

A.   They still did a good job.

Q.   You were only willing to pay $11,000 plus commissions for salespeople; is that right?

A.   That's all I could afford.

Q.   The salespeople had no knowledge of programming, did they?

A.   Sure they did.

Q.   Mr. Danielson, Drew Anderson, your manager, filed an affidavit in this proceeding; is that right?

A.   Yes.

Q.   You agreed with what he said in that affidavit, didn't you?

A.   I guess so.

Q.   In his affidavit, in paragraph 4, in reference to these salespeople, he said: "Neither of them, for example, had the slightest knowledge of computer programming." Is that a true statement?

Opposing
Counsel: Your Honor, I don't believe counsel can impeach with someone else's affidavit.

The Court: Counsel?

Counsel: Your Honor, the witness said he agreed with the affidavit. He adopted Mr. Anderson's statement.

The Court: I'll allow it.

Q.   Was Mr. Anderson's statement true, Mr. Danielson? Neither of them had the slightest knowledge of computer programming?

A.   That's his opinion.

Q.   The two people you hired had only a superficial comprehension of the computer market; is that right?

A.   I guess.

Q.   They didn't know how to operate computer programs; is that true?

A.   I guess so.

Q.   They couldn't do simple financial modeling on a computer; is that correct?

A.   I don't . . . I guess you're right.

Q.   Mr. Anderson fired them for these reasons, correct?

A.   Yes.

Q.   When you were still working at the store, Mr. Atkins repeatedly asked you to hire better personnel, didn't he?

A.   Once or twice.

Q.   He told you untrained personnel tend to depress sales; is that true?

A.   He may have said that.

Q.   He even wrote you, stating alarm that trained professionals had not been hired; is that correct?

A.   He may have written me a letter on that.

Counsel: May I approach the witness, Your Honor?

The Court: Proceed.

Q.   Mr. Danielson, I show you a letter that I've marked Defendant's Exhibit 4. Do you recognize this as a letter you received from Dale Atkins?

A.   This letter was sent to me and Margaret. It came after my heart attack.

Q.   But you read it, didn't you?

A.   Margaret showed it to me.

Counsel: With your permission, Your Honor, I wonder if Mr. Danielson could read the first sentence for the jury.

The Court: Proceed.

A.   "I note with alarm that you have yet to engage experienced computer professionals on your sales force."

Counsel: Your Honor, I'd like to offer this exhibit.

The Court: Any objection? Let it be admitted.

Q.   Mr. Danielson, Mr. Atkins also told you, you had to stock more inventory; is that right?

A.   Yes.

Q.   He told you the failure to do so would hurt your sales, didn't he?

A.   Yes.

Q.   Your franchise did not adhere to either request, did it?

A.   We couldn't.

Counsel: I'd like to refer you again to Defendant's Exhibit 4. Your Honor, this letter is only one paragraph. To save time, I wonder if Mr. Danielson could read it to the jury?

The Court: All right.

Q.   Mr. Danielson, would you read the letter?

A.   "I note with alarm that you have yet to engage experienced computer professionals on your sales force. In my experience this will likely lead to depressed sales. Also, I must remind you of the obligation to maintain sufficient inventory. As we have discussed, you are not keeping sufficient items in your stock to permit ready delivery to customers. We are doing everything we can to expedite your shipments to you, but you will lose sales if you cannot maintain some stock of the most common computers locally. Please let me know how you plan to rectify these matters."

Q.   Mr. Danielson, I'd like to turn to the subject of your location. You know that location is very important to a retail franchise; is that correct?

A.   Yes.

Q.   Dale Atkins wanted to help you find a good location; is that true?

A.   Yes.

Q.   You knew he wanted one with good demographics — meaning a population base that would provide lots of retail traffic, right?

A.   Yes.

Q.   You made your decision on location on the night you attended the first seminar, didn't you?

A.   A tentative decision.

Q.   You and your wife decided over dinner?

A.   Right.

Q.   You selected the Middletown historic shopping area; is that correct?

A.   Yes.

Q.   You based your decision on news stories that the area was being revitalized; is that right?

A.   That's right.

Q.   You did not ask for ComputerCentre's advice on the location, did you?

A.   I told them about it.

Q.   You did no demographic study, did you?

A.   We couldn't have done one.

Q.   Mr. Atkins suggested that you wait for a demographic study, didn't he?

A.   He mentioned one.

Q.   You made your decision without waiting for a study; is that right?

A.   We thought we had a good choice.

Q.   The two main choices were the Historic Mall and the Tri County Mall; is that correct?

A.   Yes.

Q.   The Tri County Mall draws from a much larger area, doesn't it?

A.   That's what Atkins said.

Q.   It draws from a population base of more than 2 million people; is that right?

A.   If you say so.

Q.   The Historic Mall draws from a base of about 76 thousand people; is that correct?

A.   Yes, but it doesn't have another computer store in it.

Q.   The Tri County Mall has twenty times the pedestrian traffic that the Historic Mall has; is that right?

A.   Perhaps.

Q.   Mr. Atkins advised you to consider the Tri County Mall; is that true?

A.   He mentioned it.

Q.   You wanted the franchise closer to home, correct?

A.   I didn't want to compete with another store in the same mall.

Q.   Mr. Atkins told you that another store would actually help your business by drawing customers, didn't he?

A.   That's what he said.

Q.   Yet you chose to stick with the Historic Mall; is that right?

A.   Yes.

Q.   I'd like to turn to the events of last summer. You are aware that Mr. Anderson began stocking computer game products last summer; is that right?

A.   I knew that.

Q.   These products were not approved by ComputerCentre; is that correct?

A.   We had to do something.

Q.   Is that a "yes"? You knew they were not approved?

A.   Yes.

Q.   You knew your franchise was not supposed to sell unapproved products; is that true?

A.   I knew that.

Q.   Would you agree that game computers are much less sophisticated than those you sold when you opened the franchise?

A.   We needed to make sales.

Q.   Is that a "yes"?

A.   Yes.

Q.   Mr. Danielson, are you familiar with the other ComputerCentre franchises?

A.   What?

Q.   You've become very aware of those franchises in this litigation, haven't you?

A.   Pretty much.

Q.   There were 41 franchises when you signed up; is that right?

A.   Yes.

Q.   There are 84 now; is that right?

A.   I think that's correct.

Q.   The vast majority of those franchises are very profitable; is that true?

A.   That's what your documents say.

Q.   Most of the stores, like your store, did not order in bulk; is that correct?

A.   That's probably right.

Q.   Those stores all paid the same mark-up that you paid; is that true?

A.   I guess so.

Q.   Still, virtually all of them were profitable; is that correct?

A.   That's what the documents say.

Q.   All those franchises had to deal with Mr. Atkins, didn't they?

A.   I guess so.

Q.   All of them had to deal with Ms. Nelsen; is that correct?

A.   Probably.

Q.   All of them had to deal with Wizard Supply; is that true?

A.   I guess so.

Q.   All of them got the same products that you got; is that correct?

A.   I suppose.

Q.   Mr. Danielson, I have one final area. Are you familiar with your franchise income statement for the last twelve months the store operated?

A.   I've seen it.

Q.   Do you know what the net loss was?

A.   I think it was $23,000.

Q.   The gross sales were about $767,000; is that right?

A.   I think that's right.

Q.   Now Mr. Danielson, you knew that you were losing money in that last year; is that correct?

A.   Yes.

Q.   But you were never involved in the day-to-day operation of the store; is that true?

A.   I think I already said that.

Q.   Yet you took a salary of $14,000; is that right?

A.   I thought I was entitled to something.

Q.   You took a bigger salary than your wife got; is that right?

A.   Yes.

Q.   And without that salary, your store would have been within $10,000 of breaking even; is that correct?

A.   That's correct arithmetic.

Q.   You had untrained personnel, you were not there to manage the store, your wife was drained, your manager couldn't keep the store open normal hours, and you still would have been within $10,000 of breaking even, right?

> A.   Under your assumptions, that's right.
>
> Counsel: I have no further questions.

§ 9-25.   Calling the Adverse Party on Direct Examination: Example.

The following are excerpts of an actual direct examination of the adverse party, an engineer, in litigation concerning runway failures at the New Orleans International Airport. The engineer claimed he was not responsible to oversee the preparation of the asphalt mixture or the quality of construction at the job site, although the contract explicitly required the engineer to perform these functions and he was paid several hundred thousand dollars to do so. He contended that a testing laboratory had orally assumed many of these duties.

In this excerpt counsel attempts to establish the lack of basis for the claim that responsibilities were transferred and the extent of the duties the engineer failed to perform. Counsel had already introduced the contracts and reviewed the fees and the contractual requirements with the witness. Notice that the witness attempts to explain virtually every answer, but the explanations do not necessarily help him.

[Engineer's familiarity with contractual responsibilities.]

Q.   Now, you wrote the specifications for the north-south and east-west runway projects using the FAA guide. Is that correct?

A.   Yes, sir.

Q.   And you are familiar with the various provisions in the specifications that you wrote concerning the responsibility of the engineer. Is that correct?

A.   I'm sorry, could you repeat that?

Q.   You are familiar with the various provisions in the specifications that you wrote concerning the responsibility of the engineer. Is that correct?

A.   No, those are the FAA standard specifications that mandatorily were to be put into the specifications. I didn't write that, and those specifications are construction documents only. That's not my document. And it's — it was written by the FAA with the understanding that the engineer in the testing lab were one and the same firm. There's very little mention of the testing lab in the specifications.

Q.   Getting back to my question, Mr. Lambert, you are familiar with the various provisions in the specifications concerning the responsibility of the engineer. Is that right?

A.   Yes, sir, I'm familiar with the — what is in the specifications, but I do differ that the term "engineer" refers to me. Where it pertains to the site or the design plans and specifications would be my responsibility. Where it pertains to the quality of materials and quality control in the plant inspection, those duties were superseded by these specifications at a later date by Delta Testing.

Q.   Mr. Lambert, in your engineering contract, who does the term "engineer" refer to?

A.   In my engineering contract, the term "engineer" refers to me, but I would like to say, at that time no testing lab was picked, and I could very well be told to do the testing, as I was on future jobs.

Q.   You remember our previous discussion about the amounts that were paid under those contracts to the engineer, sir?

A.   Yes, sir.

Q.   Those amounts were all paid to you. Is that right?

A.   Yes, sir.

Q.   None of these amounts for engineering supervisors were paid to Delta Testing. Is that right?

A.   Not through me, but none of the functions that Delta Testing did was I responsible to perform or did I perform. Otherwise, I should have been compensated for it, as I was in the future contracts.

* * *

[Engineer's attempt to shift responsibility.]

Q.   Mr. Lambert, with respect to the responsibility of the engineer in these specifications, Mr. Dale [of the FAA] specifically told you that he would not allow you to alter them. Is that right?

A.   That's correct.

Q.   And when you indicated that you wanted to alter them, he wouldn't let you do it. Is that right?

495

A. That's correct. At that time, he told me, "I may be doing the testing, and if you do the testing, then the specifications stay as they are."

Q. Well, sir, even after the north-south runway, the specs for the east-west runway were made up in the same way. Is that right?

A. Mr. Dale said there was not going to be a change on that one either.

Q. Now, I believe that you indicated that you had a conversation with Mr. Jack Meyn of Delta Testing and told him that he should handle some of the responsibilities set forth for the engineer. Is that correct?

A. I think that the — any — when Delta Testing was hired to do the testing, that the specification had to be separated as to which portion was material testing and quality control, and I gave the specifications to Mr. Meyn and recommended to Mr. Stoulig [the airport director] to enter into a contract with him that would segregate the responsibilities; that Mr. Meyn would be responsible for everything at the plant and all the materials. I have no material testing equipment.

* * *

Q. All right. Well, didn't you say in your deposition that the responsibilities were discussed in a meeting between you and Mr. Meyn?

A. Yes, sir, we had a discussion of responsibilities.

Q. And you told Mr. Meyn, according to that testimony, that he was supposed to read "testing lab" wherever the specifications said "engineer." Is that right?

A. Mr. Meyn told me he knew everything that had to be done on testing and Phil Arena would take care of that. I want to answer your question. Would you ask it again? I'm sorry.

Q. Didn't you say that he was supposed to read "testing lab" wherever the specifications said "engineer"?

A. No, sir, not just read "testing lab," but to perform that function and to take that responsibility, as it was severed from my contract and those specifications.

Q. Now, Mr. Stoulig [airport administrator] was not at this meeting between you and Mr. Meyn. Is that correct?

A.   That's correct.

Q.   No one from the New Orleans Aviation Board was present at that meeting. Is that right?

A.   There would be a lot of meetings, obviously. No, sir, but I would like to explain that. There would be a lot of meetings that I would like to have Mr. Stoulig there, that because of his workload he cannot be there, and he will ask me to do that as a courtesy, and I do it. But he has to make the final say on the contracts.

Q.   No one else was present at that meeting. Is that correct?

A.   Jack Meyn and myself, that's correct.

Q.   You did not keep any notes concerning this discussion with Mr. Meyn. Is that right?

A.   That's correct.

Q.   You have no written documents directing Delta to take the actions that you describe. Is that right?

A.   It was — no, sir, except for the proposals that Delta Testing submitted giving the responsibility of quality control and the actual responsibility as to all plant inspection.

Q.   You have no correspondence reflecting any separate agreement between you and Delta Testing. Is that correct?

A.   That's correct. I have no contractual relationship with Delta Testing.

Q.   Now, after this meeting, you placed your reliance on Delta Testing to make all determinations as to the quality of the materials. Is that correct?

A.   I think you — yes, sir, that the New Orleans Aviation Board placed that responsibility on them, and they furnished the information to the — to all parties: The Aviation Board, the FAA, and myself.

Q.   Well, were you relying on Delta Testing or not, sir?

A.   Yes, sir.

Q.   You never made any determination yourself as to the quality of the materials produced by Vicon at the plant. Is that right?

A.   That is correct. There's no way for me to do that without physically performing the same function they did, and I would have to be compensated in the same sense.

Q.   You simply accepted the assurances of Mr. Arena that the mix was all right. Is that correct?

A.   That's correct. Mr. Arena has handled more asphalt in the state of Louisiana than all of the testing laboratories in the entire state of Louisiana combined. Yes, sir, I did rely on Mr. Arena.

*   *   *

[Engineer's inaction upon contractor's noncompliance with specifications.]

Q.   All right, sir. On the base course of the north-south runway, you knew that the asphalt content was reported outside the specifications a high percentage of the time. Is that right?

A.   That's not really correct. I'd like to explain that. On the report it gives an extracted AC content. It also gives a Brodymeter set. When I called Mr. Arena about this, he told me to use the Brodymeter, that that was the best method of determining the liquid AC content, and not to pay any attention to the extracted AC contents.

Q.   Okay. Now, getting back to my question, Mr. Lambert, you knew on the base course of the north-south runway that the extracted asphalt content was outside the specification a high percentage of the time. Is that right?

A.   I cannot say that at this time without looking at the documents. There were — there were times that the extracted [asphalt cement] content was out of the job mix design as prepared by Delta Testing.

*   *   *

Q.   Well, you testified in your deposition that you discussed this matter with Mr. Arena, the fact that the extractions were out. Is that right?

A.   That is correct.

Q.   And as you just said, Mr. Arena took the position that you should ignore the extraction and rely on the Brodymeter?

A.   Yes, sir, that the Brodymeter was the best method of determining the liquid AC content, the asphalt cement content in the mix.

Q.   Now, Mr. Lambert, you knew at this time what an extraction was. Is that correct?

A.   Yes, sir.

Q.   You knew that it was designed to show the amount of material in the mixture leaving the plant. Is that correct?

A.   The extraction test, yes, sir, it is a measure of this mixture that leaves the plant, but it is a very minute sample. It would just be a fraction of the mixture. And Mr. Arena said in this type of drum dryer, that the mass of material that it can produce, the better measurement of the liquid AC content will come from the Brodymeter.

Q.   You knew that the extraction was used as a control on the calibrations of the plant. Is that right?

A.   No, sir, I did not. Everything that had to do with the asphalt plant was done by Delta Testing.

Q.   Well, you had enough experience in this area to know that a plant can be out of calibration. Is that correct?

A.   Yes, sir, anything can be, I would think, out of calibration.

Q.   Well, sir, then what was the control on the calibration of the plant as to asphalt content in this case?

A.   You have to ask Mr. Phil Arena. That was something that he dealt with.

Q.   Now, you never went to the plant to investigate the calibration of the plant. Is that right?

A.   No, sir. I would have no knowledge of how to do that, either.

Q.   You never went to investigate the methodology used in performing the extraction test. Is that correct?

A.   That's correct. The method of testing was called out in the specifications by the FAA that have been used for twenty years, so it would be a standard procedure.

Q.   You never shut the plant down for the variations in the extracted asphalt content. Is that right?

A.   That's correct. That would be the duty of Delta Testing.

Q.   Now, Mr. Lambert, under the specifications, the asphalt mixture was supposed to have a water content of no more than five-tenths of one percent. Is that correct?

A.   It could have — of no more than a half a percent. That is correct.

Q.   Under the specifications, the aggregates were supposed to be dried to this condition prior to the introduction of the asphalt cement. Is that right?

A.   Yes, sir, in accordance with the specifications. But once again, the specifications were drawn in accordance with the FAA specifications, which did not have a specific specification for drum dryer. So Mr. Meyn said that he could adapt those specifications to the drum dryer, which is a different mixing process, but that the finished product would not have more than a half a percent moisture content.

Q.   Under the addendum to the north-south runway specifications, the use of a drum dryer mixer was conditioned on the provision that the same results specified for the batch plant had to be achieved with the drum dryer mixer. Is that correct?

A.   Yes, sir, I believe that's the wording that FAA gave them to put in there.

Q.   Now, you are aware now that no moisture tests on the finished product were ever performed by Delta during the course of the north-south runway job. Is that right?

A.   I don't have the information in front of me, but I think that on the shoulder work at the end of the east-west runway that moisture tests were taken and that it was under half a percent.

Q.   Yes, sir. But I refer you to the north-south runway. You are aware that no moisture tests were ever performed on the asphalt mixture going to the north-south runway. Is that right?

A.   To the best of my knowledge, I did not receive those reports. I did — I did, I think, receive a report on the east-west, but this would be something again that Delta Testing would do at the asphalt plant that I would not have knowledge of. There's many, many tests that they performed that they do not report.

Q.   Now, when you talk about the shoulder work on the east-west runway, you're talking about some tests that were run in October of 1988 after the north-south runway began to fail. Is that correct?

A.   I think the date would be after that. I didn't ask for those tests. Those tests were reported to me by Delta Testing on their own. Probably that was something that they went into.

Q. Now, Mr. Lambert, in order to assure compliance with specifications on moisture, tests should have been performed on the finished product, the asphalt mixture. Is that correct?

A. I cannot say exactly, because Mr. Meyn told me that he would undertake that function. And on a drum dryer it's a different situation to check the moisture content.

Q. You never took any steps to ensure that the moisture tests on the finished asphalt mix were, in fact performed by Delta. Is that correct?

A. No, except to tell — to have an agreement and an understanding from Mr. Meyn that he would see to it that the half percent moisture, no more than half a percent moisture would be in the mix.

Q. And all the time during [both] jobs, up until October 1988 when you didn't receive any moisture tests, you never took any action to ensure that they were done. Is that right?

A. No, sir. Other than the fact throughout the job Mr. Arena assured me that the moisture was being removed to — down to half a percent or less.

Q. Orally?

A. Orally, right.

Q. Now, it is your opinion, Mr. Lambert, expressed in your report issued after the runway failed, the north-south runway, that one of the reasons for the failure of this pavement was the failure to remove the moisture from the mix. Is that right?

A. I would like to see the report, but that's — that sounds like one of the things that was brought up after the project was completed. Based on what expert reports were furnished me, that was one of the — one of the items that was told to be the problem.

* * *

[Engineer's practice regarding pavement testing.]

Q. All right, sir. Now, you gave certain instructions to your employees and representatives at the lay-down site concerning the proper method for the marking of locations to take cores. Is that right?

A.　Yes, sir.

Q.　Your employees were supposed to pick the locations from which the cores were to be taken. Is that correct?

A.　Yes, sir, and to get a representative to see — to locate a representative sample of that material that would be placed.

Q.　A total of two locations per day were supposed to be chosen. Is that right?

A.　A minimum of two per day.

Q.　And two cores were supposed to be taken per day. Is that correct?

A.　Yes, sir, two good cores per day.

Q.　Now, these cores were supposed to be representative of the pavement laid on the runway of its overall density. Is that right?

A.　Of that day's pour, yes, sir.

Q.　Now, you did not instruct your inspectors, however, to choose both of the cores. Is that correct?

A.　I don't — in other words, I don't know what you're talking about. There are two cores, and they would pick both. They wouldn't pick one, and someone else have to pick the other.

Q.　Well, sir, what you're saying is that your inspectors would only mark one of the locations. Is that right?

A.　No. That's not what I said. They would tell the individual that would do the core — the specifications call for the contractor to make the core, and the individual that makes the core, the general instructions that were given, if they did a thousand foot paving, they would go to the third point of each side, and that would be a representative core. And that was the function that was carried out.

Q.　Mr. Lambert, you said in your deposition that only about half the cores were actually marked by —

Opposing
Counsel:　Your Honor, could we have the date and the page, please?

Counsel:　Volume 1, page 48.

Q.　Do you recall saying that only about half the cores were marked by your employees?

A.　Yes, sir. Marking doesn't necessarily — that doesn't create a problem. If they're going down the runway, it's a straight pass. They average say a thousand or 2,000 feet, and they were instructed to go to the third point. This is the instructions they gave to Vicon, and Vicon's personnel would do that. They didn't necessarily have to be marked every time. Just as long as the inspector felt it was a representative location of that day's work.

Q.   Well, sir, I'll ask — read to you from page 47 of your deposition and ask you if you recall this. You were giving an answer: "They are supposed to take two cores, and they can pick the location. My people, I would say in general on these projects, picked the locations half the time. The other half of the time we let the contractor pick it wherever he wanted, and we would approve that location. But it would be a random pick, and it would have to be on that particular day's material."

A.   Yes, sir. Just what I told you. If you lay — it's a straight —

Court: Okay. Let's don't belabor that any longer. I think that's clear. Let's move on.

A.   It's a representative sample.

Q.   Now, Mr. Lambert, in order for Delta to relate the cores that it received to the production for the proper day for the purpose of making the comparison between the core and the Marshall briquette, it would have been necessary to know the date on which the core was taken. Is that right?

A.   Not necessarily, but that is — is — would be the most accurate way of doing it.

Q.   Well, sir, in this case you were aware that in some cases cores were taken for several days at one time. Is that right?

A.   Yes, sir, and that's allowed in the specifications. You can't — the only thing we can do is not allow the contractor to lay asphalt over an area of asphalt that has not been previously approved. He has to — since he's laying down the runway that's two miles long, it's taking that long before he gets back to lay over some existing asphalt.

Q.   So when cores were taken for several days at a time, these cores should have been marked separately so that the testing laboratory could tell which day's lay-down they came from. Is that correct?

A. Yes, sir, that would be the best way to do it. But I must say that, from my understanding of what happened in the field, that the service truck had oil can boxes, and they would separate these cores, and I never did ever receive a call back from Delta Testing saying that there was any problem in the procedure that was done. And to my knowledge, no more than three working days elapsed before a core was cut.

Q. So you did not ensure, nor did your representatives ensure, that the cores were marked and separated according to the day's production. Is that right?

A. I — I don't — would you repeat the question?

Q. You did not ensure, nor did your representatives ensure, that the cores were marked according to the day's production. Is that right?

A. I — that's correct. I don't — I can't say in all cases, and I don't believe that was my responsibility.

Q. You did not keep any records reflecting the spots where the cores were marked. Is that correct?

A. That's correct, because in all cases we could check with Mr. Arena before we overlay any asphalt that had been previously laid to make sure that everything was okay before we could do it.

* * *

Q. Now, Mr. Lambert, you never took any action to ensure that cores were cut every day. Is that correct?

A. No, sir, we can't force the contractor to do that. We can only tell him that the test has to be — test results have to be approved prior to him laying his asphalt over it.

[Other inactions of engineer.]

Q. You did not take any action yourself with respect to rolling patterns at the runway. Is that right?

A. That's correct. Mr. Arena is the expert in that field, and he was on the runway doing it. Also with the FAA expert.

Q. So in this respect, you are relying on Delta Testing not only to take care of the plant, but now you are relying on Delta Testing to take care of the field. Is that right?

A.   Mr. Arena was telling me — yes, sir, in that point, in that portion of the work Mr. Arena was establishing the rolling pattern. There's no way I can tell the contractor what to do until I get a test result back that says he's not doing it right. And Phil Arena's telling me — if you look at those reports, one of the two results is higher than ninety-eight about every fourth or fifth day. So he kept telling me he had it whipped, and it would go in and out.

Q.   Now, the contractor was permitted to continue to lay the asphalt mixture throughout this entire period. Is that right?

A.   Yes, sir, based on the information Mr. Arena gave me. I don't know why he didn't give me the written reports.

Q.   In the course of the runway jobs, you never made any inspection of the fine sand, coarse sand, or aggregates used at the asphalt plant. Is that correct?

A.   No, sir, that was not my duties.

*   *   *

Q.   You never conducted any inspection of the plant site in which you went onto the plant site during the construction of the north-south and east-west runway pavements for any reason. Is that right?

A.   That's correct, with the exception that one time I went by in the beginning of the job just to see that they had a mountain of material to use, a stockpile of material. The gate was locked, and I couldn't — as I recall that day I couldn't get in. But those materials changed daily, so that would be something that Delta Testing would have to do, and they had two men there all day every day.

Q.   And you never made any determination to shut down the job for bad asphalt production at any time, is that right, on either runway?

A.   I don't recall any specific instance at this time. But Delta Testing would have to do that, because there's no way of me knowing. They never reported anything out of the specification to me. Otherwise, I would have solved the job in my duties.

Q.   You never exercised any responsibility to determine the acceptability of the materials used on the project. Is that correct?

A.   That's correct. There's no way for me to know of the acceptability of the material other than what Delta Testing produces to me, and they produced documents of acceptable material.

* * *

Q.   Mr. Lambert, did you expect Mr. Stoulig to exercise any engineering judgment with respect to the quality of materials on this project?

A.   I cannot answer for Mr. Stoulig. But he — any time he has a question, he calls the FAA or the street department, or he would call Delta Testing, or Delta Testing would give him their advice, and he would make a decision. He doesn't always ask my opinion.

Q.   So you were expecting him on these two projects to rely on the city's street department for engineering advice rather than you; is that right?

A.   He did, and he also asked my advice. But he leaned to the FAA, I would say, more than any of them.

II. IMPEACHMENT

§ 9-26. Introduction.

Impeachment, like other cross-examination, is designed to discredit or counter the testimony of a witness.[35] In theory, impeachment discredits character, because it shows the witness is not telling the truth or is an untruthful person[36] In practice, most impeachment — based on prior statements of the witness and other documents reflecting facts — is a tool for "training" and subjugating the witness, producing the witness's agreement to your assertions. This emphasis on the facts, rather than the witness, usually is the best avenue to successful cross-examination.

You may use a number of methods to impeach a witness's credibility. Some fairly constitute an attack on character, while others might only suggest that the witness is mistaken or inadvertently colored the facts. Using one common method, you may offer the prior convictions of the witness or question her about prior bad acts showing untruthfulness. This evidence goes to character; it is designed to show the witness is the type of person who would lie on the stand.

[35] See e.g., United States v. Wilson, 985 F.2d 348 (7th Cir. 1993); United States v. Kenny, 645 F.2d 1323 (9th Cir.), *cert. denied*, 452 U.S. 910 (1981).

[36] See MARK A. DOMBROFF, DOMBROFF ON DIRECT AND CROSS EXAMINATION 7 (1985).

You may also offer direct character evidence — a witness who provides an opinion on reputation evidence that a preceding witness has an untruthful character. These methods suggest the witness may have falsely testified because she is an untruthful person.

Other methods of impeachment do not directly attack character. Using the most common impeachment technique, you would employ the witness's prior statements to contradict her trial testimony; this approach may suggest the witness is a liar, but it may also suggest only that the witness testimony was mistaken. Similarly, when you show the witness has a "mental or sensory defect" — say senility or bad eyesight — the evidence may only show the testimony lacks a solid basis.

Evidence that the witness is biased may be aimed more at the witness's testimony than her character, but it may attack character. She may have a motive to lie in this case, perhaps because her son is charged with a crime, but that does not mean she has an untruthful character in general. Or she may lie for profit, which suggests a dishonest character.

Obviously, when you offer evidence contradicting the witness's factual portrayal, you implicitly suggest the witness's testimony was incorrect. The rules of impeachment generally do not govern the admissibility of this evidence, however, because you have the right to prove relevant facts in any event. When the evidence contradicts irrelevant testimony of the witness — perhaps false testimony as to her background — the only valid reason to offer the "collateral" evidence is to attack credibility. Thus, the evidence constitutes an attack on character

Most jurors resist the suggestion that a witness is a "bad" person. If you try to demonstrate that the witness's character is flawed, and the effort fails, the jury may resent your attack. The jurors may sympathize with the witness, imagining how they would feel in the witness chair. Most jurors give credence to an attack on the witness that *succeeds*, but if the attack fails, or produces a draw, they may hold it against you. Thus, a full scale assault on the witness is dangerous.

Impeachment that goes to the facts is less risky and a good means to gain concessions. This approach says to the witness and shows the jury: "I (counsel) have my facts straight; you are mistaken." You make this point each time the witness equivocates, by using the witness's prior testimony, statement, a document or another credible basis for establishing facts. This approach shows that you had a basis for the question and the witness was not forthright in the response, but most important, it emphasizes the fact.

Material used for fact impeachment — primarily prior statements — provides the basis for virtually every cross-examination. The attorney prepares the cross-examination from the backup material available for impeachment. If the witness admits the facts, impeachment is unnecessary; if he denies the facts, the lawyer has the impeaching material ready for use. When impeachment occurs it embarrasses the witness, because no one likes to be caught telling different stories. After being impeached a few times, a witness usually becomes more cooperative. Thus, impeachment can be used to "train" the witness to say "yes."

Of course, sometimes the only recourse is to attack the witness. If the witness's testimony would be devastating if believed, your only hope may be to show he is a liar. If "character" evidence is the only, or best, basis for countering the testimony, you may have to use it. Often the defendant in a criminal case has no factual picture to present and must attack an adverse witness. You should make sure, however, that the witness is important enough to warrant a personal attack.

When you need to portray a witness or party as a bad person, as when a defendant takes the stand in a criminal trial, you should welcome the opportunity to attack character. The same is true of a party or primary actor in a civil case. But in general, you should be cautious about attacking directly the character of a witness.

The following sections discuss the rules of impeachment and effective impeachment methods. Section 9-27 addresses general rules of impeachment. Sections 9-28–9-29 discuss impeachment with prior statements that are inconsistent with trial testimony. Section 9-30 addresses impeachment with opinion or reputation evidence, § 9-31 discusses the use of prior crimes to impeach, and § 9-32 deals with impeachment with prior bad acts for which there was no conviction. Sections 9-33–9-34 address impeachment with evidence of bias and mental or sensory defects. Section 9-35 reviews the rule barring evidence of religious beliefs for impeachment, § 9-36 discusses polygraph evidence, and § 9-37 addresses rehabilitation.

§ 9-27.   Basic Rules of Impeachment (FRE 607, 608).

A party may not impeach a witness's credibility before the witness takes the stand. Once the witness testifies, counsel may attack his truthfulness while he is on the stand or afterward, as provided in FRE 607–609 and 613. A witness may be impeached by any party, including the party who called him. A party may not support a witness's credibility until after it has been attacked, either through reputation or opinion evidence or some other evidence that fairly constitutes an attack on character. The supporting evidence generally would consist of opinion or reputation evidence. You could raise truthful prior acts in cross-examining a witness who has testified to another witness's untruthful character, however, and you may be able to respond to evidence contradicting a witness's testimony on a collateral matter. Section 9-5 presents a summary of the rules concerning character evidence, including the rules governing impeachment with character evidence.

At common law, a party was forbidden to impeach a witness on direct examination. The justification was that a party vouches for the credibility of his own witnesses. Many jurisdiction, however, recognized, exceptions to the rule. Examples include rules permitting a party on direct examination to impeach an adverse party, a hostile witness, a witness who gives surprise testimony, and a witness the party is required to call.[37] The federal rules abandon the prohibition against impeaching a party's own witness. FRE 607 provides: "The credibility of a witness may be attacked by any party, including the party calling him."[38]

The Advisory Committee Note to FRE 607 states that the traditional rule was abandoned because it was based on false assumptions and impeded fairness. The note states:

> The traditional rule against impeaching one's own witness is abandoned as based on false premises. A party does not hold out his witnesses as worthy of belief, since he rarely has a free choice in selecting them. Denial of the right leaves the party at the mercy of the witness and the adversary. . . .

§ 9-28. Prior Inconsistent Statements.

The use of prior inconsistent statements differs from other methods of impeachment.[39] Determining what the witness said in the past is an excellent means of predicting what she will agree to on cross-examination. Thus, reliance on prior statements is more a tool for obtaining concessions than a method of destroying credibility. Sometimes a prior statement is an effective means to attack character, but these situations are atypical.

§ 9-28(a). Method (FRE 613(a)).

The primary method of using prior statements is to repeat them to the witness during cross-examination, when his factual assertions make impeachment appropriate. You may use prior statements to impeach testimony given on direct or during your cross, but it is most common to at least repeat the point in cross before impeaching. The prior statement may be used only if it is inconsistent with trial testimony; in other words, the witness must first assert or deny a fact, after which her prior statement that contradicts her testimony may be repeated. You should not ask about the prior statement first, as a means of securing an

---

[37] STEPHEN A. SALTZBURG, MICHAEL M. MARTIN, DANIEL J. CAPRA. FEDERAL RULES OF EVIDENCE MANUAL, VOL. 3, 607-3 (8TH EDITION, 2001).

[38] See United States v. Faymore, 736 F.2d 328 (6th Cir. 1984), *cert. denied*, 469 U.S. 868 (1984) (district court allowed government to question its own witness-informant's credibility concerning prior involvement in narcotics); Scholz Homes, Inc. v. Wallace, 590 F.2d 860 (10th Cir. 1979) (Rule 607, allowing party to attack its own witness is not limited to situations where the party calling the witness is surprised, mislead, or entrapped); see also United States v. Schatzle, 901 F.2d 252 (2d Cir. 1990).

[39] See, e.g., United States v. McLaughlin, 663 F.2d 949 (9th Cir. 1981).

admission, but must ask the fact question first. You are not required to show the statement to the witness, but on request must show it or disclose its contents to opposing counsel. FRE 613(a) provides:

(a) Examining witness concerning prior statement. In examining a witness concerning a prior statement made by the witness, whether written or not, the statement need not be shown nor its contents disclosed to the witness at that time, but on request the same shall be shown or disclosed to opposing counsel.

The following steps are appropriate when counsel seeks to establish facts and train the witness to concede them. The example assumes the attorney has taken the witness's deposition.

1. *Ask the witness to concede the point.* "The light was red when the green car approached the intersection; is that correct?" If the witness denies the fact, the exchange would occur as follows:

Q.　The light was red when the green car approached the intersection, correct?

A.　I don't believe so. The light was yellow.

---

2. *Ask if the witness recalls giving prior testimony.* "You recall giving a deposition, under oath, at my office; is that right?" This foundational reference to the occasion of the prior testimony need not be repeated once the witness has acknowledged the prior testimony. Moreover, it should not be elaborate. You should place the emphasis on the prior statement.

3. *Read the prior statement, citing the page number for opposing counsel.* At page 106, you said: "I saw the light as the green car approached. It was red." You should emphasize the key words, showing you were correct in stating the original question.

   The impeachment ordinarily would *not* involve showing the deposition or other statement to the witness. You should *read* the prior statement aloud, with appropriate emphasis. Showing the statement to the witness requires time, gives the witness a chance to concoct an explanation, and may fuzz up the contrast between the testimony and the prior statement. Further, if you read the statement, you show the basis for, and fairness of, the original question. Although you do not need to show the document to the witness, you must provide a reference to opposing counsel or show it to him if he requests to see it.

4. *Ask if the witness admits making the statement.* "You did say that; is that correct?"

5.   *If the witness admits the prior statement, the impeachment is complete.* Your reading of the statement, emphasizing its key points, tends to establish the fact and shows you had a basis for asserting it.

6.   *Do not ask the witness to explain.* There is no need to help the witness cure the inconsistency. Thus, you should not ask: "How do you explain the discrepancy?" The witness has a right to explain, but you do not have to request the explanation. Your inquiry as to whether the witness made the prior statement provides an opportunity for the witness to explain, because he can explain any response. He does not have to explain, however, and you do not want to elicit an explanation. Often your opponent will neglect to request an explanation on redirect.

7.   *If the witness denies the prior statement, show him the statement to coerce agreement or introduce extrinsic evidence to prove it was made.* If the witness testifies, "I don't remember nothing like that in my deposition," you must coerce his agreement or introduce "extrinsic evidence" of the statement — here the deposition itself. You may show the deposition to the witness and ask him to read it. This approach usually produces a concession that the witness made the statement. If the witness denies the deposition is accurate, you have to introduce the transcript by securing a stipulation as to its authenticity or calling the court reporter. Usually calling the court reporter is unnecessary, because your opponent is unlikely to dispute that the deposition is correct. For other prior statements, you must call a witness to the statement or introduce the document containing the statement.

To summarize, an appropriate fact impeachment with prior testimony might occur as follows:

Q.   The light was red when the green car approached the intersection; is that correct?

A.   I don't think so. I believe it was yellow.

Q.   You recall giving a deposition in my office?

A.   Yes.

Q.   In that deposition, at page 106, you stated: "I saw the light as the green car approached. *It was red*." You did say that; is that correct?

A.   Yes.

Subsequent impeachment would not require asking whether the witness remembers the deposition. Thus, the impeachment might take place as follows:

> Q. The green car was going way too fast; is that correct?
>
> A. I don't think it was going all that fast.
>
> Q. In your deposition, at page 84, you said, "I gotta tell you, *the green car was going way too fast*," correct?
>
> A. Yeah, I guess so.

This approach eliminates the unnecessary ceremony that often attends impeachment. It closely juxtaposes your assertion and the prior testimony. The fact gets stated and repeated; the witness in effect concedes it; your fairness in asking the question is established. In the modern era, with its huge emphasis on discovery, you are well situated to cross-examine using this method.

When your impeachment with a prior statement relates to testimony the witness gave on direct, you generally should call the witness's attention to the statement before impeaching. In doing so, be sure to disassociate yourself from the factual assertion you will contradict by making clear that the point is the witness's rather than your own. Thus, if you wanted to establish the light was red, but the witness on direct said it was yellow, you should raise the point as follows:

> Q. On direct examination you said the light was yellow for the green car when it entered the intersection; did I hear that correctly?
>
> A. Yes.

You would not want to bring up the point as if you endorsed it, as in the following example:

> Q. The light was yellow for the green car when it entered the intersection, correct?
>
> A. Yes.

This approach suggests that *you* believe the light was yellow, which may confuse your listeners and undermine your examination.

§ 9-28(b). Extrinsic Impeachment (FRE 613(b)).

The above examples illustrate *intrinsic* impeachment, where the witness is impeached during his own examination through questions and answers. If the witness fails to admit the prior statement, you then must impeach *extrinsically* — in other words, with something other than questions on cross-examination — by actually introducing the deposition or other written statement as an exhibit or calling another witness to testify to the prior statement.

Traditionally, a rigid "foundation" was required *before* extrinsic evidence of prior inconsistent statements could be introduced; counsel had to ask the witness about the statement on cross-examination. The extrinsic evidence was allowed only if the witness denied the prior statement. This foundation requirement was designed to save time and trouble. If counsel could establish the prior statement by asking about it, the courts were unwilling to tolerate the delay associated with calling another witness or burdening the record with an additional document. At the same time, asking about the statement gave the witness an opportunity to explain it during cross-examination, which obviated any need to recall him after the introduction of extrinsic evidence.

FRE 613(b) relates the foundation requirement for extrinsic impeachment with prior inconsistent statements. It provides that the witness's opportunity to explain or deny the statement need not be given before the extrinsic evidence is introduced, but can be afforded at another time during the trial. This change permits you to delay the impeachment until after the witness testifies, which permits making a big production of the "lie." It also gives a second chance to the unprepared attorney — one who is unprepared to impeach when the witness is on the stand. The lawyers may put on the extrinsic evidence later, however, only if the witness is *still available* to explain or deny the prior statement. FRE 613(b) provides:

> **(b) Extrinsic evidence of prior inconsistent statement of witness.** Extrinsic evidence of a prior inconsistent statement by a witness is not admissible unless the witness is afforded an opportunity to explain or deny the same and the opposite party is afforded an opportunity to interrogate the witness thereon, or the interests of justice otherwise require. This provision does not apply to admissions of a party-opponent as defined in rule 801(d)(2).

If the inconsistent statement involves a "collateral" matter — one not relevant to the case — extrinsic evidence may be inadmissible under FRE 403. Thus, you must confront the witness with the statement under cross-examination to ensure you can use it. As an example, suppose a witness to a car wreck mentioned on the stand that he was in church the evening before trial, but you are aware of his statement at breakfast that he was in a bar. This inconsistency would be irrelevant to the accident case. Thus, the point is "collateral"; the prior statement only shows the witness lied on an irrelevant point. You could conduct this impeachment intrinsically — by asking about it on cross-examination — but might be precluded from doing it extrinsically. If the witness denied the prior statement, you might not be able to call the witness who overheard it.

Extrinsic evidence of collateral inconsistent statements was excluded at common law. The federal rules do not explicitly exclude it, but a judge still may do so under Rule 403. Excluding this evidence avoids disputes about minor matters and saves time. The judge would weigh the importance of the inconsistency — which would depend on its relation to the issues and the importance of the witness — against the likelihood of prejudice, confusion or delay.

§ 9-28(c). Attacking Character With a Prior Statement.

Sometimes you need to make a big deal of a prior inconsistent statement, using it to show that the witness is a liar rather than to establish a fact. In that case you should *commit the witness* to the testimony, emphasizing the witness's certainty and making sure the jury understands the testimony. This action ties the witness to the testimony, setting him up for the attack on character. Additionally, you may wish to impeach extrinsically to dramatize the conflict.

The following method should be used to attack character intrinsically with a prior statement.

1.   *Ask the question.* An example:

Q.   You never got a clear look at the man holding the knife; is that correct?

A.   Sure I did. It was the defendant, the guy you represent.

---

2.   *Commit the witness.* Make sure the witness commits himself to his new version of the facts.

Q.   [Surprised] Wait a minute, let me be sure. You're saying you did get a clear look at the man holding the knife?

A.   Yes.

Q.   That clear look is your basis for identifying Mr. Smith?

A.   Yes.

---

3.   *Dramatize the impeachment.* You should make a big deal of the impeachment so that the jury focuses on the prior statement. This dramatization can occur intrinsically or extrinsically. Usually, you want to impeach while the matter is fresh in the jury's mind — intrinsically. You should bring out the circumstances, including any oath to tell the truth, on the prior occasion. A brief example follows:

> Q.   Do you remember coming to my office for a deposition?
>
> A.   Yes.
>
> Q.   Opposing counsel was there; is that correct?
>
> A.   Yes.
>
> Q.   A court reporter was there; is that right?
>
> A.   Yeah. I remember her pretty well.
>
> Q.   Do you remember she gave you an oath?
>
> A.   Oh. Yeah.
>
> Q.   You swore to tell the truth in that deposition; is that true?
>
> A.   I sure did.
>
> Q.   You did tell the truth as you remembered it; is that correct?
>
> A.   Of course I did.
>
> Q.   In that deposition, at page 86, you said: "I never did get a clear look at the man holding the knife," is that correct?
>
> A.   I guess so.

The "dramatization" process should *precede* the impeachment. Follow-up questions unnecessarily give the witness a chance to explain. Consider the following follow-up:

> Q.   You made this statement knowing you were under oath?
>
> A.   Yes, but I made a mistake. I was real scared in that deposition and wanted to stay out of the case. I really did see your client with the knife.

This method — committing the witness and dramatizing the circumstances of the prior statement — generally is overused by attorneys. If you wish to establish facts and train the witness, it is more important to closely juxtapose the fact question and the prior statement. The dramatization should be reserved for situations in which you truly need to attack character.

In some cases — particularly criminal matters — you may have to focus heavily on attacking a witness's character with a prior statement. This process requires embellishment of the dramatization effort, perhaps with further questions regarding the circumstances of the inconsistent statement and the witness's motives for changing his story. The "motive" questions could be used as follow-up. In pursuing the character issue, you would have to anticipate and prepare to counter explanations.

Rather than bringing out an inconsistency while the witness is on the stand, you may wish to end the questioning once the witness is committed. You can then wait to impeach extrinsically, offering the prior testimony or calling a witness to the prior statement. This approach dramatizes the prior statement, but necessarily delays its introduction, so that some of the impact may be lost. Usually you should impeach while the witness is on the stand. Use the extrinsic evidence if the witness denies the prior statement.

FRE 613(b)'s lenient approach, allowing the attorney to impeach at any time so long as the witness is available, helps those attorneys who are surprised by trial testimony and unprepared to impeach while the witness is on the stand. When the impeaching evidence is obtained later in the trial, the rule permits its introduction, but only if the witness is still available to explain or deny the prior statement.

§ 9-28(d).   Securing a Double Denial for Impeachment.

When a witness lies about a fact while testifying and has made an inconsistent prior statement, you sometimes can maximize the impeachment by not only committing the witness to the fact, but getting her to deny the prior inconsistent statement. When you introduce the statement, it shows the witness lied on both counts. This strategy is best served by a general to specific line of questions regarding the prior statement, each more firmly committing the witness to the second part of the lie. An example follows:

1.   *Fact question.*

> Q.   You never got a clear look at the man holding the knife; is that correct?
>
> A.   Sure I did. It was the defendant, the guy you represent.

2.   *Commit the witness.*

> Q.   Wait a minute, let me be sure. You're saying you did get a clear look at the man holding the knife?
>
> A.   Yes.

Q.   That "clear look" is your basis for identifying Mr. Smith?

A.   Yes.

3.   *Secure denial, intrinsically, of prior statement.*

Q.   You've said in the past that your view of the man was not so clear; is that right?

A.   I don't know what you're talking about.

Q.   You don't remember saying you didn't get a good look at the man?

A.   No.

Q.   Did you ever write a letter saying you never got a clear look at the man with the knife?

A.   I don't believe so.

Q.   Did you write your girlfriend, Jennifer Hayes, and tell her your view of the scene was blocked, and you didn't get a clear look at the man?

A.   Certainly not.

Q.   In a letter dated April 13, 2000, you wrote to Jennifer Hayes: "I saw a robbery last night, and a man was knifed. It was dark, and the robber was behind a car. I didn't get a clear look at him." Did you write that?

A.   No.

4.   *Offer extrinsic evidence.*

Q.   May it please the Court, I've marked a one-page letter as Defendant's Exhibit 13 for identification. Counsel? [Shows counsel]. May I approach the witness?

The Court: Yes.

Q.   This is a letter you wrote to your girlfriend, Jennifer Hayes, on April 13, 2000; is that correct?

A.   I guess so.

Q.	It is correct — you wrote this letter?
A.	Yes.
Counsel:	I offer this letter as Defendant's Exhibit 13.
The Court:	Let it be admitted.
Q.	I ask that the witness read the second paragraph.
A.	[Reading]. "I saw a robbery last night, and a man was knifed. It was dark, and the robber was behind a car. I didn't get a clear look at him."
	[Alternatively, counsel could ask that the letter [or copies] be shown to the jurors, directing their attention to Paragraph 2].

If you do not want to give the witness an opportunity to explain the letter after denying its content, you might introduce the letter through another witness. In that situation, the cross-examination on the point would conclude when the witness firmly denies making the prior statement. Since the witness had his attention called to the prior statement, and denied it, the court probably would not give him a second opportunity to explain after admitting the letter.

§ 9-29. Substantive Effect of Prior Inconsistent Statements (FRE 801(d)).

Prior statements are statements made out of court by the witness. If offered to prove the truth of the assertion — that the fact the statement describe is correct — the statement fits the traditional definition of hearsay. Therefore, at common law a party could offer the statement only to impeach the witness, not to prove a fact. For example, if the witness testified at trial that "the light was red," his prior statement that "the light was green" to show he lied in saying the light was red, but not to show the light was really green.

Obviously, a jury might have trouble distinguishing the impeachment (he is lying when he says the light was red) from the proof of a fact (the light was green). Most people might take the impeachment as establishing a fact. Nevertheless, as a technical matter the impeachment could not be used for that purpose.

If a prior statement were the only evidence of a crucial fact, counsel's proof might not withstand a motion for directed verdict or judgment notwithstanding the verdict. Thus, if the witness denied the fact, introducing the prior inconsistent statement might not satisfy the need for evidence to prove it; the advocate might be forced to ask for an explanation, hoping the witness would concede the fact. This action would break the advocacy rule against asking the witness to explain an inconsistency, but would be necessary in the circumstances.

The Federal Rules of Evidence substantially broaden the use of prior statements to prove substantive facts. Under FRE 801, a prior statement is treated as a nonhearsay "admission" if the witness is a *party*. FRE 801(d)(2). The "admission" rule follows prior law, but it expands the categories of statements treated as admissions. If the witness is a nonparty, but his prior inconsistent statement was made under oath and subject to the penalty for perjury, it is also defined as nonhearsay. In those instances the prior statements may be used to prove the truth of the fact asserted. Rule 801(d)(1) provides in pertinent part:

> **(d) Statements which are not hearsay.**
>
> A statement is not hearsay if —
>
> **(1) Prior statement by witness.** The declarant testifies at the trial or hearing and is subject to cross-examination concerning the statement, and the statement is (A) inconsistent with the declarant's testimony, and was given under oath subject to the penalty of perjury at a trial, hearing, or other proceeding, or in a deposition;. . . .

The rule would apply to deposition statements, which are a primary basis for impeachment in litigation. The requirement that the statement be made in a contested setting, under oath, eliminates disputes as to the accuracy and solemnity of the prior statement.

The traditional hearsay rule still applies to prior statements of nonparty witnesses that are not made under oath. Thus, for instance, if the prior inconsistent statement were made by a witness to an investigator, it could be used only to impeach. Again, the jurors may have difficulty making the distinction, even if they are instructed as to the limited use of the statement. Nevertheless, you must be careful to produce independent evidence of any fact needed to prove the case.

§ 9-30. Impeachment With General Character Evidence (FRE 608).

Generally, evidence of character is not admissible to show that a person acted in conformance with that character. See FRE 404 and § 5-2. One exception permits evidence of a witness's untruthful character to show that he might lie on the stand. FRE 608 and 609 govern this use of character evidence respecting witnesses.

You may impeach a witness with evidence that his *character* for truthfulness is bad: in other words, that he is a liar. One method is to call another witness to testify that the witness is untruthful. The character witness's evidence, however, must take the form of (1) opinion or (2) reputation testimony.[40]

---

[40] See United States v. Marshall, 173 F.3d 1312, 1315–16 (11th Cir. 1999) (outlining an improper way to elicit character evidence: "The question asked by the prosecutor. . .'Do you believe that Mr. Hicks acquired the crack cocaine. . .from another source?' was primarily a question regarding a fact (the source of the crack cocaine) and was only indirectly a question regarding Hicks' truthfulness. If the prosecutor was seeking evidence regarding Hicks' veracity, the question should have been phrased very differently — for example, 'What is your opinion of Hicks' character for truthfulness?'").

FRE 608(a) controls this issue. Under the rule, evidence of *truthful* character is admissible only to rebut evidence of untruthful character. Thus, the character of a witness for truth may be attacked through opinion or reputation evidence, but it may be bolstered only if it is first attacked. Once a party attacks a witness's truthfulness, the other party may introduce opinion or reputation evidence to show a truthful character.

Additionally, FRE 608(b) precludes the introduction of extrinsic evidence of specific instances of conduct to impeach credibility, other than conviction of a crime as provided in FRE 609. It permits you only to use specific instances intrinsically, meaning in the questioning of a witness who gives opinion or reputation evidence concerning another witness or in questioning the subject himself. Rule 608 provides:

Evidence of Character and Conduct of Witness

(a) Opinion and reputation evidence of character. The credibility of a witness may be attacked or supported by evidence in the form of opinion or reputation, but subject to these limitations: (1) the evidence may refer only to character for truthfulness or untruthfulness, and (2) evidence of truthful character is admissible only after the character of the witness for truthfulness has been attacked by opinion or reputation evidence or otherwise.

(b) Specific instances of conduct. Specific instances of the conduct of a witness, for the purpose of attacking or supporting the witness' character for truthfulness, other than conviction of crime as provided in rule 609, may not be proved by extrinsic evidence. They may, however, in the discretion of the court, if probative of truthfulness or untruthfulness, be inquired into on cross-examination of the witness (1) concerning the witness' character for truthfulness or untruthfulness, or (2) concerning the character for truthfulness or untruthfulness of another witness as to which character the witness being cross-examined has testified.

The giving of testimony, whether by an accused or by any other witness, does not operate as a waiver of the accused's or the witness' privilege against self-incrimination when examined with respect to matters which relate only to credibility.

Witnesses who present opinion or reputation evidence on truthfulness often have little impact. Jurors know that most people can find someone to say something good about them and that most people have an enemy who would say something bad. Because it is limited to opinion or reputation, the testimony is conclusory and often sounds hollow. Nevertheless, the testimony can be effective if you present it properly.

To testify to a person's character, a witness must have a foundation. To offer an opinion, the witness must have personal knowledge sufficient to support the opinion. To provide reputation evidence, the person must have knowledge of what others say about the person. You must elicit the foundation to support the testimony.

Under FRE 608 specific instances of conduct cannot be admitted extrinsically to prove character for truthfulness. Thus, a character witness could not testify on direct examination to specific lies or fraudulent actions. Nevertheless, in laying the foundation, you often can give the jury a clear picture of the basis for the opinion or reputation. Indeed, a specific foundation at least shows the *types* of instances with which the witness is familiar, which gives substance to the testimony.[41] Additionally, a good foundation provides punch to testimony that otherwise might sound thin. By bringing out the witness's experience with the subject, you can give weight to the witness's conclusions. Make sure the foundation is not too specific, however, because it will otherwise run afoul of the rule.

Examples of direct examinations of witnesses who would present opinion and reputation evidence are set forth below. The first example focuses on a single context for a single opinion; the second develops three areas to obtain three versions of reputation.

Opinion — Truthfulness

Q.   State your name, please.

A.   Joyce Sherman.

Q.   What is your address?

A.   122 Gibbon Street, Alexandria.

Q.   Are you familiar with James Smith, who was a witness in this case?

A.   Yes.

[Focus attention]

Q.   Are you familiar with whether he tells the truth or not?

A.   Yes, very familiar. I have ten years of unfortunate experience.

Q.   Let's back up. Tell the jury how you met James Smith.

A.   I met him in 1981. We were college students.

Q.   What business venture did you enter?

---

[41] See FED. R. EVID. 405 advisory committee's note: The foundation should "be confined to the nature and extent of observation and acquaintance upon which the opinion is based."

A.   It was a catering service. "S-S Catering."

Q.   How long were you in business together?

A.   Five years.

Q.   What was your business relationship?

A.   We were partners. He was president, and I was vice president, but we were equal partners. We both worked full time in the business.

Q.   In that connection, what opportunity did you have to observe his character for truthfulness in dealing with money?

A.   I had a very good opportunity.

Q.   Explain what areas you observed.

A.   He insisted on handling financial transactions. He took the money to the bank and kept the books. I saw the consequences of his actions.

Q.   What opportunity did you have to observe his business dealings with others?

A.   I worked with him. I saw him deal with people from other businesses and with customers.

Q.   To what extent did he make representations to you?

A.   On many occasions he made statements to me and gave explanations concerning his conduct.

Q.   What happened to the business?

A.   It failed. I lost my investment. Customers got fed up and quit using us.

Q.   What experience did you have with Mr. Smith subsequently?

A.   I have seen him from time to time. He often has some idea for a business and wants me to put up money.

Q.   Did you enter into these ventures?

A.   Absolutely not.

Q.   Do you have an opinion concerning James Smith's truthfulness?

A.   Yes.

Q.   Tell the Court and jury, please, what that opinion is.

A.   He is a habitual liar. He is very convincing but will lie about almost anything to serve his own purpose. He is not to be believed. I know.

Q.   What is the basis for your opinion?

A.   My basis is years of experience with his untruthfulness.

Reputation — Truthfulness

Q.   What is your name?

A.   Wendell Turner.

Q.   What is your address?

A.   1520 Joseph Street, Chicago.

Q.   Are you familiar with James Smith, who was a witness in this case?

A.   Yes. I'm quite familiar with him.

[Focus attention]

Q.   Are you familiar with his reputation for telling the truth?

A.   A. I'm very familiar. We have many mutual acquaintances. He's well-known, and I'm familiar with what people say.

Q.   I want to discuss your basis for knowing Mr. Smith's reputation. Do you know him personally?

A.   Yes.

Q.   How long have you known him?

A.   I guess about three years.

Q.   How do you know him?

A.   We're both members of Trinity Church. We've had some business dealings and also know each other socially.

Q.   Do you have mutual acquaintances?

A.   Yes.

Q.   Describe mutual acquaintances in your church.

A.   There are about a hundred parishioners. Most of the people know each other. There are lots of church social functions, and we both go to them.

Q.   Does Mr. Smith have a reputation for truthfulness in the congregation?

A.   He sure does.

Q.   Tell the Court and jury, please, what that reputation is.

A.   He is known as very truthful and upstanding. People have a very high opinion of him.

Q. Describe the extent of mutual acquaintances in your business.

A. Jim is a sales representative for a computer marketing firm. I sell a lot of computer software. We call on many of the same customers. I've often talked with them about Jim.

Q. Does Mr. Smith have a reputation for truthfulness in his business dealings?

A. Yes.

Q. What is his reputation?

A. Completely honest and truthful. People speak very highly of him. They comment without being asked.

Q. In what context are these statements made?

A. That he can be trusted. That he's honest about products. That he tells the truth.

Q. What mutual acquaintances do you have socially?

A. We often play in bridge tournaments. The same people usually go, and most of them know Jim and me.

Q. What kind of competition exists in that circle?

A. Believe me, it's very strong. People in tournaments take bridge seriously.

Q. Does Mr. Smith have a reputation for truthfulness in that group?

A. Yes.

Q. Tell the Court and jury, please, what that reputation is.

A. He has a very high reputation. He is known to play by the rules. People have a very good opinion of him, unlike some other players.

You cannot introduce evidence of truthful character, as in the "reputation" example above, until after a party attacks the character of the witness. The "attack" does not have to come in the form of general character testimony, however. If opposing counsel impeaches the witness with evidence of a prior crime or prior bad acts, uses prior inconsistent statements to suggest that the witness is a liar, or if the opposing counsel otherwise suggests the witness is untruthful, the court should allow you to bolster the witness's credibility with general character evidence.[42]

---

[42] See FED. R. EVID. 608(a) advisory committee's note.

Any witness who provides favorable character evidence is subject to cross-examination concerning specific prior acts that suggest untruthfulness. Similarly, an unfavorable character witness can be cross-examined with specific prior acts suggesting truthfulness. FRE 608(b) permits cross-examination of a witness on specific instances "concerning the character for truthfulness or untruthfulness of another witness as to which character the witness being cross-examined has testified." Thus, if counsel calls a witness to give reputation or opinion evidence on character, she opens the door to an inquiry about the subject's prior conduct, which may have more impact than the direct testimony. See also § 5-&3. If the subject has a record of misdeeds, it may be better to forgo calling the witness.

§ 9-31. Use of Prior Crimes to Impeach (FRE 609).

The "relevance" rules generally prohibit the admission of prior crimes evidence to show the propensity of the accused in a criminal case to commit the crime with which he is charged.[43] See § 5-2. Paradoxically, prior crimes evidence may be admissible under FRE 609 to impeach the witness.[44] This restriction of purpose is illusory, because a jury is likely to consider the evidence in determining guilt as well as credibility.[45] Indeed, because of the potential impact of prior crimes evidence, criminal defendants often do not take the stand at trial if they have previous convictions.

In effect, the rule reflects a compromise; the accused is protected from the prejudicial effect of a prior crime so long as he does not take the stand, but if he takes the stand to deny the crime with which he is accused, the court may admit the prior crime. The limiting instruction — to consider the evidence only on the issue of credibility — presumably softens the impact.[46]

Rule 609 provides detailed standards for the use of prior crimes evidence to impeach. The rule was amended in 1990: (1) to specify different standards in a criminal case for the accused and other witnesses, and (2) to permit the introduction of the evidence at times other than during cross-examination.[47] A

---

[43] FED. R. EVID. 404(a).

[44] See United States v. Harris, 738 F.2d 1068 (9th Cir. 1984); United States v. Hurst, 951 F.2d 1490 (6th Cir. 1991), *cert. denied*, 504 U.S. 915 (1991) (court allowed prior conviction of attempted bribery of a police officer to be admitted).

[45] See generally H. Richard Uviller, *Credence, Character, and the Rules of Evidence: Seeing Through the Liar's Tale*, 42 DUKE L.J. 776 (1993).

[46] In United States v. Hursh, 27 F.3d 761, 768 (7th Cir. 2000), the court cites five factors that a district court should consider in balancing the probative value of evidence of a defendant's prior conviction against the prejudicial effect of that evidence. These factors include: 1. impeachment value of the prior crime; 2. the point in time of the conviction and the witness's subsequent history; 3. the similarity between the past crime and the charged crime; 4. the importance of the defendant's testimony; 5. the centrality of the defendant's credibility.

[47] See 42 DUKE L.J. at 795–803.

party may prove the prior crime intrinsically, by asking the witness about it, or extrinsically, by introducing a public record showing the conviction.

Generally, any crime that goes to veracity is admissible to impeach, whether it is a felony or misdemeanor. Felonies that do not directly involve dishonesty or false statement are admissible against ordinary witnesses if they would be admissible under Rule 403: in other words, so long as their probative value for impeachment is not substantially outweighed by the risk of prejudice, confusion, or waste of time. For the accused in a criminal case, the felony is admissible only if its probative value on the issue of credibility outweighs the prejudicial effect.

The federal rule does not specify how much detail counsel may elicit concerning a prior crime in impeachment. Generally, you are permitted to introduce the name of the crime and the date of conviction. Usually the sentence is admissible. Other details likely are not admissible because of the potential for undue prejudice.[48]

If a witness has a criminal record, attorneys often ask about a prior crime or crimes on direct examination. This strategy of "drawing the sting" may take the wind out of any impeachment effort. If you ask for an *explanation* that mitigates the criminal act, however, you may open the door for the exposure of harmful details in cross-examination. Particularly if the prior crime is similar to that with which the defendant is accused, the impact may be devastating. The jury may find it much easier to convict once they visualize the defendant committing a similar criminal act.

When a party "draws the sting" by disclosing a criminal conviction after the court has ruled it will be admissible for impeachment, the part waives the right to challenge the evidentiary ruling on appeal, *Ohler v. United States*[49] In *Ohler*, the Court determined that any harm resulting from the adverse ruling necessarily would be speculative; by preemptively disclosing the conviction, the defendant preempted the government from deciding whether to use the conviction in cross-examination and risk reversal on appeal. The court stated: "In our view, there is nothing unfair, as petitioner puts it, about putting petitioner to her choice in accordance with the normal rules of trial."[50]

The Court's assumption that the government might not introduce a conviction once it has won the right to do so appears dubious, however, since evidence of a conviction usually is devastating to a defendant. The ruling places a huge penalty on the exercise of a time-honored method of tempering the impact of

---

[48] McCORMICK ON EVIDENCE § 42 (5th ed. 1999).

[49] 529 U.S. 753 (2000).

[50] *Id.* at 759. But see State v. Daly, 623 N.W. 2d 799 (Iowa, 2001) (declining to follow Ohler on state law grounds).

a conviction and may not realistically serve to protect a government "choice" of tactic.

FRE 609 contains the following standards for the admissibility of prior crimes to impeach:

1. If the prior crime is a felony, it is admissible if a) the court determines that balancing test of Rule 403 is satisfied — relevance is not "substantially outweighed" by prejudice — assuming the witness is not the defendant in a criminal case, or b) if the witness is the accused, its probative value on the issue of credibility outweighs prejudicial effect. In any event, if the prior crime involves dishonesty or false statement, even if it is not a felony, it "shall be admitted."

2. The evidence must involve a crime either a) for which the defendant was convicted, or b) for which the defendant was released from incarceration, whichever was later, within 10 years. A court may admit an older crime only if it determines that the probative value of the crime on the issue of credibility substantially outweighs its prejudicial effect. When a party uses crimes older then the ten-year limit, he must give the adverse party notice sufficient to allow that party to contest the use of the evidence.

3. Convictions that have been pardoned or annulled cannot be used if the action is based on a finding of innocence. Nor can a party use a conviction that has been pardoned or annulled based on or a finding of rehabilitation, if the witness has not subsequently committed a felony.

4. Juvenile adjudications generally are inadmissible. In a criminal case, the court may allow impeachment of a witness other than the defendant with a juvenile adjudication for an offense that could be used to impeach an adult, if the court believes the evidence is necessary to fairly determine the defendant's guilt or innocence.

5. The pendency of an appeal does not render the evidence inadmissible, but evidence that an appeal is pending is admissible.

The text of FRE 609 is set forth below:

Impeachment by Evidence of Conviction of Crime

(a) **General rule.** For the purpose of attacking the credibility of a witness,

(1) evidence that a witness other than an accused has been convicted of a crime shall be admitted, subject to Rule 403, if the crime was punishable by death or imprisonment in excess of one year under the law under which the witness was convicted, and evidence that an accused has been convicted of such a crime shall be admitted if the court determines that

the probative value of admitting this evidence outweighs its prejudicial effect to the accused; and

(2)   evidence that any witness has been convicted of a crime shall be admitted if it involved dishonesty or false statement, regardless of the punishment.

(b) Time limit. Evidence of a conviction under this rule is not admissible if a period of more than ten years has elapsed since the date of the conviction or of the release of the witness from the confinement imposed for that conviction, whichever is the later date, unless the court determines, in the interests of justice, that the probative value of the conviction supported by specific facts and circumstances substantially outweighs its prejudicial effect. However, evidence of a conviction more than 10 years old as calculated herein, is not admissible unless the proponent gives to the adverse party sufficient advance written notice of intent to use such evidence to provide the adverse party with a fair opportunity to contest the use of such evidence.

(c) Effect of pardon, annulment, or certificate of rehabilitation. Evidence of a conviction is not admissible under this rule if (1) the conviction has been the subject of a pardon, annulment, certificate of rehabilitation, or other equivalent procedure based on a finding of the rehabilitation of the person convicted, and that person has not been convicted of a subsequent crime which was punishable by death or imprisonment in excess of one year, or (2) the conviction has been the subject of a pardon, annulment, or other equivalent procedure based on a finding of innocence.

(d) Juvenile adjudications. Evidence of juvenile adjudications is generally not admissible under this rule. The court may, however, in a criminal case allow evidence of a juvenile adjudication of a witness other than the accused if conviction of the offense would be admissible to attack the credibility of an adult and the court is satisfied that admission in evidence is necessary for a fair determination of the issue of guilt or innocence.

(e) Pendency of appeal. The pendency of an appeal therefrom does not render evidence of a conviction inadmissible. Evidence of the pendency of an appeal is admissible.

An example of impeaching with a prior conviction is set forth below, based on the affidavit of Jene Nelsen in the *Danielson v. ComputerCentre Associates* case.[51]

> Q.   I'd like to review your criminal record, Ms. Nelsen. You were convicted of mail fraud; is that correct?

---

[51] See Appendix A, statement of Jene Nelsen.

A.   Yes.

Q.   This conviction for mail fraud occurred six years ago; is that right?

A.   I believe that's true.

Q.   The mail fraud conviction occurred in federal court in Allentown, Pennsylvania; is that true?

A.   Yes.

Q.   This conviction was for fraud in the marketing of weight-loss preparations; is that correct?

Opposing
Counsel: Objection. Counsel is outside the permissible scope of impeachment and is trying to prejudice the jury against the witness.

The Court: Sustained. Members of the jury, please disregard that last question. Counsel, are you finished?

Counsel: One more question, Your Honor, respecting the sentence.

The Court: Proceed.

Q.   You were sentenced to two years in the federal penitentiary for this mail fraud conviction; is that right?

A.   Yes.

§ 9-32. Use of Other Bad Acts to Impeach (FRE 608(b)).

Specific instances of conduct may be used to attack or support credibility only on the cross-examination of the witness who committed the act, or of a witness who has testified on the character for truthfulness of another witness, if the court in its discretion permits. The cross-examination must involve instances that are probative of truthfulness. FRE 608(b) states:

(b) **Specific instances of conduct.** Specific instances of the conduct of a witness, for the purpose of attacking or supporting the witness' credibility, other than conviction of crime as provided in rule 609, may not be proved by extrinsic evidence. They may, however, in the discretion of the court, if probative of truthfulness or untruthfulness, be inquired into on cross-examination of the witness (1) concerning the witness' character for truthfulness or untruthfulness, or (2) concerning the character for truthfulness or untruthfulness of another witness as to which character the witness being cross-examined has testified.

The giving of testimony, whether by an accused or by any other witness, does not operate as a waiver of his privilege against self-incrimination when examined with respect to matters which relate only to credibility.

This rule establishes that extrinsic evidence of bad acts may not be admitted to attack a witness's truthful character. If the witness denies the bad act on cross-examination, you are stuck with the denial. You may probe on cross-examination in an attempt to change the witness's answer, however. The witness may not know extrinsic evidence is inadmissible; thus the presence of an incriminating document or witness may convince the witness to concede the point. Indeed, if the evidence is documentary, you may show it to the witness under the guise of refreshing recollection, which may provoke a concession. In addition, the witness always is subject to prosecution for perjury. The rule does not bar the use of extrinsic evidence on other points relating to credibility, such as bias of the witness.

In some ways, the rule governing impeachment with prior acts is more lenient than that for prior crimes. The ten-year time limitation does not apply, although the court might use its discretion to bar an inquiry into a bad act that is stale. Moreover, since there is no conviction to lend a name and date to the offense, counsel necessarily has greater leeway to inquire into details. This examination may severely taint the witness in the jury's eyes.

An example of impeachment with bad act evidence is set forth below. The bad act consists of lying about a conviction; counsel could have to be sure the conviction was admissible to use the bad act.

Q.   You applied for employment at Brown and Company two years ago; is that correct?

A.   Yes.

Q.   You lied on your employment application, right?

A.   I don't know what you mean.

Q.   You stated you had never been convicted of a crime in that application; is that true?

A.   I can't remember.

Counsel: May I approach the witness?

The Court: Go ahead.

Q.   I show you your application. Do you recognize it?

A.   Yeah.

Q.   Is that your signature?

A.   Yes.

Q.   You wrote on Line 19 that you were never convicted of a crime, correct?

A.   What do you mean?

Q.   Line 19 asks if you were convicted of a crime, and you wrote "No"; is that right?

A.   Yes.

Q.   But you were convicted of mail fraud four years earlier; is that right?

A.   That was bogus.

Q.   You were convicted by a federal court jury of mail fraud; is that right?

A.   Yes.

Q.   And in response to this question — "Have you ever been convicted of a crime?" — you wrote no; is that correct?

A.   Yes.

If the witness denied the contents of the application, counsel could not introduce it. The attorney could pursue the matter on cross-examination, however, so long as the judge believed the examination was reasonable.

§ 9-33. Impeachment With Evidence of Bias.

Although not covered by a specific federal rule, evidence of bias always is admissible to impeach.[52] The right to cross-examine a witness for bias in criminal cases is protected under the confrontation clause of the Sixth Amendment.[53]

Given the rule applicable to prior inconsistent statements, you probably can introduce extrinsic evidence of bias without first asking the witness about it, so long as the witness has an opportunity at some point in the trial to explain or refute the evidence. In some state jurisdictions, however, asking the witness about his bias or interest is a necessary foundation to introducing the extrinsic evidence. You may introduce the extrinsic evidence after the witness fails to admit the bias.[54]

---

[52] See, e.g. Alford v. United States, 282 U.S. 687, 692 (1931). See also Henry v. Speckard, 22 F.3d 1209, 1214 (2nd Cir. 1994) (holding that "[t]he motivation of a witness in testifying, including her possible self-interest and any bias or prejudice against the defendant, is one of the principal subjects for cross-examination"); United States v. Keys, 899 F.2d 983 (10th Cir. 1990), cert. denied, 498 U.S. 858 (1990).

[53] See Davis v. Alaska, 415 U.S. 308 (1974).

[54] See STEPHEN A. SALTZBURG, MICHAEL M. MARTIN, DANIEL J. CAPRA. FEDERAL RULES OF EVIDENCE MANUAL, VOL. 3, 607–16 (8th Edition, 2001).

The opportunity to show "bias" provides a fruitful basis for getting some types of evidence before the jury. For instance, assume the plaintiff sues two defendants, then settles with one of them for a modest sum. The plaintiff calls the former defendant as a witness in his behalf. Under FRE 407, evidence of the prior settlement probably would not be admissible to show the former defendant was really liable for the claim.[55] It probably would be admissible, on the other hand, to show that the first defendant has reason to be biased for the plaintiff. Thus, counsel could get the modest settlement before the jury, benefitting from its tendency to show (1) the former defendant was really liable, and (2) damages were modest, as well as to show bias. Of course, counsel must take care not to argue the first two points *directly*. An example of cross-examination on bias is the following:

Q. You were involved in the accident; is that right?

A. Yes.

Q. In fact, you were the driver of the car; is that correct?

A. Yes.

Q. You made a compromise with the plaintiff, Ms. Weinstein; is that true?

A. I guess.

Q. As part of that deal, you agreed to testify for her; is that right?

A. Yes, and to tell the truth.

Q. She agreed to let you off for $500 if you agreed to testify for her; is that correct?

A. Yes, but I didn't promise to lie.

Q. Part of the settlement was that you would have to appear here, true?

A. It was.

Q. You also agreed to cooperate with her attorney if she would settle with you for $500; is that correct?

A. I met with the attorney, sure.

---

[55] See FED. R. EVID. 407.

§ 9-34. Impeachment With Mental or Sensory Defects.

Evidence of mental or sensory incapacity is admissible when probative to determine the credibility of the witness's testimony.[56] Decisions are divided as to whether a party may prove slowness of mind, less-than-average intelligence, and similar handicaps with extrinsic evidence, although he may show them on cross-examination.[57] Abnormality, as when a witness was drunk when the event occurred, is a standard basis for impeachment and usually may be shown on cross-examination or through extrinsic evidence. A tougher issue arises when counsel seeks to show alcoholism or addiction generally, without claiming that the witness was under the influence at the time of the event. The court probably would bar the evidence unless counsel could show a likely impact on the witness's power to observe or recount the event.

An examination regarding a sensory defect — drunkenness — is the following:

Q.	You say you saw two men running on Maple Street?
A.	Yes.
Q.	You saw this after an evening in Beno's Bar; is that right?
A.	Yes.
Q.	You were in Beno's for more than four hours; is that correct?
A.	Yes.
Q.	You drank beer the whole time; is that right?
A.	Most of the time.
Q.	How many pitchers did you have, Mr. Stone?
A.	I guess about two.
Q.	How many glasses of beer is that?
A.	About 15.
Q.	You had 15 glasses of beer before you saw this event on Maple; is that what you're saying?
A.	That's what I said.
Q.	You had about four glasses of beer an hour for four consecutive hours, right?

[56] See e.g., United States v. Leonard, 494 F.2d 955 (D.C. Cir. 1974).

[57] STEPHEN A. SALTZBURG, MICHAEL M. MARTIN, DANIEL J. CAPRA. FEDERAL RULES OF EVIDENCE MANUAL, VOL. 3, 607–16 (8th Edition, 2001).

> A.   I guess that's about right.
>
> Q.   Tell the jury where you slept that night.
>
> A.   In my car.
>
> Q.   You couldn't even make it home; is that right?
>
> A.   I decided not to drive.
>
> Q.   You decided not to drive because you knew you were drunk; is that true?
>
> A.   I wasn't drunk, but I might not have passed a breath test.
>
> Q.   After two pitchers of beer — 15 glasses — you knew you would not pass a sobriety test; is that correct?
>
> A.   Probably wouldn't.

§ 9-35. Rule Barring Use of Religion on Credibility (FRE 610).

FRE 610 prohibits the use of religious beliefs or opinions to attack or enhance credibility. It states:

> Evidence of the beliefs or opinions of a witness on matters of religion is not admissible for the purpose of showing that by reason of their nature the witness' credibility is impaired or enhanced.

The rule prohibits the direct use of religion on the issue of credibility. It is not intended to prevent the use of religion to show interest or bias, such as when a witness is a member of a religious organization that is also a party in the case.[58]

§ 9-36. Polygraph Evidence.

The United States Supreme Court in *United States v. Scheffer*[59] upheld the constitutionality of an evidentiary rule precluding the introduction of polygraph evidence in military trials. Military Rule of Evidence 707 establishes a *per se* rule forbidding the introduction of polygraph evidence and any reference to the polygraph examination during the trial. The defendant, who was found not deceptive in the polygraph examination, sought to introduce the polygraph evidence to support his trial testimony.

Justice Thomas delivered the judgment of the Court. In Part II(A) and (D) of his opinion, joined by seven members of the Court, he determined that polygraph evidence may constitutionally be excluded to further the objective of ensuring the introduction of reliable evidence at the trial. Since "there is simply

---

[58] FED. R. EVID. 610 advisory committee's note.

[59] 523 U.S. 303 (1998).

no consensus that polygraph evidence is reliable"[60] and "the scientific community remains extremely polarized about the reliability of polygraph techniques,"[61] it was not arbitrary or disproportionate to exclude all polygraph evidence.[62] Additionally, since the defendant was not precluded from presenting any evidence as to the facts of the case, his constitutional contention was not supported by prior rulings invalidating other provisions that restricted a defendant's right to present evidence.[63]

In portions of his opinion joined by three members of the Court, Justice Thomas identified two other government interests that justified the rule. He determined that polygraph evidence may be excluded to preserve "the jury's core function of making credibility determinations in criminal trials"[64] and to avoid "litigation over issues other than the guilt or innocence of the accused."[65] The four concurring justices did not deem it necessary to reach these grounds for decision and questioned the contention that the introduction of polygraph evidence would diminish the jury's role in determining credibility issues.[66]

The Court noted that most states preclude the introduction of polygraph evidence and one federal court of appeals maintained a per se rule against its introduction. On the other hand, some courts of appeals leave the determination to the discretion of district courts.[67]

The Fifth and Ninth Circuits have discarded *per se* rules against the introduction of polygraph evidence.[68] The Sixth Circuit has held that unilaterally scheduled polygraph examinations should not be admitted under FRE 403.[69] The Fourth Circuit, as noted in *Scheffer*, maintains a *per se* rule against the introduction of polygraph testimony.[70]

§ 9-37.   Rehabilitating With Prior Consistent Statements.

At common law, a party could introduce prior consistent statements of the witness to rebut an express or implied charge of recent fabrication or improper

---

[60] *Id.* at 309.

[61] *Id.*

[62] *Id.* at 312.

[63] *Id.* at 315–317.

[64] *Id.* at 312–13.

[65] *Id.* at 314.

[66] *Id.* at 318–20.

[67] *Id.* at 310–12.

[68] United States v. Posado, 57 F.3d 428 (5th Cir. 1995); United States v. Cordoba, 104 F.3d 225 (9th Cir. 1997), *cert denied,* 529 U.S. 1081 (2000).

[69] Conti v. Commissioner of Internal Revenue, 39 F.3d 658 (6th Cir. 1994) *cert. denied.,* 514 U.S. 1082 (1995).

[70] United States v. Sanchez, 118 F.3d 192 (4th Cir. 1997).

influence or motive. Since these statements were hearsay, they could be offered only to rebut impeachment. The federal rules adopt this approach and also provide that the prior consistent statement is excluded from hearsay and may be used to prove substantive facts.[71] See § 6-19(b).

Before you can rehabilitate with a prior consistent statement, there must be an express or implied charge that the witness was influenced or had a motive to fabricate his testimony. Simple cross-examination and occasional impeachment with prior statements probably would not suffice. Additionally, in 1995 the United States Supreme Court ruled that only prior statements made before the improper motive or influence occurred may be introduced to rehabilitate. *Tome v. United States*.[72] The Court directly dealt with whether post-motive statements are admissible as nonhearsay under FRE 801(d)(1), but its reasoning also appears to preclude their introduction to rebut impeachment. The Court found that FRE 801(d)(1) carries over the common law rule that only pre-motive prior consistent statements may be used to rebut an express or implied charge of improper motive or undue influence.[73]

Despite the Court's reliance on common law impeachment rules in deciding the hearsay issue, some courts of appeals have ruled that prior consistent statements offered solely to rehabilitate should be subjected to a more relaxed test than that provided for non-hearsay under FRE 801(d)(1).[74] In *United States v. Simonelli*[75] for instance, the First Circuit ruled that "[w]hen the prior statements are offered for credibility, the question is not governed by Rule 801."[76] Thus, a statement may be admitted even if there is no express or implied charge of recent fabrication or improper influence or motive, if the prior consistent statement tends "to show the [impeaching] statement is not really inconsistent when it is understood in its proper context,"[77] or to clarify an impeaching statement.[78] The court noted, however, that the statement must have some rehabilitating force beyond mere consistency with the trial testimony.[79]

---

[71] FED. R. EVID. 801(d)(1).

[72] 513 U.S. 150 (1995).

[73] *Id*. at 158-59.

[74] United States v. Simonelli, 237 F.3d 19 (lst Cir. 2001); United States v. Ellis, 121 F.3d 908 (4th Cir. 1997), *cert. denied*, 522 U.S. 1068 (1998).

[75] 237 F.23d 19 (1st Cir. 2001).

[76] *Id*. at 27.

[77] *Id*.

[78] *Id*. at 29.

[79] *Id*. at 28.

CHAPTER 10

EXPERT WITNESSES

537

---

§ 10-1. Introduction.

Expert witnesses have taken on a powerful role in litigation. The Federal Rules of Evidence broadened the admissibility of expert opinions and the material on which experts may rely. Modern litigation involves complex issues — relating to scientific, technical, and specialized fields — and expert testimony often aids the jury's understanding of these matters. Further, presenting an expert is often a great tool of advocacy; counsel can *use* the expert to argue his case. Thus, learning the rules governing expert testimony and the best methods for dealing with experts is important to success in litigation.

The federal rules expanded the potential areas of expert testimony and relaxed the rules governing the presentation of this testimony.[1] The welcoming approach provoked an increased use of experts in litigation to analyze and interpret facts. Some expert "fields," such as "accident reconstruction," found their primary use in litigation. In response, appellate courts began to question the permissive standards under which experts provided their opinions about litigation issues.[2] In 1993, the United States Supreme Court decided *Daubert v. Merrell Dow Pharmaceuticals, Inc.*,[3] which required trial courts to assess the relevance and reliability of expert testimony before admitting it.

Daubert spawned a huge amount of litigation over the admissibility of expert testimony. The application of *Daubert's* criteria is probably the most litigated evidentiary issue in American courts today. Particularly since proving causation often requires expert testimony in tort and products cases, and a plaintiff must prove causation to prevail, the evidentiary rulings may also determine the outcome of cases. Additionally, trial courts have considerable discretion in assessing the admissibility of expert testimony. Thus, good advocacy may influence courts' determinations regarding this evidence.

This chapter addresses the admissibility of expert testimony and techniques for dealing with this evidence in trial. Sections 10-2–10-3 discuss the importance of experts in litigation and the attorney's role in the presentation of expert testimony. Sections 10-4–10-12 discuss the rules governing expert testimony, including those set out in *Daubert*. Sections 10-13–10-23 address methods for preparing and presenting expert testimony and effective techniques for cross-examination.

---

[1] FRE 702-03.

[2] *E.g.,* In re Air Crush Disaster at New Orleans, La., 795 F.2d 1230 (5th Cir. 1986).

[3] 509 U.S. 579 (1993).

§ 10-2.   Importance of Experts in Litigation.

Expert witnesses can provide great assistance in presenting a case. They can help you formulate a principled basis for recovery. As witnesses, they may explain technical matters supporting your theory, draw conclusions on these matters and sometimes virtually testify to your theory of the case. Additionally, experts give credibility to large damage computations. Thus, attorneys in modern litigation place great reliance on experts; at times they offer experts who function primarily as advocates.

The federal rules allow experts to play a large role in analyzing and interpreting evidence. FRE 702 permits expert testimony in scientific, technical and "other specialized" areas. FRE 703 allows experts to rely on information that is not admissible, if it would reasonably be relied on in the expert's field. FRE 704 permits expert opinions that "embrace" the ultimate fact issue, so long as the opinions are helpful to the jury. The rules were amended in 2000 to include *Daubert's* "fit" and "reliability" requirements and to limit the circumstances under which an expert may reveal inadmissible evidence that he relies on to the jury, but they still permit a wide range of specialized opinion testimony. This broad acceptance of expert input provides an excellent means of influencing a jury.

The increasing use of experts has led to an explosion of "litigation support" consulting services — experts who offer their services primarily to trial attorneys. Some enterprising "experts" have created new fields of specialization for litigation. These experts essentially function as professional witnesses. Unfortunately, many of them lose any grounding in scientific or other principle as they seek ways to help their clients. Of course, many experts are not professional witnesses, and many professional witnesses adhere to accepted principles, but almost any expert in trial argues his client's case.

Daubert's requirements that trial judges assess the reliability and relevance of expert testimony has spawned substantial pretrial litigation over the admissibility of expert conclusions and theories. The judge's determination of whether this testimony is admissible decides the outcome of many cases, because expert testimony often is necessary to prove causation, fault or product defectiveness. Lawyers must gain an understanding of expert methods to litigate these issues effectively.

When experts are permitted to testify, you have to deal with them. You must find experts who can combine true expertise, and a solid grounding in fact and theory, with an ability to make points effectively. At the same time you must prepare to expose the flaws in the opposing expert's theory. These challenges arise in virtually every complicated case.

§ 10-3. Lawyer's Role in Dealing With Experts.

Experts present a great challenge in advocacy. Using experts effectively requires that you learn the field, identify and employ technical principles that support your case, and work with your expert to explain complex points. Contesting with an adverse expert requires even more skill and work; you have to think through the issues, depose him thoroughly on his positions, and devise ways to bring out the flaws in his logic. If you succeed in advocating your case through experts, you generally will win it.

Your primary function in dealing with experts is translation. You need to *explain* things to the jury. For your expert, this means devising ways to help her explain points. For the opposing expert, you must develop a cross-examination that exposes — in an understandable fashion — the flaws in his basis or logic. If you do not make your points understandable, they cannot persuade the jury.

Most experts deal in scientific or technical areas that are not familiar to most people. Expert testimony is admissible because it helps the jurors understand the issues. These specialized areas often involve terminology that lay people do not comprehend. Further, experts sometimes assume incorrectly that others are familiar with principles in the field. Thus, experts often do not explain their points adequately.

Few things are more boring than a complicated discussion of technical matters that are beyond the listener's comprehension. If he cannot understand what the expert is trying to say, he tunes out the testimony. Even if the listener tries to listen to the points, he likely will not remember them. Thus, if you fail to make the expert's testimony understandable, the evidence will not have much impact.

You must find the right expert. You need someone who is credible and understandable. You should stay away from the pure advocate — the "hired gun" who has no loyalty to principle — because a good opposing attorney often can expose him. At the same time you need someone who will help you, within reasonable limits. Your expert needs to be well prepared, not only on technical principles, but on their application to your case.

You must work with your expert. Use the expert to help you understand specialized principles. Let him help you prepare discovery and plan for trial. Work with him to develop a presentation that is effective and understandable. Seek his help in preparing cross-examination. At the same time, keep control, even if the presentation is technical. The expert cannot try your case for you.

You should thoroughly depose opposing experts and determine whether you can challenge the admissibility of their conclusions. To the extent an adverse expert cannot demonstrate, using objective criteria, that his methods are reliable, you may succeed in preventing him from testifying. Similarly, you may prevent the testimony if his assumptions do not "fit" the facts of the case. A motion in limine may resolve the case even before the trial.

If the opposing expert testifies, you must plan a cross-examination that helps your case and exposes flaws in his logic. This undertaking is not easy; usually an expert witness is a professional. Experts generally have an advocacy mindset and try to make their points no matter what you ask. Thus, you need to devise approaches that force the expert to concede your points, or at least show that he will not fairly answer your questions.

All of this requires work. You must become an "expert" to successfully present and cross-examine experts. Further, you need to understand better than anyone how the technical concepts apply to *your facts*. Even the experts cannot match you on knowledge of the facts; you can use this knowledge to your advantage. With a willingness to learn, preparation, and confidence in your strategy, you can succeed in dealing with experts.

§ 10-4. Admissibility of Expert Testimony (FRE 702).

You may offer expert testimony of any witness who is specially qualified to give opinion testimony, where the testimony will help the trier of fact understand the evidence or determine a fact in issue and the testimony reflects reliable principles reliably applied to the facts.[4] FRE 702 governs expert testimony. It states:

> If scientific, technical, or other specialized knowledge will assist the trier of fact to understand the evidence or to determine a fact in issue, a witness qualified as an expert by knowledge, skill, experience, training, or education, may testify thereto in the form of an opinion or otherwise, if (1) the testimony is based upon sufficient facts or data, (2) the testimony is the product of reliable principles and methods, and (3) the witness has applied the principles and methods reliably to the facts of the case.

The primary criterion for admitting expert testimony is a showing that specialized knowledge is needed to understand relevant facts. The issue must be sufficiently removed from common understanding that lay persons require expert help to comprehend it. Expert opinions on matters within ordinary comprehension are not admissible, because jurors can form these opinion themselves. As the Advisory Committee Note to FRE 702 states: "Whether the situation is a proper one for the use of expert testimony is to be determined on the basis of assisting the trier."

The rule suggests that expert evidence is admissible whenever the witness has specialized knowledge that reliably may help the trier. Thus, experts not only

---

[4] See generally In Re Bonham, 251 B.R. 113, 134 (Bkrpty. D. Alaska 2000). See also Nemir v. Mitsubishi Motors Corp., 2002 U.S. LEXIS 9628 (E.D. Mich. May 22, 2002).

may testify in scientific or technical fields, such as medicine, engineering, and architecture, but may present evidence in areas of "specialized" knowledge, such as banking and real estate.[5] The latitude in the rule has led to expert testimony in new and imaginative areas, such as "accident reconstruction."[6] At the same time, *Daubert* and its progeny seek to ensure that the expert testimony provides a legitimate, principled basis of analysis.[7]

Because of the requirement that an expert's testimony assist the trier, you may have to demonstrate, when presenting this testimony in areas not traditionally recognized as "expert" fields, why specialized help is needed. Thus, you might have the expert explain why technical knowledge is necessary to draw conclusions. If you present this information prior to asking for the expert's opinion, the court will better understand the need for specialized analysis.

You must satisfy certain conditions to admit expert testimony. First, you must show the expert possesses credentials in a field that has a legitimate application to the issue. An expert in astrology, a psychic, or a numerologist probably could not be qualified to provide opinions concerning the cause of a car accident, even if the witness were trained to apply the accepted methods in the field. Similarly, a purported expert in a supposed new field — say, the analysis of negligence in left hand turns at intersections — would have no principled body of knowledge on which to base his opinion. The expert's area must have recognition as a field of specialized study reflecting principled methods.

Second, the expert must have sufficient qualifications to assist the trier in analyzing specialized issues. Qualifications may come in the form of education, special training or experience. The court also must decide the expert is trustworthy; *Daubert* requires courts to give increasingly rigorous analysis to the expert's methods. In some cases evidentiary hearings may be necessary to determine the admissibility of expert testimony.

Third, to the extent that testimony reflects scientific or technical tests, you must show the expert used a reliable method. If the process has gained general acceptance in the field and the courts, courts often assume reliability — as when radar devices are used to detect speed. When a witness presents evidence based on a new technique or a novel scientific theory, however, its proponent must demonstrate reliability.

Traditionally, courts deemed scientific techniques admissible if they had gained "general acceptance" in the particular field. This test was articulated in *Frye v.*

---

[5] FED. R. EVID. 702 advisory committee's note.

[6] Rushing v. Tran-Star, Inc., 1992 WL 370500 *4 (N.D. Ill. 1992) (holding that "[t]he specialized knowledge of plaintiff's accident reconstruction expert will assist the jury to understand the evidence and to determine facts in issue. . .").

[7] Daubert v. Merrell Dow Pharmaceuticals, Inc., 509 U.S. 579 (1993).

United States.[8] *Frye* was superseded in 1993 by *Daubert v. Merrell Dow Pharmaceuticals, Inc.,*[9] discussed below, which alters the test for accepting expert evidence.

§ 10-5. *Daubert* Requirements: Reliability and Relevance.

The "general acceptance" test for novel scientific methods was announced by the United States Court of Appeals for the District of Columbia Circuit in *Frye v. United States.*[10] It held, in a case involving a polygraph analysis, that expert opinion based on a scientific technique was admissible if "generally accepted" as reliable in the relevant scientific community. The court stated: "[W]hile courts will go a long way in admitting expert testimony deduced from a well-recognized scientific principle or discovery, the thing from which the deduction is made must be sufficiently established to have gained general acceptance in the particular field in which it belongs."[11]

In 1993, the United States Supreme Court held that FRE 702 displaces the *Frye* standard. The Court found that the *Frye* test is "absent from and incompatible with the Federal Rules of Evidence, [and] should not be applied in federal trials." *Daubert v. Merrell Dow Pharmaceuticals, Inc.*[12] The Court announced a number of standards to be applied in analyzing scientific expert evidence under FRE 702.

Daubert involved proposed expert testimony based on studies of whether a link existed between the use by pregnant women of Benedictin, an anti-nausea drug, and birth defects. A large body of epidemiologic data cleared Benedictin of problems. The proffered testimony, based on cell and animal studies and recalculations of epidemiologic data, was determined inadmissible by the district court in the face of the prevailing body of evidence. The Ninth Circuit affirmed, relying on *Frye*.

The Supreme Court ruled that *Frye* no longer establishes the standard for the admission of expert testimony. It articulated the Rule 702 test as follows:

> Faced with a proffer of expert testimony, then, the trial judge must determine at the outset, pursuant to Rule 104(a), whether the expert is proposing to testify to (1) scientific knowledge that (2) will assist the trier of fact to understand or determine a fact in issue. This entails a preliminary assessment of whether that reasoning or methodology properly can be applied to the facts in issue. . . .[13]

---

[8] 293 F. 1013, 1014 (D.C. Cir. 1923).

[9] 509 U.S. 579 (1993).

[10] 293 F. 1013 (1923).

[11] *Id.* at 1014.

[12] 509 U.S. 579, 589 (1993).

[13] *Id.* at 592–93.

The court observed that "many factors" may bear on whether a method is scientifically reliable and applies to the facts in issue. Without setting out a definitive test, the Court offered its general observations as to the pertinent factors. They include:

1. *Testing.* Has the technique or knowledge been tested? The testing would determine accuracy and reliability of the method. If the technique cannot be or has not been tested, it would lack a basic indicia of scientific validity. [14]

2. *Peer review.* Has the technique or knowledge been subjected to peer review and publication? The Court said: "The fact of publication (or lack thereof) in a peer-reviewed journal thus will be a relevant, though not dispositive, consideration in assessing the scientific validity of a particular technique or methodology on which an opinion is premised." [15]

3. *Potential for error.* What is the known or potential rate of error and what standards exist to control the technique's operation? [16] This information permits the court to assess the reliability of the method.

4. *Scientific "acceptance."* As one factor, a court may consider "acceptance" of a technique in a relevant scientific community. "Widespread acceptance can be an important factor in ruling particular evidence admissible, and 'a known technique that has been able to attract only minimal support within the community' properly may be viewed with skepticism." [17] Thus, the *Frye* test survives as one factor in the new analysis. [18]

Daubert requires the trial judge to make a "preliminary assessment" pursuant to Rule 104(a) of the admissibility of expert testimony. The Court said: "This entails a preliminary assessment of whether the reasoning or methodology underlying the testimony is scientifically valid and of whether that reasoning or methodology properly can be applied to the facts in issue. We are confident that

---

[14] *Id.* at 593.

[15] *Id.* at 593–94.

[16] *Id.* at 594.

[17] *Id.* (citation omitted).

[18] In In Re Paoli Railroad Yard PCB Litg., 102 F.3d 256, 263 (7th Cir. 1996) *cert. denied*, 520 U.S. 1042 (1996), the Third Circuit suggested other factors besides those announced in *Daubert* for evaluating scientific methods. In a ruling that dealt with various types of scientific evidence, and allowed the introduction of certain testimony, it considered the following additional factors:

(1)   the existence and maintenance of standards controlling the techniques's operation;

(2)   the relationship of the technique to methods that have been established to be reliable;

(3)   the qualifications of the expert witness testifying based on the methodology;

(4)   the non-judicial uses to which the method has been put.

federal judges possess the capacity to undertake this review."[19] When the court must familiarize itself with difficult material, the best means to accomplish the assessment may be an evidentiary hearing. Of course, the court also could determine the matter on affidavits, reports and depositions.

Daubert applied to "scientific" expert testimony. The Court limited its discussion to the scientific context but implied that its observations apply to other kinds of expert testimony.[20] The *Daubert* standards are sometimes difficult to apply, however, outside the scientific realm. In scientific studies, empirical evidence typically is developed to prove or disprove the reliability of theories. In other areas, such as psychology or economics, the theories and techniques are not so easy to test and there is much more room to dispute conclusions.

On the remand of *Daubert*, the Ninth Circuit again ruled that the expert testimony proffered by the plaintiffs was inadmissible. *Daubert v. Merrell Dow Pharmaceuticals, Inc.*[21] It noted that a "very significant fact" to be considered is whether the expert's opinion grew out of independent scientific research or was developed solely for the litigation.[22] If it is developed only for the litigation, the court determined that the proffering party must produce "objective, verifiable evidence" that the testimony is based on sound scientific principles.[23] In *Daubert*, the testimony did not have an independent origin and there was no showing it was based on valid scientific principles. Additionally, the court found the evidence failed the "fit" test because it only suggested the possibility of medical causation of the birth defects in question.[24]

Daubert left unresolved a number of issues applicable to the admissibility of expert testimony. It did not determine whether the "gatekeeper" role of the trial judge in assessing expert testimony applies outside the scientific realm and, if so, whether the *Daubert* factors apply to this testimony. Additionally, while *Daubert* delegated responsibility to trial judges to scrutinize expert testimony, it did not determine the standard under which appellate courts would review their rulings. The Court resolved these issues in subsequent decisions.

§ 10-5(a).   Applicability of *Daubert* Outside the Scientific Realm.

The Supreme Court determined in 1999 that *Daubert* should be applied to all expert testimony, but that the factors for assessing the reliability of expert testimony should depend on the circumstances. In *Kuhmo Tire Co., Ltd. v.*

---

[19] 509 U.S. 579, 592–93 (1993).

[20] *Id.* at 591. (Rehnquist, C.J., concurring and dissenting).

[21] 43 F.3d 1311 (9th Cir.), *cert. denied*, 516 U.S. 869 (1995).

[22] *Id.* at 1317.

[23] *Id.* at 1318.

[24] *Id.* at 1322.

Carmichael,[25] the Court ruled that *Daubert's* requirements that the trial court test reliability and relevance applies to all expert testimony, not just scientific testimony. The Court determined that the analysis was applicable to testimony of a tire expert who offered an opinion regarding the cause of a blowout. It emphasized the flexible nature of the inquiry, however, and determined that a trial court is not bound by the *Daubert* factors in determining reliability. The Court said: "The conclusion, in our view, is that we can neither rule out, nor rule in, for all cases and for all time the applicability of the factors mentioned in *Daubert*, nor can we now do so for subsets of cases categorized by category of expert or kind of evidence. Too much depends upon the particular circumstances of the particular case at issue."[26]

The Court's ruling allows courts to develop and apply reliability standards suited to particular types of expert testimony, but still requires a standard-based preliminary assessment of reliability. The assessment presumably should determine whether the expert applies accepted methodologic criteria reliably to the facts of the case. To associate psychological symptoms with a particular disorder, for instance, a psychologist might have to demonstrate that the diagnosis is consistent with psychological practice.

Several courts of appeals have determined that a doctor's "differential diagnosis" — the process by which a physician diagnoses the cause of a patient's problems by eliminating potential causes until the likely one is isolated — satisfies the *Daubert* requirement of a reliable methodology.[27] For instance, in *Hardyman v. Norfolk & Western Railway Co.*, the Sixth Circuit held that a district court's decision to exclude testimony based on a differential diagnosis as to causation was an abuse of discretion.[28] It ruled that even though the methodology excludes alternative causes, rather than establishing a "direct link" between the alleged cause and the jury, it is still acceptable under *Daubert*.[29]

Although it upheld a district court ruling excluding expert testimony that certain organic compounds in a carpet caused the plaintiff's respiratory illness, the Third Circuit ruled in *Heller v. Shaw Industries, Inc.*,[30] that a medical expert

---

[25] 526 U.S. 137, 147 (1999).

[26] *Id.* at 150.

[27] Hardyman v. Norfolk & Western Railway Co., 243 F.3d 255, 260–61 (6th Cir. 2000); Turner v. Iowa Fire Equipment Co., 229 F. 3d 1202 (8th Cir. 2000); Baker v. Dalkon Shield Claimants Trust., 156 F.3d 248 (lst Cir. 1998).

[28] Hardyman v. Norfolk & Western Railway Co., 243 F.3d 255, 260–68 (6th Cir. 2000).

[29] *Id.*

[30] 167 F.3d 146, 155 (3rd Cir. 1999). *See also* Kennedy v. Collagen Group, 161 F.3d 1226, 1229 (9th Cir. 1998), *cert. denied*, 526 U.S. 1099 (1999) (abuse of discretion to exclude opinion based on reliable methods because there were no published epidemiological or animal studies to support it).

may offer an opinion on causation even if there are no published studies to support it. The court recognized that doctors often have to make determinations of causation without published studies. The court ruled, however, that the grounds relied on by the expert in the case did not reliably support his conclusion.

If an expert offered primarily factual testimony — for instance, a description of the mob hierarchy in a particular area — the testimony would not involve the application of a scientific or technical method. In that case, a demonstration of the expert's basis of knowledge should provide adequate assurance of reliability. The "testing" of that knowledge appropriately should occur in cross-examination.[31]

§ 10-5(b). Appellate Review of Trial Court Rulings on Expert Testimony.

A trial court's decision to exclude or admit expert testimony often determines the outcome of a case, because expert opinion is often the basis to prove causation. Thus, the desirability of consistency in case resolution suggests a need for exacting appellate review of these determinations. Nevertheless, in *General Elec. Co. v. Joiner*,[32] the Supreme Court held that the "abuse of discretion" standard should be used when appellate courts review decisions applying the *Daubert* standard. Under this standard, a trial judge's decision will not be reversed unless it has no reasonable basis. The Court overruled a ruling of the Eleventh Circuit that applied a "particularly stringent" standard of review to a decision excluding expert evidence, which formed the basis for dismissing a plaintiff's case. The Court stated:

---

[31] In United States v. Markum, 4 F.3d 891 (10th Cir. 1993), the court affirmed the district court's ruling to admit a fire chief's testimony as to probable arson. The court applied the traditional FRE 702 analysis because no methodology or technique was used. In United States v. Muldrow, 19 F.3d 1332, 1338 (10th Cir. 1994), *cert. denied*, 513 U.S. 862 (1994), the Tenth Circuit again applied the traditional FRE 702 analysis in admitting a police officer's testimony because the police officer had specialized knowledge of drug trafficking based on his experience and training. The Tenth Circuit confirmed this approach in Smith v. Ingersoll Rand, Corp., 214 F.3d 1235 (2000) (holding that "the word Daubert is not talismanic; it simply means that prior to admitting expert testimony, the court must ensure that the testimony is not only relevant, but reliable").

Other circuits have ruled similarly. *See also* United States v. Locascio 6 F.3d 924, 937 (2d Cir. 1993), *cert. denied*, 511 U.S. 1070 (1994) (allowing expert testimony on organized crime under helpfulness analysis); United States v. Sepulveda, 15 F.3d 1161 (1st Cir. 1993) *cert denied*, 512 U.S. 1223 (1994) (affirming decision to qualify expert on drug trafficking); United States v. Romero 189 F.3d 576, 585 (7th Cir. 1999) (approving decision to admit expert testimony concerning typical behavior of child molesters). The Fifth Circuit in Watkins v. Telsmith, Inc., 121 F.3d 984, 990 (5th Cir. 1997), upheld a district court ruling that excluded an engineer's testimony for lack of a reliable technical basis. It recognized that all the Daubert factors might not be applicable to engineering testimony, but the inquiry into reliability is still necessary.

[32] 522 U.S. 136, 142 (1997).

Thus, while the Federal Rules of Evidence allow district court's to admit a somewhat broader range of scientific testimony than would have been admissible under *Frye*, they leave in place the "gatekeeper" role of the trial judge in screening such evidence. A court of appeals applying "abuse of discretion" review to such rulings may not categorically distinguish between rulings allowing expert testimony and rulings which disallow it. We likewise reject respondent's argument that because the granting of summary judgment in this case was "outcome determinative," it should have been subjected to a more searching standard of review. On a motion for summary judgment, disputed issues of fact are resolved against the moving party — here, petitioners. But the question of admissibility of expert testimony is not such an issue of fact, and is reviewable under the abuse of discretion standard.[33]

The Court also determined that the district court did not abuse its discretion in excluding expert opinion that the plaintiff's exposure to certain chemicals caused him to contract lung cancer. It held that a study linking PCB exposure to cancer in infant mice was not a sufficient basis for the opinion in the absence of an explanation of how the animal study could be applied to humans. Further, the Court rejected reliance on four human studies as not sufficiently connected to the particular facts of the case.

The Court's ruling creates the potential for inconsistent case determinations and, potentially, forum shopping by plaintiffs. Under the abuse of discretion standard, an appellate court might be required to uphold inconsistent rulings on identical facts, because neither is manifestly unreasonable. The determination leaves litigants largely at the mercy of trial courts.

Paradoxically, the Supreme Court in *Weisgram v. Marley Co.*[34] ruled that a court of appeals may order the entry of a judgment after determining that a trial court should not have admitted expert evidence under *Daubert* and other evidence was not sufficient to sustain the verdict. The Court determined that verdict winners are not entitled to a second chance to present admissible expert testimony when their expert evidence on appeal is ruled inadmissible and the verdict overturned.[35] The Court relied on the proposition that proponents of expert testimony "have had notice of the exacting standards of reliability such evidence must meet.[36] It said:

> It is implausible to suggest, post-*Daubert,* that parties will initially present less than their best expert evidence in the expectation of a second chance should their first try fail. We therefore find unconvincing Weisgram's fears

---

[33] *Id.* (citations omitted).

[34] 528 U.S. 440 (2000).

[35] *Id.* at 455–56.

[36] *Id.* at 455.

that allowing courts of appeals to direct the entry of judgment for defendants will punish plaintiffs who could have shored up their cases by other means had they known their expert testimony would be found inadmissible.[37]

This lack of concern for parties who too late find out their evidence was inadmissible in seemingly inconsistent with *Joiner*. Under the abuse of discretion standard of that case, a party may expect that a trial judge's ruling on the admissibility of expert evidence will be respected absent a clear showing of error. Once a trial court indicates expert evidence is admissible, the party reasonably could determine that "shoring up" the case is unnecessary and a waste of expense. In light of *Weisgram*, however, parties should be mindful that there may be no second chance.

§ 10-5(c).   Amendment to Codify *Daubert*.

The 2000 amendment to FRE 702, designed to reflect the *Daubert* criteria, specifies three requirements for the admissibility of expert testimony: (a) a fact or data base for the opinion, (b) the use of reliable principles and methods in developing the methods in developing the opinion, and (c) a reliable application of the principles and methods to the facts of the case.

The twofold reliability requirement — a court must determine that an expert has used "reliable" principles and methods and applied them "reliably to the facts of the case" — may introduce a new level of judicial "gatekeeping" to the expert testimony problem. *Daubert* required a reliable methodology, but called for a determination "of whether the reasoning or methodology properly can be applied to the facts in issue."[38] The elevated inquiry suggested by the rule — can the reasoning or method apply "reliably" to the facts? — may lead judges to perform more than a screening function. Additionally, since the amendment appears to authorize greater intrusion into an area traditionally left to juries, it inevitably will lead to inconsistent results. Some judges may decide cases summarily based on their own determinations as to which party's expert is more persuasive; others may leave the evaluation of persuasiveness to the jury. Thus, the amendment may further and unnecessarily complicate an area that already is unpredictable.

Additionally, a 2000 amendment to FRE 701 makes it clear that expert testimony is governed by FRE 702. It establishes that the authorization to admit rationally-based opinion testimony does not extend to expert testimony.

§ 10-5(d).   Preeminence of "General Acceptance" Factor for Novel Methods.

Although *Daubert* purportedly rejected the "general acceptance" test for novel scientific methods, the test appears to have paramount status when parties rely

---

[37] *Id.* at 455–56.

[38] Daubert v. Merrell Dow Pharmaceuticals, Inc. 509 U.S. 579, 593 (1993).

on novel theories. A methodology might be published, peer-reviewed, and objectively defensible, yet fail to satisfy *Daubert* for admissibility.

In *United States v. Scheffer*,[39] the Supreme Court focused on the lack of scientific consensus on the reliability of polygraph evidence in upholding a rule barring the introduction of that evidence in military trials. The Court noted that the scientific community and the courts exhibit disagreements about the reliability of polygraph evidence. It determined: "[T]here is simply no consensus that polygraph evidence is reliable."[40] The Court did not, however, announce a rule precluding the introduction of the evidence in federal courts.[41]

In *Moore v. Ashland Chemical, Inc.*,[42] the Fifth Circuit, sitting *en banc*, determined that expert testimony on clinical medical causation should be excluded under *Daubert*. The court rejected the conclusion of a panel majority that the *Daubert* standards are inapplicable to expert testimony regarding medical causation. The court ruled that the proponent must provide "some objective, independent validation of the expert's methodology."[43] It reached this conclusion while recognizing that the standards may result in the exclusion of valid, though unproven, opinions that run against accepted views in a field:

> Scientific conclusions are subject to perpetual revision. Law, on the other hand, must resolve disputes finally and quickly. The scientific project is advanced by broad and wide-ranging consideration of a multitude of hypotheses, for those that are incorrect will eventually be shown to be so, and that in itself is an advance. Conjectures that are probably wrong are of little use, however, in the project of reaching a quick, final and binding legal judgment — often of great consequence — about a particular set of events in the past. We recognize that, in practice, a gatekeeping role for the

---

[39] 523 U.S. 303 (1998).

[40] *Id.* at 309.

[41] *Id.* at 311. The Fifth Circuit in United States v. Posado, 57 F.3d 428, 434 (5th Cir. 1995) reexamined its *per se* rule barring the use of polygraph evidence. The court recognized the increased reliability of the test since Frye. The court remanded the case to the district court to make the determination of the admissibility of polygraph evidence under Daubert. The Ninth Circuit in United States v. Cordoba, 104 F.3d 225, 228 (9th Cir. 1997) followed Posado in discarding a *per se* rule against the introduction of unstipulated polygraph testimony. In Conti v. Commissioner of Internal Revenue, 39 F.3d 658, 662–63(6th Cir. 1994), *cert. denied*, 514 U.S. 1082 (1995), the plaintiffs argued that unilaterally scheduled polygraph tests should have been admitted. The Sixth Circuit did not apply the Daubert test. It upheld the Tax Court's ruling excluding the evidence, based on FRE 403. The court found that the prejudicial effect of such polygraph evidence outweighs its probative value. The party offering the evidence would not have had anything at stake if the test results were unfavorable. The court found that a unilaterally scheduled polygraph examination is almost always inadmissible. *Id.* at 663.

[42] 151 F.3d 269 (5th Cir. 1998).

[43] *Id.* at 275–76 (quoting Daubert).

judge, no matter how flexible, inevitably on occasion will prevent the jury from learning of authentic insights and innovations.[44]

In *Allison v. McGhan Medical Corp.,*[45] the Eleventh Circuit held that peer review, publication and an explanation of the link to the facts in the case were insufficient to support the introduction of causation evidence where the expert's conclusions ran counter to a large majority of epidemiological studies. The expert's conclusions were based on animal studies and human studies that, according to the court, used potentially biased methodologies or were not sufficiently linked to the facts.[46] The court said: "We find that the district court did not abuse its discretion by considering that the proffered conclusions in studies with questionable methodologies were out of sync with the conclusions in the overwhelming majority of the epidemiological studies presented to the court."[47] The court also upheld the exclusion of other expert evidence.[48]

§ 10-5(e). Pretrial Determination of Admissibility.

The means by which expert evidence is tested generally should be an *in limine* motion. Additionally, if the admissibility ruling turns on questions of fact, the trial court may be required to conduct a hearing. In *Padillas v. Stork-Gamco, Inc.,*[49] the Third Circuit ruled that a district court abused its discretion in excluding expert evidence and granting a summary judgment because it did not conduct an evidentiary hearing, even though the losing party did not request a hearing. The court found: "[W]hen the ruling on admissibility turns on factual issues, as it does here, at least in the summary judgment context, failure to hold such a hearing may be an abuse of discretion."[50] The failure to request a hearing was deemed immaterial because: (1) the court has an independent responsibility to manage complex litigation, and (2) the plaintiff could not have known the

---

[44] *Id.* at 276.

[45] 184 F.3d 1300 (11th Cir. 1999).

[46] *Id.* at 1314–15.

[47] *Id.* at 1316.

[48] *Id.* In Ruiz-Troche v. Pepsi Cola of Puerto Rico, 161 F.3d 77 (1st Cir. 1998), however, the First Circuit reversed a district court ruling that excluded expert testimony in a collision case because it was not based on an accepted methodology. The testimony addressed the likely timing and amount of cocaine consumption by the deceased driver of a car involved in the accident, based on a toxicology report of cocaine found in his blood during an autopsy. Although the methodology for estimating the driver's cocaine consumption had achieved significant scientific acceptance, some studies showed that variances exist among individuals in the retention of cocaine in their bodies. Additionally, the effects of cocaine on individuals may vary. Thus, the district court excluded the testimony as failing the *Daubert* reliability test. The court of appeals reversed, holding that an expert's opinion that is based on "good grounds" should be admitted and tested in the adversary process. *Id.* at 85 (citations omitted).

[49] 186 F.3d 412 (3d Cir. 1999).

[50] *Id.* at 418.

district court's reasoning in advance and needed an opportunity to address the critical issues.[51]

Other cases hold, however, that a pretrial evidentiary hearing is not necessarily required and a district court's decision as to whether to conduct an admissibility hearing should be reviewed under the abuse of discretion standard.[52] For instance, in *Nelson v. Tennessee Gas Pipeline Co.*,[53] the Sixth Circuit held that a district court has flexibility in deciding how to evaluate expert testimony and may deny an evidentiary hearing on its admissibility.[54] Further, the court determined that a district court may deny a plaintiff the opportunity to cure defects in expert testimony even when the defects require dismissal of the suit.[55] In *United States v. Alatorre*,[56] the Ninth Circuit held that a district court need not hold a pretrial hearing on expert testimony, but may evaluate its admissibility during the trial.

§ 10-6. Qualifying an Expert to Give Testimony.

To qualify a witness to give an expert opinion, you must show that the witness's special knowledge permits him to draw inferences, or to draw them more truly, than the ordinary layman. You may also show that the witness can explain the evidence in a way that aids the trier's understanding.[57] The rule sets forth the means for meeting this foundation requirement; you may qualify the witness by showing "knowledge, skill, experience, training, or education." The better you qualify the witness, the more persuasive his opinion is likely to be.

Qualifying an expert not only is essential to introduce his opinion, but necessary to make him persuasive. If the expert's credentials impress the jurors, they are more likely to believe him. Additionally, if the expert has a background that specially qualifies him to deal with specific issues, his testimony may be more credible than that of other experts. Thus, qualifying an expert well is a means of making his opinions appear credible.

The following is a checklist of potential areas of inquiry to establish expertise, assuming the witness has each qualification:

---

[51] *Id.* at 417.

[52] Nelson v. Tennessee Gas Pipeline Co., 243 F.3d 244 (6th Cir. 2001); United States v. Alatorre, 222 F.3d 1098 (9th Cir. 2000); United States v. Nichols, 169 F.3d 1255 (10th Cir. 1999), *cert. denied*, 528 U.S. 924 (1999).

[53] 243 F.3d 244, 249 (6th Cir. 2001).

[54] *Id.*

[55] *Id.*

[56] 222 F.3d 1098, 1102–03 (9th Cir. 2000).

[57] See U.S. v. Hansen, 262 F.3d 1217, 1233 (11th Cir. 2001) (holding that scientific expert testimony admissible if it assists "the trier of fact, through application of scientific, technical, or specialized expertise, to understand or to determine a fact in issue"). See also Westbury v. Gislaved Gummi AB, 178 F.3d 257, 260 (4th Cir. 1999); U.S. v. Hall, 93 F.3d 1337, 1341 (7th Cir. 1996).

1. *Education.* This area includes college and postgraduate degrees. If the witness has written a thesis or dissertation in the area at issue, you should have him explain it.

2. *Professional experience.* Bring out the witness's breadth and length of experience. Emphasize special experience with matters similar to the one at issue. Develop similar projects that the witness has performed. Practical experience provides an impressive basis for explaining a matter to others.

3. *Special training.* This category includes professional seminars, on-the-job training, military or government training, and other instruction of a serious nature. Again, if the witness has special training in areas closely related to those in the case, you should develop it.

4. *Teaching experience.* If the witness has taught the subject, the jury may view him as specially qualified to give an opinion, particularly if the witness also has practical experience. Again, you should bring out the extent to which the witness has instructed others in the specific matter at issue, such as when a doctor has taught others how to perform surgery.

5. *Publications.* The witness's publications in so-called "refereed" or scholarly journals — those that select articles for their quality and contribution in a specialized field — are important to qualify him under *Daubert*. Publications on the same topic as the expert testimony are particularly relevant. The witness's books and articles on the subject should be given special emphasis. Bring out publications in trade journals and other less scholarly publications, but give them less emphasis, as these journals often do not require any particular quality.

6. *Prior qualifications.* You should review the witness's prior qualifications as an expert, especially in the same court. Technically, the qualification of the expert in another case should not influence the judge in determining whether the witness is qualified for the matter at issue. Courts usually permit the question, however, and give weight to prior qualifications. You may want to avoid establishing too many prior qualifications because they might make the expert look too much like a "hired gun."

7. *The "big number."* You should bring out the large number of times the expert has dealt with the matter in controversy. This number often has an impressive effect. An example:

> Q.   Doctor, in the course of your 50 years of professional experience, how many times have you had occasion to treat or consult with respect to ankle sprains?
>
> A.   At least 2,000 times.

8. *Reliability of method.* You should demonstrate that the expert used accepted methods in his field, such as a statistician's regression model. If the expert did not apply a model or theory, demonstrate the basis for his analysis or testimony. Remember that *Daubert* primarily requires that the testimony satisfy objective criteria for determining reliability. See § 10-5 You also need to show the expert's analysis fits the facts of the case.

Two traditional methods exist for qualifying experts.[58] In the formal method, the attorney reviews the expert's qualifications and then "tenders" her as an expert in a designated area: "Your Honor, I ask that Dr. James be recognized as an expert in the psychology of post-traumatic stress." Once counsel makes the tender, the opposing attorney is entitled to "voir dire" the expert — or cross-examine him — on his qualifications. At the close of the examination on qualifications, the court determines whether to formally designate the witness as an expert in the field.

Formally qualifying the witness has the advantage of obtaining the court's imprimatur, or approval, of the witness's credentials. Additionally, many judges are used to this practice and would not permit you to ask for opinions absent recognition of the expert's credentials. Further, the lawyer opposing the expert may insist upon the opportunity to test credentials before the expert offers opinions. Nevertheless, this procedure does not necessarily establish the expert's qualifications to answer specific questions. It also tends to break up the testimony, separating the expert's basis from his opinions.

In the second method, counsel reviews qualifications and moves to the substantive testimony without a formal request to recognize the expert. This approach is consistent with the practice for laying and testing most foundations; the foundation is presented in direct testimony and tested in cross-examination. It closely links the witness's credentials with her opinions, which strengthens their impact. Additionally, it allows you better control of the presentation. Further, it permits you to link specific qualifications to specific opinions.

Many judges may be uncomfortable with the informal method of qualifying experts. Moreover, since *Daubert v. Merrell Dow Pharmaceuticals, Inc.*[59]

---

[58] See generally Peter Murray, Basic Trial Advocacy (1995).
[59] 509 U.S. 579 (1993).

indicates the court must assess reliability before admitting expert testimony, it may require the formal practice. Further, if you try to move to substance before tendering an expert, your opponent may object that qualifications have not been tested. Nevertheless, the technique of moving directly from credentials to opinions can improve the cohesiveness of the presentation. You should find out whether the judge permits this approach and, if so, try using it. Particularly when the court determines the admissibility of testimony prior to the trial, or your opponent informs you he will stipulate to credentials, you should be able to use this approach.

In bringing out qualifications you should not neglect your witness's human side. Cover at least some background that is nontechnical. Find aspects of the expert's history that help the jurors identify with him. You are not entitled to cover extensive background, but you should be able to review some personal information. Try to make your expert seem normal and personable.

Before qualifying a witness, go over the questions and answers. You do not want to ask for a credential that the witness does not possess. Adapt your questions to portray the witness's credentials in the best possible light. Help the witness describe her credentials in an impressive way, without bragging.

Plan an examination that guides the expert through her qualifications. Do not force the witness to present monologue explaining of her own accomplishments. Break the credentials into categories and prepare specific questions that permit direct, on-point answers. An expert's review of his own achievements is inoffensive if your questions require the answers; it may seem like bragging if the expert has to do it alone. Additionally, if you use specific questions, you can ensure that a modest witness does not gloss over important qualifications.

In cross-examining on foundation, find areas in which the witness lacks qualifications. Often witnesses with practical experience lack scholarly credentials, and vice versa. Focus on qualifications the witness does not possess that are related to his conclusions. Bring out points on which your witness is better qualified than the opposing expert. Usually you will not prevent the expert from testifying, but you can lay the basis for comparing him unfavorably to your expert.

When you call an expert to testify on a number of points, you may wish to break up the foundation, relating the expert's special experience to particular opinions. This approach gives credibility to the expert's conclusions. It also focuses attention on each point. The questions that develop expertise, along with those that review the expert's factual basis, provide the "step-step-step" leading to his opinion. Further, breaking the expert's testimony into areas makes it more understandable.

Under the formal method of establishing qualifications, counsel usually reviews all the credentials before tendering the witness. Nevertheless, even if you have conducted a general review of qualifications, you can ask a few questions in each part of the substantive presentation to bring out special credentials. This approach provides some linkage between special qualifications and the expert's testimony.

An example of an examination that breaks up an expert's qualifications and links them to separate subjects is presented in § 10-21. The following example follows the formal approach of qualifying an expert. It assumes the expert testifies primarily from a base of knowledge on a technical subject rather than on the application of method or process. The example assumes a nonjury trial before an administrative law judge. The review, however, would not differ significantly in a jury trial.

Q. State your name, please.

A. Louis Bruce.

Q. What is your occupation?

A. I'm a public utility consultant.

Q. Did I ask you to appear here to present testimony?

A. Yes, you did.

Q. Could you explain briefly the areas that I asked you to address?

A. You asked me to give my opinion regarding the standards to be applied in determining whether a utility's conduct was prudent. You also asked that I give my conclusions on whether the Big Bend nuclear unit has been operated in a prudent and reasonable manner.

Q. Where are you from, Mr. Bruce?

A. McLean, Virginia.

Q. How long have you lived there?

A. About 30 years.

Q. What is your current occupation?

A. I'm president of a consulting firm — Economics, Inc.

Q. What sort of consulting does Economics, Inc. engage in?

A. We consult on matters involving economic theory and regulatory analysis. We specialize in the area of public utility regulation.

Q. How long have you been with that firm?

A.   Well, with that firm and its predecessor, almost three decades.

Q.   Could you tell the judge what educational degrees you hold?

A.   I have a degree in economics from Georgetown University, received in 1965. I also received a juris doctor degree from the Yale Law School.

Q.   You're a lawyer?

A.   Yes, but I haven't practiced.

Q.   Have you pursued any other professional training?

A.   Yes. I've attended a number of professional seminars and training courses.

Q.   To what extent have these courses dealt with prudent utility practice?

A.   Most utility regulation courses deal with that to some extent. I've been to a number that concentrated on prudence issues.

Q.   What about prudence in the operation of generating plants?

A.   I've been to several that dealt with that subject.

Q.   What courses have you taught in the area of public utility regulation?

A.   Yes. I was a lecturer at the George Washington School of Business Administration.

Q.   What did you teach?

A.   I taught Public Utility Economics.

Q.   To what extent did that course address prudence issues?

A.   It was a big part of the course. We dealt with the prudent utility practice standard and its application in various contexts.

Q.   Have you lectured on public utility regulation?

A.   Yes. At the NARUC-sponsored Regulatory Studies Program at Michigan State University, and at the Canadian Bar Association's Public Utility Seminar.

Q.   What is NARUC?

A.   National Association of Regulatory Utility Commissioners. It's the association of State Commissioners.

Q.   What papers you prepared for professional groups?

A.   I presented a paper on rate design to the Southern Economics Association.

Q.   What consulting services have you provided to regulatory commissions?

A.   Yes.

Q.   Would you describe your experience in that area?

A.   For about 20 years I worked primarily for state commissions and public consumer advocates. I provided consulting and expert testimony on many issues, including rate base determinations, revenue requirements, fair rate of return, and cost allocations.

Q.   To what extent were you required to apply standards for prudent utility practice?

A.   That issue comes up frequently when you determine the rate base and revenue requirements. Any time you examine a utility's costs you have to determine whether they are prudent.

Q.   Have you testified for other parties?

A.   In the past 10 years I've worked both for state commissions and for utilities. I've testified for several utilities in recent years.

Q.   Have you provided testimony on prudence issues for utilities?

A.   Yes. Again, my testimony often deals with the application of the prudence standard.

Q.   Have you ever been qualified as an expert in utility regulation, and particularly in applying prudence criteria?

A.   Oh, yes.

Q.   Where?

A.   Let's see. The Federal Energy Regulatory Commission, the states of New York, New Jersey, Louisiana, Maine, Minnesota, Maryland, Florida, North Carolina, Ohio, Washington, District of Columbia . . . Canadian National Energy Board. I suspect there are others.

Q.   Approximately how many times have you been qualified to give opinions on public utility issues?

A.   At least 200.

Q.	How many times have you been qualified to testify on issues of prudent utility practice?
A.	Probably close to 200.
Q.	Your Honor, I tender Mr. Bruce as an expert in the field of public utility regulation, and particularly in the area of prudent utility practice.

For the same witness, the following is an example of a cross-examination on qualifications, designed to bring out the areas where the credentials are weak. Here the examination focuses on scholarly credentials.

Q.	Mr. Bruce, I believe it's true that you have no engineering degree, is that correct?
A.	Correct.
Q.	And you have no experience in the profession of engineering, is that right?
A.	Right.
Q.	You have no special expertise on the subject of nuclear physics, is that correct?
A.	Correct.
Q.	You have no specialized knowledge on the operation of nuclear power plants, is that right?
A.	Correct.
Q.	Now, Mr. Bruce, how old are you?
A.	51.
Q.	So, you're in the prime of your professional life, is that correct?
A.	I'll let you decide that, counsel.
Q.	Well, you do have a history of testifying in the utility field, is that true?
A.	I have many years experience in that area, yes, sir.
Q.	Once upon a time, you consulted for state commissions, is that right?
A.	Yes.

*   *   *

Q.   Now, Mr. Bruce, you have not been engaged as a consultant for state commissions since 1985, is that right?

A.   I believe that is correct.

Q.   So, what I'd like to do, just in the next few minutes is catch up on your professional accomplishments since 1985. I believe you went to work for some of the companies in the Powerco System, is that true?

A.   When?

Q.   Around 1985.

A.   No, I went to work for Electrico.

Q.   Is that a company in the Powerco System?

A.   It is — it's one of them.

Q.   Well, since the time you went to work for Electrico, have you worked for any of the other companies in the Powerco System?

A.   Yes, sir, but your question was in 1985, did I go to work for some of them, and that's why I answered, no.

Q.   Well, let's see if we can get it correct. In 1985, you went to work for one of the companies in the Powerco System.

A.   Correct.

Q.   And since that time, you have worked for other companies in the Powerco System, is that true?

A.   Yes, sir.

Q.   Now, Mr. Bruce, in this period since 1985, have you had an occasion to write a book on utility regulation?

A.   No, sir.

Q.   Have you had an occasion in the last ten years to write a book on the subject of public utility economics?

A.   No, sir.

Q.   Have you had an occasion to write a book or a treatise on the subject of economics in the last ten years?

A.   No.

Q.   As a matter of fact, you haven't written a book on utility regulation or public utility economics any time in your career?

A.   That's correct.

Q.   Now, in the last ten years, Mr. Bruce, have you had occasion to be a professor, a regular professor in charge of teaching a course on public utility regulation at an accredited institution?

A.   Not in the last ten years.

Q.   In the last ten years, have you had occasion to be a professor in charge of teaching a course on economics at an accredited institution?

A.   Not in the last ten years.

Q.   In the last ten years have you taught a course on public utility accounting at an accredited institution?

A.   No, sir.

Q.   In the last ten years, Mr. Bruce, have you written an article on public utility regulation published by a scholarly journal?

A.   No, sir.

Q.   In the last ten years, have you written an article on public utility economics published in a scholarly journal?

A.   No, sir.

Q.   Well, in the last ten years, have you had occasion to write an article on public utility regulation published in a trade journal?

A.   No, sir.

Q.   Well, in the last ten years, have you published an article on public utility regulation or economics, perhaps for the Powerco Newsletter?

A.   It's not my understanding that such material goes into the Powerco Newsletter.

Q.   So, is the answer no?

A.   The answer is no.

Q.   Well, in the last ten years, have you written articles on public utility regulation for any kind of publication?

A.   Oh, I have had a number of testimonies presented on issues involving public utility regulation, accounting, and economics that have been published in the sense that they have been filed in official proceedings in various jurisdictions.

Q. I'm talking about one that was published in even a newspaper or a magazine or a journal reviewed by professionals in the field, or a scholarly journal or a referee journal, or a book, or a compilation of articles, have you done that in the last ten years?

A. No, sir, I've already answered that question.

Q. Well, you're aware that, you know what NARUC is?

A. Yes.

Q. National Association of Regulatory Utility Commissioners?

A. Yes.

Q. And you know that NARUC occasionally has conventions and seminars and things like that, don't you?

A. I'm aware of that.

Q. In the last ten years, have you had occasion to give a speech at a NARUC convention?

A. No, counsel, I don't do conventions.

Q. In the last ten years, have you had occasion to give a speech on public utility regulation to a NARUC seminar?

A. No, sir, I don't believe in the last ten years.

Q. In the last ten years, have you had occasion to give a speech on economics at a NARUC seminar?

A. No, sir.

Q. Have you appeared to give any kind of speech at a NARUC seminar?

A. No, sir.

Q. Well, there is a NARUC Public Utility School, is there not?

A. Yes.

Q. In the last ten years, have you taught at NARUC's Public Utility School?

A. Not in the last ten years, prior to that, but not in the last ten years.

Q. You know the Federal Energy Bar Association?

A. I'm aware of it.

Q. It has seminars and meetings on public utility regulation, does it not?

A.   Yes.

Q.   It's located right up in your bailiwick, is it not?

A.   Yes, sir.

Q.   In the last ten years, have you had occasion to give a speech to the Federal Energy Bar Association on public utility regulation?

A.   I've had the occasion; I rejected it.

Q.   Did you give a speech?

A.   No, I had the opportunity, and I refused.

Q.   Have you lectured on economics before the Federal Energy Bar Association or any seminar put on by the Federal Energy Bar Association?

A.   Well, it would be the same answer to your last question.

Q.   The Edison Electric Institute has seminars and programs, does it not?

A.   I assume they do, yes.

Q.   Have you had occasion in the last ten years to speak to the Edison Electric Institute?

A.   No, I have not.

Q.   Have you appeared on a panel at a regulatory seminar in the last ten years?

A.   Yes, sir.

Q.   And what was the nature of your appearance on the panel?

A.   It had to do with municipalization of public utilities.

Q.   And what was the panel?

A.   It was a panel of individuals discussing that matter.

Q.   At which regulatory seminar?

A.   Now, wait, if you go back and read your question back, you'll find you didn't add the words, "regulatory seminar."

Q.   Oh, I'm certain the question was, "Have you appeared on a panel —"

A.   — no, your written —

Q.   "— at a regulatory seminar in the last ten years?"

A.   My recollection is your written words may have that down, but your spoken words did not include the words "regulatory panel," that's why I answered the question as I did. If you want to amend it, and exclude the "regulatory panel," or include only "regulatory panel," then the answer would be no. If it was as you originally phrased the question, the answer is yes.

Q.   Well, let's just forget the word "regulatory." Have you appeared on a panel at a seminar that was designed to educate those in the profession of regulation in the last ten years?

A.   Yes, sir.

Q.   What was the group you appeared before?

A.   What was the group, you asked?

Q.   Yes.

A.   I can't remember the exact title, it had initials, but it was public administrators, an organization of —.

Q.   These were professionals in the field of regulation?

A.   Professionals in the field of public administration, which is a subject matter of municipalities, generally.

Q.   Have you received — are you a member of any professional groups other than attorney groups?

A.   No.

Q.   So there's no group of economists that you're a member of?

A.   No, not me, personally.

Q.   Accountants?

A.   No.

Q.   Have you received an award from a professional group in the last ten years?

A.   No.

Q.   Have you organized any meetings or seminars of public utility consultants in the last ten years?

A.   Yes — I mean I've organized meetings of public utility consultants, yes.

Q.   Like a professional meeting?

A.   Well, they are professionals, and we met to discuss topics that were of importance to us in terms of serving the needs of our clients.

> Q. Meaning?
>
> A. They were specific.
>
> Q. Consultants for Powerco?
>
> A. Yes, sir.
>
> Q. All right. No further questions.

§ 10-7. Stipulating Expert Credentials.

In order to avoid an extensive review of the opposing expert's credentials, attorneys often offer to stipulate that the witness is an expert. This tactic presumably is designed to keep the jury from hearing all the expert's accomplishments. The strategy usually does not work, however, and you should not use it absent special circumstances.

First, a stipulation is not likely to stop your opponent from reviewing the expert's credentials. Counsel still has a right to provide the jury with a basis for evaluating the expert's opinion. Your opponent might decide to shorten the review — or the court may require it — but the court will permit him at least to review the high points. Thus, the jury still will hear the most impressive aspects of the expert's background.

Second, the stipulation places you at a disadvantage. Your opponent can argue in closing argument that you agreed that his expert was qualified; if he does not do the same for your expert, you give him an edge. Additionally, once you stipulate that the witness is an expert, you may have difficulty winning an objection that specific testimony is beyond the witness's qualifications. You do not want to give away an objection before it arises.

In a judge trial stipulations to credentials sometimes shorten the presentation. The judge may be familiar with the experts and may not need an extensive presentation. Before agreeing to a stipulation, however, make sure a review of qualifications is unnecessary. Moreover, ensure the stipulations are mutual. If the opposing party brings out qualifications, you should too.

In a jury trial you should enter a mutual stipulation only if you are sure this action will not hurt the presentation. Generally you can do better by making points on cross-examination that undercut the opposing expert in comparison to your witness. Additionally, if entering a stipulation also gives up the chance to link the expert's special qualifications and conclusions, it may detract from your presentation. Thus, this approach generally is inadvisable.

§ 10-8. Expert Opinion Embracing Ultimate Issue (FRE 704).

The expert opinion may embrace an ultimate factual issue — a departure from the rule in some jurisdictions. An "ultimate issue" is a conclusion of fact that makes a difference in the application of the law: say, an opinion that an accident caused a back injury. FRE 704(a) states:

> Except as provided in subdivision (b), testimony in the form of an opinion or inference otherwise admissible is not objectionable because it embraces an ultimate issue to be decided by the trier of fact.

FRE 704(b) prevents an expert from offering an opinion that a criminal defendant did or did not have the mental state constituting an element of the offense or an affirmative defense. It provides:

> No expert witness testifying with respect to the mental state or condition of a defendant in a criminal case may state an opinion or inference as to whether the defendant did or did not have the mental state or condition constituting an element of the crime charged or of a defense thereto. Such ultimate issues are mattes for the trier of fact alone.

Even when the issue is not the mental state of the accused, expert opinions are not always admissible. The opinions must actually help the trier of fact. The court may exclude opinions that embrace legal as well as factual conclusions and opinions that do not require expertise. The Advisory Committee Note to FRE 704 states:

> The abolition of the ultimate issue rule does not lower the bars so as to admit all opinions. Under Rules 701 and 702, opinions must be helpful to the trier of fact, and Rule 403 provides for exclusion of evidence which wastes time. These provisions afford ample assurances against the admission of opinions which would merely tell the jury what result to reach, somewhat in the manner of the oath-helpers of an earlier day. . . .

The lenient approach toward opinions embracing ultimate conclusions allows an expert flexibility for advocacy. The expert may testify to conclusions that counsel can state only in argument; she can also provide technical reasons why they are correct. Additionally, the expert's endorsement of ultimate conclusions provides a thematic link with counsel's presentation.

To curb expert advocacy, courts enforce the helpfulness requirement. Some courts have come to view many experts as "hired guns," offered primarily to advocate a result. Their conclusions often require little more analytic training than that possessed by laymen. Although the expert's opinion may not run afoul of the *Daubert* criteria because it is so basic, the jury may not need the expert's opinion to interpret the facts. Additionally, courts are suspicious of "professional experts" who appear in litigation as quasi-advocates. These views were expressed by the United States Court of Appeals for the Fifth Circuit in *In re Air Crash Disaster at New Orleans, La.*[60] The court said:

---

[60] 795 F.2d 1230 (5th Cir. 1986).

[T]he ultimate issue in such cases can too easily become whatever an expert witness says it is, and trial courts must be wary lest the expert become nothing more than an advocate of policy before the jury. Stated more directly, the trial judge ought to insist that a proffered expert bring to the jury more than the lawyers can offer in argument. Indeed, the premise of receiving expert testimony is that it will assist the trier of fact to understand the evidence or to determine a fact in issue. . . .[61]

Courts may enforce the helpfulness requirement in two ways. First, the court may exclude an opinion that does not require specialized expertise: in other words, the jury could draw the same inference for itself. An example is a situation in which an "expert" in "accident reconstruction" opines on the cause of a crash. If the opinion does not require specialized knowledge, it should be excluded as unhelpful.

Second, although the expert's opinion may "embrace" the ultimate issue, the expert should not apply the law to the facts, effectively advising the jury how to vote. Thus, an expert might testify on why a piece of machinery was unsafe, but could not conclude it was "defective" or "dangerous" in the sense to be determined by the jury. The advisory committee provides the following example:

[The criteria in FRE 701, 702 and 403] stand ready to exclude opinions phrased in terms of inadequately explored legal criteria. Thus, the question, "Did T have the capacity to make a will?" would be excluded, while the question, "Did T have sufficient capacity to know the nature and extent of his property and the natural objects of his bounty and to formulate a rational scheme of distribution?" would be allowed.[62]

The phrasing of the example is a bit complicated, but illustrates the dividing line between legal and fact conclusions. The expert can opine on ultimate facts, but cannot directly state how legal rules control the facts.[63]

An expert may not give legal opinions. Witnesses generally address fact issues; the court has the function of instructing the jury on the law. Thus, if a lawyer were called to testify about the law, the testimony would invade the province of the court.[64] In rare situations — such as when the law of a foreign country

---

[61] *Id.* at 1233 (citations omitted).

[62] FED. R. EVID. 704, advisory committee's note (citation omitted).

[63] Specht v. Jensen, 853 F.2d 805, 808 (10th Cir., *en banc*, 1988). The court stated: "The basis for this distinction is that testimony on the ultimate factual questions aids the jury in reaching a verdict; testimony which articulates and applies the relevant law, however, circumvents the jury's decision making function by telling it how to decide the case." *Id.* at 808 (citing Stoebuck, *Opinions on Ultimate Facts: Status, Trends, and a Note of Caution*, 41 Den. L. Cent. J. 226, 234 (1964) (footnote omitted)).

[64] *Id.*

is at issue — an expert may be called to aid the court, but probably could not give legal opinions to a jury.

You should be mindful of the helpfulness requirement in preparing expert testimony. Making the testimony helpful renders it more vivid, because the expert provides the basis for conclusions and does so in more concrete terms. The more concrete a presentation, the easier it is for people to understand.

§ 10-9.   Expert Testimony on Facts.

Experts are not confined to giving opinions. If the expert has personal knowledge, she may provide testimony like any other witness, even if she also provides opinions. For instance, a doctor who actually treats a victim may describe the injuries as well as opine on their cause. Similarly, experts are well suited to provide factual testimony concerning accepted practices in a profession, the effect of drugs, the meaning of special terminology, and similar matters. As long as the facts are relevant and within the expert's knowledge, they are admissible.

An expert's knowledge of facts is a powerful factor supporting his conclusions. Many experts base their conclusions on secondhand information and are disadvantaged compared to someone with firsthand knowledge. A doctor who examined a patient is in a better position to give an opinion on her injury, for instance, than one who merely reviewed a chart. Thus, you should help the expert obtain firsthand knowledge and review this knowledge as a basis for the expert's opinions.

As discussed in § 10-10, an expert may rely on facts not within his knowledge in forming an opinion if they are of a type reasonably relied on by experts in the field. The expert's reliance of a secondhand factual basis does not prove the facts, however, and the expert generally may not disclose her basis if it is not otherwise admissible. See § 10-10. Expert testimony based on personal knowledge does tend to prove facts, just like the testimony of any other witness.

§ 10-10.   Basis for Expert's Opinion (FRE 703).

Traditionally, advocates were required to conform to rigid formats in providing experts the factual basis for opinions. The commonly accepted methods included: (1) using an expert with personal knowledge, such as a treating physician; (2) asking an expert without personal knowledge to respond to a hypothetical question; and (3) allowing an expert to listen to the testimony and offer an opinion based on it.

In many courts, experts were precluded from offering opinions based on their own review of secondhand information. For example, if a doctor had not examined a patient, he could not offer an opinion based on medical reports but was required to answer a hypothetical reflecting facts in evidence. Otherwise, the opinion would be based on hearsay. FRE 703 eliminates the requirement of personal knowledge, so long as the expert relies on material reasonably relied on by experts in the field. If the expert's basis is inadmissible, however, he generally may not disclose it to the jury on direct examination. FRE 703 states:

> The facts or data in the particular case upon which an expert bases an opinion or inference may be those perceived by or made known to the expert at or before the hearing. If of a type reasonably relied upon by experts in the particular field in forming opinions or inferences upon the subject, the facts or data need not be admissible in evidence in order for the opinion or inference to be admitted. Facts or data that are otherwise inadmissible shall not be disclosed to the jury by the proponent of the opinion or inference unless the court determines that their probative value in assisting the jury to evaluate the expert's opinion substantially outweighs their prejudicial effect.

The expert may rely on records, reports, studies and any other information that reasonably could be relied on in his field, even if the evidence would not be admissible in court.[65] Additionally, the expert may accumulate the information informally, outside the courtroom setting. This permissive approach gives the "professional" expert — the expert who advocates as well as opines — substantial leeway in formulating opinions and places greater pressure on counsel to discover the basis for opinions.

The relaxed rule does not eliminate the traditional methods of providing facts to experts. Obviously, an expert with personal knowledge can still offer an opinion based on that knowledge. You may still pose hypothetical questions to experts. An expert may also base an opinion on facts he hears presented at the trial.

The expert's ability to rely on inadmissible evidence does *not* mean that his testimony proves the facts. Even if the court permits the expert to explain the basis for his opinion, the jury should be instructed not to consider the testimony — to the extent it relies on inadmissible evidence — as proof of facts. On an important matter, you may wish to file a motion in limine to make sure the expert does not disclose inadmissible facts on direct examination. If you succeed in keeping the evidence out, be careful not to elicit it in cross-examination.

Although the rule expands the permissible basis for expert opinions, the limitation to material "reasonably relied on by experts in the particular field" has more substance than most attorneys think. Experts often offer opinions based on flimsy support — perhaps relying on the reports of others. Yet few doctors,

---

[65] See In Re Lake States Commodities, Inc., 271 B.R. 575, 585 (Bankr. N.D. Ill. 2002) (holding that an expert can rely on inadmissible evidence). See also Black v. M&W Gear Co., 269 F.3d 1220, 1229 (10th Cir. 2001); U.S. v. Corey, 207 F.3d 84, 89 (1st Cir. 2000).

accountants, or other professionals would issue a formal opinion on this basis alone. You should find it fruitful to examine the witness in discovery as to the basis ordinarily required for a professional opinion. If you do not reveal your strategy, the expert may describe rigid requirements as to the basis supporting a professional opinion, providing the means to exclude his opinion in court.

You can also use the expert's reliance on secondhand information against him. Hearsay reports often seem flimsy when offered as support for conclusions. If you can dramatize the expert's lack of personal knowledge in cross-examination, you may weaken the expert's persuasiveness. Bringing out the secondhand basis for opinions may also make the expert appear unprofessional. This approach may involve a discussion of inadmissible evidence, thus permitting its disclosure, but showing the expert's flimsy basis may outweigh any harm from disclosing the inadmissible material.

§ 10-11. Expert's Ability to Offer an Opinion Without Disclosing Basis (FRE 705).

Under FRE 705 the expert may offer an opinion without disclosing beforehand the underlying facts.[66] In other words, you may call the expert, qualify him, and ask him to give his opinion without explaining its basis. The expert must disclose the basis if the adverse attorney inquires into it on cross-examination.[67] The rule provides:

> The expert may testify in terms of opinion or inference and give reasons therefor without first testifying to the underlying facts or data, unless the court requires otherwise. The expert may in any event be required to disclose the underlying facts or data on cross-examination.

This provision permits the introduction of an opinion without a factual basis. If cross-examination showed the expert lacked a basis for his opinion, the court would strike it. It accommodates FRE 703, which permits an expert to rely on inadmissible evidence in reaching an opinion, but generally prevents him from disclosing the evidence on direct examination. Counsel on cross-examination may determine whether to probe the inadmissible basis for the opinion. Cross-examination may reveal that the expert relied on incorrect facts, used material *not* ordinarily relied on in the field, or relied on a novel technique not generally accepted in the field. The lack of basis might never come out, however, if counsel failed to cross-examine.

Permitting the expert to offer an opinion without disclosing its factual basis places pressure on the cross-examiner. The rule shifts the burden from the proponent of the opinion to the opponent to show whether it is well grounded.

---

[66] See University of Rhode Island v. A.W. Chesterton Co., 2 F.3d 1200, 1217–19 (5th Cir. 1993).
[67] *Id.*

Since an expert can make a groundless opinion sound as if it has a basis, counsel faces a difficult task in supporting a motion to strike.

On the other hand, an opinion without a fact basis has less impact than an opinion supported by facts and data. Facts are concrete and give credibility to conclusory assertions. In argument, you can attack an expert's conclusory opinion, especially if your own expert provided a well-supported opinion. Thus, in the "battle of experts," offering an opinion without disclosing its basis does not provide an advantage.

§ 10-12. Use of Hypothetical Questions.

Although FRE 703 broadens the permissible basis for expert opinions, it does not necessarily displace the use of hypothetical questions. The hypothetical has been criticized as unwieldy and confusing, especially when lengthy questions are interrupted by objections.[68] Given the relaxed rules governing expert testimony, attorneys now rarely use hypotheticals. Nevertheless, the hypothetical can be an effective method for restating the factual theory of the case and arguing conclusions.[69]

The facts in a hypothetical must be supported by evidence, although the evidence need not be uncontradicted. In addition, the facts may be reasonable inferences drawn from the evidence. The facts need not be proven before an opinion is rendered, although proving facts first is desirable. This action eliminates confusion and avoids the embarrassment of having an opinion stricken after it is rendered, when evidence is not introduced to support the hypothetical. Proving the facts first also tends to eliminate "facts not in evidence" objections. You may ask a hypothetical question even if the expert knows some or all the facts.

Preparation is the key to using a hypothetical question. The "word picture" in the hypothetical should fairly reflect facts and inferences reasonably flowing from the evidence. You should not weigh down the hypothetical with needless detail; emphasize the facts supporting the expert's opinion. Make sure there are no mistakes in the factual rendition. Outline or write out the hypothetical in advance so that you do not muddle it. The crisper the presentation, the less likely the hypothetical will evoke an objection.

Stated properly, a hypothetical can be a good tool of argument. Consider the following example:

---

[68] See U.S. v. Reno, 992 F.2d 739, 734 (7th Cir. Ill. 1993) (holding that hypothetical questions that did not reach the ultimate issue of the defendant's mental state did not violate FRE 704(b)). See also Fluckey v. Chicago & Northwestern Transp. Co., 838 F.2d 302, 303 (8th Cir. 1988) (hypothetical questions should contain only facts that are supported by evidence).

[69] See Specht v. Jensen, 832 F.2d 1516, 1526 (10th Cir. 1987) (court allowed testimony of expert concerning the constitutionality of a search and seizure to be structured around hypothetical questions).

> Q. Mr. Cunningham, I'd like to ask you a hypothetical relating to this case. Please assume the following facts: The airport aviation authority hired a contractor — ABC Corp. — to renovate the east-west runway with an asphalt overlay. The job was conducted over the months June to October, 1988. During the course of the job, large amounts of black smoke were frequently emitted from the smokestack at the asphalt mixing plant. Additionally, diesel fuel was used to clean the truckbeds used to transport the asphalt mixture to the runways, and this fuel frequently was not removed from the beds prior to loading the asphalt.
>
> Within a few weeks after laydown of the asphalt, the runways experienced raveling. Tests established that the asphalt was not adhering completely to the aggregate, so that the mixture came apart. Holes began developing in the pavement. Within a few months there was widespread deterioration of the runway, so that it could not be used for takeoffs and landings of planes. Assume the condition of the runway was the same as that you described today in your testimony, based on your inspection. Do you have an opinion of the cause of the failure of the runway?
>
> A. Yes, I do.
>
> Q. Tell the Court and jury, please, what that opinion is.
>
> A. In my opinion the cause was poor workmanship.
>
> Q. What are your reasons for that opinion?
>
> A. In particular, the asphalt was burned in the mixing process, limiting its ability to adhere to the aggregate and hold it in place. The diesel fuel made this situation worse because it dissolved the bond between the asphalt and the aggregate when it got into the mix. Neither of these conditions would have occurred if the job had been performed properly.

§ 10-13. Choosing the Right Expert.

Selecting the right expert is perhaps the most important element of a good technical presentation. You need to make sure the expert has the qualifications to provide opinions on the specific issues. This trait requires more than expertise in a general field. For example, an economist may be "expert" in the general sense but have no experience analyzing competition in a particular industry. He thus might be unsuited to testify in an antitrust case. You must make sure the expert has the ability to address the issues in the case.

You should identify, with some precision, the technical issues. In interviewing experts, probe the candidate's specific experience in those areas. Remember that most experts want jobs and may try to "sell" themselves. Unless you probe the candidate's qualifications, you may be fooled by a smooth talker who wants a fee.

One method of finding the right expert is to inquire with other attorneys. Lawyers experienced in the area may provide insights concerning the strengths and weaknesses of those who often testify. Additionally, you should ask your client — or others with experience in the area — for the names of knowledgeable professionals. You may also consult with experts in related fields. Again, these professionals can help you assess candidates.

Make sure the expert can provide testimony that does not conflict with his prior positions. In some fields, experts testify on a regular basis. Usually they testify for the same side, partly to avoid conflicts. For instance, economists consistently provide damage computations for the same side; in public utility cases, pro-consumer experts testify for consumer advocates, while pro-utility experts testify for utilities. Yet even when an expert stays with one side, his prior testimony on a particular issue may raise a conflict. If so, the prior testimony may dilute the expert's enthusiasm and provide ammunition for cross-examination. Thus, you should explore this matter before retaining the expert.

You also should make sure the expert's prior testimony does not conflict with the client's position on other technical issues. Often a party retains an expert to address one issue, but his field overlaps with other matters. A skillful lawyer may discover the conflicts and turn the expert into a favorable witness on matters he was not retained to address.

An expert who is not a "professional witness" may have more credibility than one with experience testifying. An expert who has not often testified brings an objective appearance and a fresh outlook to a case. The expert may be uncomfortable with litigation, however, and may appear nervous in presenting testimony. He may also have difficulty withstanding a vigorous cross-examination. Additionally, the inexperienced witness may be less helpful than the professional expert in preparing for trial. You must balance these considerations in choosing an expert.

You should weigh these considerations, but in the final analysis the choice depends on an assessment of the person's abilities. Find an expert who makes a good impression, works well with you, and is accessible. Obviously, the fee is an issue, but the fee should be weighed against the potential gain or loss at trial. You should try to get the best expert, not the least costly one.

§ 10-14. Use of Experts.

Experts can be valuable throughout the litigation. An expert may help formulate discovery requests, analyze technical issues, and plan the trial. The expert also can help counter the opposition's expert, including helping prepare cross-examination. Thus, you should retain an expert early in the litigation and use him to prepare for trial.

In dealing with specialized issues, you should use the expert's technical knowledge, but remember that you — not the expert — have paramount responsibility for the litigation. Often experts, especially those who testify frequently, try to take over trial preparation. You should not cede control to the expert. You should remain in charge of all trial preparation, including the examination of your expert and the opposing technical witness.

One good use of an expert is to help you understand the issues. A major role of the attorney is the translation of technical matters: making them understandable to average people. You must make your expert's presentation understandable and explain weaknesses in the opposing expert's testimony. Thus, you should discuss the issues with the expert, review explanatory material, and acquire a working understanding of the technical concepts.

Use the expert in pretrial preparation. The expert should help you formulate requests for discovery and prepare for depositions. Consult with the expert to identify important facts. Keep control of the process, but use the expert as a resource. Work with the expert in preparing testimony, seeking a way to bring out points in a manner that the expert can endorse. Ask for the expert's input for cross-examination.

You should not abandon the technical field to the experts. Too often, attorneys do not understand the technical issues and rely on the experts to guide the presentation of evidence. The advocate becomes a reader, repeating questions prepared by the expert without comprehending their meaning. This approach places the attorney at a grave disadvantage, especially in cross-examination. An experienced witness can virtually toy with counsel, asking that he define terminology or rephrase questions, and making it obvious that the attorney is dependent on his expert.

Further, depending on an expert to prepare an interrogation and whisper follow-up questions rarely works; the expert usually cannot pin down a witness because he has no training as an attorney. Additionally, this approach often deteriorates into an incomprehensible battle of jargon; the experts joust as everyone wonders what they are fighting about. The examination has meaning only if counsel gets involved and translates concepts.

You should be careful about sharing privileged information with an expert. If he uses the information to prepare testimony, you may waive the privilege and subject the information to discovery. You have greater protection in sharing privileged information with a non-testifying expert, but the opposing side still may obtain it in special circumstances. These issues are discussed further in § 11-6.

§ 10-15. Need to Take Discovery of Experts.

Exhaustive discovery of the opposing expert is essential in trial preparation. The evidence rules, which permit the expert to rely on evidence outside the record and state conclusions without disclosing the basis, place pressure on you to uncover the expert's weaknesses in cross-examination. In the process, you must avoid giving the expert a chance to cause damage. Only through extensive discovery — including a thorough deposition — can you succeed at this task.

Written discovery of experts usually is not very useful. As quasi-advocates, experts are adept at avoiding disclosure of harmful information. Moreover, their responses typically are filled with self-serving conclusions. Thus, interrogatories usually do not produce much helpful data. In a deposition, with the ability to follow up, you can pin down the expert and obtain specific concessions.

Unlike interrogatories, requests for prior reports and testimony may produce helpful material. If the expert previously has testified on a related issue, you may benefit from the concessions obtained by other attorneys. Further, you may find it fruitful to review the expert's publications. These documents may contain statements of principle that can be used to obtain concessions.

Depositions provide the best opportunity to obtain useful material for cross-examining experts. The following suggestions may help you depose experts effectively.

1. *Pursue explanations.* The guiding rule in deposing experts is to keep them talking. You should make the expert explain, explain, explain. You may appear dumb in the deposition, but you will look much smarter at the trial. Ask the expert to describe points in common, everyday language, drawing him away from specialized jargon. You should also follow up until you are sure you fully understand every point.

   This advice is difficult for many people to follow. If a witness makes a technical statement you do not understand, and everyone else appears to follow it, your natural inclination is to *act like* you do also. Young attorneys especially are reluctant to admit they do not understand points. But you cannot conduct an effective cross-examination without finding out what the expert is trying to say. If you do not understand a point, you cannot show why it is wrong. Even if you think you understand, you must make sure that the expert's meaning does not differ from your interpretation. Thus, the most effective way to depose an expert is to play dumb, asking continually for explanations.

575

2.   *Explore expert's credentials.* Find out the expert's credentials. Use the checklist presented in § 10-6 to find out what the expert has, and has not, accomplished. Think of professional credentials that might be distinctly suited to the facts; ask if the expert possesses them. Try to think of credentials you do not believe the expert will have. Asking about them will lay a foundation for cross-examination and may make the expert defensive.

3.   *Determine expert's method and its acceptance.* Early in the deposition, explore how the expert ordinarily arrives at conclusions in her profession. Determine the factual predicate and the types of evidence that she would require to support a conclusion. You might try intimating that the expert would offer an opinion without much support, which should produce assurances that the expert would require extensive support. This testimony may come in handy in attacking the expert's basis. It may even support exclusion of the expert's opinions if the expert relies on a basis for the litigation that she would not accept in her professional practice.

   If the expert uses a novel method or theory in drawing conclusions, explore the extent to which the method is accepted in the field. Pursue the issues of testability and accuracy. Determine whether the method was created for litigation. Find out the extent to which it is peer-reviewed. You may be able to exclude th expert's testimony if the method is not well accepted.

4.   *Explore application of principles.* General principles provide a fruitful area in deposing experts. Often an expert is prepared to support his position on the issue in the case but does not think through the theoretical underpinnings for that position. If you start with the theory, before addressing the particular issue, the expert may offer potentially damaging opinions. You must be knowledgeable to use this strategy, however, because you cannot follow up on theories without understanding them. Further, knowledge helps you mask your true objectives.

   Asking about principles in different contexts from that in the case is a good deposition strategy. Identify the principle in an expert's opinion and see how well it works in other situations. Think of hypotheticals in which the principle leads to an unfair result for the expert's client. In the deposition you can ask the hypothetical *without linking the matter to your facts*. Often the expert will select a competing principle to produce a favorable outcome for his side. You then can ask all his reasons, again without linkage to the case. The expert's explanations may supply a great basis for cross-examination.

   You can also approach the matter more directly, asking the expert to apply his principles in different situations. Often experts create "hybrid principles" for litigation; these rules are similar to the accepted principles in the field, but are adjusted to support a party's theory. The expert may admit the principle leads to an unfair result in a different context. If so, you can ask him to give all the reasons it should not be applied. Alternatively, the expert may defend applying the principle in the parallel situation, which forces him to support an unfair outcome. Again, the testimony provides useful material for cross-examination.

You also should ask the expert about the principles supporting your position. Get him to explain the principle, its justification, and when it should be applied. Go ahead and ask why it should not govern your case; the deposition is the place to let the expert attack your position. If you get the expert to discuss your principles, you may obtain material for making positive points in cross-examination. At worst, you can anticipate the expert's reasons for rejecting your position and plan to counter them.

Often the principles espoused by experts cut different ways on different issues. You can get the expert in the deposition to provide all the reasons supporting the application of the principle where it helps him, then use it in cross-examination where it hurts him. This approach requires thinking through the issues and planning a deft approach, but it can provide good material for cross-examination.

5. *Explore expert's method.* Experts often play the role of advocates. If an expert thinks you are trying to get him to say something, he has an urge to offer reasons why you are wrong. The expert may not realize how these statements can be turned around. Try a bit of acting, suggesting the expert should accept a conclusion you really want him to reject. You will be surprised how often he will argue against a principle that supports his own position. For this tactic to work, however, the questioning must be conceptual, and you must thoroughly understand the area.

6. *Explore related issues.* Often a case involves a number of related technical issues. A party may hire several experts to address individual points without preparing each expert on the overall theory. Thus, in deposition you may entice an expert to provide reasons why his own client's position is wrong on related issues. Cross-examination at trial on separate issues may be limited by the scope-of-direct rule, but often leeway to cross-examine is allowed on theoretical issues. If necessary, you can recall the expert in your case to support you on new points. Thus, an examination on related, technical points in the deposition may prove fruitful.

7. *Determine expert's preparation.* Experts, like other people, often procrastinate. They may delay full preparation until the time of trial. If you examine the expert on what he has done to reach his conclusions, you

may find his preparation scanty. You need to think of things that he logically should have done, or might have done, to reach opinions. Additionally, you might first ask what actions are normal in the expert's field to render opinions, without specifically referring to his preparation in the case. After the expert endorses various actions, you can determine whether he accomplished them in the litigation. Even if the expert "catches up" for trial, you can bring out in cross-examination that he reached initial conclusions without a comprehensive analysis.

8. *Explore factual predicates.* Find out the factual grounds on which the expert relies and her basis for identifying these facts. Sometimes experts learn the facts from counsel and are not aware of facts that support your position. Determine whether hypothetical changes in the factual predicate would alter the expert's opinion. If the expert is not well prepared, you may secure concessions that will help you at trial. Alternatively, if the expert is unsure of her basis, she may equivocate enough to undermine her conclusions that do apply to the facts.

9. *Nail down points in agreement.* Some expert fields are governed by well-accepted principles. A doctor, engineer, or scientist usually must adhere to governing precepts in the field. Thus, you often can elicit concessions that statements in authoritative publications are correct, even if they support your position. Moreover, you can use the authorities themselves as evidence if the expert accepts them or another expert testifies they are authoritative. See § 6-31.

10. *Determine expert's compensation.* Find out in the deposition how the expert is being compensated. An extremely high hourly rate or an outcome-based fee can be a basis for cross-examining on motive for testifying, but you need to find out the fee basis in advance. You do not want to be surprised by the expert's response.

Some jurisdictions traditionally limited expert discovery to protect "work product." The evidence rules make these limitations obsolete, however, because the rules place the burden on the attorney to reveal the holes in an expert's opinion through cross-examination. In 1993, the discovery provisions of the Federal Rules of Civil Procedure were amended to substantially broaden a party's right to obtain discovery from an opposing expert. Rule 26(a)(2) requires a party to disclose the identity of any expert witness and unless otherwise stipulated or provided by the court, a report containing his opinions, basis, reasons, the data he considered, and other information. Additionally, Rule 26(b)(4) provides a right to depose an opposing expert who will appear at trial. Rule 26(b)(4) provides:

> (A) A party may depose any person who has been identified as an expert whose opinions may be presented at trial. If a report from the expert is required under [Rule 26(a)(2)(B), providing for pretrial disclosure of expert

testimony], the deposition shall not be conducted until after the report is provided.

§ 10-16.   Direct Examination of Experts.

The same general rules apply to the direct examination of experts as other witnesses. Counsel should try for a good start, focusing attention through a thematic question or one that stresses the expert's special vantage point. Counsel should use signposts to focus attention on upcoming subjects. The "step-step-step-whirr!-replay-replay-replay" method is effective with experts, because it allows counsel to control the examination and follow up to ensure the testimony is understandable, but permits the expert to display his knowledge. See § 7-13.

In preparing the expert, you should stress the need for an understandable presentation. Technical jargon may seem impressive, but it does little good if no one can understand what the expert is saying. Your effort to translate technical terms can succeed only if the expert cooperates. You need to get the expert's help in developing simple explanations, examples, and analogies. The expert must make a special effort to avoid jargon, because technical terms are part of his everyday language.

Caution the expert to be responsive. Experts — especially academicians — have a natural tendency to launch into lecture-like explanations. To the expert, this approach seems a good way to cover everything; since he conceives the explanation, it all seems clear to him. Your goal, in contrast, is to break the testimony into understandable parts and focus on one point at a time. In particular, you need to emphasize the points that best support your theme. Thus, you should go over the testimony, hear the expert's answers, and train him to be responsive.

Make sure the expert checks his computations, ensures the accuracy of exhibits, and can explain technical terms. Your opponent can unnerve your expert if he exposes mathematical errors and other mistakes, even if the errors are not that important. Experts hate to admit that their computations are inaccurate, yet they often leave it to someone else to check them. You and the expert need to make sure the material is accurate.

Help the expert appear congenial. Experts often display attitudes that appear arrogant. Particularly if an expert is sensitive to weaknesses in his position, he may become caustic and condescending. You cannot change the expert's personality, but you can adjust it. Caution the expert to keep his cool and retain a pleasant appearance. The more an expert displays a disagreeable disposition, the more the listeners will sense he is getting hurt.

Develop a presentation that is straightforward and logical. If the expert has more than one main point, cover the basis, opinion and reasons for each point separately; in other words, make a comprehensive presentation of each point. A suggested sequence for the direct examination is discussed in § 10-19.

§ 10-17. Use of Leading Questions With Experts.

In many jurisdictions, the rule against leading in direct examination tradition-ally did not apply to the questioning of experts. Apparently, it was believed leading was required to bring out technical and conceptual points. Moreover, counsel must suggest facts to an expert in a hypothetical question, although he need not suggest conclusions. In any event, many courts still recognize an unwritten rule permitting counsel to lead an expert.

The Federal Rules of Evidence make no exception to the rule against leading for expert examinations. FRE 611(c) does recognize, however, that leading is permissible if necessary to develop the testimony of the witness. Presumably on technical issues this exception permits you some leeway. Additionally, the traditional permissive approach may influence many judges to permit leading. Further, as noted in § 10-12, courts still permit the hypothetical as a means to pose a basis for an expert's conclusion.

Even if the jurisdiction permits leading of experts, or the judge allows leading, the leading should be limited to the examination on the expert's conclusions and theories. An attorney should not be allowed in direct examination to lead an expert on fact testimony. Moreover, if factual material, such as a data compilation, forms a basis for the expert's conclusions, the court generally should not allow leading in the development of this information. Most experts do not need this help in getting their points across.

§ 10-18. Translating Expert Testimony.

One of the advocate's main functions with experts is to make the direct examination understandable to listeners who have no special expertise. You also must make your points understandable on cross-examination. If jurors can comprehend your technical case, but not the adverse party's, you should prevail on that aspect of the case.

Translating is not easy. Attorneys fall into the same traps that entangle experts — after grappling with complex issues for years, lawyers often use the same jargon that the experts employ. Further, you may forget how hard it was to understand specialized concepts when you first encountered them. You can be effective only if you back up, put yourself in the listener's place, and make the material understandable.

To explain points, you have to figure them out. You need to understand your own expert's theory and that of the opposing expert. Once you comprehend the material, you should devise clear explanations. You need to cover the basics, avoid jargon, and keep your explanations uncomplicated.

Means of making technical information understandable in direct examination include the following.

1. *Use common language.* Have the expert explain her points in terms that are familiar to everyone. If the expert must use technical terms, have her explain them. Try to avoid jargon as you develop the expert's points.

2. *Break up the subjects.* Cover one point at a time. If you break matters up, allowing the listeners to absorb technical information in pieces, you make it easier for them to keep up. You might first provide an overall view of the testimony, which provides context, but cover the underlying information in comprehensible parts.

3. *Use examples.* One way to help listeners understand technical points is through examples. Experts often testify in the abstract, explaining principles and theories without relating them to facts. Unfortunately, listeners often have difficulty following an abstract presentation. If you have the expert provide examples of how theories work, testimony takes on meaning. An example follows:

Q. Mr. Louiselle, can you describe a seller's ability to influence price in perfect competition?

A. All sellers are price takers in perfect competition.

Q. What is a price taker?

A. A price taker is someone who can't influence price by increasing or decreasing his supply.

Q. Can you give the jury an example?

A. Well, one example that is often used is the farmers' market — say, corn. There are so many suppliers of corn and so many buyers that the market really sets the price. No one buyer or seller is large enough to affect the price by changing the amount he's willing to sell or buy. An individual farmer couldn't drive the price up, for instance, by withholding his corn.

---

4. *Use analogies.* Sometimes a concept that seems difficult when applied in a complex case can be simplified through the use of an analogy. Have the expert provide an analogy that demonstrates his point. An analogy is another form of example, parallel to the expert's application of principle to facts. An example follows:

Q. Mr. Baron, what did you conclude about Monocorp's price?

A. I concluded it was set artificially low to drive other suppliers out of business.

Q. On what basis did you form this conclusion?

A. The price was below Monocorp's incremental cost of making digital switches.

Q. What conclusion can you draw from that finding?

A. No reasonable seller would sell his product for less than his marginal cost of making it unless he had some ulterior or unusual reason.

Q. How did you determine Monocorp's marginal cost?

A. I had to separate the fixed costs of production from the variable, or marginal costs, of making additional switches.

Q. Can you give a simple example, or analogy, to explain your reasoning?

A. Well, let's say you have a popcorn vendor in a shopping center. Now, let's say he's already bought a stand and a popcorn machine — he has to pay those costs whether or not he sells any popcorn. When he makes popcorn, he needs some electricity, oil, corn, a box, and salt. Let's say those items cost ten cents a box. Now the popcorn vender obviously would like to get more than ten cents a box — say fifty cents — because he would like to pay off the cost of his stand. But if competition drove the price down to eleven cents, he still has a reason to make and sell popcorn — he can make a penny on each box.

One thing he probably wouldn't do is sell the popcorn for five cents. If he did, he would not only have to eat the cost of his stand, but he would lose a nickel for each new box of popcorn he sold. That would be irrational behavior. He would only do that if he had some other reason besides making money on each box of popcorn. For instance, he might do it to try to drive another popcorn stand out of business by taking away all its customers.

5. *Use demonstrative aids.* A great way to explain technical concepts is through visual aids. A chart or graph may demonstrate the factual basis

for an expert's conclusions. A model can help her describe how a complex process works. These tools provide concreteness to an abstract explanation. Thus, they are especially helpful with experts. You should make sure, however, that demonstrative exhibits actually add to the presentation. Too many demonstrative aids can be disruptive.

6. *Explain the basis of cross-examination.* Translation is also important to an effective cross-examination. You need to get the expert to agree to your explanations of technical terms. Use lay language in your questions. You can use models and charts in cross-examination as well as in direct, so long as the process does not become too time consuming. Your overall goal should be to make *your points* understandable; do not worry about translating material that hurts you. An example of translating in cross-examination follows.

Q.   Mr. Kahal, do you know what a "price taker" is?

A.   I know the term. I'm not sure how you're using it.

Q.   Would you agree that the term "price taker" is sometimes used to describe a seller in perfect competition?

A.   Yes, if such a market exists.

Q.   A price taker is a firm that can't affect the price by changing his supply, correct?

A.   Yes, that's true.

Q.   For instance, if a farmers' market for corn had so many sellers and so many buyers that any one farmer could not affect the price by increasing or decreasing his supply, he would be a price taker, right?

A.   That's one example.

Q.   He could withhold all his corn, and still the price wouldn't go up, because of all the other sellers, correct?

A.   In combination with all the buyers, yes.

---

§ 10-19. Sequence of Direct Examination of an Expert.

The sequence of direct examination for an expert witness should reflect the basic principles governing any direct examination. First, you want to focus attention by achieving a thematic beginning or highlighting the importance of the witness. Second, you need an orderly, understandable presentation. Third, you need to stay in control while allowing the expert to present the material.

Fourth, you need to highlight and support your main points. The following organization is a good means to accomplish these goals.

§ 10-19(a). Focus Attention on the Witness.

You need to start strong, letting the jury know why the witness is important. One good way to achieve this aim is to ask the expert to describe the general purpose of her testimony, before reviewing her background. This action makes qualifications and other background more meaningful. An example of an introduction that focuses attention is the following:

> Q.   State your name, please.
>
> A.   Dr. Renee Williams.
>
> Q.   Dr. Williams, what is your occupation?
>
> A.   I am an assistant coroner with the County Coroner's Office. I am a pathologist by profession.
>
> Q.   To what extent were you involved in examining the corpse of a person identified as Bruce Begonia?
>
> A.   I was the pathologist who examined the body and determined the cause of death.
>
> Q.   All right, doctor. I'd like to back up and discuss your background. . ..

---

§ 10-19(b). Lay the Groundwork for the Expert's Opinion.

The foundation for the expert's opinion consists of two elements: his expertise and his factual basis. You need to review both before presenting the opinion. If you decide to qualify and tender the witness as an expert before getting to substance, you must review qualifications first. For a single issue expert, you then would move on to the factual basis for his opinion, and, if applicable, the method he used to reach it.

If the expert testifies on multiple points, you may want to review some special aspect of his expertise in laying the basis for a related opinion, even if he is already qualified. This action establishes specific credentials to give an individual opinion. Once you review specific qualifications, you should review the expert's relevant factual knowledge in connection with each main point he addresses. The approach of combining qualifications, factual basis, and opinion works especially well with experts who address multiple topics. The linkage gives credibility to the expert's conclusions.

§ 10-19(c). Ask for the Expert's Opinion.

Once you review the basis, ask for the expert's opinion. When the expert has a single opinion that you wish to dramatize, this request is best accomplished in two steps: first, you ask the expert if she has an opinion, to which she answers "yes"; and second, you ask the expert to "tell the court and jury" the opinion. This procedure announces that an opinion is coming and, hopefully, wakes everyone up. An example follows:

Q. Dr. Williams, do you have an opinion as to what caused the death of Bruce Begonia?

A. I do.

Q. Tell the court and jury, please, what that opinion is.

A. The cause of death was the gunshot wound to the chest, in which the bullet pierced the upper left portion of the heart.

When the expert offers multiple opinions, dramatizing each may give the impression that the expert offers mostly opinions without a solid basis. In that situation you should ask for the conclusions without characterizing them as opinion:

Q. Mr. Kollen, how did Monocorp's price compare to its marginal cost of producing products?

A. It was below marginal cost.

Q. What was the effect of charging prices below marginal cost?

A. The effect was to drive Littlecorp out of business.

Q. How did Monocorp's pricing do that?

A. The prices were also below Littlecorp's marginal cost. Both companies were incurring greater losses with each new sale. Littlecorp did not have the financial wealth of Monocorp and went bankrupt shortly after the price war began.

---

§ 10-19(d). Review the Expert's Reasons.

You can emphasize the opinion and further support it by asking the expert to explain her reasons. This technique allows the expert to advocate her conclusion and, in the process, your case. Ask follow-up questions that permit the expert to elaborate on individual reasons. In each case, show how the reason leads back to the expert's conclusion.

An example of the direct examination of an expert is provided in § 10-21.

§ 10-20. Use of Demonstrative Exhibits in Presenting Expert Testimony.

Demonstrative exhibits provide an excellent means of communicating technical points. Charts, diagrams, and models may facilitate the expert's explanation of complex matters. Moreover, if an expert has accumulated data in support of her position, a chart or graph may dramatize the supporting evidence. You should seek ways to use demonstrative exhibits with expert testimony but should remember to use them sparingly — to illustrate the testimony and emphasize major points.

You should ensure that the sponsoring expert can testify from personal knowledge to the accuracy of demonstrative exhibits. Too often testifying experts delegate the task of preparing exhibits and sponsor them as prepared under the expert's "supervision." This indirect foundation may not be enough to admit the exhibit, although many judges are lenient on the admissibility issue. Nevertheless, the expert's lack of personal knowledge may expose her to effective cross-examination, especially if the exhibit contains errors. If the expert checks the exhibit to ensure personal knowledge, she will uncover most errors.

§ 10-21. Example of Direct Examination of an Expert Witness.

The following is an example of a direct examination that employs the method of moving from qualifications and basis to opinions within subject areas. The testimony is presented in a case for defamation. Mr. Paves, an architect, claims that Mr. Johnstone, another architect, defamed him by saying that his fee was too high, his credentials poor, and his work shoddy on a municipal project, which caused him to lose the job. Here, the expert testifies for the plaintiff. Counsel attempts to show that no basis existed for the alleged defamatory statements.

The example is based on a demonstration at an advocacy institute. The reader will note that the opposing party examines the same witness in the example of direct examination presented in § 7-20. Both examinations were based on the witness script reproduced in Appendix B. The examples demonstrate how selection and emphasis can change the character of testimony, even using the same script. Obviously, with a script there is more room to fill in facts, but the techniques work with any witness.

Q.   Will you state your name for the jury, please.

A.   My name is Aubrey Robinson.

Q.   What is your occupation?

A.   My occupation is an architect.

Q.   Where do you practice architecture?

A.   I practice in Fredericksburg, Virginia.

Q.   Do you know the plaintiff in this case, John Paves?

A.   Yes, I do.

Q.   How do you know John Paves?

A.   I know Mr. Paves through my association in the Spotsylvania County Association of Architects and he is an architect here in Fredericksburg, and I've known him the entire time I've been here.

Q.   How long is that?

A.   Approximately 10½ years.

Q.   Do you know the defendant in this case, Mr. Johnstone?

A.   Yes, I do.

Q.   How long have you known Mr. Johnstone?

A.   I have known Mr. Johnstone also about 10½ years, since I came to Fredericksburg.

Q.   Now, Mr. Robinson, did I ask you to come here today to give some testimony on certain matters for the jury?

A.   Yes, you did.

Q.   What did I ask you to come and testify about?

A.   You asked me to testify as to Mr. Paves' reputation as an architect. You asked me to testify as to the fees charged by Mr. Paves in this post office project, and you also asked me to testify as to his work on the post office project.

Q.   Thank you very much. I'd like to turn first of all to the fee question, and I'll ask you just a few preliminary questions with regard to your knowledge in this area. Could you tell the jury the nature of your practice?

A.   I work in a firm, Robinson and Jones. I primarily deal with large construction projects — schools, large office buildings, other large government buildings, and whatnot.

Q.   How long have you been engaged in a practice that mainly deals with large construction?

A.   Since 1985.

Q.   How does the kind of job that you typically do compare to, say, the post office renovation job that's at issue in this case?

A.   The post office job is right up the alley of what I do.

Q.   To what extent, if any, have you had occasion to deal with jobs for which there was some kind of a bid process?

A.   Very often.

Q.   Would you explain to the jury a little bit about your experience in that area.

A.   About five to ten times a year I submit bids for publicly bidded projects. That averages out — I've probably done several dozen bids over the years. In addition, I review bids when a project is bidded upon and I have not personally submitted a bid, oftentimes whoever solicits and receives the bids asks me to review those that are received.

Q.   Do you do that — what — for the purpose of providing advice on which bid to select?

A.   Precisely. Whoever as solicitor received the bids comes to me and asks me to look over the costs of the project, the quality of the proposals, the fees charged, whatnot.

Q.   To what extent do the fees being quoted by the architects enter into that analysis?

A.   It is a very important part of the evaluation of any bid.

Q.   In the course of your ten years or so of experience in Spotsylvania County, about how many jobs would you say involving large construction, and by that I mean nonresidential jobs, that you've either been involved in as the architect or supporting the architect or reviewing a bid or giving advice with respect to the project?

A.   Since 1985, I would have to say scores — probably close to 100.

Q.   Now, Mr. Robinson, are you generally familiar with the fees that are customarily charged on large construction projects in Spotsylvania County, the area around Fredericksburg?

A.   Yes, I am.

Q.   Would you tell the jury how it is that you're familiar with the customary fees?

A.   In Spotsylvania County, I'm familiar with the fees due to my association with other architects through the Spotsylvania County Association of Architects. There are about twenty of us here in Spotsylvania County. I know them both professionally and socially, and we get together, and through our discussions I've become familiar with fees charged. And in addition, for three years I sat on the fee resolution, fee grievance council, of the Spotsylvania County Architecture Association.

Q. Are there any standard references that are used by architects in determining fees?

A. Yes. The most popular standard reference is something called the NS Data Book. I call it The Data Book. Also, there's something called the Governor's Capital Outlay Book. Those are standard references.

Q. How are they used?

A. They are used, again, as reference sources. When you have a project that comes in, and you understand exactly what is being done on the project, the materials, the size, whatnot, you refer to these manuals, and it gives you — at least in the case of the cost data book — it gives you a range, a general range of architectural fees that are normally charged for a project.

Q. Now you have an understanding that one of the issues in this case relates to Mr. Paves' fee that he was charging on the post office renovation, do you not?

A. Yes.

Q. Are you familiar with the post office renovation project?

A. Yes, I am.

Q. How are you familiar with it?

A. I was initially interested in the project. I wanted to — originally had planned to submit a bid. I expressed my interest to the council, I took a tour of the old post office with the City Manager, Mr. Knowles. I decided that based upon what was needed to be done I did not have the time, and so I did not submit a bid. Since that time I have reviewed the fact statements and also the drawings done by Mr. Paves on this project.

Q. Mr. Robinson, is there a customary or typical fee or range of fees that one might expect for a job of that type in Spotsylvania County?

A. Yes, there is.

Q.   Would you tell the jury please what is the typical range of
      that fee?

A.   The range is about 9 to 12 percent.

Q.   Are you familiar with the fee that was stated by Mr. Paves
      in his proposal that he gave to the city and was accepted
      by the city?

A.   Yes, I am.

Q.   What was that fee?

A.   Ten percent.

Q.   How does Mr. Paves' fee quotation, which was accepted,
      compare to the standard or typical fee as you know it?

A.   Well within the range of what I would consider a typical,
      reasonable fee.

Q.   Based on your experience, Mr. Robinson, would it be typical
      or normal to charge a fee 50% less than what Mr. Paves
      charged?

A.   No, it would not.

Q.   Would you say that Mr. Paves charged 50% more than what
      could be considered reasonable?

A.   No.

Q.   Would you, an architect in the Fredericksburg area, consider
      the fee charged by Mr. Paves to be unreasonably or unjusti-
      fiably high?

A.   No, not at all.

Q.   Would you explain to the jury the basis for your determina-
      tion that Mr. Paves' fee was not unjustifiably high but in
      fact was reasonable?

A.   Again, through my association with other architects in the
      area and through my conversations with them and through
      my membership in the Spotsylvania County Association of
      Architects, and also through my experience on the grievance
      board, I have come to understand what the fees are in this
      area. Also in reviewing bid proposals I stay current on the
      fees that are being charged for projects around here.

Q.   Thank you. Now the next thing I'd like to discuss — have
      you discuss with the jury — is the issue of Mr. Paves'
      reputation and experience. I believe you indicated earlier
      that you're generally familiar with Mr. Paves?

A. Yes, I am.

Q. Well, would you tell the jury how you know him and how well you know him, please?

A. Mr. Paves and I first met at an alumni-student mixer at the School of Architecture at UVa. When I graduated and came to Fredericksburg about 10½ years ago, I was pleased to see that he was just moving back to the area after having spent some time in Washington. And so, in my entire time in Fredericksburg as an architect, I have known Mr. Paves both professionally and personally.

Q. To what extent, if any, have you had any professional interaction with Mr. Paves?

A. I've had a number of instances in which I have gone to Mr. Paves professionally, and he has come to me. We exchange ideas, sometimes we get like an architectural block, like a writer's block, and we need somebody to jar us, and so I go to Mr. Paves, Mr. Paves comes to me, and so we exchange ideas and also work product.

Q. Are architects in the Fredericksburg area fairly up to speed or familiar with the qualifications and abilities of the other architects here?

A. Yes. Again, there aren't very many of us here.

Q. Would you explain how architects interact and the basis for that familiarity?

A. Again, through the association here in Spotsylvania County, we have a number of functions throughout the year. Also, Fredericksburg is not that big. We see each other socially out, and also we see each other when we submit bids for works, and we talk to each other about what each is doing and the fees each are charging and movements in the field.

Q. Did Mr. Paves have a reputation among other architects in the Fredericksburg area with regard to his experience and his work abilities?

A. Yes.

Q. Would you tell the jury what Mr. Paves' reputation was with respect to his architectural experience?

A. He had a very good reputation in terms of his experience. His work experience was well-known.

Q. What was his reputation with respect to his experience in dealing with the larger construction projects, say, on the order of the post office renovation?

A. Again, he had a very good reputation.

Q. And what was the basis for that reputation, if you know?

A. I do know Mr. Paves did a number of large projects in Washington, D.C. before he came to Fredericksburg. His renovation and conversion work at the White House is well-known. One of his designs won an award for an office building in Tyson's Corner. Since he has been in Fredericksburg, he has done a number of projects at Mary Washington College that are well-known throughout the architectural community as being of excellent quality.

Q. Let me ask you this: Was it Mr. Paves' reputation in Fredericksburg that he was an inexperienced architect?

A. No, not at all.

Q. Was it Mr. Paves' reputation in Fredericksburg that he was inexperienced in jobs of the type of the City Hall renovation?

A. No, not at all.

Q. Do you have knowledge yourself concerning Mr. Paves' experience, was that, what you described earlier, was that also . . . ?

A. Yes. Yes, I do. Again, I'm familiar with his work in Washington; I went and visited those places and also here in Fredericksburg.

Q. To your knowledge, Mr. Robinson, was Mr. Paves inexperienced in jobs like the City Hall project?

A. No, not at all.

Q. Would you consider him experienced?

A. Yes, I would.

Q. And what is the basis for that experience?

A. Again, the work he has done here in Fredericksburg at Mary Washington College and also the size of the projects that he has completed in Washington, D.C., and also some of the projects he has been working on and continues to work on today.

Q. All right. Now, I'd next like to turn to the performance question in this case with respect to what Mr. Paves actually did for the city. And I'd like to ask you some questions preliminary to that, with respect to your specific experience. Have you had experience, since your graduation from Virginia, in jobs involving space allocation and schematic design?

A. Yes, I've had extensive experience in that field.

Q. Would you tell the jury, please, what your experience is in the areas of space allocation and schematic design?

A. In large construction and design projects, there is a floor plan of each floor if it's multi-level, or one ground floor, and in those particular projects what is absolutely crucial is the ratio of one need to another. For instance, if one room has a particular need, what is the ratio of that need and that floor space to all the other needs of that particular floor. And that continues throughout the building. And crucial to that, obviously, are floor plans, and jotting down exactly the ratio of where you're going to put the walls, the ratio of the rooms to each other.

Q. Approximately how many times in your experience would you say that you've dealt with these issues of space allocation and schematic design?

A. Virtually every large project upon which I've worked.

Q. Have you ever done any teaching in the area of architecture with particular respect to space allocation or schematic design?

A. Yes, sir, I have. I've taught some classes at Mary Washington College; I've also taught some classes at Northern Virginia Community College in Fairfax, Virginia, on schematic design, and it's kind of an introduction to architecture course.

Q. Have you ever had occasion to have a publication or publications in the area of space allocation and schematic design?

A. Yes sir, I have had, I believe, four publications in *Architectural Digest* on that field.

Q. Have you had other publications as well?

A. There were three others that I published that were more of a historical nature.

Q. Have you ever won an award in the area of space allocation and schematic design?

A. I won one award two years ago from the Spotsylvania County association for the work I did on a building at Mary Washington College.

Q. Was that in the area of space allocation and schematic design?

A. Yes. Yes, it was.

Q. Have you ever been qualified as an expert witness to testify with particular reference to space allocation and schematic design?

A. Yes, about two weeks ago, I think, I was here in Judge Wolf's court and was so qualified.

Q. Now, did I ask you to review the drawings that were prepared by Mr. Paves in connection with the post office project?

A. Yes, you did.

Q. And what did you do? Just tell the jury briefly what it is you took a look at.

A. Well, I looked at the contract, I looked at the proposal put out by the city, I looked at the preliminary drawings and schematic designs of Mr. Paves, and also the fee schedule that had been set up, and also his, he did a space study.

Q. Do you have an opinion, sir, as to the professional quality of the drawings that were prepared by Mr. Paves for that project?

A. Yes, I do.

Q. Tell the court and the jury, please, what your opinion is.

A. My opinion was that the concept employed by Mr. Paves was sound. My opinion was the drawings were very well done, very professional, and that the functional and aesthetic layout that he had proposed were very good.

Q. Mr. Robinson, knowing what you know, that Mr. Paves made a submission that was accepted by the city; that he made a study and that he submitted the drawings that you've described to the jury; to your knowledge, was there any professional basis that would have justified his dismissal?

A. None that I can see. No.

Q. No further questions, Your Honor.

§ 10-22. Cross-Examination of Expert Witnesses.

Effective cross-examination of experts requires extensive preparation. You must understand the technical area, the precise issue in the case, and how its outcome is influenced by technical factors. You must take extensive discovery, including a deposition, and thoroughly review the discovery to find avenues for attacking the expert's position. You must thoroughly plan the cross-examination, anticipating the expert's responses and limiting the opportunities for escape.[70]

Generally, the techniques that are effective in cross-examining other witnesses work well with experts. You should abstract the experts' prior assertions from a deposition, prior testimony, responses to discovery, and other material. Organize potential points into subject areas, making notes as to how the points might be developed. These categories can then be translated into cross-examination areas and questions. See § 9-10.

You should not expect an expert, however, to be as compliant as the average witness. Experts are paid to get their points across. They often stretch the bounds of questions to give mini-lectures supporting their points. Many experts are professionals at litigation and see cross-examination as a challenge to their abilities at advocacy. Thus, you must expect an expert to volunteer information.

You usually cannot stop an expert from volunteering points, but you can make him look bad doing it. If you use specific questions, long-winded answers appear gratuitous. The expert's lectures may frustrate the jurors as much as you. Additionally, you need not depend on the expert to make your points. If your questions have a solid basis and lead to logical conclusions, and the expert's points are hard to follow, you will accomplish much of your objective.

Part of the secret of cross-examining an expert is not to meet him on his home field. Take him out of the confines of his presentation. Make him concede *your* basic principles. Examine him with examples in which his principles produce unfair or illogical results. Force him to explain the matters that support your case in common, understandable language. Figure out how his points can be turned around. Try to accomplish something positive with the expert, in addition to attacking his position.

The following strategies work well with experts on cross-examination:

1. *Use lay language.* You should use lay language as much as possible, drawing the expert away from technical jargon. Translate technical language through questions, establishing that you understand the area

---

[70] See generally Margaret S. Gibbs et al., *Cross-Examination of the Expert Witness: Do Hostile Tactics Affect Impressions of a Simulated Jury?*, 7 BEHAVIORAL SCI. & L. 275 (1989).

and making the cross-examination points more real. Many experts feel more comfortable in the technical realm and may be less impressive if required to agree to everyday descriptions.

2. *Use the facts.* You know the facts better than the expert. In many cases, some facts support the expert's conclusion, while other facts support a contrary conclusion. For instance, some patient symptoms may support a particular medical diagnosis, while other symptoms indicate the diagnosis is wrong. You can use the facts that do not support the expert's conclusion, breaking the facts down to gain momentum through the "mountain out of a molehill" approach.

Additionally, just because an expert analyzes the facts does not mean that lay people cannot also interpret them. Often an expert's conclusion does not comport with ordinary reason. If you develop facts that point to a common sense conclusion, you undermine an expert's opinion that conflicts with it.

3. *Get agreement on positive points.* In many cases, the disagreements between opposing experts are fairly narrow. You should bring out — in elaborate detail — all the points on which the opposing expert agrees with your own expert. These concessions can prove valuable in closing argument.

4. *Point up absurdities.* It is surprising how often experts — motivated by their own economic interests and feeling protected from scrutiny in a technical area — offer up absurd positions in litigation. By translating the expert's opinion and basis, bringing out countervailing facts, and juxtaposing the opinion with the facts, you often can show the absurdity of the testimony. For instance, if a psychiatrist testified a rape victim did not suffer much psychological damage from the rape, the attorney could use the facts, and the normal psychological effect of these facts, to dramatize the unlikely nature of the expert's conclusion.

5. *Attack the expert's basis.* Many experts justify unrealistic conclusions by assuming unrealistic facts. The expert maintains his "integrity" because the conclusion is correct if one accepts the assumptions. Obviously, in this scenario, the weakness is in the assumptions, not necessarily the expert's logic. You may be able to exclude the expert's testimony if his assumptions do not "fit" the facts. If the expert does testify, point up the ways in which the assumptions diverge from the facts, using the "mountain out of a molehill" approach. Further, if the expert's assumptions are speculative, you should show that they are unlikely.

Sometimes experts draw conclusions for litigation based on scanty information. The expert may rely on reports of others, for instance, without checking the underlying facts. You should bring out this secondhand basis in cross-examination. You may also show that the expert would not rely on secondhand data in the professional world.

The expert may also employ incorrect facts in drawing his conclusions. If the factual basis conflicts with the evidence, you need to bring out the inconsistency. You may be able to demonstrate the expert's reliance on an incorrect fact, and its importance as a basis for his conclusion, before he realizes he made a mistake. If you start by demonstrating the mistake, he will say it is not important to his opinion.

6.   *Cover the "didn't do's."* A specialized version of attacking the expert's basis is an examination of "didn't do's" — the things the expert omitted from his review. If the opposition's expert made a less comprehensive study than your own expert, you should bring out the differences. Again, you should break these points down, so it seems that the expert missed a lot of information. Thus, for example, you might bring out the lack of personal examination of a patient, failure to review health history, or non-attendance at a surgical procedure.

7.   *Bring out financial and other loyalties.* You sometimes can undercut an expert by showing that she is biased. Bringing out the expert's fee or a long tradition of testifying only for one side suggests that the expert is not objective. This approach is double-edged, however; both side's experts usually get a fee and often tend to be associated with particular views. You may wish to bring out the point in a low-key fashion: "Hello again, Mr. Catlin. I guess this is about the twelfth time we've met in court, right?"

8.   *Lay your foundations first.* Often you can obtain concessions from an expert before she knows where you are going. Cross-examining on general points first can establish principles that later prove useful on the precise issue. The expert may quibble about a well-accepted point if he knows how you will use it.

Of course, the place to examine basic principles is in a deposition. If the expert concedes the principles, however, you need to get him to do so before the jury. If you wait until the point comes up in context, the expert may try to explain it away. Thus, you may want to get a straightforward concession of the principle before you place it in context; this approach makes it difficult for the expert to recant.

9.   *Use scholarly and technical authorities.* You can obtain concessions on fundamental points by referring the expert to technical authorities. This approach also may tell the expert that you are prepared, reducing his tendency to quibble. If the expert (or another expert) testifies the authority

is reliable, you may read its content to the jury.[71] An expert who repeatedly denies that authorities are reliable quickly loses credibility. Thus, faced with an argumentative expert, you may want to come prepared with a stack of authorities for the expert to reject. You can make a show of reviewing each author's qualifications and laying aside the publications as the expert denies their reliability.

10.   *Check the expert's numbers.* Experts make a surprising number of mathematical errors, either because they do sloppy work, fail to check numbers, or delegate mathematical tasks. Thus, a fruitful means to embarrass the expert is to find the errors. Experts are often masters of evasion, but they rarely can evade admitting an obvious mistake. Experts hate to have their mistakes pointed out, even on small matters, so doing it at the beginning may rattle the witness, paving the way for an effective cross-examination.

§ 10-23.   Examples of Expert Cross-Examination.

The following examples demonstrate some of the tactics of expert cross-examination.

§ 10-23(a).   Making Positive Points With an Expert.

The following example is an excerpt from a cross-examination of an economic expert in a utility merger case. The witness testified that the merger — between two large public utilities, Entergy Corp. and Gulf States Utilities Co. — should be allowed to proceed only if the projected benefits of the merger were redistributed to make them more proportional among all the companies, including Gulf States and several companies owned by Entergy. In the example counsel elicits agreement to the proposition that the merger should be approved in theory if it produces a net economic benefit. The attorney also reviews the basis for proving a net benefit.

Q.   Now, before we get to the conditions, I want to address the issue of whether the merger should be approved at all. Would you agree that setting aside the issue of what conditions to attach, that a merger should be approved if it is in the public interest?

A.   Yes.

Q.   Again, with the same caveat, setting aside the conditions, a merger between two public utilities is desirable if it will produce a net economic benefit?

---

[71] FED. R. EVID. 803(18).

A.   What is your question? I'm sorry.

Q.   Would you agree with that proposition that if we put the conditions aside for a second, the merger is desirable if it will produce a net economic benefit?

A.   I don't think that is sufficient.

Q.   Okay. What else do you need?

A.   I think the resultant rates applicable to the companies should be just and reasonable.

Q.   Okay, well, let us assume that we can get the rate through a condition, get the rates that would be just and reasonable. That's what I meant by setting aside.

A.   Okay, I'm sorry.

Q.   Now, if we can get a net economic benefit, we should go forward with the merger, right?

A.   And the rates are just and reasonable applied to the different operating companies?

Q.   Yes.

A.   Yes.

*   *   *

Q.   I think we just agreed, Dr. Berry, that if we can keep the rates just and reasonable, the merger is desirable if it will produce a net economic benefit?

A.   Yes.

Q.   In determining this economic benefit, the issue is whether the merger would result in a net reduction in cost for the utilities combined, as compared to the two entities in a stand-alone mode; is that right?

A.   Yes.

Q.   In other words, it would be whether the merger will produce a benefit to the economic welfare through an efficiency gain; is that right?

A.   Yes.

Q.   In the case of electricity, that would mean allowing the supply of electricity to customers at lower costs; would you agree with that?

A.   Yes.

> Q. Now, in your basic presentation, you have accepted most of the projections of Entergy that savings will be produced from the merger; is that right?
>
> A. Yes.
>
> Q. So, I take it that you agree that the delivery of electricity by Entergy to customers, the combined customers of Entergy and GSU, will be less costly with the merger than without the merger?
>
> A. Yes.
>
> Q. So, you have no dispute that there will be a net economic gain from the merger; is that right?
>
> A. That's correct.

§ 10-23(b).   Turning Points Around.

The following example is from a case in which a party attacked a state's "Cash Beer Law," which precluded beer wholesalers from extending credit to retailers. The plaintiffs claimed the law was anticompetitive in that it protected wholesalers from competing in offering credit terms and thus was preempted by federal antitrust laws. An expert for the defense asserted that the wholesale beer market was competitive because customers' needs were being met, based on a survey he reviewed. He also asserted that wholesalers would raise their prices if they had to extend credit, to cover the costs of additional working capital. Counsel attempted to turn around the expert's conclusions to support the view that the market was not competitive, and credit was a customer need.

> Q. Can you tell me, sir, what the economist's definition of a competitive market is?
>
> A. Yes. The economist's definition of a competitive market is that it is a marketplace in which there are many buyers and many sellers and that they assume perfect information, but quite frankly it often doesn't exist.
>
> Q. Well, is there any other part to the definition of the economist's, sir?
>
> A. Well, in instances that's sometimes defined as a situation where the prices are not controlled by any individual.
>
> Q. Everybody in the market is a price taker in a purely competitive market, is that right?

A. Everybody is a price taker. I'm not sure what you mean by that statement.

Q. You've never heard the term "price taker"?

A. I've heard of the term, but I'm not sure how you're using it.

Q. Well, do you know what the term "price taker" means?

A. I would assume that what you're talking about is an individual is looking at price and taking advantage of it wherever possible.

Q. Well, let's see about whether this definition rings a bell. "In a competitive market, since no supplier of goods is able to influence the price by how much of the goods he puts on the market, he is subject to taking the market price, and so therefore, he is a price taker." Have you heard that definition?

A. In a purely competitive market, that is true.

Q. And isn't it true that in pure competition all of the sellers in the market are deemed to be price takers?

A. Sounds logical.

Q. Isn't it also true, Professor Hair, that in a competitive market . . . as a seller's costs go up, he still — if he wants to sell — he has to sell at the market price?

A. If you're in a purely competitive market, he does. But we are dealing only with theory there, and in practice we very seldom have a purely competitive market. So I would say that in a real live market that does not necessarily hold true.

Q. Isn't it true, sir, that the economists' definition of competition depends on how much a party is incapable of influencing price himself?

A. The economists' definition of pure competition.

Q. And as you get closer to pure competition, it's more difficult for any individual supplier in the market to change his price and still sell his goods. Is that right?

A. Based upon my reading, I would say yes.

Q. And as his costs change, go up or down — or particularly up — it's more difficult for him to react to those cost changes by changing his price. Is that true?

A. Correct.

Q.   And as you've moved toward anticompetitive markets — monopolistic markets — the economist says that the person with more market power is able to change the price as he wishes to and still makes sales. Is that right?

A.   Correct.

Q.   In fact, in the case of the monopolist, the only limitation on the monopolist — according to market theory — is the demand curve. Is that right?

A.   Correct.

Q.   So the monopolist can charge any amount that he wants, the only thing that's going to cause him to make fewer sales is that the consumers just can't bear the price in that instance. Is that right?

A.   That's right.

Q.   It drives them out of the market. Is that correct?

A.   Correct.

Q.   Now let's see about your assumption in this case, sir. You've assumed that we have a market here in which every seller can pass through every penny of every cost increase. Is that right?

A.   No.

Q.   Did you believe Mr. Mariner, Professor Hair?

A.   Did I believe him? Can you be specific?

Q.   Well, you relied on his questionnaire, didn't you?

A.   I certainly did.

Q.   He sent you a questionnaire, and you relied on it. Is that right?

A.   In that particular instance, I did.

Q.   And Mr. Mariner said he was going to raise the price of a case of beer for the full cost of any additional credit transactions.

A.   My recollection is that he said he was going to raise the price within 24 hours and that he would leave it at that level as long as he could.

Q.   Didn't you hear him say that he was going to, he has a categorical fact that the cost of a case of beer was going to go up 40¢ ?

A.   I did. . . .

Q.   Forty cents was his calculation of every penny of the added costs. Is that right?

A.   Well, he said that there were some things that he could not put a price on, but that was his calculation of everything that he could put a price on.

Q.   So Mr. Mariner operates in a very unusual market, doesn't he, Professor Hair?

A.   Not necessarily. That is his intention. We don't know what all the rest of them are going to do.

Q.   Professor, is it true that you believe that many sellers is consistent with lots of competition?

A.   Generally, yes. Many sellers would indicate a high level of competition.

Q.   And fewer sellers is consistent with less competition?

A.   As a general principle, that would be true. The opportunity would be much greater for higher competition with many sellers, I would assume.

Q.   You've discerned a trend in Louisiana toward fewer whole-sale sellers?

A.   Correct.

Q.   And fewer wholesalers is consistent with less competition?

A.   Since we do have fewer, and since we are dealing with that particular aspect, I think that if you want to say that, that's fine. I think that, in fact, in order to conclude that directly, we would have to go beyond the specific size. But that is one dimension, the number per capita, yes.

Q.   Sir, it didn't bother you a bit to make an analysis of the number per capita of retailers and introduce into the court here based on that number alone your conclusions about what kind of a market the retailers operate in. Is that right?

A.   That's correct.

Q.   But now when we look at a definite trend, according to you, a trend toward fewer wholesalers, a trend based on a study you did, you can't conclude that that's toward less competition. Is that correct?

A.   I concluded that it is in all likelihood towards that, but it's not a, you know, a complete and final answer.

Q. And that trend towards fewer wholesalers came about when the Cash Beer Law was in effect. Is that right?

A. It certainly did.

Q. Is it true, sir, that in your view, the competitiveness of a market depends in part on how well customer needs are being met?

A. Yes.

Q. Well, I want to ask you. You made a calculation of the working capital difference in this case, and I believe it's about $5 million. Right? For the wholesalers?

A. The cost of interest plus opportunity cost.

Q. And I saw. . . .

A. Working capital.

Q. I gather you're here to tell the court that that is a cost that actually will occur to the wholesalers if the Cash Beer Law goes away. Is that right?

A. I certainly, you know, there's no such thing as a free lunch. We've got the cost of interest presently for retailers. We've got the cost of interest for wholesalers. Somebody in the long run has got to absorb that, and I. . . .

Q. So it's your, it's your sworn view that if the Cash Beer Law goes away that those costs actually will come about. Is that right?

A. I am convinced that those costs, that's the time value of money. It's got to be there.

Q. And that begins on your assumption, doesn't it, that 90% of all retailers are going to demand credit in such a way that the wholesalers will have to give it to them.

A. That is correct.

Q. Which means that 90% of all retailers have a customer need that is not being met right now. Is that right, sir?

A. Well, we look at customer needs that may be in the area of credit, but there are a lot of other needs. And when we look at the final analysis of customer needs there are a lot of dimensions to it.

Q. The question was "And that means that 90% of all retailers have a customer need that is not being met." Is that right, sir?

A.   I'm not sure that it's a need. I haven't done a study to determine that it's a need.

Q.   Well, it's certainly something that — in your view, categorically, according to your sworn testimony — 90% of them will want and find a way to get, if the Cash Beer Law goes away.

A.   If I testified that they will want, I testified incorrectly. Because I haven't talked to any retailers.

Q.   Well, shall we throw out the $5 million right now. . . .

A.   No, no. I testified according to 90% based upon information provided to me from Anheuser Busch about their experience in the market.

Q.   Well, is the 90% number a good number or not?

A.   Actually the 90% number is conservative. Anheuser Busch indicates to me that their experience is 95%.

Q.   Ninety-five percent of customers in markets where it's possible, can be done, where freedom exists, 95% of the customers want, demand, get credit. According to what you find out. Is that right?

A.   Correct.

Q.   But you're unwilling to call that a customer need, Dr. Hair?

A.   I haven't done a survey.

§ 10-23(c).   Covering the "Didn't Do's."

The following example relates to an engineer's basis for providing testimony concerning the cause of cracks in concrete and other alleged deficiencies in liquid retaining tanks at a sewage treatment plant. The engineer offered opinions based on a report of another firm and general standards applicable to the project. He performed an analysis concerning the bending strength of a wall, but no other diagnostic studies.

Q.   Now, Mr. Aderman, I think you said you had made six visits at the plant?

A.   Yes, sir, I believe that's correct.

Q.   And one of those visits was yesterday?

A.   Yes, sir.

Q.   At the time of your deposition you had made four visits to the plant?

A.   I had recorded four visits. I believe that I had made five at the time of the deposition. I will correct that. I have field reports from four times that I was there. I was also there prior to my first field report that I did not make a record of.

Q.   Well, you made those visits primarily in connection with setting and reading deflection gauges; is that true?

A.   Yes, sir, that's correct.

Q.   As a matter of fact, when you went out there to that plant site it was your understanding that your undertaking out there was to measure the deflection of that center wall. Wasn't that your understanding?

A.   Yes, sir, that is correct.

Q.   You didn't have an understanding that somebody was going to ask you to appraise the width or normality of the cracks within the clarifier tank; did you?

A.   No, I didn't go out there for that purpose.

Q.   As a matter of fact, being a professional and being somebody who tries to do things right I assume that if somebody told you he was going to ask for your expert opinion on the normality or expectability of the cracks in that tank, you probably would have gotten in the tank and looked at it; wouldn't you?

A.   Probably so, or made some record of it or some survey of it.

Q.   Probably would actually have been measuring those cracks; wouldn't you have?

A.   No. But under your hypothesis I would have made some type of record of their location and their length and what they looked like; yes.

Q.   And if you thought somebody was going to ask you about the extent to which there's observable distress or observable honeycombing on the wall as a professional, as somebody who tries to do things right, do it correctly, you probably would have gotten in the tank and looked for that too; right?

A.   Yes, sir. If I had been asked to do a structural survey of that tank I would have spent quit a bit of time looking at it; yes.

Q. And as a matter of fact you didn't spend quite a bit of time looking —

A. I was not asked to do that; no sir.

Q. Now, the first time you were there you were at the site — well, I say the first time. The first time you made an actual recording you were at the site for about two hours; right?

A. I think that's right.

Q. And during that two hours you were primarily engaged in setting up these gauges between the common wall and this other wall in the chlorine contact chamber; is that true?

A. That's true.

Q. So you weren't primarily engaged in looking over the rest of the structure to see what the cracks looked like; were you?

A. On that date, no, I was not.

Q. And as a matter of fact, Mr. Aderman, is this true; you've never been on the slab in the clarifier tank?

A. I believe that is correct. I do not think I've ever been down on that floor. I could be wrong, but I don't think so.

Q. You've never been on the bottom of the chlorine contact chamber; is that true?

A. I don't think so.

Q. You've never observed cracks except from the top of the structure looking down; is that correct?

A. That's correct.

Q. Construction Technology Laboratories had actually out-line[d] in chalk the visible areas of leakage on the common wall that were coming through the wall?

A. I don't know that I was aware of that. I mean, I had seen CTL's report and their records and their documentation of the cracks, and I didn't take any exception to it I believe.

Q. Okay, but I'm not asking you about that, Mr. Aderman. I'm asking you about [your] test. [You] were allowed into Plaquemine's plant for a period of about six weeks; weren't you?

A. Yes, sir.

Q. And during the course of [your] test when you — you arranged for these gauges to be put on and put water in the clarifier tank and so on, CTL also had somebody out there to kind of watch what was going on; didn't they?

A.   Yes, sir.

Q.   And I'm asking you if — tell me if this is true. You didn't even look at the walls of the chlorine contact chamber closely enough to be able to tell whether the visible areas of leakage were outlined in chalk?

A.   No, sir. That would be a correct statement.

Q.   You never measured the width of a crack in the clarifier tank or the chlorine contact chamber; is that true?

A.   That is true.

Q.   You never measured the depth of a crack in the clarifier tank or the chlorine contact chamber; is that right?

A.   That is correct.

Q.   You never made any attempt to determine whether any of the cracks and which of the cracks went all the way through the wall, is that true?

A.   I agree. I believe that is true.

Q.   You never tried to measure the distance between cracks yourself; is that right?

A.   I don't think I ever did; no, sir.

Q.   You never got into the tank to look at the cracks over on the west wall that's against the earth; did you?

A.   No sir.

Q.   And you didn't ever measure any of the cracks on the west wall, did you?

A.   No, sir.

Q.   You never got into the excavation to measure the cracks on the outside of the west wall; did you?

A.   No sir.

Q.   You never measured any of the cracks on the north wall, did you?

A.   No sir.

Q.   You never measured any of the cracks on the south wall; is that true?

A.   No, sir, I did not.

Q.   You never personally made an inspection under the sludge trough looking up at the bottom of the sludge trough to see that the extent of proper formation, whether it was nice smooth surface like it should be; did you?

A.   No, sir.

Q.   You were not part of any effort by North America Constructors to document leaks at the plant; is that right?

A.   No, sir, I was not.

Q.   And as a matter of fact, Mr. Aderman, is this true; with regard to this entire project you gathered no empirical information? Do you understand what I mean about "empirical?"

A.   Yes, sir.

Q.   In other words, information that's actually based on physical tests or visual observation, something documented. You gathered no empirical information of your own except for these deflection readings; right?

A.   Except for the deflection readings; that is correct.

Q.   You didn't try to make any tests to see what honeycombs or voids existed within the walls; did you?

A.   No, sir.

Q.   So in the six weeks that North American had the opportunity to be on the plant site to do whatever it wanted to do to see how many voids or honeycombs existed in the wall and where they existed, you didn't try to do that at all; did you?

A.   No, sir, I didn't need to.

Q.   You didn't make any extensive observation of the videos that Plaquemine made of the results of the dye test, where water was injected into the cracks; did you?

A.   No, sir, I didn't.

Q.   Did you do an aerometer test out at the site?

A.   No, sir, I did not.

Q.   A half cell test reading out at the site?

A.   Again, I didn't need to.

Q.   Is that because CTL did?

A.   Yes, sir.

Q. Okay, but I'm asking you if you did?

A. No, I did not.

Q. Did you make any petrographic examinations?

A. No, sir. I performed no test on any of the materials on any of the walls or any part of that plant.

* * *

Q. And you didn't make any comprehensive analysis of the extent to which all of the Pittsburgh Testing Lab's slump results fit outside or inside the specifications; did you?

A. No, sir. I did not have a lot of interest in the slump results or the slump tickets, no.

Q. You made no analysis of your own to try to determine the extent to which the steel in the wall varies from the specifications in terms of cover; did you?

A. No, I did not.

Q. You're accepting CTL on that?

A. Yes, sir.

Q. You made no analysis of your own of any core or any piece of concrete, any concrete sample to try to determine whether the concrete was air entrained; is that right?

A. That's correct.

Q. You're accepting CTL on that?

A. Yes, sir.

Q. You made no analysis to try to determine or back out the water/cement ratios; is that true?

A. I'm sorry, I — believe it is true, but would you repeat that?

Q. Sure. Okay, the water/cement ratio; you didn't try to make any sort of a calculation . . . from the slumps or from the . . . after construction core samples to try to determine what the water/cement ratio in the concrete was; is that true?

A. No, sir. I accepted CTL's petrographic results.

§ 10-23(d). Attacking Expert's Basis.

In the following example an expert presented testimony opposing the proposed merger between Entergy Corp. and Gulf States Utilities Co. He relied in part on studies, which he claimed showed that mergers between large companies do not lower overall costs. The expert recommended that the Federal Energy Regulatory Commission establish a presumption that large mergers would not produce a public benefit. This part of the cross-examination attacks the basis for his conclusion about the cost effectiveness of large mergers.

Q. What I would like to do first . . . is to focus on your direct testimony, and what you provide to the FERC and the judge in your direct testimony. One of the things that you do is report the findings of some published literature, is that right?

A. That's correct.

Q. You read the published literature that you cite to suggest that proposed mergers sometimes don't produce the efficiencies that are expected; is that right?

A. That's correct, more than sometimes — most often.

Q. You, yourself, did not participate in any of these studies reflected in the published literature; is that correct?

A. I did write a comment to one of the articles that is part of this literature, yes, which has been submitted in this case.

Q. A comment?

A. Yes.

Q. You mean your comment was incorporated in the article?

A. No, in the literature in the economics journals. Often [someone] writes an article. Then there are comments that are published at later times that take — that criticize or comment on the findings of the person who wrote the original article. So, that's part of the literature.

Q. Well, Dr. Stoner, do you regard commenting on somebody else's article as the same thing as participating in his study?

A. I regard it as less than writing an initial article, but depending on the incisiveness of the comment, it could be more important than the original article.

Q. Well, I'm not asking you whether it's more important, less important, or whatever. My original question was: Did you participate in any of these studies you cite? I gather you're saying yes because you wrote a comment on one of them; is that your view?

A.   I'm simply saying I wrote a comment on one of the studies.

Q.   Okay. As far as the studies that you cite in your testimony, were you an active participant in analyzing, reviewing the empirical data, and reporting the results in the literature?

A.   In my comment, I carefully read and digest the way a certain individual looked at that literature, and found it wanting. So, yes, I participated in that literature. Did I do a regression analysis myself? Is that the standard you now hold one up to, that it has to be a statistical analysis? I mean, I wrote a comment.

Q.   Well, are you saying that with regard to one of the nine articles that you cite in supporting your testimony, you wrote a comment that criticized that article?

A.   No, I'm not saying that.

Q.   Did you criticize it?

A.   No.

Q.   Did you find it wanting?

A.   Not one of these articles, no.

Q.   Okay. One of these articles, then — have you written any comments on any of these articles?

A.   No, I have not.

Q.   Okay. So then did you participate in any of these articles?

A.   No, I did not.

Q.   Okay. So you are reporting to the judge nine articles that you did not participate in any of them? That will never pass an English test. But nevertheless, is that what you are doing?

A.   That's correct. That's one of the things I'm doing, yes.

Q.   Now, I assume that if you did not participate in any of these studies, you cannot personally attest to the truth or accuracy of the empirical data that underlay the study.

A.   Personally?

Q.   Yes, sir, personally; in other words, beyond the fact that you know how to read, and you read it in the literature.

A.   And that the literature appeared in journals that are generally considered to be extremely high quality.

Q.   Right.

A.   And that I know some of these individuals to be fine economists.

Q.   Right.

A.   Other than that, can I personally attest that these numbers weren't cooked?

Q.   Right.

A.   The best answer to that is that the overwhelming — the fact that so many of the articles report the same findings makes one think very strongly that the results are not cooked.

Q.   Well, I had a little bit different question, though. It was, "Can you personally attest, raise your hand and swear under penalty of perjury, this data is correct?"

A.   No, I cannot.

Q.   Okay. So then what you are doing is coming before the judge with someone else's findings that have been reported in some literature and reporting to the judge what someone else found in somebody else's study; is that true?

A.   That's one of the things I'm doing, as I pointed out.

Q.   Do you know if Occidental intends to call these experts in for me to get the chance to ask them questions about their studies?

A.   Many of the studies have been provided already in this case, and you can ask all the questions you want.

*   *   *

Q.   Do you know if Occidental intends to provide the people who do have firsthand knowledge of the data recorded in the studies that are reported in the literature that you have surveyed to make your recommendations to the judge?

A.   No, I don't know.

Q.   Okay. Now, based on the — I think one of the things that you have concluded — for instance, at page 9 of your testimony, you say that many participants anticipate that a merger will yield cost savings and efficiencies, but other studies demonstrate that it is relatively rare for such expectations to be fulfilled, and then you cite three studies for the second point; is that right?

A.   That's correct.

Q. Now, is it true that one of these studies was published in 1921?

A. That's correct.

Q. And the study that was published in 1921 relied on data that was modern up until the year 1903; is that right?

A. That's absolutely correct. I just would like to add for the purposes of not appearing to be ridiculous that the reason that that study was included was to show that this — there is a long history of articles that have shown the same thing. If I was just reporting from a study from 1921 using 1903 data and nothing else, I would agree with you that's ridiculous, but to show that studies done in previous merger waves — this was looking at an earlier merger wave — found X result and that studies done later found the same X result I think is quite interesting.

Q. Well, let me ask you this more specific question, because I am interested in it too, but I'd rather have you answer this. Do you think a merger that may have occurred, say, in 1880 is good evidence of whether there will be efficiencies in a merger that's planned in 1994?

A. Clearly you would want to look at the more recent studies and put more weight on those, and they are cited here. But this study was cited because it speaks to the proposition that for a long time now, merger applicants have been coming forward saying there are going to be big savings, just you wait, and then ex-post, it doesn't happen, and I just wanted to point out that there is a rich history here and that we shouldn't turn our backs on this and ignore it and say this one is automatically going to be different, because it might not be.

* * *

Q. Dr. Stoner, I want to return to the three studies because I believe I had a question pending that at least I am not satisfied with the answer, and the question was, do you believe that a merger that occurs in the 1880s is a good guide to determine the efficiency of a merger that is planned in 1994?

A. If you are talking about a specific merger, of course not. Looking at a specific merger in 1880 will give us guidance for a specific merger in 1993, but that is not what this is designed to show. It is designed to show that over time there is a tendency, a very strong tendency, for merger applicants to exaggerate the savings that they expect to get from the merger, and that the ex post facto evidence indicates that it doesn't happen. I think that is extremely probative, whether the evidence comes from merger applicants in 1888, and you look at what happened to those mergers, and you see that they didn't get the savings they said, or the evidence comes from 1988. I think it still — maybe it tells you less, or says less, and you wouldn't want to depend on it alone, but viewed together, I think it does add value.

Q. Dr. Stoner, is it true that the authors of the 1921 article that relied on the data up to 1903 stated that their results were attainable only by using a large amount of guessing?

A. If you want to read me a precise line from their testimony. . . .

Q. Did you review their article?

A. I absolutely did.

Q. And you cited it as being a credible valid article?

A. Yes, I did.

Counsel: May I approach, Your Honor?

The Court: Yes, you may.

Q. I am going to show you a copy, Dr. Stoner. Do you have the article?

A. Yes. Are you talking about the Dewing article?

Q. The *Quarterly Journal of Economics* article, a statistical test of the success of consolidations. I can show you my copy, if you would like.

A. Can I see it, please?

Q. Sure. Would you just read the sentence that begins "Owing"?

A. "Owing to the merger data ordinarily furnished by the different corporations, especially those obviously unsuccessful, results were obtainable only by using a large amount of guessing."

Q. Did you recall that that was in there?

A. I don't recall that specific reference.

*   *   *

Q.   Have you found that in your book, Dr. Stoner?

A.   Yes, I have.

Q.   Does it say the same thing in your article?

A.   Yes, it does.

*   *   *

Q.   Dr. Stoner, with regard to the second article you cite, "The Bottom Line On Ten Big Mergers," that was published in *Fortune Magazine*; is that right?

A.   That's correct.

Q.   Is that one of the scholarly high class journals that leads you to believe that you can rely unequivocally on the comments of the authors?

A.   It is a different sort of article in evidence, but it is nonetheless probative.

Q.   "The Bottom Line On Ten Big Mergers" examined, for instance, the Heublein and Kentucky Fried Chicken merger; is that right?

A.   That's correct.

Q.   That was a merger of alcoholic beverages and fast food outlets; is that true?

A.   It would appear so.

Q.   It examined the RCA and Coronet Industries merger, which combined electronics with carpets; is that right?

A.   That's correct.

Q.   It took a look at the Schering and Plough merger, which combined drugs with cosmetics; is that true?

A.   Again, the point is that no matter what the industry, no matter what the products, no matter what the time period it appears, that mergers don't achieve what their negotiators and practitioners expect them to do, that is the whole point.

Q.   Isn't the whole point of "The Bottom Line On Ten Big Mergers" that mergers of different industries, conglomerates, didn't work too well?

A.   That's correct.

Q.   Do you think that GSU is in a different industry than Entergy?

A.   No, it is not.

Q.   Dr. Stoner, I believe you do come forward with six articles on electric matters; is that right?

A.   That's correct. That is what I was just going to say.

Q.   Those six articles on electric matters deal with data from the 1950s and the 1960s; is that right?

A.   And the 1970s and the 1980s.

Q.   Well, isn't the vast majority of the data reflected in those articles pre-1972?

A.   Hartman has basically replicated the studies that were done in the '70s and early '80s based on '70s data. He's basically replicated those studies in 1990 based '87 data.

Q.   So you've got one that replicates prior studies; is that what you're saying?

A.   I'm saying, he applied similar techniques to different data so as to test whether the results still [held].

Q.   So the initial results all reflect data from the '50s and the '60s and the first two years of the '70s?

A.   Which studies are you referring to?

Q.   I'm referring to the studies that you are bringing in here, sir. Can you answer the question?

A.   The reason I asked for a clarification is because Hartman — one of the Hartman articles — one of the seven articles is a summary article that talks about many, many different studies, some that go beyond the —

                        *   *   *

A.   Thank you. Some that go beyond — there is mention of more than just the six, that's all I'm saying.

Q.   Well, Dr. Stoner, you know the difference between an empirical study —

A.   Yes.

Q.   — and a study that just tells you about what other studies say?

A.   Yes.

> Q.   Now, the empirical data is — the empirical study looks at data and draws conclusions; is that right?
>
> A.   Correct.
>
> Q.   Now, the data from which conclusions are drawn about actual mergers is '50s and '60s data?
>
> A.   And early '70s, yes.

§ 10-23(e). Limiting the Expert's Testimony: "Don't Knows."

The following example is from a telephone rate case in which an expert testified in favor of a telephone company's "incentive regulation" plan. The company argued that the plan would promote productivity and new investment as it permitted higher earnings. The cross-examination attempts to demonstrate that the witness cannot support many of the company's claims and that he is not familiar with the regulated industry.

> Q.   Would you agree that one of the purposes of your testimony is to give general support for incentive regulation as being an appropriate way of regulating South Central Bell?
>
> *   *   *
>
> A.   Yes, that's right. Yes, ma'am.
>
> Q.   You played no role in developing Bell's incentive plan, is that correct?
>
> A.   I did not develop it at all.
>
> Q.   You have a general idea of how Bell's plan would operate, but you are not aware of the details of the plan, is that correct?
>
> A.   I'm not aware of all the specifics of the plan, yes, ma'am.
>
> Q.   You have not made a study in terms of quantifying the impact of putting in Bell's incentive plan, the impact on the Louisiana economy, is that correct?
>
> A.   I have not made a quantitative study of that, no, ma'am.
>
> Q.   You don't know how Bell's plan would affect employee productivity, is that correct?
>
> A.   I cannot make a statement to that effect, no, ma'am.

* * *

Q. You do not know whether Bell has declined to make some investment in Louisiana that it otherwise would have made if its rate of return had been higher, is that correct?

A. I do not know.

Q. You cannot tell us what investments Bell will make if we implement the incentive regulation plan, is that correct?

A. No. No, ma'am, I cannot.

Q. Is the following an accurate characterization of your testimony? Your testimony is limited to stating that Bell's plan sets up the environment for innovation to occur. You are not stating that there would be any particular type of innovation or how much it would be at any particular point in time.

A. That is correct.

Q. You, additionally, do not know if there would be any innovation if the incentive plan were implemented that would not occur under traditional regulation, is that correct?

A. I cannot — yes, that is correct. It would be my hypothesis that there would be more, but I cannot say that.

Q. And it is also your understanding that South Central Bell cannot identify precisely what investment might occur if their plan is implemented, is that correct?

A. It is my understanding that — right. That is correct.

Q. Innovation does not necessarily require new investment. Is that an accurate statement?

A. It could be a reorganization. That is correct. It could be a reorganization of things such as that.

Q. You cannot state whether additional investment of any type would make Bell more efficient, is that an accurate statement?

A. Again, under new investment — I cannot state that specifically — but under new investment, you anticipate that there's a reason for the investment, so it has some productive result.

Q. You have not made a study of the areas of South Central Bell services that are or are not competitive, is that correct?

A. That is right.

Q. You don't know where the customer line and local usage services of South Central Bell are competitive, is that correct?

A. No, I do not know.

Q. You don't know whether local service is a monopoly service or a competitive service, is that correct?

A. I cannot say in every case, that's right.

Q. Additionally, you don't know whether anyone other than Bell in any given franchise area is providing local telephone service, is that correct?

A. That is correct.

Q. You don't know whether intraLATA toll is monopoly or competitive, is that correct?

A. That's right.

Q. Additionally, you don't know if any other company is entitled to receive intraLATA and intrastate access charges from the interexchange carriers other than Bell for the areas that Bell serves.

A. That's right.

§ 10-23(f). Illustrating Absence of Principle With a Hypothetical.

In the utility merger case referred to in §§ 10-23(a) and 10-23(d), counsel seeks to show that an expert's recommendation to redistribute benefits from the merger is driven not by an economic principle, but by a concept of "fairness" that has no grounding in principle and could be used to produce varying results. The examination uses a hypothetical that was put forth in the expert's deposition to evaluate the principles on which he relied.

Q. Well, is it true that the principle that you are applying is a fairness principle, rather than an economic principle?

A. I'd say it is more of a fairness principle. When we think about economic principles, we usually think in terms of economic efficiency, and this has little to do, if any, with economic efficiency.

Q. Isn't it true that you don't know if there is an economic definition of what is fair?

A. I think in my reading of the literature that putting economic efficiencies aside, fairness is a judgmental concept.

Q. Remember the question? You don't know if there is an economic definition of what is fair.

A. I don't know that there is an economic definition of what is fair.

Q. In your view, fairness is in the eye of the beholder, is that right?

A. That's correct.

Q. Is this a true statement — what you are referring to in your proposal is the concept of fairness. You don't know if there is one economic definition of what is fair. It's going to be in the eye of the beholder.

A. That's correct.

Q. Okay, and it is based upon this concept of what is fair that you proposed the various conditions that you put forth, is that right?

A. Based on my conception of what is fair.

Q. Okay, I understand that. Now, Dr. Berry, just as a matter of getting some basic I guess principles set forth for examining your proposal, I would like to ask you a hypothetical. I know you have heard it.

A. I have got my airline ticket here.

Q. Okay, I know. You have got a ticket to San Francisco for $70. I have a ticket for $60. The airline offers two for $100 so we could each go if we split it for $50 and they allow us to cash in our prior tickets. Now you would agree as a matter of economics we each have sufficient economic incentive to merge if we split the $100 price. Is that true?

A. Yes.

Q. My saving of $10 in that hypothetical should be sufficient as a matter of economics for me to go forward, is that true?

A. I'm not sure if I would agree with the use of the word "sufficient" for you to go forward. I would say that there are some economic benefits to you in going forward.

Q.   Well, is this true — each of us have sufficient but differing levels of incentive to go forward at a $50 price for each of us?

A.   That might be true.

Q.   Well, that's exactly how you would describe it, is that right?

A.   They may be equal incentives. They may be differing, I don't know.

Q.   Okay. Now . . . we know that as a matter of economics we each have a sufficient economic incentive to go forward. I can save $10; you can save $20. That does not tell us whether Dr. Berry's fairness principle would be satisfied, is that right?

A.   That's correct.

Q.   Now if we assume that I demanded $5 of your benefit so that it would cost you in total $55 to go to San Francisco and it would allow me to go for $45, in your view that might be fair and reasonable, is that right?

A.   Yes.

Q.   To know if that was fair, you would have to know how much I want to get to San Francisco and how much you want to get to San Francisco, is that right?

A.   The value of the benefits associated between — as compared between the two parties.

Q.   In my hypo it is how much we want to get to San Francisco, is that right?

A.   Which ties in with the value, the value that the two parties separately put on going to San Francisco.

Q.   And that is over and above our savings from our prior ticket, right?

A.   Well, that is a separate issue. I don't know if it is over and above, but it is a separate issue.

Q.   Okay, it's something associated with who is waiting for us in San Francisco.

A.   Maybe.

Q.   Yes?

A.   I said maybe — I'm not sure about the idea of who is waiting for us.

Q.   A restaurant, or whatever.

A.   That's right.

Q.   Now, is this true: You think, to the extent possible, the person who wants to get to San Francisco the most should pay the most cost?

A.   Assuming agreement can't be reached, I think that would be a reasonable approach.

Q.   Okay. And that would be the fair way to do it; is that right?

A.   I don't think there is one fair way. That would be a fair way.

Q.   Okay. Now, is this true: If I said I don't think $5 is going to do it, I want $6, that might be reasonable depending on how much we want to get to San Francisco; is that true?

A.   In terms of fairness, yes.

Q.   If I said $6 isn't going to do it, I want $8, in your view that might satisfy the fairness principle?

A.   Yes.

Q.   If I said $8 isn't going to do it, I want $10, that might satisfy the fairness principle depending on how much we want to get to San Francisco; is that true?

A.   Let me think about that just a second. What's the starting price on your ticket before the merged ticket scenario?

Q.   Sixty dollars.

A.   And mine is $70.

Q.   Right.

A.   And —

Q.   Fifty dollars, $50 to go, plus whatever I make you pay me.

A.   And you would argue that after the merger, I should pay $60 and you should pay $40. Is that what you're saying with the $10?

Q.   Right.

A.   Okay. That could be fair.

Q.   Okay. Six, 8, 10, 12, any of those might be fair?

A.   Yes.

Q.   Depending on how much we want to get to San Francisco?

> A. Depending on the value associated with going to San Francisco.
>
> Q. So your fairness principle in my hypo doesn't tell you, unless you actually get into an analysis of what we're going to do at the end of the trip, what is the correct amount that I could demand of you in order to do the deal?
>
> A. Well, I'm not sure if "correct" is the word, but that's the fair amount.

§ 10-23(g). Pointing Up Absurdities.

In the merger case from previous examples a witness for a group of industrial consumers in Arkansas opposed the merger between Entergy Corp., which served parts of Arkansas through a subsidiary, and Gulf States Utilities Co. The witness testified that a merger might ultimately force ratepayers in Arkansas to bear the costs of a potential judgment against Gulf States for alleged fraud relating to its participation with Cajun Electric Power Coop. in the River Bend nuclear power plant. Cajun's suit against Gulf States was pending at the time. The attorney tries to show that the witness's asserted concern is implausible.

> Q. Now, let's take these risks one by one if we could, Dr. Roach. The biggest risk is the Cajun lawsuit, is that right?
>
> A. Correct.
>
> Q. And that risk is $1.6 billion, is that true?
>
> A. That's the number I've used, yes.
>
> Q. Well, have you reviewed the complaint in the Cajun lawsuit?
>
> A. I read it.
>
> Q. You did? Okay, well, then, you know that Cajun alleged that GSU induced its participation in River Bend by fraud, is that right?
>
> A. I don't recall the details. I'm not a lawyer able to judge it. I read it, but I don't have an opinion on the legal merit of the case.
>
> Q. Well, I am not asking you for an opinion on the legal merit. I know you haven't made that analysis, didn't think it necessary to do that, but can you remember when you read

the lawsuit that the lawsuit says that GSU told a bunch of lies that got Cajun to be a part of River Bend?

A. I generally remember.

Q. Okay, and you are familiar with the fact that it's referred to as "Cajun's fraud lawsuit against GSU"?

A. As I recall, I think there are two lawsuits, and I am not sure exactly the legal consequences, a rescission lawsuit — is that separate from the fraud lawsuit?

Q. The rescission lawsuit is the fraud lawsuit. You defrauded us to get into it, therefore give us $1.6 billion back, right? Does that refresh your recollection?

A. Okay.

Q. Okay. Now in your regulatory experience, Dr. Roach — I know you've been around — is the cost of a fraud judgment against a company for the deceitful misrepresentations of its management ordinarily allowed in the cost of service?

A. I don't know.

Q. Do you know of any jurisdiction that has ever included in the cost of service a judgment against a company for the deceitful misrepresentations of its management against a third party?

A. I don't know.

Q. Okay. Well, in any event, the scenario of the risk turning into a cost, the $1.6 billion demand of Cajun, in your view, there is some possibility, may turn into a judgment in which a court of final resort says, "Indeed, GSU did defraud Cajun; it must pay X," right?

A. Yes, there is some judgment that leads to the payment of the $1.6 billion.

Q. And then this judgment, this fraud judgment — let's say it's a $1 billion fraud judgment — is spun off into a wholesale rate base. That's Step 2, right?

A. Well, there is some — the matter of timing is important. Whether it occurs prior to the decision or after the decision I don't think is crucial. The point is that these actions would be taken so as to protect stockholders. If Entergy needs to anticipate the decision and do the spinoff prior to that, they can do it that way.

* * *

Q.　Dr. Roach, I'd like to focus on this question of the River Bend fraud litigation and see if we can exactly figure out how it will be transferred over to the Arkansas ratepayer under your clear vision of what will happen.

Let's assume that the River Bend fraud lawsuit produces a judgment of, let's say, $500 million against GSU for management's fraud, but no transfer back of capacity. Are you with me?

A.　Yes, sir.

Q.　All right. Now in your view, would that judgment for $500 million that has no capacity associated with it be spun off into a wholesale rate base?

A.　I'm not sure that it's impossible, but it's less likely than if capacity were associated with it, and the $500 million would therefore not be a direct effect. It would result in the indirect or cost of capital.

Q.　Okay. Well, let's talk about — so it is possible in your view that the $500 million fraud judgment that has no capacity associated with it would be spun off into the wholesale rate base?

A.　I don't think that is likely. I think you need capacity to have a spin-off, as in my four-point, four-step action.

Q.　Okay. I won't quarrel with you that it's not likely, Dr. Roach, at all, but I am asking you if this is part of your scenario that that's possible that that might happen.

A.　No, that scenario speaks to literally transferring capacity, megawatts, along with costs.

* * *

Q.　Let's try Scenario 2. The Court rules that GSU has to pay $1.6 billion, and it gets back a couple of hundred megawatts of capacity, okay, that might be worth three or four hundred million dollars, all right? It's your scenario that the mega-watts of capacity would be spun off into a wholesale rate base and with it would go the fraud judgment cost of $1.6 billion, right?

A.　Yes, in the sense that that is what Entergy would have an interest to do. They got 300 megawatts or 30 percent share of River Bend. It cost them $1.6 billion in cash to protect their shareholders. They have a significant motive to get that into rate base. Whether they get it all in, again that speaks to the probability, so maybe we get in, you know, some certain number.

Q.   Okay, now they try to spin it off into a wholesale rate base. They still have to come into FERC to get approval of passing that over to the Arkansas ratepayer, right?

A.   Correct.

Q.   And they are trying to get, you think they will be trying to get $1.6 billion, which equals this fraud judgment, right?

A.   I think they have the incentive to do that to protect their shareholders.

Q.   And you understand they'll have to get by an administrative law judge with this idea and the FERC before it will happen?

A.   Yes, I do. I am not saying it is going to be snuck by anyone, and I am not saying that it's easy. I'm saying that it's plausible.

Q.   Okay — plausible. All right, now you've . . . had an opportunity to gaze at this judge for some extended periods. Does he look like a judge . . . for whom it would be plausible to expect that he would pass through a $1.6 billion fraud judgment incurred by GSU's management for its deceit and misrepresentations to innocent Arkansas ratepayers?

Mr. Hertz: Objection, Your Honor. The question is irrelevant, the question is inflammatory. The case is not about that you're going to be sitting on the panel which decides whether Arkansas or some other Entergy company would have to decide the case. If he would like to ask a question about whether it's plausible that a judge might do so, that's . . .

Counsel: I'll rephrase it.

*   *   *

Q.   Well, let me try and rephrase it, Dr. Roach.

In your experience with regulation, would a reasonable FERC judge pass a $1.6 billion fraud judgment assessed against GSU for the deceit and misrepresentations of its management through a FERC tariff and assess it to innocent Arkansas ratepayers? Is it plausible?

* * *

A.   What is plausible is that Entergy to protect its shareholders will attempt to put that $1.6 billion with capacity — it's not a decision, it's a $1.6 billion price with megawatts — and why I say Entergy says that, again when asked the CEO of Entergy would not indemnify existing Entergy ratepayers against that risk.

He said I don't want to do it, but I want to have the option of imposing River Bend capacity and cost on Arkansas or any existing Entergy ratepayer against the will of the local regulators.

It is going to — it is plausible in the sense that there is motive and there's a method for Entergy to do it.

I don't agree with these arguments. I hope it doesn't happen, but I am concerned that if such an allocation doesn't make sense today prior to the merger, I'm concerned that with the merger it makes a ruling plausible down the road.

§ 10-23(h). Making Positive Points and Attacking Expert's Basis.

The following example is from a regulatory proceeding involving an examination of a telephone company's profits on its Yellow Page sales. Yellow Page transactions were transferred from the telephone company to a separate subsidiary of the holding company named "BAPCO." To assure that Yellow Page profits continued to support local telephone service, the regulatory agency "imputed" BAPCO's profits back to the telephone company. The profits thus reduced the total cost of service and lowered rates.

A report prepared by a consultant for the regulatory agency, Kennedy & Associates, contended that BAPCO entered into transactions with other subsidiaries of the holding company, incurring "expenses" that reduced the profits imputed into regulation and increased the separate profits of the holding company. An expert for the telephone company disputed these conclusions.

In the following excerpt, counsel examines the telephone company expert in a manner that supports the contention that profits were siphoned away from regulation and attacks the expert's basis for contrary conclusions.

Q. Have you read the divestiture decree relating to Yellow Pages?

A. Yes, I have.

Q. The divestiture decree was issued in 1982; is that right?

A. Yes.

Q. I would like you to read the paragraph that Judge Greene wrote with regard to Yellow Pages that begins "in addition."

A. "In addition to these factors directly related to competition, there are other reasons why the prohibition and publication of the Yellow Pages by the operating companies is not in the public interest. All those who have commented on or who have studied the issue agree that the Yellow Pages provide a significant subsidy to local telephone rates. This subsidy will most likely continue if the operating companies were permitted to continue to publish Yellow Pages."

Q. I would like you to read the footnote that is dropped right there with regard to Yellow Pages operations.

A. "The assets used in the production of these printed directories will accordingly have to be allocated to the operating companies."

Q. Does it say Regional Holding Companies or subsidiaries of the Regional Holding Companies?

A. Operating companies.

Q. Have you read the opinion that was issued two years later by Judge Greene regarding what the Regional Holding Companies did?

A. I am not sure.

Q. I would like you to read — I am calling your attention [to] *United States v. Western Electric*, the cite is 592 Fed. Supp., and I would like you to begin with page 865, "When the court required," please.

A. "When the court required AT&T to turn over its Yellow Pages operations to the operating companies, it assumed that the revenues from directory advertising would continue to be included in the rate base of the operating companies providing a subsidy to local rates.

"Yet the Regional Holding Companies, or some of them, had breached that understanding. Instead of funneling Yellow Pages revenues to the operating companies, they have created separate subsidiaries to handle their directory publishing operations which do not feed the revenues from these operations into the rate base."

* * *

Q. Now, Mr. Warnement, you are aware that BAPCO is not an operating company; is that true?

A. It's not an operating company in the same context as referred to in that document; that is correct.

Q. Does your team of experts know when BAPCO was created?

A. BAPCO was created effective January 1st, 1984.

Q. BAPCO was created effective January 1st, 1984, at divestiture, to receive the assets that Judge Greene had said should be given to the operating companies; is that right?

A. I think he stated allocated to the operating companies.

Q. Well, allocated to the operating companies. Is there a difference between "allocated to the operating companies" and "give it to the operating companies"?

A. I believe there is a subtle distinction, yes.

Q. Does that distinction mean you can give it to a separate subsidiary or allocate it to a separate subsidiary?

A. I think you can place the assets to a separate subsidiary as long as you allocate the effect of those assets back to the telephone company, yes. That's correct.

Q. Were you aware that Judge Greene issued that decree, and Judge Greene made those comments when you appeared here before the Commission to talk about Yellow Pages?

A. Yes.

Q. Do you know if BellSouth ever came to this Commission and asked for approval to put the Yellow Pages assets in a separate subsidiary?

A. Can you ask that once more?

Q. Are you aware of whether BellSouth Telecommunications, South Central Bell, ever came to this Commission and asked for approval for putting Yellow Pages operations in the separate subsidiary?

A. I am aware there were communications with the Commission with respect to what they were doing. Whether or not they were seeking approval, I don't know.

Q. Did you meet with some commissioners regarding what they were doing?

A. No.

Q. Is there a document that you reviewed that said that Bell-South or South Central Bell had met with commissioners regarding what they were doing?

A. No.

Q. From where do you get an understanding that somebody from South Central Bell met with commissioners regarding what they were doing?

A. I don't know if they met with commissioners. I did ask whether or not there was communication to the Commission regarding what they were doing in terms of transferring those assets and assuring that there was some form of maintaining that subsidy back to ratepayers, and they replied, "Yes, we did . . . that."

Q. Who is "they" — the lawyers?

A. I am not sure if it was just the lawyers.

Q. Were the lawyers included in the ones that gave you that understanding?

A. I think there was a lawyer or two that would have been participating in that communication.

Q. Did you have that understanding when you came before the Commission and made your report on September 15th?

A. No. I was operating on the assumption the company did communicate that similar to what they did in other jurisdictions that we looked at.

Q. Did you . . . obtain that understanding prior to September 15th from the company?

A. No.

Q. Were you aware that the Commission issued an order relating to the spin-off in 1984?

A.   Not in Louisiana. When you say "the Commission" — the Louisiana Commission?

Q.   Yes.

A.   Not before September 15th, no.

Q.   I am going to show you order U-15955-A, which was issued by the Commission on October 1st, 1984. I ask you to read the paragraph beginning "South Central Bell recently spun off"?

A.   "South Central Bell recently spun off its directory assistance operation to a subsidiary of BellSouth. The consultants of the Commission indicated even though South Central Bell will receive a percentage of directory assistance revenues, these revenues will decrease. Pursuant to their recommendation, South Central Bell is directed to maintain its records in a manner that will permit the Commission to determine in the future the revenues lost because of the spin-off. For the test year, only an adjustment to working capital is required to achieve the proper ratemaking treatment of the directory assistant matter."

Q.   Mr. Warnement, did you make any review of South Central Bell's records to see if indeed South Central Bell maintains on its books adequate records to determine the revenues lost because of the spin-off?

A.   Not if it wasn't included in the Kennedy and Associates data responses, no.

Q.   You are aware, are you not, Mr. Warnement, South Central Bell doesn't keep any of the BAPCO book numbers on its own records?

A.   I am not — I have not looked into that matter.

Q.   Now, you are aware that there is a negotiated contract between BAPCO and South Central Bell for sharing publishing revenues; are you not?

A.   Yes.

Q.   Mr. Abbott made a presentation here today about the revenues that are shared under the publishing agreement; is that correct?

A.   Yes.

Q.   That contract was negotiated by two affiliates owned by the same parent; is that right?

A.   That is correct.

Q.   Would you agree with this: So-called negotiations between two subsidiaries owned by a parent could not be deemed arm's length?

A.   Not purely arm's length.

Q.   Would you agree with this: You would not accept assurances from the two parties owned by the same parent that it was arm's length?

A.   I don't think I would ever depend on assurances from those folks, no.

Q.   I believe we established a few minutes ago that the Joint Cost Order . . . establishes a pricing hierarchy for transactions between affiliates; is that right?

A.   Establishes a direct — a pricing hierarchy in direct transactions between affiliates; that is correct.

Q.   Would you agree with this: The negotiated contract between South Central Bell and BAPCO does not fit any of the three pricing methods in the pricing hierarchy?

A.   Yes.

Q.   Are you aware that there are hundreds of millions of dollars of costs, for 1990, I believe 240-some-odd million dollars of costs, that are recorded on the books of BAPCO for transactions with other affiliates?

A.   I am aware of that, yes.

Q.   You did not report to the Commission any of those 240-some-odd million-plus dollars of cost; is that true?

A.   That is correct.

Q.   You reported $4.7 million of cost that flow through for non-Yellow Page transactions; is that right?

A.   For services directly offered from BAPCO to South Central Bell; that is correct.

Q.   When you reported that only $4.7 million of cost coming through BAPCO were relevant for the pricing hierarchy, or for your analysis, you were aware of the additional 240-some-odd million dollars of revenues covered by the publishing contract, were you not?

A.   I was aware that there were other significant transactions, but none for which there needed to be compliance to the pricing hierarchy.

Q.   Do you believe that $240 million is material, sir?

A.   Yes, it is.

CHAPTER 11

PRIVILEGES

---

§ 11-1.   Introduction.

A privilege protects a person from disclosing information. Usually the privilege protects information obtained in a personal or professional relationship, such as the attorney-client relationship. Sometimes it protects a party from testifying at all; examples are the privilege against self-incrimination and the spousal immunity, which protects a married person from testifying against a spouse. The number of recognized privileges varies from jurisdiction to jurisdiction. Additionally, some privileges are qualified and must yield to a compelling need for information.

This chapter addresses the privileges recognized in the federal courts. Congress did not enact the rules proposed to govern privileges; instead, it determined that the courts should apply common law principles in deciding privilege issues. Nevertheless, this chapter uses the proposed rules as a basis for explaining various privileges, as they provide a good summary of many common law principles. Section 11-2 discusses the purposes supporting privileges. Section 11-3 addresses the rejection of the proposed federal rules, while § 11-4 discusses the rule Congress adopted to replace them. Sections 11-5–11-19 discuss various privileges and potential privileges.

§ 11-2.   Purposes of Privilege Rules.

Privileges differ from many rules of evidence in that they are not designed to promote fair fact finding. A privilege denies information to the fact finder, even if it is relevant and reliable, and thus impedes the search for truth. Privileges generally promote social goals that are unrelated to just decisionmaking.[1] In creating and applying privileges, courts balance these social goals against the need for relevant information.

One justification for privileges is the promotion of valued relationships. According to this theory, courts recognize privileges to promote special relationships in which private information is shared. Examples include the attorney-client, husband-wife, priest-penitent, and doctor-patient relationships. Proponents of these privileges argue that they are necessary to the existence of the relationships; in other words, if courts compelled disclosure of private information shared in these relationships, the relationships themselves would be threatened. Critics argue that these relationships would exist regardless of privileges and the impact on the relationships does not justify denying information to litigants.

With the exception of the attorney-client privilege, the link between privilege rules and the success of relationships appears a tenuous basis for inhibiting fact

---

[1] See GRAHAM C. LILLY, AN INTRODUCTION TO THE LAW OF EVIDENCE 437 (3d ed. 1996).

finding.[2] Even if evidentiary privileges did not exist, men and women would marry, priests would hear confessions and patients would confide in their doctors. Nor would the quality of these relationships be substantially diminished. The attorney-client privilege is different because it allows a client to confide facts to counsel for litigation; if the confidences were subject to disclosure, information might not be shared, impeding counsel's ability to represent the client.

Privacy provides a second rationale for relational privileges. The intimacy of some relationships makes it unseemly for the government to compel disclosure of confidences shared in them. Safeguarding confidences may not be necessary to preserve the relationship, but it does protect participants from an intrusive airing of their intimate secrets.

A practical consideration provides additional support for some privileges: many persons would disobey an order to disclose information from confidential relationships. These people view the commitment of confidentiality or the relationship as more important than a court order, and would endure penalties to honor their commitments. For instance, a priest likely would defy an order to disclose a penitent's confession and a husband might refuse to testify against his wife. Rather than punishing persons for honoring duties of confidentiality, the courts create privileges that protect the information.

Although privileges originated as rules of evidence, they usually are more important in discovery than trial. Modern discovery rules permit parties to obtain information, including some that is inadmissible, prior to trial. Privileges often are asserted as the grounds for withholding material. The validity of the claim often is determined before the trial begins.

The earliest recognized privileges were judicially created. According to *McCormick*, the development of these common law privileges "virtually halted over a century ago,"[3] perhaps because judges did not want to expand the grounds for withholding evidence. Additional privileges were recognized in statutes, which legislatures often passed in response to the lobbying efforts of interests seeking to protect sensitive information.[4] Most jurisdictions today codify privileges, including the common law privileges, in statutes or evidence codes. The legislative process has produced varied results, so that "the various states differ substantially in the numbers and varieties of the privileges which they recognize."[5]

A privilege generally does not limit the issues or facts at trial; instead, the privilege protects information. If a party obtains other, unprotected evidence to

---

[2] *Id.*

[3] McCormick on Evidence § 75 (5th ed. 1999).

[4] *Id.*

[5] *Id.*

prove the facts, the privilege does not exclude it. Moreover, only the person who holds a privilege, or someone acting on her behalf; ordinarily may assert it;[6] if the party does not claim the privilege, the information may be disclosed. Further, a party may waive a privilege by disclosing protected information to third parties or offering some of it as evidence.

A party who is not the holder of a privilege often is denied standing to assert privilege issues on appeal. If the trial court erroneously compels disclosure from a nonparty, the losing party at trial generally may not appeal the point because it was not his privilege to assert. The introduction of probative evidence is not an error affecting the litigant's right to a fair trial. If the trial court erroneously protects nonprivileged information, on the other hand, the losing party may appeal; the ruling denies him relevant evidence and thus affects his rights, regardless of who holds the privilege.[7]

Some privileges are conditional and may be overcome by a compelling need for the privileged information. For example, in *United States v. Nixon*,[8] the United States Supreme Court ruled that a demonstrated, specific need for evidence in a pending criminal proceeding overcame the privilege for executive communications. In criminal cases the right of confrontation or due process may allow the defendant to compel disclosure of information that would otherwise be privileged. In *Davis v. Alaska*,[9] the Supreme Court ruled that a state could not protect the juvenile records of a critical state witness, where the information was necessary for cross-examination.

Courts often conduct *in camera* inspections of material for which a party claims a privilege, to determine whether the privilege applies and whether the material is needed by the party requesting it. Need depends on whether the material is the only reasonably available evidence of crucial facts. Requiring disclosure to the court in a sense breaches the privilege, but this action is necessary to resolve privilege disputes and is less intrusive than mandating disclosure to a party. The *in camera* device inhibits parties from making false claims of privilege and permits courts to rule with precision on the information that should be disclosed.

§ 11-3. Proposed Federal Rules on Privileges (FRE 501-13).

The proposed federal rules, as approved by the United States Supreme Court and submitted to Congress, contained thirteen rules to govern privileges. They

---

[6] GRAHAM C. LILLY, AN INTRODUCTION TO THE LAW OF EVIDENCE 439 (3d ed. 1996): "The privilege thus is reserved for the holder, who may or may not wish to exercise it. Sometimes, however, a party or some other person is permitted to claim the privilege in a representative capacity on behalf of the absent holder."

[7] *Id.*

[8] 418 U.S. 683 (1974).

[9] 415 U.S. 308 (1974).

recognized nine separate privileges and contained provisions for applying the privilege rules. The proposed rules provoked considerable criticism, both from commentators who opposed the enactment of specific privileges and others who believed the rules should recognize additional privileges,[10] and Congress did not enact them. Instead, the proposed rules were replaced with FRE 501, which provides that courts should apply common law principles in determining privilege issues in cases involving federal questions, and state rules of privilege in cases governed by state law. See § 11-4.

Although Congress did not adopt them, the proposed federal rules and advisory committee comments are a useful guide in determining the common law of privileges. Generally, the proposed rules were distilled from cases and statutes on privileges,[11] although they did contain a few intentional departures from prevailing law.[12] With the exception of these changes, the proposed rules are good summations of the law and the courts often treat them as persuasive.[13] The proposed rules obviously do not take account of legal developments since they were put forth, however, so they only provide a starting point in determining the law.

Additionally, many jurisdictions have adopted rules based on the proposed privilege rules. Rules of privilege were included in the Revised Uniform Rules of Evidence; these rules generally reflect the content of the proposed federal rules. Many state enactments also alter the proposed federal rules to reflect preexisting differences in state law.[14]

§ 11-4. Federal Rule Governing Privileges (FRE 501).

Rather than enact the proposed rules on privileges, Congress adopted FRE 501. This provision establishes that in federal law cases a court generally should use the federal common law in deciding privilege issues. When state law controls substantive issues, FRE 501 directs the court to apply state privilege rules. It provides:

> Except as otherwise required by the Constitution of the United States or provided by Act of Congress or in rules prescribed by the Supreme Court

---

[10] See STEPHEN A. SALTZBURG, MICHAEL M. MARTIN AND DANIEL J. CAPRA FEDERAL RULES OF EVIDENCE MANUAL 501-13 (8th ed. 2001).

[11] GRAHAM C. LILLY, AN INTRODUCTION TO THE LAW OF EVIDENCE 442 (3d ed. 1996).

[12] See Proposed FED. R. EVID. 505, which did not recognize a privilege for marital communications.

[13] United States v. McPartlin, 595 F.2d 1321 (7th Cir. 1979), *cert. denied*, 444 U.S. 833 (1979); but see United States v. Bizzard, 674 F.2d 1382, 1386 (11th Cir. 1982), *cert. denied*, 459 U.S. 973 (1982). Also see GRAHAM C. LILLY, AN INTRODUCTION TO THE LAW OF EVIDENCE 441 (3d ed. 1996).

[14] McCORMICK ON EVIDENCE § 75 (5th ed. 1999).

pursuant to statutory authority, the privilege of a witness, person, government, State or political subdivision thereof shall be governed by the principles of the common law as they may be interpreted by the courts of the United States in the light of reason and experience. However, in civil actions and proceedings, with respect to a claim or defense as to which State law supplies the rule of decision, the privileges of a witness, person, government, State or political subdivision thereof shall be determined in accordance with State law.

FRE 501 does not establish whether federal or state privilege rules should govern cases in which federal and state issues are tried together. Applying different privilege rules in the same case would have little point. Mandating disclosure for only part of the case still breaches the privilege and obviates any societal interest in protecting the information. Additionally, this approach probably would be unworkable. Even with a limiting instruction, the jury would have difficulty considering the evidence for one purpose and not for another. Thus, if there is a conflict between federal and state privilege rules, only one rule should apply.

When confronted with conflicting privilege rules, the courts generally have used the federal privilege rule.[15] This approach makes sense because federal claims usually are primary when federal and state claims are tried together; pendent state claims are tried with federal claims in the interest of judicial economy.

Some commentators argue, however, that the courts should balance federal and state interests in these cases. Generally, conflicts are likely when state law contains a privilege not recognized in the federal common law.[16] The commentators contend that if a strong state interest supports a privilege, that interest should prevail unless counterbalanced by an equally strong federal interest in disclosure of the information.[17]

A balancing approach would lead to conflicting results, however, because "interests" are difficult to weigh except in the context of specific cases. Additionally, it eventually might lead to federal recognition of additional privileges; recognizing state law privileges in cases involving mixed issues might introduce the state privileges into the federal common law. This expansion of the federally recognized privileges may unduly limit the evidence available in federal trials.

---

[15] See Virmani v. Novant Health Inc., 259 F.3d 284, 287 (4th Cir. 2001); Hancock v. Hobbs, 967 F.2d 462, 463 (11th Cir. 1992).

[16] See Virmani v. Novant Health Inc., 259 F.3d 284, 287 (4th Cir. 2001); Hancock v. Hobbs, 967 F.2d 462, 463 (11th Cir. 1992).

[17] Stephen A. Saltzburg, Michael M. Martin & Daniel J. Capra, Federal Rules of Evidence Manual 501-15 (8th ed. 2001).

FRE 501 does not provide whether federal courts may recognize new privileges in applying the common law. The Supreme Court determined in *Jaffee v. Redmond*,[18] however, that the federal courts may recognize new privileges; in doing so, the court specifically recognized a psychotherapist-patient privilege. The Court noted that FRE 501 allows the courts to define new privileges by interpreting "common law principles . . . in the light of reason and experience."[19] The rule "thus did not freeze the law governing the privileges of witnesses in federal trials at a particular point in our history, but rather directed federal courts to 'continue the evolutionary development of testimonial privileges.' "[20] Reason and experience persuaded the Court to recognize a privilege protecting confidential communications between a psychotherapist and her patient because the privilege " 'promotes sufficiently important interests to outweigh the need for probative evidence. . . .'"[21] See § 11-14.

Despite the Court's ruling, a strong showing still is required for the adoption of a new privilege.[22] If the courts recognize a new privilege, they are likely to qualify it, so that the privilege may be overcome by a showing of need. Of course, interest groups still may seek legislation to recognize privileges. Because privileges are often based on social policy, Congress may be in the best position to determine these issues.

Even when privileges are not formally recognized, the courts retain considerable power to protect privacy and prevent the disclosure of sensitive information. Whenever discovery disputes arise, the courts consider whether requiring disclosure of the requested information would be burdensome.[23] A claim that evidence should be privileged usually embodies a contention that disclosure

---

[18] 518 U.S. 1 (1996).

[19] *Id.* at 8–9.

[20] *Id.* at 9 (quoting Trammel v. United States, 445 U.S. 40, 47 (1980).

[21] *Id.*

[22] The Third Circuit declined to recognize a parent-child privilege in In re Grand Jury, 103 F.3d 1140 (3d Cir. 1997). The court noted that it had the authority to create a new privilege, but refused to do so because the privilege was not generally recognized and would not benefit the parent-child relationship or serve social policy. The court ruled that new privileges in general should be recognized by Congress rather than courts. In Pearson v. Miller, 211 F.3d 57 (3d Cir. 2000), the Third Circuit declined to recognize a federal privilege for information contained in the records of a Pennsylvania county youth services agency, where the agency claimed the information was confidential under state law. The person whose records were requested had consented to disclosure, but the agency sought the recognition of its own privilege based on state laws providing for confidentiality of the records. The court held that recognition of an agency privilege would be inappropriate because numerous beneficiaries of the privilege would be dependent on the government to assert or waive it. On the other hand, the court directed the district court to balance the interests in confidentiality and disclosure through appropriate protective provisions under FRCP 26(c).

[23] FED. R. CIV. PROC. 26(b)(2).

would be vexatious. Therefore, the courts may protect sensitive information even if they do not adopt new privileges.

§ 11-5. Attorney-Client Privilege.

The attorney-client privilege is the most well-entrenched of the common law privileges and undoubtedly receives the greatest deference from the courts. The high regard for the privilege undoubtedly results from the fact that judges, in their former careers, were lawyers. They generally ascribe to the belief that clients should feel free to "tell all" to their counsel. Additionally, judges see the importance of the privilege in promoting adequate assistance of counsel, which is essential to the adversary system.

The attorney-client privilege at its core is rather limited; it protects communications made in confidence by a client to a lawyer for the purpose of obtaining legal services. [24] For practical reasons — to ensure that core confidences are protected — the privilege has been extended to confidential communications of the lawyer to the client, among lawyers for the client, among representatives of the client and lawyer, and among different clients and their lawyers regarding a matter of common interest. [25] The privilege overlaps the attorney's work product privilege, and the two privileges strengthen each other. It belongs to the client but the lawyer may claim it on his behalf. There are several exceptions to the privilege, and in certain circumstances a party may waive it.

The primary justification for the privilege is to promote full disclosure from clients to their counsel. [26] This disclosure promotes just legal results, since lawyers who have all the facts are better equipped to help their clients. [27] If the privilege did not exist, clients would withhold information they perceived as damaging. Indeed, to adequately represent the client, the attorney might be required to caution against disclosure of damaging facts, since he might be required to reveal them.

The privilege also is justified by the adversary system. In a lawsuit, the lawyer has an ethical obligation to advocate the client's cause. Both lawyer and client must work together to present the best possible case. If the privilege did not exist, this teamwork would be difficult. The attorney might not have access to relevant information, could not develop a complete factual picture, and might not be able to anticipate harmful evidence. Thus, lawyers would be handicapped in arguing the facts for their clients.

---

[24] See GRAHAM C. LILLY, AN INTRODUCTION TO THE LAW OF EVIDENCE 452 (3d ed. 1996): Analysis begins "with the recognition that the privilege *protects only the narrow right of a client to communicate confidentially with his lawyer about a legal problem.*" (Emphasis in original.)

[25] See Proposed FED. R. EVID. 503.

[26] See MCCORMICK ON EVIDENCE § 87 (5th ed. 1996).

[27] *Id.*; GRAHAM C. LILLY, AN INTRODUCTION TO THE LAW OF EVIDENCE 451 (3d ed. 1996).

Additionally, the privilege accommodates ethical obligations of the profession. Whether or not an evidentiary privilege exists, attorneys are supposed to maintain client confidences.[28] Moreover, attorneys would be faced with recurring conflicts absent the privilege, because they could be called upon to testify against the persons they were hired to represent — raising a choice between self or client.[29] Further, the attorneys who testified would run afoul of the rule prohibiting a witness from acting as trial counsel.[30] For these reasons, many attorneys would refuse an order to testify, so the privilege probably does not cause the loss of much information.

Proposed FRE 503, which was approved by the Supreme Court but deleted by Congress, restates the common law attorney-client rule and is generally accepted in the federal courts.[31] The proposed rule contains a detailed summary of the privilege and its exceptions. It provides:

Rule 503. Lawyer-Client Privilege. [Not enacted.]

(a) **Definitions.** As used in this rule:

(1) A "client" is a person, public officer, or corporation, association, or other organization or entity, either public or private, who is rendered professional legal services by a lawyer, or who consults a lawyer with a view to obtaining professional legal services from him.

(2) A "lawyer" is a person authorized, or reasonably believed by the client to be authorized, to practice law in any state or nation.

(3) A "representative of the lawyer" is one employed to assist the lawyer in the rendition of professional legal services.

(4) A communication is "confidential" if not intended to be disclosed to third persons other than those to whom disclosure is in furtherance of the rendition of professional legal services to the client or those reasonably necessary for the transmission of the communication.

(b) **General rule of privilege.** A client has a privilege to refuse to disclose and to prevent any other person from disclosing confidential communications made for the purpose of facilitating the rendition of professional

---

[28] MODEL RULES OF PROFESSIONAL CONDUCT RULE 1.6.

[29] MODEL RULES OF PROFESSIONAL CONDUCT RULE 1.7(b).

[30] MODEL RULES OF PROFESSIONAL CONDUCT RULE 3.7.

[31] See GRAHAM C. LILLY, AN INTRODUCTION TO THE LAW OF EVIDENCE 453 (3d ed. 1996):

> Although not law, the Supreme Court [attorney-client] standard is cited with approval throughout the federal system. Most of the states that have adopted the Federal Rules of Evidence have patterned their Attorney-Client Rule on the detailed standard.

legal services to the client, (1) between himself or his representative and his lawyer or his lawyer's representative, or (2) between his lawyer and the lawyer's representative, or (3) by him or his lawyer to a lawyer representing another in a matter of common interest, or (4) between representatives of the client or between the client and a representative of the client, or (5) between lawyers representing the client.

(c)   **Who may claim the privilege.** The privilege may be claimed by the client, his guardian or conservator, the personal representative of a deceased client, or the successor, trustee, or similar representative of a corporation, association, or other organization, whether or not in existence. The person who was the lawyer at the time of the communication may claim the privilege but only on behalf of the client. His authority to do so is presumed in the absence of evidence to the contrary.

(d)   **Exceptions.** There is no privilege under this rule:

    (1)   *Furtherance of crime or fraud.* If the services of the lawyer were sought or obtained to enable or aid anyone to commit or plan to commit what the client knew or reasonably should have known to be a crime or fraud; or

    (2)   *Claimants through same deceased client.* As to a communication relevant to an issue between parties who claim through the same deceased client, regardless of whether the claims are by testate or intestate succession or by *inter vivos* transaction; or

    (3)   *Breach of duty by lawyer or client.* As to a communication relevant to an issue of breach of duty by the lawyer to his client or by the client to his lawyer; or

    (4)   *Document attested by lawyer.* As to a communication relevant to an issue concerning an attested document to which the lawyer is an attesting witness; or

    (5)   *Joint clients.* As to a communication relevant to a matter of common interest between two or more clients if the communication was made by any of them to a lawyer retained or consulted in common, when offered in an action between any of the clients.

The components of the privilege and significant aspects of its application are discussed below.

§ 11-5(a).   Information Protected by the Privilege.

The privilege applies to confidential *communications* between a client and his lawyer. Although its theoretical justifications apply primarily to communications of the client, it has been extended to lawyers' communications because they often tend to reveal clients' confidences.[32] Thus, confidential communications of both client and lawyer are protected.

The privileged communications are those exchanged so that the lawyer may render legal services. The privilege extends to preliminary communications made when the client seeks representation, even if the client has not formally retained the attorney.[33] The communication must actually relate to a professional legal service; if the attorney acts only as a friend, messenger, business associate, or in another non-legal capacity, the privilege does not apply. When a lawyer acts in mixed capacities, courts generally require that the attorney role predominate before recognizing the privilege.[34]

The privilege only protects communications; if the client discloses facts to the attorney that are provable independently — such as the content of preexisting documents — the privilege does not protect independent evidence of the facts. In other words, a client may not cloak otherwise discoverable evidence with the privilege by discussing it with her lawyer. Similarly, if documents are prepared outside the attorney-client relationship, the client may not protect them from discovery by giving them to her lawyer.[35] Nor can the client protect physical evidence from discovery by placing it in the lawyer's possession. The client's communications regarding physical evidence — say, as to its location — would be protected, but not the evidence itself.

For the privilege to apply, the client or lawyer must have a reasonable expectation of confidentiality. If the client speaks with the lawyer when others can overhear the conversation, it is not privileged. Similarly, if information is given to the lawyer with the expectation that it will be provided to third parties, the privilege is inapplicable. Of course, a client often provides information to her attorney with the expectation that counsel will *choose* what to publish and keep the rest confidential; the privilege applies to the communication unless the attorney decides to disclose it.[36]

Generally, the fact of legal employment, identity of the client, and terms of employment are not protected by the privilege.[37] This view is sensible, because

---

[32] McCORMICK ON EVIDENCE § 89 (5th ed. 1999); see Proposed FED. R. EVID. 503(b).

[33] In re Auclair, 961 F.2d 65 (5th Cir. 1992).

[34] See Boca Investing Partnership v. United States, 31 F. Supp. 2d 9, 11–12 (D.D. C. 1998) ("[T]he lawyer must not only be functioning as an advisor, but the advice given must be predominantly legal, as opposed to business, in nature"); see also Matter of Feldberg, 862 F.2d 622 (7th Cir. 1988).

[35] See In re Grand Jury, 959 F.2d 1158 (2d Cir. 1992).

[36] United States v. (Under Seal), 748 F.2d 871, 875–76 (4th Cir. 1984): "Only when the attorney has been authorized to perform services that demonstrate the client's intent to have his communications published will the client lose the right to assert the privilege. . . ."

[37] See In Re Subpoena to Testify Before the Grand Jury v. United States, 39 F.3d 14 (9th Cir. 1994) *cert. denied sub nom,* Alexiou v. United States, 514 U.S. 1097 (1995); McCORMICK ON EVIDENCE § 90 (5th ed. 1999).

these facts are not communications *per se* and usually must be disclosed so a court can determine whether the privilege exists. The privilege may apply, however, if revealing the client's identity would link him to activity that is known to others except for the client's involvement. For example, if a lawyer filed a late, anonymous tax return on behalf of a client, he later could refuse to reveal the client's identity.[38]

In *In re Bruce R. Lindsey* (*Grand Jury Testimony*),[39] the United States Court of Appeals for the District of Columbia Circuit held that the attorney-client privilege does not protect information relating to criminal conduct sought by a grand jury from government attorneys. In a 2-1 ruling, the court held that the primary duty of government attorneys is to uphold the law, which requires disclosure of information relating to illegal conduct. It said: "Unlike a private practitioner, the loyalties of a government lawyer therefore cannot and must not lie solely with his or her client agency."[40]

§ 11-5(b).   Persons Whose Communications Are Protected.

The privilege protects confidential communications from the client to the lawyer. The attorney's communications to the client are also protected, since allowing disclosure of this information could reveal the client's confidences. Additionally, communications made between client and lawyer through their representatives are protected. Persons who act on behalf of the lawyer in providing legal services, such as clerks, secretaries, paralegals and investigators, are within the scope of the privilege. Persons authorized by the client to communicate confidential information, such as a family member or business advisor, also are protected.[41]

For the privilege to apply, the representative must be acting on behalf of the lawyer or client in connection with legal services. If a client consulted a doctor independent of the lawyer-client relationship and the doctor's report were later sent to the lawyer, the privilege would not apply. On the other hand, if the attorney obtained the doctor's help to evaluate the client's condition for the purpose of rendering legal services, communications among the client, doctor and lawyer would be protected.[42] The attorney can protect some communications between the client and other advisers by structuring the relationship so that the advisers act on counsel's behalf.

Although communications to professionals acting for the lawyer are protected, their independent observations are not.[43] If an opinion is based on a confidential

---

[38] Baird v. Koerner, 279 F.2d 623 (9th Cir. 1960).

[39] 148 F. 3d 1100 (D.C. Cir. 1998).

[40] *Id.* at 1108.

[41] See Proposed FED. R. EVID. 503(a), (b); REV. UNIF. R. EVID. 502(a)(2), (4).

[42] GRAHAM C. LILLY, AN INTRODUCTION TO THE LAW OF EVIDENCE 465 (3d ed. 1996).

[43] *Id.*

communication, the privilege applies, but not if it is based on independent information. The professional's opinion may be subject to the work product privilege, however, so it may receive conditional protection. See § 11-6.

When multiple clients jointly seek the services of a lawyer, their confidential communications are protected. Since the clients seek representation on a matter of common interest, the fact that they overhear each others' statements does not breach the confidentiality requirement. Each client may invoke the privilege to protect the communications from disclosure outside the attorney-client relationship.

If the clients later become adversaries with respect to the same subject matter, the privilege does not apply between them. The information was not intended to be confidential as between the joint clients, so they may use it against each other.[44] In the absence of adversary litigation between the joint clients, however, the privilege remains effective even if their interests conflict in other ways.[45]

Communications among lawyers for different clients with respect to common interests generally are protected. Additionally, if a client discloses information to a lawyer for an allied party at the direction of his own lawyer in pursuit of a common interest, the privilege attaches. This approach allows lawyers and clients to pool their information in matters on which they are allied.

If parties to an arrangement for pooling information or services have potential conflicts, each client has a privilege only as to information he or his lawyer discloses to others in the pool; he cannot invoke the privilege against outsiders to protect information disclosed by another party.[46] To protect the information, the disclosing party has to claim the privilege. Additionally, if a client discloses information extraneous to the common interest, it is not protected. Further, if he gives information to another attorney without being asked to do so by his own counsel, it may be deemed unprotected. Absent advice of counsel to reveal information, the communication may fall outside a joint interest strategy.[47]

§ 11-5(c). Persons Who May Claim the Privilege.

The privilege belongs to the client; it is his to claim. The lawyer may claim the privilege on the client's behalf, however, and is presumed to have authority

---

[44] See Proposed FED. R. EVID. 503(d)(5).

[45] STEPHEN A. SALTZBURG, MICHAEL M. MARTIN AND DANIEL J. CAPRA, FEDERAL RULES OF EVIDENCE MANUAL 501-32, 33 (8th ed. 2001).

[46] Proposed FED. R. EVID. 503(b) advisory committee's note: ·Allowing any client to invoke the privilege against other parties to the pooling arrangement overlooks "actually or potentially conflicting interests in addition to the common interest which brings them together. The needs of these cases seem to be better met by allowing each client a privilege as to his own statements."

[47] United States v. Bay State Ambulance & Hospital Rental Serv., Inc., 874 F.2d 20, 29 (1st Cir. 1989).

to do so unless there is evidence that the client does not wish to claim it. The Advisory Committee Note to Proposed FRE 503 observes that counsel ordinarily would be obliged ethically to claim the privilege for the client. A person who serves in a representative capacity for the client, such as a guardian, may claim the privilege on his behalf.

A party to litigation may not claim the privilege for a witness; the witness must claim it himself. Additionally, a party may not appeal a court's decision to compel disclosure from a different party or witness. When a privilege is erroneously sustained, a party may appeal if the ruling denies her access to probative evidence.[48]

§ 11-5(d). Duration of the Privilege.

The privilege still applies after the attorney-client relationship is terminated. It also survives the death of the client. In *Swidler & Berlin v. United States*,[49] the United States Supreme Court ruled that the attorney-client privilege survives the client's death, rejecting arguments of the Office of Independent Counsel for an exception to the privilege when the client has died and the information is relevant to a criminal proceeding. The case involved handwritten notes taken by an attorney during an interview with Vincent W. Foster, Jr., who was Deputy White House Counsel when certain employees were dismissed at the White House Travel Office. Foster committed suicide nine days after the interview. The Independent Counsel sought the notes in an investigation of whether various persons obstructed justice when the firings themselves were investigated.

The Court held that inadequate justification had been provided for narrowing "one of the oldest recognized privileges for confidential communications."[50] It noted that many court decisions assume the attorney-client privilege survives the client's death. Moreover, it determined that the purpose of the privilege — to promote full and frank disclosure of client confidences relevant to the attorney-client relationship — is promoted by applying the privilege after the client's death. The Court said:

> Knowing that communications will remain confidential even after death encourages the client to communicate fully and frankly with counsel. While the fear of disclosure, and the consequent withholding of information from counsel, may be reduced if disclosure is limited to posthumous disclosure in a criminal context, it seems unreasonable to assume that it vanishes altogether.[51]

---

[48] McCORMICK ON EVIDENCE § 92 (5th ed. 1999).

[49] 524 U.S. 399 (1998).

[50] *Id.* at 403.

[51] *Id.* at 407.

The Court concluded that it "has been generally, if not universally, accepted, for well over a century, that the attorney-client privilege survives the death of the client in a case such as this."[52] Since the Independent Counsel's arguments for an exception were based only on "thoughtful speculation" that the exception would not impede full communication, the court concluded that the "Independent Counsel has simply not made a sufficient showing to overturn the common law rule embodied in the prevailing caselaw."[53]

Given the precept that the privilege belongs to the client, recognizing it after death is questionable. The privilege would promote client-lawyer confidences even if they could be revealed after the client died. Nevertheless, the permanence of the privilege is well accepted.[54] This aspect of the privilege is probably an accommodation of the lawyer's ethical obligation rather than an attempt to promote the attorney-client relationship. If lawyers feel compelled to keep information from a deceased client confidential, judges are naturally reluctant to compel its disclosure.

§ 11-5(e). Exceptions.

There are a number of well-recognized exceptions to the rule, five of which were embodied in Proposed FRE 503(d). The exceptions include the following:

§ 11-5(e)(1). Communications in Furtherance of Crime or Fraud.

When the lawyer's services are sought in furtherance of a plan that the client reasonably should know is criminal or fraudulent, the privilege is inapplicable. The exception is limited to conduct that a reasonable person would know is unlawful; otherwise, consultation to find out whether conduct is permissible might not be protected. Additionally, consultation regarding past misconduct is not covered by the exception.

The client's actual or imputed knowledge that a plan is criminal or fraudulent is essential to the exception. If the lawyer knows the plan is illegal, but the client is innocent, no reason exists to deny the client the privilege. If the lawyer is innocent and the client guilty, the exception applies because it is meant to prevent clients from misusing legal services.

A party may establish a basis for the exception by making out a *prima facie* case that it applies.[55] Conflicts exist regarding the level of proof needed to meet the *prima facie* standard and whether a court needs to give the party claiming the privilege an opportunity to rebut the *prima facie* case. These matters were

---

[52] *Id.* at 410.

[53] *Id.* at 411.

[54] Stephen A. Saltzburg, Michael M. Martin and Daniel J. Capra, Federal Rules of Evidence Manual 501-45, 46 (8th ed. 2001).

[55] See United States v. Reeder, 170 F.3d 93 (1st Cir. 1999).

left unresolved in *United States v. Zolin*,[56] which held that a court could consider the alleged privileged statements in determining whether the privilege applies.

Cases requiring only a *prima facie* showing, without opportunity for rebuttal, place little burden on the party seeking disclosure, but he is not in a good position to produce evidence on an adverse party's intent in consulting with counsel. Thus, the relaxed burden is fair. Moreover, a more difficult burden could place the courts in the position of shielding criminal schemes. Additionally, courts still must limit disclosure to matters within the exception, so there should be little disclosure of matters that are legitimately privileged.

Some courts have extended the exception to consultations that further intentional tortious conduct, such as the intentional infliction of emotional distress. This extension was not recognized, however, in Proposed FRE 503. When consultation promotes conduct that the client reasonably knows is wrongful, the extension makes good sense. The purpose of the exception is to eliminate the cloak of confidentiality when a client misuses the lawyer's service. An intentionally tortious plan should qualify.

§ 11-5(e)(2).　Claimants Through the Same Deceased Client.

When more than one party claims to be the rightful successor to a deceased client — as in a will contest — the lawyer may possess information needed to determine who is correct. Additionally, a court can determine the person who might rightfully claim the privilege — the legitimate successor to the deceased client — only by resolving the dispute.[57] Therefore, an exception permits the disclosure of the deceased client's communications. The Advisory Committee Note to Proposed FRE 503(d)(2) states: "The choice is thus between allowing both sides or neither to assert the privilege, with authority and reason favoring the latter view."

§ 11-5(e)(3).　Breach of Duty by Lawyer or Client.

When a claim exists that the lawyer breached a professional obligation, that the lawyer or client breached the fee agreement, or that some other violation of the attorney-client relationship occurred, "considerations of fairness and policy"[58] require that their relevant communications be excepted from the privilege. Of course, when a client sues an attorney regarding his representation, the suit generally would also waive the privilege.

§ 11-5(e)(4).　Document Attested by Lawyer.

When a lawyer signs a document as a witness, the client is presumed to waive any privilege as to communications regarding the document.

---

[56] 491 U.S. 554 (1989).

[57] Proposed FED. R. EVID. 503(d)(2) advisory committee's note.

[58] Proposed FED. R. EVID. 503(d)(3) advisory committee's note.

§ 11-5(e)(5).   Action Between Joint Clients.

If multiple clients consult an attorney on a matter of common interest and subsequently become involved in a lawsuit over the same matter, relevant communications are excepted from the privilege. The clients already have shared the information with each other and their common representative; it can be protected from outsiders, but no reason exists to prevent its use in litigation between the clients.[59]

§ 11-5(e)(6).   Fiduciaries.

In *Garner v. Wolfenbarger,*[60] the Fifth Circuit established the so-called "*Garner* doctrine," which provides that shareholders in a corporate derivative suit may obtain access to communications between the corporation's counsel and management upon showing "good cause" for the disclosure. The theory for the exception is that management communicates with counsel on behalf of the shareholders. Allowing full access to the communications would permit minority shareholders to disrupt management's legitimate access to counsel, however, so the "good cause" showing is required.

To determine good cause, the court considers the strength of the claim, need for the information, relevance, and the particularity of the request. As with the crime-fraud category, the communications must precede the claimed fiduciary violation to fall within the exception; allowing inquiry into communications occurring after the violation might infringe management's right to defend itself. *Garner* has been extended to other fiduciary situations, but also has received considerable criticism.[61] Some courts limit it to shareholder derivative suits.

The Ninth Circuit discussed the scope of the fiduciary exception to the attorney-client privilege in *United States v. Mett,*[62] an ERISA case. The court determined that the exception does not apply when an attorney provides advice to a plan trustee in the course of defending against potential liabilities to plan fiduciaries. The court found the information in question was defensive and thus protected by the privilege.

§ 11-5(f).   Waiver.

The attorney-client privilege can be waived, expressly or impliedly. The client may waive the privilege by saying so, by directing the attorney to make use of

---

[59] GRAHAM C. LILLY, AN INTRODUCTION TO THE LAW OF EVIDENCE 469-470 (3d ed. 1996): "The rule in such situations protects the statements of both the clients and the lawyer, and allows *any of the clients* to invoke the privilege against outsiders. The privilege is lost, however, in subsequent litigation between the clients themselves." (emphasis in original).

[60] 430 F.2d 1093 (5th Cir. 1970), *cert. denied,* 401 U.S. 974 (1971).

[61] Stephen A. Saltzburg, *Corporate Attorney-Client Privilege in Shareholder Litigation and Similar Cases: Garner Revisited,* 12 HOFSTRA L. REV. 817, 846 (1984).

[62] 178 F.3d 1058 (9th Cir. 1999).

information in a manner that entails publication, by voluntarily disclosing significant parts of communications, and by placing the communications in issue in a dispute with the lawyer or a third party.[63]

An express or implied authorization to publish information makes the privilege inapplicable. If the client does not give information to the lawyer with the expectation of confidentiality, the privilege does not apply at all. On the other hand, a client may authorize the attorney to share information that initially was communicated in confidence. That action constitutes a waiver.

A client also may waive the privilege by disclosing a significant part of the confidential information. If partial disclosure were not a waiver, a client could use portions of confidential communications to his benefit, while unfairly shielding harmful communications. Thus, courts generally do not permit a client to disclose confidential information selectively.[64]

When a party inadvertently discloses confidential information, the revelation is less likely to be a waiver.[65] In an era of wholesale discovery, attorneys face an enormous task in weeding out privileged documents from the thousands that often are exchanged. Courts are likely to be sympathetic with the red-faced associate who mistakenly allows a privileged communication through his screen. Additionally, this sort of disclosure usually is not an attempt to gain a litigation advantage. Thus, courts generally do not treat the revelation as a general waiver so long as the mistake is excusable and there is no unfairness to the opposing party.[66] If the privileged information reveals the existence of previously undisclosed evidence that may help resolve the issues, however, the inadvertent disclosure may open the door to further inquiry.[67]

When a client puts confidential communications in issue, her action generally constitutes a waiver. Thus, for instance, if the client asserts that she relied on advice of counsel as a defense to a charge, she may not shield relevant attorney-client communications from disclosure. Similarly, if she sues her lawyer for malpractice, she waives the privilege as to relevant communications.[68] Obviously, it would be unfair to admit the client's version of her lawyer's advice without permitting a response.

---

[63] See United States v. Mass. Inst. of Tech., 129 F.3d 681, 684–86 (1st. Cir. 1997) (holding that contractor's disclosure of documents to government auditor forfeited attorney-client privilege covering such documents). See generally MCCORMICK ON EVIDENCE § 93 (5th ed. 1999); JOHN W. GERGACZ, ATTORNEY-CORPORATE CLIENT PRIVILEGE ¶ 2.03 (2d ed. 1990).

[64] Westinghouse Electric Corp. v. Republic of the Philippines, 951 F.2d 1414 (3d Cir. 1991); Permian Corp. v. United States, 655 F.2d 1214 (D.C. Cir. 1981); but see Diversified Industries, Inc. v. Meredith, 572 F.2d 596 (8th Cir. 1978) (*en banc*).

[65] See Hydraflow, Inc. V. Enidine, Inc., 145 F.R.D. 626, 638 (W.D.N.Y. 1993).

[66] *Id.*

[67] See Alldread v. City of Grenada, 988 F.2d 1425 (5th Cir. 1993).

[68] See Proposed FED. R. EVID. 503(d)(3).

An important issue for the trial lawyer is the possibility that the client may waive the privilege by relying in testimony on information prepared by counsel. FRE 612 provides that when a witness uses a writing to refresh her memory while on the stand, it must be turned over to the opposing counsel, who is entitled to cross-examine the witness on it. This provision indicates that showing a testifying witness a document prepared by counsel is a waiver as to that document. Additionally, the court in its discretion may require the disclosure of documents used to refresh the witness's recollection before she testifies. The exercise of discretion may be influenced by a claim of privilege, but the court may require the disclosure of privileged documents if they are important in testing the witness's recollection. [69]

FRE 612 does not by its terms extend to conversations with counsel. In theory, if the attorney tells the witness facts that are incorporated into testimony, the privilege would be waived as to that information; if the attorney's statement merely refreshes recollection, the testimony would not be a waiver. Determining the extent to which counsel influenced the testimony would be difficult, however, without an examination that intruded into privileged areas. Thus, courts are unlikely to authorize much inquiry into the witness's conversations with counsel.

If circumstances indicate that counsel suggested facts to the witness that were repeated in testimony — as when the witness's memory revives after consultation — some probing of the foundation may be allowed. A court probably would require the adverse lawyer to first gain a concession that the testimony was based on counsel's suggestion before allowing an examination of the communications themselves.

§ 11-5(g).   Corporate Clients.

Corporations, like individuals, are clients, and are covered by the attorney-client privilege. [70] Applying the privilege to persons who work for the corporation, however, presents a dilemma. On the one hand, an overbroad privilege for communications between corporate employees and their lawyers might deny important information to adverse parties. These communications — particularly reports that compile relevant information — might save the adverse party a huge expenditure of time and money. On the other hand, an overly restrictive privilege could prevent corporate employees from engaging in frank discussions with counsel. [71]

· Prior to 1981 some courts used a "control group" test in determining the scope of the attorney-client privilege for corporations. This test required that an employee not only have authority to seek legal advice for the corporation, but

---

[69] See FED. R. EVID. 612.

[70] JOHN W. GERGACZ, ATTORNEY-CORPORATE CLIENT PRIVILEGE ¶ 1.04 (2d ed. 1990).

[71] GRAHAM C. LILLY, AN INTRODUCTION TO THE LAW OF EVIDENCE 472 (3d ed. 1996).

power to influence the corporation's response to that advice, before the privilege applied to his communications.[72] The Supreme Court rejected that test in *Upjohn Co. v. United States*[73] and substantially broadened the scope of the corporate privilege.

The Court's opinion suggests that the privilege applies to employee communications when (1) the communication is made by the employee for the purpose of obtaining legal advice or services for the corporation, (2) the communication relates to matters within the employee's duties, and (3) the corporation keeps the information confidential. The Court did not further define the privilege's scope.

The requirement of corporate confidentiality has two aspects. First, the corporation cannot disclose the information to outsiders. Second, widespread dissemination of confidential information *within the corporation* may make the privilege inapplicable. If the corporation gives employees who have no "need to know" access to the communications, the information may be deemed non-confidential.[74] Thus, corporate management should limit access within the corporation to information it believes is privileged.

§ 11-6. Attorney Work Product Privilege (FRCP 26(b)(3), (4)).

The attorney work product privilege is closely related to that for confidential communications. It applies to material prepared in anticipation of litigation by the attorney, the client, or someone acting on their behalf. The privilege is conditional as to most trial preparation materials; the adverse party may obtain it by showing he has substantial need for the material and could not obtain it by other means without undue hardship. When a court requires a lawyer to produce work product, it still must protect the mental impressions, conclusions, and legal theories of the attorney concerning the litigation.[75]

The work product rule was established by the Supreme Court in *Hickman v. Taylor*.[76] The Court determined that liberal discovery of a lawyer's trial strategy, witness interviews, and other material would unduly deter and interfere with trial preparation.[77] Therefore, it found that this discovery should be permitted only on a strong showing of need.

---

[72] See City of Philadelphia v. Westinghouse Electric Corp., 210 F. Supp. 483, 484–86 (E.D. Pa. 1962).

[73] 449 U.S. 383 (1981).

[74] JACK B. WEINSTEIN & MARGARET A. BERGER, WEINSTEIN'S EVIDENCE § 503(b)[04](19) (1994).

[75] ROGER C. PARK, DAVID P. LEONARD, STEVEN H. GOLDBERG, EVIDENCE LAW 401 (1998).

[76] 329 U.S. 495 (1947).

[77] *Id.* at 512.

The work product doctrine is now codified in FRCP 26(b). The rule limits discovery of "documents and tangible things" prepared in anticipation of litigation by another party or his representative "only upon a showing that the party seeking discovery has substantial need of the materials in the preparation of the party's case and that the party is unable without undue hardship to obtain the substantial equivalent of the materials by other means." The rule provides that mental impressions and conclusions should be given absolute protection. It says: "In ordering discovery of such materials when the required showing has been made, the court shall protect against disclosure of the mental impressions, conclusions, opinions, or legal theories of an attorney or other representative of a party concerning the litigation."

This provision grants a conditional privilege for work product to the attorney, the client, and persons preparing for litigation on their behalf. It accords an unconditional privilege to the attorney's mental impressions incorporated in documents. These impressions should be excised from documents that a court requires a party to produce.

Further, FRCP 26(b)(4) extends the conditional privilege to nontestifying experts. To obtain discovery from these experts, a party must show "exceptional circumstances under which it is impracticable for the party seeking discovery to obtain facts or opinions on the same subject by other means." Similar provisions are contained in statutes or court rules in most of the states.

The attorney-client and work product privileges overlap. Obviously the attorney's conclusions often are built on information communicated by the client. The client's communications to counsel in preparing for trial may qualify for both privileges. At the same time, each privilege encompasses information that the other does not, and thus extends the protection afforded attorney-client material.

The work product doctrine is more limited than the attorney-client privilege because it applies only to material prepared in anticipation of litigation. As set out in FRCP 26(b), it applies only to documents and tangible items. Nevertheless, the principle undoubtedly would be extended to verbal work product — say, oral reports communicated to the attorney by an investigator.[78]

§ 11-7. Attorney's Ethical Obligation of Confidentiality.

The lawyer has an ethical duty not to reveal information relating to the representation of a client. This obligation is independent of, and broader than, the evidentiary privilege for attorney-client communications. It applies not only to communications, but to all information relating to the representation, even if it comes from a third party. The attorney may disclose information only when: (1) the client expressly or impliedly consents, (2) the lawyer reasonably believes

---

[78] See MCCORMICK ON EVIDENCE § 96 (5th ed. 1999).

the action is necessary to prevent a crime likely to result in imminent death or substantial bodily harm, or (3) disclosure is reasonably necessary in a lawsuit relating to the representation.

Rule 1.6 of the Model Rules of Professional Conduct sets forth the obligation of confidentiality. It provides:

Confidentiality of Information

(a)   A lawyer shall not reveal information relating to representation of a client unless the client consents after consultation, except for disclosures that are impliedly authorized in order to carry out the representation, and except as stated in paragraph (b).

(b)   A lawyer may reveal such information to the extent the lawyer reasonably believes necessary:

   (1)   to prevent the client from committing a criminal act that the lawyer believes is likely to result in imminent death or substantial bodily harm; or

   (2)   to establish a claim or defense on behalf of the lawyer in a controversy between the lawyer and the client, to establish a defense to a criminal charge or civil claim against the lawyer based upon conduct in which the client was involved, or to respond to allegations in any proceeding concerning the lawyer's representation of the client.

The requirement of confidentiality is abrogated when it conflicts with the duty of candor toward the court or other tribunal. Under Rule 3.3(a)(2) of the Model Rules, the attorney must disclose a material fact to a tribunal if that action is necessary to "avoid assisting a criminal or fraudulent act by the client." Additionally, Rule 3.3(a)(4) precludes the attorney from offering evidence she knows to be false and requires remedial measures if she later learns evidence she offered was false. These rules trump Rule 1.6; Rule 3.3(b) states the duties apply "even if compliance requires disclosure of information otherwise protected by Rule 1.6."

The ethical duties differ from the evidentiary privilege in several ways. First, they apply to all information relating to the representation, whether communicated confidentially or not. Second, they preclude disclosure of information relating to most crimes; an attorney may "blow the whistle" on a client only to prevent imminent death, bodily injury or fraud on a tribunal. Third, the attorney must disclose that a client defrauded a tribunal, even if counsel learned it in a confidential communication.

If counsel knows in advance of a client's plan to defraud the tribunal, she must attempt to dissuade the client from proceeding. If this effort fails, she generally may satisfy Rule 3.3 by withdrawing. If she is not permitted to withdraw, she faces an ethical dilemma in criminal cases — disclosing a client's plan to commit perjury conflicts with the duty of effective representation. The prevailing view would prevent the attorney from putting on perjured testimony, but some authorities have approved putting on a witness to "tell his story," without active participation from the lawyer.[79] In civil cases the lawyer at least must withdraw and may be required to inform the court of the intended perjury.[80]

§ 11-8. Marital Privileges.

There are two generally recognized marital privileges. One permits a spouse to refuse to testify against the other in a criminal case. The second protects confidential communications between spouses during their marriage. The privileges are designed to protect the marital relationship by avoiding spousal confrontations and preserving intimacies.[81] They are discussed below.

§ 11-8(a). Spousal Immunity.

The privilege against testifying originated in the common law rule disqualifying persons from testifying *for or against* their marriage partners. This ancient rule of witness "competency" was based on the proposition that a spouse could not testify objectively.[82] As time passed the rule that a witness could not testify for a spouse was discarded, but the privilege to prevent adverse testimony was retained.

The privilege is aimed at preserving harmony within marriages. If one spouse testified against the other, the adversarial overtones could cause ill feelings. Further, the testifying spouse would be subject to cross-examination and impeachment, causing further hostility. Additionally, the privilege protects the right of privacy. Compelling a person to testify against a spouse may be seen as an undue government intrusion into the intimacy of marriage.

The privilege also reflects the practical difficulties of compelling spousal testimony. Some spouses would refuse to testify even if there were no privilege. A spouse who gives testimony may color it in favor of her partner, impairing its helpfulness. If the spouse willingly gives adverse testimony, it often is motivated by negative bias. Thus, when spousal testimony is elicited, it rarely is objective.

At common law the privilege allowed the criminal defendant to prevent a spouse from testifying against her.[83] A number of jurisdictions allowed both the

---

[79] ANNOTATED MODEL RULES OF PROFESSIONAL CONDUCT 340-41 (2d ed. 1992).

[80] *Id.* at 342–43.

[81] David Farnham, *The Marital Privilege*, LITIG. 34 (Winter 1992).

[82] McCORMICK ON EVIDENCE § 66 (5th ed. 1999).

[83] GRAHAM C. LILLY, AN INTRODUCTION TO THE LAW OF EVIDENCE 447–48 (3d ed. 1996).

accused and the testifying spouse to claim the privilege.[84] In *Trammel v. United States*,[85] however, the Supreme Court ruled that in federal prosecutions only the testifying spouse may claim the privilege. The Court reasoned that if a spouse is willing to give adverse testimony, there is little to protect in the marriage relationship; thus, the defendant should not be able to keep her spouse off the stand.[86] *Trammel* is inconsistent with the proposed federal rule on spousal immunity, which would have made the criminal defendant the sole holder of the privilege.[87] Since the proposed rule was not adopted, *Trammel* prevails.

The spousal immunity privilege applies only during the marriage.[88] There is no spousal immunity if the parties are divorced, but they are still subject to the privilege for marital communications. If the marriage is a sham — entered primarily to obtain the privilege — spousal immunity may not be granted. Additionally, the courts may deny the privilege if the spouses participated jointly in the crime charged against the defendant.[89]

§ 11-8(b). Marital Communications.

The marital communications privilege protects confidential communications between spouses that occur during the marriage. As to those communications, the privilege survives the termination of the marriage. Communications made

---

[84] *Id.*

[85] 445 U.S. 40 (1980).

[86] *Id.* at 46.

[87] Proposed FED. R. EVID. 505 provided:

> **Rule 505. Husband-Wife Privilege. [Not enacted.]**
>
> **(a) General rule of privilege.** An accused in a criminal proceeding has a privilege to prevent his spouse from testifying against him.
>
> **(b) Who may claim the privilege.** The privilege may be claimed by the accused or by the spouse on his behalf. The authority of the spouse to do so is presumed in the absence of evidence to the contrary.
>
> **(c) Exceptions.** There is no privilege under this rule (1) in proceedings in which one spouse is charged with a crime against the person or property of the other or of a child of either, or with a crime against the person or property of a third person committed in the course of committing a crime against the other, or (2) as to matters occurring prior to the marriage, or (3) in proceedings in which a spouse is charged with importing an alien for prostitution or other immoral purpose in violation of 8 U.S.C. § 1328, with transporting a female in interstate commerce for immoral purposes or other offenses in violation of 18 U.S.C. §§ 2421-2424, or with violation of other similar statutes.

[88] See United States v. Porter, 286 F.2d 1014, 1019 (6th Cir. 1993) (privilege does not apply to statements made by one spouse to the other after the spouses have permantely separated); United States v. Hamilton, 19 F.3d 350, 354 (7th Cir. 1994) (privilege only exists within a valid marriage). See also McCORMICK ON EVIDENCE § 66 (5th ed. 1999).

[89] See McCORMICK ON EVIDENCE § 81 (5th ed. 1999); STEPHEN A. SALTZBURG, MICHAEL M. MARTIN AND DANIEL J. CAPRA, FEDERAL RULES OF EVIDENCE MANUAL 501-81 (2001).

after the marriage are not protected; the date of divorce is generally recognized as the time the privilege ends. Generally, the communicating spouse — the one who provided confidential information to his married partner — holds the privilege and may enforce it against the other spouse. In some jurisdictions either spouse may claim the privilege.[90]

The privilege is intended to foster and protect intimate marital communications. Since married persons often do not even know the privilege exists, however, it probably does little to promote these communications. The privilege also recognizes the legitimate privacy interests in marriage and the indelicacy of compelling disclosure of intimate communications. It thus is consistent with constitutional cases recognizing a right of privacy in marriage.[91]

The spousal communication must be confidential to be protected. If the information is shared in the presence of a third person — even a child old enough to understand it — the privilege does not apply. The communication is not privileged if it was never intended to remain confidential; confidential intent is presumed by many courts, but the circumstances may overcome this presumption. Generally, if third parties overhear or learn of marital confidences, the privilege does not prevent the third parties from testifying.

If a spouse discloses a marital communication to a third party, the disclosure may be a basis for finding that it was not intended to be confidential. The privilege is not abridged, however, by a disclosure that breaches the trust of the other party — for instance, when a divorced person tells marital secrets to embarrass his former spouse.[92]

Continuing the privilege in this circumstance avoids rewarding spousal betrayal[93] but has little justification under the rationales for the privilege — protecting privacy and promoting marital communications. Once a communication is disclosed, there is no privacy to protect. Additionally, admitting marital communications after they are disclosed to third parties would not deter the communications themselves. A married person might worry that his spouse would reveal a confidence but probably would assume the communication could be used in court once it was revealed to others.

The privilege may not apply in cases involving the marriage, such as a prosecution for a crime committed by one spouse against the other or a civil action between the spouses. It also may be inapplicable in a suit by a spouse

---

[90] GRAHAM C. LILLY, AN INTRODUCTION TO THE LAW OF EVIDENCE 447–451 (3d ed. 1996).

[91] Roe v. Wade, 410 U.S. 113 (1973); Griswold v. Connecticut, 381 U.S. 479 (1965).

[92] GRAHAM C. LILLY, AN INTRODUCTION TO THE LAW OF EVIDENCE 445 (3d ed. 1996).

[93] McCORMICK ON EVIDENCE § 82 (5th ed. 1999): "Just as that spouse would not be permitted, against the will of the communicating spouse, to betray the confidence by testifying in court to the message, so he or she may not effectively destroy the privilege by out-of-court betrayal."

against a third party for intentional injury to the marriage.[94] The privilege should not attach if a marital communication is intended to further a crime or fraud — just as it does not in the attorney-client setting.[95]

The proposed privilege rules in the Federal Rules of Evidence would not have recognized a privilege for marital communications. Since these rules were not adopted, however, the common law privilege still applies in federal courts.

§ 11-9. Self-Incrimination.

The privilege against self-incrimination is established by the Fifth Amendment to the United States Constitution, which provides that "[n]o person . . . shall be compelled in any criminal case to be a witness against himself." Originally a restraint on the federal government, the provision has been applied to the states as a right "incorporated" into the due process guarantee of the Fourteenth Amendment.[96] The privilege protects individuals from being compelled by the government to give testimony that might subject them to criminal prosecution.

The self-incrimination privilege raises numerous issues of constitutional law and criminal procedure, which can more effectively be reviewed in texts devoted to those subjects. The purpose of this section is to note the existence of the privilege and discuss its primary attributes.

The constitution bars the government from compelling a person to testify against himself. The courts enforce this prohibition through an exclusionary rule, which bars the introduction of certain statements given involuntarily to law enforcement officials. Additionally, to ensure that statements are not coerced, the Supreme Court has required that a person in police custody be told that he has a right to remain silent and obtain a lawyer before being interrogated — the so-called *Miranda* warnings.[97]

The privilege against self-incrimination belongs only to individuals. It cannot be claimed on behalf of an organization, partnership, labor union or similar organization.[98] The privilege can be claimed only by the holder; an individual may not claim the privilege for another or refuse to provide information on the ground that it will incriminate someone else. Generally, a criminal defendant may not complain that someone else's right against self-incrimination was violated in a criminal investigation or trial. A lawyer generally may invoke the privilege for his client, but the decision to invoke it must be made by the client.

---

[94] MCCORMICK ON EVIDENCE § 84 (5th ed. 1999).

[95] STEPHEN A. SALTZBURG, MICHAEL M. MARTIN AND DANIEL J. CAPRA, FEDERAL RULES OF EVIDENCE MANUAL 501-81 (8th ed. 2001).

[96] Malloy v. Hogan, 378 U.S. 1 (1964).

[97] Miranda v. Arizona, 384 U.S. 436 (1966).

[98] United States v. White, 322 U.S. 694, 701 (1944).

Although the Fifth Amendment refers to "any criminal case," a witness may assert the privilege in any proceeding so long as the testimony tends to incriminate him. Thus, a witness may invoke the privilege in a civil or administrative proceeding. For the privilege to apply, there must be an actual risk of *legal* criminal liability. If the revelations would expose the speaker to public scorn or ridicule, but not to criminal sanction, the privilege is inapplicable. The privilege may be invoked in one jurisdiction even if the testimony would subject the speaker to criminal liability in a different jurisdiction.[99]

The risk that the statements will tend to incriminate the witness must be real rather than fanciful. This requirement is satisfied so long as the testimony would implicate the witness in activity prohibited by a criminal provision, even if the crime is rarely prosecuted.[100]

The privilege protects the individual from being compelled to communicate — generally to provide an oral or written statement. It does not protect him from providing physical evidence, such as a fingerprint or blood sample, taking part in a line-up, or submitting to physical examination.[101] Similarly, an individual may be compelled to provide a handwriting sample or speak aloud for a voice identification.

Additionally, the privilege does not protect against the production of preexisting documents, even if the documents contain testimonial disclosures. Documents may be protected, however, if the act of producing them or acknowledging their existence would be self-incriminating.[102] Of course, compelled disclosure or seizure of documents by the government may raise Fourth Amendment issues.

A person in custody has the right to remain silent. In a criminal case the defendant need not take the stand and the prosecution may not comment on his failure to testify.[103] Persons who are not yet criminal defendants, such as a witness called before a grand jury, may not refuse to take the stand on the basis of the Fifth Amendment. Instead, they must assert the privilege in response to individual inquiries.

Under *Miranda v. Arizona*,[104] a person in police custody must be warned of his constitutional rights before being interrogated. *Miranda* requires that the suspect be told he has a right to remain silent, a right to be represented by an

---

[99] Murphy v. Waterfront Commission of New York Harbor, 378 U.S. 52 (1964).

[100] MᶜCORMICK ON EVIDENCE § 122 (5th ed. 1999).

[101] Schmerber v. California, 384 U.S. 757 (1966).

[102] United States v. Doe, 465 U.S. 605 (1984); Fisher v. United States, 424 U.S. 382 (1976). See also In Re Grand Jury Proceedings, 173 F.R.D. 336, 337 (D.Mass. 1997) (holding that personal business records are not protected by Fifth Amendment privilege, but that affidavit prepared in attorney's office had a "real and appreciable tendency" to incriminate and thus was protected).

[103] Griffin v. California, 380 U.S. 609 (1965).

[104] 384 U.S. 436 (1966).

attorney, a right to have counsel appointed for him if he is unable to pay for a lawyer, and a right to have counsel present at the interrogation. If the suspect is not told of his rights, his incriminating statements are inadmissible in the prosecution's case. If the defendant takes the stand at trial, however, his statements may be used for impeachment even if the warnings were not provided.[105]

A person may waive the privilege by voluntarily giving testimony, at least as to the subject matter of the testimony. For instance, if the accused takes the stand to assert his innocence, he is subject to cross-examination on matters fairly relevant to his testimony; questions that tend to refute, undermine or contradict the testimony are permissible. Some jurisdictions may view trial testimony as a waiver for all offenses with which the defendant is charged in the case.[106]

FRE 608(b) provides that a defendant who takes the stand does not waive the privilege with respect to past acts that might be used to impeach. Thus, he may refuse to answer questions with respect to those acts. It provides:

> The giving of testimony, whether by an accused or by any other witness, does not operate as a waiver of the accused's or the witness' privilege against self-incrimination when examined with respect to matters which relate only to credibility.

The Advisory Committee Note to FRE 608(b) states that the no-waiver rule is necessary to preserve the privilege. It explains:

> While it is clear that an ordinary witness cannot make a partial disclosure of incriminating matter and then invoke the privilege on cross-examination, no tenable contention can be made that merely by testifying he waives his right to foreclose inquiry in cross-examination into criminal activities for the purpose of attacking his credibility. So to hold would reduce the privilege to a nullity. While it is true that an accused, unlike an ordinary witness, has an option whether to testify, if the option can be exercised only at the price of opening up inquiry as to any and all criminal acts committed during his lifetime, the right to testify could scarcely be said to possess much vitality.

Of course, refusing to answer questions concerning prior crimes likely will undermine the accused's chance of acquittal.

When an ordinary witness voluntarily testifies on a subject, the testimony generally waives the privilege as to that matter. The questioner is permitted to obtain details regarding the testimony or to interrogate the witness on closely

---

[105] Harris v. New York, 401 U.S. 222 (1971).

[106] GRAHAM C. LILLY, AN INTRODUCTION TO THE LAW OF EVIDENCE 499 (3d ed. 1996).

related matters. If further responses would significantly add to the risk of self-incrimination, however, the witness may claim the privilege.[107] Presumably the witness would be protected from disclosing new facts subjecting her to criminal liability.

Since the privilege protects the individual only from self-incrimination, the Government may compel testimony when the risk has been eliminated. Thus, if a prosecution for the relevant offense has already occurred, immunizing the defendant from further liability, he may be required to testify. Additionally, the prosecution may compel testimony by granting immunity to the witness.

Generally, immunity can only be granted pursuant to statutory authority and procedures. Two types of immunity exist: "Transactional immunity" protects the witness from prosecution for the transactions that are the subject matter of the testimony; "use immunity," which is more limited, protects the witness from the use of his incriminating statements and other evidence obtained by virtue of those statements. Thus, the defendant could still be prosecuted for the underlying transactions based on evidence obtained independently. The Supreme Court has held that use immunity is sufficient to compel testimony, despite potential difficulties in determining what evidence may eventually be discovered by the prosecution because of compelled statements.[108]

§ 11-10.   Trade Secrets (FRCP 26(c)(7)).

The term "trade secrets" refers to confidential information that would expose a commercial entity to economic harm if it were revealed. Trade secrets include the fruits of research and development, chemical and physical formulas, mechanical plans and structures, customer lists, confidential data relating to the prices and services provided customers, production expense data, and similar information.[109] Trade secrets constitute the commercial work product of a firm; their revelation would subject the business to a competitive disadvantage. The trade secrets privilege is based on the unfairness of requiring a party who has produced valuable data to disclose it for free to economical rivals.

The trade secrets privilege is conditional. It is embodied in FRCP 26(c)(7) and numerous statutes and authorities.[110] FRCP 26(c)(7) states that a court may grant a protective order to provide "that a trade secret or other confidential research, development, or commercial information not be revealed or be revealed only in a designated way." In applying the privilege, the court balances the need to protect confidential information against the need for disclosure of relevant

---

[107] *Id.* "The test appears to be whether further revelations significantly would add to the risk of prosecution."

[108] Counselman v. Hitchcock, 142 U.S. 547 (1892).

[109] MICHAEL H. GRAHAM, HANDBOOK OF FEDERAL EVIDENCE § 508.1 (3d ed. 1991).

[110] See Proposed FED. R. EVID. 508 advisory committee's note.

facts.[111] Ordinarily, the court should limit the disclosure to information that is truly necessary.[112]

Trial judges often conduct *in camera* reviews of evidence in balancing the competing considerations. This review permits the judge to select material that is necessary to the case and protect other information. Additionally, the judge may adopt other protections — for instance, allowing only the attorneys to review the privileged information, providing it only to experts in the case, or requiring the persons who review it to execute confidentiality agreements.

Often parties assert the trade secrets privilege for information that is not truly confidential or presents no serious risk of competitive injury. The unclear contours of the trade secret category give counsel considerable flexibility to claim it. Thus, the courts must take care to ensure that the privilege is not given too broad an application.

Proposed FRE 508 would have established a qualified privilege for trade secrets so long as "allowance of the privilege will not tend to conceal fraud or otherwise work injustice." It also provided that the judge should take protective measures to protect the legitimate interests of the holder if the judge required disclosure of the privileged information.[113]

§ 11-11. Identity of Informer.

When a confidential informant provides information to law enforcement officials regarding a possible violation of law, disclosure of his identity could lead to reprisals. Additionally, the fear of retaliation would deter people from providing valuable information if an informer's identity could be discovered. Thus, the courts have recognized a privilege to protect the identities of inform-ers.[114]

---

[111] See e.g., Star Scientific, Inc. v. Carter, 204 F.R.D. 410, 415 (S.D. Indiana 2001); Computer Economics Inc. v. Gartner Group, Inc., 50 F.Supp.2d 980, 988 (S.D. Calif. 1999).

[112] Hartley Pen Co. v. United States District Court, 287 F.2d 324, 328 (9th Cir. 1961):

> A trade secret must and should be disclosed when upon a proper showing it is made to appear that such disclosure is relevant and necessary to the proper presentation of a plaintiff's or defendant's case. The delicate problem is to secure the right of one litigant to get relevant and necessary evidence and to protect the other litigant from disclosing secrets which are not relevant and necessary.

[113] Proposed FED. R. EVID. 508 provided:

> A person has a privilege, which may be claimed by him or his agent or employee, to refuse to disclose and to prevent other persons from disclosing a trade secret owned by him, if the allowance of the privilege will not tend to conceal fraud or otherwise work injustice. When disclosure is directed, the judge shall take such protective measure as the interests of the holder of the privilege and of the parties and the furtherance of justice may require.

[114] Proposed FED. R. EVID. 510, which was not enacted, provided:

(Text continued on page 666)

Rule 510. Identity of Informer [Not Enacted].

(a) Rule of privilege. The government or a state or subdivision thereof has a privilege to refuse to disclose the identity of a person who has furnished information relating to or assisting in an investigation of a possible violation of law to a law enforcement officer or member of a legislative committee or its staff conducting an investigation.

(b) Who may claim. The privilege may be claimed by an appropriate representative of the government, regardless of whether the information was furnished to an officer of the government or of a state or subdivision thereof. The privilege may be claimed by an appropriate representative of a state or subdivision if the information was furnished to an officer thereof, except that in criminal cases the privilege shall not be allowed if the government objects.

(c) Exceptions.

(1) Voluntary disclosure; informer a witness. No privilege exists under this rule if the identity of the informer or his interest in the subject matter of his communication has been disclosed to those who would have cause to resent the communication by a holder of the privilege or by the informer's own action, or if the informer appears as a witness for the government.

(2) Testimony on merits. If it appears from the evidence in the case or from other showing by a party that an informer may be able to give testimony necessary to a fair determination of the issue of guilt or innocence in a criminal case or of a material issue on the merits in a civil case to which the government is a party, and the government invokes the privilege, the judge shall give the government an opportunity to show in camera facts relevant to determining whether the informer can, in fact, supply that testimony. The showing will ordinarily be in the form of affidavits, but the judge may direct that testimony be taken if he finds that the matter cannot be resolved satisfactorily upon affidavit. If the judge finds that there is a reasonable probability that the informer can give the testimony, and the government elects not to disclose his identity, the judge on motion of the defendant in a criminal case shall dismiss the charges to which the testimony would relate, and the judge may do so on his own motion. In civil cases, he may make any order that justice requires. Evidence submitted to the judge shall be sealed and preserved to be made available to the appellate court in the event of an appeal, and the contents shall not otherwise be revealed without consent of the government. All counsel and parties shall be permitted to be present at every stage of proceedings under this subdivision except a showing in camera, at which no counsel or party shall be permitted to be present.

(3) Legality of obtaining evidence. If information from an informer is relied upon to establish the legality of the means by which evidence was obtained and the judge is not satisfied that the information was received from an informer reasonably believed to be reliable or credible, he may require the identity of the informer to be disclosed. The judge shall, on request of the government, direct that the disclosure be made in camera. All counsel and parties concerned with the issue of legality shall be permitted to be present at every stage of proceedings under this subdivision except a disclosure in camera, at which no counsel or party shall be permitted to be present. If disclosure of the identity of the informer is made in camera, the record thereof shall be sealed and preserved to be made available to the appellate court in the event of an appeal, and the contents shall not otherwise be revealed without consent of the government.

The privilege is well established at common law.[115] Generally, it belongs to the government and may be claimed by counsel or some other representative of the government. Although the privilege usually is invoked in criminal cases, litigants in civil suits also may claim it.[116] The privilege terminates if disclosure is voluntarily made to persons who would resent the informer's action.[117]

The privilege is qualified and must yield to the need of an accused for information to prepare her defense. The Supreme Court held in *Roviaro v. United States*[118] that a court should balance "the public interest in protecting the flow of information against the individual's right to prepare his defense" and should consider "the crime charged, the possible defenses, the possible significance of the informer's testimony, and other relevant factors."[119] The party opposing the privilege must show that the need for the information is greater than the government's need to invoke the privilege.[120]

The courts have held that the protected information must be important to the defendant's case to outweigh the strong policy considerations supporting the privilege.[121] Disclosure usually is required if the informer is a key witness in the case — for example, an eyewitness to, or a participant in, the crime.[122] Disclosure normally is not required when the information consists only of "tips" that assist investigations or provide support for search warrants.[123]

The privilege does not apply unless the government establishes that the informant provided information with an expectation of anonymity. In *United States Department of Justice v. Landano*,[124] the Supreme Court held that the government has the burden of establishing that the informant expected his identity to be kept confidential; it may not rely on a general presumption that this expectation exists. Particular circumstances such as a high risk of reprisal, however, may justify a presumption that anonymity is expected.

---

[115] Proposed FED. R. EVID. 510 advisory committee's note.

[116] United States v. One 1986 Chevrolet Van, 927 F.2d 39, 43 (1st Cir. 1991).

[117] Roviaro v. United States, 353 U.S. 53 (1957).

[118] *Id*. at 62.

[119] *Id*. See also United States v. Lapsley, 263 F.3d 839, 843 (8th Cir. 2001) (remanding case to trial court for *in camera* hearing to determine if informant's testimony was material enough to require disclosure of his identity).

[120] See, e.g., Emmons v. McLaughlin, 874 F.2d 351 (6th Cir. 1989).

[121] See, e.g., United States v. Spires, 3 F.3d 1234, 1238 (9th. Cir. 1993); United States v. Prueitt, 540 F.2d 995, 1003 (9th Cir. 1976), *cert. denied*, 429 U.S. 1063 (1977).

[122] See, e.g., United States v. Moralez, 917 F.2d 18, 19 (10th Cir. 1990) (disclosure not required where informant was not present during the offense).

[123] See, e.g., United States v. Sanchez, 988 F.2d 1384, 1391 (5th Cir. 1993); United States v. Fryar, 867 F.2d 850, 856 (5th Cir. 1989); United States v. Sherman, 576 F.2d 292 (10th Cir. 1978), *cert. denied*, 439 U.S. 913 (1978).

[124] 508 U.S. 165 (1993).

§ 11-12. State Secrets.

Three types of government privileges are generally recognized in the law. The "state secrets" privilege applies to secrets of the federal government affecting the national defense or international relations. "Executive privilege" protects high level communications among persons responsible for decisions within the executive branch. The deliberative process privilege protects communications within a government department or agency for the purpose of formulating policy. These privileges are discussed below.[125]

---

[125] Proposed FED. R. EVID. 509 would have established government privileges as follows:

Rule 509. Secrets of State and Other Official Information [Not Enacted]

(a) Definitions.

(1) Secret of state. A "secret of state" is a governmental secret relating to the national defense or the international relations of the United States.

(2) Official information. "Official information" is information within the custody or control of a department or agency of the government the disclosure of which is shown to be contrary to the public interest and which consists of: (A) intragovernmental opinions or recommendations submitted for consideration in the performance of decisional or policymaking functions, or (B) subject to the provisions of 18 U.S.C. § 3500, investigatory files compiled for law enforcement purposes and not otherwise available, or (C) information within the custody or control of a governmental department or agency whether initiated within the department or agency or acquired by it in its exercise of its official responsibilities and not otherwise available to the public pursuant to 5 U.S.C. § 552.

(b) General rule of privilege. The government has a privilege to refuse to give evidence and to prevent any person from giving evidence upon a showing of reasonable likelihood of danger that the evidence will disclose a secret of state or official information as defined in this rule.

(c) Procedures. The privilege for secrets of state may be claimed only by the chief officer of the government agency or department administering the subject matter which the secret information sought concerns, but the privilege for official information may be asserted by any attorney representing the government. The required showing may be made in whole or in part in the form of a written statement. The judge may hear the matter in chambers, but all counsel are entitled to inspect the claim and showing and to be heard thereon, except that, in the case of secrets of state, the judge upon motion of the government, may permit the government to make the required showing in the above form in camera. If the judge sustains the privilege upon a showing in camera, the entire text of the government's statements shall be sealed and preserved in the court's records in the event of appeal. In the case of privilege claimed for official information the court may require examination in camera of the information itself. The judge may take any protective measure which the interests of the government and the furtherance of justice may require.

(d) Notice to government. If the circumstances of the case indicate a substantial possibility that a claim of privilege would be appropriate but has not been made because of oversight or lack of knowledge, the judge shall give or cause notice to be given to the officer entitled to claim the privilege and shall stay further proceedings a reasonable time to afford opportunity to assert a claim of privilege.

(e) Effect of sustaining claim. If a claim of privilege is sustained in a proceeding to

§ 11-12(a).   State Secrets.

The privilege for state secrets is absolute when a showing is made that the requested information involves confidential matters of state security.[126] Additionally, the courts generally show great deference to the government when it claims the privilege. If convinced the material is particularly sensitive, the judge should not even inspect it himself.[127]

In *Reynolds v. United States*,[128] the Supreme Court recognized the privilege and established its requirements. The Court determined that the privilege must be claimed by the government officer or supervisor who has control over the requested information; the officer is supposed to consider the privilege issues personally to ensure that the government reasonably invokes the privilege.

The court determines if the government's claim of privilege is reasonable, that is, whether "there is a reasonable danger that disclosure of the particular facts in litigation will jeopardize national security."[129] While performing this analysis, the court must be careful not to "forc[e] a disclosure of the very thing the privilege is designed to protect."[130] An *in camera* review may be conducted so long as the action will not expose information that is too sensitive even for court review. The court must show deference to the government's assertion of privilege in reviewing the material, and "even the most compelling necessity cannot overcome the claim of privilege if the court is ultimately satisfied that military secrets are at stake."[131]

If upholding the privilege prevents the plaintiff from stating a prima facie claim or may cause the jury to reach an erroneous verdict, the court may dismiss the plaintiff's case.[132] The government is not required to subject itself to liability as the price for asserting the state secrets privilege.[133] A claim of privilege may also result in dismissal when the government is prosecutor or plaintiff. Upholding the privilege may force dismissal of a criminal prosecution when the information

---

which the government is a party and it appears that another party is thereby deprived of material evidence, the judge shall make any further orders which the interests of justice require, including striking the testimony of a witness, declaring a mistrial, finding against the government upon an issue as to which the evidence is relevant, or dismissing the action.

[126] United States v. Reynolds, 345 U.S. 1 (1953).

[127] *Id.* at 7–8.

[128] 345 U.S. (1953).

[129] Zuckerbraum v. General Dynamics Corp., 935 F.2d 544, 547 (2d Cir. 1991).

[130] United States v. Reynolds, 345 U.S. 1, 8 (1953).

[131] *Id.* at 11.

[132] Kasza v. Browner, 133 F.3d 1159, 1170–71 (9thCir. 1998) *cert. denied* 525 U.S. 967 (1998); Farnsworth Cannon, Inc. v. Grimes, 635 F.2d 268, 281 (4th Cir. 1980); United States v. Wilson, 586 F. Supp. 1011 (S.D.N.Y. 1983).

[133] McCormick on Evidence § 109 (5th ed. 1999).

is reasonably necessary to the defense.[134] In a civil action, if the plaintiff is the government and withholding the information would deny the defendant due process, the suit may be dismissed.[135] The courts usually attempt to avoid complete dismissal against either side, however, and are increasingly willing to review evidence *in camera* to determine whether sufficient information may be disclosed to avoid this extreme remedy.[136]

§ 11-12(b). Executive Privilege.

The privilege protecting confidential communications of the president and his advisors — and presumably other policymaking officials of the executive branch — is based on the separation of powers doctrine. The privilege was recognized by the Supreme Court in *United States v. Nixon*,[137] where the president claimed the privilege against requests for information in the Watergate prosecution, but it was found to be qualified. The Court determined that the privilege may be overcome by a showing that the requested information is needed for a criminal prosecution.

Because few cases have dealt with the privilege, its scope and application are not well defined. Its purpose is to promote the free flow of information between the president and his advisors. Since the privilege is qualified, an *in camera* inspection and redaction of sensitive material is an appropriate means to balance competing interests. *Nixon* held that the privilege must give way to a need for information in a criminal case, but the same result is likely in civil cases.[138] Indeed, the Freedom of Information Act suggests a legislative trend toward more open public access to information the executive branch may view as sensitive.[139]

In *In re Sealed Case*,[140] the United States Court of Appeals for the District of Columbia Circuit rejected a contention by Secret Service agents and the Secretary of the Treasury that the agents were protected by a "protective function privilege" from disclosing certain information learned in guarding the President. The court determined that the Secret Service "failed to carry its heavy burden under Rule 501 of establishing the need for the protective function privilege" and left "to Congress the question whether a protective function privilege is appropriate . . . and, if so, what the contours of that privilege should be."[141]

---

[134] *Id.*

[135] *Id.*

[136] GRAHAM C. LILLY, AN INTRODUCTION TO THE LAW OF EVIDENCE 515 (3d ed. 1996).

[137] 418 U.S. 683 (1974).

[138] See Dellums v. Powell, 561 F.2d 242 (D.C. Cir. 1977), *cert. denied*, 434 U.S. 880 (1977).

[139] 5 U.S.C. § 552.

[140] 148 F.3d 1078 (D.C. Cir. 1998).

[141] *Id.* at 1079.

The privilege proposed by the Secret Service would have protected "information obtained by Secret Service personnel while performing their protective function in physical proximity to the President," except for observations of activity providing reasonable grounds that a felony has been, is being or will be committed.[142] According to the Secret Service, the privilege is necessary to avoid giving the President reason to push away his protectors because of concerns about confidentiality.

Since the Secret Service requested the recognition of a new privilege, the court of appeals applied the following test: "The Supreme Court requires that a party seeking judicial recognition of a new evidentiary privilege under Rule 501 demonstrate with a high degree of clarity and certainty that the proposed privilege will effectively advance a public good."[143] The Court found that the arguments favoring the privilege were based largely on speculation. Further, it relied on the fact that the Secret Service does not require its agents to keep information confidential after they leave the Secret Service. Additionally, it pointed out that the information protected by the proposed privilege likely would be revealed in private, when the President faced the least danger. Finally, the Court noted a strong Congressional policy, reflected in 28 U.S.C. § 535, indicating that executive officers should reveal criminal misconduct.

In a different, earlier *In re Sealed Case*,[144] the United States Court of Appeals for the District of Columbia Circuit clarified the scope of the executive privilege and the showing of need required to overcome it. In deciding whether the White House was required to turn over to a grand jury documents relating to a White House investigation of allegedly improper conduct by a former Secretary of Agriculture, the Court determined: (a) that executive privilege extends to documents prepared by or for White House staff empowered to advise the President regarding the issues addressed in the documents, even if the documents are not directly reviewed by the President; and (b) to overcome the privilege, the Independent Prosecutor appointed to investigate the alleged improprieties needed to show the documents contained important evidence not available from another source.

The Court held that executive process privilege is not waived by the release of some material on a subject, except as to the released materials.[145] It determined that documents containing statements of the Secretary or his counsel in the course of the White House investigation were not available elsewhere and should be produced.[146] It also ruled that the Independent Counsel on remand

---

[142] *Id.* at 1075.

[143] *Id.* at 1076.

[144] 121 F.3d 729 (D.C. Cir. 1997).

[145] *Id.* at 741.

[146] *Id.* at 762.

should be given an opportunity to make out a showing of need as to other documents.[147]

The Court limited its ruling to material sought in a judicial proceeding; it did not decide "how the institutional needs of Congress and the President should be balanced."[148] Additionally, since the deliberative process privilege provides less protection to executive documents than executive privilege, the Court deemed it unnecessary to address the contours of that privilege.[149]

§ 11-12(c). Deliberative Process Privilege.

The deliberative process privilege is related to, but broader than, executive privilege. It protects the process by which government agencies and other decisionmakers formulate their decisions. The privilege promotes frank communication and consideration of competing arguments within the deliberative process; without the privilege, this give-and-take might later be used against the policy makers in an attack on their decision.[150] Additionally, the privilege shields government decisionmakers from submitting to interrogation regarding their mental processes and deliberations.[151] The privilege is based in part on the theory that agency orders should be reviewed on their merit rather than on the process by which they are reached.

The Freedom of Information Act and Administrative Procedure Act sharply reduce the scope of the deliberative process privilege. The Freedom of Information Act opens the door to discovery of information within government files and, although it excepts from discovery certain deliberative information, prevents a claim of privilege as to data that must be revealed under the statute.[152] The Administrative Procedure Act[153] establishes rules for reaching agency decisions and necessarily contemplates discovery on whether the rules were obeyed. Nevertheless, neither act requires disclosure of true deliberative processes.

The privilege is qualified. In applying it, a court should balance the need for and importance of the information against the potential effect on the deliberative

---

[147] *Id.*

[148] *Id.* at 753.

[149] *Id.* at 740, 758.

[150] See Hinckley v. United States, 140 F.3d 277, 284 (D.C. Cir. 1998) (court defines communications as "deliberative" if they are " 'part of the agency give and take by which the decision itself is made.' "). See also Carl Zeiss Shiftung v. V.E.B. Carl Zeizz, Jena, 40 F.R.D. 318, 325–26 (D.D.C. 1966), *aff'd*, 384 F.2d 979 (D.C. Cir. 1967), *cert. denied*, 389 U.S. 952 (1976).

[151] United States v. Morgan, 313 U.S. 409 (1941).

[152] MCCORMICK ON EVIDENCE § 108 (5th ed. 1999): "[I]t would be anomalous in the extreme to deny evidentiary admission on grounds of confidentiality to material available on request to even the casually interested."

[153] 5 U.S.C. 551 *et seq.* and 701 *et seq.*

process.[154] Generally, the privilege does not extend to purely factual information compiled by an agency.[155] If the compilation involves selection of relevant data or an evaluation of the data, however, it is covered by the privilege.[156]

§ 11-13. Communications to Clergymen.

A privilege for communications with clergy was not firmly recognized at common law but has been codified by statute and recognized in decisions in most of the United States.[157] The Supreme Court endorsed the privilege in *Trammel v. United States*,[158] when it stated that the privilege protects the individual's need for a confidential exchange with a spiritual counselor regarding human flaws. The Court said:

> The privileges between priest and penitent, attorney and client, and physician and patient . . . are rooted in the imperative need for confidence and trust. The priest-penitent privilege recognizes the human need to disclose to a spiritual counselor, in total and absolute confidence, what are believed to be flawed acts or thoughts and to receive priestly consolation and guidance in return.[159]

The privilege also has a practical basis. Spiritual counselors answer to a higher power than the law and are not likely to disclose information privately confided to them. They should not be subject to sanctions for obeying their consciences.

Generally, the clergy-communicant privilege has been recognized and approved by the federal courts.[160] Following *Trammel*, the Seventh Circuit

---

[154] See Abramson v. United States, 39 Fed. Cl. 290 (Fed. Cl. 1997); STEPHEN A. SALTZBURG, MICHAEL M. MARTIN, AND DANIEL J. CAPRA, FEDERAL RULES OF EVIDENCE MANUAL 501-71, 72 (8th ed. 2001).

[155] STEPHEN A. SALTZBURG, MICHAEL M. MARTIN, AND DANIEL J. CAPRA, FEDERAL RULES OF EVIDENCE MANUAL 501-71, 72 (8th ed. 2001).

[156] *Id.*

[157] Proposed FED. R. EVID. 506 advisory committee's note: "In this country . . . the privilege has been recognized by statute in about two-thirds of the states and occasionally by the common law process of decision." JOHN C. BUSH & WILLIAM H. TIEMANN, THE RIGHT TO SILENCE 111 (3d ed. 1989).

[158] 445 U.S. 40 (1980).

[159] *Id.* at 51.

[160] Proposed FED. R. EVID. 506 would have established a privilege as follows:

Rule 506. Communications to Clergymen [Not Enacted]

(a) Definitions. As used in this rule:

(1) A "clergyman" is a minister, priest, rabbi, or other similar functionary of a religious organization, or an individual reasonably believed so to be by the person consulting him.

(2) A communication is "confidential" if made privately and not intended for further disclosure except to other persons present in the furtherance of the purpose of the communication.

approved of the clergy-communicant privilege; upholding its use concerning religious counseling and communications but not business communications with a clergyman.[161] The Third Circuit more specifically defined the parameters of the privilege in *In re Grand Jury Investigation.*[162] It held that the privilege applies to communications made "(1) to a clergyperson (2) in his or her spiritual and professional capacity (3) with a reasonable expectation of confidentiality."[163] The court stressed that "the presence of third parties, if essential to and in furtherance of the communication, should not void the privilege"[164] and held the privilege should cover communications between communicants and clergy of all denominations.[165] The court left for case-by-case evaluation questions such as whether a clergyperson must disclose to authorities communications that involve threatened and imminent harm to third parties.[166] In *Eckmann v. Board of Education,*[167] the court said "[t]he 'priest-penitent' privilege has clearly been recognized by federal courts" and that it could be utilized by a Catholic nun to shield communications she received while serving as a spiritual advisor.[168]

The privilege belongs to the individual who communicates confidential information to a member of the clergy. The clergyperson can claim the privilege on his behalf, however, and the authority to do so should be presumed.[169]

(b) General rule of privilege. A person has a privilege to refuse to disclose and to prevent another from disclosing a confidential communication by the person to a clergyman in his professional character as spiritual adviser.

(c) Who may claim the privilege. The privilege may be claimed by the person, by his guardian or conservator, or by his personal representative if he is deceased. The clergyman may claim the privilege on behalf of the person. His authority so to do is presumed in the absence of evidence to the contrary.

[161] United States v. Dube, 820 F.2d 886 (7th Cir. 1987); see also United States v. Gordon, 655 F.2d 478 (2d Cir. 1981).

[162] 918 F.2d 374 (3d Cir. 1990).

[163] *Id.* at 384 (footnote omitted).

[164] *Id.*

[165] *Id.* at 385.

[166] *Id.*; see also 8 WIGMORE ON EVIDENCE § 2285 (McNaughton rev. ed. 1961); Yellin, *History and Current Status of the Clergy-Penitent Privilege*, 42 SANTA CLARA L. REV. 95 (1983).

[167] 106 F.R.D. 70 (E.D. Mo. 1985).

[168] *Id.* at 72; In Seidman v. Fishburn-Hudgins Educational Foundation, however, the Fourth Circuit held that the decedent's relative could not invoke the privilege on the decedent's behalf, and stated that the privilege "has no firm foundation in common law." 724 F.2d 413, 415 (4th Cir. 1984).

[169] See Proposed FED. R. EVID. 506(c) advisory committee's note. The committee states that the privilege belongs to the communicator, but "a prima facie authority on the part of the clergyman to claim the privilege is recognized."

§ 11-14. Psychotherapist-Patient Communications.

Virtually all the states recognize a psychotherapist-patient privilege by statute or rule.[170] The privilege did not exist at common law, however, and initially received mixed acceptance in the federal courts. The proposed federal rules contained a provision establishing the privilege, but it was not adopted by Congress.[171]

---

[170] See Proposed FED. R. EVID. 504 advisory committee's note.

[171] Proposed FED. R. EVID. 504 provided:

Rule 504. Psychotherapist-patient Privilege [Not Enacted]

(a) Definitions.

(1) A "patient" is a person who consults or is examined or interviewed by a psychotherapist.

(2) A "psychotherapist" is (A) a person authorized to practice medicine in any state or nation, or reasonably believed by the patient so to be, while engaged in the diagnosis or treatment of a mental or emotional condition, including drug addiction, or (B) a person licensed or certified as a psychologist under the laws of any state or nation, while similarly engaged.

(3) A communication is "confidential" if not intended to be disclosed to third persons other than those present to further the interest of the patient in the consultation, examination, or interview, or persons reasonably necessary for the transmission of the communication, or persons who are participating in the diagnosis and treatment under the direction of the psychotherapist, including members of the patient's family.

(b) General rule of privilege. A patient has a privilege to refuse to disclose and to prevent any other person from disclosing confidential communications, made for the purposes of diagnosis or treatment of his mental or emotional condition, including drug addiction, among himself, his psychotherapist, or persons who are participating in the diagnosis or treatment under the direction of the psychotherapists, including members of the patient's family.

(c) Who may claim the privilege. The privilege may be claimed by the patient, by his guardian or conservator, or by the personal representative of a deceased patient. The person who was the psychotherapist may claim the privilege but only on behalf of the patient. His authority to do so is presumed in the absence of evidence to the contrary.

(d) Exceptions.

(1) Proceedings for hospitalization. There is no privilege under this rule for communications relevant to an issue in proceedings to hospitalize the patient for mental illness, if the psychotherapist in the course of diagnosis or treatment has determined that the patient is in need of hospitalization.

(2) Examination by order of judge. If the judge orders an examination of the mental or emotional condition of the patient, communications made in the course thereof are not privileged under this rule with respect to the particular purpose for which the examination is ordered unless the judge orders otherwise.

(3) Condition an element of claim or defense. There is no privilege under this rule as to communications relevant to an issue of the mental or emotional condition of the

In *Jaffee v. Redmond*,[172] the Supreme Court recognized a psychotherapist-patient privilege. The Court analogized the psychotherapist-patient privilege to the attorney-client privilege and the spousal privilege. All these privileges are "rooted in the imperative need for confidence and trust."[173]

The Court gave two primary reasons for recognizing the privilege. First, the privilege allows the psychotherapist to successfully treat his patient's mental or emotional needs. "Effective psychotherapy . . . depends upon an atmosphere of confidence and trust in which the patient is willing to make a frank and complete disclosure of facts, emotions, memories, and fears."[174] The psychiatrist's ability to help her patients is dependent on their belief that the communications will be confidential. The mere possibility that others could learn of their communications would shut down the utility of their relationship. Without frank and complete communication, the psychiatrist's ability to give a successful treatment of her patient's mental or emotional needs would be diminished. Second, "[t]he psychotherapist privilege serves the public interest by facilitating the provision of appropriate treatment for individuals suffering the effects of a mental or emotional problem. The mental health of our citizenry, no less than its physical health, is a public good of transcendent importance."[175]

The Court explained that the privilege covers statements to licensed psychiatrists, psychologists and licensed social workers. It also determined the privilege should not be subject to a balancing test, adopted by the court of appeal, which weighed the patient's interest in preventing disclosure versus the need for the information. The court indicated the privilege is more absolute, but did not define its contours.[176]

The Ninth Circuit held in *Oleszko v. State Compensation Insurance Fund*[177] that communications between employees and unlicenced counselors employed by Employee Assistance Programs are covered by the privilege. Communications between these counselors play an important role in increasing access to mental health treatment. The court concluded that confidentiality was necessary for these counselors and programs to function effectively.

---

patient in any proceeding in which he relies upon the condition as an element of his claim or defense, or, after the patient's death, in any proceeding in which any party relies upon the condition as an element of his claim or defense.

[172] 518 U.S. 1 (1996).

[173] *Id.* at 9 (quoting Trammel v. United States, 445 U.S. 40, 51 (1980).

[174] *Id.*

[175] *Id.* at 11.

[176] *Id.* at 17-18. But see Schoffstall v. Henderson, 233 F.3d 818, 823 (8th Cir. 2000) (holding that by putting his or her mental health at issue, a defendant waives the psychotherapist-patient privilege).

[177] 243 F.3d. 1154 (9th Cir. 2000).

The Sixth Circuit in *United States v. Hayes*[178] rejected the contention that the Supreme Court intended a "dangerous patient" exception to the psychotherapist-patient privilege. The Government in Hayes relied on the following passage from the footnote in *Jaffe v. Redmond*[179] in contending that a psychotherapist could testify in a prosecution against the defendant for threats made during therapy: "We do not doubt that there are situations in which the privilege must give way, for example, if a serious threat of harm to the patient or to others can be averted only by means of disclosure by the therapist."[180] The Sixth Circuit ruled, however, that the Supreme Court's statement was an "aside" that simply recognized the therapist's professional duty to disclose communications when necessary to protect the patient or third persons from harm — for example, in commitment proceedings.[181] It determined that there is insufficient justification for recognizing the exception in a subsequent prosecution of the patient. In doing so, the court rejected an approach taken by the Tenth Circuit, which recognized the exception but narrowed it to situations where the threat is serious when made and disclosure is the only means of preventing harm.[182]

§ 11-15. Doctor-Patient Privilege.

Many states recognize a privilege for statements from a patient to a physician for the purpose of treatment. Although recognized in dicta in *Trammel v. United States*,[183] the doctor-patient privilege generally has not received acceptance in the federal courts.[184] The proposed federal rules did not contain a provision to establish a doctor-patient privilege.

The privilege varies among jurisdictions, but it usually protects information given a doctor for treatment and information obtained by the doctor through examination and tests.[185] It would not typically protect information communicated for some other purpose, such as a life insurance examination. The privilege promotes full disclosure of potentially embarrassing information between patient and physician. It is probably unnecessary to ensure that a sick person is frank with his doctor, however, and therefore must be justified on privacy grounds.[186]

The biggest problem with a doctor-patient privilege is the need for doctor testimony in many cases and the extensive use of physicians as experts. A large

---

[178] 227 F.3d 578 (6th Cir. 2000).

[179] 518 U.S. 1 (1996).

[180] *Id.* at 18 n.19.

[181] 227 F.3d at 585.

[182] United States v. Glass, 133 F.3d 1356 (10th Cir. 1998).

[183] 445 U.S. 40, 45 (1980).

[184] See e.g., United States v. Moore, 970 F.2d 48, 50 (5th Cir. 1992); United States v. Barker, 848 F.2d 917 (8th Cir. 1988).

[185] GRAHAM C. LILLY, AN INTRODUCTION TO THE LAW OF EVIDENCE 480 (3d ed. 1996).

[186] *Id.*

number of lawsuits involve personal injuries; a diagnosis often is essential to determine causation and both diagnosis and treatment are relevant to damages. Doctors necessarily rely on patients' statements in forming their opinions, so it is unfair to protect these communications from disclosure if the doctor testifies. Additionally, since a non-testifying physician may know facts important to deciding liability or causation, it may be unfair to deny his testimony to the adverse party. Doctors often are central players in the litigation process.

If communications to doctors are made accessible in cases in which their testimony is relevant, a general rule of privilege protecting the communications makes little sense. Instead, courts can protect irrelevant and sensitive communications under the general burdensomeness test in FRCP 26(b)(2).

§ 11-16. Reports Required and Privileged by Statute.

Often the government requires a person or organization to submit reports, but at the same time provides that the reports are confidential. The required reports privilege protects the person who makes the report from being required to produce it in a lawsuit and from production of the report by the government. The privilege coordinates the evidentiary rules with statutory provisions, promotes compliance with statutes, preserves a citizen's reasonable expectation of confidentiality, and may avoid conflicts between reporting requirements and the privilege against self-incrimination.[187]

The proposed federal privilege rules contained a required reports privilege, based in part on a "reluctance to compel disclosure" manifested in the authorities.[188] The authorities suggest that the privilege extends not only to reports protected by federal law, but to those made confidential by state law. The case law does not extend absolute protection to the reports, however; the privilege may be overcome by need. As an example, when the federal government asserts the need for a state to disclose privileged information relevant to a federal prosecution, the federal courts generally weigh the potential benefits of disclosure

---

[187] Proposed FED. R. EVID. 502 advisory committee's note.

[188] *Id.* Proposed FED. R. EVID. 502 provided:

Rule 502. Required Reports Privileged by Statute [Not Enacted]

A person, corporation, association, or other organization or entity, either public or private, making a return or report required by law to be made has a privilege to refuse to disclose and to prevent any other person from disclosing the return or report, if the law requiring it to be made so provides. A public officer or agency to whom a return or report is required by law to be made has a privilege to refuse to disclose the return or report if the law requiring it to be made so provides. No privilege exists under this rule in actions involving perjury, false statements, fraud in the return or report, or other failure to comply with the law in questions.

against its potential damage.[189] If the need outweighs the state's interest in protecting the information, the state must disclose it.

§ 11-17. Political Vote.

A privilege of a citizen not to disclose his vote is essential to democratic government.[190] Therefore, "a privilege has long been recognized for a voter to decline to disclose how he voted."[191] The privilege does not extend, however, to ballots that are cast illegally.[192] In appropriate circumstances, an illegal voter may still claim the privilege against self-incrimination.[193]

§ 11-18. Journalistic Privilege.

In *Brownsburg v. Hayes*,[194] the Supreme Court rejected the argument that the First Amendment protects a journalist's sources from government inquiry. Nor was a newsperson's privilege included in the proposed federal rules. Nevertheless, many federal courts recognize a qualified privilege that protects journalists' sources and unpublished resource materials from disclosure.[195] The privilege must yield when a party demonstrates "a sufficiently compelling need for the journalist's materials to overcome the privilege."[196]

The privilege avoids an undue interference with journalists' access to sources; if government could easily compel disclosure of the identities of informers, press scrutiny of government would diminish. Additionally, the privilege limits the instances in which the judiciary imposes its will on the press, which necessarily

---

[189] See, e.g., In Re Grand Jury Subpoena, 596 F.2d 630, 632 (4th Cir. 1979); Matter of Special April 1977 Grand Jury, 581 F.2d 589, 592–93 (7th Cir. 1978), *cert. denied*, 439 U.S. 1046 (1978); Matter of Grand Jury Impaneled Jan. 21, 1975, 541 F.2d 373, 378–83 (3d Cir. 1976)). See In Re Hampers, 651 F.2d 19, 22 (1st Cir. 1981).

[190] Proposed FED. R. EVID. provided:

> **Rule 507. Political Vote [Not Enacted]**
>
> Every person has a privilege to refuse to disclose the tenor of his vote at a political election conducted by secret ballot unless the vote was cast illegally.

See also Charles B. Nutting, *Freedom of Silence: Constitutional Protection Against Governmental Intrusions in Political Affairs*, 47 MICH. L. REV. 181, 193–95 (1948).

[191] Proposed FED. R. EVID. 507 advisory committee's note.

[192] *Id.*

[193] *Id.*

[194] 408 U.S. 665 (1972).

[195] E.g., United States v. LaRouche Campaign, 841 F.2d 1176, 1182 (1st Cir. 1988). See GRAHAM C. LILLY, AN INTRODUCTION TO THE LAW OF EVIDENCE 491 (3d ed. 1996): "[A] qualified privilege protecting not only the identity of sources, but unpublished information gained in the course of journalistic investigation is now widely accepted under the federal common law under Rule 50."

[196] Shoen v. Shoen, 5 F.3d 1289, 1296 (9th Cir. 1993).

creates a First Amendment tension. The privilege also reflects a practical reality: many journalists would not divulge their sources even if ordered to do so. News organizations may be expected to fight disclosure of confidential information, consuming the resources of both the press and the judiciary. Thus, a qualified evidentiary privilege promotes strong policies, especially in a society that depends on the press to curb the excesses of government.

§ 11-19. Other Potential Privileges.

Claims have been made for the establishment of other privileges, but they generally have not been adopted by the federal courts.[197] The asserted privileges include accountant-client, parent-child, bank-depositor, researcher, and institutional self-evaluation. While reluctant to adopt new privileges, the courts may indirectly recognize the considerations supporting them by giving special content to the burdensomeness of disclosure under FRCP 26(b)(2). Thus, a reasonable claim of privilege may aid a party in protecting sensitive information.

---

[197] STEPHEN A. SALTZBURG, MICHAEL M. MARTIN, AND DANIEL J. CAPRA, FEDERAL RULES OF EVIDENCE MANUAL 501-89 (8th ed. 2001).

CHAPTER 12

CLOSING ARGUMENT

---

§ 12-1.   Introduction.

Closing argument, or summation, is often thought of as a dramatic, theatrical oration. Young lawyers and students dream of winning cases in summation through the force of their speaking skills. In movies and the theater, the hero's summation often carries a reluctant or undecided jury to a favorable verdict. Sometimes a lawyer is portrayed as winning with a new and amazing explanation of the facts. The fictional summation usually depends as much on personal appeal as a compelling case.

In practice, the closing argument usually is not so dramatic. A lawyer does not have to be a genius at oration to be effective. A good closing need not be theatrical; a methodical discussion of evidence, fact, and law is even more persuasive. Indeed, a solid, fact-based presentation is essential to convincing jurors who have seen the evidence.

At the same time, closing arguments have a special place in advocacy. The summation is counsel's chance to wrap up the case, explain the evidence, synthesize conflicting facts, and tie together the facts and the law. It provides the attorney's last chance to speak with the jury. This part of the trial is also a contest, in which the opposing attorneys openly attack each others' arguments. A juror justifiably may expect the summations to be interesting, adversary, and compelling. Thus, the jurors may perk up for the summations.

This chapter discusses the appropriate content and delivery of the Closing Argument, Sections 12-3–12-5 address the purpose of the Closing Argument and the rules governing this presentation, §§ 12-6–12-12 discusses the content and delivery of the closing argument, and §§ 12-13–12-15 provide a sample outline and examples of Closing Arguments. Sections 12-16–12-17 address post-trial submissions.

§ 12-2.   Importance of Closing Argument.

Just as the first impression is important in persuasion, so is the last. Listeners often give close attention to the last thing a speaker has to say. The closing is your formal opportunity to persuade the jury. The focus on argument, the conflict between the parties, and the finality of the event should provide a good forum for argument. Thus, the closing provides a great opportunity to make a last impression.

Many jurors have reached tentative conclusions by the time of the closing arguments, but some often are undecided. Convincing these "swing votes" may make the difference between victory and defeat. The closing argument also may solidify those jurors who are leaning toward voting in your favor. The closing is the chance to complete logical connections that may not be apparent, answer lingering questions, and refute the arguments of the opposing party.

Additionally, the closing argument provides the jurors' first exposure to the jury instructions. Most jurors try to fulfill their duty to comply with legal requirements. The jury instructions often are lengthy, boring, and full of legalese, however, and laymen do not easily absorb them. Thus, if you emphasize a key instruction, blending a favorable legal principle with your factual theme, you may convince wavering jurors.[1]

The closing arguments come at a time when the jurors have heard the evidence. Most likely, they are eager to begin deliberations. Many jurors probably are thinking of arguments they can use to lead others to conclusions. In this situation you have an opportunity to lead the deliberations. By providing the basis for a favorable decision, linking the evidence to fact conclusions and reasoning with the jury about conflicting arguments, you start the deliberative process. If you document your conclusions effectively, your arguments will be repeated in the jury room.

In most jurisdictions the closing arguments follow the order in which the parties present evidence. The party with the burden — the plaintiff or prosecution — goes first, followed by the defendant, after which the plaintiff or prosecution provides rebuttal. In some jurisdictions there are only two presentations; the defendant goes first and the plaintiff or prosecutor speaks last. In either case, the party with the main burden has the last word.

Closing argument is a special, compelling event in advocacy. It is the climactic act in the trial drama. You must assimilate the evidence, mix the facts with the law, advocate the justness of the cause, and combat the arguments of the opposing attorney. In the process, you must show the belief and conviction necessary to persuade others. This endeavor is not easy, requiring skill and hard work, and a good closing argument is a high professional achievement.

---

[1] See HARRY KALVEN, JR. AND HANS ZEISEL, THE AMERICAN JURY (1966); Valerie P. Hans and Neil Vidmar, *The American Jury at Twenty-five Years,* 16 LAW AND SOC. INQUIRY 323 (1991); Norbert L. Kerr, *Trial Participants' Behaviors and Jury Verdicts: An Explanatory Field Study,* in THE CRIMINAL JUSTICE SYSTEM: A SOCIAL-PSYCHOLOGICAL ANALYSIS 261, 268 (Vladimir J. Konecni and Ebbe B. Ebbensen eds., 1982).

§ 12-3. Purposes of Closing Argument.

Unlike the opening statement, the closing argument *is* designed to permit you to argue your case. In closing, you explain the reasons why the evidence supports your factual contentions, argue the credibility of witnesses, and show why the facts and the law require a favorable verdict. The closing argument is a mix of facts, inferences, equity, and law, and requires a simple and logical blend of these elements into a forceful theme.[2] Additionally, it is an opportunity to display, with sincerity and emotion, your total belief in the client's case.

Paradoxically, the closing argument comes at a time when most of the jurors at least are leaning toward one side or the other. The average person would have a difficult time sitting through an entire trial without forming a conclusion as to who should prevail. Thus, you generally do not argue to jurors with open minds.

The closing argument serves two primary purposes. The first, of course, is persuasion. Even if most of the jurors have a favorite, some still may be undecided. Additionally, the jurors who already are leaning may still be subject to persuasion; most people see some merit in both sides of a case, and a strong closing may change their view of which party is "more right." Further, jurors sometimes miss essential points during the trial and explaining these matters may change their opinions.

The second purpose of the summation is to document the basis for a favorable verdict. You should support your factual claims with evidence and show that the evidence does not support the opposing party. This approach gives ammunition to those on the jury who support your position. The jurors can use these arguments in deliberations to persuade undecided jurors and counter the contentions of those who support your opponent.

Documenting a position is more methodical than dramatic. You need to show the jurors how the evidence supports fact conclusions. You must refer specifically to testimony and documents, reading or showing key material to the jurors. Rather than depending on rhetoric, you must demonstrate the evidentiary basis for winning. Your logic should be direct and easy to follow. One-step logic, in which the conclusion flows directly from each ground, serves this purpose.

Fortunately, persuading the jurors and documenting a position are compatible. A strong evidentiary basis gives credibility and power to a fact portrayal. You can combine a dramatic "word picture" with a step-by-step explanation of why

---

[2] See Craig Lee Monitz, *Why Lawyers Continue to Cross the Line in Closing Argument.* 28 Ohio N.U.L. Rev. 67, 73 (2001) ("Proper jury argument consists of: '(1) summation of the evidence, (2) reasonable deductions from the evidence, (3) an answer to the argument of opposing counsel. . .' ."(citing Felder v. State, 848 S.W. 2nd 85, 94-5 (Tex. Crim. App.1992) *cert denied* 528 U.S. 1067 (1999)). See also John J. Cleary, *The Final Argument in a Criminal Case,* 27 Prac. Law 39-53 (1981); William R. Colson, *Final Argument,* 36 Miss. L.J. 500-04 (1964-65).

it is the only justified interpretation of the evidence. In pursuing both goals of a closing argument, you should achieve a compelling presentation.

In the closing, you "sum up" the trial, showing how the evidence supports a fact picture and why the law ordains a favorable result. You should "tie the knots," explaining the *reasons* for your conclusions. Use simple logic, employ a factual theme, and call on accepted views of fairness. You also must apply the law, based on the court's instructions, but in most cases the facts are the most important factor in the verdict. Thus, documenting the word picture should be your primary goal.

§ 12-4. Improper or Questionable Practices in Closing Argument.

The following practices are improper or require cautionary instructions if they are used in closing argument.

1. *"Golden rule" argument.* You may not ask the jurors to put themselves in the place of a party or treat the party as the jurors would like to be treated themselves.[3] An acceptable technique is to ask how "any reasonable person" would feel, react, or respond. Because jurors believe themselves to be "reasonable," the technique should accomplish your purpose.

2. *Personal attestation.* You may not express a personal belief in the credibility of a witness, the justness of a cause, or the validity of the case.[4] Thus, you may not state: "I believe the plaintiff, and you should too." Nevertheless, you may unequivocally state that the witness is telling the truth: "You should believe Ms. Brown because she is telling the truth."

    Attorneys often use phrases such as "I think" or "I believe" as part of everyday conversation. Some find it difficult to eradicate this terminology at trial. The rule really is not designed to prevent this sort of conversational filler, but the true attestation: "I can tell you from the bottom of my heart that Ms. Baron is telling the truth."[5] Nevertheless, you should stay away from "attestation" terminology to the extent possible.

3. *"Conscience of the community" argument.* You may not rely on the parties' relative popular appeal, identities, or geographical location to

---

[3] See Whitehead v. Food Max of Mississippi, 163 F.3d 265, 278 (5th Cir. 1998) (holding "[s]uch [golden rule] arguments encourage the jury to 'decide the case on the basis of personal interest and bias rather than on the evidence.' "(citing Loose v. Offshore Navigation, 670 F.2d 495, 496 (5th Cir. 1982)).

[4] MODEL RULES OF PROFESSIONAL CONDUCT RULE 3.7.

[5] See Robert L. Carlson and Michael S. Carlson, *"Over the Top" Final Arguments: How Far is Too Far?* 49-JAN FED. LAW. 37, 38 (2002) ("While a few 'I believe' statements mark most attorneys' arguments, they only become inappropriate when they refer to the guilt or fault of an opposing party or the credibility of witnesses. . . .").

prejudice the viewpoint of jurors. Thus, for example, it would be improper to argue that the jury should favor the hometown corporation over an out-of-state corporation.[6]

4.　*Inflammatory comments.* You should not engage in personal attacks or inflammatory rhetoric regarding a party or opposing counsel.[7] This sort of conduct often is prohibited by rules of court. Additionally, it often distracts the jurors from the issues and places them in the difficult position of choosing between counsel. A professional approach is best.

5.　*Limitation on "unit of time" argument.* Many jurisdictions permit "unit of time" arguments, but courts generally view the arguments as potentially prejudicial. The "unit of time" argument invites the jury to compensate the plaintiff for each day, hour, heartbeat, or other time unit that the plaintiff has suffered or will suffer. This approach can build to astronomical totals. The court may give a cautionary instruction to ameliorate the impact of the argument.[8]

6.　*Personal knowledge of counsel.* Generally, you may not argue facts that are matters of personal knowledge or opinion. You may refer, however, to matters that are general knowledge. Thus, the attorney could refer to Louisiana as a southern state even if this fact had not been proven; you might not be able to describe the appearance of a particular street.

7.　*Reference to evidence not admitted.* It is improper to refer to evidence that was excluded by the court.

8.　*Misstating the law.* You should be careful to accurately paraphrase the jury instructions. It is improper to state the law inaccurately. Of course, you should also acknowledge the court's lawgiving role when referring to instructions.

9.　*Comments upon court's rulings.* You may not suggest that the court's evidentiary rulings were improper.

§ 12-5.　Objections During the Closing Argument.

Objections should be relatively infrequent during closing arguments, but if they are necessary, you should not be afraid to assert them. You should phrase the objection to explain in lay terms the unfairness of the opposing lawyer's action, so that the jury will know there is good reason for the interruption. If the objection is not that important, however, you may wish to pass it up. Objections are likely

---

[6] See Guaranty Serv. Corp. v. American Employers' Ins. Co., 893 F.2d 725 (5th Cir. 1990).

[7] See Fineman v. Armstrong World Indus., Inc., 774 F.Supp. 266, 271 (D.N.J. 1991) (in granting new trial on defense motion based on plaintiff attorney's misconduct, court found "[p]erhaps most troubling . . . the unadorned, disparaging attack upon defense counsel through [plaintiff attorney's] closing argument.").

[8] See Colburn v. Bunge Towing, Inc., 883 F.2d 372 (5th Cir. 1989).

to produce retaliation, and you want to speak unimpeded during your own closing. Also, you should consider whether the objection will unduly emphasize harmful material.

§ 12-6. Essentials of a Good Closing Argument.

A good closing argument serves the twin purposes of persuasion and documentation. You should for a time enter the deliberative process, reasoning with the jurors about the meaning of the evidence. You should provide a simple, logical basis for a favorable ruling. The attributes needed to achieve these goals include the following.

§ 12-6(a). Efficiency.

The summations occur at the end of the trial, when the jurors are tired. They want to get into deliberations and decide the case. You should use time efficiently, making them feel that listening is productive. Do not take too much time. Generally, you should argue the facts, with an occasional use of the law. Stay away from "boilerplate" civics lessons; the judge can tell the jury its role in deciding the case. For a criminal defendant, you may have to rely on burdens or presumptions, but most litigants should argue a version of the facts.

Choose a simple, direct organization and follow it. In a simple trial, the summation should not be longer than about 30 minutes. Most people have difficulty paying attention to any speaker for a more extended period, so you do not lose anything by planning a crisp summation.

§ 12-6(b). Theme.

A theme is just as important in the closing argument as it is in the opening statement. The *same theme* should run throughout the trial.[9] The theme usually reflects central facts. You should build your closing argument around the theme, calling attention to it at the beginning, dramatizing it in the word picture, using it to argue evidence and inferences, and referring to it at the end. A theme gives staying power to any presentation.

§ 12-6(c). Documentation.

Since a major function of the closing argument is to demonstrate how the evidence supports your version of the facts, you should openly document your

---

[9] See Costopoulos, *Commentaries: Persuasion in the Courtroom,* 10 DUQ. L. REV. 384 (1972). See also Ervin A. Gonzalez, *Winning Trail Themes When Representing Ethnic Clients*, 1 Ann. 2000 ATLA CLE 593 (2000) ("It is important to discover the heart of the case early enough in the litigation so that the winning theme may be developed through discovery and properly presented to the jury. Once established, the theme should tell the jury in very few words what the case is really about."); Jim M. Perdue, Sr. and Jim M. Perdue, Jr. *Trial Themes: Winning Jurors' Minds and Hearts*, 34-APR TRIAL 34, 37 (1998) ("A theme must incorporate ideas and values that achieve the widest level of acceptance. Research suggests that jurors deliberate in themes.").

points. Rather than merely paraphrasing the evidence, you should use exhibits, charts, and actual testimony. Demonstrate how pieces of hard evidence establish facts or refute opposing points. This approach gives a concrete quality to your arguments.

You should use demonstrative exhibits to grab the jury's attention and illustrate general points. The demonstrative exhibits often do not have the same concreteness, however, as real evidence. Bringing out fingerprint samples, blood specimens, and similar solid items, and using them to support fact conclusions, gives your contentions an air of substance. You should exhibit the key items — holding them in front of the jurors — in reviewing how they prove your assertions.

Reading back key portions of testimony is another way to document a point. If a transcript is available, you can read important passages to drive home the witness's actual words. You should keep it short, however; nothing turns listeners off more quickly than reading a lengthy discourse. Another effective approach is to use notes made during the trial that summarize testimony. You can refer to the notes as you describe what the witness said, giving credibility to your description. You must, of course, be accurate in depicting the testimony.

By documenting your claims, you give content to your points and provide evidentiary keys for the jurors to discuss in deliberations. Thus, you serve the goal of persuasion while providing the basis on which the jurors can reason to a favorable conclusion.

§ 12-6(d).   Simplicity.

The closing argument should be simple and easy to follow. The spoken word is elusive; listeners rarely remember details of an oral presentation, or exact words, for more than a few moments. Thus, you should build the closing around main thematic points. You should have a simple overall structure. Your logical connections should be direct and understandable. You should use signposts to signal transitions and focus attention on important matters. "Lay out" what you are trying to say, so that the jurors do not have to work to follow your presentation.

§ 12-6(e).   Conviction.

In summation, you should demonstrate a total belief in this client's case. You are *supposed* to argue in closing argument; the judge and jurors expect it. Further, you can expect the jurors to accept your conclusions only if you appear to believe in them. An attorney who distances himself from client or phrases arguments as if they are doubtful cannot persuade others that his client is right. You are not allowed to personally attest to your client's position — by saying the words "I believe" — but your manner should say it for you. See § 12-4.

§ 12-6(f).   Spontaneity.

The closing argument provides an opportunity to reason with the jurors. In a good summation, you figuratively act as the jury's discussion leader for deliberations. To accomplish this goal you need a conversational style. You have to look at the jurors, hold their interest, and conduct a lively one-way "discussion." A prepared script does not allow this spontaneity. You need a well-prepared closing argument — preferably, one you have rehearsed — but it must permit a lively, conversational presentation.

§ 12-7.   Preparation of the Closing Argument.

You should begin the preparation of the closing argument even before the beginning of the trial. Indeed, your "word picture" and theme should be the same as those you present in your opening statement. The common theme has the advantage of facilitating preparation. In most cases, you know essential contentions — and those of your opponent — before the trial begins. Thus, you can outline and rehearse the closing before the trial and "fine tune" it for consistency with the evidence as the trial proceeds. At the least, you should prepare the closing well before you deliver it, not the evening before it is scheduled.

The extemporaneous method is the best method of delivery, just as it is with the opening statement. You need to look the jurors in the eye and speak in a lively, spontaneous manner. You must show your belief in the closing; exhibiting conviction is easiest if you can look at, and relate to, the jurors. Constant eye contact with the entire jury is essential to persuasive communication.

At the same time, you should have full control of the closing; it should be well-organized, easy to follow, direct, and forceful. Only a well-planned and rehearsed argument fills these requirements. You may feel the need to have notes during the closing argument, but try not to rely on them. Once you begin looking down at notes, the written entries act as a magnet for the eyes, even if you can speak without them. Your repeated references to notes may interfere with effective communication.

A good method for preparing an extemporaneous presentation is set forth in § 1-14. To review, the extemporaneous approach requires that you first prepare an outline of the closing argument. You may incorporate the word picture and evidentiary points from the opening statement into the outline. Think through the points and then practice the summation, start to finish, without looking at the notes. The importance of completing the presentation without resorting to the outline is discussed in § 1-14. Rehearse the summation until you can deliver it in a smooth, controlled fashion.

You should rehearse the argument prior to the trial and again when possible during the trial. An advantage to the extemporaneous approach is its flexibility; even with the substance of the argument fixed in your mind, you easily can adjust the presentation to conform to surprises in the evidence. Thus, you can change the argument as needed right up to the time of delivery. Additionally, the extemporaneous approach allows you to discuss the issues in a spontaneous, lively manner.

§ 12-8. General Outline for Closing Argument.

The following is a general outline of a closing argument. You should adapt it as necessary for specific cases.

§ 12-8(a). The Introduction.

At the beginning of the closing, you should refer to the central issue in a way that captures the jury's attention. The first impression is crucial, so you should not beat around the bush. You may want to refer briefly to the key general thematic point of the opening statement, arguing that you "delivered" the evidence to support the point.

> I told you the Danielsons were defrauded through the repeated misrepresentations of ComputerCentre Associates, and we have proven that the fraud occurred.

Alternatively, you may have to clear up or refute a point right at the beginning. An example for the defendant in *Danielson v. ComputerCentre Associates* follows:

> Let's get something straight right off the bat. Dale Atkins did not cause Mr. Danielson to have a heart attack. As Mr. Danielson stated, he had blockages in his arteries that required surgery. He did not get those blockages from talking to Mr. Atkins. We're all sorry about Mr. Danielson's heart attack, but nothing in this case caused his heart condition.

Having addressed a troublesome issue, you then should move to a main theme, as follows:

> This case is not about Mr. Danielson's heart attack, but about the cause of the Danielsons' failure. That was the fault of the Danielsons, not ComputerCentre. The Danielsons failed to follow sound advice, made poor business decisions, and did not pay attention to their store. Unlike other franchises across the country, they failed to follow ComputerCentre's proven methods for success.

Additionally, you should briefly list the points to be covered in the closing. This action helps the jury follow the argument:

I will first review the facts that have been proven in this trial, showing that the Danielsons were defrauded. I will then discuss the evidence supporting our positions on the key issues, along with the legal instructions the court will render. Finally, I will review the damages suffered by the Danielsons as the result of the fraud.

The introduction generally should consist of only a few sentences and should be accomplished within the first minute.

§ 12-8(b). Word Picture.

You should again provide a word picture of the facts, similar to the word picture in the opening. In the closing, you should be able to develop facts in the word picture in conformance with the evidence. As in the opening statement, the word picture should not involve repeated references to witnesses' testimony but should describe the crucial events in narrative fashion. The word picture again permits you to subtly turn inferences into facts. In a civil case, the word picture generally should include the "what happened afterward" that provides the basis for damages.

§ 12-8(c). Argument of Evidence and Law.

After the word picture, you should discuss the witnesses and exhibits and show that the evidence supports your version of the facts. You should also review the opponent's contentions and show why the evidence does not support these claims. You may cite to key jury instructions, perhaps using a legal principle as a reference point for discussing the evidence, but do not discuss too many instructions. Mix the parties' contentions, the evidence, and the law in a way that emphasizes your theme. Use a simple structure so the jury can easily follow your logic.

One good way to discuss the evidence is to juxtapose the competing claims of the parties and demonstrate why the evidence, sound logic or fairness supports your position. This approach allows you to use one-step logic, in which each of your grounds directly shows why you are right or your opponent is wrong. Offering multiple grounds to support your position, or refute your opponent's, should have a cumulative persuasive impact.

This approach is illustrated below:

What do each of the parties contend in this case? The Danielsons say that ComputerCentre's delays in providing support and the decision to charge them the standard markup caused them to fail. We contend that the

> Danielsons caused their own failure by failing to accept advice, choosing the wrong location and failing to pay attention to their business. Now let's see which picture the evidence and common sense supports. . . .

Generally, you should first discuss support for your own case, showing how the main parts of your word picture are supported by the testimony and exhibits. You should then demonstrate why contentions of the opposing side that conflict with key parts of this picture are not supported by the evidence. This approach, which starts positive and then refutes the negative, is simple and easy to follow. In complicated cases you may want to discuss the evidence topically, using the suggested structure within each topic.

Some legal instructions provide the general rules for deciding the case in light of fact determinations. For instance, if a jury finds a party defrauded another, it can hold him liable for the damages from the fraud. This type of instruction provides an overlay to the argument and usually should be discussed near the beginning. You should use an important evidentiary instruction — for instance, that a fact may be presumed from proof of another fact — as you discuss the evidence.

§ 12-8(d). Damages.

In most civil cases, you need to specially discuss damages. The attorney for the plaintiff should find ways to dramatize the damages and bring out the need for compensation; one effective means of doing so is to break the damages into categories. Counsel for the defendant may wish to recast the damage issue as a single item for compensation.

§ 12-8(e). Conclusion.

In the conclusion, restate the theme of the argument and tell the jurors exactly what verdict you want them to reach.

§ 12-9. References to Jury Instructions.

Closing argument does not just involve a discussion of evidence and fact; it also involves the law. You must show that the legal rules, as applied to the facts, require a favorable verdict. Usually this effort is fact-focused; you characterize the facts so that they fit within a favorable rule. The wording of the legal standard may make a difference, however, in fitting it with the facts. Additionally, the applicable rules on presumptions and burdens may influence the jury's fact determinations.

In most jurisdictions the court delivers the instructions after the closing arguments. Instructing the jury is the sole province of the court; to use a legal point in argument, you must ensure that the judge includes it in the instructions.

Thus, you must find out what instructions the judge intends to give. Of course, in using an instruction, you must depict it accurately.

The best way to obtain a favorable instruction is to request that the judge include it. Usually the judge has a general form instruction adapted to the type of case — say civil or criminal — but the form does not deal with specific issues. The parties request additional instructions, which are incorporated into the form if the judge adopts them. Often counsel must brief the propriety of these instructions, as the parties dispute their applicability.

A book of form instructions based on the law of the jurisdiction provides a source of jury instructions. Often these instructions are too general, however, since they are not drafted for specific facts. Holdings in favorable, closely related cases provide a better source. You should use statements of principle from these authorities that fit the facts. If you rely on authoritative cases — rendered by the court itself or an appellate court with jurisdiction over the trial court — the judge should accept the instructions.

Instructions should be understandable. Usually legal instructions are complex, twisting, and filled with legalese. Judges often read them in rote fashion, which makes it harder to comprehend them. For an instruction to have an impact, it needs to be clearly phrased. Thus, you should select clear statements of legal principles or rephrase them — fairly — for clarity.

In referring to the law in closing argument, you should acknowledge the court's role as law-giver: "As the court will instruct you, . . ." Citing to the instruction avoids an objection that "the court, not counsel, is supposed to instruct the jury." Further, the reference to the court's instruction gives weight to the argument by placing the court's credibility behind your statement of principle.

Generally, you should refer to only one or two — no more than a few — jury instructions. Because jury instructions are inherently confusing, the jurors may have a hard time remembering many of them. If you urge the jurors to focus on a single instruction, it may stand out when the judge recites it. The combination of your reference and the judge's recitation should underscore the point for the jurors. At the same time, the less favorable instructions should have less impact.

§ 12-10. Arguing the Evidence.

The most important aspect of summation is establishing that your version of the facts is correct. Most verdicts are driven by facts rather than law; indeed, a successful characterization of the facts usually takes it within a favorable rule of law. Thus, you need to show how the evidence supports your factual theory. The following techniques should help this effort.

§ 12-10(a). Using the Evidence.

A good way to give credibility to factual claims is to link them directly with supporting evidence. You need to *use* the statements of witnesses, contents of documents, and pieces of real evidence. Show how they directly prove key aspects of your word picture. This direct documentation of your factual claims gives the jurors a concrete basis to accept them. An example, using the *Danielson v. ComputerCentre Associates* problem:

> How do we know that Mr. Atkins made these promises regarding training? Well, we have the testimony of Mr. Danielson. I have the transcript of what he said on Monday. He testified:
>
> "Atkins promised that we would have technical assistance. He said they would provide us with training. He promised to train our salespeople. He also said they had a training facility to train our technician. He said ComputerCentre would totally take care of our need for training."

§ 12-10(b). Using the Opposing Party's Evidence.

One of the best ways to establish a fact is to document it with evidence offered by or conceded by witnesses for the opposing party. Using testimony elicited on cross-examination, documents prepared or adopted by the adverse party, and your opponent's exhibits eliminates disputes. If both sides support or concede a point, nothing remains for the jurors to decide. Thus, you should show that the adverse party's evidence supports your arguments. An example:

> What else do we have? Well, we have Mr. Atkins's own agenda for the meeting. What does it say? "We train you to make even more." It also specifically refers to "technical facilities."

§ 12-10(c). Absence of Opposing Evidence.

If you produce evidence to establish a fact and the other party fails to refute it, your evidence is the only proof on the point. You should call attention to the adverse party's failure to address it. A "don't know" or "can't remember" from the opposing party's witness makes the point even more forceful, because it suggests that the point is correct and the opposing witness was not forthright enough to admit it. The following is an example:

> Jack Danielson very clearly testified that Jene Nelsen promised to train him at that seminar in Middletown. ComputerCentre never tried to refute the evidence that she made that promise. What did Jene Nelsen say? "I can't remember what I said." Whether she can't remember or doesn't want to remember, there's nothing to deny Jack Danielson's testimony.

§ 12-10(d). Inconsistencies in Opposing Evidence.

A good way to attack the credibility of opposing evidence is to point out its inconsistencies. If a witness's testimony contains conflicts, it is less credible than a consistent portrayal because it cannot all be true. Similarly, inconsistencies in the stories of different opposing witnesses show that someone is incorrect. Thus, you should review conflicts on significant points. An example:

> Dale Atkins said that only high volume outlets paid the 20 percent markup. But this claim is refuted by his own franchise status survey. It showed that some franchises with high volume didn't get the 20 percent markup and some with low volume did. Let's look at Defense Exhibit 6. Philadelphia got the 20 percent markup with $790,000 of sales. The Danielsons had about the same sales — $767,000 — and got a 40 percent markup. Denver, Peoria, Phoenix, San Diego, Seattle and others all had higher sales than Philadelphia and got the 40 percent markup. Obviously, Mr. Atkins did not have any consistent standard for providing the 20 percent versus the double markup. His testimony conflicts with his own document.

§ 12-10(e). Weight of the Evidence.

If a witness makes a claim that is inconsistent with much of the other evidence, you can refute it by arguing that one person is more likely to be wrong than many. The following is an example that uses evidence of both sides:

> What does ComputerCentre have to support its claim that technical assistance was available to the Danielsons? Terry Johansen's statement that he would have gone to Middletown to provide assistance if they had asked for it. Yet Mr. Danielson said he did ask for technical assistance and no one offered to do anything. Margaret Danielson said the same thing. Drew Anderson testified he asked for technical support and got no help whatsoever. Plus, Dale Atkins wrote a memorandum in July, 1993, right after the Danielsons opened, saying all service rep training was put off. It was Plaintiffs' Exhibit 16. What does it say? "I've encouraged all of the franchises to make arrangements by contracting with outsiders like RCA Service Corp., Honeywell or Xerox to carry out warranty service or other work on units they sell." All this evidence refutes Terry Johansen's supposed willingness to train the Danielsons.

§ 12-10(f). Objectivity of Witness.

Each party in any case wants to win. The parties, and those closely identified with them, have a strong reason to stretch the truth. An objective third party generally has no reason to do so. Thus, you can add credibility to your claims if you can substantiate them with third party testimony. An example:

> There is no doubt that the loss of sales was caused by delays in deliveries by ComputerCentre and Wizard. Remember the testimony of Loren Walsh, a customer who has no allegiance at all in this case? He said he waited more than three weeks for his order and then canceled it. Why did he cancel it? Because of the long delay.

§ 12-10(g).   Concrete Nature of Documents and Exhibits.

Documents and exhibits have a solid quality that gives them credibility. The written words seem more concrete than oral testimony; things the jurors can hold and see irrefutably exist. Thus, this evidence lends strength to an argument. You should use documents and real evidence to establish your points, as in the following example:

> Can there be any doubt that ComputerCentre promised training, computer selection, inventory management, shipping and advertising to the Danielsons? There isn't any doubt. Look at the contract both parties signed [holding exhibit]. It says the Danielsons paid their franchise fee for "attendant training, accounting support, computer selection, technical services, inventory management program, shipping and advertising. . . ." This document is the agreement between the parties. . . .

§ 12-10(h).   Credibility of Witnesses.

Sometimes you must argue that a witness simply was not credible. You can cite inconsistencies in his testimony and conflicts with other evidence for this purpose, as described above. Additionally, you can use the means ordinarily relied on to attack credibility: motive, bias, appearance, history, and other factors. Link the reason for not believing the witness to his testimony. An example:

> Can we believe Dale Atkins' claim that he thought technical services would be available to the Danielsons even though there was no service facility? Did you see him as he made that statement? He was fidgeting and couldn't even look his own counsel in the eye. He has every reason to stretch the truth because he doesn't want to lose this case. We just can't believe that claim. . . .

§ 12-11. Argumentative Techniques.

The most important attribute of the closing argument is a consistent, coherent theme that makes sense of the evidence. A good "word picture" is the key to this effort, because in developing the word picture you need to consider how it accommodates the evidence. Once you develop a consistent word picture, the facts and the evidence naturally work together to support your theme.

The key requirement for the theme is that it be real, drawn from the facts. An artificial theme — perhaps an allegorical overlay forced onto the facts — often seems a diversion from the issues. Additionally, an artificial theme may provide a weapon to your opponent, because superficial points often can be turned against you. Thus, you should find the theme in the case rather than imposing it on the case.

Belief and conviction also are essential in convincing a jury. Unless you obviously believe in your client's case, there is little likelihood that the jury will do so. You should identify completely with the client's cause in thought and manner. You may not use the words "I believe," but the entire presentation should communicate this thought to the jury.

Some techniques often used in closing argument include the following.

§ 12-11(a). Dramatic Recitation of Events.

A dramatic description of your version of events is a great way to fix that story in the jurors' minds. Thus, the word picture should be a central part of the closing argument. The word picture allows you to fill in inferences for the jury without referring to the evidence at all. Once you depict a story it seems more real, and the jurors are more likely to accept the facts you infer from the evidence. Further, in arguing the evidence you can replay parts of the word picture, which reestablishes that your version fits well with the evidence.

§ 12-11(b). Reasoning With, Rather Than at, the Jury.

In keeping with the "discussion leader" approach to persuasion, you should assume a manner that places you in a discussion "with" the jurors in reasoning through the issues. You cannot climb into the jury box, but you can use language that figuratively places you there. One method is to use "we" rather than "you" in leading the jurors to conclusions. The following are examples of the two approaches:

> How do we know that Atkins lied? Well, let's look at what he said versus what he knew the facts to be. . . .

> How do you know that Atkins lied? You can look at what he said versus what he knew the facts to be. . . .

The difference is subtle, but the first may place you in a better posture to lead the jury.

§ 12-11(c). One-Step Logic.

You should employ one-step logic. The link between a conclusion and the underlying basis, if possible, should require only a single logical leap. Several reasons for the conclusion may exist, but you should argue that each supports it independently. Thus, the identity of the killer might independently be supported by: (1) fingerprint evidence, (2) an identification, (3) blood stains, and (4) his possession of a weapon. One-step logic is easy to follow and gives the impression of cumulative support for a point. A more complex argument, requiring multiple steps to draw a single conclusion, is harder to follow. It may also be easier to refute, because a single slip destroys the conclusion.

In employing one-step logic you should state the conclusion first, followed by a discussion of each point supporting it. This method ensures that the jurors follow the argument and see the reasons accumulate in support of the point. It also helps you avoid more complex logic.

Of course, a more complex argument may be necessitated by the facts or evidence. The "one-step" approach is a rule of preference, subject to the requirements of the case. Regardless of the number of steps, you should strive to make your arguments as simple as possible. An example of one-step logic follows:

> How do we know that Dale Atkins knew he was lying? First, he said he would provide technical training, but he had no technical facility. Certainly he knew that was a lie. Second, he said he would provide sales training, but he had no one but Jene Nelsen to do that, and she was busy marketing franchises. He knew that promise was untrue. Third, he promised prompt delivery of supplies, but he knew full well that Wizard was habitually late in getting needed products to franchises. Since he planned to keep using his family's business, he knew that was a lie. Fourth, he told Mr. Danielson all about the San Francisco franchise and its 19 percent profit, but he knew that franchise had the normal markup. Since he planned to give the Danielsons a 40 percent markup — because they were "yokels" in his view — he knew they would never do as well as San Francisco.

§ 12-11(d). Using Common Knowledge and Experience.

Common knowledge, experience, and old-fashioned "common sense" are means to demonstrate that your claims are valid and your opponent's incredible. You need to ask yourself whether contentions are consistent with normal experience. Use the "normal" response to a situation to show that a claim differing from the norm is incredible. An example:

Jene Nelsen says that she tried to train the Danielsons but they wouldn't listen and made her leave. Now, does that make sense? Here are the Danielsons, opening a franchise with little prior knowledge of the business, who are desperate for training. They were promised training. They paid for training. They expected training. According to Jene Nelson, however, they refused to take training.

On the other hand, Jene Nelsen was busy selling computer franchises at $50,000 a pop. She was eager to get on the road and make money. Yet she says she wanted to stay and train the Danielsons.

Ladies and gentlemen, we know that someone who pays for training ordinarily accepts it. We know that someone making lots of money ordinarily doesn't like distractions. Jene Nelsen's version just isn't reasonable, is it?

---

§ 12-11(e). Arguing Implications of Opposing Contentions.

Sometimes the fallacy in a contention can be exposed by extending the underlying principle to another situation in which its unfairness is apparent. The technique works best if the principle is applied in a situation familiar to the jurors. The following is an example:

Counsel for ComputerCentre keeps saying that other franchises did well, as if that were a reason to ignore the harm to the Danielsons. What if a used car salesman used that argument? I sold 20 cars today, and only one didn't have an engine, so how can that one complain? Would that be a fair defense? What if one person's steak came to the table too rare to eat, but the others at the table decided theirs were okay? Would he have a right to complain about the blood red steak? Of course he would. This case is about the Danielsons, not about the other franchises. We need to focus on what the Danielsons were promised and what they got.

---

§ 12-11(f). Analogies and Anecdotes.

You may wish to use analogies and anecdotes to emphasize points. The focus, however, should be on the facts and the theme. Make sure the analogy or story fits with the theme. You should develop the theme first; do not choose an analogy, perhaps a successful one from a past case, and try to make the facts fit it. Opposing counsel can show the case doesn't fit the analogy, or worse, show the analogy really supports her.

Despite the risk, a good story or analogy is often a way to illustrate a point. Jurors perk up when presented with a story, especially when it involves common experience. Just do not try to do too much with the analogy. An example follows:

> Jene Nelsen's story is like an apple with a worm in it. On the surface it looks great. She's cool and calm — a pro at convincing people she's right. But when you get beneath the surface you notice the contents are a little brown and mushy. If you cut deep, you find that her whole story is rotten. Jene Nelsen is a born liar. She may be smooth on the outside, but she has a worm on the inside.

§ 12-11(g). Candor.

The most effective weapon you have is your credibility. You should confront weaknesses and provide explanations that draw the sting from your opponent's arguments. Of course, your discussion of weaknesses should be secondary to your main presentation, so that they do not take on undue importance. Nevertheless, a discussion of a weak point enhances the impression that you are fair and candid.

One good method of demonstrating your candor is to concede harmless points. If the opposing party makes a claim that fits well within your word picture, concede and use it. This action gives you an appearance of fairness while emphasizing that your theory accommodates all the evidence. An example:

> What does Mr. Atkins say on the issue of technician training? He says he didn't have a facility to provide training. That's true. But the point is he knew he didn't have a facility when he made his promise to the Danielsons. Thus, he knew his promise was false. . . .

§ 12-11(h). Rhetorical Questions.

An effective technique of argument is to employ rhetorical questions. Examples: "What would a reasonable person do in these circumstances?" "What is a fair amount of compensation in these circumstances?" "Was that a just thing to do?" Jurors believe themselves to be "reasonable," "fair," and "just," and these inquiries can subtly draw them to the conclusion that the advocate's position is "reasonable," "fair" or "just."

One good method of argument is to let the jurors draw conclusions that seem harsh. The rhetorical question is a good way to lead them to the desired point.

You avoid the role of hangman, yet establish your point. You need to make sure, of course, that the answer to the rhetorical question is obvious. An example:

> Dale Atkins promised technical training when he knew he had no training facility. He promised prompt delivery when he knew Wizard almost never provided prompt delivery. He promised attendant training when he knew his trainer — Jene Nelsen — was too busy selling franchises to provide it. He promised the profits of a franchise getting a 20 percent markup when he planned to give the Danielsons a 40 percent markup. He promised software accounting support when the software was nowhere near ready. I ask you, did Dale Atkins tell the truth, or did he lie?

§ 12-11(i). Phrasing Points to Reflect Conviction.

You need to describe your own contentions in a manner that reflects your conviction they are true, while describing opposing arguments as mere contentions. Keep yourself identified with your client. Do not be afraid to use "we" in describing your claims. If you say "my client contends," it sounds like you are not totally supportive of the assertion.

Do not use phrases that make your points sound tentative. "We submit that . . . ," "we contend that . . . ," and similar phrases suggest that a point is nothing but a contention. If you make a point, say it as a fact. Thus, "Atkins lied" shows greater belief than "We submit that Atkins lied."

Make sure you do not appear to endorse something you really do not agree with. Rather than referring to your opponent's contentions as fact, describe them as contentions. Consider the following examples:

> [By the Danielsons' attorney.] Consider Mr. Atkins' story. He told the truth. He didn't know of the difficulties with Wizard. He tried to help the Danielsons but they wouldn't listen.

The phraseology here suggests that counsel adopts Atkins's story. But counsel for the Danielsons would want to separate himself from those contentions, as follows:

> [By the Danielsons' attorney.] What did Mr. Atkins say? He claimed he told the truth. According to him, he didn't know of the difficulties with Wizard. He says he tried to help the Danielsons but they wouldn't listen.

The second approach eliminates the chance that the jurors believe counsel endorses parts of the other side's story.

§ 12-11(j).   Challenging the Opponent.

You may be able to impair your opponent's argument by posing questions for her to answer. If you do, make sure the answers are not easy. Find weaknesses in the opposing case and demand that counsel address them. This approach may force your opponent to spend time on points she would rather gloss over. An example:

> We'll see if counsel for ComputerCentre can explain why Mr. Atkins used a franchise that had a 20 percent markup as an example of profitability if he knew a new franchise would get a 40 percent markup. Let's pay special attention to see if counsel addresses that point.

§ 12-11(k).   Humor.

Humor can be a great means of persuasion, but the humor should be real. Trying to force a joke often has a deadening impact on your momentum. Some people are natural storytellers and can get away with a lot, but most lawyers should venture into this area with care. Trying to get too many laughs can be counterproductive.

The best ammunition for humor should come from the trial itself. If a witness adopts a particularly absurd position, you might get a laugh by dramatizing the absurdity. If the opposition uses an inapt analogy, you may be able to exaggerate it, using humor to show its inapplicability. Humor is uniquely dependent on the circumstances; what works in one situation often does not work in another. To use it effectively you must have a sense of humor and employ it at the right time.

One tip in using humor: if it involves personal appearance, traits, or style, self-deprecation is much safer than attack humor. You can still make your point. Compare the attack humor in the following example with the self-deprecating humor in the second:

Now we know where Jene Nelsen got that long, pointy nose. It's been growing all her life, just like Pinocchio, because she's such a liar. Her nose got even longer, if that's possible, in this trial.

I'm sure you've noticed my rather large nose. It's really something, isn't it? I'll tell ya, it was a burden in high school. Well, we've finally found someone who deserves my long nose. Jene Nelsen deserves it, as far from the truth as she was in this case. Her nose should be bigger than mine by now. . . .

§ 12-12. Stylistic Suggestions for the Closing.

The following practical and stylistic pointers are helpful in presenting an effective closing argument.

1. *Be yourself.* Every person has something special to offer in argument. The shy individual often has a special credibility that cannot be duplicated by someone with a strong personality. The effervescent type usually finds it easy to capture and hold attention. No one can change his basic traits, but you can capitalize on your best attributes and improve the rest. Thus, the shy person can make a special attempt to inject life into the argument, while the effervescent type should adopt a more serious tone. These adjustments of style should improve your presentation, but do not overdo them.[10] Your core strategy should be to rely on your natural qualities.

2. *Use the conversational style.* Speak to the jurors as if you were having a conversation. Maintain eye contact with the entire jury, allowing your eyes to move from juror to juror, securing brief eye contact with each. Speak in an authoritative fashion, but avoid a patronizing or condescending tone. Your air should be that of a discussion leader.

3. *Avoid overstatement.* Overstatement is not necessarily good argument. You seem much more credible if you employ slight understatement. Rhetoric alone often sounds empty. If you employ the facts and evidence to build a theme, your argument will have plenty of strength. It is easier to be persuasive if the jury believes everything you say, and that is possible only if you avoid overstatement.

---

[10] See G. Ross Anderson, Jr. *ALI-ABA Course of Study: Closing Argument,* SG045 ALI-ABA 1317 ("Underlying the jury's acceptance of closing arguments is the jurors' perceptions of the lawyer's honesty and sincerity. Be yourself." See generally, Stephen Feldman and Kent Wilson, *The Value of Interpersonal Skills in Lawyering,* 5 LAW & HUM. BEHAV. 311 (1981).

4.   *Show emotion.* Although you should not make excessive statements, your delivery should make it clear that you believe in your client's position. You should show some righteous indignation on occasion. Your entire manner should communicate a commitment to your client's cause.[11]

5.   *Vary your style.* Vary your voice pitch, volume, speech rate, and rhythm to help inject life into the presentation. An occasional pause is a great attention-getter. Avoid a monotonous delivery in speech or gestures.

6.   *Stand where the jury can see you.* As the discussion leader, you need to stand where you can speak with, rather than at, the jurors. Try to stand about 8 to 12 feet from the jury box. If you use documents or exhibits, approach the jurors so they can see. If the court requires you to stand at a podium, try to move a bit to the side so the jurors can see you; impediments get in the way of communication.

7.   *Use gestures naturally.* You should employ gestures that flow naturally with your argument. Thus, if you describe a stabbing, you might make a stabbing motion with your arm. "Act" a bit as you portray events. Your gestures should not be forced, however; gestures that are not part of the message may seem unnatural.

§ 12-13. Outline of a Closing Argument: *Danielson v. ComputerCentre Associates.*

The following is an outline of a closing argument for ComputerCentre Associates in the *Danielson* case. Notice that the outline generally contains the same word picture as the opening statement. You must adjust the word picture for surprises in the evidence, but ideally the word pictures should be consistent. Of course, you may hold back some points from the opening statement so you can use them effectively at trial, and you need to incorporate these facts into the word picture in the summation. The outline is more detailed than you would need after presenting a case, so it will be clear.

A.   Introduction.

    1.   *Theme statement.* As I told you at the beginning of this trial, the Danielsons did not fail because ComputerCentre Associates did anything wrong. We experienced a few temporary problems in serving our franchises, but we fixed those problems. The Danielsons failed because of their failure to accept the advice

---

[11] See Murray Ogburn, *Making Your Case Come to Life: Storytelling and Theme Creation,* 1 ANN. 2001 ATLA-CLE 189 (2001). See also Robert V. Wells, *Lawyer Credibility,* 21 TRIAL 69 (1985); P. TAYLOR, R. BUCHANAN AND D. STRAWN, COMMUNICATION STRATEGIES FOR TRIAL ATTORNEYS (1984).

of ComputerCentre, their poor business decisions, and their failure to pay attention to the business.

At the close of this trial the judge will instruct you that you can find against ComputerCentre only if you determine that its actions caused losses to the Danielsons. I want you to listen to that instruction. You cannot award damages against ComputerCentre for losses the Danielsons caused by their own actions.

2. *I will cover:*

    (a)   the facts that were proven,

    (b)   why the evidence supports those facts,

    (c)   the contentions of the Danielsons, and

    (d)   the damage claim of the Danielsons.

B.   Word Picture.

   1. *ComputerCentre's national success.*

      — 84 franchises nationwide.

      — Grown by 43 franchises in two years.

      — Franchises are lucrative.

      — ComputerCentre methods successful nationwide.

      — Virtually all franchises profitable.

      — ComputerCentre methods very popular.

      — Only one failure ever — Middletown.

      — Danielsons didn't follow proven methods.

      — Failed to adjust even to small problems.

   2. *Danielsons sought ComputerCentre franchise.*

      — Mr. Danielson called ComputerCentre.

      — Wanted to get into a franchise.

      — He came to Middletown meeting.

      — Mr. Danielson knew it was a meeting to interest prospects and sell franchises.

      — Decided the very next day.

      — Pushed to sign up to a franchise.

   3. *ComputerCentre representations were accurate.*

      — These were long-term commitments.

      — All have been fulfilled.

      — ComputerCentre made same commitments to all franchises.

      — Atkins/Nelsen never said success is guaranteed.

4. *Danielsons ignored ComputerCentre advice in choosing location.*

   — Location is very important to a franchise.
   — ComputerCentre offered studies of population and traffic to help find the best spot.
   — Danielsons chose location before even signing up.
   — Selected Middletown Historic Mall.
   — Less than one-twentieth the annual traffic of Tri-County Mall.
   — Danielsons ignored request to reconsider.
   — Did not even wait for demographic study.

5. *Danielsons consistently made poor business decisions.*

   (a) *Failed to hire knowledgeable sales reps.*

   — Knowledgeable reps are essential.
   — Explain computers to customers.
   — In hiring inexperienced people, Danielsons ignored advice.
   — Their sales reps could not even explain the most basic steps in dealing with computers.

   (b) *Danielsons ordered inventory late.*

   — They knew Wizard was having difficulty.
   — Could have corrected by ordering earlier.
   — Danielsons never took this action.
   — Failed to adjust to a temporary problem.
   — When they opened, ordered only *two weeks* prior to the opening.

   (c) *Danielsons refused training.*

   — Jene Nelsen went to Middletown.
   — Tried to provide training.
   — They failed to show up.
   — Would not listen to her advice.

   (d) *Refused to keep adequate inventory.*

   — You have to have products on hand.
   — Danielsons refused to keep supplies available.
   — Failed to order more even when they knew of potential delays.

   (e) *Ignored Mr. Atkins' pleas to correct mismanagement.*

   — Even ignored his letter.

6. *Danielsons failed to participate in their own business.*
   — Jack Danielson — refused to be involved after heart attack.
   — Refused his own wife's pleas for help.
   — Even after recovery, would not go to store.
   — Margaret Danielson could not handle decisions.
   — She completely withdrew.
   — Hired friend of a friend to run the store — a man with no sales experience.

7. *Stocked inferior products in violation of agreement.*
   — Brought in games and low quality products rather than high tech equipment.
   — Inconsistent with ComputerCentre standards.
   — Cheapened their store.

8. *Failed to pay royalties.*
   — Agreement *and* addendum call for royalties.
   — They never paid.

9. *Store failed at a time of total inattention.*
   — Neither Danielson was involved.
   — Store was not even open full hours.
   — It was selling different, cheaper products.
   — No one with experience to run it.
   — Still paying salaries to the Danielsons.

C. Evidence shows the Danielsons failed solely because of their own poor performance.

1. *Heart attack: not caused by ComputerCentre.*
   — Mr. Danielson said it was from a blockage problem.
   — Needed heart surgery.
   — Blockages are physical, long-standing problems.
   — Can't come from a telephone conversation.

2. *Danielsons admit the key points.*
   (a) *Danielsons admit failure to be involved with business.*
   — Even after recovery, he refused to be involved.
   — Would not even respond to pleas of his wife.
   — Neither even went to the store last summer.
   — Mr. Danielson testimony (cross).
   — Mrs. Danielson testimony (cross).

    (b)   *Anderson and Danielsons admit they employed inexperi-enced salespeople.*

       — Anderson testimony.

       — Danielson concession.

    (c)   *Danielsons admit they chose location without study.*

       — Mr. Danielson testimony.

       — Chose before even signing up.

       — One-twentieth the traffic.

       — Impact: $$ thousands.

  3.   *Danielsons couldn't deny other points.*

    (a)   *Mr. Danielson didn't order the inventory; left it to the salespeople.*

       — Mrs. Danielson didn't know how.

       — Salespeople waited until orders were placed (Johansen testimony).

    (b)   *Danielsons admit receiving Mr. Atkins's letter, asking them to correct problems* (letter).

  4.   *Danielsons admit they weren't involved last summer, when the losses really mounted.*

       — Mr. Danielson testimony (cross).

       — Mrs. Danielson testimony (cross).

D.   **Compare the Danielsons' claims.**

  1.   *Their main claims are side issues.*

    (a)   *The "yokel" and "clown" letter is by a man frustrated with dealing with people who would not listen.*

       — It does not say anything about the case.

    (b)   *Jene Nelsen's prior conviction is irrelevant.*

       — Judge will instruct you that it has nothing to do with the merits.

       — She was given a chance by Mr. Atkins.

       — Has made a lot of people successful.

    (c)   *Let's stick with the merits.*

  2.   *Danielsons contend Atkins intentionally defrauded them.*

       — Runs against common sense.

       — Atkins is successful if franchises are successful.

       — No reason at all to hurt the Danielsons.

  3.   *Danielsons claim misrepresentations.*

— The representations were long term.

— Today, they all have been fulfilled for franchises.

— Admittedly everything didn't come true at once.

— There were temporary problems.

— The other franchises adjusted.

— The Danielsons refused advice to adjust.

(a) *Sales/attendant training.*

— Jene Nelsen said she went to train.

— The Danielsons don't deny this point.

— They just wouldn't accept her help.

— Look at their action, using inexperienced sales personnel against her advice.

— Refusing to order early, against her advice.

— Why didn't they ever document a lack of training?

(b) *Technician training.*

— This was a temporary delay.

— The facility now is finished.

— Outside services cost the Danielsons only $2,000 (income statement).

— A full-time technician would have cost much more.

— Actually saved them money!

(c) *Advertising.*

— No particular level was promised.

— Danielsons admit they were told it might have to be cut back.

— The Danielsons were given some support.

— But they refused to pay royalties on sales.

— Without royalties, it would be crazy for ComputerCentre to support advertising.

(d) *Double markup.*

— There is no double markup.

— Bulk purchase gets a discount.

— Drew Anderson had no basis for his comment on "normal markup."

— He admitted total lack of knowledge of industry.

— Every franchise that got 20 percent had a proven record of bulk purchase.

— The Danielsons knew this from Day One, yet they never said a word.

(e) *Fraud in preparing addendum.*

— This one is the most amazing.

— The franchise agreement calls for a royalty.

— Danielsons admit they signed that.

— Royalty is same as all other franchises.

— If the signatures are incorrect, why haven't the Danielsons produced an expert?

— Why would they think they don't have to pay a royalty?

(f) *Their case just doesn't make sense.*

— People do not go into franchises expecting instant success with no work, or to get service with no payment.

E.   Damages.

1. *There is no liability.*

2. *If you find liability, damages are zero.*

— Net debt is only $11,000.

— Mr. Danielson took a salary of $14,000 for doing no work last year.

— Mrs. Danielson took $11,500 even though she did not work for the last several months.

— Since neither is willing to work in the business, they have no right to lost profits.

— Only damages could be the franchise fee of $52,000.

— That is set off by unpaid royalties:

$33,355 — last 12 mos.

$20,000 — approximate amount for prior 6 months

$53,335

— Additionally, advertising support provided.

— Nothing is owed.

F.   Conclusion.

The Danielsons have no valid claim. They caused their own losses and now expect you to make someone else pay. Under the law and any reasonable view of fairness, you can't require ComputerCentre to pay for the Danielsons' failure. You should bring back a verdict of no liability. That means checking no on the form when it asks: "Is ComputerCentre liable to the Danielsons for fraud?"

§ 12-14. Example of a Closing Argument: *Danielson v. ComputerCentre Associates*.

The following is a sample closing argument for the Danielson case on behalf of ComputerCentre, based on the outline in § 12-13.

We have come to the end of this case, and I, too, want to thank you for your patience as we have reviewed the evidence. As I told you at the beginning of this trial, the Danielsons did not fail because ComputerCentre Associates defrauded them or did anything else that was wrong. The Danielsons failed because of their own failures — their failure to accept good advice, their poor business decisions, and their failure to pay attention to their own business. We admit that ComputerCentre experienced temporary problems in serving our franchises in a few areas, but we fixed those problems, and none of the other ComputerCentre franchises failed.

After these closing arguments the judge will give you your instructions as to the law. I want you to remember one particular instruction that the judge will give you. He will tell you that you can find against Computer-Centre only if you determine that its actions actually caused the losses that the Danielsons say they suffered. You may not award damages against ComputerCentre for losses that the Danielsons suffered as a result of their own actions. This is the central issue in this case: What caused the Danielsons' failure?

In reviewing these matters with you, I would like to cover four areas. First, I would like to discuss with you the facts that were proven in the trial. Second, we will review how the evidence supports these facts. Third, we will discuss the contentions that the Danielsons have raised against ComputerCentre. Finally, we will review the damage claim of the Danielsons. Again, as to all of these matters, the key issue is causation — what caused the Danielsons to fail?

Now, let's discuss what was proven in this case. First, the evidence showed that ComputerCentre is a nationally renowned, successful franchising operation. Mr. Atkins' operation had 41 franchises two years ago; it has 84 successful franchises today. People all over the country want to be a part of the ComputerCentre operation. Virtually all of the ComputerCentre franchises are profitable, and they get more profitable all the time. There is only one failure that has ever occurred, and that is the Danielsons' franchise. The Danielsons didn't follow the proven, accepted methods of ComputerCentre, and they failed to adjust even to small problems. Additionally, the Danielsons failed to take a strong role in operating their own business.

Let us recall the background in which the Danielsons sought out a ComputerCentre franchise. ComputerCentre didn't go looking for the Danielsons. It merely ran an ad, advertising the availability of a franchise opportunity, in the Wall Street Journal. The Danielsons saw that ad, and they came to ComputerCentre. They wanted to get into a franchise. Mr. Danielson came voluntarily to the meeting in Middletown. He knew it was a meeting in which Mr. Atkins and Ms. Nelsen would review the benefits of a ComputerCentre franchise. Surely he knew that they would be telling him good things — in this case, good things that were true across the country. It was Mr. Danielson who decided the very next day, after discussing the matter with his wife, to sign up for a franchise. It was Mr. Danielson who called Mr. Atkins and said he wanted to sign up right away.

Now, let's talk about that meeting. Everything that Jene Nelsen and Dale Atkins said in that meeting was true. They were making long-term commitments to potential franchisees, and those long-term commitments have been fulfilled. ComputerCentre made the very same commitments to its other franchisees across the country. All of those franchisees have been successful. ComputerCentre does provide training to its franchises; it does provide technical training; it does provide advertising help; it does provide inventory selection; it does provide prompt delivery. Mr. Atkins and Ms. Nelsen did not say that there would never be a problem or there would never be a delay or that success would be guaranteed. All the Danielsons have focused on are temporary problems that were corrected as soon as possible by ComputerCentre Associates.

What about the Danielsons? Let's talk about how they went about operating their business. First of all, let's look at their choice of location. As you know, location is very important to any business. Location is the key to getting customers in the door. Many businesses fail or succeed on the basis of location alone.

What did the Danielsons do, knowing that ComputerCentre wanted to help them find a good location? Well, they chose a location themselves, even before they signed up for a franchise. They selected the Middletown Historic Mall, a small shopping center that was only 1/20 the size of the Tri-County Mall. When Mr. Atkins found out that the Danielsons had already selected a location, he was very surprised. He asked them to reconsider. He asked them at least to wait for a demographic study. But did the Danielsons wait? No, they were sure they were right, and they went ahead and signed a lease for a store in a center with 1/20 the traffic of the Tri-County Mall.

Let's talk about the Danielsons' business decisions. First, we know that they failed to hire knowledgeable sales representatives. Mr. Atkins told them that knowledgeable representatives are essential. Jene Nelsen told them that people with experience are essential. Any reasonable person knows that in dealing with a computer, you need someone who can explain how the machine operates, how to program it, and how to get the best results. Yet the Danielsons hired people to explain their computers who knew nothing about computers. They did so to save money because they didn't want to pay for experience.

Next, the Danielsons ordered inventory when it was too late to achieve delivery by their opening day. Jene Nelsen told them that they needed to order earlier because of problems that Wizard was experiencing in making deliveries, but the Danielsons didn't listen. Mr. Danielson left it to the sales representatives to order the inventory, and they failed to do so until the last minute. As a result, the computers didn't arrive in time for the opening day.

The Danielsons also refused training from Jene Nelsen. She went to Middletown to try to help them, but after three days she was forced to leave. She found that they were late in arriving for meetings, that they often were missing from the store, and they didn't want to sit down and listen to her when they did come. Finally, she had a falling out with them and left. She was a very frustrated person when she left.

What else do we know? Well, we know the Danielsons failed to keep an adequate inventory. They didn't want to pay to have stock on hand. Further, Mr. Danielson left it to the sales representatives to do the ordering, and they rarely ordered until a customer had already purchased a product. Mr. Danielson did this knowing that Wizard was having supply problems and that there might be delays. He just refused or failed to adjust to the temporary supply problem.

Additionally, Mr. Danielson and Mrs. Danielson ignored the pleas of Mr. Atkins to correct their management problems. They even ignored his January letter asking them to get experienced sales representatives and to maintain an adequate inventory. The Danielsons never even responded to that letter.

What about the Danielsons' participation in their own business? Well, we know that Jack Danielson lasted for about five months. As he told you, he had a heart attack in September. But at that time, he was not even a strong enough participant in the process to know whether his own store was profitable. After his heart attack Mr. Danielson was not involved in the business at all. The franchise went on for nearly a year without any participation from Mr. Danielson whatsoever.

Mr. Danielson recovered by February and was able to engage in all sorts of activities, but he couldn't even give advice to his wife. He wouldn't help her with decisions, he wouldn't help her operate the store, and he wouldn't listen to her when she asked him for help. In the end, Mrs. Danielson had to withdraw also. She was completely overwhelmed because she had no idea how to operate a computer franchise. Last May, she wound up hiring a friend of a friend — someone who had no sales experience — to take over the store.

What else did the Danielsons do? Well, their store stocked inferior supplies. Mr. Anderson decided that game computers might increase sales so he brought in a line of low quality, low priced games and other pieces of equipment. This action was completely inconsistent with Computer-Centre's high standards and it led to a loss of business. Obviously, people did not want to go to a high quality computer franchise that did not stock high quality equipment.

The Danielsons also failed to pay royalties from the day they opened to the day they closed. When they signed up, they agreed to pay royalties. Their franchise agreement says that they will pay royalties. The addendum they signed at the same time as they executed the franchise agreement also calls for a 5% royalty. But the Danielsons never made one payment to ComputerCentre.

Finally, as we know, the store failed last summer at a time when the Danielsons were providing it no attention at all. Mr. Danielson did not set foot inside the store during the entire time Drew Anderson was the manager. Mrs. Danielson rarely went to the store. Even though Drew Anderson was trying to run the store alone, even though there were no salesmen, even though Mr. Anderson had to shorten the hours, even though there was no one there with any sales experience, Mr. Danielson never went into the store once to provide some help or to extend the hours so that more sales could be made. And during all that time, Mr. Danielson continued to accept his salary from the store.

Now, let's talk about the evidence. What does the evidence show with respect to the issue of causation? The evidence shows that the Danielsons failed because of their own poor performance, not because of any problem experienced by ComputerCentre.

First, let's get one thing straight. We know Mr. Danielson had a heart attack, but that heart attack was not caused by ComputerCentre. Mr. Danielson himself testified that his heart attack was caused by a blockage in his arteries. He said he needed heart surgery to repair that blockage. Now regardless of what counsel might imply, and has attempted to imply, a blockage does not come from a telephone conversation. Blockages in the arteries are physical and are the result of long-standing health problems or genetics or personal history. We all know that. One phone call cannot cause a heart blockage, and Mr. Danielson's telephone conversation with Mr. Atkins did not cause his heart blockage. So let's put that aside.

Second, the key points on causation are all admitted by the Danielsons. The most important point — the failure of the Danielsons to be involved in their own business — was admitted by both Mr. and Mrs. Danielson. Mr. Danielson conceded, right here on the stand, that he would not be involved in the business at all after his heart attack. We all heard him say that he would not even respond to the pleas of his own wife to help her, to give her advice, or to come to the store.

What did Mr. Danielson say? You'll recall what he said on Tuesday afternoon. He admitted that she told him she was desperate for help. He admitted that she asked him to help with decisions. He admitted that she begged him to give her relief. But what did he say? He said he was afraid that it might give him some stress if he helped her. So he wouldn't help her. Indeed, Mr. Danielson admitted that he never even went to the store last summer, when there were not enough people to run it and not enough people to keep normal hours. He couldn't even be bothered to go down there to help with selling computers.

What about the issue of the experience of the sales people? There's no dispute on this point. Mr. Anderson — the Danielsons' manager — said it best. He said that the salespeople didn't even have a minimal knowledge of the operation of computers. That was the reason he fired the salespeople. Think of that — for more than a year, the Danielsons had salespeople operating their franchise who did not even understand the most basic aspects of operating and programming computers.

What about the question of location? Well, we heard Mr. Danielson's testimony that he didn't think he needed any help in choosing a location. He admitted that he chose the location before ever signing up with ComputerCentre. He admitted that he decided not to wait for a location study from ComputerCentre. The Danielsons made a choice to go to a mall with 1/20 the traffic of the Tri-County Mall. Just think of that. With even double the traffic, or even triple the traffic, the Danielsons surely would have had sales of well over $1 million. If they had higher sales, they might have qualified for the lower markup they now say they wanted.

Additionally, the Danielsons couldn't deny the other reasons for their failure. Mr. Danielson conceded that he left it to the salespeople to order inventory. He wasn't involved at all in the business after September, and he really didn't remember ordering inventory before that point. Mrs. Danielson admitted that she didn't really know how to order inventory.

And so what happened? The salespeople waited until orders were placed before sending in the orders for inventory. Remember Terry Johansen's testimony? His frustration with the Danielsons for making the same

715

mistakes, over and over? Well, they made the same mistakes because they left it to someone else to do the ordering.

The Danielsons admit they received Mr. Atkins' letter last January, begging them to correct their problems. Mr. Atkins testified that he asked the Danielsons repeatedly to get experienced personnel, that he asked them repeatedly to stock adequate inventory — particularly while Wizard was having problems — but they never responded. Nor did the Danielsons ever respond to his letter.

Most important, the Danielsons admit that they weren't involved at all last summer, when they really suffered the losses that brought their store down. At that time, neither Mr. Danielson nor Mrs. Danielson even went to the store on a regular basis. Both of them admitted that on the stand. What did Mr. Danielson say? It might have been stressful to go to the store. Well, of course it might have been stressful, but we all know that nothing good comes for free. You have to work to get ahead.

So, we have evidence that supports every aspect of ComputerCentre's case. The Danielsons really don't deny that they failed to operate their own business. How then can they blame their failure on ComputerCentre?

Let's compare the evidence with respect to the Danielsons' claims. What do the Danielsons say? Well, their case is about alleged misrepresentations, but their lawyer talks mostly about side issues.

Let's deal with the side issues first. Counsel tells you all about the letter that describes the Danielsons as "yokels" and "clowns." He acts like calling someone a yokel or a clown is the same thing as fraud or the same thing as making a misrepresentation, but it's not.

Mr. Atkins described to you in vivid detail why he made that statement. He was seething with anger. For two weeks Mr. Atkins had been trying to get the Danielsons to hold up on locating a franchise, but they wouldn't listen. He kept telling them to wait for a demographic study, but they decided to go ahead with the Middletown Mall. Additionally, they wouldn't listen to him on a strategy for hiring employees. He was furious, and so he referred to them as "yokels." But that is a perfectly natural reaction in the circumstances.

The other side issue that counsel wants to talk about is Jene Nelsen's prior conviction. As the judge will instruct you — and I hope you pay attention to that instruction — her prior conviction can be considered on the issue of her credibility, but it has absolutely nothing to do with the merits of this case. It does not prove anything about ComputerCentre's conduct in this case. All it proves is that Mr. Atkins gave her a chance after she paid her debt to society. Since that time, Jene Nelsen has made a lot of people successful. This is just another effort by my opponent to bolster a very weak case with an irrelevant point. But as I think we all know, in deciding this case we have to stick with the merits.

Now, let's talk about the Danielsons' claim. And when you get right down to it, their basic claim is that Mr. Atkins and Ms. Nelsen intentionally defrauded them to get their money and make them fail. Let's ask ourselves, does that make sense? Why would Mr. Atkins want to make one of his own franchisees fail? Mr. Atkins is in the business of developing successful franchises, not failing franchises. He gets a heck of a lot more money from successful franchises than he does from failed franchises.

The whole basic underlying concept of the Danielsons' theory just makes no sense. And if it did make sense, it would show that Mr. Atkins doesn't know what he's doing, because all the other franchises succeeded. If he's trying to make franchises fail, how did he make all the franchises in the country except for the Danielsons' succeed? Let's be serious — it's just a bogus concept.

So let's take this claim of misrepresentations. First of all, we'll admit that everything the Danielsons were told two years ago didn't come true at once. ComputerCentre did experience temporary problems in providing technical training and in providing prompt shipment of inventory. But those representations were commitments that ComputerCentre was making to its franchises for the long run, and they have all turned out to be true.

ComputerCentre does provide advertising. ComputerCentre does provide prompt delivery. ComputerCentre does provide technician training. Additionally, the temporary problems were not that difficult. All it took was simple adjustments, ordering a little earlier and working out ways to get technical assistance. The other franchises handled it just fine. The Danielsons didn't handle it just fine because they weren't paying attention to their business.

What about the training of the Danielsons and the sales personnel? Jene Nelsen said she went to train the Danielsons, and the Danielsons didn't deny it. The problem was that the Danielsons didn't want to accept her help. She said use experienced personnel; they said they wanted to use inexperienced personnel. She told them to order early; they decided to order late. She showed up for meetings; they didn't show up on time for meetings. It's certainly no wonder that Jene Nelsen didn't last the full ten days.

Let's talk about technician training. Sure, there was a temporary delay in getting the technical facility up and going, we admit that. But the facility has been finished, and people are being trained there today. What about the impact on the Danielsons? Well, their own income statement shows that over the last year they spent $2,000 on outside technical services. Let's ask ourselves — what would it have cost them to have a full-time technical assistant? Would it have been $15,000 for that year? Would it have been $20,000? The Danielsons actually *saved money* by using outside services.

What about this claim regarding advertising? Well, first of all, we know that no particular level of advertising was promised. Mr. Atkins said, and the Danielsons admitted, that they were told the advertising might have to be cut back. The Danielsons were given the same advertising support that every other franchise in the country received.

But that's not the important thing about advertising. Think about it, ladies and gentlemen, this is a franchise that wasn't paying a dime of royalties to ComputerCentre. For the entire time that the Danielsons were in operation, they did not provide one royalty payment. How could the Danielsons expect advertising support from ComputerCentre when they weren't even paying royalties?

Quite obviously, advertising support comes out of the royalties received for new sales. No one would ever agree to pay advertising support forever based on a one-time payment of a franchise fee. Yet what did Computer-Centre do? It did provide advertising support; it did send advertising checks to the Danielsons; it just didn't send as many checks as they wanted.

This point, as much as any point, illustrates the good faith of Computer-Centre and the total lack of common sense of the Danielsons. Here these people are, actually expecting ComputerCentre to send them advertising dollars when they won't send ComputerCentre royalty dollars. They just plain wanted a free lunch.

What about this issue of the double markup? Well, there is no double markup. As Mr. Atkins explained, if someone purchases in bulk, he gets a discount. Every franchise that got the 20% markup had a proven record of bulk purchases. The Danielsons have not claimed that they could qualify as a bulk purchaser. Their sales were less than the franchises that got the 20% markup. The Danielsons knew this from day one and never made a complaint about the markup they received.

Drew Anderson had absolutely no basis for his comment that the markup the Danielsons received was higher than normal. As you heard him admit, he had no experience in computer sales and no knowledge on which to base his opinion.

Now let's turn to the so-called fraud in preparing the addendum. The Danielsons try to get out of their royalty commitment by saying Computer-Centre prepared a fraudulent addendum. This one is perhaps their most amazing claim. Ladies and gentlemen, you recall the franchise agreement. Let's take a look at the franchise agreement. The Danielsons admit they signed this document. What does it say? It says that they "agree to pay to ComputerCentre Associates the sum of $52,000, and thereafter to pay a royalty to ComputerCentre Associates on a previously agreed scale, for the life of the contract." These people admit they read that agreement, they knew what it said, and they signed it. Therefore, they knew they agreed to pay a royalty.

What about the addendum? The addendum is the same as the contract addendum for all the other franchises. The royalty is the same — Mr. Atkins told you it's the same. As Mr. Atkins and Ms. Nelsen stated, the Danielsons signed that addendum at the same time they signed their franchise agreement. Those documents just had to be called up from storage, but they were signed on March 10, two years ago.

If those signatures aren't genuine, why haven't the Danielsons produced an expert to say so? And how can they come before you and actually make the amazing claim that they never expected to have to pay a royalty, when they admit they signed an agreement that provided for them to pay a royalty?

The fact is that the Danielsons' claims just don't make sense. You can't be a success in this world without working — everyone knows that. If you don't know what you're doing, you have to follow advice — everyone knows that. You can't ignore a business operation — totally ignore it — and expect it to be successful on its own. Everyone knows that. Yet the Danielsons ask us to pretend we don't know it. Their request just isn't reasonable. There's no basis to hold ComputerCentre liable for the problems they had.

The evidence in this case just doesn't support a finding of liability. But my opponent has addressed the issue of damages, so I want to address it too, just for a minute. He has made a huge claim of many hundreds of thousands of dollars, against my client. Let's take a look at that claim for just a minute.

First, we can forget this point of lost future profits. Lost future profits assumes that someone would want to continue working at the computer store, to run it, and to make it a success. Both of the Danielsons told us very clearly that they could not possibly continue to work at the Computer-Centre franchise. Therefore, there is absolutely no basis to give them anything for lost future profits.

If you take out lost profits, that leaves the net debt, as shown on their own operating statement, of $11,000. But their own statements also show that Mr. Danielson took a salary of $14,000 last year for doing no work. Additionally, Mrs. Danielson took a salary — several thousand dollars — even after she didn't work. Certainly ComputerCentre couldn't be required to pay the Danielsons for not working, and these salaries cancel out that debt.

That leaves us with one other point — the franchise fee of $52,000. But as we know, the Danielsons also agreed to pay royalties to ComputerCentre, which they did not pay. For the last twelve months, the royalty at 5% on sales of $767,000 is over $33,000. In the prior six months we know they did even better, so the royalty would be at least $20,000. Thus, the unpaid royalties are more than $52,000 and cancel out the one payment they did make. This doesn't even count all the advertising dollars sent to the Danielsons by ComputerCentre.

Nothing is owed to the Danielsons. Nothing is owed because Computer-Centre is not liable, but even if ComputerCentre were liable, there are no damages to pay.

In conclusion, ladies and gentlemen, let's think about this case in reason and in fairness. We might feel sorry for the Danielsons, but that's not a reason to impose an unjustified harm on someone else. There is no doubt that the Danielsons caused their own losses, and they now expect you to make someone else pay. Under the law and under any reasonable view of fairness, you can't require ComputerCentre to pay for the Danielsons' failure. They caused their own loss, and they should have to bear that loss.

Therefore, we ask that you bring back a verdict of no liability. That means you should check the box for "no" on the verdict form next to the question that asks: "Is ComputerCentre liable to the Danielsons for fraud?" The answer to that question is no, and that is the answer that you should give. Thank you.

§ 12-15. Example of Closing Argument: Wrongful Death Case.

The following example of a summation is based on a demonstration from a wrongful death case involving a student who was shot by a police officer. The summation deals only with liability.

As I said to you at the beginning of the trial, this is a case in which the wanton and negligent use of violence by a police officer whose senses were impaired by alcohol led to the death of an innocent victim. That victim was a bright, energetic, personable college student who deserved to live. Today his mother comes before you asking for compensation for the terrible fact that her son's life was taken from her.

What I'd like to do is talk about three basic things with you. First of all, I'd like to talk to you about what we believe the facts and the reasonable inferences to be drawn from those facts have proven in this case. Secondly, I'll discuss very briefly your role in deciding the case and what you are required to do. And thirdly, I'm going to talk about the disputes in the evidence, and which side, which version of the facts the evidence actually supports in light of those disputes.

First, what has the evidence shown in this case and the reasonable inferences that can be drawn therefrom? One thing that has been shown is a story about John Killeen, who at the age of twenty-one years was a very admirable young man in every way. In fact, he gave substance and meaning to the idea of the all-American person in many ways. As his mother testified, he was a loving son, a son who was liked by most people, who supported his mother, who got along well with his mother and others, who was admirable in the sense of social inter-relationships and in every way. But in addition to that, he was an achiever in his scholarship and in his other activities.

You heard that at the age of fourteen, he began winning scholarships for the grades that he made at St. Mary's School; that by the time he was seventeen, he had won a National Merit Scholarship, an additional scholarship to Coolidge College, and that despite winning these scholarships he had continued to support his mother while he went to school. That his other activities in high school led him to be honored by being admitted into *Who's Who in American High Schools*.

That subsequent to that, even at Coolidge College, where he took a very hard and arduous pre-med curriculum, he never made anything but an "A." Straight A's for three semesters. He did so well that he was an early admittance to medical school and that the medical school gave him a full scholarship, a very, very unusual thing, with the proviso that of course he would still be able to work to support his mother. Now you've heard that that person, who had his entire life ahead, and I think had a life that was unusually full of promise, had that life snuffed out by a bullet.

Now there are some other aspects to the evidence in this case surrounding the events that have become the focus of attention here. Officer Gunny, who had to go to a demonstration at Coolidge College, was a person who had been a patrolman in this city for approximately ten years. Officer Gunny was a habitual drinker. Every day before going on duty, he drank. He drank martinis. One, two or three martinis every day. And on the day in question, Officer Gunny, in the afternoon, prior to 4:00 p.m., a 4:00 p.m. shift and in fact any day prior to a 4:00 p.m. shift, but this day especially, consumed *some* martinis — two or three, or even more, martinis, prior to the events in question.

He then went on duty with his partner, and they received a call to go to a demonstration at Coolidge College, where they proceeded. They arrived at the university and they observed, off in the distance, a large crowd of people milling around, or actually observing some other people. At that time, knowing that a demonstration was existing there, they made no call for help. They split up. The partner going on, Officer Gunny proceeding forward toward this crowd of people. Officer Gunny proceeded to the crowd where he observed that there was a semi-circle of students, and he did indicate that in his view most of the students at Coolidge College were straight, serious students. And there was a semi-circle of about one hundred onlookers, and then within the semi-circle and off a little bit near the corner of the ROTC building, thirty demonstrators.

Officer Gunny pressed forward through the onlookers into this inner area where he was then facing — by himself, with his partner not there, no one else there — the thirty demonstrators. Officer Gunny then observed a man who he knew as a person who he had arrested previously for breaking windows and being involved as a troublemaker, take a bottle, apparently filled with gasoline, throw it against the corner of the building where it made a "bang" and some fire, but not enough to cause the people watching to leave.

And in the meantime, John Killeen and his friend Terry Ire, moved by curiosity as to what was going on near the ROTC building, just as a hundred other straight and serious students had been moved by curiosity as to what was going on around the ROTC building, they went over to look. And they had moved into a position where they could see what was going on. In fact they were near the front of the onlookers.

After the bottle hit the ROTC building, Officer Gunny tried to arrest this head demonstrator, the leader. Although there were thirty demonstrators and only one of him, in Clint Eastwood style, he moved forward to arrest a 6'4" husky demonstrator. And they began to grapple. They rolled on the ground. They exchanged blows. We know that Officer Gunny with his nightstick delivered a blow to the side of Mark Rider. We know that Mark Rider delivered some blows to the head of Officer Gunny.

We know that at the end they wound up separated, approximately ten feet apart, with Rider crouched — he wasn't even kneeling — in pain from what happened to his side; the police officer standing up with blood on his face, facing Rider. Rider said "Get out of here!" but Officer Gunny didn't leave, though he was still facing thirty demonstrators and felt that he was having problems with blood and so on; he stayed.

Now at this point, Officer Gunny drew his gun. And these demonstrators, or onlookers, who had stayed when an explosion occurred and stayed during the altercation, were moved to fear by the manner in which he was holding and waving that gun to such an extent that everyone turned and ran. Before a shot was fired, that crowd of onlookers was running. Rider was in his crouch. The officer was holding the gun and waving it. Three bullets — "BANG, BANG, BANG" — were fired by the officer.

We know that Rider was hit by at least two and probably all three of those bullets. One bullet entered his chest, exited almost behind it at a downward angle, almost directly behind [gesturing]. Another bullet entered the chest and exited almost directly behind but slightly further left, as the gun moved to the right in double action firing, but again, a downward angle. A third bullet entered the side of the chest and exited slightly below, a quarter inch below, one inch behind, according to the autopsy report, but at that angle it was moving down at the rate of one inch for four inches, three inches per foot, and within twenty feet would have been in the ground. All three bullets discharged, BANG, BANG, BANG.

At that point, John Killeen and Terry Ire turned, looked back, and what did they see? What at least did Terry Ire see? He saw Rider, clutching his stomach, bent over; obviously having received three bullets through the body he would be in that situation. Rider at that point, in fact, was about to fall over. Killeen, also looking back and seeing this, stopped. Obviously this altercation was over. Killeen turned, turned back, to look, in fact, may have started back toward the scene.

Now Officer Gunny at this point had the opportunity to stop again for the third time, to back away. But did he do so? No. Again he fired. BANG, BANG, BANG [gesturing]. And this time, he hit, probably with the first shot a falling man, a man who had an entry wound in the left chest and an exit wound in the right, below it to the right of the chest on the side. He could only have been shot as he fell to the ground.

The second shot: BANG! — probably killed or mortally wounded John Killeen [gesturing].

A third shot: BANG! — may have been the one stray bullet.

John Killeen was mortally wounded. He didn't die immediately — he was taken to the hospital where the records show he was writhing in such pain that they had to strap him down. But he did eventually die and that is the subject of this case, this lawsuit.

Now that leads me to the second part of what I have to say, because it's your job to evaluate the evidence. The judge is going to instruct you as to the law, and you are going to apply that law to the facts of this case. The judge is going to tell you that if the officer in this case used excessive force, was negligent, that Mary Killeen is entitled to a judgment against the officer. And if the officer was acting in accordance with, or within the scope and course of his normal duties as a police officer while under active duty, which he was, that the city and the police department are also liable.

He will instruct you that we have the burden of proof and must prove our case by a preponderance of the evidence, which means that it must be more than a tie. We have to have a little bit more credible and believable evidence, in your view, than the defense has credible and believable evidence. The judge will explain all that to you. It will be your job to evaluate the evidence to see what the facts are. But in this case it's nothing close to a tie, ladies and gentlemen of the jury. The evidence very, very much favors Mary Killeen's version of this case.

You've heard two versions. You heard our version, and you heard Officer Gunny's version. Now what supports our version? One thing that supports it is the testimony of the bartender, Mr. Gus Rizzuto, who is a friend of Officer Gunny's and has known him for years and has every reason to be on his side or friendly to him. What did he say? That he had a habit of drinking prior to going on duty. That he was an afternoon drinker when he went on afternoon shift. That on this day in question, he had *some* martinis. Two or three or more martinis. Any logical person knows that to some extent, a person's judgment is impaired if that person has had *some* martinis.

In addition to that, you have the testimony of Terry Ire, who described to you what occurred in this case, described going over out of curiosity to view with the other onlookers who had gone to see this demonstration, and observing what occurred. Observing Rider in his crouch. Observing the police officer pulling the gun out, and the people starting to run.

And then BANG, BANG, BANG! A series of three shots, and then a pause, and then turning back, and Killeen turning back, and apparently Killeen turning to look. And then, despite the fact that everything appeared to have been over, BANG, BANG, BANG again. And seeing his friend on the ground, mortally wounded.

You have some testimony pertaining to the admissions of Officer Gunny. Officer Gunny admitted that he pressed forward through these crowds of onlookers. He admitted that he didn't call for further help. He admitted that he didn't wait for his partner. He admitted that he didn't take Mark Rider's invitation to leave. He admitted that he fired until his gun was empty — six shots. He admitted to all of that.

Perhaps most importantly you have the autopsy report. Autopsy reports don't lie. The autopsy report says that there were ten bullet holes. There was entry wound and an exit wound. An entry wound and an exit wound [gesturing]. An entry wound and an exit wound in Mark Rider, consistent with BANG, BANG, BANG, as the double-action gun moves to the right. An entry wound and an exit wound consistent with a man shot as he's falling to the ground, after already being wounded, made helpless. They don't lie.

And you have another autopsy report that says that there was an entry wound and an exit wound in John Killeen that was the cause of his death.

Now against all that evidence you have the version of Officer Gunny, which is not supported by the evidence. Officer Gunny says that he had one beer, or maybe one drink, on this occasion, which is contradicted by his own friend, Mr. Gus Rizzuto. Officer Gunny says that Mark Rider had some sort of a razor in his hand, but Terry Ire says he didn't see a razor. And in addition to that, even Gunny admits that Mark Rider was saying "get out of here," and he didn't accept that invitation to get out of there or avoid trouble; he claims — with style — he was alone against thirty demonstrators.

And Officer Gunny, and this is perhaps one of the most important things, says that he was being attacked as he shot Mark Rider. Well, if the man is 6'4" tall — lunges at you, and you shoot, would you expect the bullets to go down? And yet the autopsy report shows that *every bullet* entered at a higher level than it exited Mark Rider's body, consistent with the man being in a crouch after being injured in the side by a blow from a nightstick, just as Jerry Ire described. And of course at that point, certainly there's no way that the man could be attacking as he fell to the ground.

And in addition to that, one last important thing, Officer Gunny says that he fired into the air and that he ran into the back as he parried a blow from the razor blade, and the gun went off a second time. And that he fired, then he fired double-action four times. And of course then the bullet magically under that version being sent up into the air, and entered the body and passed directly through it, it's just not possible that that version of events occurred. It's also not possible with double-action — bang, bang, bang, bang — that a person could get three bullets straight on but then quickly move to the side as if falling down to receive the fourth one. Those autopsy facts are consistent only with one version of the events: Jerry Ire's version, the plaintiff's version.

And as he fell to the ground, Officer Gunny decided to finish the job. He fired a bullet into the falling man, a second bullet that hit John Killeen, and a third bullet that went astray. And that, ladies and gentlemen of the jury, is what is known as excessive force and negligence. It's the single cause of death of that bright hope, and Mrs. Killeen is entitled to recover for her loss.

* * *

§ 12-16. Post-Trial Memoranda.

When the judge must decide some or all of the issues, and takes the matter under submission, you usually should submit a post-trial memorandum. You can use the memorandum to argue the meaning of evidence and the application of the law to the evidence. Thus, the memorandum may serve as a written closing argument. The memorandum should be aimed at persuasion, although the court usually has a good idea of the appropriate outcome by the close of the trial. The memorandum also should help the court prepare a well-reasoned decision, which makes it more likely to stand up on appeal.

In most post-trial memoranda, there is no need for an objective statement of the facts. Once the trial is complete, the court should be familiar with the facts. The primary objective is to argue the inferences and conclusions to be drawn from the evidence. Additionally, the memorandum should show that the authorities, when applied to the factual conclusions, require a favorable decision.

The basic parts of a post-trial memorandum should include: (1) an introduction, (2) an argument of facts and authorities, and (3) a conclusion. The introduction briefly should describe the purpose of the memorandum in a manner that captures the theme:

> This post-trial memorandum is submitted on behalf of Jack and Margaret Danielson, plaintiffs, to review the facts and authorities establishing that the Danielsons are entitled to recover for the misrepresentations that led them to purchase a franchise from ComputerCentre Associates ("ComputerCentre"), defendant, and for the failure of ComputerCentre to fulfill its promises.

In the argument, you should draw factual conclusions and show how the evidence supports these conclusions. If a transcript is available, you should provide transcript references to support factual claims. If the transcript is not available, provide references to witnesses' testimony or exhibits. Set off these references by brackets or parentheses: [Test. of Mary Jones; pl. ex. 2; test. of Ron Smith]. Place them at the ends of paragraphs, or the ends of sentences, to avoid disrupting the readability of the text.

In making factual arguments, move from the general to the specific, drawing conclusions and then providing evidentiary support. Indeed, use introductory paragraphs to describe ultimate factual and legal conclusions. The argument should document the factual claims and show how these contentions, combined with the applicable legal principles, support a favorable result. Moving from the general to the specific makes it easy for the judge to understand the context of the arguments and follow their logic.

The post-trial memorandum also should discuss the failure of the opposing party to prove its case. Review the absence of evidence to support your opponent's factual contentions, along with factual inconsistencies and logical flaws in her case. Again, the memorandum serves as a written, formal closing argument.

The legal discussion should explain how the ultimate facts are controlled by favorable authorities. The court should have a good understanding of the applicable legal principles, either through experience with similar cases or from pre-trial memoranda. Thus, you may be able to briefly set out the principles and concentrate on the evidentiary arguments. In some cases, however, you must develop the nuances in the authorities for their application to particular facts. Once a judge has heard the entire case, he may more easily see the importance of legal fine points.

The post-trial memorandum also should address any outstanding issues, such as unresolved evidentiary motions. This action helps ensure that they are actually resolved, and resolved correctly, by the court.

§ 12-17. Proposed Findings of Fact and Conclusions of Law.

Some courts require the submission of proposed findings of fact and conclusions of law in nonjury cases. The findings and conclusions serve as the basis for the court to prepare a written decision.

Take advantage of the opportunity to submit findings and conclusions. When the court does not explicitly require their submission, inquire as to whether the court wishes to receive them. Although the findings and conclusions are no more persuasive than the post-trial memorandum, submitting them has benefits. First, if the judge's decision is favorable, the findings and conclusions help ensure that the opinion has a solid basis. Second, proposed findings and conclusions help the judge provide a speedy decision. Third, if the findings and conclusions are better prepared than those of your opponent, they may provide the easiest path to a decision. Thus, they may influence the result.

The following techniques should be used in preparing proposed findings of fact and conclusions of law:

1. *Use the objective style.* You should write the findings and conclusions in the style that would be used by an unbiased third party. Their purpose is to serve as a basis for the court's opinion. A judge is more likely to adopt your submissions if they are phrased as they would be in the opinion. Numbering the paragraphs enhances the appearance of objectivity. Each paragraph should provide a factual or legal conclusion and its basis, so that the judge can pick out findings and conclusions for incorporation into the opinion.

2. *Provide detailed findings of fact.* Too often advocates submit proposed findings that are nothing more than ultimate factual contentions. This approach provides little help to the court and is not likely to have persuasive impact. You should provide findings not only for ultimate facts, but for any facts on which ultimate conclusions are based. Additionally, provide references to the evidence supporting these factual claims. Remember that fact findings are presumed correct on appeal. A favorable decision is less subject to reversal if the court supports it by well-documented fact findings.

3. *Move from the general to the specific.* You should provide general conclusions first, followed by specific supporting facts or evidence. If the finding contains an ultimate point, state that point first, followed by its factual basis. More specific findings should be stated in separate paragraphs, with the underlying specific factual basis. This approach facilitates an understanding of the proposed findings and conclusions and makes it easy for the court to incorporate them in an opinion.

4. *Document the factual claims and legal conclusions.* You should provide the evidentiary basis for factual claims and citations for legal conclusions. If they are available, provide transcript references for factual assertions. Indeed, you may wish to quote key statements of witnesses and important documents. If a transcript is unavailable, cite to the testimony of witnesses. Place record references between sentences or group them at the end of paragraphs. The conclusions of law should state principles from the authorities. Provide a statutory or case citation, with reference to the relevant page of the court's opinion, for each conclusion. Argument concerning the meaning of cases usually should be provided in the post-trial memorandum.[12]

---

[12] For a more detailed discussion of the post-trial memorandum, see MICHAEL R. FONTHAM, MICHAEL VITIELLO AND DAVID W. MILLER, PERSUASIVE WRITTEN AND ORAL ADVOCACY IN TRIAL AND APPELLATE COURTS § 8.8 (2002).

APPENDIX A

DANIELSON v. COMPUTERCENTRE ASSOCIATES

The following case file is reproduced with the permission of the Practicing Law Institute and the author, Professor Kent Sinclair.

APPENDIX A

Danielson v. ComputerCentre Associates

Statement of the Case:

This is a civil action brought on behalf of Jack and Margaret Danielson, husband and wife, following their purchase of a franchise to run a computer store under arrangements with defendant ComputerCentre Associates. The store opened in May, two years ago, and closed fifteen months later, in September of last year. Plaintiffs allege violations of the Federal Trade Commission Act, common-law fraud in the misrepresenting of the arrangements for running this franchise, the capacities of defendants, and the financial attractiveness of the franchise itself, as well as breach of fiduciary duty and conflict of interest. There are five core witnesses and two optional witnesses in the discretion of the instructor:

Plaintiffs' Witnesses:

    Jack Danielson (proprietor)
    Margaret Danielson (co-proprietor)
    Drew Anderson (interim manager of the franchise)
    — optional witness: Loren Walsh (customer)

Defendant's Witnesses:

    Dale Atkins (principal of ComputerCentre Associates)
    Terry Johansen (technical services manager, ComputerCentre Associates)
    — optional witness: Jene Nelsen (sales manager, ComputerCentre Associates)

APPENDIX A

UNITED STATES DISTRICT COURT
CENTRAL DISTRICT OF THE STATE OF EAST

JACK DANIELSON, et al.,
 	
               Plaintiffs
 	
      -against-
 	
COMPUTERCENTRE
ASSOCIATES,
  and DALE ATKINS,
 	
               Defendants
	Civil Action No. 99-7201
	
	COMPLAINT

Plaintiffs, by their attorneys, for their complaint, aver:

1. This action is brought in the United States District Court for the Central District of East by and through the undersigned attorneys on behalf of all plaintiffs in this action.

2. This action is brought under the antifraud provisions of the Federal Trade Commission Act, 15 U.S.C. 13(c) and, as an action under the provisions of diversity of citizenship, 28 U.S.C. 1332, on grounds of common law fraud and fraud in the marketing of a franchise.

The Parties

3. Plaintiff Jack Danielson is a resident of the State of East, with a domicile at 1234 Barstow Avenue, Middletown. He is the co-owner with his wife of "The Middletown ComputerCentre," located at 1330 Main Street Plaza, Middletown.

4. Plaintiff Margaret Danielson is the wife of Jack Danielson, and resides at the same address. She is a co-owner of "The Middletown ComputerCentre," located at the address above.

Defendants

5. Defendant ComputerCentre Associates is, upon information and belief, a corporation or limited partnership headquartered in Boston, Massachusetts and engaged principally in the business of marketing nationwide the franchises for "ComputerCentre." The headquarters and principal place of business of ComputerCentre Associates is 1710 Shore Drive, Boston, Massachusetts. Upon information and belief, ComputerCentre Associates is registered and doing business under the laws of Massachusetts.

6. Defendant Dale Atkins is, upon information and belief, a domiciliary of the State of Massachusetts with an office address at 1710 Shore Drive, Boston,

APPENDIX A

Massachusetts. Defendant Dale Atkins is the principal of ComputerCentre Associates and, upon information and belief, is either the general partner or president of the organization.

The Facts

7. On or about January 15th, two years ago, plaintiffs Jack and Margaret Danielson read an advertisement published in the January 12th issue of The Wall Street Journal advertising franchises being offered by ComputerCentre Associates. The advertisement, attached and annexed hereto as Exhibit A and incorporated by reference in this paragraph, set forth certain of the terms of an offering of franchises in ComputerCentre Associates and, further, provided an "800 number" to call for further information.

8. On or about January 16th, two years ago, plaintiffs Jack and Margaret Danielson called the toll-free number provided in The Wall Street Journal advertisement for ComputerCentre Associates. At that time plaintiff Jack Danielson spoke with an individual who identified herself as Sherry, and who advised plaintiffs that a "public forum" on the ComputerCentre franchises was going to be offered in early February at the Holiday Inn in Middletown, State of East, to provide further information and answer questions from those interested in learning more about franchises for ComputerCentres. *acting as agent?*

9. The woman identifying herself as "Sherry" told plaintiff Jack Danielson that, while she did not have the full information packet, ComputerCentre franchises were "going like hotcakes" and were "really a good deal."

10. On or about February 12th, two years ago, plaintiff Jack Danielson attended a presentation made at the Holiday Inn in Middletown on behalf of ComputerCentre Associates. Such presentation was attended by defendant Dale Atkins and an assistant to Atkins by the name of Jene Nelsen. There were, in addition, one or two clerical personnel on behalf of ComputerCentre there, taking information, including financial background sheets from each of the attending parties.

11. In addition to the individual plaintiffs herein, the presentation was attended by some 13 persons from a 300-mile radius in the State of East.

12. Plaintiffs filled out the "financial background sheet" requested by defendants. A copy of the information sheet was left with plaintiffs and is annexed hereto as Exhibit B to this complain, incorporated by reference herein to the same extent as though set forth in haec verba. *(in these exact words)*

13. The presentation on February 12th, two years ago, lasted six hours. It included a videotape showing ComputerCentres in such major cities as Los Angeles, San Francisco and Chicago. The program featured speeches by defendant Dale Atkins and the assistant, Jene Nelsen.

732

APPENDIX A

14. In the course of the public presentation on February 12, two years ago, the following representations were made in the knowledge and on the expectation that plaintiffs would rely thereon:

a. that ComputerCentres was an attractive investment opportunity for the small investor;

b. that ComputerCentres did not require technical expertise, an electronics degree, or other advanced training in order to engage in the business profitably;

c. that ComputerCentres required only a modest financial commitment;

d. that large numbers of persons without prior experience in the mini- or micro-computer field had opened ComputerCentres successfully;

e. that all ComputerCentre franchises in existence at the time of the February 12 program were being operated at a substantial profit to their owners;

f. that no difficulties had evolved in the marketing of computers through the ComputerCentre network;

g. that ComputerCentre Associates had the inventory to supply computers promptly to fill orders at each ComputerCentre franchise location;

h. that ComputerCentre Associates would maintain a technical backup facility capable of prompt repair of computers marketed by the franchises;

i. that ComputerCentre Associates would maintain a technical training facility such that each franchise would be entitled to have its computer repair personnel trained at the headquarters free of charge and thus be equipped to provide local repair for the brands and models of computers being handled by the franchise;

j. that ComputerCentre Associates would provide expert selection of computer models to be carried in each franchise;

k. that ComputerCentre Associates would carry sufficient inventory of the models being carried to provide rapid supply of equipment to each franchisee;

l. that ComputerCentre Associates would supply technical assistance to each franchisee in setting up the accounting systems and other arrangements necessary to operate a computer store sales facility.

15. On or about March 10, two years ago, plaintiffs Jack and Margaret Danielson met in Conference Room C of the Marriott Hotel in downtown Middletown with defendant Dale Atkins and the assistant, Jene Nelsen. No other persons attended this meeting. At that time plaintiffs expressed their interest in pursuing arrangements to become the ComputerCentre Associates franchisee for the Middletown area.

16. During the course of the March 10 meeting, defendant Dale Atkins, Jene Nelsen, or both, reiterated each and every representation set forth in the preceding paragraphs and, in addition, made the following additional representations:

a. that ComputerCentre Associates would supply plaintiffs with adequate stocks of brochures, flyers, and promotional handouts;

b. that ComputerCentre Associates would supply "camera ready" artwork for use in local newspaper advertising campaigns;

c. that ComputerCentre Associates would engage in a program of "institutional advertising" in the national print and video media to create public awareness of the ComputerCentre franchises and the facilities and equipment being carried by those franchises;

d. that ComputerCentre Associates would, on a cooperative basis, pay 50% of the advertising cost for local television and radio "spot advertisements" using either materials developed by ComputerCentre Associates or the local franchise;

e. that each of the franchises in existence at March 10, two years ago, was "highly profitable" and that operating a ComputerCentre was "goldmine";

f. that Middletown had the demographic characteristics to make it a successful franchise area;

g. that towns smaller and hence "worse" as a market for mini- and micro-computers were presently the locations for several of the ComputerCentre franchises and that each of these locations had been "a cash cow to be milked by the owners."

17. At the meeting on March 10, two years ago, defendant Dale Atkins specifically represented that he possessed the experience in micro-computer marketing necessary to assure that the product lines carried by ComputerCentres would be "top of the line" and "the fastest moving products in the business." Atkins further represented that a broad spectrum of price ranges would be represented in the products carried and the "the necessary inventory would be slight because of the ability of ComputerCentre Associates headquarters to dropship equipment on 24 hours notice."

18. On March 10, two years ago, plaintiffs received a Franchise Disclosure Statement from defendants, annexed here as Exhibit C and incorporated by reference herein, which utterly failed to provide any concrete information despite its purported compliance with 16 CFR 436. Thereafter plaintiffs Jack and Margaret Danielson signed a "franchise agreement" annexed hereto as Exhibit D and incorporated by reference herein. Also on March 10, two years ago, plaintiffs tendered to defendant Atkins their check in the amount of $52,000 as the full and complete payment of the franchise fee called for in the franchise agreement, Exhibit D. A photocopy of this check is annexed hereto as Exhibit E and is incorporated by reference herein. Further, at the March 10 meeting, plaintiffs displayed to defendants and delivered to them a photocopy of a "letter of credit" running to the benefit of plaintiffs, and obtained by plaintiffs by the

Central National Bank in Middletown. A copy of this letter of credit is set forth as Exhibit F hereto. The purpose of this letter was to finance the inventory of computer equipment to be maintained at the premises of the Middletown ComputerCentre.

19. All of the representations by defendants Dale Atkins and Computer-Centre Associates, set forth in paragraphs 14, 16 and 17 above, were false and misleading. Defendants Atkins and ComputerCentre Associates knew, or in the exercise of reasonable diligence should have known, that each and every representation set forth in paragraphs 14, 16 and 17 above were false and would be relied on by plaintiffs to their substantial financial and emotional detriment.

20. Following the meeting of March 10, two years ago, plaintiffs on March 17 and 19 signed leases for retail space at 1330 Main Street Plaza, Middletown and warehouse storage space at 1130 Prospect Avenue, Middletown.

21. In further reliance on the representations and arrangements struck with ComputerCentre Associates, plaintiffs on March 27 and April 10, two years ago, placed ads in the local newspapers in Middletown and in April, hired two salesmen to assist them in the operation of the Middletown ComputerCentre.

22. The Middletown ComputerCentre opened in May, two years ago.

23. During the start-up period plaintiffs experienced the following difficulties in their relationship with ComputerCentre Associates:

a. initial inventory was late in arriving for the May opening ceremonies, such that the advertisements for local papers promised more equipment than was actually on hand at the time of the opening;

b. the "accounting software" which was to be provided to the Middletown ComputerCentre for its own bookkeeping purposes did not arrive until October;

c. instead of the ten-day to two-week "training program" plaintiffs were led to expect, Jene Nelsen visited Middletown on behalf of ComputerCentre Associates for a total of three days during late April, two years ago, to work with plaintiffs on the subject of how to actually operate the franchise.

24. In or about September, two years ago, plaintiff Jack Danielson had a telephone conversation with defendant Dale Atkins in which plaintiffs demanded immediate delivery of the "accounting software" for operation of the franchise itself and prompt delivery of the order forms and inventory records necessary to obtain equipment for customers from the ComputerCentre Associates Depot in Boston, Massachusetts. Defendant Atkins took a very "haughty" attitude during this telephone conversation and belittled the business acumen of plaintiffs, commenting "Can't you guys do anything for yourself?" During this telephone call defendant Atkins became abusive and threatened to revoke the Middletown franchise agreement. At that moment in the telephone conversation plaintiff Jack Danielson suffered a major heart attack and was hospitalized under a diagnosis

of "acute myocardiac infarction" in the intensive care unit at the Middletown General Hospital.

25. During the three weeks plaintiff Jack Danielson spent in the hospital plaintiff Margaret Danielson ran the Middletown ComputerCentre. After consultation with cardiovascular experts, plaintiff Jack Danielson underwent open-heart surgery October 2, two years ago, and began a successful four-month recuperative period.

26. During the period November 1, two years ago, through June last year, plaintiff Margaret Danielson ran the franchise, and plaintiffs experienced, among many others, the following difficulties caused by defendants:

a. On six occasions defendants refused to answer the phone or return telephone calls from plaintiffs;

b. Thirteen sales were lost by plaintiffs because the delay of defendants in shipping order equipment was so significant that the customers withdrew their orders;

c. Plaintiffs were compelled to send their technician to an RCA computer technician academy in Lexington, Kentucky for training because the defendants' technical center was not established in time to provide the requisite electronics training for the franchise personnel;

d. Throughout its operation the franchise was charged a 40% mark-up on all items ordered, literally twice the industry standard 20% mark-up. This increased cost rendered the franchise, which otherwise would have made money, unable to turn a profit. This charge was caused due to the conflict of interest of defendant Atkins, who owns an interest in the wholesaler.

27. On June 23, last year, plaintiff Margaret Danielson, acting on behalf of the Middletown ComputerCentre, employed Drew Anderson to serve as the manager for the franchise.

28. Throughout the remainder of the summer last year, Drew Anderson made every effort to keep the Middletown franchise solvent. To this end, Anderson fired all other salesmen, reduced the business hours of the Centre to the period from 10:00 a.m. to 6:00 p.m. Monday through Saturday, increased local advertising expenditures, and, in an effort to improve weekly sales, stocked a series of low-cost computers to supplement the product lines being fostered by defendants.

29. Nevertheless, on August 29, last year, the financial position of the Middletown ComputerCentre had reached the state reflected in Exhibit G to this Complaint, annexed and incorporated herein by reference.

30. On August 30, last year, plaintiff Margaret Danielson called defendants. In response to her request for financial, management, and technical assistance

to keep the franchise afloat, defendant Dale Atkins, on behalf of Atkins and ComputerCentre Associates, told plaintiffs to "stuff it." Further, defendant Dale Atkins demanded payment of an additional $18,000 franchise fee within 10 days and, further, advised Margaret Danielson that in the event that defendants did not receive a check for an additional amount equaling 5% of the gross sales experienced by the franchise from the date of the telephone call, that he would "take legal action" to "close you down."

31. On September 6, last year, plaintiff Margaret Danielson closed the Middletown ComputerCentre.

Claims for Relief

32. Each of the foregoing paragraphs of this Complaint is reincorporated and realleged with full force and effect.

33. The conduct of defendants herein violates the franchising and antifraud provisions of the Federal Trade Commission Act, 15 U.S.C. 13(c) and 16 CFR 436. Defendants are jointly and severally liable to plaintiffs therefor.

34. In addition, the conduct of defendants as set forth in the preceding paragraphs of this Complaint, constitutes fraudulent misrepresentations made in the knowledge that plaintiffs would rely to their detriment thereon, and plaintiffs, as shown above, did in fact rely to their extreme financial, emotional, and physical detriment, on these misrepresentations. Therefore, plaintiffs are entitled to damages of common law fraud.

WHEREFORE:

Plaintiffs demand judgment on the foregoing theories in the following amounts:

a. $52,000, in the form of the franchise fee paid by the check set forth as Exhibit E hereto.

b. $112,715.37, being the amount by which plaintiffs' expenses, and existing debts, arising out of the operation of the Middletown ComputerCentre exceeded all income and other monies derived from operation of the franchise.

c. The profits plaintiffs would have earned over the first 10 years of franchise operation had the defendants purchased computers from a truly independent wholesaler and charged plaintiffs only 20% markup, such profits estimated to exceed $100,000 annually.

d. Such doubling, trebling, or quadrupling of damages as may be permitted under pertinent law.

e. $5,000,000, as punitive damages for the intentional, wanton, malicious, and fraudulent conduct engaged in by these defendants.

f. Attorneys' fees to plaintiffs' counsel, in an amount yet to be determined but estimated to exceed $42,000.

g. Such other and further relief as the premises may warrant and may to the court appear just.

36. Plaintiff reserves the right to amend and supplement its damage claims as the final expenses, returns, and claims — including customer suits and warranty claims — are received, processed, settled, or paid.

Dated: December 15, last year   _____
               Middletown, State of East   Counsel for Plaintiffs
                                                                  4321 Northcross Circle
                                                                  Middletown, East
                                                                  (800) 987-6543

Verification

We, the undersigned, are the individual plaintiffs named in the foregoing complaint in this action. We, and each of us, have read the foregoing complaint and know the contents thereof to be true. Thus, with the exception of the portions of the complaint averred with knowledge and belief, we hereby affirm, under penalties of perjury, that the foregoing complaint is true and correct to the best of our knowledge.

_____
Jack T. Danielson

_____
Margaret M. Danielson

Sworn to before me this 15th day of December,

_____
Notary Public

UNITED STATES DISTRICT COURT
CENTRAL DISTRICT OF THE STATE OF EAST

JACK DANIELSON, et al.,

                Plaintiffs

       -against-

COMPUTERCENTRE
ASSOCIATES,
  and DALE ATKINS,

                Defendants

Civil Action No. 99-7201
DEFENDANTS' ANSWER

Defendants ComputerCentre Associates and Dale Atkins, by and through their attorneys, for their answer, respond and aver as follows:

1. Defendants deem paragraphs 1 and 2 to allege matter as to which no responsive pleading is required.

2. Defendants deny information sufficient to form a belief as to the following paragraphs of the Complaint: paragraphs 3, 4, 7, 8, 20, 21, 25, 27, 28, 29, 30, and 31.

3. Defendants admit the allegations of paragraphs 5, 6, 8, 10, 11, 12, 13, 15, and 22.

4. Defendants deny each and every avowment in paragraphs 14, 16, 17, 19, 23, 24, 26, 32, 33, 34, 35, and 36.

5. Defendants admit the amounts of paragraph 18 of the complaint, except denies the characterization in the complaint as to Exhibit C, the Franchise Disclosure Statement.

Defendants' Answer

As and For a First Affirmative Defense, Defendants Allege:

6. Plaintiff lacked the requisite expertise to run a small business and caused their own insolvency.

As and For a Second Affirmative Defense, Defendants Allege:

7. Plaintiffs' personal circumstances, including health, caused the closure of the Middletown ComputerCentre, Inc. The necessity of hiring an independent manager, at a high salary, caused any financial difficulties which plaintiffs experienced and defendants are not responsible therefor.

As and For a Third Affirmative Defense, Defendants Allege:

8. Plaintiffs violated the terms of the franchise agreement herein by stocking throughout the summer last year, supplies and equipment not approved or selected by ComputerCentre Associates and which demeaned and degraded the character of the franchise. Such "cheap" or "low-end" equipment as the Commodore "VIC-20" and "TI99" home computers were inconsistent with the image of professionalism which was to characterize the ComputerCentre franchise operation and thus contributed to the failure of the Middletown franchise to establish itself as a competent provided of quality micro- and mini-computer equipment.

As and For a Fourth Affirmative Defense, Defendants Allege:

9. At no time did plaintiffs employ a trained or educated computer technician capable of learning computer repair techniques. Therefore, plaintiffs were and are at all times relevant to this action, in default of the provision of their franchise obligation requiring them to have available sufficient and technically qualified personnel to provide routine maintenance at a "shop" desk in support of warranty and other service obligations of the franchise.

As and For a Fifth Affirmative Defense, Defendants Allege:

10. Plaintiffs failed to obtain the services of experienced personnel capable of encouraging and closing sales for sophisticated micro-computer equipment.

As and For a Sixth Affirmative Defense, Defendants Allege:

11. Plaintiffs failed to take advantage of the defendants' cooperative advertising campaign and, upon information and belief, failed adequately to advertise the availability of the services and equipment in the territory.

As and For a Seventh Affirmative Defense, Defendants Allege:

12. Plaintiffs lacked the requisite financial resources to carry an adequate inventory to serve the population in the Middletown area. This financial capacity, represented to the defendants in a letter of credit and oral statements by the plaintiffs to the effect that they would be able to maintain an adequate inventory to provide immediate delivery of the most common sales items, was lacking throughout the period that the franchise was in operation. Moreover, after plaintiff Jack Danielson experienced physical ailment early during the course of the franchise's operations, assets of the franchise were devoted to the payment of medical expenses of Jack Danielson and, therefore, the inventory available during the last year of its operation was inadequate to provide customer satisfaction.

As and For an Eighth Affirmative Defense, Defendants Allege:

13. Of the 47 ComputerCentre franchises around the United States, only one has become insolvent or closed its doors: plaintiff herein. Under the doctrine of res ipsa loquitur, it is obvious that any difficulties encountered by the plaintiffs herein were as a result of their own lack of business experience, improvident decisions made during the course of the franchise, health difficulties for which

740

defendants are not responsible, breaches of the franchise agreement by the plaintiff, and other causes for which defendants carry no responsibility whatsoever.

As and For a First Counterclaim Defendants Allege:

14. On or about March 10, two years ago, plaintiffs undertook to pay a franchise fee for the right to open an establishment under the marque of ComputerCentre. This franchise fee was reflected in a check received from plaintiffs in the amount of $52,000, annexed as Exhibit E to the Complaint, and a promissory note payable 12 months after commencement of operation of the franchise in the amount of $18,000. A copy of this promissory note is attached to this Answer as Exhibit 1 and is incorporated herein by reference.

15. Upon the failure of plaintiffs to effect payment of the principal amount of the promissory note on or about May 15, last year, defendants duly made demand for payment of the full amount of said note.

16. From the date of demand to and including the day and date of this Answer and Counterclaim, plaintiffs have paid no part of the principal or interest due under the promissory note attached to this Answer as Exhibit 1.

17. Wherefore defendants demand judgment in the amount of $18,000 plus interest at the rate of 18% as provided in paragraph 3 of the promissory note, and attorneys' fees in the amount of $10,000 as provided in paragraph 4 of the promissory note, Exhibit 1 to this Answer and Counterclaim.

As and For a Second Counterclaim Defendants Allege:

18. As part of its franchise obligations under the franchise agreement dated March 10 and set forth, in partial form, as Exhibit D to the Complaint herein, plaintiffs undertook to pay defendants an additional sum equal to 5% of the gross selling price for all merchandise sold during the first five years of operation of the Middletown ComputerCentre and 2 1/2% of the gross selling price for sales thereafter. This agreement was embodied in an "Addendum" to the franchise agreement executed by the parties on March 10, two years ago. Such addendum is attached to this Answer and Counterclaim as Exhibit 2 and is incorporated by reference herein.

19. By virtue of the franchise agreement and the integral addendum thereto, plaintiffs are indebted to defendants in an amount as yet to be determined but which appears, based on the financial statements set forth as Exhibit G to the Complain herein, to exceed $35,000 (5% of at least $720,000 in gross sales).

Wherefore,

20. Defendants demand judgment dismissing plaintiffs' complaint, awarding defendants judgment on each of their counterclaims set forth for the sums requested therein, and such other and additional relief as may to the court appear warranted in the circumstances.

APPENDIX A

Defendants, by Dale Atkins, aver that the foregoing Answer and Counterclaims are true to the best of their personal knowledge.

Date:

Sworn to before

on this ———— day

of   .

_____

Notary Public

APPENDIX A

AFFIDAVIT OF JACK DANIELSON IN SUPPORT OF PLAINTIFFS' MOTION FOR SUMMARY JUDGMENT

1. Three years ago I retired from the Middletown Police force after twenty years. Since I am only in my forties my wife and I set about the prospect of finding a business in which we could engage to supplement my retirement benefits from the police force. We investigated a number of franchises and attended a regional "franchise show" held in a large coliseum at which about 10,000 people were in attendance. We walked from booth to booth and picked up literature on literally dozens of possible franchises, attempting to figure out what the minimum capital investment was and what it would be like to operate each of the franchises. It was not, however, until January two years ago that we saw an advertisement in the Wall Street Journal offering the franchises for a "ComputerCentre," a retail sales operation selling micro and mini-computers.

2. I had some experience with small computers while working on the police force. The Criminal Information Network (CIN) for our state has a central records data bank containing the criminal records of all convicts and ex-convicts in the state. Further we link up to the FBI public information network (PIN) on criminal records. From time to time in my duties as an officer in the racket and fraud bureau of the department during my last three years on the force, I used a computer terminal located at the station house to communicate, through a "modem" attached to a telephone line, to obtain information from the state CIN and the FBI PIN information computers. Thus, I became familiar with computer operation in a general sense by using the terminal at the station. Among other things I learned how to turn the computer on, type instructions to "log on" to a communications program, used the modem and communications "software," to instruct the computer to dial the numbers I wished to reach, and to follow the "menus" displayed on the screen in order to obtain information from the distant computer data banks available to us at the police station. The communication software used at the police station was contained on a 5 and 1/4 inch floppy disk and therefore I was required to learn a modest amount about the handling of disks, how to insert them in the computer and to remove them, and general care of the disks and computer hardware. I had no formal training in dealing with the computer; one of the other officers simply explained to me the procedure we use to obtain the criminal record information which was required for our work.

3. When my wife and I saw the advertisement in the Wall Street Journal for the ComputerCentre franchises, we discussed the matter of opening a store to sell micro and mini-computers. We thought that was a timely business, with a rapidly expanding market, and that we could be part of the so-called "high tech" revolution without having to go back to school for extensive retraining, be means of purchasing a franchise.

4. We recognized that a substantial amount of cash would be required to go into any business, especially one with expensive products to sell such as small

computers. We owned our house free and clear, however, and we decided that having a productive business was sufficiently important that we take out a mortgage on the house to finance the commencement of our business. My wife is my partner in life and fully supported the idea of opening a franchise. A couple of days after we saw the ad in the Wall Street Journal I called the "800" number listed there to ask about the availability of the franchises and what the financial terms were. A woman answered the phone and identified herself as "Sherry." She was unable to give me more than a sketch of the financial information I was seeking. She did say, however, that the franchises were "going like hotcakes" and that most people thought that they were "really a good deal." I asked her how I might get further information about the ComputerCentre franchises. She told me that there would be a "public forum" at the Holiday Inn in Middletown for a number of persons who had expressed interest in the franchises. I asked her when the forum was to take place and she told me it would be February 12.

5. I attended the presentation on February 12 at the Holiday Inn in Middletown. There were perhaps 12 or 13 other people present, some married couples and some individuals. It was at this meeting that I first made the acquaintance of Dale Atkins, the head of ComputerCentre. There were other people at the meeting from ComputerCentre. One I remember was named Jene Nelsen, an incredibly pushy and insistent salesperson. Nelsen was in attendance throughout the presentation and was constantly asking us personal questions and insisting on our agreement with every tiny fact which was mentioned about the nature of the computer revolution, the amount of money that people were making in marketing computers, the wisdom of the concept of franchise sales, the need for expert assistance in the marketing of a complex technological device like a computer, and virtually every other statement which was made. If we did not nod our head or indicate our assent verbally, Nelsen would specifically ask us if we did not agree with the observation which has been made in the sales presentation. I found Nelsen's presence quite eerie and after a while it became nerve-wracking to do anything other than agree with the fact that Nelsen wanted us to accept. Particularly in the group setting with others present we felt that to deny these facts, most of which seemed to be correct, would have been disruptive on our part and might have been embarrassing.

6. I felt quite relieved when the day was over. It was a very long presentation and by the end of it constant reinforcement of the statements of Atkins had left me quite drained. I felt I had no opportunity to reflect on the presentation because of the moment a statement was made we had been asked to assent to it. Before I was allowed to leave the conference room at the Holiday Inn, around 4:00 p.m. Nelsen came around to get our agreement to meet on a further occasion to take further steps to sign up to become owners of a franchise for a ComputerCentre.

Solely in order to get out of that room, I signed the paper agreeing to meet the following month to obtain further information toward obtaining a franchise.

7. After I left the Holiday Inn, my wife and I met at a local restaurant and had dinner. Over the course of dinner we discussed the presentations I had heard and, despite the obnoxious indoctrination I had obtained from Jene Nelsen, we both felt that there was a core of truth to the observation that the sales of micro- and mini-computers would become a very profitable and growing part of the economy. We both observed that other than the Computerland franchise out at the Tri-County Shopping Mall, there was no store selling small computers in the Middletown area. She and I discussed the vitality of the "historic shopping area" in downtown Middletown and our recollection that news stories in recent years had indicated that the area was becoming revitalized and that the shops there were experiencing sufficient pedestrian traffic to make them profitable. It seemed to us, therefore, that a store located in the historic downtown shopping area would be a most viable operation. I was impressed, too, by the seeming expertise of Atkins and Nelsen in the small computer area. I had been told of their activities going back many years in the marketing of Apple computers and similar devices.

8. The next morning at breakfast I was still somewhat groggy from the intense presentation and the echoing catechism of Jene Nelsen. Over coffee, my wife and I discussed the seeming completeness of the plans which Computer-Centre Associates had made for the management of the franchises. It seemed like all of the difficult technical decisions in figuring out which computers to stock would be handled by Atkins and his experienced assistant Nelsen. Since the shipping arrangements would be very fast from the ComputerCentre Associates depot in Boston, we would not be required to maintain a huge inventory locally. Thus, we thought that we would not have to take out too large a mortgage on our house, which we felt had an equity value of approximately $90,000. The presentation the prior day had also promised training for a technician to be our repair person, and complete "accounting software" for operating our business; we would get all of the computer programs necessary to set up our own books of account to handle invoices and inventory without creating an entire set of books and paperwork on our own. Since neither of us had previously owned a business we both felt that this was a very important part of the package of services which ComputerCentre Associates was promising. I know it sounds silly to have decided so quickly, but right after breakfast we decided to go ahead with the venture. The presentations had been so compelling that we were convinced it was a safe and sound idea. So about 10 o'clock that morning I again called the 800 number and this time reached Dale Atkins personally. I told Atkins that we wanted to go ahead with the purchase of the franchise if the franchise fee was not exorbitant. He told me that their standard fee was $50,000 plus a $2,000 training fee which was to cover a seven to ten day orientation program for my wife and me in the

operation of a small retail business selling computers. I asked whether the training of our technician would be an additional charge and was told that the technician training came free as part of the package. Atkins asked where we proposed to locate the franchise and I said the historic mall in downtown Middletown. Atkins indicated that the staff would examine the "demographics" to help assure us that this was a good choice of location. At the end of the telephone call we agreed to meet on March 10 to sign the papers. At the end of this telephone call I felt very relieved, as though I had followed instructions which had been given to us and satisfied duties imposed upon us. We both also thought that the franchise would provide a lifetime of income and security to us.

9. During the next four weeks we visited two local banks and eventually obtained a mortgage on our house in the amount of $55,000. We put $3,000 into our checking account and obtained a certified check for $52,000 payable to ComputerCentre Associates. Probably the only negative that happened during that month was when we learned the cost of local advertising. My wife called the TV and radio stations nearby and also got a price sheet from the Daily Press, our local newspaper.

10. When we went to the meeting on March 10th, we asked about advertising because it seemed possible to us that the great cost of the ads might reduce our profits substantially. We were told, once again, that all ComputerCentre franchises in operation were profitable (just as I had been told at the February meeting) and that there were ways to reduce the advertising burden. First, we were told that ComputerCentre Associates itself would run a series of ads which Atkins called "institutional ads" in nationwide media, such as national magazines like Time and Newsweek and over network television. Purpose of these ads, we were told, would be to "raise the consciousness of the American public to the existence of high quality computer sales franchises under the mark 'Computer-Centre.' " Also at the March 10 meeting Jene Nelsen explained the Computer-Centre Associates cooperative advertising program. We were told that this program involved a fifty/fifty split of advertising cost between a local franchise such as the one we were discussing and ComputerCentre Associates. I asked what the budget for such advertising was, and Nelsen told me that there was "no limit" to the amount of cooperative advertising. She said: "Oh sure, if everybody started running thousands of dollars worth of ads every week we would have to set a limit. But right now, we are able to match all of the forty-seven franchises in splitting advertising costs on a cooperative basis; I don't foresee any problem in helping you out on a one to one basis for any ads you wish to run."

11. At the same March 10 meeting, Dale Atkins represented to us: "we have a whole collection of pre-taped video spots advertising ComputerCentre, and a large file of 'camera-ready' artwork for use in local newspaper advertisements so there is a big pool of ready-made advertising materials; you won't even have to write the copy yourself."

APPENDIX A

12. After all these assurances and more talk about how all of the Computer-Centre franchises were "gold mines," we agreed orally to proceed with the purchase of a franchise. After we expressed our agreement Atkins asked again where we proposed to put the franchise. I told him, again, that it would be in the historic downtown shopping area., probably on Main Street if we could find a vacant storefront. At that time Atkins asked whether we had considered placing the franchise at the Tri-County Shopping Mall in Hudson County. We told him that we preferred to have the franchise closer to home and there already was one computer store in the Tri-County Center, a Computerland franchise that had opened a year previously. Atkins shrugged and said, "well, it's your money, and I am sure that you are making a wise choice." At no time did Atkins tell us he thought that our chosen location was a bad one or show use any documentation about the population of possible customers that would be available at another location from the one we had chosen. Nor do I recall seeing any charts or diagrams about this subject. At the end of the March 10 meeting we signed all the papers. My wife and I both signed the franchise agreement and we turned over the certified check for $52,000 to Atkins. In addition, we gave them a copy of the letter of credit we had obtained at Central National Bank here in Middletown in order to finance the limited quantity of inventory we were obligated to maintain in order to run the franchise.

location

13. After signing the papers my wife and I were quite elated. Atkins had promised use so much and seemed to be so knowledgeable in the computer area that we were quite sure the venture would be successful. We even joked about leaving it to our children or grandchildren.

14. Shortly after the franchise agreement was signed we rented space on Main Street in the historic shopping area in downtown Middletown. We placed ads in the Daily Press and eventually hired two salesmen to assist us in selling the computers. As the arrangement evolved we adopted a date in mid May for the formal opening. We placed ads in the Daily Press and also in the Wednesday Shopper, a local newspaper, advertising our gala opening with free refreshments.

15. Unfortunately, most of the merchandise we ordered to have on display at the opening did not arrive by the date we had advertised. Those people who came to the store saw a fairly sparse set-up table and I don't think they came away with the feeling that we had much equipment available for them. We did make one sale the first day which made us very happy, but things moved slowly in the days that followed.

16. Over the course of that first summer, two years ago, we had a number of difficulties in our relationship with ComputerCentre Associates. These include failure to deliver ordered merchandise, failure to provide use with accounting software for running our own books and records, and failure to give us the 10 day training session promised (Jene Nelsen visited us for 3 days in Middletown instead).

747

17. In the early fall I had a telephone conversation with Dale Atkins in which I demanded that we be sent immediately the accounting software necessary so that we could maintain the operations of the franchise on a computerized basis without having to continue the hand creation of books and ledger sheets, invoices and other records. Atkins made several abusive comments in response, including: "Can't you guys do anything for yourselves?" During the course of this conversation I began to feel extreme pain in my left upper chest, radiating down my left forearm from my armpit to my elbow on the inside. I was forced to hang up fairly abruptly. I lay down and shouted for Margaret to come help me. The next thing I knew I must have blacked out because I woke up in the hospital in the Intensive Care ward. The cardiologist who was attending me told me that I had suffered a severe myocardial infarction and that they were running tests on me to determine what the best course of treatment would be. After a couple of weeks in Intensive Care I was told by two physicians that open heart surgery was required to "bypass" some damaged arteries leading to the heart. After Margaret and I discussed this matter for a short time we agreed to go ahead with the surgery. I had the surgery in October and began a four month recuperation thereafter.

18. My day to day contact with the work of the franchise ended in or about mid-September when I had my phone call with Atkins and the resulting heart attack. Many times during the ensuing months as I recovered from the heart surgery Margaret discussed the business of the franchise with me and the difficulties we were experiencing. I tried to share with her the decisions that she was wrestling with in an effort to make the franchise productive, but to no avail. When it became clear that she was no longer able to manage all of the operations of the franchise herself we hired Drew Anderson to become the franchise manager and for the last few months Drew attempted to streamline the operation to make the arrangements pay. Drew fired the two salesmen and handled the office hours of the store alone, 10 to 6 Monday through Saturday. In addition Drew ordered a number of cheap micro-computers outside the product line of ComputerCentre Associates in the hope that the sale of few of these so-called "game machines" would improve our cash flow. During that period last year, Drew was stocking in addition to the ComputerCentre Associates computers (IBM PCs, Epsons, Kaypros) such shelf items as the Commodore VIC 20 (priced at $89.00) and a large number of Texas Instruments TI-99 computers purchased on close-out from the manufacturer which were sold in our franchise for $49.99 with plug-in program modules selling for $19.00 a piece. While I was not in the store during this time period Margaret told me that the shop was also carrying low-end Atari computers such as the Atari 400 and straight game machines such as the Intelevision and the Coleco "game computers."

19. As Margaret could tell you, none of these efforts were able to overcome the basic defect in the product choice and inventory management systems of

ComputerCentre Associates, er lost many large sales as a result of delays in shipping and none of the support, technical or otherwise, that we had been led to expect was forthcoming. Margaret told me at the end of August last year it looked like we would have to close the franchise. I suggested that she cal Atkins to obtain some stop-gap help. She did that and told me afterwards that he had offered nothing and in fact requested a payment of an additional $18,000 franchise fee and something, I think it was 5%, by way of "royalties" based on all of the dollar value of the sales that we had made during the fifteen months the franchise was in operation. We were very despondent after this call and agreed to close the franchise on September 6 of last year.

20. As part of the preparations for trial in this case I have studied the financial statements which Drew Anderson prepared for use at the end of last summer. It is clear to me that we were being overcharged for the computer merchandise which we were ordering through ComputerCentre Associates and that, if we had received the normal industry markup of twenty percent on products we purchased from the wholesalers, we would not have lost money but in fact would have earned well over a $100,000 dollars in the last year of our operation. Thus, it seems to me that over the next twenty years we would have earned at least two million dollars in excess of all expenses, salaries and other costs.

21. My attorney advises me that during the preparation for this case it has been learned that Atkins was getting kickbacks from the wholesale supplier of the computers, or maybe he was an owner of that company too, and was pocketing the extra markup we had to pay to order computers. It seems highly improper to me, that on the one hand as the head of ComputerCentre Associates he can promise us to make product selection decisions and give us a good deal, and on the other hand place the orders with the company that he has some sort of interest in and pocket the extra profits himself when the supplier charges us double the industry standard as a markup over the manufacturers price. All this and lousy shipping speed too meant the downfall of our business.

22. Thus we are left with a $55,000 mortgage on our house and no assets to show for it. I am a partial "cardiac cripple" as a result of my heart attack and am receiving Social Security disability. It does not appear that I will be able to obtain any other employment.

23. In retrospect it seems that every single and important representation which they made to us at the February and March meetings has proven to be false and it seems to us that they knew they were false statements when they were made. Something should be done to punish these people and to prevent them from hoodwinking others into investing their life savings in a program which in no way lives up to the promises which are made for it.

Sworn to this
14th day of January

749

_____   _____
Notary Public   Jack E. Danielson

AFFIDAVIT OF MARGARET DANIELSON IN SUPPORT OF PLAINTIFF'S MOTION FOR SUMMARY JUDGMENT

1. I have read Jack Danielson's affidavit and believe it to be true in all respects.

2. After Jack's heart attack in September, two years ago, I hardly knew what to do. There was a period of several weeks when he was on medication in the Intensive Care Unit and then after his surgery was being medicated for the pain, where I had no assistance or advice whatsoever. I am a college graduate, but I have never run my own business and this period in October and November of last year was a very difficult one for me. I worked in the store from September through almost June covering hours when the salesmen were not there and processing the paperwork was necessary because we never got the "accounting software" to computerize our own records and invoicing. I also maintained the books of the Middletown ComputerCentre during this period.

3. We had a number of serious problems during the period from the fall two years ago through last June. These included: late delivery of items ordered; lack of technical support; failure on 6 occasions to return phone calls; loss of 13 sales dues to non-shipment or late shipment of goods ordered; failure to establish a program to train our technicians at defendant's expense (so we contracted with a nearby RCA facility to do the service on our products); and charging us a 40% markup on all products, twice the "industry standard" of 20%. In June of last year, it became clear to me that Jack was not going to be able to return to full strength in operating the store. He had been awarded a period of disability from the Social Security Administration and the doctors' instructions indicated that he should not maintain a full work schedule even at a relatively sedentary position such as running the store.

4. I feel funny saying it, but I also felt that Jack had a mental block about focusing on the problems of the store during this period. I don't know whether his heart attack affected his ability to concentrate or whether he was so fearful that re-immersing himself in the problems of the store would trigger another heart attack just as it triggered the attack in September two years ago. Whatever the reason, I had difficulty last spring in getting Jack to focus on the problems we were having and he was, frankly, not much help in coming up with concrete suggestions of how to improve our sales or find a way to improve our profit margin on the sales we were making. Part of the frustration was that we did seem to be selling the computers, but we paid so much for them that there was nothing left after we paid the salesmen salaries and commissions.

5. I cannot blame the salesmen for the problems we had last year. It is true that we could not find two people with experience selling mini or micro computers who were willing to work for the $11,000 salary that we had available. But then, in an emerging field like small computers there really aren't that many

people who have experience selling this exact product. Both of the men seemed to me to be knowledgeable about technical things and were not intimidated by the electronic jargon which characterized so much of computer marketing today. Each of the two men did have some sales experience and, as I watched them in operation in the store, I felt they were doing a good job.

6. Early in the spring last year I asked the salesmen to take a salary cut and neither of them was willing to do that, although I did obtain a reduction in the bonus we were paying for sales. We had started out in May two years ago paying a bonus equal to five percent of the total purchase price on any sales over $1,000. Last spring the salesmen were willing to agree to reduce that to a token one percent so long as their basic salary was kept intact.

7. By June of last year I was feeling overwhelmed, both with the personal frustration of Jack's extended recuperation and his unwillingness to help with the operation of the Centre, and with the financial difficulties which the ComputerCentre continued to experience. We also had a number of very irate customers who took out their unhappiness on me both in person and by letter. These problems were mainly in the area of delayed delivery caused by Computer-Centre Associates and we lost many sales, totaling at least $30,000, because of withdrawn orders after ComputerCentre Associates failed to deliver merchandise in the time frame we had been promised.

8. Through a personal friend I met Drew Anderson in the late spring of last year. Drew had recently retired as a Commander in the United States Navy and had experience in the office of naval supply in Washington. When I chatted with Drew I was impressed with Drew's knowledge of financial management and office procedures. Drew was looking for a civilian occupation and I fairly promptly offered Drew the opportunity to work as the office manager for the ComputerCentre in an effort to see if some bold tactical strokes could save it. I explained that throughout this period we were dipping into savings and taking additional loans in order to pay expenses as they accrued and that despite the fact that we were having some success in building a customer base in the community we were losing money.

9. Drew accepted the position of manager for the franchise and throughout the summer of last year made every effort to keep it afloat.

10. I was, frankly, physically and emotionally exhausted last summer and thus I did not go into the franchise on a daily basis. I did visit the shop at least once a week however during last summer and I had several meetings with Drew over lunch and at our house to discuss the ongoing efforts. I approved the firing of the two salesmen and agreed to cover the store on odd hours during the week so that Drew would not be single-handedly responsible for a six-day-a-week, eight-hour day. I was not consulted about the decision Drew made to stock a lot of game computers during the summer last year, but I did not disagree with

the thought when I saw them sitting there on the shelves in June, July, and August last year. It seemed to me that anything we could do to increase our cash flow was beneficial. I only wish it had been enough to keep us solvent.

11. Throughout the summer last year we obtained no help whatsoever from ComputerCentre Associates. After Drew prepared some financial statements at the end of August it was hard to avoid seeing the handwriting on the wall. But before we decided to close the franchise I placed one final call to Dale Atkins at ComputerCentre Associates. I asked for help from a managerial standpoint in figuring ways to improve our profit margin and in the technical vein to help us do a better job of handling customer questions and servicing equipment to build better visibility in the community and better customer referrals on a continuing sales basis. Not only was my request for assistance completely shunned by Atkins, but he made the startling and, to me, phenomenal request that we pay to him an additional $18,000 franchise fee and, on top of that, he said that we owed them 5% of the gross selling price for all of the equipment that we had sold during the fifteen months the franchise had been in operation. Now I think we may have signed some sort of promissory note to the effect that if were profitable at the end of the first year that we owe them an additional franchise fee, but we obviously weren't profitable so we couldn't possibly have owed them some more money. And I have no recollection whatsoever about any "royalty" which we owe to them. In preparation for this case I have seen a document shown to me by attorney in which looks like a promissory note and another one which is called an "Addendum" to the Franchise Agreement. It looks like my signature on both of these documents but as I say I have only limited recollection of the promissory note and absolutely no recollection of the royalty addendum.

[handwritten marginal note: not Profitable]

[handwritten marginal mark: ✳]

12. I feel bitter and quite sad about the entire experience with Computer-Centre Associates. None of the promises which they made to us at the February and March meetings two years ago was true and we invested essentially our life savings by taking out a mortgage on our house which we had owned free and clear prior to purchasing this franchise. We have lost that investment and we have lost a substantial amount of cash savings funds which we had to use to pay expenses as they accrued last year. I feel, moreover, that I have lost my husband as a result of trauma involved in attempting to make a go of this franchise. After his heart attack he has not been the same person and, as you may know, he is not physically able to engage in any other profession because of his cardiac disability. I feel that the defendants in this case should be punished for their lies and for their disruption of our life.

Sworn to this
15th day of January

_____   _____
Notary Public   Margaret Danielson

APPENDIX A

AFFIDAVIT OF DREW ANDERSON IN SUPPORT OF PLAINTIFFS' MOTION FOR SUMMARY JUDGMENT

1. I retired last April 30 after 21 years in the United States Navy. During most of the last three or four years of my tour of duty I was assigned to the Office of Naval Supply in Bethesda, Maryland. During this time I had substantial experience in running a large office with thirty-seven employees and detailed accounting responsibilities for the purchase of goods used in navy offices around the world. Our responsibilities included purchasing, invoicing and accounting for supplies and equipment in a wide variety of subject areas. I was responsible for the total of approximately four hundred million dollars each year in supplies purchased for various navy facilities.

2. Some of the items purchased in the last three or four years of my naval duty were computers and computer peripheral equipment as well as software to run on the computers. While most of these computer purchases were large units such as IBM 360 or VAX units and "Prime" computers, each year for the last three or four years of my naval service, I supervised the purchase of at least 200 micro or mini-computers. We purchases a large variety of these computers from a number of vendors and wholesalers and during this period I became quite familiar with the pricing practices of the micro- and mini-computer industry.

3. Among the computers which I purchased or supervised the purchase for the Office of Naval Supply were IBM PCs, DEC, Rainbow computers, Epson micro computers, Kaypro computers, Northstar computer equipment, TRS-80 and many others. Similarly, I became familiar with the purchase of such peripheral equipment as printers, "modems" for telecommunications over telephone lines, and a host of current software offerings for micro and mini-computers such as "spread sheets," word processing software and other programs. When I returned to Middletown, where I had grown up, in May of last year I was approached by Margaret Danielson and offered the opportunity to manage the Middletown ComputerCentre in the downtown shopping area. Since this job seemed to call on the managerial and accounting expertise I had developed over twenty years in the navy and particularly in the last few years of duty, and also placed me in an evolving area of technology that I had become somewhat familiar with in my purchasing capacity for the navy, I accepted the position. My salary was set at $4,000 each month, out of which I had to pay my own benefits. I know this is a high salary for a small company that was in serious financial trouble, on the other hand I was required to give up other employment opportunities I might have found during the summer and it seemed like a fair compensation for the full time six day a week commitment that was required to try to save this business.

4. One of the first things I did as manager of the Middletown Computer-Centre was to terminate the two salesmen that were working there. In my opinion,

neither of the two men had much more than a superficial comprehension of the micro- or mini-computer market and they were simply "mouthing the words" that appear in the glossy literature advertising these computers. Neither of them, for example, had the slightest knowledge of computer programming. More importantly, I was not convinced that either of these two men knew how to operate the most common programs that ran on the computers that were being carried by the Centre. For example, they did not seem to be able to manipulate a "spread sheet" program to do simple financial modeling. Not being able to perform these simple program manipulations would make it very difficult in my view for them to explain to a prospective customer the advantages of purchasing a small computer. Thus, from June through August I was the sole salesman as well as the manager of the franchise. This required me to put in long hours before and after the open hours of 10 to 6 for the franchise store itself to maintain minimum accounting records, perform invoicing and to bug ComputerCentre Associates to ship equipment on a timely basis. Among the difficulties I observed from a financial standpoint was the fact that the Middletown Centre did not have its own service representative. A contract with RCA Service Corp. had been entered so that all equipment which needed warranty service was paid for on an hourly rate at a nearby RCA Center. This expense contributed to the poor cash flow of the business.

5. By far the most important problem that I observed during the summer of last year was the fact that the Middletown ComputerCentre was being ripped off on the sales price of computers it ordered. Based on my last three or four years of experience in the micro- and mini-computer market it was obvious to me that the wholesalers from whom ComputerCentre Associates were obtaining computers to fill orders which we forwarded, were charging the Middletown ComputerCentre substantially more markup than was common in the aspects of the industry I had seen in recent years. On one occasion I called the 800 number for ComputerCentre Associates and spoke to a Jene Nelsen. Nelsen told me that we had a small franchise and thus the mark-up on each individual item would be higher. I told Nelsen I thought that was ridiculous and asked that we be given a rate of twenty percent mark up in line with the normal industry practice rather than the forty percent which we seemed to be paying on all of the equipment which we obtained. I was told by Nelsen that ComputerCentre Associates had a long term arrangement with "Wizard Computer Supply" in Bala Cynwyd, Pennsylvania, and that forty percent was the standard rate being charged for products ordered under the ComputerCentre arrangements for smaller franchises.

6. Several times during the summer I was required to ask Mrs. Danielson to find money from her savings or by borrowing it from a bank in order to pay the rent and to make payments for equipment which was purchased. I found a beleaguered and frightened woman in these dealings and did not feel that she

was capable of providing any professional assistance to me. Certainly, Computer-Centre Associates provided none either.

7. I made the decision early in the summer last year to augment the product lines which were being foisted upon us by ComputerCentre Associates. The products which ComputerCentre Associates had selected were all top-of-the-line items averaging $3000 and up for a system composed of a keyboard, processing unit and video monitor. Obviously the number of persons in the Middletown area who were ready and able to spend $3000 or more for a small computer was limited. I decided therefore to add to the store a number of "low-end" or "game computers" which frequently provide a first vehicle for people becoming exposed to small computer technology. It was my hope that we would have two advantages from doing this. First, we would improve the immediate cash flow of the business by selling these computers. Even the though the TI-99 computers which I ordered in bulk on the manufacturers only sold for $49.95 we made a substantial profit on each one. Similarly, the Commodore "Vic-20" which sold $89.00, had a profit for us of about 50% of its sales price. Second, I hoped that by introducing our customers to the computer world through these inexpensive vehicles we would be the store of choice when these customers decided to "move up" to a full function micro or mini-computer with floppy disk drives and the computer power necessary to perform sophisticated program functions. I have since been told that stocking items not approved by ComputerCentre Associates is in violation of the franchise agreement under which the Danielsons were operating the franchise. To me, however, it seemed like an essential step to try to keep the business afloat and I hardly see how anyone was harmed by it.

8. The finances of the Middletown ComputerCentre were so precarious throughout the summer that I kept virtually a daily log of cash flow and financial position. I prepared in late August a complete statement of income for the prior twelve months and a statement of position at around August 29th of last year. My purpose in doing this was for my own understanding of whether the continued operation of the franchise was viable and secondly to present to the Danielsons a picture so they might decide what course to take. I prepared these financial statements using the handwritten accounting records which had been maintained first by Jack Danielson and then by his wife during his period of recuperation from his heart attack and later his surgery, and also from the records that I maintained during the early part of the summer last year. They are, to the best of my ability, a fair and accurate portrayal in summary form of the information found in the invoices, ledger sheets and other records in the files of the Middletown ComputerCentre.

9. The August 29th financial statements which I prepared showed me that the business was losing money at a rapid rate. Interestingly, however, it was obvious that the cause of the financial crisis was the excessive markup being

charged on the equipment through ComputerCentre Associates. The forty percent markup was double what the industry normally charges and, in my analysis of the figures, it looked to me as though the franchise would have made a profit of over $100,000 for the last twelve months if it had been paying a twenty percent markup rather than a forty percent markup imposed by the ComputerCentre Associates' supplier "Wizard Computer Products." This excessive cost was compounded by the problems of late delivery of equipment and lack of technical support such that, I reluctantly concluded, the franchise was not viable. After I had discussed this with Margaret Danielson she had a telephone call in my presence with someone at ComputerCentre Associates and they refused to offer her any help. As I understand it, they actually asked for more money from the Danielsons under some agreement which must have happened when the franchise was opened. I have no knowledge of those agreements and during my three month period in the office I saw no paperwork to indicate that any further payments were due by the Danielsons to the ComputerCentre Associates as part of the franchise arrangements. It is true, however, that the basic paperwork for the franchise must have been kept by the Danielsons at their house because I didn't see it anywhere at the franchise office itself.

10. I have learned from the lawyers who have asked me testify at trial that one of the leaders of ComputerCentre Associates has a financial stake in the Wizard Computer Supply Corporation. I know that this kind of arrangement would have been barred by federal statute in the procurement arrangements which I supervised at the Office of Naval Supply. I do not know whether it violates the antitrust laws or the antifraud provisions of any of the consumer protection statutes. But it seems to me that it ill behooves a person like Atkins, who lures private investors to take franchises, to milk them for excessive mark-ups on supplies through shell corporations which are owned by the same people. I hope and trust that the court will render judgment in favor of the Danielsons, who seem to me to have been in over their heads, both technically and financially, and to have been hurt severely by the conduct of Atkins and ComputerCentre Associates.

Sworn to this
17th day of January

_____   _____
Notary Public   Drew Anderson

Witness Statement

I entered the Middletown ComputerCentre store on the downtown mall shopping area early last year, I think it was mid January, and spent some time looking at the micro computers on sale there. Eventually I ordered an IBM PC personal computer. The salesman assured my that I would obtain the computer within ten days from their central warehouse depot in Boston and that I shouldn't worry about it. After two weeks I visited the store and was told they had not received the computer but that it was expected any day.

After another week went by I returned to the store and was told they had not yet received it. I told the salesman that the Computerland in the Tri-County shopping center had the same computer I was ordering at about twenty percent less cost and they had it in stock and that if the ComputerCentre did not make delivery within three days I intended to withdraw my order. Three days later I returned to the ComputerCentre and was told that they had not yet received the equipment. I then withdrew my order and traveled to the Computerland at the Tri-County center where I purchased an identical model, outfitted with the same peripheral equipment, for about twenty percent less than the Computer-Centre was charging me; they loaded it in the back of my car that very day and I took it home.

Date:　　January 12
　　　　　Middletown　　　　　　　　　　　　　　Loren Walsh

APPENDIX A

AFFIDAVIT OF DALE ATKINS
IN OPPOSITION TO PLAINTIFFS'
MOTION FOR SUMMARY JUDGMENT

1. I have a bachelor's degree in economics from the University of Pennsylvania and a master's degree in business administration from Cleveland State University. For several years during the 1970s I was the manager of a small computer store in Cleveland which carried mainly Apple brand computers. During this time I studied and learned everything there was to know about the small computer business. By the end of the 1970s I was teaching basic computer use courses in local community colleges and adult education seminars. It became clear to me through the course of these programs that there was a tremendous, untapped market for sales of mini- and micro-computers.

2. With the advent of two or three spectacularly successful programs for micro computers, the sales for sophisticated small computer machines really began to take off. The programs which turned national attention to these computers were of three types. First, the spread-sheet programs came on the scene. These programs allow a lay person to develop a financial "model" to analyze such things as tax deductions, real estate investments, home purchases and any situation where one financial effect will change other figures in a complex financial statement. Spread sheets thus allow the person using the computer to say "what if" and change one or more of the figures, allowing the computer to recalculate all of the other numbers. They permit creation in minutes of financial analyses which would have taken hours or days otherwise. The second development was word processing programs compact enough to run on very small computers. By far the most common of these is WordStar, but numerous other programs with similar capabilities have come on the market. Anyone who does a modest amount of writing will find these programs very beneficial. Thirdly, data base management programs have been developed which allow a lay person, with no computer programming training, to develop systems for records management ranging from simple mailing lists of clubs or groups to a specific office or profession and handle all aspects of the financial work entailed.

3. With the explosion of these programs and the increasing awareness of the general public that there are actually advantages to the micro computer world which can be enjoyed by one who does not have extensive computer training, it became very clear to me that the sale of micro computers themselves — along with these software programs which run on them — would be the most lucrative field of endeavor in the 1980s and '90s. In the early 1980s, therefore, I founded ComputerCentre Associates. I am the principal owner of ComputerCentre Associates and the chief executive officer. I am assisted by the Director of Marketing, Jene Nelsen. We have a staff of eighteen persons in supporting positions in general offices on Shore Drive in Boston, Massachusetts.

4. Commencing in the early 1980s and continuing to the day of this trial, ComputerCentre Associates has marketed franchises for the sale of mini- and micro-computers under the mark "ComputerCentre." In January, two years ago, when the Danielsons saw the Wall Street Journal ad and first contacted ComputerCentre Associates, we had 41 franchises in existence. Today, that number is 84 and is growing each month. The franchises are generally quite lucrative and many of our franchisees tell me they have become millionaires solely as a result of the successful operation of their ComputerCentre franchise.

5. The marketing of franchises is heavily restricted by federal and state laws. The marketing program adopted by ComputerCentre Associates is based on the advice of our attorneys and complies with each and every regulation of the Federal Trade Commission and all states in which we operate. Because of the regulations imposed by these bodies, the agreements are all in writing, and are accompanied by a franchise disclosure statement and other information. Also, in accord with the prevailing law, the disclosure statement must be shown to a franchisee before he or she signs a franchise agreement and all of the fees and charges must be spelled out.

6. As the figures mentioned above imply, interest in ComputerCentre franchises has been high. In response to ads in the Wall Street Journal and other publications, a sufficient number of inquiries have been received by Computer-Centre Associates to cause us to establish a system of "introductory seminars" for interested persons. In these programs we outline for a group of people in a given geographical area the nature of the operation of a ComputerCentre franchise. One such program was held on February 12 two years ago at the Holiday Inn in Middletown for about 13 people from the central part of the state of East. All of these persons had seen advertisements placed ComputerCentre Associates in the national media and all had requested the opportunity to meet with representatives of ComputerCentre Associates for a more complete description of the franchise system.

7. In the meeting of February 12, two years ago, as in our other general marketing seminars on an introductory basis, the investors in attendance were given a complete and candid description of the means by which the Computer-Centres are marketed and operate. This description includes, for example, the services provided by ComputerCentre Associates and the commitments and undertakings expected of the investors themselves.

8. Essentially, ComputerCentre Associates provides the following services to the franchises: institutional advertising (national ads designed to create awareness of the franchises), cooperation in underwriting local advertising campaigns, selection of leading computer models to be supported under the franchise, national technical assistance and training, training and the operation of a franchise retail computer sales outlet, wholesale ordering of computers and related supplies and equipment and similar devices.

760

9. Each ComputerCentre franchise is expected to perform a number of functions itself. These include: recruiting and training sales personnel knowledgeable in the area of micro-and mini-computers; obtaining adequate technical assistance for a repair and warranty service station; maintaining adequate inventory for local sales needs (to be supplemented by "drop ship" service from the ComputerCentre Associates warehouse in Massachusetts); local advertising and public relations services; customer relations and normal small business practices.

10. In compliance with federal law, ComputerCentre Associates explains at each of the regional seminars it holds each year the financial arrangements which govern the sale of franchises. Thus, at the February 12 meeting, two years ago, all of the attending prospective investors were told that there would be a franchise fee payable in respect to any franchise in an amount ranging from 50,000 to 75,000 dollars depending on the size and nature of the geographic area allotted to the franchise. Moreover, each of the investors who attend such a seminar is told that there is a continuing "royalty fee" payable by the franchisees to ComputerCentre Associates for the life of the contract. This fee is also subject to negotiation and ranges from 2 1/2% in the longer term, to 10%.

11. I have attended upwards of 50 regional sales seminars for persons who have expressed interest in ComputerCentre Associates franchises. In almost all of these trips, my assistant Jene Nelsen has accompanied me. We also normally take a handful of clerical and support personnel to make the conference run smoothly. As you might imagine, I cannot remember specifically the presentation which was made on February 12, two years ago. As part of the preparation of this law suit I have seen a document collected by my attorneys which looks like the agenda for the February 12 meeting. I do recall that the subjects listed there were normally on the agenda for any of our public marketing seminars during the period two years ago. I have no reason to think we would have changed any of the general subjects listed there or that any major new topic which is not listed on the agenda was discussed at any length, at least, at the February 12th meeting two years ago.

12. I do recall that the following morning, February 13th, I received a telephone call from Mr. Danielson indicating they had decided they wanted to purchase a ComputerCentre franchise. I was fearful that the Danielsons were leaping at the franchise, which is an attractive investment and has been highly successful for many, without adequately considering their own circumstances. Thus on the telephone that morning I inquired about the plans which they had in mind and specifically the location proposed for the ComputerCentre outlet. Mr. Danielson told me they were thinking of placing the franchise on Main Street in downtown Middletown. I told him at that time I was not sure that the "demographics" (the population pattern) of Middletown was the most propitious

for a new franchise but that we would check the census figures. Despite my warning, Danielson appeared to have his mind made up that they wanted to go ahead with a purchase of a franchise. Thus I agreed to his suggestion that we set a date in March for a final meeting to review the proposed arrangements.

13. On March 10th two years ago Jene Nelsen and I met with Danielsons at the Marriott Hotel in Middletown. At that meeting I presented the Danielsons with our franchise disclosure statement and a copy of the blank franchise agreement and we spent perhaps an hour going over the basic documents so that they would fully understand the commitments and obligations which these papers embody. The Danielsons were quite concerned about the financial arrangements. Nelsen and I reviewed with them the information concerning national advertising and cooperative local advertising and, I think this allayed their fears about the staggering burden of advertising expenses. Also at this meeting I explained the financial commitment they would be making. This was in three parts. First, the Danielsons had brought with them a certified check in the amount of $52,000 as the initial franchise fee payment. Second, they were to sign an $18,000 promissory note at 18% interest which had no explicit due date, but which I advised them would be called for payment twelve months after the franchise went operational, a date tentatively scheduled in mid-May. Third, I reminded the Danielsons that all franchises in the ComputerCentre system pay a monthly or quarterly franchise fee equal to a percentage of the gross receipts of the franchise. They indicated to me that they understood this from the advertisement they had read and from the presentation on February 12. I told them they were getting the lowest royalty rate of any class of franchises: 5 percent for the first 5 years of the franchise's life, and 2 1/2 percent for the remainder of the years in which the franchise is operated.

14. We spent some time in the meeting of March 10 two years ago discussing the location for the ComputerCentre franchise the Danielsons were buying. I tried to encourage them to locate the franchise at the Tri-County Shopping Mall in Hudson County. When the Danielsons mentioned there was already a Computerland franchise at the Tri-County Centre, I told them that we have generally found that such "head to head" competition is beneficial for a franchise's sales. Consumers seem to find it convenient to be able to comparison shop quickly at one location and few customers will make a substantial purchase in one computer on a mall without having at least visited for a few minutes the other store. In this way an established franchise like the one which previously existed at the Tri-County Shopping Mall can provide an immediate flow of customers by way of comparison when a new ComputerCentre franchise is opened. These arguments fell on deaf ears with the Danielsons. They were convinced that being the exclusive location in "historic" downtown Middletown would provide a greater volume of serious customers than being in the shopping mall with a large number of transients who had come to the mall for other purposes entirely. I

displayed to the Danielsons the demographic chart prepared by my staff based on the most recent census data for this state. That chart demonstrates that there is a much larger population base who regularly travel to the Tri-County Shopping Mall, from a larger geographic radius than is the case at the downtown shopping area in Middletown. Despite the fact that a smaller geographic area regularly travels to central Middletown, and fewer people reside in that geographic area than in the one served by the Tri-County Shopping Mall, the Danielsons insisted that they wanted to go forward with a franchise in downtown Middletown. I told them that we would be willing to place a franchise in the location of their choice but that they bore the risk that the location might not be viable. I told them that we do everything in our power to assist them in making a go of it.

15. After these discussions all of the papers mentioned were duly executed and completed by all sides. The Danielsons indicated that they expected to be able to rent space and hire sales personnel for a May 15th opening date and I assigned Jene Nelsen the task of arranging for a training session, expected to last 10 days or two weeks, for Mr. and Mrs. Danielson in the operation of a ComputerCentre franchise. I further instructed Jene Nelsen to take an initial set of product orders from the Danielsons so that they would have sufficient inventory to commence on the target date in May.

16. Since the Danielsons had essentially made up their mind prior to meeting with us to go ahead with the franchise purchase, there was nothing else to negotiate at the March 10 meeting two years ago. In fact, there was no need of any supplemental meeting other than the training session to be conducted by Jene Nelsen. Therefore, I thanked the Danielsons for joining the ComputerCentre team. I told them that the other ComputerCentre franchises were profitable and that I hoped and trusted that theirs would be as well.

17. I understand from Jene Nelsen that the Danielsons' franchise did open in mid-May in the downtown area of Middletown, though we were not able to deliver the full compliment of equipment requested because their invoices for the initial inventory were late in arriving at our offices.

18. During the summer and fall two years ago, we had a number of interactions with the Danielsons. Both Jack and Margaret Danielson called headquarters betraying a complete lack of common business understanding. It became very clear, for example, that they had no understanding of such basic tax concepts as depreciation and investment credit. On the computer front they were continually misusing such terms as bytes and bits, and Mrs. Danielson kept referring to the television monitors as "CPU," a term properly reserved for the main computer enclosure in a small system. Contrary to my explicit suggestions to them at the March 10 meeting, it did not appear that they hired a sales personnel who had any experience in the micro-computer area. For a couple with such limited technical capacities I felt this was a serious impediment to successful

operation of the franchise. I mentioned to them more than once during the summer two years ago that they should continue to look for sales personnel with computer experience to replace the two fellows they had initially taken on board. Since they did not have lengthy employment contracts with these people it would have been feasible, at any time, to replace them with more well equipped personnel.

19. One complaint which the Danielsons reiterated through out the summer, two years ago, was the delay we experienced in delivering to them the proprietary software for doing the actual bookkeeping of the franchise on a computerized basis. I explained to them repeatedly that this was not our fault. Indeed ComputerCentre Associates had invested some $47,000 in retaining the services of a software development concern on State Street in Boston to develop business management programs tailored expressly for the needs of a ComputerCentre Franchise. For reasons solely in the sphere of the software company with whom we were dealing, they were not able to complete the programming of these items until late last summer, about a year after they were promised to us. As a result, all of our franchises, including the Danielsons, had to wait for late delivery of the computerization program. I am not aware of any instance among any of our franchisees where this delay cost as much as a penny to the franchise. Granted, the bookkeeping required before the programs became available last summer was laborious. The franchisees had to maintain their books by hand, as books have always been maintained by businesses. But there is no expense which the franchise faced because of using bookkeeping by hand, and no financial saving is achieved under the computer programs even in their refined form today. Rather, the program simply makes it easier and less time-consuming to keep the books of a busy small company.

20. Thus when Jack Danielson called me in September of two years ago and started in for about the sixth time bemoaning the lack of the business operation software for the franchise itself I may have lost patience with him for a moment. I believe I did tell him at that time "You guys will simply have to do these records" and slammed down the phone. I learned only much later that he claims to have suffered a heart attack shortly after this conversation and became hospitalized for an extended period. Indeed, I understand that eventually he underwent by-pass surgery for a long-standing deterioration in the arteries serving his heart.

21. I attribute much of the difficulty which the Middletown franchise had in the ensuing year to Jack Danielson's medical problem. First of all, Margaret Danielson was the least business experienced of the couple and had less computer experience. Jack, at least, had worked with computers while he was on the police force. Mrs. Danielson, on the other hand, was equipped only with her college degree and not with much intuitive understanding of complex machinery. Secondly, Mrs. Danielson was obviously and quite understandably upset by this

serious medical condition of her husband. She was not able, in conversations with me during the winter a year and a half ago, to deal concretely with the problems which were facing her in operating the franchise. She was distracted, perhaps understandably again, and did not bring full attention to this problem. Third, she confided in me that she felt that her husband had suffered psychological damage from the fact of the heart attack. When I asked her why she could not turn to him for advice in the management of the business she broke down. After crying for a while on the telephone she told me in, I believe, January of last year, that she was having difficulty getting Jack to focus on any of the practical questions of operating the business. She said "it's as though he is afraid that thinking about the franchise will bring on another heart attack; I can't get him to pay attention to the business anymore." And she said: "I think I am going to ask Jack to see a psychiatrist."

22. By the spring of last year relations had deteriorated even further and it was apparent to me that Mrs. Danielson was not making a go of the business. In a telephone conversation I had with her in March or April I suggested that she consider selling the franchise. She told me she would rather have someone else run it but to retain ownership of it. I gave her several names but she declined to contact them. I learned in or about May last year, that she had fired the two salesmen working for her and retained a custodian to hold the business together and attempt to restructure it. When Mrs. Danielson finally called in early September of last year she made it clear that the franchise was on the verge of closing. I reminded her at that time that the $18,000 promissory note had come due in May and was beginning to accrue interest. I had not wanted to press her on that note at the time it first became due in May because of the extreme pressure she was obviously under and the major transition which was taking place to the administration of the franchise by Drew Anderson, the manager Mrs. Danielson hired. Since, however, it was becoming clear that the franchise would fold and many creditors would be seeking to realize upon the assets of the franchise, I felt it important that we make it clear that we were not waiving the debt which the Danielsons had undertaken at the time of the closing on March 10 two years ago. Further, I had learned from my staff, shortly before her call, that the Danielsons had never paid a single payment toward the sales royalties which each franchisee is obligated to remit to ComputerCentre Associates. I told her that this obligation was an extremely serious one and that we took a dim view of the failure of the franchise to make these payments. A few days later I learned that the Middletown ComputerCentre had folded. To this day we have not been paid the $18,000 reflected in the promissory note or the $35,000 (or more) which we are due under the royalty agreement pegged at 5% of gross sales.

23. As part of the preparations of this lawsuit I have seen the scurrilous allegations in the plaintiffs' papers challenging the wholesaler arrangements used by ComputerCentre Associates. It is true that throughout the period in question

in this lawsuit purchases, at least for the smaller franchises such as Middletown, were placed through a company in Bala Cynwyd, Pennsylvania, known as Wizard Computer Supply. There were several reasons for using Wizard Supply. I knew of this company because my brother was employed there. In many conversations with him I learned that they were able to negotiate extremely favorable supply arrangements with Original Equipment Manufacturers (OEMs) and that they bought in such large bulk that they obtained from the OEMs the best available commercial rates for micro and mini-computers. At one point about a year before the Danielsons purchased their franchise, my brother came to me and indicated that the employees of Wizard Computer Supply were attempting to purchase the company from the owner. He told me that if I would help him put up some of the money he and several of the employees would, in effect, take over their own business and become co-owners. My brother has never had much success in the business world and this seemed like an excellent opportunity to help him get on his feet in a permanent way. Thus I invested $22,000 of my own money in the purchase of Wizard Computer Supply. Most of this was intended as a gift to my brother since he is financially much less well off than my wife and I. As a result, I asked him to arrange it so that I became a limited partner with only a 5% interest in the company while he became a general partner with a 17% interest in the operation.

24. I did not establish the pricing policies of Wizard Computer Supply. It is not unknown in the industry for smaller orders from a distributor or middle-man such as Wizard to receive a mark-up higher than larger or "bulk" orders placed by high-volume purchasers. I do not think, therefore, that the Danielsons were treated unfairly or illegally.

Sworn to this
22nd day of February.

_____
Dale Atkins

_____
Notary Public

APPENDIX A

AFFIDAVIT OF TERRY JOHANSEN
IN OPPOSITION TO PLAINTIFFS'
MOTION FOR SUMMARY JUDGMENT

1. I am the technical services manager for ComputerCentre Associates. I have held this position for five years and my duties include managing the inventory and drop shipment activities of ComputerCentre Associates as well as the "technical support" function.

2. My inventory and shipping responsibilities involve supervision of a staff of three persons in our warehouse near Boston, MA. This staff maintains a current inventory of micro and mini-computers and ships these items to our franchisees upon receipt of appropriate written orders. I am responsible for ordering our supply of inventory for the warehouse from a variety of wholesalers, principally Wizard Computer Supply Company in Bala Cynwyd, PA. Until recently, that is for about three years prior to the present calendar year, almost all of our purchases were through Wizard Computer Supply. During this period orders earmarked for our smaller and middle size franchises were billed at a markup of approximately 40% by Wizard Computer Supply over the manufacturer's cost. Our larger franchises, which ordered in bulk or carload lots, were billed at a markup of only 20% over the manufacturer's cost as a reflection of the economies involved in shipping large quantities.

3. I had several contacts with Jack and Margaret Danielson, proprietors of the Middletown ComputerCentre franchise, during the 15 months that their franchise was in operation, from May two years ago through last August. I recall that, as a small franchise, they paid the 40% markup rate on goods we ordered for them through Wizard Computer Supply. The Danielsons did not complain to me about the prices of goods they obtained, though I do recall a couple of telephone calls complaining about the late delivery of these items. On one of these occasions I think the responsibility was that of ComputerCentre Associates, since we had a turnover of two of the three persons on my staff at the warehouse, and for a period of six weeks during the first summer that the Middletown franchise was in operation, we had significant shipping delays due to understaffing. The Danielsons also complained during the fall and winter of that year, but I do not believe that any delays we experienced were the fault of Computer-Centre Associates. Rather, during this period we seemed to be experiencing a "stretch-out" of delivery times of goods ordered through Wizard Computer Supply in Pennsylvania. Several times during that period and continuing through last summer I suggested to our President, Dale Atkins, that we switch wholesalers in order to improve our delivery positions. It was obvious to me that many of our franchisees around the country were losing sales. I knew this because items we placed on back order with Wizard Computer Supply were subsequently withdrawn by a number of the franchisees with angry notes or telephone calls

767

informing me that the failure to deliver the products timely had resulted in cancellation of the purchaser's order and a resulting loss of sales. Mr. Atkins told me that he did not wish to change suppliers but wanted to keep the source of supply "in the family." Finally, last summer, Mr. Atkins did authorize me to obtain alternative sources of wholesale supply for the equipment we were carrying for our franchises. Since that time I have established a diversified group of four suppliers and our average shipping time has been reduced from the five weeks we experienced during the time the Danielsons held a franchise in Middletown to ten days at present. Even today, however, Mr. Atkins insists that we place a volume of long term orders with Wizard Computer Supply. I am able to accomplish this safely by relying on the other suppliers to fill in for unusual items or items with a rapid "turn around" obligation.

4. I know that the Danielsons maintain that the failure of their franchise in Middletown was a result of our inability to ship computers in less than five weeks pursuant to their orders. I have two responses: (1) At least with respect to the "opening day fiasco" the fault lies with the Danielsons. They failed to send me orders for the equipment they wanted to have on hand for their opening day around mid-May, two years ago, until about two weeks beforehand. This delay made it impossible, at least under the supply arrangements we had at that time, to accommodate their request. My guess is that we sent only about a quarter of the items they requested to have on hand for the opening ceremonies. (2) The real cause, in my view, of the demise of the Danielsons' Middletown franchise was the total lack of technical capability of the Danielsons.

5. It was obvious to me in telephone conversations with both Mr. and Mrs. Danielson that they were completely lacking in any technical understanding of the operation of micro computers. They frequently misused basic computer terminology and gave no indication whatsoever that they understood the technical aspects of the business sufficient to even hire an adequate sales staff.

6. I further understand that the Danielsons never did hire a technician to have on their premises so that they might have offered customers rapid repair or upgrading of products they listed for sale. Rather, they relied on a local RCA repair facility on a contract basis, with the necessary delays involved in shipping computers to an outside facility for repair and maintenance.

7. It is true that ComputerCentre Associates did not have its technicians' training facility in operation until last July or August, about the time the Middletown franchise closed. But I personally would have been willing to travel to Middletown to train the technician they were supposed to hire to assure that they were able to offer this kind of support to customers. I have a Bachelors Degree in Electronic Engineering and spent seven years repairing Apple and TRS-80 mini computers before assuming my duties for ComputerCentre Associates. I have taught computer electronics courses for several correspondence

schools and am presently in charge of the ComputerCentre Associates technician training program. Starting this past fall we have had two instructors on the staff in Boston and all new franchisees are requested to send their technical personnel to Boston for a free one week technical training program.

Sworn to before me
this 23rd day of February.
_____

Notary Public

_____

Terry Johansen

APPENDIX A

Statement of Witness Jene Nelsen

I am the Sales Manager of ComputerCentre Associates. I have held this position for four years. Prior to that I spent two years in the Federal Penitentiary at Allentown, PA for mail fraud arising out of bogus charges against me concerning the marketing of weight-loss preparations.

My duties as Sales Manager for ComputerCentre Associates involve relations with prospective franchisees, creation of an agenda for seminars for interested franchise investors and assisting Dale Atkins, the President of ComputerCentre Associates, in sales presentations and late creating the documentation for franchise arrangements.

In connection with my duties I attended the introductory seminar February 12 two years ago and I also met with Atkins and the Danielsons on March 10, two years ago, during the finalization of their arrangements to purchase a franchise for a ComputerCentre in Middletown.

In my opinion the Danielsons are, or were, very headstrong individuals in the early months two years ago. Despite their lack of experience in technological employment, both were quite confident that they could "make a killing" in the computer sales field. I thought that Jack Danielson in particular overrated the utility of his experience at the police department as a means of being prepared for sales of micro-computers. I do not have any specific recall at this point of the financial terms that were struck with the Danielsons at March 10 two years ago. It would of been normal for us to accept a certified check for the bulk of a franchise fee with a smaller personal note being accepted with payment deferred for a year to permit the franchisees to earn additional funds with which to pay the note. All of the personal notes we were taking during this period, two years ago, carried interest at the rate of 18% per annum on the unpaid balance.

While I do not recall the financial terms agreed to on March 10 I have some recollection that several weeks after that Dale Atkins requested me to prepare papers, including a personal note in the amount of $18,000 for the Danielsons to sign in connection with their franchise.

I did the research and the census records which led to the preparation of the exhibit attached to the materials showing the population patterns in the Middletown vicinity and those surrounding the Tri Counties Shopping Center in Hudson County. To the best of my knowledge these statistics are accurately reflected on the diagram.

March 1

Jene Nelsen

APPENDIX A

Atkins Copy

Promotional Meeting

AGENDA

February 12 -- Holiday Inn, Middletown

9:00   1. Introduction of CCA concept & staff

          2. History of CCA

          3. Technical facilities

          4. Life of the Franchisee

[Luncheon talk]

12:00   5. How the Profits Mount (use Frisco as example; 19%)

          6. We train you to make even more

[Classroom again]

2:00   7. Inventory and the CCA approach

          8. We'll do 37 National Ads each year/help with local
              advertisers (co-op sharing costs)

          9. How to get more information: (800) 987-6543

                  -- use forms we gave you

                  -- we'll be calling you soon

4:00   10. Join us now for cocktails on Mezzanine level; thank you.

APPENDIX A

TO: Atkins

From: Nelson

March 2, two years ago

Attached is the annual franchisee status report for this fiscal year.
For your info, the high-volume outlets paying 20% markup are numbers 1,
2,3,4,8,9,15,23,27,33 and 42. All the rest are paying us 40%.

APPENDIX A

Annual Franchisee Status Survey

This Report prepared by:

Date: March 1, two years ago.
Number of Franchisees: 42

Code	Location	Sales in Last 12 Mo.	Profit (loss) reported to us	Profit (loss) as % of gross sales
1	San Francisco	1,450,699	275,823	19%
2	New York	2,899,400	434,910	15
3	Atlanta	989,333	168,186	17
4	Chicago	1,780,433	195,847	11
5	Denver	877,020	21,400	2
6	Peoria	925,430	66,232	7
7	Richmond	655,244	11,200	1.5
8	Philadelphia	790,340	268,501	15
9	Los Angeles	3,950,324	474,044	12
10	Phoenix	800,210	47,432	6
11	Portland	544,290	(17,400)	(3)
12	Detroit	777,188	35,200	5
13	Sioux City	444,266	7,490	1.5
14	San Diego	810,001	88,200	10
15	Dallas	1,490,200	238,402	16
16	Nashville	669,500	37,250	5
17	Fairbanks	227,800	6,450	3
18	Kansas City	707,290	14,395	2
19	Pittsburgh	566,435	27,810	5
20	Seattle	944,166	88,202	9
21	Butte	166,900	5,305	3
22	Charleston	644,888	54,300	8
23	Minneapolis	1,375,400	192,521	14
24	Cincinatti	760,380	19,230	2.5
25	Buffalo	922,450	125,378	14
26	Huntsville	556,399	42,800	8
27	Houston	2,455,240	303,202	12
28	Lansing	766,244	32,300	4
29	Indianapolis	810,420	66,488	9.5
30	Hartford	450,388	22,100	5
31	Reno	660,200	38,100	6
32	Caspar	422,180	9,422	2
33	Miami	1,477,207	177,241	12
34	Durham	689,400	23,604	3
35	Keokuk	499,370	17,355	3
36	Sacramento	700,340	29,802	6
37	Morgantown	454,390	11,408	2
38	Dayton	644,950	(24,236)	(4)
39	New Orleans	872,300	(14,557)	(1.5)
40	Honolulu	566,240	19,898	3
41	Cleveland	780,800	26,477	3
42	Baltimore	924,655	127,250	14

New Prospects: Albequerque; Middletown, Jacksonville

APPENDIX A

Financial Background Sheet

NOTE: Please press hard, you are making a carbon copy for your own records. Thank You.

Name(s): *Mr./Mrs. Jack Danielson*

Address: *1234 Barstow Ave., Middletown, Eq*

Telephone: (555) *979-2628*

Present Business(es): *Police Dept (Retired)*

Prior Business Experience: *see above*

Bank Accounts: *Central Nat. Bank, Middletown, Eq*
checking Act # 57-71963

Approximate Investable Cash: *savings Act # 10-1047*
$50,000

Stocks, bonds and liquidatable assets: *None*

Equity in Home or other Property: *$50,000 - $60,000*   Location: *Middletown*

Debts (please include credit cards and revolving charge accounts):
Minor Charge Accounts

Have you ever filed for Bankruptcy?:

No

Site Selection Data
Potential Geographical Market

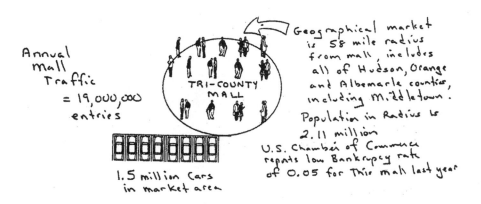

Annual
Mall
Traffic
= 19,000,000
entries

TRI-COUNTY
MALL

Geographical market
is 58 mile radius
from mall, includes
all of Hudson, Orange
and Albemarle counties,
including Middletown.
Population in Radius is
2.11 million
U.S. Chamber of Commerce
reports low Bankrupcy rate
of 0.05 for This mall last year

1.5 million Cars
in market area

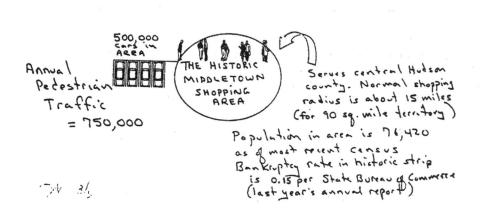

500,000
cars in
AREA

Annual
Pedestrian
Traffic
= 750,000

THE HISTORIC
MIDDLETOWN
SHOPPING
AREA

Serves central Hudson
county. Normal shopping
radius is about 15 miles
(for 90 sq. mile territory)

Population in area is 76,420
as of most recent census
Bankruptcy rate in historic strip
is 0.15 per State Bureau of Commerce
(last year's annual report)

ComputerCentre Associates ..

Franchise Disclosure Statement

Pursuant to 16 C.F.R. section 436, implementing obligations under the Federal Trade Commission Act, 15 U.S.C. 13(c), this document sets forth the background of *ComputerCentre Associates* as it pertains to the offering of franchises for sale in inter-state commerce.

Business and Experience.

The business of *ComputerCentre Associates* is the marketing of computers in the micro- or mini- market, for home and professional or business use, and the administration of a system of franchises to that end. *ComputerCentre Associates* was formed four years ago and is substantially controlled by Dale Atkins. Atkins is an experienced businessman, a citizen of the United States, residing near Boston, Massachusetts. Neither *ComputerCentre Associates* nor Atkins has filed for relief under the Bankruptcy Code of the United States within the past five (5) years.

Contractual Rights.

The franchisee(s)' rights under the form Franchise Agreement being marketed by *ComputerCentre Associates* include use of the licensed mark and benefit from a number of services of the franchisor as set forth therein and negotiated individually with each franchisee. Such rights as are conferred on the franchisee are subject to termination for non-payment of franchise fees or contractual royalties, failure to maintain a high-quality franchise location, failure to stock items prescribed by the franchisor, or stocking inferior merchandise not approved by the franchisor. The contract does not require periodic renewals; instead it runs until terminated by either party and the financial obligations of the franchisee(s) continue throughout its lifetime.

Franchisor's Financial Condition.

The financial condition of *ComputerCentre Associates* is sound, and fully adequate to operate the franchise system. As at December 31, for the most recent fiscal year, the balance sheet for *ComputerCentre Associates* showed a net equilty of $ 13 million and the income statement for the same period showed a net income after all expenses of $522,780 on annual sales of $8,652,720. There are no material undisclosed liabilities known to management. The books of *ComputerCentre Associates* are audited annually by the Boston office of Messrs. Haskins & Lybrand, CPA's, and receive a "clean opinion" each year as having been prepared consistent with accepted accounting practices and having been tested by the auditors consistent with generally accepted auditing standards.

Franchisee Payments.

Franchisee(s) are obligated to make an initial payment of a franchise fee to obtain the rights noted herein and within the Franchise Agreement. This payment initially shall be $ In addition, franchisee(s) are responsible for remitting to *ComputerCentre Associates* monthly a royalty fee predicated on the volume of gross monthly sales of covered merchandise. The percentage of such fee shall be negotiated at the time the Franchise Agreement is signed and shall range from 2 and 1/2 percent to 12 and 1/2 percent of gross selling price. "Covered merchandise" shall mean computers, peripheral equipment such as printers, cables, modems and the like, as well as programs, other software and books.

Resale of the Franchise.

Franchisee(s) are free to re-sell the franchise, subject only to these conditions: (1) *ComputerCentre Associates* shall be given the right of first refusal to consider purchasing the franchise itself for operation as a company-owned facility; (2) franchisee(s) shall give the franchisor ninety (90) days' notice of the intention to re-sell a franchise; (3) after agreement with a purchaser, franchisee(s) must allow franchisor thirty (30) days

in which to satisfy itself as to the credit and expertise of the ·
proposed purchaser; and (4) franchisor must consent to the transfer
-- such consent not to be unreasonably withheld; (5) Upon the
transfer the transferror franchisee(s), transferree
franchisee(s), or a combination as they may agree, shall be
liable to *Computer Centre Associates* for a franchise
transfer fee in the amount of $15,000.

Representations.

There are no representations other than those contained in
this disclosure document and the franchise agreement itself.

QUALITY and PROFESSIONALISM -- the *Computer Centre* way!

I certify that I have read the foregoing prior to signing any
franchise agreement:

_Jack Danielson_____ Date:_3/10_____

_Margaret Danielson_____ Date:_March 10_____

Franchise Agreement

KNOW ALL PERSONS by these presents that *ComputerCentre Associates* hereby licenses Jack and Margaret Danielson as franchisee(s) to use the *ComputerCentre* mark in connection with establishment and operation of a retail computer sales store to be located at Middletown Historic Mall and to be opened on or before July 15th of this year. In exchange for this right, and the attendant training, accounting support, computer selection, technical services, inventory management program, shipping and advertising to be provided by *ComputerCentre Associates*, the named franchisee(s) agree to pay to *Computer Centre Associates* the sum of $ 52,000 , and thereafter to pay a royalty to *ComputerCentre Associates* on a previously agreed scale, for the life of this contract. Failure of the named franchisee(s) to make such payments shall void this agreement. Should *ComputerCentre Associates* be obliged to take legal action to enforce its rights hereunder, franchisee(s) agree to pay attorneys fees at the liquidated and reasonable amount of $10,000.

This agreement shall be deemed made pursuant to the laws of the State of Massachusetts and the laws of that state shall apply to its construction and enforcement.

DATED this 10th day of March and signed by

(print) Dale Atkins on behalf of

ComputerCentre Associates and (print) Jack Danielson

and Margaret Danielson on behalf of the named

franchisee(s).

ComputerCentre Associates

Dale Atkins

Franchisee(s)

Jack Danielson

Margaret Danielson

Jack or Margaret Danielson
1234 Barstow Avenue
Middletown, BA 23134

157-62
97

No. 427

Date: March 10

Pay to the order of: Computer Centre Assoc.

The sum of: Fifty two thousand and no/100 ———— $ 52,000.00

Central National Bank
Main Street Tower ·
Middletown, BA 23134

Memo: Franchise fee

Jack Danielson

Promissory Note

We the undersigned hereby agree to pay to *ComputerCentre Associates* the sum of $18,000 (eighteen thousand dollars) in connection with the Franchise Agreement between the parties dated March 10th of this year.

Payment hereunder shall be made within ten (10) days after demand therefor by an authorized representative of *ComputerCentre Associates* orally in writing to the undersigned, or either of them.

Upon the failure of the undersigned to make payment within the 10 day period specified above, interest shall accrue on this note at the rate of eighteen percent (18%) per annum on the unpaid amount until the principal shall have been paid in full.

In the event of any default of payment under this note, or any other circumstances reasonably requiring *ComputerCentre Associates* to retain counsel, the undersigned shall be liable for reasonable counsel fees, hereby fixed in the fair liquidated amount of $10,000.

WHEREUNTO we have this 10th of March set our hands,

Jack Danielson _____   _____

ComputerCentre Associates

1710 Shore Drive
Boston, Massachusetts

March 25, two years ago.

Wizard Computer Supply Company
Industrial Park
Bala Cynwyd, PA

    Attn: Frank Atkins

Dear Frank:

    Mom says hello and is expecting all of us kids for dinner over the holidays.

    Down to business. We've added two more franchisees, bringing our total to 47 at the moment. Some of these yokels can't resist the "Reverand Moon" tactics of Jene Nelson! Please forward starter sets (the $20,000 version) with one IBM-PC, one DEC-Rainbow 100, one Epson QX-10, one KayPro Model 4 and one of the PC clones (your choice), to

Kansas City ComputerCentre	Middletown ComputerCentre
1457 Alderman Blvd.	Historic Downtown Mall
Kansas City, MO 69696	Middletown, EA 99301

I think you can charge double mark-up to both of these clowns. They wont recognize the difference. Maybe you could enclose some standard software literature for them: WordStar, Calcstar, Multiplan, Visicalc, Lotus 1,2,3, and so on. I trust you like a brother to do a good job (get it?).

      Love,

      Dale

        PS: Mom wants one of those ferns you got Sally at the Bala Cynwyd nursery. Could you pick one up before driving up next time? We're all looking forward to having all of the kids under one roof again over Memorial Day.
        PSS: could you bring my check for the Wizard dividends with you when you come? I never thought that my investment in Wizard would start to pay off so soon, but with CCA ordering from you, and some hefty markups to some of my lesser franchisees, I profit both ways. See you soon, love, Dale.

*** LETTER OF CREDIT ***

The bearer(s) of this letter, Jack & Margaret Danielson have this 5 th day of April, two years ago established an irrevocable line of credit in the amount of $ 75,000 and valid for ninety (90) days, subject to renewal. Such credit shall be secured by a security interest in the inventory or other property of the bearers and they shall cooperate in perfecting such a security interest in response to reasonable requests of the bank.

D. E. Twerpskopf
Vice—President

Central National Bank
Main Street Tower
Middletown, EA 23134

ComputerCentre Associates

1710 Shore Drive
Boston, Massachusetts

Internal Memoranda

FROM: Paul Hobart, Asst. to the Principal

TO: Dale Atkins, Principal - CCA

DATE: July, two years ago.

We have continued to suffer delays in obtaining coverage for the Technical Services Department under Terry Johansen's direction. We've put off all service rep training until we find a guy who can handle all the common PC's and our typical installation problems. I've encouraged all of the franchises to make arrangements by contracting with outsiders like RCA Service Corp., Honeywell or Xerox to carry out warranty service or other work on units they sell. Some of them are bitching that we should bear the cost of these arrangements, but nobody is going to sue over this, I don't think.

ComputerCentre Associates

1710 Shore Drive
Boston, Massachusetts

From: Nelsen Jr

To: Atkins

Date: January 17, last year.

    I've cut our nationwide ad spots for this year from the 37 we'd planned to 12. The networks just hit us with new rate schedules, averaging $65,000 a minute off-peak! We'll have to concentrate more on co-ops with the local franchisees' regular media. I think all but the marginal franchisees will be able to take up the obvious slack from our national cuts and increase local exposure to compensate. Seattle, Cleveland and Middletown may be a problem since they're giving us the poor mouth, but I'll try to lean on them. They'll sure go under if they <u>don't</u> up their local ads.

ComputerCentre Associates

1710 Shore Drive
Boston, Massachusetts

Jack Danielson
Margaret Danielson
Middletown ComputerCentre
Middletown, EA

January 30, last year

Dear Jack and Margaret:

I note with alarm that you have yet to engage experienced computer professionals on your sales force. In our experience this will lead to greatly depressed sales. Also, I must remind you of the obligation to maintain suffient inventory. As we have discussed, you are not keeping sufficient items in your stock to permit ready delivery to customers. We are doing everything we can to expedite shipments to you, but you will lose sales if you cannot maintain some stock of the most common computers locally. Please let me know how you plan to rectify these matters.

Very Truly Yours,

Dale Atkins

Dale Atkins
Principal

APPENDIX A

Central National Bank
Main Street Tower
Middletown, EA 23134

May 7, last year.

Jack Danielson
Middletown ComputerCentre
Historic Downtown Mall
Middletown, EA

Dear Mr. Danielson:

Our Credit Department has completed a regularly scheduled quarterly evaluation on our letters of credit, including the one we issued to your company last April 5th.

Since you have depleted your savings account with us during the past 14 months from $57,000 to $5,000 and failed to show outside guarantees of income, we are constrained to reduce the line of credit outstanding to you to a level more proportional with our security protections under our agreement. We have decided to fix that level at $25,000, at least until there is a demonstrated earnings stream from your new franchise.

Hope this letter finds you well and that the business venture is going well.

Cordially,

D. E. Twerpskopf
Assistant Vice-President

ComputerCentre Associates

1710 Shore Drive
Boston, Massachusetts

Internal Memoranda

FROM: Dale Atkins ʰᵏ

TO: Jene Nelsen

DATE: May 19, last year.

Jene, please complete the paperwork right away on the Kansas City and Middletown contract Addenda. I don't want any gaps when we start requesting the baloon payments pretty soon. Do you have to be creative to come up with these? Attached are clear copies of the Thomases' and Danielsons' signatures from the contracts. Let me know when you've worked them up so I can "remind" these franchisees.

ComputerCentre Associates

1710 Shore Drive
Boston, Massachusetts

Jack Danielson
Margaret Danielson
Middletown ComputerCentre
Middletown, EA

May 30, last year

Dear Jack and Margaret:

Now that one year of operation has been completed, please remit to CCA your check for the remainder of the franchise fee, as agreed at the closing.

Very Truly Yours,

Dale Atkins
Principal

ComputerCentre Associates

1710 Shore Drive
Boston, Massachusetts

Internal Memoranda

From: Nelsen

To: Dale Atkins

Date: June 2, last year.

    Enclosed are the newly completed addenda for Kansas City and Middletown per your request.

APPENDIX A

A D D E N D U M

Further to the Franchise Agreement being entered by the parties on this day, the signatories below hereby set forth their agreement to an addendum to such agreement. It is hereby stipulated and agreed that the franchisees listed below, as consideration for creation of the franchise arrangements between the parties and as further compensation to ComputerCentre Associates, all of which shall be deemed reasonable and in proportion to value conferred by said ComputerCentre Associates, do hereby agree to pay to ComputerCentre Associates a royalty fee on the gross dollar value of all sales made by the franchise, to be computed at __5__ percent (%) for the first five years from the date the franchise enters into business, and __2½__ percent (%) of gross sales volume thereafter. Such payments shall be due upon demand by ComputerCentre Associates and any delay or forebearance permitted by ComputerCentre Associates shall not operate to relieve the franchisee of the obligation to make such payments retroactively thereafter. If legal action is required to enforce this Addendum to the Franchise Agreement, the franchisees signing below agree to be responsible, jointly and severally, for reimbursement of any and all reasonable attorneys' fees incurred by ComputerCentre Associates in enforcing its rights hereunder.

DATED: March 10, two years ago
      Middletown

Franchisees: _Jack Danielson_

              Margaret Danielson

      Accepted: _Dale Akins_

              ComputerCentre Associates

Central National Bank
Main Street Tower
Middletown, EA 23134

June 30, last year.

Jack Danielson
Middletown ComputerCentre
Historic Downtown Mall
Middletown, EA

Dear Mr. Danielson:

Your line of credit with us, opened 15 months ago on March 6th last year, is overdrawn. The outstanding balance has reached $44,020.00. While some or all of this debt is secured by our lien interest in your inventory, <u>it is imperative</u> that you reduce this debt to $25,000 within five (5) business days or we will be compelled to take legal steps to protect our interests.

Please deliver the balance to the bank immediately.

I trust that you will comply with this formal written demand forthwith and that we may continue a productive professional relationship in the future.

Cordially,

D. E. Twerpskopf
Vice-President

Sent registered mail, return receipt required.

APPENDIX A

Interim Financial Statement
prepared by
Drew Anderson; August 29th DA

Assets

Cash on Hand	857.50
Checking balance	2726.87

Accounts Receivable
    Total: 13,202.12
    Doubtful: 4,512.00

                    8,690.12

Inventory
    Computers: 37,006.12
    Other: 17,210.30

                  54,216.42

           TOTAL   66,490.91

Liabilities

Accounts Payable	32,607.20
Salaries Due	4,110.52
Rent Past Due	2,440.00
Royalty Owed CCA	38,355.00

        TOTAL   77,512.72

NET EQUITY (DEBT)   (11,021.81)

APPENDIX A

```
              12 Months Income Statement
              September 1 thru August 29
                   by Drew Anderson  DA
```

Income

```
     Sales#
          Gross:  767,100.22
          Returns: 46,056.10

                                      721,044.12

     Instructional Class Tuitions       1,201.00

     Checking Account Interest          1,711.39

                    TOTAL                              723,956.51
```

Expenses

```
     Cost of Goods Sold                664,400.20

     Salaries
          Mr. Danielson:    14,000
          Ms. Danielson:     8,500
          Johnson (sales):  11,500
          Hadden (sales):   11,500
          Anderson:          8,000
                                       53,500.00

     Rent                              12,000.00

     Utilities & Telephone              2,110.12

     Delivery Services                    400.60

     Other Shipping                     1,107.10

     Outside Repair Service on
        warranted items (RCA)           2,000.00

     Advertising                       12,375.00
                    TOTAL                              747,893.02


     PROFIT (LOSS)                                     (23,436.51)
```

```
* Almost all items purchased
from Wizard/CCA at 40% markup
```

APPENDIX B

PAVES v. JOHNSTONE

The following witness script from the trial advocacy case file in *Paves v. Johnstone* is reproduced with the permission of Professor Stephen A. Saltzburg.

Aubrey Robinson

I have been an architect in the Fredericksburg area for the last ten years, having begun my practice after graduating from the University of Virginia with a B.S. in architecture in YR-11. I am a member of the American Institute of Architects, am 34 years old, and have known both the plaintiff and the defendant for the years I have been in practice. Both the plaintiff and the defendant have reputations as competent architects.

When the council was thinking of redoing the post office and converting it into a city hall, I was one of four architects who were invited to tour the post office and speak with the City Manager, Mr. Noles. The plaintiff was one of the other four, but I did not see the defendant present.

In the end I decided not to submit a proposal on the post office because I was so busy with major jobs that I could not spare the time. I never bothered to inquire about how many proposals were received.

When I compute the fee that I will charge, I consult the R.S. Means Cost Data Book. It is a very useful compilation of square footage costs for various kinds of buildings based on the average of construction costs around the country. It is widely used around the United States and has been a leading authority since YR-15. One can also examine the Governor's Capital Outlay Manual to see how much an architect would be paid on a similar state building. In this case, the state fee for renovation of the post office would have been 9.918%. State fees might be higher sometimes than other fees, because there is a good bit of red tape associated with the state. You have to go to Richmond, you have to fill out a mass of paperwork, and you have to deal with bureaucrats who are a real pain.

The Data Book also indicates what the standard charges are for architectural services. The standard fees for offices and municipal buildings are reported to be 10.5% for a $500,000 project, with 50% added to the fee if alterations are to be done and 25% more (i.e., 25% of the 10.5%) for any additional costs over $500,000. Any fee of 9–12% would have been reasonable for the post office project, in my opinion. I would never charge less, and I would regard a lower fee as unreasonable.

There are different degrees of difficulty in designing buildings. The easiest is a warehouse. An office building is next. Retail stores are more difficult, and hospitals are the most difficult of all. Obviously, refurbishing or renovating an old building can be difficult, depending on what is going to be done. One would consider the need to hire consultants, travel, etc. in arriving at a fee.

APPENDIX C

FEDERAL RULES OF EVIDENCE

Federal Rules of Evidence

ARTICLE I.   GENERAL PROVISIONS

Rule 101.   Scope.

These rules govern proceedings in the courts of the United States and before the United States bankruptcy judges and United States magistrate judges, to the extent and with the exceptions stated in rule 1101. [*Adopted Jan. 2, 1975, effective July 1, 1975; amended Mar. 2, 1987, effective Oct. 1, 1987; Apr. 25, 1988, effective Nov. 1, 1988; Apr. 22, 1993, effective Dec. 1, 1993.*]

Rule 102.   Purpose and Construction.

These rules shall be construed to secure fairness in administration, elimination of unjustifiable expense and delay, and promotion of growth and development of the law of evidence to the end that the truth may be ascertained and proceedings justly determined. [*Adopted Jan. 2, 1975, effective July 1, 1975.*]

Rule 103.   Rulings on Evidence.

(a) Effect of erroneous ruling.—Error may not be predicated upon a ruling which admits or excludes evidence unless a substantial right of the party is affected, and

   (1) Objection.—In case the ruling is one admitting evidence, a timely objection or motion to strike appears of record, stating the specific ground of objection, if the specific ground was not apparent from the context; or

   (2) Offer of proof.—In case the ruling is one excluding evidence, the substance of the evidence was made known to the court by offer or was apparent from the context within which questions were asked.

Once the court makes a definitive ruling on the record admitting or excluding evidence, either at or before trial, a party need not renew an objection or offer of proof to preserve a claim of error for appeal.

(b) Record of offer and ruling.—The court may add any other or further statement which shows the character of the evidence, the form in which it was offered, the objection made, and the ruling thereon. It may direct the making of an offer in question and answer form.

(c) Hearing of jury.—In jury cases, proceedings shall be conducted, to the extent practicable, so as to prevent inadmissible evidence from being suggested to the jury by any means, such as making statements or offers of proof or asking questions in the hearing of the jury.

(d) Plain error.—Nothing in this rule precludes taking notice of plain errors affecting substantial rights although they were not brought to the attention of the court. [*Adopted Jan. 2, 1975, effective July 1, 1975; amended Apr. 17, 2000, effective Dec. 1, 2000.*]

Rule 104. Preliminary Questions.

(a) Questions of admissibility generally.—Preliminary questions concerning the qualification of a person to be a witness, the existence of a privilege, or the admissibility of evidence shall be determined by the court, subject to the provisions of subdivision (b). In making its determination it is not bound by the rules of evidence except those with respect to privileges.

(b) Relevancy conditioned on fact.—When the relevancy of evidence depends upon the fulfillment of a condition of fact, the court shall admit it upon, or subject to, the introduction of evidence sufficient to support a finding of the fulfillment of the condition.

(c) Hearing of jury.—Hearings on the admissibility of confessions shall in all cases be conducted out of the hearing of the jury. Hearings on other preliminary matters shall be so conducted when the interests of justice require, or when an accused is a witness and so requests.

(d) Testimony by accused.—The accused does not, by testifying upon a preliminary matter, become subject to cross-examination as to other issues in the case.

(e) Weight and credibility.—This rule does not limit the right of a party to introduce before the jury evidence relevant to weight or credibility. [*Adopted Jan. 2, 1975, effective July 1, 1975; amended Mar. 2, 1987, effective Oct. 1, 1987.*]

Rule 105. Limited Admissibility.

When evidence which is admissible as to one party or for one purpose but not admissible as to another party or for another purpose is admitted, the court, upon request, shall restrict the evidence to its proper scope and instruct the jury accordingly. [*Adopted Jan. 2, 1975, effective July 1, 1975.*]

Rule 106. Remainder of or Related Writings or Recorded Statements.

When a writing or recorded statement or part thereof is introduced by a party, an adverse party may require the introduction at that time of any other part or any other writing or recorded statement which ought in fairness to be considered contemporaneously with it. [*Adopted Jan. 2, 1975, effective July 1, 1975; amended Mar. 2, 1987, effective Oct. 1, 1987.*]

ARTICLE II. JUDICIAL NOTICE

Rule 201. Judicial Notice of Adjudicative Facts.

(a) Scope of rule.—This rule governs only judicial notice of adjudicative facts.

(b) Kinds of facts.—A judicially noticed fact must be one not subject to reasonable dispute in that it is either (1) generally known within the territorial jurisdiction of the trial court or (2) capable of accurate and ready determination by resort to sources whose accuracy cannot reasonably be questioned.

(c) When discretionary.—A court may take judicial notice, whether requested or not.

(d) When mandatory.—A court shall take judicial notice if requested by a party and supplied with the necessary information.

(e) Opportunity to be heard.—A party is entitled upon timely request to an opportunity to be heard as to the propriety of taking judicial notice and the tenor of the matter noticed. In the absence of prior notification, the request may be made after judicial notice has been taken.

(f) Time of taking notice.—Judicial notice may be taken at any stage of the proceeding.

(g) Instructing jury.—In a civil action or proceeding, the court shall instruct the jury to accept as conclusive any fact judicially noticed. In a criminal case, the court shall instruct the jury that it may, but is not required to, accept as conclusive any fact judicially noticed. [*Adopted Jan. 2, 1975, effective July 1, 1975.*]

ARTICLE III.   PRESUMPTIONS IN CIVIL ACTIONS AND PROCEEDINGS

Rule 301.   Presumptions in General in Civil Actions and Proceedings.

In all civil actions and proceedings not otherwise provided for by Act of Congress or by these rules, a presumption imposes on the party against whom it is directed the burden of going forward with evidence to rebut or meet the presumption, but does not shift to such party the burden of proof in the sense of the risk of nonpersuasion, which remains throughout the trial upon the party on whom it was originally cast. [*Adopted Jan. 2, 1975, effective July 1, 1975.*]

Rule 302.   Applicability of State Law in Civil Actions and Proceedings.

In civil actions and proceedings, the effect of a presumption respecting a fact which is an element of a claim or defense as to which State law supplies the rule of decision is determined in accordance with State law. [*Adopted Jan. 2, 1975, effective July 1, 1975.*]

ARTICLE IV.   RELEVANCY AND ITS LIMITS

Rule 401.   Definition of "Relevant Evidence."

"Relevant evidence" means evidence having any tendency to make the existence of any fact that is of consequence to the determination of the action more probable or less probable than it would be without the evidence. [*Adopted Jan. 2, 1975, effective July 1, 1975.*]

Rule 402.   Relevant Evidence Generally Admissible; Irrelevant Evidence Inadmissible.

All relevant evidence is admissible, except as otherwise provided by the Constitution of the United States, by Act of Congress, by these rules, or by other rules prescribed by the Supreme Court pursuant to statutory authority. Evidence which is not relevant is not admissible. [*Adopted Jan. 2, 1975, effective July 1, 1975.*]

Rule 403. Exclusion of Relevant Evidence on Grounds of Prejudice, Confusion, or Waste of Time.

Although relevant, evidence may be excluded if its probative value is substantially outweighed by the danger of unfair prejudice, confusion of the issues, or misleading the jury, or by considerations of undue delay, waste of time, or needless presentation of cumulative evidence. [*Adopted Jan. 2, 1975, effective July 1, 1975.*]

Rule 404. Character Evidence Not Admissible to Prove Conduct; Exceptions; Other Crimes.

(a) Character evidence generally.—Evidence of a person's character or a trait of character is not admissible for the purpose of proving action in conformity therewith on a particular occasion, except:

(1) Character of accused.—Evidence of a pertinent trait of character offered by an accused, or by the prosecution to rebut the same, or if evidence of a trait of character of the alleged victim of the crime is offered by an accused and admitted under Rule 404(a)(2), evidence of the same trait of character of the accused offered by the prosecution;

(2) Character of alleged victim.—Evidence of a pertinent trait of character of the alleged victim of the crime offered by an accused, or by the prosecution to rebut the same, or evidence of a character trait of peacefulness of the alleged victim offered by the prosecution in a homicide case to rebut evidence that the alleged victim was the first aggressor;

(3) Character of witness.—Evidence of the character of a witness, as provided in rules 607, 608, and 609.

(b) Other crimes, wrongs, or acts.—Evidence of other crimes, wrongs, or acts is not admissible to prove the character of a person in order to show action in conformity therewith. It may, however, be admissible for other purposes, such as proof of motive, opportunity, intent, preparation, plan, knowledge, identity, or absence of mistake or accident, provided that upon request by the accused, the prosecution in a criminal case shall provide reasonable notice in advance of trial, or during trial if the court excuses pretrial notice on good cause shown, of the general nature of any such evidence it intends to introduce at trial. [*Adopted Jan. 2, 1975, effective July 1, 1975; amended Mar. 2, 1987, effective Oct. 1, 1987; Apr. 30, 1991, effective Dec. 1, 1991; Apr. 17, 2000, effective Dec. 1, 2000.*]

Rule 405.   Methods of Proving Character.

(a) Reputation or opinion.—In all cases in which evidence of character or a trait of character of a person is admissible, proof may be made by testimony as to reputation or by testimony in the form of an opinion. On cross-examination, inquiry is allowable into relevant specific instances of conduct.

(b) Specific instances of conduct.—In cases in which character or a trait of character of a person is an essential element of a charge, claim, or defense, proof may also be made of specific instances of that person's conduct. *[Adopted Jan. 2, 1975, effective July 1, 1975; amended Mar. 2, 1987, effective Oct. 1, 1987.]*

Rule 406.   Habit; Routine Practice.

Evidence of the habit of a person or of the routine practice of an organization, whether corroborated or not and regardless of the presence of eyewitnesses, is relevant to prove that the conduct of the person or organization on a particular occasion was in conformity with the habit or routine practice. *[Adopted Jan. 2, 1975, effective July 1, 1975.]*

Rule 407.   Subsequent Remedial Measures.

When, after an injury or harm allegedly caused by an event, measures are taken that, if taken previously, would have made the injury or harm less likely to occur, evidence of the subsequent measures is not admissible to prove negligence, culpable conduct, a defect in a product, a defect in a product's design, or a need for a warning or instruction. This rule does not require the exclusion of evidence of subsequent measures when offered for another purpose, such as proving ownership, control, or feasibility of precautionary measures, if controverted, or impeachment. *[Adopted Jan. 2, 1975, effective July 1, 1975; amended Apr. 11, 1997, effective Dec. 1, 1997.]*

Rule 408.   Compromise and Offers To Compromise.

Evidence of (1) furnishing or offering or promising to furnish, or (2) accepting or offering or promising to accept, a valuable consideration in compromising or attempting to compromise a claim which was disputed as to either validity or amount, is not admissible to prove liability for or invalidity of the claim or its amount. Evidence of conduct or statements made in compromise negotiations is likewise not admissible. This rule does not require the exclusion of any evidence otherwise discoverable merely because it is presented in the course of compromise negotiations. This rule also does not require exclusion when the evidence is offered for another purpose, such as proving bias or prejudice of a witness, negativing a contention of undue delay, or proving an effort to obstruct a criminal investigation or prosecution. [*Adopted Jan. 2, 1975, effective July 1, 1975.*]

Rule 409. Payment of Medical and Similar Expenses.

Evidence of furnishing or offering or promising to pay medical, hospital, or similar expenses occasioned by an injury is not admissible to prove liability for the injury. [*Adopted Jan. 2, 1975, effective July 1, 1975.*]

Rule 410. Inadmissibility of Pleas, Plea Discussions, and Related Statements.

Except as otherwise provided in this rule, evidence of the following is not, in any civil or criminal proceeding, admissible against the defendant who made the plea or was a participant in the plea discussions:

(1) a plea of guilty which was later withdrawn;

(2) a plea of nolo contendere;

(3) any statement made in the course of any proceedings under Rule 11 of the Federal Rules of Criminal Procedure or comparable state procedure regarding either of the foregoing pleas; or

(4) any statement made in the course of plea discussions with an attorney for the prosecuting authority which do not result in a plea of guilty or which result in a plea of guilty later withdrawn.

However, such a statement is admissible (i) in any proceeding wherein another statement made in the course of the same plea or plea discussions has been introduced and the statement ought in fairness be considered contemporaneously with it, or (ii) in a criminal proceeding for perjury or false statement if the statement was made by the defendant under oath, on the record and in the presence of counsel. [*Adopted Jan. 2, 1975, effective July 1, 1975; amended Dec. 12, 1975; Apr. 30, 1979, effective Dec. 1, 1980.*]

Rule 411. Liability Insurance.

Evidence that a person was or was not insured against liability is not admissible upon the issue whether the person acted negligently or otherwise wrongfully.

This rule does not require the exclusion of evidence of insurance against liability when offered for another purpose, such as proof of agency, ownership, or control, or bias or prejudice of a witness. [*Adopted Jan. 2, 1975, effective July 1, 1975; amended Mar. 2, 1987, effective Oct. 1, 1987.*]

Rule 412. Sex Offense Cases; Relevance of Alleged Victim's Past Sexual Behavior or Alleged Sexual Predisposition.

(a) Evidence Generally Inadmissible.—The following evidence is not admissible in any civil or criminal proceeding involving alleged sexual misconduct except as provided in subdivisions (b) and (c):

    (1) Evidence offered to prove that any alleged victim engaged in other sexual behavior.

    (2) Evidence offered to prove any alleged victim's sexual predisposition.

(b) Exceptions.

    (1) In a criminal case, the following evidence is admissible, if otherwise admissible under these rules:

        (A) evidence of specific instances of sexual behavior by the alleged victim offered to prove that a person other than the accused was the source of semen, injury or other physical evidence;

        (B) evidence of specific instances of sexual behavior by the alleged victim with respect to the person accused of the sexual misconduct offered by the accused to prove consent or by the prosecution; and

        (C) evidence the exclusion of which would violate the constitutional rights of the defendant.

    (2) In a civil case, evidence offered to prove the sexual behavior or sexual predisposition of any alleged victim is admissible if it is otherwise admissible under these rules and its probative value substantially outweighs the danger of harm to any victim and of unfair prejudice to any party. Evidence of an alleged victim's reputation is admissible only if it has been placed in controversy by the alleged victim.

(c) Procedure to Determine Admissibility.

    (1) A party intending to offer evidence under subdivision (b) must—

        (A) file a written motion at least 14 days before trial specifically describing the evidence and stating the purpose for which it is offered unless the court, for good cause requires a different time for filing or permits filing during trial; and

(B) serve the motion on all parties and notify the alleged victim or, when appropriate, the alleged victim's guardian or representative.

(2) Before admitting evidence under this rule the court must conduct a hearing in camera and afford the victim and parties a right to attend and be heard. The motion, related papers, and the record of the hearing must be sealed and remain under seal unless the court orders otherwise. [*Adopted Oct. 28, 1978, effective Nov. 28, 1978; amended Nov. 18, 1988; Apr. 29, 1994, effective Dec. 1, 1994; Sept. 13, 1994, effective Dec. 1, 1994.*]

Rule 413. Evidence of Similar Crimes in Sexual Assault Cases.

(a) In a criminal case in which the defendant is accused of an offense of sexual assault, evidence of the defendant's commission of another offense or offenses of sexual assault is admissible, and may be considered for its bearing on any matter to which it is relevant.

(b) In a case in which the Government intends to offer evidence under this rule, the attorney for the Government shall disclose the evidence to the defendant, including statements of witnesses or a summary of the substance of any testimony that is expected to be offered, at least fifteen days before the scheduled date of trial or at such later time as the court may allow for good cause.

(c) This rule shall not be construed to limit the admission or consideration of evidence under any other rule.

(d) For purposes of this rule and Rule 415, "offense of sexual assault" means a crime under Federal law or the law of a State (as defined in section 513 of title 18, United States Code) that involved—

(1) any conduct proscribed by chapter 109A of title 18, United States Code;

(2) contact, without consent, between any part of the defendant's body or an object and the genitals or anus of another person;

(3) contact, without consent, between the genitals or anus of the defendant and any part of another person's body;

(4) deriving sexual pleasure or gratification from the infliction of death, bodily injury, or physical pain on another person; or

(5) an attempt or conspiracy to engage in conduct described in paragraphs (1)–(4). [*Adopted Sept. 13, 1994, effective July 9, 1995.*]

Rule 414. Evidence of Similar Crimes in Child Molestation Cases.

(a) In a criminal case in which the defendant is accused of an offense of child molestation, evidence of the defendant's commission of another offense or offenses of child molestation is admissible, and may be considered for its bearing on any matter to which it is relevant.

(b) In a case in which the Government intends to offer evidence under this rule, the attorney for the Government shall disclose the evidence to the defendant, including statements of witnesses or a summary of the substance of any testimony that is expected to be offered, at least fifteen days before the scheduled date of trial or at such later time as the court may allow for good cause.

(c) This rule shall not be construed to limit the admission or consideration of evidence under any other rule.

(d) For purposes of this rule and Rule 415, "child" means a person below the age of fourteen, and "offense of child molestation" means a crime under Federal law or the law of a State (as defined in section 513 of title 18, United States Code) that involved—

(1) any conduct proscribed by chapter 109A of title 18, United States Code, that was committed in relation to a child;

(2) any conduct proscribed by chapter 110 of title 18, United States Code:

(3) contact between any part of the defendant's body or an object and the genitals of the body of a child;

(4) contact between the genitals or anus of the defendant and any part of the body of a child;

(5) deriving sexual pleasure or gratification from the infliction of death, bodily injury, or physical pain on a child; or

(6) an attempt or conspiracy to engage in conduct described in paragraphs (1)–(5). [*Adopted Sept. 13, 1994, effective July 9, 1995.*]

Rule 415.   Evidence of Similar Acts in Civil Cases Concerning Sexual Assault or Child Molestation.

(a) In a civil case in which a claim for damages or other relief is predicated on a party's alleged commission of conduct constituting an offense of sexual assault or child molestation, evidence of that party's commission of another offense or offenses of sexual assault or child molestation is admissible and may be considered as provided in Rule 413 and Rule 414 of these rules.

(b) A party who intends to offer evidence under this Rule shall disclose the evidence to the party against whom it will be offered, including statements of witnesses or a summary of the substance of any testimony that is expected to be offered, at least fifteen days before the scheduled date of trial or at such later time as the court may allow for good cause.

(c) This rule shall not be construed to limit the admission or consideration of evidence under any other rule. [*Adopted Sept. 13, 1994, effective July 9, 1995.*]

ARTICLE V.   PRIVILEGES

Rule 501.   General Rule.

Except as otherwise required by the Constitution of the United States or provided by Act of Congress or in rules prescribed by the Supreme Court pursuant to statutory authority, the privilege of a witness, person, government, State, or political subdivision thereof shall be governed by the principles of the common law as they may be interpreted by the courts of the United States in the light of reason and experience. However, in civil actions and proceedings, with respect to an element of a claim or defense as to which State law supplies the rule of decision, the privilege of a witness, person, government, State, or political subdivision thereof shall be determined in accordance with State law. [*Adopted Jan. 2, 1975, effective July 1, 1975.*]

ARTICLE VI.   WITNESSES

Rule 601.   General Rule of Competency.

Every person is competent to be a witness except as otherwise provided in these rules. However, in civil actions and proceedings, with respect to an element of a claim or defense as to which State law supplies the rule of decision, the competency of a witness shall be determined in accordance with State law. [*Adopted Jan. 2, 1975, effective July 1, 1975.*]

Rule 602. Lack of Personal Knowledge.

A witness may not testify to a matter unless evidence is introduced sufficient to support a finding that the witness has personal knowledge of the matter. Evidence to prove personal knowledge may, but need not, consist of the witness' own testimony. This rule is subject to the provisions of rule 703, relating to opinion testimony by expert witnesses. [*Adopted Jan. 2, 1975, effective July 1, 1975; amended Mar. 2, 1987, effective Oct. 1, 1987; Apr. 25, 1988, effective Nov. 1, 1988.*]

Rule 603. Oath or Affirmation.

Before testifying, every witness shall be required to declare that the witness will testify truthfully, by oath or affirmation administered in a form calculated to awaken the witness' conscience and impress the witness' mind with the duty to do so. [*Adopted Jan. 2, 1975, effective July 1, 1975; amended Mar. 2, 1987, effective Oct. 1, 1987.*]

Rule 604. Interpreters.

An interpreter is subject to the provisions of these rules relating to qualification as an expert and the administration of an oath or affirmation to make a true translation. [*Adopted Jan. 2, 1975, effective July 1, 1975; amended Mar. 2, 1987, effective Oct. 1. 1987.*]

Rule 605. Competency of Judge as Witness.

The judge presiding at the trial may not testify in that trial as a witness. No objection need be made in order to preserve the point. [*Adopted Jan. 2, 1975, effective July 1, 1975.*]

Rule 606. Competency of Juror as Witness.

(a) At the trial.—A member of the jury may not testify as a witness before that jury in the trial of the case in which the juror is sitting. If the juror is called so to testify, the opposing party shall be afforded an opportunity to object out of the presence of the jury.

(b) Inquiry into validity of verdict or indictment.—Upon an inquiry into the validity of a verdict or indictment, a juror may not testify as to any matter or statement occurring during the course of the jury's deliberations or to the effect of anything upon that or any other juror's mind or emotions as influencing the juror to assent to or dissent from the verdict or indictment or concerning the juror's mental processes in connection therewith, except that a juror may testify on the question whether extraneous prejudicial information was improperly brought to the jury's attention or whether any outside influence was improperly brought to bear upon any juror. Nor may a juror's affidavit or evidence of any statement by the juror concerning a matter about which the juror would be precluded from testifying be received for these purposes. [*Adopted Jan. 2, 1975, effective July 1, 1975; amended Dec. 12, 1975; Mar. 2, 1987, effective Oct. 1, 1987.*]

Rule 607.   Who May Impeach.

The credibility of a witness may be attacked by any party, including the party calling the witness. [*Adopted Jan. 2, 1975, effective July 1, 1975; amended Mar. 2, 1987, effective Oct. 1, 1987.*]

Rule 608.   Evidence of Character and Conduct of Witness.

(a) Opinion and reputation evidence of character.—The credibility of a witness may be attacked or supported by evidence in the form of opinion or reputation, but subject to these limitations: (1) the evidence may refer only to character for truthfulness or untruthfulness, and (2) evidence of truthful character is admissible only after the character of the witness for truthfulness has been attacked by opinion or reputation evidence or otherwise.

(b) Specific instances of conduct.—Specific instances of the conduct of a witness, for the purpose of attacking or supporting the witness' credibility, other than conviction of crime as provided in rule 609, may not be proved by extrinsic evidence. They may, however, in the discretion of the court, if probative of truthfulness or untruthfulness, be inquired into on cross-examination of the witness (1) concerning the witness' character for truthfulness or untruthfulness, or (2) concerning the character for truthfulness or untruthfulness of another witness as to which character the witness being cross-examined has testified.

The giving of testimony, whether by an accused or by any other witness, does not operate as a waiver of the accused's or the witness' privilege against self-incrimination when examined with respect to matters which relate only to credibility. [*Adopted Jan. 2, 1975, effective July 1, 1975; amended Mar. 2, 1987, effective Oct. 1, 1987; Apr. 25, 1988, effective Nov. 1, 1988.*]

Rule 609. Impeachment by Evidence of Conviction of Crime.

(a) General rule.—For the purpose of attacking the credibility of a witness,

> (1) evidence that a witness other than an accused has been convicted of a crime shall be admitted, subject to Rule 403, if the crime was punishable by death or imprisonment in excess of one year under the law under which the witness was convicted, and evidence that an accused has been convicted of such a crime shall be admitted if the court determines that the probative value of admitting this evidence outweighs its prejudicial effect to the accused; and

> (2) evidence that any witness has been convicted of a crime shall be admitted if it involved dishonesty or false statement, regardless of the punishment.

(b) Time limit.—Evidence of a conviction under this rule is not admissible if a period of more than ten years has elapsed since the date of the conviction or of the release of the witness from the confinement imposed for that conviction, whichever is the later date, unless the court determines, in the interests of justice, that the probative value of the conviction supported by specific facts and circumstances substantially outweighs its prejudicial effect. However, evidence of a conviction more than ten years old as calculated herein, is not admissible unless the proponent gives to the adverse party sufficient advance written notice of intent to use such evidence to provide the adverse party with a fair opportunity to contest the use of such evidence.

(c) Effect of pardon, annulment, or certificate of rehabilitation.—Evidence of a conviction is not admissible under this rule if (1) the conviction has been the subject of a pardon, annulment, certificate of rehabilitation, or other equivalent procedure based on a finding of the rehabilitation of the person convicted, and that person has not been convicted of a subsequent crime which was punishable by death or imprisonment in excess of one year, or (2) the conviction has been the subject of a pardon, annulment, or other equivalent procedure based on a finding of innocence.

(d) Juvenile adjudications.—Evidence of juvenile adjudications is generally not admissible under this rule. The court may, however, in a criminal case allow evidence of a juvenile adjudication of a witness other than the accused if conviction of the offense would be admissible to attack the credibility of an adult and the court is satisfied that admission in evidence is necessary for a fair determination of the issue of guilt or innocence.

(e) Pendency of appeal.—The pendency of an appeal therefrom does not render evidence of a conviction inadmissible. Evidence of the pendency of an appeal is admissible. [*Adopted Jan. 2, 1975, effective July 1, 1975; amended Mar. 2, 1987, effective Oct. 1, 1987; Jan. 26, 1990, effective Dec. 1, 1990.*]

Rule 610.   Religious Beliefs or Opinions.

Evidence of the beliefs or opinions of a witness on matters of religion is not admissible for the purpose of showing that by reason of their nature the witness' credibility is impaired or enhanced. [*Adopted Jan. 2, 1975, effective July 1, 1975; amended Mar. 2, 1987, effective Oct. 1, 1987.*]

Rule 611.   Mode and Order of Interrogation and Presentation.

(a) Control by court.—The court shall exercise reasonable control over the mode and order of interrogating witnesses and presenting evidence so as to (1) make the interrogation and presentation effective for the ascertainment of the truth, (2) avoid needless consumption of time, and (3) protect witnesses from harassment or undue embarrassment.

(b) Scope of cross-examination.—Cross-examination should be limited to the subject matter of the direct examination and matters affecting the credibility of the witness. The court may, in the exercise of discretion, permit inquiry into additional matters as if on direct examination.

(c) Leading questions.—Leading questions should not be used on the direct examination of a witness except as may be necessary to develop the witness' testimony. Ordinarily leading questions should be permitted on cross-examination. When a party calls a hostile witness, an adverse party, or a witness identified with an adverse party, interrogation may be by leading questions. [*Adopted Jan. 2, 1975, effective July 1, 1975; amended Mar. 2, 1987, effective Oct. 1, 1987.*]

Rule 612.   Writing Used To Refresh Memory.

Except as otherwise provided in criminal proceedings by section 3500 of title 18, United States Code, if a witness uses a writing to refresh memory for the purpose of testifying, either—

(1) while testifying, or

(2) before testifying, if the court in its discretion determines it is necessary in the interests of justice,

an adverse party is entitled to have the writing produced at the hearing, to inspect it, to cross-examine the witness thereon, and to introduce in evidence those portions which relate to the testimony of the witness. If it is claimed that the writing contains matters not related to the subject matter of the testimony the court shall examine the writing in camera, excise any portions not so related, and order delivery of the remainder to the party entitled thereto. Any portion withheld over objections shall be preserved and made available to the appellate court in the event of an appeal. If a writing is not produced or delivered pursuant to order under this rule, the court shall make any order justice requires, except that in criminal cases when the prosecution elects not to comply, the order shall be one striking the testimony or, if the court in its discretion determines that the interests of justice so require, declaring a mistrial. [*Adopted Jan. 2, 1975, effective July 1, 1975; amended Mar. 2, 1987, effective Oct. 1, 1987.*]

Rule 613. Prior Statements of Witnesses.

(a) Examining witness concerning prior statement.—In examining a witness concerning a prior statement made by the witness, whether written or not, the statement need not be shown nor its contents disclosed to the witness at that time, but on request the same shall be shown or disclosed to opposing counsel.

(b) Extrinsic evidence of prior inconsistent statement of witness.—Extrinsic evidence of a prior inconsistent statement by a witness is not admissible unless the witness is afforded an opportunity to explain or deny the same and the opposite party is afforded an opportunity to interrogate the witness thereon, or the interests of justice otherwise require. This provision does not apply to admissions of a party-opponent as defined in rule 801(d)(2). [*Adopted Jan. 2, 1975, effective July 1, 1975; amended Mar. 2, 1987, effective Oct. 1, 1987; Apr. 25, 1988, effective Nov. 1, 1988.*]

Rule 614. Calling and Interrogation of Witnesses by Court.

(a) Calling by court.—The court may, on its own motion or at the suggestion of a party, call witnesses, and all parties are entitled to cross-examine witnesses thus called.

(b) Interrogation by court.—The court may interrogate witnesses, whether called by itself or by a party.

(c) Objections.—Objections to the calling of witnesses by the court or to interrogation by it may be made at the time or at the next available opportunity when the jury is not present. [*Adopted Jan. 2, 1975, effective July 1, 1975.*]

Rule 615. Exclusion of Witnesses.

At the request of a party the court shall order witnesses excluded so that they cannot hear the testimony of other witnesses, and it may make the order of its own motion. This rule does not authorize exclusion of (1) a party who is a natural person, or (2) an officer or employee of a party which is not a natural person designated as its representative by its attorney, or (3) a person whose presence is shown by a party to be essential to the presentation of the party's cause, or (4) a person authorized by statute to be present. [*Adopted Jan. 2, 1975, effective July 1, 1975; amended Mar. 2, 1987, effective Oct. 1, 1987; Apr. 25, 1988, effective Nov. 1, 1988; Nov. 18, 1988; Apr. 24, 1998, effective Dec. 1, 1998.*]

ARTICLE VII. OPINIONS AND EXPERT TESTIMONY

Rule 701. Opinion Testimony by Lay Witnesses.

If the witness is not testifying as an expert, the witness' testimony in the form of opinions or inferences is limited to those opinions or inferences which are (a) rationally based on the perception of the witness, (b) helpful to a clear understanding of the witness' testimony or the determination of a fact in issue, and (c) not based on scientific, technical, or other specialized knowledge within the scope of Rule 702. [*Adopted Jan. 2, 1975, effective July 1, 1975; amended Mar. 2, 1987, effective Oct. 1, 1987; Apr. 17, 2000, effective Dec. 1, 2000.*]

Rule 702. Testimony by Experts.

If scientific, technical, or other specialized knowledge will assist the trier of fact to understand the evidence or to determine a fact in issue, a witness qualified as an expert by knowledge, skill, experience, training, or education, may testify thereto in the form of an opinion or otherwise, if (1) the testimony is based upon sufficient facts or data, (2) the testimony is the product of reliable principles and methods, and (3) the witness has applied the principles and methods reliably to the facts of the case. [*Adopted Jan. 2, 1975, effective July 1, 1975; amended Apr. 17, 2000, effective Dec. 1, 2000.*]

Rule 703. Bases of Opinion Testimony by Experts.

The facts or data in the particular case upon which an expert bases an opinion or inference may be those perceived by or made known to the expert at or before the hearing. If of a type reasonably relied upon by experts in the particular field in forming opinions or inferences upon the subject, the facts or data need not be admissible in evidence in order for the opinion or inference to be admitted. Facts or data that are otherwise inadmissible shall not be disclosed to the jury by the proponent of the opinion or inference unless the court determines that their probative value in assisting the jury to evaluate the expert's opinion substantially outweighs their prejudicial effect. [*Adopted Jan. 2, 1975, effective July 1, 1975; amended Mar. 2, 1987, effective Oct. 1, 1987; Apr. 17, 2000, effective Dec. 1, 2000.*]

Rule 704. Opinion on Ultimate Issue.

(a) Except as provided in subdivision (b), testimony in the form of an opinion or inference otherwise admissible is not objectionable because it embraces an ultimate issue to be decided by the trier of fact.

(b) No expert witness testifying with respect to the mental state or condition of a defendant in a criminal case may state an opinion or inference as to whether the defendant did or did not have the mental state or condition constituting an element of the crime charged or of a defense thereto. Such ultimate issues are matters for the trier of fact alone. [*Adopted Jan. 2, 1975, effective July 1, 1975; amended Oct. 12, 1984.*]

Rule 705. Disclosure of Facts or Data Underlying Expert Opinion.

The expert may testify in terms of opinion or inference and give reasons therefor without first testifying to the underlying facts or data, unless the court requires otherwise. The expert may in any event be required to disclose the underlying facts or data on cross-examination. [*Adopted Jan. 2, 1975, effective July 1, 1975; amended Mar. 2, 1987, effective Oct. 1, 1987; Apr. 22, 1993, effective Dec. 1, 1993.*]

Rule 706. Court Appointed Experts.

(a) Appointment.—The court may on its own motion or on the motion of any party enter an order to show cause why expert witnesses should not be appointed, and may request the parties to submit nominations. The court may appoint any expert witnesses agreed upon by the parties, and may appoint expert witnesses of its own selection. An expert witness shall not be appointed by the court unless the witness consents to act. A witness so appointed shall be informed of the witness' duties by the court in writing, a copy of which shall be filed with the clerk, or at a conference in which the parties shall have opportunity to participate. A witness so appointed shall advise the parties of the witness' findings, if any; the witness' deposition may be taken by any party; and the witness may be called to testify by the court or any party. The witness shall be subject to cross-examination by each party, including a party calling the witness.

(b) Compensation.—Expert witnesses so appointed are entitled to reasonable compensation in whatever sum the court may allow. The compensation thus fixed is payable from funds which may be provided by law in criminal cases and civil actions and proceedings involving just compensation under the fifth amendment. In other civil actions and proceedings the compensation shall be paid by the parties in such proportion and at such time as the court directs, and thereafter charged in like manner as other costs.

(c) Disclosure of appointment.—In the exercise of its discretion, the court may authorize disclosure to the jury of the fact that the court appointed the expert witness.

(d) Parties' experts of own selection.—Nothing in this rule limits the parties in calling expert witnesses of their own selection. [*Adopted Jan. 2, 1975, effective July 1, 1975; amended Mar. 2, 1987, effective Oct. 1, 1987.*]

ARTICLE VIII.   HEARSAY

Rule 801.   Definitions.

The following definitions apply under this article:

(a) Statement.—A "statement" is (1) an oral or written assertion or (2) nonverbal conduct of a person, if it is intended by the person as an assertion.

(b) Declarant.—A "declarant" is a person who makes a statement.

(c) Hearsay.—"Hearsay" is a statement, other than one made by the declarant while testifying at the trial or hearing, offered in evidence to prove the truth of the matter asserted.

(d) Statements which are not hearsay.—A statement is not hearsay if—

> (1) Prior statement by witness.—The declarant testifies at the trial or hearing and is subject to cross-examination concerning the statement, and the

statement is (A) inconsistent with the declarant's testimony, and was given under oath subject to the penalty of perjury at a trial, hearing, or other proceeding, or in a deposition, or (B) consistent with the declarant's testimony and is offered to rebut an express or implied charge against the declarant of recent fabrication or improper influence or motive, or (C) one of identification of a person made after perceiving the person; or

(2) *Admission by party-opponent.*—The statement is offered against a party and is (A) the party's own statement, in either an individual or a representative capacity or (B) a statement of which the party has manifested an adoption or belief in its truth, or (C) a statement by a person authorized by the party to make a statement concerning the subject, or (D) a statement by the party's agent or servant concerning a matter within the scope of the agency or employment, made during the existence of the relationship, or (E) a statement by a coconspirator of a party during the course and in furtherance of the conspiracy. The contents of the statement shall be considered but are not alone sufficient to establish the declarant's authority under subdivision (C), the agency or employment relationship and scope thereof under subdivision (D), or the existence of the conspiracy and the participation therein of the declarant and the party against whom the statement is offered under subdivision (E). [*Adopted Jan. 2, 1975, effective July 1, 1975; amended Oct. 16, 1975, effective Oct. 31, 1975; Mar. 2, 1987, effective Oct. 1, 1987; Apr. 11, 1997, effective Dec. 1, 1997.*]

Rule 802. Hearsay Rule.

Hearsay is not admissible except as provided by these rules or by other rules prescribed by the Supreme Court pursuant to statutory authority or by Act of Congress. [*Adopted Jan. 2, 1975, effective July 1, 1975.*]

Rule 803. Hearsay Exceptions; Availability of Declarant Immaterial.

The following are not excluded by the hearsay rule, even though the declarant is available as a witness:

(1) *Present sense impression.*—A statement describing or explaining an event or condition made while the declarant was perceiving the event or condition, or immediately thereafter.

(2) *Excited utterance.*—A statement relating to a startling event or condition made while the declarant was under the stress of excitement caused by the event or condition.

(3) Then existing mental, emotional, or physical condition.—A statement of the declarant's then existing state of mind, emotion, sensation, or physical condition (such as intent, plan, motive, design, mental feeling, pain, and bodily health), but not including a statement of memory or belief to prove the fact remembered or believed unless it relates to the execution, revocation, identification, or terms of declarant's will.

(4) Statements for purposes of medical diagnosis or treatment.—Statements made for purposes of medical diagnosis or treatment and describing medical history, or past or present symptoms, pain, or sensations, or the inception or general character of the cause or external source thereof insofar as reasonably pertinent to diagnosis or treatment.

(5) Recorded recollection.—A memorandum or record concerning a matter about which a witness once had knowledge but now has insufficient recollection to enable the witness to testify fully and accurately, shown to have been made or adopted by the witness when the matter was fresh in the witness' memory and to reflect that knowledge correctly. If admitted, the memorandum or record may be read into evidence but may not itself be received as an exhibit unless offered by an adverse party.

(6) Records of regularly conducted activity.—A memorandum, report, record, or data compilation, in any form, of acts, events, conditions, opinions, or diagnoses, made at or near the time by, or from information transmitted by, a person with knowledge, if kept in the course of a regularly conducted business activity, and if it was the regular practice of that business activity to make the memorandum, report, record or data compilation, all as shown by the testimony of the custodian or other qualified witness, or by certification that complies with Rule 902(11), Rule 902(12), or a statute permitting certification, unless the source of information or the method or circumstances of preparation indicate lack of trustworthiness. The term "business" as used in this paragraph includes business, institution, association, profession, occupation, and calling of every kind, whether or not conducted for profit.

(7) Absence of entry in records kept in accordance with the provisions of paragraph (6).—Evidence that a matter is not included in the memoranda reports, records, or data compilations, in any form, kept in accordance with the provisions of paragraph (6), to prove the nonoccurrence or nonexistence of the matter, if the matter was of a kind of which a memorandum, report, record, or data compilation was regularly made and preserved, unless the sources of information or other circumstances indicate lack of trustworthiness.

(8) Public records and reports.—Records, reports, statements, or data compilations, in any form, of public offices or agencies, setting forth (A) the activities of the office or agency, or (B) matters observed pursuant to duty imposed by law as to which matters there was a duty to report, excluding, however, in criminal cases matters observed by police officers and other law enforcement personnel, or (C) in civil actions and proceedings and against the Government in criminal cases, factual findings resulting from an investigation made pursuant to authority granted by law, unless the sources of information or other circumstances indicate lack of trustworthiness.

(9) Records of vital statistics.—Records or data compilations, in any form, of births, fetal deaths, deaths, or marriages, if the report thereof was made to a public office pursuant to requirements of law.

(10) Absence of public record or entry.—To prove the absence of a record, report, statement, or data compilation, in any form, or the nonoccurrence or nonexistence of a matter of which a record, report, statement, or data compilation, in any form, was regularly made and preserved by a public office or agency, evidence in the form of a certification in accordance with rule 902, or testimony, that diligent search failed to disclose the record, report, statement, or data compilation, or entry.

(11) Records of religious organizations.—Statements of births, marriages, divorces, deaths, legitimacy, ancestry, relationship by blood or marriage, or other similar facts of personal or family history, contained in a regularly kept record of a religious organization.

(12) Marriage, baptismal, and similar certificates.—Statements of fact contained in a certificate that the maker performed a marriage or other ceremony or administered a sacrament, made by a clergyman, public official, or other person authorized by the rules or practices of a religious organization or by law to perform the act certified, and purporting to have been issued at the time of the act or within a reasonable time thereafter.

(13) Family records.—Statements of fact concerning personal or family history contained in family Bibles, genealogies, charts, engravings on rings, inscriptions on family portraits, engravings on urns, crypts, or tombstones, or the like.

(14) Records of documents affecting an interest in property.—The record of a document purporting to establish or affect an interest in property, as proof of the content of the original recorded document and its execution and delivery by each person by whom it purports to have been executed, if the

record is a record of a public office and an applicable statute authorizes the recording of documents of that kind in that office.

(15) Statements in documents affecting an interest in property.—A statement contained in a document purporting to establish or affect an interest in property if the matter stated was relevant to the purpose of the document, unless dealings with the property since the document was made have been inconsistent with the truth of the statement or the purport of the document.

(16) Statements in ancient documents.—Statements in a document in existence twenty years or more the authenticity of which is established.

(17) Market reports, commercial publications.—Market quotations, tabulations, lists, directories, or other published compilations, generally used and relied upon by the public or by persons in particular occupations.

(18) Learned treatises.—To the extent called to the attention of an expert witness upon cross-examination or relied upon by the expert witness in direct examination, statements contained in published treatises, periodicals, or pamphlets on a subject of history, medicine, or other science or art, established as a reliable authority by the testimony or admission of the witness or by other expert testimony or by judicial notice. If admitted, the statements may be read into evidence but may not be received as exhibits.

(19) Reputation concerning personal or family history.—Reputation among members of a person's family by blood, adoption, or marriage, or among a person's associates, or in the community, concerning a person's birth, adoption, marriage, divorce, death, legitimacy, relationship by blood, adoption, or marriage, ancestry, or other similar fact of personal or family history.

(20) Reputation concerning boundaries or general history.—Reputation in a community, arising before the controversy, as to boundaries of or customs affecting lands in the community, and reputation as to events of general history important to the community or State or nation in which located.

(21) Reputation as to character.—Reputation of a person's character among associates or in the community.

(22) Judgment of previous conviction.—Evidence of a final judgment, entered after a trial or upon a plea of guilty (but not upon a plea of nolo contendere), adjudging a person guilty of a crime punishable by death or imprisonment in excess of one year, to prove any fact essential to sustain the judgment, but not including, when offered by the Government in a criminal prosecution for purposes other than impeachment, judgments against persons other than

the accused. The pendency of an appeal may be shown but does not affect admissibility.

(23) Judgment as to personal, family, or general history or boundaries.— Judgments as proof of matters of personal, family or general history, or boundaries, essential to the judgment, if the same would be provable by evidence of reputation.

(24) (Transferred to Rule 807.]
(*Adopted Jan. 2, 1975, effective July 1, 1975; amended Dec. 12, 1975; Mar. 2, 1987, effective Oct. 1, 1987; Apr. 11, 1997, effective Dec. 1, 1997; Apr. 17, 2000, effective Dec. 1, 2000.*]

Rule 804. Hearsay Exceptions; Declarant Unavailable.

(a) Definition of unavailability.—"Unavailability as a witness" includes situations in which the declarant—

   (1) is exempted by ruling of the court on the ground of privilege from testifying concerning the subject matter of the declarant's statement; or

   (2) persists in refusing to testify concerning the subject matter of the declarant's statement despite an order of the court to do so; or

   (3) testifies to a lack of memory of the subject matter of the declarant's statement; or

   (4) is unable to be present or to testify at the hearing because of death or then existing physical or mental illness or infirmity; or

   (5) is absent from the hearing and the proponent of a statement has been unable to procure the declarant's attendance (or in the case of a hearsay exception under subdivision (b)(2), (3), or (4), the declarant's attendance or testimony) by process or other reasonable means.

   A declarant is not unavailable as a witness if exemption, refusal, claim of lack of memory, inability, or absence is due to the procurement or wrongdoing of the proponent of a statement for the purpose of preventing the witness from attending or testifying.

(b) Hearsay exceptions.—The following are not excluded by the hearsay rule if the declarant is unavailable as a witness:

   (1) Former testimony.—Testimony given as a witness at another hearing of the same or a different proceeding, or in a deposition taken in

compliance with law in the course of the same or another proceeding, if the party against whom the testimony is now offered, or, in a civil action or proceeding, a predecessor in interest, had an opportunity and similar motive to develop the testimony by direct, cross, or redirect examination.

(2) Statement under belief of impending death.—In a prosecution for homicide or in a civil action or proceeding, a statement made by a declarant while believing that the declarant's death was imminent, concerning the cause or circumstances of what the declarant believed to be impending death.

(3) Statement against interest.—A statement which was at the time of its making so far contrary to the declarant's pecuniary or proprietary interest, or so far tended to subject the declarant to civil or criminal liability, or to render invalid a claim by the declarant against another, that a reasonable person in the declarant's position would not have made the statement unless believing it to be true. A statement tending to expose the declarant to criminal liability and offered to exculpate the accused is not admissible unless corroborating circumstances clearly indicate the trustworthiness of the statement.

(4) Statement of personal or family history.—(A) A statement concerning the declarant's own birth, adoption, marriage, divorce, legitimacy, relationship by blood, adoption, or marriage, ancestry, or other similar fact of personal or family history, even though declarant had no means of acquiring personal knowledge of the matter stated; or (B) a statement concerning the foregoing matters, and death also, of another person, if the declarant was related to the other by blood, adoption, or marriage or was so intimately associated with the other's family as to be likely to have accurate information concerning the matter declared.

(5) (Transferred to Rule 807.]

(6) Forfeiture by wrongdoing.—A statement offered against a party that has engaged or acquiesced in wrongdoing that was intended to, and did, procure the unavailability of the declarant as a witness. [*Adopted Jan. 2, 1975, effective July 1, 1975; amended Dec. 12, 1975; Mar. 2, 1987, effective Oct. 1, 1987; Nov. 18, 1988; Apr. 11, 1997, effective Dec. 1, 1997.*]

Rule 805.   Hearsay Within Hearsay.

Hearsay included within hearsay is not excluded under the hearsay rule if each part of the combined statements conforms with an exception to the hearsay rule provided in these rules. [*Adopted Jan. 2, 1975, effective July 1, 1975.*]

Rule 806.   Attacking and Supporting Credibility of Declarant.

When a hearsay statement, or a statement defined in Rule 801(d)(2)(C), (D), or (E), has been admitted in evidence, the credibility of the declarant may be attacked, and if attacked may be supported, by any evidence which would be admissible for those purposes if declarant had testified as a witness. Evidence of a statement or conduct by the declarant at any time, inconsistent with the declarant's hearsay statement, is not subject to any requirement that the declarant may have been afforded an opportunity to deny or explain. If the party against whom a hearsay statement has been admitted calls the declarant as a witness, the party is entitled to examine the declarant on the statement as if under cross-examination. [*Adopted Jan. 2, 1975, effective July 1, 1975; amended Mar. 2, 1987, effective Oct. 1, 1987; Apr. 11, 1997, effective Dec. 1, 1997.*]

Rule 807.   Residual Exception.

A statement not specifically covered by Rule 803 or 804 but having equivalent circumstantial guarantees of trustworthiness, is not excluded by the hearsay rule, if the court determines that (A) the statement is offered as evidence of a material fact; (B) the statement is more probative on the point for which it is offered than any other evidence which the proponent can procure through reasonable efforts; and (C) the general purposes of these rules and the interests of justice will best be served by admission of the statement into evidence. However, a statement may not be admitted under this exception unless the proponent of it makes known to the adverse party sufficiently in advance of the trial or hearing to provide the adverse party with a fair opportunity to prepare to meet it, the proponent's intention to offer the statement and the particulars of it, including the name and address of the declarant. [*Adopted Apr. 11, 1997, effective Dec. 1, 1997.*]

ARTICLE IX.   AUTHENTICATION AND IDENTIFICATION

Rule 901.   Requirement of Authentication or Identification.

(a) General provision.—The requirement of authentication or identification as a condition precedent to admissibility is satisfied by evidence sufficient to support a finding that the matter in question is what its proponent claims.

(b) Illustrations.—By way of illustration only, and not by way of limitation, the following are examples of authentication or identification conforming with the requirements of this rule:

(1) Testimony of witness with knowledge.—Testimony that a matter is what it is claimed to be.

(2) Nonexpert opinion on handwriting.—Nonexpert opinion as to the genuineness of handwriting, based upon familiarity not acquired for purposes of the litigation.

(3) Comparison by trier or expert witness.—Comparison by the trier of fact or by expert witnesses with specimens which have been authenticated.

(4) Distinctive characteristics and the like.—Appearance, contents, substance, internal patterns, or other distinctive characteristics, taken in conjunction with circumstances.

(5) Voice identification.—Identification of a voice, whether heard firsthand or through mechanical or electronic transmission or recording, by opinion based upon hearing the voice at any time under circumstances connecting it with the alleged speaker.

(6) Telephone conversations.—Telephone conversations, by evidence that a call was made to the number assigned at the time by the telephone company to a particular person or business, if (A) in the case of a person, circumstances, including self-identification, show the person answering to be the one called, or (B) in the case of a business, the call was made to a place of business and the conversation related to business reasonably transacted over the telephone.

(7) Public records or reports.—Evidence that a writing authorized by law to be recorded or filed and in fact recorded or filed in a public office, or a purported public record, report, statement, or data compilation, in any form, is from the public office where items of this nature are kept.

(8) Ancient documents or data compilation.—Evidence that a document or data compilation, in any form, (A) is in such condition as to create no

suspicion concerning its authenticity, (B) was in a place where it, if authentic, would likely be, and (C) has been in existence 20 years or more at the time it is offered.

(9) Process or system.—Evidence describing a process or system used to produce a result and showing that the process or system produces an accurate result.

(10) Methods provided by statute or rule.—Any method of authentication or identification provided by Act of Congress or by other rules prescribed by the Supreme Court pursuant to statutory authority. [*Adopted Jan. 2, 1975, effective July 1, 1975.*]

Rule 902. Self-Authentication.

Extrinsic evidence of authenticity as a condition precedent to admissibility is not required with respect to the following:

(1) Domestic public documents under seal.—A document bearing a seal purporting to be that of the United States, or of any State, district, Commonwealth, territory, or insular possession thereof, or the Panama Canal Zone, or the Trust Territory of the Pacific Islands, or of a political subdivision, department, officer, or agency thereof, and a signature purporting to be an attestation or execution.

(2) Domestic public documents not under seal.—A document purporting to bear the signature in the official capacity of an officer or employee of any entity included in paragraph (1) hereof, having no seal, if a public officer having a seal and having official duties in the district or political subdivision of the officer or employee certifies under seal that the signer has the official capacity and that the signature is genuine.

(3) Foreign public documents.—A document purporting to be executed or attested in an official capacity by a person authorized by the laws of a foreign country to make the execution or attestation, and accompanied by a final certification as to the genuineness of the signature and official position (A) of the executing or attesting person, or (B) of any foreign official whose certificate of genuineness of signature and official position relates to the execution or attestation or is in a chain of certificates of genuineness of signature and official position relating to the execution or attestation. A final certification may be made by a secretary of an embassy or legation, consul general, consul, vice consul, or consular agent of the United States, or a diplomatic or consular official of the foreign country assigned or accredited to the United States. If reasonable opportunity has been given to all parties

to investigate the authenticity and accuracy of official documents, the court may, for good cause shown, order that they be treated as presumptively authentic without final certification or permit them to be evidenced by an attested summary with or without final certification.

(4) Certified copies of public records.—A copy of an official record or report or entry therein, or of a document authorized by law to be recorded or filed and actually recorded or filed in a public office, including data compilations in any form, certified as correct by the custodian or other person authorized to make the certification, by certificate complying with paragraph (1), (2), or (3) of this rule or complying with any Act of Congress or rule prescribed by the Supreme Court pursuant to statutory authority.

(5) Official publications.—Books, pamphlets, or other publications purporting to be issued by public authority.

(6) Newspapers and periodicals.—Printed materials purporting to be newspapers or periodicals.

(7) Trade inscriptions and the like.—Inscriptions, signs, tags, or labels purporting to have been affixed in the course of business and indicating ownership, control, or origin.

(8) Acknowledged documents.—Documents accompanied by a certificate of acknowledgment executed in the manner provided by law by a notary public or other officer authorized by law to take acknowledgments.

(9) Commercial paper and related documents.—Commercial paper, signatures thereon, and documents relating thereto to the extent provided by general commercial law.

(10) Presumptions under Acts of Congress.—Any signature, document, or other matter declared by Act of Congress to be presumptively or prima facie genuine or authentic.

(11) Certified domestic records of regularly conducted activity.—The original or a duplicate of a domestic record of regularly conducted activity that would be admissible under Rule 803(6) if accompanied by a written declaration of its custodian or other qualified person, in a manner complying with any Act of Congress or rule prescribed by the Supreme Court pursuant to statutory authority, certifying that the record —

(A) was made at or near the time of the occurrence of the matters set forth by, or from information transmitted by, a person with knowledge of those matters;

(B) was kept in the course of the regularly conducted activity; and

(C) was made by the regularly conducted activity as a regular practice.

A party intending to offer a record into evidence under this paragraph must provide written notice of that intention to all adverse parties, and must make the record and declaration available for inspection sufficiently in advance of their offer into evidence to provide an adverse party with a fair opportunity to challenge them.

(12) Certified foreign records of regularly conducted activity.—In a civil case, the original or a duplicate of a foreign record of regularly conducted activity that would be admissible under Rule 803(6) if accompanied by a written declaration by its custodian or other qualified person certifying that the record —

(A) was made at or near the time of the occurrence of the matters set forth by, or from information transmitted by, a person with knowledge of those matters;

(B) was kept in the course of the regularly conducted activity; and

(C) was made by the regularly conducted activity as a regular practice.

The declaration must be signed in a manner that, if falsely made, would subject the maker to criminal penalty under the laws of the country where the declaration is signed. A party intending to offer a record into evidence under this paragraph must provide written notice of that intention to all adverse parties, and must make the record and declaration available for inspection sufficiently in advance of their offer into evidence to provide an adverse party with a fair opportunity to challenge them. [*Adopted Jan. 2, 1975, effective July 1, 1975; amended Mar. 2, 1987, effective Oct. 1, 1987; Apr. 25, 1988, effective Nov. 1, 1988; Apr. 17, 2000, effective Dec. 1, 2000.*]

Rule 903. Subscribing Witness' Testimony Unnecessary.

The testimony of a subscribing witness is not necessary to authenticate a writing unless required by the laws of the jurisdiction whose laws govern the validity of the writing. [*Adopted Jan. 2, 1975, effective July 1, 1975.*]

ARTICLE X.   CONTENTS OF WRITINGS, RECORDINGS, AND PHOTOGRAPHS

Rule 1001.   Definitions.

For purposes of this article the following definitions are applicable:

(1) Writings and recordings.—"Writings" and "recordings" consist of letters, words, or numbers, or their equivalent, set down by handwriting, typewriting, printing, photostating, photographing, magnetic impulse, mechanical or electronic recording, or other form of data compilation.

(2) Photographs.—"Photographs" include still photographs, X-ray films, video tapes, and motion pictures.

(3) Original.—An "original" of a writing or recording is the writing or recording itself or any counterpart intended to have the same effect by a person executing or issuing it. An "original" of a photograph includes the negative or any print therefrom. If data are stored in a computer or similar device, any printout or other output readable by sight, shown to reflect the data accurately, is an "original."

(4) Duplicate.—A "duplicate" is a counterpart produced by the same impression as the original, or from the same matrix, or by means of photography, including enlargements and miniatures, or by mechanical or electronic re-recording, or by chemical reproduction, or by other equivalent techniques which accurately reproduces the original. [*Adopted Jan. 2, 1975, effective July 1, 1975.*]

Rule 1002. Requirement of Original.

To prove the content of a writing, recording, or photograph, the original writing, recording, or photograph is required, except as otherwise provided in these rules or by Act of Congress. [*Adopted Jan. 2, 1975, effective July 1, 1975.*]

Rule 1003. Admissibility of Duplicates.

A duplicate is admissible to the same extent as an original unless (1) a genuine question is raised as to the authenticity of the original or (2) in the circumstances it would be unfair to admit the duplicate in lieu of the original. [*Adopted Jan. 2, 1975, effective July 1, 1975.*]

Rule 1004. Admissibility of Other Evidence of Contents.

The original is not required, and other evidence of the contents of a writing, recording, or photograph is admissible if—

(1) Originals lost or destroyed.—All originals are lost or have been destroyed, unless the proponent lost or destroyed them in bad faith; or

(2) Original not obtainable.—No original can be obtained by any available judicial process or procedure; or

(3) Original in possession of opponent.—At a time when an original was under the control of the party against whom offered, that party was put on notice, by the pleadings or otherwise, that the contents would be a subject of proof at the hearing, and that party does not produce the original at the hearing; or

(4) Collateral matters.—The writing, recording, or photograph is not closely related to a controlling issue. [*Adopted Jan. 2, 1975, effective July 1, 1975; amended Mar. 2, 1987, effective Oct. 1, 1987.*]

Rule 1005.   Public Records.

The contents of an official record, or of a document authorized to be recorded or filed and actually recorded or filed, including data compilations in any form, if otherwise admissible, may be proved by copy, certified as correct in accordance with rule 902 or testified to be correct by a witness who has compared it with the original. If a copy which complies with the foregoing cannot be obtained by the exercise of reasonable diligence, then other evidence of the contents may be given. [*Adopted Jan. 2, 1975, effective July 1, 1975.*]

Rule 1006.   Summaries.

The contents of voluminous writings, recordings, or photographs which cannot conveniently be examined in court may be presented in the form of a chart, summary, or calculation. The originals, or duplicates, shall be made available for examination or copying, or both, by other parties at [a] reasonable time and place. The court may order that they be produced in court. [*Adopted Jan. 2, 1975, effective July 1, 1975.*]

Rule 1007.   Testimony or Written Admission of Party.

Contents of writings, recordings, or photographs may be proved by the testimony or deposition of the party against whom offered or by that party's written admission, without accounting for the nonproduction of the original. [*Adopted Jan. 2, 1975, effective July 1, 1975; amended Mar. 2, 1987, effective Oct. 1, 1987.*]

Rule 1008. Functions of Court and Jury.

When the admissibility of other evidence of contents of writings, recordings, or photographs under these rules depends upon the fulfillment of a condition of fact, the question whether the condition has been fulfilled is ordinarily for the court to determine in accordance with the provisions of rule 104. However, when an issue is raised (a) whether the asserted writing ever existed, or (b) whether another writing, recording, or photograph produced at the trial is the original, or (c) whether other evidence of contents correctly reflects the contents, the issue is for the trier of fact to determine as in the case of other issues of fact. [*Adopted Jan. 2, 1975, effective July 1, 1975.*]

ARTICLE XI.   MISCELLANEOUS RULES

Rule 1101.   Applicability of Rules.

(a) Courts and judges.—These rules apply to the United States district courts, the District Court of Guam, the District Court of the Virgin Islands, the District Court for the Northern Mariana Islands, the United States courts of appeals, the United States Claims Court, and to United States bankruptcy judges and United States magistrate judges, in the actions, cases, and proceedings and to the extent hereinafter set forth. The terms "judge" and "court" in these rules include United States bankruptcy judges and United States magistrate judges.

(b) Proceedings generally.—These rules apply generally to civil actions and proceedings, including admiralty and maritime cases, to criminal cases and proceedings, to contempt proceedings except those in which the court may act summarily, and to proceedings and cases under title 11, United States Code.

(c) Rule of privilege.—The rule with respect to privileges applies at all stages of all actions, cases, and proceedings.

(d) Rules inapplicable.—The rules (other than with respect to privileges) do not apply in the following situations:

(1) Preliminary questions of fact.—The determination of questions of fact preliminary to admissibility of evidence when the issue is to be determined by the court under rule 104.

(2) Grand jury.—Proceedings before grand juries.

(3) Miscellaneous proceedings.—Proceedings for extradition or rendition; preliminary examinations in criminal cases; sentencing, or granting or revoking probation; issuance of warrants for arrest, criminal summonses, and search warrants; and proceedings with respect to release on bail or otherwise.

(e) Rules applicable in part. In the following proceedings these rules apply to the extent that matters of evidence are not provided for in the statutes which govern procedure therein or in other rules prescribed by the Supreme Court pursuant to statutory authority: the trial of misdemeanors and other petty offenses before United States magistrate judges; review of agency actions when the facts are subject to trial de novo under section 706(2)(F) of title 5, United States Code; review of orders of the Secretary of Agriculture under section 2 of the Act entitled "An Act to authorize association of producers of agricultural products" approved February 18, 1922 (7 U.S.C. 292), and under sections 6 and 7(c) of the Perishable Agricultural Commodities Act, 1930 (7 U.S.C. 499f, 499g(c)); naturalization and revocation of naturalization under sections 310–318 of the Immigration and Nationality Act (8 U.S.C. 1421–1429); prize proceedings in admiralty under sections 7651–7681 of title 10, United States Code; review of orders of the Secretary of the Interior under section 2 of the Act entitled "An Act authorizing associations of producers of aquatic products" approved June 25, 1934 (15 U.S.C. 522); review of orders of petroleum control boards under section 5 of the Act entitled "An Act to regulate interstate and foreign commerce in petroleum and its products by prohibiting the shipment in such commerce of petroleum and its products produced in violation of State law, and for other purposes," approved February 22, 1935 (15 U.S.C. 715d); actions for fines, penalties, or forfeitures under part V of title IV of the Tariff Act of 1930 (19 U.S.C. 1581–1624), or under the Anti-Smuggling Act (19 U.S.C. 1701–1711); criminal libel for condemnation, exclusion of imports, or other proceedings under the Federal Food, Drug, and Cosmetic Act (21 U.S.C. 301–392); disputes between seamen under sections 4079, 4080, and 4081 of the Revised Statutes (22 U.S.C. 256–258); habeas corpus under sections 2241–2254 of title 28, United States Code; motions to vacate, set aside or correct sentence under section 2255 of title 28, United States Code; actions for penalties for refusal to transport destitute seamen under section 4578 of the Revised Statutes (46 U.S.C. 679); actions against the United States under the Act entitled "An Act authorizing suits against the United States in admiralty for damage caused by and salvage service rendered to public vessels belonging to the United States, and for other purposes," approved March 3, 1925 (46 U.S.C. 781–790), as implemented by section 7730 of title 10, United States Code. [*Adopted Jan. 2, 1975, effective July 1, 1975; amended Dec. 12, 1975; Nov. 6, 1978, effective Oct. 1, 1979; Apr. 2, 1982, effective Oct. 1, 1982; Mar. 2, 1987, effective Oct. 1, 1987; Apr. 25, 1988, effective Nov. 1, 1988; Apr. 22, 1993, effective Dec. 1, 1993.*]

Rule 1102. Amendments.

Amendments to the Federal Rules of Evidence may be made as provided in Section 2072 of title 28 of the United States Code. [*Adopted Jan. 2, 1975, effective July 1, 1975; amended Apr. 30, 1991, effective Dec. 1, 1991.*]

Rule 1103. Title.

These rules may be known and cited as the Federal Rules of Evidence. [*Adopted Jan. 2, 1975, effective July 1, 1975.*]

INDEX

[References are to section numbers.]

[References are to section numbers.]

[References are to section numbers.]

[References are to section numbers.]

[References are to section numbers.]

[References are to section numbers.]

[References are to section numbers.]

[References are to section numbers.]

[References are to section numbers.]

[References are to section numbers.]

IMPEACHMENT OF WITNESSES—Cont.
Prior inconsistent statements—Cont.
    General discussion . . . 9-26; 9-28
    Intrinsic impeachment under FRE 613(a)
      . . . 9-28(a)
    Substantive facts under FRE 801(d) . .
      9-29
Rehabilitating witness with prior consistent
    statements . . . 9-37
Religious beliefs or opinions, FRE 610 barring
    use of . . . 9-35
Specific instances of conduct . . . 9-30; 9-32

INFERENCES
Criminal cases . . . 4-13(c)
Lay opinions . . . 4-3
Opening statement . . . 3-4

INFORMANTS
Privilege to protect identity of informer . . .
    11-11

***IN LIMINE* MOTION**
Expert evidence . . . 10-5(e)

INSURANCE
Evidence of insured or uninsured status . . .
    5-14

INTERNET
Hearsay rule . . . 6-9

INTERPRETERS
Qualifications . . . 4-6(e)

J

JOURNALISTIC PRIVILEGE
General discussion of . . . 11-18

JUDGES
Competence to be witness . . . 4-6(b)
Original writing rule, judge's role concerning
    proof of contents . . . 8-28
Witness, judge as . . . 4-6(b)

JURY
Comparison by jury to determine identification
    of exhibit . . . 8-9(c)
Deliberations (See JURY DELIBERATIONS)
Exhibits, showing to jury (See EXHIBITS)
Original writing rule, jury's role concerning
    proof of contents . . . 8-28
Witnesses, juror as . . . 4-6(c)

JURY DELIBERATIONS
Closing argument . . . 12-2
Exhibits, submission of (See EXHIBITS)

JURY INSTRUCTIONS
Closing argument . . . 12-2; 12-9

K

KNOWLEDGE (See PERSONAL KNOWL-
EDGE)

L

LAW ENFORCEMENT REPORTS
Public records hearsay exception . . 6-27(b);
    6-27(d)
Regularly kept records hearsay exception . .
    6-26(f)

LAY OPINIONS
Factual testimony, need to emphasize . . 4-5
Handwriting, nonexpert to identify . . 8-9(b)
Regularly kept records, hearsay exception for
    . . . 6-26(d)
Standards for admitting under FRE 701 . . .
    4-4
Traditional rule . . . 4-3
Voice identification . . . 8-9(e)

LEADING QUESTIONS
Cross-examination . . . 9-4; 9-12; 9-23
Direct examination . . . 7-4; 7-6(a)
Expert witnesses . . . 10-17
Explanation of FRE 611(c) . . . 7-4
Objections to . . . 7-6(a)

LEARNED TREATISES
Hearsay exception . . . 6-31

LIABILITY INSURANCE
Evidence of insured or uninsured status . . .
    5-14

LIBEL AND SLANDER
Expert witnesses, direct examination of . . .
    10-21
Hearsay rule and defamatory statements . . .
    6-5(a)

M

MAPS (See DEMONSTRATIVE EXHIBITS)

[References are to section numbers.]

[References are to section numbers.]

[References are to section numbers.]

[References are to section numbers.]

[References are to section numbers.]